THE
ENCYCLOPEDIA
OF
CANADA

ALBERTA

SPLENDOR SINE OCCASU

BRITISH COLUMBIA

COAT OF ARMS OF THE
PROVINCES OF ALBERTA AND BRITISH COLUMBIA.

The
ENCYCLOPEDIA
of
CANADA

GENERAL EDITOR

W. STEWART WALLACE, M.A. (Oxon.), F.R.S.C.
Librarian, University of Toronto

Volume VI
SILLERY — ZURICH

UNIVERSITY ASSOCIATES OF CANADA
Limited
TORONTO

1937

PRINTED IN CANADA BY
MURRAY PRINTING COMPANY, LIMITED, TORONTO

CONTRIBUTORS OF SPECIAL ARTICLES

VOLUME VI

Sisters of Charity—Sister MAURA, Mount St. Vincent College, Halifax, Nova Scotia.

Sisters of the Joan of Arc Institute—Mother ST. THOMAS AQUINAS, Officier d'Académie, founder of the community.

Sisters of Our Lady of Charity of Refuge—Rev. EDMOND LEMIEUX, O.M.I.

Sisters of Service—Sister C. ALBURY, S.O.S., Local Superior, Mother House, Wellesley Place, Toronto.

Sulpicians—Mgr. OLIVIER MAURAULT, LL.D., F.R.S.C., Rector of the University of Montreal.

Tariffs—Professor K. W. TAYLOR, Department of Political Economy, McMaster University, Hamilton.

Taxation—Miss M. L. NEWTON, M.A., Head of the Circulation Department, University of Toronto Library.

Telegraphs and **Telephones**—Miss M. L. NEWTON, M.A., University of Toronto Library.

Textile Industries—Miss M. L. NEWTON, M.A., University of Toronto Library.

Theatre—Miss AGATHA LEONARD, B.A., University of Toronto Library.

Toronto—PERCY J. ROBINSON, Esq., LL.D., author of *Toronto during the French régime*.

Trade, External—Professor HUMPHREY MICHELL, M.A., Head of the Department of Political Economy, McMaster University, Hamilton.

Transportation—Professor GEORGE GLAZEBROOK, M.A., Department of Modern History, University of Toronto.

Tunkers—Rev. W. G. Wallace, D.D., Toronto.

United Empire Loyalists—W. S. WALLACE, Esq., M.A., F.R.S.C., author of *The United Empire Loyalists*.

Upper Canada Bible Society—Rev. J. B. M. ARMOUR, M.A., General Secretary of the British and Foreign Bible Society in Canada.

Ursulines—Rev. Father AUGUSTE MORISSET, O.M.I., Librarian, University of Ottawa.

Water-Powers—Miss IRENE BISS, M.A., Department of Political Economy, University of Toronto.

World War—Lieut.-Col. WILFRID BOVEY, O.B.E., LL.D., McGill University, Montreal.

KEY TO ABBREVIATIONS

Bull. rech. hist.—Bulletin des recherches historiques (Lévis, P.Q., 1895—).

Can. hist. rev.—The Canadian historical review (Toronto, 1920—).

Can. mag.—The Canadian magazine (Toronto, 1893—).

Coll. Nova Scotia Hist. Soc.—Collections of the Nova Scotia Historical Society (Halifax, 1880—).

Dict. nat. biog.—Leslie Stephen and Sidney Lee (eds.), *Dictionary of national biography* (63 vols. and supplements, London, 1885-1912).

fl.—floruit (flourished).

n.d.—no date.

n.p.—no place of publication.

Ont. Hist. Soc. papers and records—Ontario Historical Society, papers and records (Toronto, 1899—).

q.v.—*quod vide* (which see).

Trans. Roy. Soc. Can.—Transactions of the Royal Society of Canada (Ottawa, 1883—).

S

Sillery, a village in Quebec county, Quebec, on the north shore of the St. Lawrence river, 4 miles west of the city of Quebec. It is named after Noël Brulart de Sillery, a partner in the Company of New France who established here a seminary for the Indians. From 1680 to 1700, about 500 Abnaki were settled here, before they removed to the banks of the St. Francis river in Yamaska county. The population of the parish, which is known as St. Colomb de Sillery, is over 2,000. See Abbé H. A. Scott, *La bourgade Saint-Joseph de Sillery après 1670* (La Nouvelle France, 1911).

Sillimanite, a rock-forming mineral which chemically is a silicate of aluminum. It commonly occurs on long slender crystals, which are not distinctly terminated, and often is in close parallel groups grading into fibrous and columnar forms. It is commonly found in gneisses and schists as a result of metamorphism, and is looked upon as an indication that the rock in which it occurs contained a large percentage of kaolin.

Sillitoe, Acton Windeyer (1841-1894), first Anglican bishop of New Westminster (1879-94), was born in Australia in 1841, and was educated at Pembroke College, Cambridge (B.A., 1862). He was ordained a priest of the Church of England in 1870; and in 1879 he was consecrated bishop of the new diocese of New Westminster, British Columbia. He reached New Westminster in 1880, and he administered the diocese until his death, at New Westminster, on June 9, 1894. He was a D.C.L. of the University of Trinity College, Toronto. See Rev. H. H. Gowen, *Church work in British Columbia, being a memoir of the episcopate of Acton Windeyer Sillitoe* (London, 1899).

Silver, Arthur Peters (1851-1908), author, was born in Halifax, Nova Scotia, in 1851; and died near Halifax on February 14, 1908. He was the author of *Farm, cottage, camp, and canoe in maritime Canada* (London, 1908).

Silver, a soft white metal which is ductile and malleable, but not elastic. It has a brilliant metallic lustre and a specific gravity of 10.5. On exposure, particularly to gases containing sulphur, it turns brown and finally black. It occurs in nature as native silver, and frequently contains small percentages of gold and mercury, in the latter case giving a natural amalgam. It is one of the precious metals, and is used extensively for coinage and in the arts, particularly for jewellery, tableware, and toiletware. There is also a large consumption of silver in certain chemical industries, and it is largely used in photography. Native silver has been found in abundance in Canada in the mines near Port Arthur and in the celebrated Cobalt, Gowganda, and South Lorrain silver districts in Ontario. The largest single mass of native silver ever taken from the ground is probably a block weighing about 4,400 lbs. from the Keeley mine in South Lorrain.

In addition to native silver, there are many compounds occurring in nature. Dyscrasite is a silver-white antimonide of silver which is comparatively brittle, but otherwise would be mistaken for silver. This was found in some quantity in the mines at Cobalt.

Argentite is a sulphide of silver consisting of silver 87.1 per cent, sulphur 12.9 per cent. It crystallizes in cubes and octahedrons, but recent investigation has shown that they have an inner structure corresponding to the orthorhombic system. This suggests that the mineral was formed at high temperature, and has undergone a molecular change on cooling. It is one of the important sources of silver and was quite prominent in the mines around Port Arthur and in some of the mines of British Columbia, but was extremely rare in the Cobalt district of Ontario.

Proustite, the light ruby silver, is a sulpharsenide of silver and pyargyrite. The dark ruby silver is a sulphantimonide of silver. Both these occurred in considerable quantity in the Cobalt district, and are important in many of the mines in British Columbia.

Stephanite, or brittle silver, is a black sulphantimonide of silver which occurs with the ruby silvers in Cobalt and South Lorrain.

Cerargyrite, the chloride of silver, while important in other countries is not recorded as a Canadian mineral.

See W. G. Miller, *The Cobalt nickel arsenides and silver deposits of Temiskaming* (Ontario Department of Mines, Toronto, 1913), and C. W. Knight, *Cobalt and South Lorrain silver areas* (Ontario Department of Mines, Toronto, 1924).

Silverdale, a village in the New Westminster district of British Columbia, on the main line of the Canadian Pacific Railway, 4 miles west of Mission. Pop. (1931), 325.

Silver Heights, a suburb of Winnipeg, Manitoba, on the left bank of the Assiniboine river. The name was applied as early as 1869 to "a gentle knoll of the prairie which used to shine as with a silver rim when the sun was reflected from the polished culms of the buffalo grass." The site was acquired by Lord Strathcona (q.v.), as a farm when he was in Winnipeg in 1870, and the existing log farm-house was enlarged into a mansion, to which the name Silver Heights was given.

Silver islet, a small island in lake Superior, 22 miles from Port Arthur, Ontario. A silver mine was discovered on this island in 1870, and in the subsequent fifteen years yielded over $3,000,-000 in silver. The mine is now inactive.

Silverton, a mining village in the Kootenay district of British Columbia, on the east side of Slocan lake. It has a steamer landing. Pop. (1931), 272.

Silvy, Antoine (1638-1711), missionary and author, was born at Aix in Provence, France, on October 16, 1638. In 1658 he entered the Society of Jesus as a novice, and in 1673 he was sent to Canada. He was employed as a missionary successively at Michilimackinac and Tadoussac from 1674 to 1684. In 1684 he accompanied a French expedition to Hudson bay as chaplain; and in 1686 he accompanied Troyes (q.v.) as a chaplain on his overland journey to Hudson bay. He remained at Fort Albany till 1693, when he returned to Quebec; and in his later years he taught mathematics at the Jesuit College in Quebec. He died at Quebec on May 8, 1711. His journal of the expedition to Hudson bay in 1684-5 has been published by C. de Rochemonteix in the preface to his *Relation par lettres de l'Amérique septentrionale* (Paris, 1904), and has been republished, with English translation, in J. B. Tyrrell (ed.), *Documents relating to the early history of Hudson bay* (Toronto, The Champlain Society, 1931).

Simcoe, John Graves (1752-1806), lieutenant-governor of Upper Canada (1791-6), was born at Cotterstock, Northamptonshire, England, on February 25, 1752, the son of Captain John Simcoe, R.N. He was educated at Eton and at Merton College, Oxford; and in

1771 he entered the British army as an ensign in the 35th Regiment. He served in America throughout the American Revolutionary War; and from 1777 to 1781 he commanded the Queen's Rangers, a corps of provincial troops, which he brought to a high state of efficiency. In 1781 he was invalided back to England; and for several years he lived on his estate at Wolford the life of a country gentleman. In 1790 he was elected to the House of Commons as member for St. Mawe's, Cornwall; and in 1791, on the passage of the Constitutional Act, he was appointed first lieutenant-governor of Upper Canada. He arrived in Canada in 1792, and chose Newark (Niagara) as the capital of his government. Later, in 1794, he moved the government offices to York (Toronto). His régime was notable for his efforts to open up the province by means of the building of roads and the encouragement of immigration; and in some ways his policy was remarkably farsighted. His views in regard to the relations of church and state, and his failure to allow for forces at work in a new country, contained, however, the seeds for future trouble. In 1794 he was promoted to be major-general; and, on leaving Canada in 1796, he was appointed governor and commander-in-chief of San Domingo, with the local rank of lieutenant-general. He returned to England in 1797, and in 1801 he was in command at Plymouth, when the French invasion of England was expected. In 1806 he was appointed commander-in-chief in India; but was directed first to proceed on a special mission to Lisbon. He was taken ill on the voyage, and returned home—but only to die at Exeter on October 26, 1806. In 1782 he married Elizabeth Posthuma, daughter of Lieut.-Col. Thomas Gwillim, of Old Court, Hereford; and by her he had two sons and seven daughters. He wrote and printed for private distribution a *History of the operations of a partisan corps called the Queen's Rangers* (Exeter, 1787; reprinted, with a memoir of the author, New York, 1844). His *Correspondence* has been edited for the Ontario Historical Society by Brig.-Gen. E. A. Cruikshank (4 vols., Toronto, 1921-6).

See W. R. Riddell, *Life of John Graves Simcoe* (Toronto, 1926); D. C. Scott, *John Graves Simcoe* (Toronto, 1905); D. B. Read, *Life and times of Major-Gen. John Graves Simcoe* (Toronto, 1890), and *The lieutenant-governors of Upper Canada* (Toronto, 1900); and J. Ross Robertson, *The diary of Mrs. Simcoe* (Toronto, 1911).

Simcoe, a county in Ontario, is bounded on the north by the Georgian bay and Muskoka county, on the east by lakes Simcoe and Couchiching, on the south by Peel and York counties, and on the west by Dufferin and Grey counties and Nottawassaga bay. It was named by Colonel John Graves Simcoe (q.v.) after his father. About 1,592,000 acres of land were bought from the Chippewa Indians by treaties dated 1798, 1815, and 1818; and by the Municipal Act of 1849 part of this district was erected into the county of Simcoe. A few refugees from the Red River Settlement came to Simcoe in 1819, but the first considerable immigration was in the years 1831-5, from England. The county town is Barrie. The county is about 50 miles long, and has an average width of about 20 miles. Pop. (1931), 83,667. See A. F. Hunter, *History of Simcoe county* (2 vols., Barrie, 1909).

Simcoe, a town in Norfolk county, Ontario, on the river Lynn, and on the Canadian National Railway, 22 miles south of Brantford, and 8 miles north of Port Dover. It was first settled before the end of the eighteenth century, and was named after John Graves Simcoe (q.v.), lieutenant-governor of Upper Canada. It was incorporated as a town in 1875. Situated in an excellent farming district, it does a large business in dairy and meat products and in canned fruits and vegetables. It has canning and jam factories, an ice-cream plant, textile mills and factories, a glove factory, and flour and saw mills. In it are found a high school, a county hospital, a public library, and a weekly newspaper (*Reformer*), founded in 1858. It has not only hydro-electric power, but in addition a plentiful supply of natural gas. Pop. (1931), 5,226. See L. Brown, *A history of Simcoe* (Simcoe, 1929).

Simcoe, lake, is in Ontario, between Georgian bay and lake Ontario. It discharges into Georgian bay by Couchiching bay and the Severn river. The lake was discovered by Champlain (q.v.) in 1615, but is named after John Graves Simcoe (q.v.), lieutenant-governor of Upper Canada (1791-6). In some parts it is of considerable depth and contains numerous islands. Some of these are of large size, but are not permanently inhabited, except by Indians. Barrie, Orillia, Jackson's Point, Beaverton, and the other ports on the lake were formerly connected with each other by steamers; but the motor-car has put the steamship on lake Simcoe out of business. The banks of the lake are generally wooded down to the water's edge. The lake is 30 miles long, about 18 broad, and has an area of 280 square miles. See Stephen Leacock, *The lake Simcoe country* (Can. Geog. Journal, 1935).

Similkameen river, in the Similkameen district of British Columbia, rises in the United States and flows in a northerly direction for 39 miles to Princeton, British Columbia, and thence in a south-east direction for 56 miles, crossing the boundary into the United States 11½ miles west of Osoyoos lake. Continuing in a south and east direction, it joins the Okanagan river 2 miles south of Osoyoos lake. The length of the river in British Columbia is 95 miles. The Similkameen valley has been an important copper and gold-producing area.

Simpson, Sir George (1792-1860), governor-in-chief of Rupert's Land, was born at Loch Broom, Ross-shire, Scotland, in 1792, the illegitimate son of George Simpson. In 1809 he entered the employ of a firm in London engaged in the West India trade; but in 1820 he took service with the Hudson's Bay Company, and was sent to Canada. He was influential in bringing about the union of the Hudson's Bay and North West Companies in 1821, and was soon afterward appointed governor of the northern department of the united company. Later he became governor-in-chief of Rupert's Land, and general superintendent of the Hudson's Bay Company in North America. His administration of the affairs of the company was marked by great firmness; and he was notable also for the encouragement he gave to geographical exploration. In 1841-2 he crossed the continent, and made a trip around the world, an account of which is contained in his *Narrative of an overland journey around the world* (2 vols., London, 1847). During the later years of his life he lived at Lachine, near Montreal; and here he died, on September 7, 1860. He married, in 1827, Frances Ramsay, daughter of Geddes M. Simpson, of London; and by her he had one son and three daughters. In 1841 he was created a K.B. See G. Bryce, *Mackenzie, Selkirk, Simpson* (Toronto, 1905); and F. Merk (ed.), *Fur trade and empire: George Simpson's journal* (Cambridge, Mass., 1931).

Simpson, John (1788-1873), member of parliament, was born in England in 1788, and emigrated to Canada in 1815 with his wife and the children she had had by a previous marriage. One of these children, John Arthur Roebuck (q.v.), was afterwards a member of the British House of Commons, and agent of the Lower Canadian Assembly in London. In 1822 Simpson was appointed collector of customs at Coteau du Lac; and he retained this post for many years. From 1824 to 1827 he also represented the county of York in the Legislative Assembly of Lower Canada; and from 1841 to 1844 he represented Vaudreuil in the Legislative Assembly of United Canada. He died at Brockville, Ontario, in 1873. See F. J. Audet, *John Simpson* (Can. Hist. Association, Report, 1936).

Simpson, John (1807-1878), provincial secretary of Canada (1864), was born at Helmsley, Blackmoor, Yorkshire, England, on December 27, 1807. He carried on business as a linen-draper in London, England, for several years; but about 1835 he came to Canada, and settled at Niagara, Upper Canada. Here he established the *Chronicle*, a weekly newspaper, and kept a bookshop. Later he founded at Niagara a woollen factory. In 1857 he was elected to represent Niagara in the Legislative Assembly of Canada, and he continued to sit for this constituency until 1864. For three months in 1864 he was provincial secretary in the Taché-Macdonald government; but on the formation of the Brown-Macdonald coalition, he was appointed assistant auditor-general of Canada—a position which he held until his death at Ottawa, on September 19, 1878. He published *The Canadian forget-me-not for 1837* (Niagara, 1837), and *The Canadian mercantile almanack* (Niagara, 1844).

Simpson, John (1812-1885), senator of Canada, was born at Rothes, near Elgin, Scotland, in May, 1812. He was brought to Canada by his parents in 1816, and began life in 1825 as a clerk at Darlington, Upper Canada. He became a successful general merchant; and in 1848 he opened a branch of the Bank of Montreal at Bowmanville, and later another branch at Whitby. In 1857 he was one of the founders of the Ontario Bank, and he became president of this bank. From 1856 to 1867 he represented the Queen's division as a Liberal in the Legislative Council of Canada; and in 1867 he was called to the Senate of Canada by royal proclamation. He died at Bowmanville, Ontario, on March 21, 1885.

Simpson, Thomas (1808-1840), explorer, was born at Dingwall, Ross-shire, Scotland, on July 2, 1808, the son of Alexander Simpson, and the nephew of Sir George Simpson (q.v.). He was educated at the University of Aberdeen (B.A., 1828; M.A., 1829), and in 1829 he entered the service of the Hudson's Bay Company. In 1836-40 he commanded an important expedition which explored the Arctic coast of North America. On his return from this expedition, he was killed, or else committed suicide, near Turtle river, in the Hudson's Bay Company territories, on June 14, 1840. His *Narrative of the discoveries on the north coast of America . . . during the years of 1836-39* was published posthumously (London, 1843). See A. Simpson, *The life and travels of Thomas Simpson* (London, 1845).

Simpson. See **Fort Simpson.**

Simpson pass is in the Rocky mountains, on the boundary between British Columbia and Alberta, about 25 miles north-west of White Man pass, and has an altitude of 6,914 feet. It divides the waters flowing into Bow river from those flowing into the Kootenay river. The first recorded crossing was made by Sir George Simpson (q.v.) in 1841, when on his famous trip around the world.

Simpson strait, the passage between King William island and Adelaide peninsula, in the Franklin district of the North West Territories. It was named after Thomas Simpson (q.v.), the head of the Simpson-Dease expedition of 1836-40.

Sinclair, Alexander (1818-1897), pioneer and author, was born in Scotland in 1818, emigrated to Canada in 1831, settled in the western part of Upper Canada, and died near Ridgetown, Ontario, on December 17, 1897.

He was the author of a pamphlet, *Pioneer reminiscences* (Toronto, 1898).

Sinclair, Alexander Maclean (1840-1924), clergyman and Gaelic scholar, was born near Antigonish, Nova Scotia, in 1840. He was educated at Pictou Academy, and at the Presbyterian College, Halifax; and was ordained a minister of the Presbyterian Church in 1866. He held various pastoral charges in Nova Scotia and Prince Edward Island; and he came to be recognized in Canada as an outstanding authority on the Gaelic language and literature. Among the books published by him were *Peoples and languages of the world* (Charlottetown, Prince Edward Island, 1894), *Clan Gillean* (Charlottetown, Prince Edward Island, 1899), and *Mactalla nan tur* (Sydney, Nova Scotia, 1901), the last a collection of Gaelic poetry. In 1907 he was appointed lecturer on the Gaelic language and literature at Dalhousie University, Halifax. He died on February 14, 1924.

Sinclair, Samuel Bower (1855-1933), educationist and author, was born at Ridgetown, Ontario, in 1855. He was educated at Victoria University (B.A., 1889), at the University of Toronto (M.A., 1893), and at Chicago University (Ph.D., 1901). He was one of the pioneers in teacher-training in Canada, having been appointed principle of the Teachers' Training School in Hamilton in 1886. For many years he was dean of the Teachers' Training School at Macdonald College. He died in Toronto on December 20, 1933. He was the author of *First years at school* (New York, 1894), *The possibility of a science of education* (Toronto, 1903), *Brilliant and backward children* (Toronto, 1931), and, with Frederick Tracy, was joint author of *Introductory educational psychology* (Toronto, 1909).

Sintaluta, a village in the Qu'Appelle district, Saskatchewan, on the main line of the Canadian Pacific Railway, 50 miles east of Regina. It is in a mixed farming district, and has five grain elevators and a weekly newspaper (*Times and Fort Qu'Appelle Gazette*). Pop. (1931), 333.

Sioux, the most numerous linguistic family of Indians north of Mexico, next to the Algonkian family. The name is an abbreviation of the term "Nadowessioux", a French corruption of *Nadowe-is-iw* (meaning "rattle-snake" or "enemy"), the name applied to the Sioux by the Chippewa. The Sioux occupied originally the territory stretching from the valley of the upper Mississippi to the Rocky mountains, and they even extended northward into the Red river valley; but they cannot be described strictly as Canadian Indians. A few of them are found to-day on reserves in Manitoba and Saskatchewan, descendants of the bands that in 1876, under Sitting Bull, annihilated the force of General Custer, and then sought refuge in Canada.

Sioux Lookout, a town in Kenora district, Ontario, on the transcontinental line of the Canadian National Railways, south-east of lac Seul, and 250 miles east of Winnipeg. It is a railway divisional point, a distributing centre for the Red lake mining district, and an outfitting point for hunters, fishermen, and trappers. It has also a large creosote plant, lumber mills, and a weekly newspaper (*Northern Observer*), established in 1930. Pop. (1931), 2,088.

Sipiwesk, a station on the Hudson's Bay Railway, on Sipiwesk lake, 180 miles north-east of The Pas. Sipiwesk House of the Hudson's Bay Company was built here in 1792.

Sipiwesk lake, in northern Manitoba, is an extension of the Nelson river, in 97° 30′ west longitude. The name is Cree Indian for "lake of channels." The lake has an area of 201 square miles.

Sir Alexander, mount, is in the Cariboo district of British Columbia, about lat. 54°, long. 120° 15′, and has an altitude of 11,000 feet. It was named after Sir Alexander Mackenzie (q.v.), who crossed the Rockies to the Pacific in 1793 near this mountain.

Sir Donald, mount, is in the Kootenay district of British Columbia, in the Sir Donald range of the Selkirk mountains. It is in lat. 51° 16′, long. 117° 25′, and has an altitude of 10,808 feet. It was named by order-in-council in 1885 after Lord Strathcona (q.v.), then Sir Donald A. Smith.

Sir Douglas, mount, is on the boundary between Alberta and British Columbia. It is in lat. 50° 43½′, long. 150° 20′, and has an altitude of 11,174 feet. It may be the mountain that was named Robinson by Captain Palliser (q.v.). It is named after Field Marshal Sir Douglas Haig (later Earl Haig of Bemersyde), commander-in-chief of the British armies in France during the World War.

Sir George Williams College, an educational institution founded in Montreal by the Young Men's Christian Association. It is named after Sir George Williams (1821-1905), the founder of the Young Men's Christian Association in England; and it is situated on Drummond street, Montreal. Since 1873 the Young Men's Christian Association in Montreal has carried on educational classes; and in 1920 it inaugurated the Evening High School. In 1926 the board of directors of this school adopted the name "Sir George Williams College" to designate their expanding educational programme. The College was made co-educational in 1926; a building campaign was held, and a large endowment was obtained; the plant and the equipment were enlarged; in 1929 the curriculum was extended to include first year university work in arts, science, commerce, and engineering; in 1931 a junior college of arts, science, and commerce was organized, covering two years of college work; and in 1934 the junior college was expanded into a faculty of

arts, science, and commerce. The principal of the college is K. E. Norris.

Sir Sandford, mount, is in the Kootenay district of British Columbia. It is one of the Sir Sandford range, north of Gold river in the Selkirk mountains. It is in lat. 51° 39′, long. 117° 52′, and has an altitude of 11,590 feet. It was named after Sir Sandford Fleming (q.v.).

Sisters Antoniennes of Mary (Sisters of St. Anthony of Padua). This order was founded in 1904; and like many other orders it owes its existence to local events and to some new needs. For many years the Seminary of Chicoutimi had recourse to the good services in housekeeping of the Sisters of Good Counsel of Chicoutimi. These Sisters, whose principal work was teaching, could not continue this work indefinitely. The Seminary was authorized by the bishop of Chicoutimi to found a new congregation, whose special work would be the interior housekeeping of the Seminaries and all other spiritual or temporal works that could contribute to the recruiting of the clergy. In 1917 the Rev. Father M. P. Hudon, pastor of Murray Bay, with the help of the Sisters Antoniennes, founded an apostolic orphanage at Murray Bay. In 1918 the Seminary of Chicoutimi confided its preparatory class, which became the Apostolic School, to the Sisters. In March, 1924, the Sisters Antoniennes took charge of the housekeeping of the Canadian Seminary of Foreign Missions at Pont Viau. In 1931, they were called to Worcester, Massachusetts, by the Augustinian Fathers of Assumption. The Fathers entrusted them with the housekeeping of their Franco-American College. Lastly, in 1934, the Sisters Antoniennes accepted the housekeeping of the agricultural school at St. Martine, Châteauguay. The principal aim of the institute, as of all other religious institutes, is the sanctification of its members. Its second purpose is to lend a humble but useful service to the clergy in the work of sacerdotal recruitment. The Institute devotes itself to foreign missions; it also assumes the care of retired priests, the housekeeping of the episcopal houses, and other houses under the direction of the clergy.

Sister-Servants of the Immaculate Heart of Mary.

The Congregation of the Sister-Servants of the Immaculate Heart of Mary, incorporated under the title of Good Shepherd Asylum, Quebec, was founded by Sir George Manly Muir, barrister and clerk of the Legislative Assembly, Quebec, and also a zealous member of the Society of St. Vincent de Paul. A poor widow, Mrs. F. X. Roy, was the instrument chosen by Providence to effect the execution of his pious project. Under the name of Mother Mary of the Sacred Heart, Mrs. Roy became the first superioress of the new institute. On January 11, 1850, the first refuge, first called St. Magdalen, was opened in a dilapidated tenement building in one of the poorest districts of Quebec; and the very next day, January 12, the first penitent was admitted.

The aim of the Institute was twofold: first came "the conversion of wayward girls and the preservation of children by means of education"; then, as a secondary aim, teaching was added. These very modest beginnings were followed by a gradual, but steady period of development. In 1855, the Institute was incorporated under the name of Good Shepherd Asylum of Quebec; in 1856, it was raised to a religious community by the archbishop of Quebec, under the title of the Congregation of the Sister-Servants of the Immaculate Heart of Mary. Since then, the Congregation has made marvellous headway; at present (1935), it numbers 963 sisters, shelters 3,662 inmates, and gives instruction to 13,057 children. A maternity hospital and a foundling home receive yearly approximately 700 new-born infants; these are provided for from birth until adopted by some charitable persons. There is, furthermore, a kindergarten, or Hospice of Holy Angels, for these same children from the ages of 2 to 7. An industrial school, the Hospice St. Charles, cares for girls from 7 to 14. The St. Geneviève Protectory completes the first period of education by a practical training in house-keeping, culinary, and other domestic arts. In fine, the St. Magdalen's Home houses wayward girls and repentant women. Bethany solidifies their conversion, assures their perseverance by their consecration for life under the name of Magdalens. For some years past, the sisters have had charge of the women's jail or Refuge of Our Lady of Mercy, and of two orphanages for abandoned boys and girls. The work of education counts numerous establishments such as boarding-schools, day-schools, academies, a school of home economics, and a normal school. These houses extend their beneficial work to the regions of Chicoutimi, Gaspé, and the United States.

Sisters of Charity. See Grey Nuns.

Sisters of Charity,

of Halifax, Nova Scotia. When Elizabeth Bayley Seton, the founder of this community first thought of becoming a religious, she looked at first towards Canada, where native communities of women flourished; but through the advice of Bishop Carroll of Baltimore, she remained at home and founded her own mother house and girls' academy in St. Joseph's valley, Emmitsburg, Maryland, in 1809. In 1849, however, one of her spiritual daughters, Sister Basilia McCann, came to Halifax at Bishop Walsh's request, and established the first religious community in that city at St. Mary's Convent. As early as 1856, St. Mary's was raised to the rank of an independent mother house, and the little congregation grew and flourished. In 1873, through the beneficence of Archbishop Connolly (q.v.), a new mother house, Mount St. Vincent, was erected on a beautiful property overlooking Bedford basin, which is one arm of Halifax harbour. Here Mount St. Vincent Academy, a boarding school for girls, was opened at the same time. From the beginning the standard set for this school has been "a liberal education", and many of its daughters have played a worthy part upon the Canadian scene and elsewhere. In 1894, thanks to a memorial prepared by the Hon. L. G. Power and presented by the supervisor of schools, the Council of Public Instruction recognized Mount St. Vincent training school for teachers as a provincial normal school for Sisters. The Mount edifice of to-day consists of three main buildings and two wings.

At present, the Sisters conduct twenty-seven schools, grammar and high, in Nova Scotia, and maintain a residence for normal school students in Truro. In the sister province of New Brunswick, they have a grammar and a high school in Bathurst, and another grammar school around the head of Chaleur bay, in Bathurst West. In Hamilton, Bermuda, they conduct a very successful academy, Mount St. Agnes.

By 1887, the Sisters' activities in Halifax had become, as they continue to be, widely varied. St. Joseph's Orphanage, a bright spacious building, surrounded by ample grounds, looks after the welfare, physical, intellectual, and moral of two hundred and more boys and girls. The Home of the Angel Guardian shelters foundlings, and helps unmarried mothers. Recently, the Home had a record of only one death among infants in two years. St. Teresa's Retreat, established originally as a home for working girls, has become also a haven for old ladies who wish to spend their last days under the Sisters' care. The Halifax Infirmary outgrew its earlier domicile, and to-day, the new Infirmary, a last work in hospital beauty, comfort, and efficiency, has prospered beyond expectation ever since it opened its doors to patients in January, 1933.

In 1887, with the establishment of St. Parrick's Parochial School—later a high school—in Boston, a southward expansion began. Now, the community has six flourishing schools in and around Boston, including three high schools and a large boarding academy for girls, with another for young boys, both delightfully situated in the township of Wellesley Hills. The opening of the School of Our Lady of the Angels, at Brooklyn, New York, in 1924, marked a still more southerly expansion. At present, the Congregation has seven schools in New York state, and two in New Jersey.

In 1923, the Sisters accepted the far-flung parish of Ladysmith, British Columbia. To-day they have six excellent schools on the Pacific coast, among them Seton Academy on Vancouver Heights, a boarding school for girls. Schools in Edmonton, hospitals in Westlock, Hardisty, Jasper Park, Alberta, and Swan River, Manitoba, form the stepping-stones of the community from sea to sea.

By 1917, higher education having become a necessity for young women, the Hon. L. G. Power introduced into the legislature of Nova Scotia a bill granting Mount St. Vincent a college charter. He secured its passage through the House of Assembly, but failed in the now non-existent Legislative Council. In 1925, however, influential friends finally secured the passing of a bill which empowered Mount St. Vincent to grant college degrees. The College has already five degree-granting departments, namely: arts, science, secretarial science, household science, and music. In 1932-3, the first course in journalism ever taught in Halifax was given by a Sister professor.

During the years from 1856 to 1935, the Institute of the Sisters of Charity of Halifax has opened houses in five provinces of the Dominion (Nova Scotia, New Brunswick, Manitoba, Alberta, and British Columbia), in four states of the Union (Massachusetts, New York, New Jersey, and Washington), and in Bermuda. The Sisters maintain forty-three houses in Canada, sixteen in the United States, and one in Bermuda; they teach in fifty-eight schools, and administer six hospitals. In 1908, Pius X raised the Sisterhood to the rank of a papal community; its present protector is Cardinal Sbaretti, sometime apostolic delegate to Canada. The Congregation now numbers, as professed members and novices, 1,190 women who devote their lives entirely to public and private good.

Sisters of Charity of Notre Dame d'Evron. This Congregation was founded in 1861 in the diocese of Le Mans, France, for the purpose of educating children and nursing the sick. The first sisters arrived in Canada in 1909, and established themselves in Saskatchewan.

Sisters of Charity of Providence (Montreal). The Institute of the Sisters of Charity of Providence was founded at Montreal, Canada, in 1843, by Bishop Bourget (q.v.) and the venerated Mother Gamelin (q.v.), first superior-general of the Institute. The principal end of the Institute is the sanctification of its members by the practice of the vows of religion and the observance of its constitutions, definitely approved on September 12, 1900, by the Holy See. The secondary and specific aim of the Institute is to serve God in the person of the poor, the homeless, and the aged, the sick and the infirm, the mentally afflicted, deaf-mute girls, and orphan children of both sexes, and in giving Christian education from kindergarten to college in its various schools in Canada and the States, as well as in many Indian missions. The Institute of Providence has grown remarkably strong and vigorous, extending west-ward to the Pacific ocean, as far south as Oakland, California, and as far north as Fairbanks, Alaska, and Fort Ver-milion, Alberta, close to the Arctic circle. It is also in different parts of the

east, and from New Brunswick and Nova Scotia to Jersey city, New Jersey, on the Atlantic coast. At present the Institute has a personnel of 3,120 members, apart from 250 novices in training, both in the eastern and western noviti-ates of the Institute.

Sisters of Charity of St. Louis. This congregation was founded in Brittany, in 1803, for the education of poor girls in orphanages and parochial schools. In 1903, the Sisters came to Canada, where they met with a hospitable reception and spread very rapidly. In 1934, the Canadian province adminis-tered 50 houses distributed from Quebec city to Calgary, Alberta. In 1910, the Congregation inaugurated its educa-tional activities in the United States of America. The Canadian mother-house is at Bienville, Lévis, Quebec.

Sisters of Hope (Sœurs de l'Espérance). The Sisters of Hope are a branch of the Holy Family of Bordeaux, founded in 1820 by Canon Pierre Bienvenu Noailles. Their mission is to nurse the sick in their own homes. These Sisters were called to Montreal in 1901 by Mgr. Bruchési, and to Quebec in 1903 by Cardinal Bégin (q.v.). They had in 1935 five houses in Canada.

Sisters of Jesus-Mary. The Congregation of Jesus and Mary comprises two groups of religious: choir religious, to whom is confined the education of youth, and auxiliary sisters, who, in the different houses, take charge of the manual labour. In some countries, as in India, where the customs of the people are entirely different from those of Europeans, the religious of Jesus-Mary have been authorized to accept a third class, the associated native Sisters, whose knowledge of the native dialects makes them invaluable to the missions, especially for catechism and religious instruction and in dispensary work. The education of youth is the first duty of the religious of Jesus-Mary. The Congregation has 12 houses in

Canada, 10 in the United States, 6 in England, 2 in Ireland, 12 in Spain, and 4 in South America. The Sisters have in these various countries flourishing boarding schools where young girls receive secular training and a solid knowledge of their religion. In the New England states, they conduct several vast parochial schools, where thousands of children are taught.

The Congregation of Jesus-Mary was founded at Lyons, France, in 1818, by Claudine Thevenet, under the direction of Father Coindre. Claudine Thevenet, daughter of a wealthy silk merchant of Lyons, was but nineteen when the French Revolution broke out in 1793. During the days of the "Terror" she became a veritable apostle of charity, gaining access to the prisons, and encouraging the prisoners among whom were two of her own brothers, who were martyred. Later, aided by a number of other young women, she formed a charitable association, the aim of which was the religious instruction of the poor children of Lyons. She was seconded in her zealous work by Father André Coindre, a priest of Lyons, who became protector of the little society. He confided to her his plans of founding a community of religious for the education of the young girls of the poorer classes. On October 6, 1818, Claudine Thevenet left home, and occupied a miserable dwelling under the shadow of Notre Dame de Fourvières, where she assumed the care of orphans. It was on this same hill of Fourvières that, in 1821, the first boarding school for young ladies of the higher class was opened. Thus the little Congregation, from the outset, united the teaching of the poorer with that of the higher class.

In 1855, Mother St. Cyprien at the head of a colony of religious left France to establish the first house in Canada, at St. Joseph de Lévis. There are at present 12 houses in Canada, the principal one and provincialate being at Sillery near Quebec. For a few years,

Sillery has offered the advantage of a college course to both French and English-speaking students, and the degree of B.A. is conferred by Laval University. Here also, as in New York and in different cities, the religious of Jesus-Mary conduct a residence for ladies, where the latter may enjoy the benefits of a home atmosphere along with the charms of solitude as desired. Other houses in Canada are at Trois-Pistoles, St. Michel, St. Gervais, Beauceville (which has a normal school for girls), and Lameque, New Brunswick. The Convent of Gravelbourg, Saskatchewan, opened in 1915, now has its own novitiate for the west of Canada, and dependent on it are two parochial schools.

In 1896 Pope Leo XIII permitted the foundation of a house in Rome; and later the mother house of the Congregation was removed from Fourvières to Rome. The present mother-general is Mother Borgia; Cardinal Marchetti Selvaggiani is protector of the Congregation. Besides the Mother House, there is also, in Rome, situated on the Via Nomentana, just opposite the Villa Mirafiori, a college under the direction of the religious of Jesus-Mary which offers young ladies who have enjoyed a liberal education in their own country the opportunity of perfecting themselves in foreign languages and specializing in music and art, under professors of high repute in the schools of Rome.

After an existence of 100 years, the Congregation counts at present over 1,500 religious spread throughout Europe, Asia, and America, in 60 houses, with an attendance of 15,000 pupils.

Sisters of Mercy (Miséricorde). This community was founded in Montreal in 1848 by Mgr. Bourget (q.v.) and by Madame Rosalie Jetté, Sœur de la Nativité. In addition to its special work, which is the reclamation of sinners, it has established and operated a number of hospitals throughout Canada and parts of the United States.

Sisters of Our Lady of Angels.
This Institute was founded in 1919, by
Mlle. Florina Gervais (Mother Marie du
Sacré-Cœur), who is still alive. Its aim
was to offer to Chinese girls the
advantage of religious apostolic life.
The Institute has 3 houses in Canada:
the mother-house, at Lennoxville, Quebec; the Home of Our Lady of Angels,
at Victoriaville; a school at Beebe
Plain in China; and it has 7 mission
stations. The Chinese and Canadian
Sisters are occupied in the following
works in their different Missions: Five
dispensaries, two orphanages, three
cribs, two normal schools, three English
schools, and two workhouses. On an
average, the Sisters care for over
300,000 sick *per annum.*

Sisters of Our Lady of Chambriac.
This congregation originated in 1732.
At Usson-en-Forez, France, there is an
antique sanctuary dedicated to Notre
Dame de Chambriac; and it was here
that four pious young girls joined in
1732 to devote themselves to good works
and to found a religious family under the
auspices of the Blessed Virgin. About
1845, a series of circumstances led to
the division of the Institute into two
branches: one known under the name
of Notre Dame de Clermont, with its
mother-house at Chamalières; the other
known as Notre Dame de Fourvières,
with its mother-house at Lyons. The
two communities, which had always
remained united by the same rule and
the links of the most fraternal affection,
were re-united in 1928, and a decree of
the Sacred Congregation has consecrated their union under their original
title, "Congregation de Notre Dame de
Chambriac". The aims of the Congregation are the education of children and
the care of the sick in hospitals, dispensaries, home visits, etc. The Congregation has houses in several dioceses of
France, in Switzerland, and in Canada.
In 1913, accepting the invitation of
late Rev. Father Albert Royer, founder
of the parish of Notre Dame d'Auvergne,

Ponteix, Saskatchewan, six sisters left
France for Canada. They immediately
opened a school at Ponteix. In 1918 the
sisters opened also a small hospital at
Ponteix; and in 1930 this hospital was
enlarged and equipped with modern
X-ray equipment.

**Sisters of Our Lady of Charity of
Refuge.** The Order of Our Lady of
Charity of Refuge was founded at
Caën, France, in 1641, by a missionary,
St. Jean Eudes. The constitutions of the
order received the approbation of the
bishop of Bayeux, in 1670, in accordance
with the authority he had received from
Pope Alexander VII in 1666. Its
general end, in common with that of
all other congregations in the Catholic
Church, is to serve God by a perfect
imitation of the virtues of Our Lord and
His Blessed Mother. But the special
and peculiar aim of the Daughters of
Our Lady of Charity, whereby they are
distinguished from others, is to imitate,
as exactly as possible, the ardent
charity of Jesus by the rehabilitation of
young girls and women fallen into licen-
tiousness, the preservation of young girls
who are exposed to moral dangers, the
correction of young girls, sent by civil
or family authorities, and the sanctification of those who willingly accept a life
of penance in imitation of Mary
Magdalen. The order has five mon-
asteries in Canada and two in the
United States.

**Sisters of Our Lady of Charity of
the Good Shepherd.** The founder of
this community was St. Jean Eudes
(1601-1680), a great missionary who
established the Congregation of Jesus
and Mary (Eudist Fathers) in 1643,
and the Sisters of Our Lady of Charity
in 1641, at Caën, France. In 1815, Rose
Virginia Pelletier (1796-1868) entered
the community of Our Lady of Charity,
which had been founded at Tours,
France. She became superior at the
early age of 29, and in 1829 she was
called to Angers, France, to found a
convent there. In 1844, four zealous

religious were sent from Angers to Montreal on the request of Mgr. Bourget (q.v.), bishop of Montreal. This little branch became later on a large tree. It is the provincial monastery situated at 104 East Sherbrooke Street, to which is attached a novitiate. Three hundred protected girls find shelter under the maternal care of the devoted daughters of Blessed Mother Pelletier. From this house have spread the following foundations in Canada: Asile Ste. Darie (Female Jail and St. Helen's Home for Protected Girls), 1730 Fullum Street, Montreal; Maison Ste. Domitille (Industrial School and Solitude of the Magdalens), Laval-des-Rapides, near Montreal; Maison de Lorette (Reformatory School), Laval-des-Rapides; at Halifax, Nova Scotia, a refuge, an industrial school, a reformatory, a solitude for Magdalens, and also an English novitiate; at Saint John, New Brunswick, a refuge, industrial school, and reformatory; at West Kildonan, near Winnipeg, Manitoba, a reformatory, a refuge, and an industrial school; and at St. Hubert, Quebec, and at St. Louis-de-Gonzague, Montreal, boarding convents for young ladies.

Sisters of Our Lady of Good Counsel. This sisterhood was founded and erected canonically in 1923 by Mgr. Gauthier, coadjutor archbishop of Montreal, with the approbation of the Sacred Congregation of Religious Institutions, and the blessing of Pope Pius XI. The members are trained to become competent in several employments, such as (a) domestic and industrial occupations; (b) such social service works as hostels, free employment bureaux, and recreational centres for young girls; (c) educational works of a three-fold character, religious, social, and home-making, through study guilds, evening classes, etc. The object of these Sisters is to offer their fellow-women in different walks of life the opportunity of acquiring what their early training may have lacked; and to help them to remain staunch in their faith, and better able to do their part in the lay-apostolate that each one is called upon to exercise in her own sphere. The Sisters help the parochial clergy in organizing groups of feminine Catholic Action, or in training its leaders. The mother-house is situated at 5035 De-Laroche Street, Montreal. The Sisters have also been actively engaged since 1930 in the towns of St. Jérôme and St. Hyacinthe, Quebec.

Sisters of Our Lady of Good Counsel. The Institute of the Sisters of Our Lady of Good Counsel was founded in Canada in 1894. The foundress and first superior was Frances Simard, a pious person possessing the qualities required for this purpose. The congregation comprises sisters devoting their life to the instruction of children, and lay sisters occupied with domestic work, without any difference regarding rank or habits. The teaching sisters study to form the heart and mind of their scholars by inculcating in them principles of Christian life. When leaving school, students are prepared to represent Catholic thought, to develop personally along Catholic lines, and to live up to their belief. The Institute numbers at present (1935) 198 professed sisters and 30 novices and postulants. It has 16 mission houses located in the counties of Quebec, Saguenay, and Lake St. John. There are 4,335 children taught in the 16 convents, under the control of the Catholic Committee of Public Instruction.

Sisters of Our Lady of Mont Laurier. This congregation was founded in 1921 for teaching purposes, as well as for the material care of sanctuaries and colleges. To-day the sisters number 62, distributed in three schools and three other establishments, located in the Mont-Laurier diocese and in Boston, Massachusetts.

Sisters of Our Lady of Perpetual Help. The Order of the Sisters of Our

Lady of Perpetual Help was founded in 1892 by the Rev. Joseph Onésime Brousseau, who was at that time parish priest at St. Damien of Buckland, Bellechasse county, Quebec. It was incorporated in 1894 by the Canadian parliament. Its works of philanthropy to-day are limited to the following: asylums for the poor, agricultural orphanages, domestic science schools, and parochial schools. The Sisters of Our Lady of Perpetual Help have given primary agricultural and domestic science instruction to more than 100,000 boys and girls. At present they are teaching in 27 parochial schools of Quebec and one in Northern Ontario. Father Brousseau's ideal was to promote greater love for agriculture, and thereby to induce people to return to their abandoned farms. He wished also to prevent Canadian immigration to the United States.

Sisters of Our Lady of Sion. The Sisters of Our Lady of Sion owe their foundation to Fathers Alphonse and Théodore Ratisbouce, two Hebrew converts, who destined the small community to the Christian education of Jewish girls. To-day the sisters are found throughout the world. Canada has four houses in Saskatchewan, with a novitiate at Prince Albert.

Sisters of Our Lady of the Cross of Murinais. The Community of "Les Religieuses de Notre Dame de la Croix," was founded in 1832, by the Abbé Buisson and Mlle. Odèle d'Auberjon de Murinais at Murinais, France. Its members have a two-fold aim: to sanctify themselves and to serve their neighbours by the performance of every possible act of charity, but chiefly by the education and instruction of youth and the care of the sick, whether at home or in hospitals. In 1902, several members of the Institute founded colonies in Belgium. In 1905, another group crossed the seas, and settled themselves in Forget, Saskatchewan. There a flourishing academy and a novitiate have grown up. In 1907, the small community of Forget sent two of its members to St. Hubert's Mission, near Whitewood, Saskatchewan, to help the Sons of Mary Immaculate in their mission work. Here they founded Joan of Arc Home. Wauchope, Montmartre, and Estevan, all in Saskatchewan, claim other establishments of the order, where the same work is being accomplished as at Forget. In Regina, a group of Sisters have been in charge of the domestic interests of the "Regina Cleri Seminary" since 1930. The constitutions of the Congregation were definitely approved by the Holy See in 1929.

Sisters of Our Lady of the Holy Rosary. The Congregation of the Sisters of Our Lady of the Holy Rosary was founded in 1874 in the city of Rimouski, by the Most Rev. J. Langevin, first bishop of the diocese of Rimouski, and Elizabeth Turgeon, with the special aim of the Christian instruction and education of children in parochial schools. The Sisters of Our Lady of the Holy Rosary are now directing 33 schools distributed in the dioceses of Rimouski, Gaspé, Quebec, and Chicoutimi, in Canada, and Portland, Maine, in the United States. Everywhere they settle they prove very helpful to all parochial works: not only do they teach, but they also take special care to impart to young girls domestic economy both theoretically and practically. Moreover, they are helpful to the clergy by taking care of the sacristy and altar linens.

Sisters of Our Lady of the Missions. The Institute of Our Lady of the Missions was founded at Lyons, France, in 1861, by the Very Rev. Mother Marie du Cœur de Jésus. Three years later, in 1864, four sisters from the young Institute embarked at London for New Zealand, and after a voyage of five months landed at Napier, Hawkes bay, where they opened the first missionary convent of their Congregation. There are now over thirty houses of the

Institute in New Zealand. Soon the order spread to other countries so that, at the present day, Sisters of Our Lady of Missions have establishments in England, Ireland, France, Switzerland, East and West Australia, New Zealand, British India, Indo-China, and Canada. The Institute was established in Canada in August, 1898, at Grande Clairière, Manitoba. Fourteen houses now exist in the provinces of Manitoba, Saskatchewan, and Ontario. In 1910 the Institute was incorporated by Act of the Dominion parliament. The provincial house of Manitoba and Ontario is at Letellier, Manitoba; that of Saskatchewan is the Sacred Heart College, at Regina. This College is affiliated with the Universities of Saskatchewan and Ottawa, for courses leading to the degree of bachelor of Arts. Besides the College, there is in Regina the Sacred Heart Academy and St. Mary's Convent. The primary work of the Institute of Our Lady of the Missions is education, whether in elementary schools, academies, or colleges. Where necessary, the Sisters visit the poor and the sick. In missionary countries, the Sisters have orphanages, workrooms, hospitals, dispensaries, etc. In 1934, they took charge of a government leper-hospital in Indo-China. The general house was in 1901 transferred to Hastings, Sussex, England.

Sisters of Our Lady of the Sacred Heart. The Congregation of Our Lady of the Sacred Heart was founded on February 17, 1924, by the bishop of St. John, New Brunswick. It is a detached branch of the English-speaking community of the Reverend Sisters of Charity of the Immaculate Conception, founded in 1854 by Bishop Connolly (q.v.), then bishop of St. John. On February 17, 1924, the new congregation was recognized by Rome under the name of "Our Lady of the Sacred Heart". It is now composed of nearly 200 sisters, and operates four boarding-schools and four day-schools, where both French and English are taught. The Sisters of Our Lady of the Sacred Heart are principally teaching sisters. Their work, however, includes also hospitals and orphan's homes. Theirs is the first French-Acadian community founded in the Maritime provinces. In 1931, they opened a mission in Louisiana, where they are actively engaged in the educational interests of the descendants of the exiles of 1755.

Sisters of Service (S.O.S.). The Institute of the Sisters of Service was founded in August, 1922. Its foundation was the result of religious problems arising from the immigration into Canada of Catholics from the British isles and continental Europe. The care of immigrants, from the moment of their arrival until they are happily settled, is the special work of the Sisters of Service. This work has various phases. It includes the meeting of immigrants at the ports, and looking after them in the hostels in large cities. The Sisters conduct hospitals for the care of the immigrant, and they also have charge of schools, where the pupils are all children of Catholic immigrants, who would not otherwise receive any religious training. A most important branch of their work is the teaching of the catechism by mail. Over 10,000 children receive religious instruction from catechetical centres in Alberta and Saskatchewan. During the summer months the Sisters get in personal touch with the pupils by means of catechism tours. Although canonically erected according to all the laws of the Church, the Community of the Sisters of Service differs somewhat in outward appearance from other communities. The habit of the Sisters is not strictly religious, but rather a uniform, somewhat like that of a nurse. This is found more convenient for the work they are called to do. The Sisters receive two and a half years' training to fit them for the religious life and the special work of their vocation before being sent to the missions. Their missions are in the provinces of Nova Scotia, Quebec, Ontario, Manitoba, Saskatchewan, Alberta, and British Columbia. Their headquarters are in Toronto.

Sisters of St. Anne (S.S.A.), a religious congregation devoted to the education of youth and to works of charity, which was founded on September 8, 1850, at Vaudreuil, Quebec, by Bishop Bourget (q.v.), of Montreal, and Marie Esther Sureau-Blondin, venerated by her spiritual daughters as Mother Mary Ann. In 1853, the community was transferred to St. Jacques l'Achigan. The Sisters accepted the direction of a boarding school, already established by the Ladies of the Sacred Heart, and also taught the children of the village. In all, they numbered 24 professed sisters and 12 novices. Four remained to conduct the convent at Vaudreuil; three stayed at St. Geneviève, a branch house opened in 1851. At Lachine, in 1861, the residence of the late governor of the Hudson's Bay Company, Sir George Simpson (q.v.), was purchased to found a boarding-school for the education of young ladies. This institution, opened in September of the same year, progressed rapidly, and is still flourishing. Finding it expedient to be nearer Montreal, the mother-house and the novitiate were removed from St. Jacques to Lachine in 1864, and the present large edifice was erected in 1870. Subsequently, Governor Simpson's house was demolished, and was replaced by the Community's chapel, known as the Sanctuary of St. Anne. Since 1909, the general administration and the novitiate have occupied a spacious building about a mile distant, on an elevation called Mount St. Anne. Here are the headquarters of the whole Institute.

As early as 1858, Sisters of St. Anne crossed the continent, and opened schools, hospitals, and a novitiate, in Victoria, British Columbia, in 1889. From here branches have stretched north to beneath the Arctic Circle, to Alaska, and in the far east to Japan. The work of the Sisters has so expanded that to-day they number 2,309, and conduct nearly 100 institutions, scattered throughout the archdioceses of Montreal, Ottawa, Vancouver, and Boston, the dioceses of Joliette, Valleyfield, Mont-Laurier, Saint-Jean, Victoria, Springfield, Providence, Albany, Seattle, the apostolic vicariates of Alaska and Prince Rupert, and the prefecture of Kagoshima. Whether in day or boarding schools, the course of studies includes kindergartens, primary, grammar, commercial, and high school subjects. Among the 50 residential and day academies in Montreal and its vicinity, may be mentioned St. Anne's Boarding School, Lachine; St. Angela's, St. Cunégonde; Guarding Angel, St. Henry; Luke Callaghan Memorial School, Montreal; Holy Angel's Academy, St. Jérôme; and St. Anne's, Rigaud. These are high schools affiliated with Montreal University. The Sisters of St. Anne have also the direction of a regional domestic science school at St. Jacques de Montcalm, a normal school at St. Jérôme de Terrebonne, and a classical college at St. Henri, Montreal. In the eastern States, the Congregation has charge of many Franco-American parochial schools. It also conducts St. Anne's Academy, Malborough, Massachusetts, a select boarding school, affiliated with the Catholic University of Washington. In British Columbia, the humble "log cabin", half of which served as a "school" and half as a "convent", has expanded to an imposing chain of modern schools and academies, such as St. Anne's Academy, Victoria; Little Flower Academy, Vancouver; St. Anne's Academies of New Westminster and Kamloops, respectively.

The objective of these establishments is to prepare cultured and practical Christian women for society. To this the Sisters direct their efforts by giving moral, intellectual, and physical training to their pupils. The buildings are well located and modernly equipped, and the curriculum includes music, art, and domestic science.

The *alumnae* of these institutions belong to "St. Anne's Association of Former Pupils," which has for its aim to stimulate Catholic action by study circles, social works of charity, and mission activities. Lay retreats are given twice a year at the mother-house, and annually in the boarding schools.

A few Indian industrial schools, orphanages, private sanitaria, hospitals, and nurses' training schools are conducted by the Sisterhood. Though hospital work is not the specific end of the Institute, it is undertaken at the request of the bishops, and principally in far-away mission regions, where there are no nursing congregations. See the Rev. E. J. Auclair, *Histoire des Sœurs de Sainte-Anne, 1850-1900* (Montreal, 1922).

Sisters of St. Anthony of Padua. See **Sisters Antoniennes of Mary.**

Sisters of Ste. Jean d'Arc. The Congregation of the Sisters of Ste. Jeanne d'Arc was founded on Christmas day, 1914, at Worcester, Massachusetts, by the Rev. Father M. Clement, A.A. Three years later (on September 29, 1917), the centre of the Congregation was transferred to Quebec. The following year, the mother-house was established at Bergerville, near Quebec. The Congregation devotes itself to the sanctification of its members and the spiritual and temporal service of the priesthood. It serves the priesthood in a spiritual way by prayer and in a material way by taking charge of domestic work in rectories, seminaries, ecclesiastical colleges, and apostolic schools. The Institute is ready to accept houses in which aged or retired priests may live a life of prayer and of peace, receiving the care which their age and condition of health demand. The Institute has 30 foundations, with 225 Sisters, of whom 148 are professed.

Sisters of St. Elizabeth. The Canadian mother-house of the Sisters of St. Elizabeth is situated at Humboldt, Saskatchewan, in the territory of the Abbey Nullius of St. Peter. It traces its origin to the Convent of St. Elizabeth (Elizabethinnen-Kloster), at Klagenfurt, Austria, in the diocese of Gurk. With the sanction of the bishop of Prince Albert, and at the urgent invitation of the abbot of St. Peter's Abbey, Muenster, Saskatchewan, three sisters of the convent at Klagenfurt undertook to make a new foundation on Canadian soil in order to provide hospital care among the German-speaking Catholic settlers of western Canada. They arrived at Humboldt, on May 14, 1911. In 1913 the Holy See declared them an autonomous community. In addition to the mother-house, there are at present, in Saskatchewan, four hospitals and one home for the aged, belonging to this community.

Sisters of St. Francis of Assisi. This Congregation was founded at Lyon, France, in 1838, by Anne Rollet. It undertakes the education of young girls, the direction of orphanages, and the care of the sick. The congregation was first established in Canada in 1904. It has several houses in the province of Quebec.

Sisters of St. Joseph. This Congregation was founded in 1650 at Le Puy, France, by a Jesuit father. Originally the Sisters conducted orphanages, as well as schools for the education of young girls. In 1851 the Congregation sent its first members in Canada. They were established in Toronto, and soon were in charge of schools, orphanages, hospitals, and homes for the aged. Today this Congregation has in Canada five independent branches, at Hamilton, London, Peterborough, and Pembroke, with the mother-house at Toronto.

Sisters of St. Joseph (Little Daughters of St. Joseph). The Little Daughters of St. Joseph, established at 2,333 West

Sherbrooke street, Montreal, were founded by the Sulpician, Antoine Mercier, with the object of aiding in spiritual and temporal matters, both by the ministry of prayer and by discharging certain manual services, such as the confection of liturgical vestments and ornaments, the mending and bleaching of the linen used in the altar service, etc. This congregation also helps poor seminaries and missionaries. At present it numbers 10 houses and 180 members.

Sisters of St. Joseph of Newark. The Sisters of St. Joseph of Newark, founded in 1884 at Nottingham, England, have for their object the domestic and industrial training of girls of the working class. In 1885 the first foundation in America was established at Newark, New Jersey. From the American province, some foundations have been made in British Columbia, namely, a hospital at Rossland, a day and boarding school at Nelson, and another at Fernie. The western houses now constitute a province.

Sisters of St. Joseph of St. Hyacinthe. This Institute was founded on September 12, 1877, by Mgr. Louis Zéphirin Moreau, fourth bishop of St. Hyacinthe. At the very beginning of his episcopate, this saintly bishop had turned his attention to the foundation of a teaching institution under whose care a sound Christian education would be given to the children of his diocese. A small school-house in the village of Providence, in the suburbs of the city, was the cradle of the new order. Here four young ladies consecrated themselves to the service of God, and were accepted as teachers. To-day, the Institute comprises 35 parochial schools in the diocese of St. Hyacinthe, 4 industrial Indian schools and 3 parochial schools in western Canada, and a day-school in the state of New Hampshire. In 1881, the little school-house being insufficient, the Sisters took possession of a larger building near the cathedral, and finally, twelve years later, a mother-house was

erected for the Community. In 1935 there were 517 professed sisters, 52 novices, and 63 juvenates, and these had 4,100 pupils under their direction. Like all religious, the Sisters of St. Joseph have specially in view their own perfection, without neglecting to give themselves up to works of apostleship; outside their teaching hours, they visit the sick and assist the dying in the localities where they have schools; consequently, their time is spent in prayer, study, and manual works. The Institute was canonically erected on March 19, 1880, and civil incorporation was granted on June 30, 1881. It has two classes of members. The first class of Sisters are possessors of professional diplomas, and are especially devoted to teaching; the other sisters share in the missionary life by domestic care of their respective religious houses and by devoting themselves to the service of the altar. All the members, however, unite in one family under the same rule, and wear the same habit.

Sisters of St. Joseph of St. Valier. The Congregation of the Sisters of St. Joseph of St. Valier was founded in the city of Le Puy-en-Velay, Haute Loire, France, in 1650. The annals of the order show that on October 15, 1650, the first daughters of St. Joseph were presented by Father Jean Paul Medaille, a famous Jesuit missionary, to the bishop of Le Puy. These young ladies had been already formed by Father Medaille on his ideal, that of realizing the original plan of St. Francis de Sales. They received from the bishop on that same day the holy habit of the Sisters of St. Joseph. The care of destitute children, the charge of hospitals, and the education of youth became the Sisters' first steps in the public life of charity. In 1683 the house of the Sisters of St. Joseph was established at St. Valier. Bishop St. Valier (q.v.), the second bishop of Quebec, desirous of having nuns to take charge of a hospital he had recently founded in that town, obtained from Le Puy Convent the Sisters he required. From the date of their foundation up to the present day the Sisters of St. Joseph of St. Valier have never ceased to devote themselves both to hospital work and to a variety of labours in accord with the spirit of their founders. Later, the establishment in St. Valier became a mother-house, to which was attached a novitiate; and on September 27, 1890, the rules and constitutions of that Institute were definitely approved by Pope Leo XIII. In 1903 the Sisters of St. Joseph of St. Valier came to Canada, where they have a number of convents in the diocese of Quebec. The principal apostolate of the Sisters of St. Joseph in that diocese has been and is to the present day the teaching of parochial schools. Their educational houses are affiliated with Laval University. Their provincial house is in the city of Quebec.

Sisters of St. Martha of St. Hyacinthe). This Community was founded as an institute in 1883 by Rev. Canon J. R. Ouellette, superior of the Seminary of St. Hyacinthe, and by the Rev. Mother St. Martha (Eléanore Charron). It was canonically established as a Congregation in 1890. The articles of its constitutions were approved by the Holy See in 1926. The purpose of this Community is to perform the general household tasks required in seminaries, bishop's palaces, schools, and colleges. It also administers charity. It has eleven establishments, with 137 active members, in eastern Canada and in the United States.

Sisters of Mary (Antigonish). This Community was founded at Antigonish, Nova Scotia, by Mgr. Cameron in 1900. It is engaged in the household duties connected with the diocesan university, in the care of the sick, in the education of youth, and in the direction of orphanages.

Sisters of Mary (Namur). This Congregation was founded at Namur,

Belgium, in 1819, by Dom Gérôme Minsart. It carries on its work of education in convents and in parish schools. The Sisters have establishments in Canada at Vankleek Hill, St. Eugène, Masson, Ottawa, Chapleau, and Ste. Rose de Lima.

Sisters of St. Mary of the Presentation, a Congregation founded in France in 1826 for teaching and charitable purposes. Since then they have added to their aims the domestic care of colleges and rectories. This Congregation has been established at Chicoutimi, Quebec, since 1925.

Sisters of St. Paul. The Community of the Sisters of St. Paul of Chartres was founded in 1694 in a little village of the French Beauce by a modest county parish priest. From the beginning the Sisters have taken care of the poor, the sick, and the education of children. A few years later, the bishop of Chartres called them to his episcopal city; and thirty years after the foundation, the first Sisters left for the missions in Cayenne. The community counts houses in nearly every part of the world. France, Switzerland, England, Ireland, Italy, Antilles, Guiana, Canada, and in the far East China, Cochin, China, Siam, Laos, Annam and Tonking, Japan, Korea, and the Philippine islands. In 1930 they founded an hospice-hospital at Ste. Anne des Monts-Nord, Quebec, and here they take care of the sick and aged, and help in all the other parish work.

Sisters of the Congregation de Notre-Dame. This community was the first religious institute founded in North America for the Christian education of youth and for the work of retreats. It grew and developed at the very origin of New France and of Ville Marie (Montreal). Marguerite Bourgeoys (q. v.), under the direction of the Sulpicians, modeled it after that of the Canonesses of Mattaincourt, to whose extern sodality she had belonged at Troyes. The Congregation may be said to have begun in a stone stable, where she opened her first school, on April 30. 1657.

Unable to continue the work alone, she crossed over to France, and returned with four companions. In spite of untold poverty, uninterrupted toil, and continual danger of attack from the Indians, her heroic task was successfully carried on. Children were received at a very early age. The first of Mother Bourgeoys's charges was not yet five years old. A few little Indian girls were adopted, baptized, and educated by the Sisters. Two of them became nuns, and spent several years instructing their fellow-Indians. Both boys and girls were taught in the school until the Sulpicians took over the former. In order to provide for the instruction of the well-to-do colonists, a boarding-school was opened, where for many years nearly all the girls of Ville-Marie and the surrounding country were taught. Great attention was given not only to religious and secular education, but also to manual training. What is known as domestic economy was a favourite item of Mother Bourgeoys's curriculum. The poorer children were gathered into an industrial school, where they taught how to work and to sanctify manual labour by prayer.

In 1670, the foundress went back to France, and returned in 1672 with six companions and bringing letters patent, signed by Louis XIV. In 1675, she built a stone chapel dedicated to Notre Dame de Bon Secours, a little outside of the settlement, as a place of pilgrimage and to receive the young girls of her sodality.

The Sulpicians, in 1676, opened an Indian mission on the slope of mount Royal. They undertook to teach boys, and asked Sister Bourgeoys to take charge of the girls. Two Sisters were lodged in wigwams, until M. de Belmont, superior of the seminary, gave them the two stone towers which may still be seen in the garden of the Grand Séminaire. In 1676, Mgr. de Laval allowed the

Congregation, now canonically recognized, to admit subjects to religious profession. Its members were to take simple vows and to be uncloistered. They were among the first to adopt a mode of life which is now the most customary among religious women.

In 1683, the Congregation's convent, with all it contained was burned to the ground. The community seemed in danger of dissolution. Mgr. de Laval (q.v.) decided to unite it with the Ursuline order, but Mother Bourgeoys firmly rejected this proposition as being utterly opposed to the specific mission of her little community. The bishop yielded to her wishes, and Providence interposed to save it from destruction. New members came in such numbers that within two years forty had been received. This facilitated the foundation of schools far and near. At first, the Sisters lived with the settlers, and travelled about from village to village, often on horseback, teaching the catechism, till their convents were built. Houses were begun at Pointe-aux-Trembles near Montreal, at Lachine, Champlain, Château Richer, and Ste. Famille, on the island of Orleans.

In 1693, Jeanne Le Ber, daughter of a rich merchant, offered a generous sum of money for the erection of a chapel. One condition was laid down, that a little cell be built behind the altar where she might spend the rest of her life in prayer and retirement. On August 6, two years later, mass was offered for the first time in the Congregation church. From that period dates the perpetual adoration of the Blessed Sacrament, which still continues in the chapel of the mother-house.

The rule, however, was not yet approved. After being modified by the superior of St. Sulpice, it was finally approved and given to the Sisters, on June 24, 1698, when Sister of the Assumption (Barbier) was superior. Mother Bourgeoys had spent six years as an ordinary member of the community in heroic obedience to her rule, when her conscience and her superiors imposed on her the obligation of writing an account of the graces she had received during her long lifetime. The book she thus composed at the age of seventy-eight, besides autobiographical notes of rare charm, contains a treasury of the maxims which had guided her.

In 1701 the Community numbered fifty-four members. The nuns were self-supporting, and, in consideration of this fact, the number of members was not limited by the French government, as was the case with all the other religious communities.

The convent at Louisbourg, in Cape Breton, fell into the hands of the English. The Sisters were twice exiled to France, where they suffered many hardships. After the conquest, the house at Point St. Charles was directly in the path of the advancing army. Two Sisters walked down the road to meet the van-guard, and asked for the commanding officer. They placed themselves and their house under his protection, and invited him and his men to come in for refreshments. Consequently, the Sisters there and in Montreal were unmolested. Though the increase of the community was much impeded by the conquest, in the latter half of the nineteenth century many foundations were made, not only near Montreal, but also in Ontario, the Maritime provinces, and the United States.

The conflagration which ravaged Montreal in 1768 destroyed the mother-house, built eighty-five years before. The convent erected after this fire, with money furnished by one of the Sulpician priests, was demolished in 1844 to give place to a larger building. A still more commodious one was built, at the foot of the mountain, in 1880. This was burned in 1893, obliging the community to return to the old house on St. John Baptist street. Since 1908 the Sisters have occupied a new building on Sherbrooke street.

The schools of the Congregation of Notre Dame give instruction in all the fundamental branches. Their educational system begins with the kindergarten. The courses are afterwards graded as elementary, model, commercial, and academic. The first college was opened in 1899 at Antigonish, in Nova Scotia, and is affiliated with St. Francis Xavier University. In 1909, the Notre Dame Ladies' College (now Marguerite Bourgeoys), in affiliation with Laval, was opened in Montreal. Colleges have since been founded in Ottawa and Staten island, New York.

At the present time, the Institute includes 145 houses, and 2,656 nuns. (1) In the diocese of Montreal are the mother-house and novitiate for the whole Institute, with the Tabernacle Society, Sodality of Children of Mary and Chief Centre for the Alumnæ; the Jacques Cartier Normal School (1899); the Teacher-Training College (1926); and Marguerite Bourgeoys College (1909), a bilingual institute affiliated to the University of Montreal; 32 city schools, including high schools, boarding-schools, academies, and graded schools; 9 in the outskirts, 14 in the country; 4 farms, 2 sanatoriums. (2) In the diocese of Quebec are 18 houses, of the same standing as those in Montreal. (3) In the diocese of Sherbrooke are 14 houses, including a normal school. (4) In the diocese of Ottawa are a bilingual college, a boarding-school, and 4 graded schools. (5) In the diocese of Charlottetown are 8 houses, boarding-schools, high schools, and graded schools. (6) In the dioceses of Alexandria, Chatham, Chicoutimi, Joliette, Kingston, Nicolet, St. Hyacinthe, Three Rivers, Toronto, and Valleyfield, are from one to five houses. Joliette and St. Pascal have normal schools. There are fifteen teaching institutions in the United States.

Sisters of the Cross of St. Andrew (Sœurs de St. André). This Congregation was founded in 1805 at St. Pierre de

Maille, France, by the Blessed Andrew Hubert Fournet and the Ven. Jeanne-Elizabeth-Marie-Lucie Bicker des Ages. It was canonically approved by Pope Pius IX in 1867, and its rules were finally approved by Pope Pius X in 1911. The Sisters of the Cross educate children and especially orphans, and care for the poor and the sick. Several houses of this Congregation have been established in Manitoba and Saskatchewan.

Sisters of the Holy Childhood of Jesus and Mary (Sainte-Chrétienne). This Congregation was founded by Mgr. Jouffret and Mme. de Mejanès at Metz, Lorraine, in 1807. It is engaged in education, and administers charity. At the request of the Abbé Lapointe of St. Malachy, Quebec, the Congregation obtained, in 1914, permission from Cardinal Bégin (q.v.) to establish a house in Canada.

Sisters of the Holy Cross and the Seven Dolours. The Congregation of the Sisters of the Holy Cross was founded in 1841 at Ste. Croix du Mans, France, by the Very Rev. Father Moreau. It was first established in Canada at St. Laurent in 1847 through the efforts of Mgr. Bourget (q.v.). It is engaged in education.

Sisters of the Holy Names of Jesus and Mary. This Congregation was founded at Longueuil, Quebec, in 1843, by Mgr. Ignace Bourget, the Rev. Father Allard, O.M.I., and Mother Marie-Rose. It plays an important part in the field of Catholic education in Canada, and conducts a large number of schools throughout the Dominion. Its activities extend also to the United States, to Basutoland, and to Japan. The mother-house was transferred in 1860 to Hochelaga, and in 1925 to Outremont, Montreal.

Sisters of the Holy Hearts of Jesus and Mary. The "Congregation des Sœurs des Saints Cœurs de Jésus et de Marie" was founded at Paramé, near St.

Malo, France, in 1853, by Amélie-Virginie Fristel. Her charity excited the admiration of all who came in contact with her. A rich and charitable gentleman of Paramé, seeing the good works done by Amélie, left her by will a large property where she could receive the old and poor. On Christmas, 1846, she took possession of her new home with one companion. The first poor were received on that day. This new institution was named Notre-Dame des Chênes. In 1856 at the request of the bishop, the Sisters took charge of the teaching in country schools in France, and they founded establishments in Guernsey, Canada, Belgium and Holland. The Sisters arrived in Canada in 1891. They first established themselves at Church Point, New Brunswick. In 1903, they took charge of the auxiliary work at the Seminary of Joliette, Quebec, and a novitiate was opened in Joliette in 1905. That same year, the Congregation opened its first school in Canada. The Congregation counts (1935) 22 parochial schools, 9 colleges or seminaries, an institution for the aged, a boarding school, and a juvenile house.

Sisters of the Infant Jesus, once known as "Ladies of Instruction", originated in France, where they conducted schools, catechism classes, hospitals, and orphanages in the second half of the seventeenth century. In 1896, these Sisters came to Canada, at the invitation of Bishop Durieu, O.M.I. They have specialized in the training of Indian children. To-day they conduct 8 schools in British Columbia and Saskatchewan, the provincial house being at North Vancouver.

Sisters of the Joan of Arc Institute. The Congregation of the Sisters of the Joan of Arc Institute, who have their mother house and novitiate in Ottawa, is both a civil corporation, chartered by the Ontario government, and a religious Congregation, founded on October 7, 1919, with the approbation of the Holy See, through His

Grace Archbishop Gauthier and Rev. Canon Plantin. It is under the direction of the Rev. Mother St. Thomas Aquinas, the foundress and first superior-general. The Congregation comprises (1935) 70 members. This Congregation has charge of the protection and education of youth. Its chief aim is the protection of young girls away from home. To them and to ladies travelling it offers room and board in a homelike atmosphere, where everything contributes to their physical and moral well-being and to their health and happiness. Through the employment bureau the Sisters help to find work for those who are unemployed. The second aim of the Congregation is education. A course of studies comprising elementary, intermediate, and high school classes is given to day pupils and boarders. The Congregation has three houses in the archdiocese of Boston, where the sisters took charge of St. Anthony's Parochial School in Shirley, Mass., in 1921, and of St. Aloysius of Gonzaga's in Newburyport, Mass., in 1923. St. Theresa's for young ladies in Newburyport, Mass., was opened in 1927. To favour health through recreation, the Congregation offers ladies two summer houses, Villa Lorraine on lake Wakefield, Quebec, in the Laurentian hills, and Villa Bellerive at Wychwood on the shore of the Ottawa river, only seven miles from the capital. In July, 1934, at Westboro, Ontario, on the outskirts of Ottawa, the Congregation built and opened the "Joan of Arc House", a beautiful residence for convalescent ladies and children, and a school for convalescent and retarded children.

Sisters of the Most Holy Sacrament (Servants of the Most Blessed Sacrament). The Congregation of the Servants of the Most Blessed Sacrament was founded in France in 1858, two years after that of the Fathers of the Blessed Sacrament, by Blessed Peter Julian Eymard, with the coöperation of the venerated Mother Margaret of the Blessed Sacrament. It was definitely approved by Pope Leo XIII in 1885. The Congregation is cloistered and contemplative. Their chief duty is perpetual adoration of the Blessed Sacrament, exposed day and night in their chapels. The religious are divided into two classes, choir and lay sisters. Their time is devoted to prayer, labour, and the fabrication of all that pertains to the altar. The mother house is in Paris, France; the Canadian novitiate is at 291 La Canardière, Quebec.

Sisters of the Presentation of Mary (St. Hyacinthe). This Congregation was founded in 1796 at Thueyts, France, by the Ven. Marie Rivier for the instruction of poor girls. It soon spread over France, and in 1853 a first house was established in Canada. Today the Sisters are distributed in 84 establishments, 37 being located in the United States, and the others in western as well as in eastern Canada. In both large cities and modest villages, the Sisters of the Presentation further the cause of secondary and primary education among the Indian children. Their normal, vocational, and industrial schools are particularly notable. The mother-house of this Congregation is established at St. Hyacinthe, Quebec.

Sisters of the Sacred Heart. The Congregation of the Sisters of the Sacred Heart was founded in 1817 by a pious parish priest, the Rev. Father Barbe, from the diocese of Vannes, Brittany. It soon became authorized as a religious society, and it was honoured by a royal charter granted by the king of France, Charles X. At present, besides a great number of houses in France, among which is the mother house, the Sisters are established in England, Belgium, the United States, and Canada. The first Sisters of the Sacred Heart to come to Canada arrived in Ottawa in 1902. Their services were required by the Oblate Fathers for the manual labour in the St. Joseph Scholasticate. The Sisters also have the care of schools in the dioceses of Ottawa, Mount-Laurier, Montreal, and Pembroke. This Congregation has a two-fold aim: first, the education of children, especially in rural schools; second, various works of charity, such as the upkeep of hospitals and orphan homes, visiting the sick in their homes, the direction of domestic economy schools, etc. The sisters are divided into two classes: the chorist sisters and the lay sisters.

Sisters of the Sacred Hearts of Jesus and Mary constitute a teaching and nursing Congregation. In Canada this Congregation conducts three establishments, one at Ironside, Quebec, one at Parent, Ontario, and one at Senneterre, Ontario.

Sisters Servant of the Holy Heart of Mary (Limoilou). The Congregation of the Sisters Servant of the Holy Heart of Mary was founded at Paris, France, by the Rev. Father Delaplace, of the Congregation of the Holy Ghost and the Holy Heart of Mary. Its first origin goes back to the establishment of the orphans' institute of the Holy Family, opened on March 19, 1860, for young orphan girls or girls of poor families. The founder was helped by Jeanne Marie Moisan, a native of Vannes diocese, Brittany. She became the first general-superior under the name of Mother Marie du St. Sacrement. The Congregation comprises but one category of members. The different functions are portioned out among them according to the physical strength and the intellectual and moral aptitudes of the members.

The Congregation has for its first and general end the glory of God and the sanctification of its members; and its secondary and particular end is the salvation of souls by (1) the instruction and education of youth in boarding schools, orphans' institutes, patronages, etc., and (2) works of mercy towards the infirm and sick, either by domiciliary visits or in hospitals. After having received the blessings of Pope Leo XIII, the institute opened houses in different dioceses of France; and in 1930 the mother house was transferred from Paris to Montgéron, Seine et Oise, in Versailles diocese. In 1889 the institute founded parish schools in the United States. This province has now many academies with boarders and day-pupils of both sexes, kindergartens, and two hospitals. The provincial house, with the novitiate, is at Beaverville, Illinois. In 1892 four French nuns were called in Canada to direct the small convent of St. Ephrem, Beauce county. In 1903 the Provincial House was fixed at Limoilou, Quebec. The Congregation received from Pope Puis X its definitive approbation in 1913.

Siveright, John (1779?-1856), furtrader, was born in Scotland about 1779, and entered the service of the XY Company in 1799, and that of the North West Company in 1805. Sir George Simpson (q.v.) wrote in 1832 that he "was promoted to the rank of clerk from being a gentleman's body servant". In 1815 he was at Portage la Prairie, and he became implicated in the Selkirk trials. From 1813 to 1823 he was in charge at Sault Ste. Marie; and from 1824 to 1847 he was in charge at Fort Coulonge on the Ottawa, and at lake Timiskaming. He was promoted to the rank of chief trader in the Hudson's Bay Company in 1828, and to that of chief factor in 1846. He went on furlough in 1847; and he retired from the Company's service in 1849. He died at Edinburgh, Scotland, on September 4, 1856.

Siwash, a word of the Chinook jargon (q.v.), meaning an Indian of any tribe or race. It is a corruption of the French word *sauvage*, and is sometimes wrongly used to qualify the word Indian, as though it were the name of a group or family.

VICTORY JUMP
Alf Engen, Salt Lake City, jumped 194 and 208 feet to win the Canadian
jumping championship at Banff.

BANFF CROWDS
Skiers from Canada, United States and Europe at Mount Norquay, Banff.

Skates, as well as rays, are related to the sharks and dogfishes, differing from them in having the body greatly flattened from above downwards in accordance with their ground-feeding habits. Half a dozen species are found in Canadian waters, about equally distributed between the Atlantic and Pacific coasts. In England, where immense quantities of skates and rays are sold in the markets, the long-snouted ones are called skates, the short-snouted ones rays. There is little or no use made of these fish as food in Canada.

Skead, James (1817-1884), senator of Canada, was born at Calder Hall, Moresby, Cumberland, England, on December 31, 1817. He came to Canada with his parents in 1832, and settled at Bytown (Ottawa), Upper Canada. Here he became a timber merchant and manufacturer. From 1862 to 1867 he represented the Rideau division in the Legislative Council of Canada as a Conservative; and in 1867 he was called to the Senate of Canada. He died at Ottawa on July 5, 1884.

Skeena river, in the Coast and Cassiar districts of British Columbia, rises north of the 57th parallel of latitude and between the 128th and 129th meridians of west longitude. It flows in a southerly direction for 175 miles to Hazelton, and thence for 150 miles in a south-west direction; and it empties into Chatham sound, about 16 miles south of Prince Rupert. It is ascended by steamer for nearly 100 miles. Nine miles from Hazelton is located the property of the Omineca Mining and Milling Company, a silver-lead-zinc-antimony prospect. The river is 325 miles in length.

Skene, George Munroe (1819?-1863), fur-trader, was born in Nairnshire, Scotland, about 1819, and entered the service of the Hudson's Bay Company. He rose to the rank of chief trader, and died at Metabetchouan, on lake St. John, Lower Canada, on March 22, 1863.

Skidegate, a village in Queen Charlotte islands district of British Columbia, on Graham island, and on the north shore of Skidegate inlet, 120 miles from Prince Rupert. The name is an adaptation of an Haida word meaning "Red paint stone", and was the name of a chief residing here. Pop. (1934), 125.

Ski-ing, a sport which consists in gliding over a snow-clad surface on a pair of skis (strips of wood four or more inches wide, and from five to eight feet long) bound one to each foot. The sport originated in Norway and Sweden, but has now become so popular in Canada that it is an important factor in the development of the tourist trade. It is said that skis were first used by miners near Rossland, British Columbia, in the seventies of last century, as a means of transportation during the winter months. In any case, skis were certainly used in Montreal as early as 1881. It was not, however, until 1904 that the Montreal Ski Club, the first regularly constituted organization of this kind in North America, was incorporated. Other clubs followed in rapid succession, the Quebec Ski Club in 1908, the Ottawa Ski Club in 1910, and the Winnipeg Ski Club in 1913. Ski-ing has entered on a period of increasing popularity in the Rocky mountain area; and even in Ontario, which is almost wholly lacking in mountains, the Toronto Ski Club has built up a membership of over 3,000—a figure believed to be a record for any local ski club in the world. A Canadian Amateur Ski Association has been formed; and a *Canadian Ski Year Book* is published in Montreal. See Dudley E. Batchelor and others, *Ski-ing in Canada* (Can. Geog. Journal, February, 1937).

Skunk. All the members of the weasel family (*Mustelidae*) have scent glands at the base of the tail, but in the skunk these have developed to such a degree that a jet of powerful scent may be thrown a distance of fifteen feet, should its possessor be annoyed or frightened.

This fact is known to many people who would not know the animal if they met it. The big striped skunk (genus *Mephitis*) is the size of a large house cat, but of sturdier build; the tail is large and bushy, with a black tip; and the general colour of the animal is a glossy black, with two white stripes extending backward from the neck. This skunk is found throughout Canada, as far north as the 60th parallel of latitude. The little spotted skunk (genus *Spilogale*) is found in Canada only in the south-western part of British Columbia. It is about the size of a half-grown house cat, and has a colour pattern of black and white in conspicuous stripes or connected spots. Both these skunks are slow-moving animals, with vast reliance on their powers of defence. They are inoffensive creatures, only utilizing their defensive barrage as a last resort. They root and dig under the sod after the fashion of pigs, and obtain much of their food in this way. Like many of the carnivores, they will eat anything they are fortunate enough to catch, and in the skunk's case, since it is neither a runner, a swimmer, or a climber, insects form a large part of its food. The den may be in a burrow, among rocks or under a stump. The litter may contain as many as ten young, but four to six is the usual number. Skunks hibernate during the cold weather, and do not appear till the warm days of early spring. Occasionally skunks become a nuisance around poultry yards, especially when young chicks are being raised. While the pelt is not a highly valued fur, it is widely used in trimming garments, and the fact that the skunk persists even in thickly settled areas has made it an item of some importance in the fur-trade. See N. E. Tantz, *Economic value of North American skunks* (U.S. Dept. of Agriculture, Farmers' Bulletins, 5 and 7, 1914), and H. E. Anthony, *Fieldbook of North American mammals* (New York, 1928).

Skunk Cabbage (*Symplocarpus foetidus* (L.) Nutt., *Araceae*). This is the very first of Canadian spring flowers, and may be found in low wet woods and swamps almost before the snow is gone. It is characterized by a cluster of large ovate or heart-shaped leaves, which appear after the flower is over. The true flowers are small and inconspicuous in themselves, but they are borne on a fleshy stalk and enfolded by a leaflike spathe, which is a greenish-yellow, striped with purple. The plant has a rank odour when mature, which accounts for its common name.

Slate, a partially metamorphosed clay rock which has developed a good cleavage along parallel planes. This results from the application of pressure on the original rock, and the slaty cleavage is at right angles to the direction in which the pressure is applied. In addition to the development of the slaty cleavage, the clay undergoes a loss of water with a change in mineral composition, while being converted to slate. Slate is utilized extensively as roofing material and for many other uses in the building trade.

Slave Indians, a tribe belonging to the Athapaskan family (q.v.). In the first half of the eighteenth century they seem to have inhabited the region of lake Athabaska, the Slave river, and the western half of Great Slave lake; but when the Cree invaded this region, they retreated down the Mackenzie river, and at the end of the eighteenth century they occupied the country on both sides of the Mackenzie from Great Slave lake to the basin of the lower Liard river. Their name was given to them by the Cree, in contempt for their peaceable and inoffensive character. Unlike the Chipewyan, they never ventured out into the barren lands, but confined themselves to the forests and the river banks. A large part of their subsistence was derived from fishing; but they also hunted the woodland caribou and the moose, running these animals down on snow shoes in the spring or snaring them with the help of dogs during the summer and winter. From the caribou and the moose they derived also clothing, bags, and babiche. Their clothing was similar to that of the Chipewyan, but was more heavily ornamented with moose hair and porcupine quills. In summer, they lived in tipis built of brush and spruce bark, though the more prosperous sometimes had tipis covered with caribou hides; but in winter they built long, low cabins of poles, with walls chinked with moss, and with roofs of spruce boughs. Before they obtained steel axes and knives from the white man, they used stone adzes for cutting down trees, and beaver-tooth blades for whittling wood and bone. Their weapons were chiefly of caribou antler or bone.

Their social organization was primitive. They were divided into independent bands, each of which chose a leader in war-time to lead its war-party, but in peace-time was virtually leaderless. Disputes were settled by an informal council of the hunters. Unlike the Chipewyan, they treated their women with great kindness, and the men took on themselves the hardest work, even the procuring of firewood. They were sometimes guilty of destroying female infants at birth; but they never abandoned the aged and infirm.

They believed in a guardian spirit, and they attributed sickness and death to sorcery. Lacking herbal remedies, they placed great reliance in their medicine men; and the surrounding tribes attributed to them great skill in witchcraft. The dead they either placed on scaffolds or covered with small huts to protect them from wild animals. They believed that the souls of the dead passed through the earth, crossed a great lake, and began life anew in another world.

It is estimated that the Slave Indians numbered 1,250 when they first came into touch with the white man. To-day they number less than 800.

Slave river, the part of the Mackenzie system which flows from lake Athabaska to Great Slave lake. Lake Athabaska is drained by two channels: the main channel joins the Peace river, while the rivière des Roches, after being joined by the Peace, continues in a north-westerly direction as the Slave river until it enters Great Slave lake by two mouths near Fort Resolution. The river was discovered in the winter of 1771-2 by Samuel Hearne (q.v.), and in 1789 Alexander Mackenzie (q.v.) descended it on his journey to the mouth of the Mackenzie. It was named after the Slave Indians, who were driven from this region by the Cree; the term did not denote servitude, but was one of reproach and implied a more than common savageness. Magnificent scenery skirts the banks of the river which are, in many parts, well-wooded. For most of the 60 miles between the junction of the Peace river and Fitzgerald, the Slave is confined between rocky banks; its average width is therefore less than half of that of the Peace for an equal distance above the junction. Above Fitzgerald is a broad, lake-like reach. A buffalo reserve of the Canadian government is located at the junction of the Peace with the Slave river. The Slave is navigable for steamers, except for the rapids between Fitzgerald and Fort Smith, which is on the northern boundary of Alberta. It is 258 miles in length. See Lewis R. Freeman, *The nearing north* (New York, 1928).

Slavery. The institution of slavery never obtained a deep foothold in Canada, partly because of the climate, which was not deemed suitable for negro slaves, and partly because there seems to have been, even in early times, a strong under-current of hostility to it. That slavery existed, and indeed flourished, in Canada in former times cannot, however, be denied. Most of the Indian tribes had slaves, generally captives taken from other tribes with which they were at war; and the French in Canada early began to buy such slaves from the Indians. These slaves were known as *panis*, from the fact that some of them belonged to the Pawnee tribe. Later, negro and Carib slaves from the West Indies and elsewhere were imported into New France; and one of the clauses of the articles of the capitulation of Montreal in 1760 was that "the Negroes and Panis of both sexes shall remain in the possession of the French and Canadians to whom they belong".

After the British conquest, slavery threatened for a time to become a well-entrenched institution. Many well-to-do people in Nova Scotia and Quebec acquired slaves; and many of the better class of United Empire Loyalists brought slaves north with them. Not a few fur-traders, moreover, continued to acquire *panis* from the Indians. There is little evidence to show that these slaves were not well treated as a rule; and there is ample evidence to show that they were sometimes treated with kindness and even affection. Numbers of them were freed by their masters, as a reward for faithful service, and were even treated as if they had been members of the family. When Charles Paterson (q.v.), the director of the south-west fur-trade from Michilimachinac, was drowned in 1788 off the north shore of lake Michigan, he was found afterwards in the sand, clutching his *panise* (female slave), whose life he had tried to save. That the slave was regarded as a chattel cannot, however, be denied; and the sale of slaves was in the eighteenth century in Canada a not infrequent occurrence.

It is to John Graves Simcoe (q.v.) that must go the credit of sounding the death-knell of slavery in Canada. He was largely responsible for the passing in the legislature of Upper Canada in 1793 of an Act forbidding the introduction of slaves into Upper Canada after that date. As a concession to vested

interests, those who possessed slaves were permitted to retain them; but the children of these slaves were to be free on reaching the age of maturity. Upper Canada was thus the first British possession to provide by legislation for the abolition of slavery, even though that abolition was to be gradual. In Lower Canada, there were attempts to abolish slavery, but no legislation was passed. The courts, however, decided here, in effect if not in form, that a master had no rights over his slave; and this decision was tantamount to the abolition of slavery. In Nova Scotia and New Brunswick also, though no legislation was passed, juries were almost uniformly against the rights claimed by a master over his slave; and here, too, slavery gradually disappeared. When, therefore, the British parliament passed an Act abolishing slavery in the British Empire in 1833, slavery was almost non-existent in the British North American colonies.

In the years between 1833 and the American civil war, when slavery was abolished in the United States, Canada became a haven of refuge for escaped slaves from the South. Hundreds of these escaped to Canada by way of what was known as "the underground railroad". An Anti-Slavery Society was formed in Canada in 1851; and during the American civil war feeling in Canada was strongly in favour of the North as against the South, mainly because of the strong prejudice in Canada against slavery.

See T. Watson Smith, *The slave in Canada* (Coll. Nova Scotia Hist. Soc., 1899); B. Sulte, *L'Esclavage en Canada* (Revue Canadienne, 1911); Mgr. L. A. Paquet, *L'Esclavage au Canada* (Trans. Roy. Soc. Can., 1914); Mrs. W. T. Hallam, *Slave days in Canada* (Toronto, 1919); F. Landon, *The fugitive slave in Canada* (University Magazine, 1919); and the Hon. W. R. Riddell, *The slave in Upper Canada* (Trans. Roy. Soc. Can., 1919), *The slave in Canada* (Journal of Negro History, 1920), and *Notes on the slave in Nouvelle-France* (Journal of Negro History, 1923).

Slender Nettle. See **Nettle.**

Slight, Benjamin (1798?-1858), clergyman and author, was born about 1798, and was ordained in 1835 a minister of the Wesleyan Methodist Conference in Upper Canada. He died at Napanee, Canada West, on January 16, 1858. He was the author of *Indian researches, or facts concerning the North American Indians* (Montreal, 1844) and *The apocalypse explained* (Montreal, 1855).

Slocan, a city in the Kootenay district of British Columbia, at the south end of Slocan lake, and on the Canadian Pacific Railway. It is a mining town. Pop. (1934), 400. See C. E. Cairnes, *Slocan mining camp, British Columbia* (Ottawa, Can. Geol. Survey, Memoir 173, 1934).

Small, Ambrose (1867-1919?), theatre-owner, was born at Bradford, Ontario, on January 11, 1867. He became the manager of the Toronto Opera House, and later the owner of the Grand Opera House, Toronto; and eventually he came to control a chain of theatres throughout Canada. In 1919 he sold his theatrical interests to the Trans-Canada Theatres for one million dollars; and on the day on which he received payment of this amount, he disappeared. The probability is that he was murdered; but no trace of his body has ever been found and his disappearance is one of the most intriguing mysteries in Canadian history. See "The mystery of Ambrose Small" in W. S. Wallace, *Murders and mysteries* (Toronto, 1931).

Small, James Edward (d. 1869), solicitor-general of Upper Canada (1842-3), was born in York, Upper Canada before 1800, the second son of John Small (q.v.). He was called to the bar of Upper Canada in 1821, and practised law in York. He was counsel for the defendants in the suit which W. L.

Mackenzie (q.v.) brought in 1826 against those who had destroyed his printing press. In 1836 he was a member of the Constitutional Reform Association; and in 1839 he was elected to represent the third riding of York in the Legislative Assembly of Upper Canada. He represented the same constituency from 1841 to 1848 in the Legislative Assembly of united Canada; and from 1842 to 1843 he was a member of the executive council and solicitor-general for Upper Canada in the first Baldwin-Lafontaine administration. In 1849 he was appointed county judge of Middlesex, and he held this post until his death in 1869.

Small, John (1746-1831), clerk of the executive council of Upper Canada (1793-1831), was born in Gloucestershire, England, in 1746. He came to Canada in 1792; and in 1793 he was appointed clerk of the executive council of Upper Canada. This position he held until his death at York (Toronto) on July 18, 1831. He married Eliza Goldsmith, a native of Kent, England; and by her he had three sons.

Small, Patrick (d. 1810?), fur-trader, was probably born near Perth, Scotland, the son of John Small, and the grandnephew of General John Small (1730-1796), lieutenant-governor of Guernsey. Through the influence of General Small, who had been an officer in the British army at the battle of Bunker's Hill, who had later been stationed in Nova Scotia, and who was a friend of Simon McTavish (q.v.), he, like his relative, John McDonald of Garth (q.v.), became a clerk in the service of the North West Company. He first appears in the West in 1779, when he wintered on the Churchill river. For a number of years he was in charge at Isle à la Crosse. He became a partner in the North West Company in 1783; but he retired from the fur-trade in 1791, and returned to Great Britain. In 1794 he was "residing in Wood Street, London", and he is described in the London directory of that year as a partner of the firm of Small and Young

"Scotch factors". In 1794 he was adopted by his grand-uncle, General Small, and in 1796, at the latter's death, he was left by his will, which is to be seen in Somerset House, London, a large part of his estate, including his property in Nova Scotia. He seems to have died about 1810, since, in the minutes of the Beaver Club of Montreal (of which he became a member in 1789), he is described as among the members "in England" in 1809-10, but disappears in the list for 1810-11. By a Cree woman at Isle à la Crosse he had one son, Patrick (q.v.), and at least two daughters, one of whom married David Thompson (q.v.), and the other of whom was the "Indian wife" of John McDonald of Garth (q.v.).

Small, Patrick (1785?-1846), fur-trader, was born, probably at Fort Isle à la Crosse, about 1785, the son of Patrick Small (q.v.) and a woman of the Cree tribe. He entered the service of the North West Company as a clerk in 1804, and was taken over as a clerk by the Hudson's Bay Company in 1821. From 1822 to 1830 he was on the Saskatchewan. He died in the West on January 18, 1846; and his will is preserved in Hudson's Bay House in London.

Smallpox. This disease has played an important and sometimes crucial part in the history of Canada. It was introduced into North America and began its ravages among the Indians, who proved exceptionally susceptible to it, before the Pilgrim Fathers even landed at Plymouth Rock in 1620; and the hostility of the Indians to the Pilgrim Fathers has been attributed to their fear of this disease. It appeared first among the Indians of Canada when the Montagnais of the lower St. Lawrence fell victims to it in 1635-6; and from that time onward its ravages in New France were severe. It wrought havoc among the Hurons in Huronia, and seriously interfered with the work of the Jesuit missionaries, who were accused by the Hurons of having introduced it among them; and the virtual obliteration of the Hurons by the Iroquois in 1649 is partially explained by the inroads of smallpox among the Hurons. Later, the Iroquois suffered severely from the disease; and the gradual cessation of Iroquois attacks on New France after 1666 is explained not only by the defence of the Long Sault by Dollard (q.v.), or by the military operations of the Carignan-Salières regiment, or even by the policy of Frontenac (q.v.), but also by the fact that the Iroquois were being decimated by the smallpox. Smallpox seriously interfered with effectiveness of the French forces in North America during the Seven Years' War, and to a smaller degree that of the English forces; and Colonel Bouquet (q.v.) actually proposed spreading smallpox among the Indians adhering to the French, as a measure of warfare. In 1776 the Americans besieging Quebec were attacked by smallpox, and this, as much as the appearance of the British fleet in the St. Lawrence, caused their retirement from before Quebec and their evacuation of the province. In the Canadian west, smallpox appeared almost as soon as the white man did. There seems to have been a serious epidemic of it there in 1736, only a few years after the La Vérendryes reached the Red river; and a still more devastating epidemic occurred in 1780 and subsequent years, when whole bands of the Indians were wiped out, and even some of the English fur-traders succumbed.

It was about the time of the British conquest of Canada that inoculation with smallpox as a preventive of smallpox was introduced; and this treatment proved efficacious in some cases, though there was decided antipathy to it. Shortly after the year 1800, vaccination by cow-pox was introduced into Canada, the famous Dr. Jenner having sent some of his vaccine to a friend in Nova Scotia. For many years, however, opposition to vaccination was widespread in Canada, with the result that repeated epidemics swept the country. In the winter of 1885-6 there died in Montreal alone a total of 3,164 persons, of whom over 2,000 were children under 10 years of age; and as recently as 1921 there were 1,352 cases of smallpox in Ottawa, though the type of disease was mild in nature, and only a few deaths occurred. In 1924 there was an outbreak of smallpox in Windsor, Ontario; and among 67 cases there were 32 deaths, all of them of unvaccinated persons. When vaccination was widely applied, the epidemic promptly subsided. If the anti-vaccinationists had not been so vociferous and so successful in Canada in the nineteenth century, it is probable that the population of Canada in the twentieth century would have been appreciably larger than it is. See John J. Heagerty, *Four centuries of medical history in Canada* (2 vols., Toronto, 1928).

Smallwood, Charles (1812-1873), meteorologist, was born in Birmingham, England, in 1812. He became a physician, and in 1853 emigrated to Canada. He settled at St. Martin, Isle Jésus, Lower Canada, and acquired here a large medical practice. He established a meteorological observatory; and in 1858 he became professor of meteorology and astronomy at McGill University. He died at Montreal, Quebec, on December 22, 1873. He was an LL.D. of McGill University (1858).

Smaltite. See **Cobalt.**

Smart, William (1788-1876), clergyman, was born in Edinburgh, Scotland, on September 14, 1788. He was educated in England, and in 1811 he was ordained a minister of the Presbyterian Church. The same year he was sent by the London Missionary Society to Elizabethtown (Brockville), Upper Canada; and he was pastor of the First Presbyterian Church in that place until his resignation in 1849. He died at

Gananoque, Ontario, on September 9, 1876. He was twice married, (1) in 1816 to Philena (d. 1855), widow of Israel Jones, of Brockville; and (2) in 1862 to Mrs. Bush, of Gananoque. See Holly S. Seaman, *The Rev. William Smart* (Ont. Hist. Soc., Papers and Records, vol. v, 1904).

Smartweed (*Polygonum Persicaria* L., *Polygonaceae*), a very common weed everywhere, growing in low fields and wet meadows. It is a smooth-stemmed, erect annual, with simple or branched stems and lance-shaped, sharply pointed leaves. The flowers are small and borne in slender, densely flowered spikes, pink to purplish in colour, blooming from July to September.

Smelt. The smelts are a group of small fishes related to the great salmon family. Most of them are strictly marine, but a few ascend rivers to spawn, and some are land-locked. The common smelt of the Atlantic area (*Osmerus mordax*) is found from the St. Lawrence southward to the Delaware. It is essentially a shore fish, but in late winter and spring it enters rivers to spawn. It is then taken in considerable numbers for the markets. The common smelt of British Columbia is *Hypomesus pretiosus*. Smelts very similar to, if not identical with, the marine form live permanently in some fresh-water lakes, notably in lake Champlain and in certain New Brunswick lakes. The smelt fisheries of Canada are normally worth more than a million dollars a year.

Smelting. See **Mining Industry.**

Smet, Pierre Jean de (1801-1873), missionary, was born in Flanders in 1801, the son of Joost de Smet. He was educated by the Jesuits, and in 1821 emigrated to America, where he entered the novitiate of the Jesuits at Georgetown. In 1838 he went west as a missionary, and in 1841 he began his life's work among the Indians of Oregon. In 1842 he visited Fort Vancouver, and in 1845

Fort Edmonton. He died at St. Louis, Missouri, on May 23, 1873. See R. P. Laveille, *Le Père de Smet* (Liège, 1913; 4th ed., Louvain and Paris, 1928).

Smilax (*Smilax rotundifolia* L. var. *quadrangularis* (Muhl.) Wood, *Liliaceae*), a smooth, woody, climbing plant which supports itself by means of its twisting leaf stalks. The stem, branches, and especially the branchlets are 4-angled, and are armed with scattered prickles. The leaves are thickish, ovate, broader than long, with an abrupt point, and with 7-9 prominent ribs or nerves. The flowers are in axillary clusters, and are small, greenish or yellowish, with a flattened stalk. The fruit is a blue-black berry with a bloom. It grows in moist thickets from Nova Scotia westward.

Smith, Sir Albert James (1822-1883), minister of marine and fisheries for Canada (1873-8), was born at Shediac, New Brunswick, on March 12, 1822, the son of T. E. Smith. He was educated at the Westmorland county grammar school; and was called to the bar of New Brunswick in 1847 (Q.C., 1861). From 1851 to 1867 he sat in the Legislative Assembly of New Brunswick for Westmorland; and from 1867 to 1868 he represented Westmorland in the Canadian House of Commons. In 1856 he became a member without portfolio of the first Liberal administration formed in New Brunswick; he was a member of several subsequent governments; and in 1865-6 he was president of the council in the Smith-Wilmot administration formed to oppose the inclusion of New Brunswick in Confederation. After Confederation he held for a time aloof from both parties; but in 1873 he became minister of marine and fisheries in the Mackenzie government, and he held this office until his defeat in the elections of 1878. He died at Dorchester, New Brunswick, on June 30, 1883. In 1868 he married June, daughter of J. W. Young, of Halifax, Nova Scotia. He was created

a K.C.M.G. in 1878, in recognition of services rendered by him in connection with the Halifax Fishery Commission under the Treaty of Washington.

Smith, Charles Douglas (*fl.* 1812-1824), lieutenant-governor of Prince Edward Island, was a brother of Admiral Sir Sidney Smith (1764-1840). He was appointed lieutenant-governor of Prince Edward Island in 1812; and for over ten years he exercised in the colony an arbitrary and high-handed rule. In 1823 a largely signed petition for his recall was forwarded to London, and in 1824 he was replaced by Lieut.-Col. Ready (q.v.).

Smith, or **Smyth, Sir David William, Bart.** (1764-1837), surveyor-general of Upper Canada, was born in England on September 4, 1764, the only son of Major John Smith, of the 5th Regiment. He obtained a commission in his father's regiment, and came to Canada about 1790. In 1792 he was elected to the Legislative Assembly of Upper Canada, probably for Essex; and in 1796 he was elected to represent Lincoln. He was speaker of the second and third parliaments of Upper Canada. He was appointed also surveyor-general of the province; and in 1796 he was sworn of the Executive Council. In 1804 he went to England; and here he became agent for the Duke of Northumberland. He died in England, near Alnwick, on May 9, 1837. He married (1) in 1788 Anne (d. 1798), daughter of John O'Reilly, of Ballykilchrist, county Longford, Ireland, by whom he had eight children; and (2) in 1803 Mary, daughter of John Tyler, of Devizes, England, by whom he had one daughter. In 1821 he was created a baronet of the United Kingdom. He was the author of *A short topographical description of His Majesty's province of Upper Canada* (London, 1799; 2nd ed., 1813), the second edition of which is said to have been revised by Francis Gore (q.v.). His papers are in the

Toronto Public Library. See C. C. James, *The first legislators of Upper Canada* (Trans. Roy. Soc. Can., 1902), *The second legislature of Upper Canada* (Trans. Roy. Soc. Can., 1903), and *David William Smith* (Trans. Roy. Soc. Can., 1913).

Smith, Edward (d. 1849), fur-trader, entered the service of the North West Company prior to 1806, when he appears as a clerk in the Athabaska department. He was employed for many years in the Athabaska and Mackenzie River departments; and in 1814 he was made a partner of the North West Company. At the union of 1821, he was made a chief factor of the Hudson's Bay Company; and from 1821 to 1823 he was in charge at Fort Chipewyan, from 1823 to 1832 at Fort Simpson, and from 1834 to 1837 again at Fort Chipewyan. He was granted furlough in 1837, and shortly afterwards retired from the Company's service. He died in 1849.

Smith, Sir Donald Alexander. See **Strathcona and Mount Royal, Baron.**

Smith, Sir Frank (1822-1901), minister of public works for Canada (1891-2), was born at Richhill, Armagh, Ireland, in 1822, and came to Canada when ten years of age. In 1849 he set up in business as a grocer in London, Upper Canada, and in 1866 he was elected mayor of London. In 1867 he removed to Toronto, and he became there an outstanding merchant and capitalist. He was president of the Dominion Bank, of the Niagara Navigation Company, of the Northern Railway Company, of the Toronto Street Railway Company, and other companies. In 1871 he was called to the Senate of Canada; and from 1882 to 1896 he was almost continuously a member without portfolio of the successive Conservative governments. He was one of the founders of the Ontario Catholic League; and in 1891-2 he was for a few months minister of public

works in the Abbott administration. He died at Toronto on January 17, 1901. He married the daughter of John O'Higgins, of Stratford, Ontario. In 1894 he was created a knight bachelor.

Smith, Goldwin (1823-1910), author and journalist, was born in Reading, Oxfordshire, England, on August 13, 1823, the son of Richard Pritchard Smith, M.D., and Elizabeth Breton. He was educated at Eton and at Magdalen College, Oxford (B.A., 1845; M.A., 1848). In 1846 he was elected Stowell law professor, and later tutor, of University College; in 1854 he was secretary of the Oxford University Commission; and from 1858 to 1866 he was regius professor of modern history at Oxford. During the American civil war he visited the United States, and in 1868 he accepted the professorship of English and constitutional history at Cornell University, Ithaca, New York. He came to Canada in 1871, and settled in Toronto; and here he spent the remainder of his life.

He took in Canadian affairs a lively interest. He allied himself with the "Canada First" party, and in 1875 was the first president of the National Club in Toronto. Later he became an advocate of commercial union with the United States, and though he was never an advocate of "annexation", he did not conceal his view that political union with the United States was the ultimate destiny of Canada—a view that earned for him much unpopularity. In Canadian journalism he took an active part. In 1872 he contributed to the *Canadian Monthly* the first of a series of papers by "A Bystander"; and under this *nom-de-plume* he continued to write, at intervals, for over thirty years. He wrote, first, occasional papers for the *Canadian Monthly* (1872-8) and the *Nation* (1874-6); then he wrote and published himself a little journal entitled *The Bystander* (first series, monthly, January, 1880 to June, 1881; second series, quarterly, 1883; third series, monthly,

October, 1889 to September, 1890); in 1884 he began contributing a weekly article to the *Week* (1883-90); and, lastly, he contributed for many years (1896-1909) a weekly *causerie* to the *Farmer's Sun* (later the *Weekly Sun*). To most of these journals he lent also his financial support.

Although a master of English style, Goldwin Smith did not fulfill in Canada his early promise of literary achievement. A bibliography of his writings would fill many pages; yet nothing he wrote is likely to occupy a permanent place in literature. His chief publications, apart from journalism, were *Lectures on modern history* (Oxford, 1861), republished as *Lectures on the study of history* (Toronto, 1883), *Irish history and Irish character* (Oxford 1861), *Does the Bible sanction American, slavery?* (Oxford, 1863), *The empire* (Oxford, 1863), *Three English statesmen* (London, 1867), *Cowper* (London, 1881), *Lectures and essays* (New York, 1881), *Jane Austen* (London, 1890), *Canada and the Canadian question* (London, 1891), *William Lloyd Garrison* (Toronto, 1892), *Bay leaves* (New York, 1893), *Essays on questions of the day* (New York, 1893), *The United States, a political history* (New York, 1893), *Guesses at the riddle of existence* (New York, 1897), *Shakespeare the man* (Toronto, 1899), *The United Kingdom* (2 vols., London, 1899), *Commonwealth or empire* (New York, 1902), *In the court of history* (Toronto, 1902), *The founder of Christendom* (Toronto, 1903), *My memory of Gladstone* (London, 1904), *Irish history and the Irish question* (Toronto, 1905), *In quest of light* (Toronto, 1906), *Oxford and her colleges* (New York, 1906), and *No refuge but in truth* (Toronto, 1908).

He died at Toronto on June 7, 1910. In 1875 he married Harriet (d. 1909), daughter of Thomas Dixon, and widow of Henry Boulton of The Grange, Toronto. By her he had no children.

See Goldwin Smith, *Reminiscences* (Toronto, 1912), ed. by A. Haultain;
A. Haultain, *Goldwin Smith's correspondence* (Toronto, n.d.) and *Goldwin Smith, his life and opinions* (Toronto, n.d.); J. J. Cooper, *Goldwin Smith, D.C.L.* (pamphlet, Reading, 1912), with bibliography; W. L. Grant, *Goldwin Smith at Oxford* (Can. mag., 1910); A. H. U. Colquhoun, *Goldwin Smith in Canada* (Can. mag., 1910); and W. S. Wallace, *The Bystander and Canadian journalism* (Can. mag., 1910).

Smith, Sir Henry (1812-1868), solicitor-general for Upper Canada (1854-8), was born in London, England, on April 23, 1812. He emigrated to Canada with his parents about 1820, and was educated, first at an academy in Montreal, and then at the royal grammar school in Kingston, Upper Canada. He was called to the bar of Upper Canada in 1836 (Q.C., 1846); and from 1841 to 1861 he represented Frontenac in the Legislative Assembly of Canada. From 1854 to 1858 he was solicitor-general west in successive Liberal-Conservative governments; and from 1858 to 1861 he was speaker of the Legislative Assembly. In 1867 he was elected to represent Frontenac in the Legislative Assembly of Ontario; but he died at Kingston, Ontario, in September, 1868. He was knighted on the occasion of the visit of the Prince of Wales to Canada in 1860.

Smith, James (1808-1868), attorney-general for Lower Canada (1844-7), was born in Montreal in 1808. He was educated in Scotland, but returned to Canada in 1823, and was called to the bar of Lower Canada in 1828. In 1844 he was elected to represent Missisquoi in the Legislative Assembly of Canada, and was appointed attorney-general for Lower Canada in the Viger-Draper administration. In 1847 he resigned office to accept appointment as a judge of the court of Queen's Bench in Lower Canada; and in 1850 he was appointed a judge of the Superior Court. He died on November 29, 1868.

Smith, James (1821-1888), author, was born at Caraquet, New Brunswick, on September 5, 1821, and was educated at the Quebec Seminary. He was a school-teacher in Lower Canada, New Brunswick, and the United States; and for several years he was a farmer at Causapscal, New Brunswick. He died at St. Laurent de Matapédia on May 18, 1888. He published *Havre de refuge: Rimouski vs. Bic* (Quebec, 1856), *Les éléments d'agriculture* (Quebec, 1862), *Les soirées de la Baie de Chaleurs* (1883), and *Un calomniateur démasqué per lui-même* (n.d.).

Smith, Samuel (1756-1826), administrator of Upper Canada (1817-18 and 1820), was born at Hempstead, New York, on December 27, 1756. He served during the American revolutionary war as an officer in the Queen's Rangers, under Simcoe (q.v.); and at the close of the war he settled in New Brunswick. After Simcoe was appointed lieutenant-governor of Upper Canada, he came to Upper Canada, and took up a grant of land. In 1815 he was appointed a member of the Executive Council of the province, and on two occasions (1817-18 and 1820) he was appointed administrator of the government. He died at York (Toronto) on October 20, 1826. In 1799 he married Jane Isabella Clarke (d. 1826); and by her he had two sons and six daughters. See D. B. Read, *Lieutenant-governors of Upper Canada* (Toronto, 1900).

Smith, Sidney (1823-1889), postmaster-general of Canada (1858-62), was born in Port Hope, Upper Canada, on October 16, 1823. He was educated at Cobourg and Port Hope, Upper Canada, and was called to the bar in 1844. He began the practice of law in Cobourg; and in 1854 he was elected to represent the west riding of Northumberland in the Legislative Assembly. From 1858 to 1862 he was postmaster-general in the Cartier-Macdonald administration, and a member of the board of railway commissioners. In 1861 he was elected to the Legislative Council; but he resigned in 1863 to contest the constituency of Victoria in the Assembly. He was defeated, and thereupon retired from political life. In 1866 he was appointed inspector of registry offices for Upper Canada. He died on September 27, 1889.

Smith, Thomas Watson (1835?-1902), clergyman and author, was born about 1835, and was ordained a minister of the Methodist Church in New Brunswick in 1857. From 1881 to 1886 he was the editor of the Halifax *Wesleyan;* and in 1890 he was president of the Nova Scotia Conference. He died on March 8, 1902, aged 66 years. In 1891 he received the degree of D.D. from Mount Allison University, and in 1901 the degree of LL.D. from Dalhousie University. He was the author of a *History of Methodism in Eastern British America* (2 vols., Halifax, 1877-90).

Smith, William (1728-1793), chief justice of Quebec and of Lower Canada (1786-93), was born in New York on June 18, 1728, the son of William Smith, a judge of the court of King's Bench for New York. He was educated at Yale College (B.A., 1745), and was called to the bar. In 1769 he was appointed a member of the Executive Council of New York, and in 1780 chief justice of the province. During the Revolution, he was a staunch loyalist and in 1784 he left New York for England with Carleton (q.v.). When Carleton returned to Canada in 1786 as governor-in-chief of British North America, Smith came with him as chief justice of Quebec. As such, he had much to do with the framing of the Constitutional Act of 1791. Under the Act he became chief justice of Lower Canada, and speaker of the Legislative Council; but he died shortly afterwards at Quebec, on December 6, 1793. He married in 1752 Janet, daughter of James Livingstone, of New York. He was the author of a *History of the province of New York* (London, 1757). See F. J. Audet, *Les juges en chef de la province de Québec* (Revue du Droit, 1925); and P. G. Roy, *Les juges de la province de Québec* (Quebec, 1933).

Smith, William (1769-1847), historian, was born in New York on February 7, 1769, the second son of William Smith (q.v.), afterwards chief justice of Quebec. He was educated at the Kensington Grammar School, London, England, and came to Canada with his father in 1786. In 1791 he was appointed clerk of the Legislative Assembly of Lower Canada, and later master in chancery for the province. From 1817 to 1837 he was a member of the Executive Council of Lower Canada. He was the author of a *History of Canada* (2 vols., Quebec, 1815 [actually 1826]), the first connected history of Canada in English. He died at Quebec on December 16, 1847. He married Susan, daughter of Admiral Charles Webber of Hampshire, England; and by her he had two sons and three daughters.

Smith, William (1859-1932), historian, was born in Hamilton, Ontario, on January 31, 1859, the son of Thomas Smith and Margaret Summerville. He was educated at the Hamilton Collegiate Institute and at the University of Toronto (B.A., 1883); and he entered the Canadian civil service. In 1902 he became secretary of the Post Office department; and in 1913 deputy keeper of public records in the Public Archives of Canada. He died in Ottawa on January 28, 1932. In 1911 he was invested with the Imperial Service Order. He was the author of a *History of the Post Office in British North America* (Cambridge, 1920), *The evolution of government in Canada* (Ottawa, 1928), and *Political leaders of Upper Canada* (Toronto, 1932).

Smith, William Henry (*fl.* 1846-1851), author, compiled *Smith's Canadian gazetteer* (Toronto, 1846) and *Canada: past, present, and future, being a historical, geographical, geological and statistical account of Canada West* (2 vols., Toronto, 1851). He appears to have been an English ship's surgeon who came to Canada, and became a travelling surgeon-dentist; and he apparently collected the information embodied in his books while making his professional journeys. He was evidently a man of excellent education; but his identity has remained, in spite of extensive research, a mystery.

Smith, William Wye (1827-1917), clergyman and poet, was born in Jedburgh, Scotland, on March 18, 1827, the son of John Smith and Sarah Veitch. He was brought by his parents to the United States in 1830, and to Canada in 1837. Educated in New York, he returned to Canada in 1849. He engaged successively in school-teaching, business, and journalism; and in 1865 he became a minister of the Congregational Church. He retired from active parochial work in 1907; and he died at Burford, Ontario, on January 6, 1917. He published several volumes of poetry, *Alazon and other poems* (Toronto, 1850), *Poems* (Toronto, 1888), and *Selected poems* (Toronto, 1908). He published also *The New Testament in braid Scots* (Toronto, 1896; new ed., 1901).

Smithers, Charles F. (1822-1887), banker, was born in London, England, on November 25, 1822. He emigrated to Canada in 1847, and entered the service of the Bank of British North America. In 1858 he entered the employ of the Bank of Montreal; and in 1879 he was appointed general manager of this bank. In 1881 he succeeded Sir George Stephen (q.v.) in the presidency of the bank; and he died at Montreal on May 20, 1887.

Smithers, a village in British Columbia, is situated on the Bulkley river, 226 miles east of Prince Rupert. It is a divisional point of the Canadian National Railway and an important agricultural centre. Its main industries are mining, lumbering, and trapping. The townsite was cleared in 1912, and the first building erected in 1913. It was incorporated in 1921, being the first village, in British Columbia, to incorporate under the Village Incorporation Act. The place was named in honour of Sir Alfred Smithers, the president of the Grand Trunk Pacific Railway Company. It has a high school and a weekly newspaper (*Interior News*). Pop. (1935), 1,000.

Smith Landing. See **Fitzgerald.**

Smith's Falls, a town in Lanark county, Ontario, situated on the Rideau river and canal, and on the Canadian Pacific and Canadian National Railways, 46 miles south-west of Ottawa. The town owes its name to an enterprising Canadian, named Smythe, who built a mill here on a waterfall of the river, the site of which is now occupied by canal locks. A settlement was established about the year 1836, and the town was incorporated in 1883. Smith's Falls is a divisional point of the Canadian Pacific Railway, employing 1,000 men. It contains several churches, a collegiate institute, public and separate schools, and a public library. The industrial establishments include farm-implement works, grist-mills, baking-powder works, a malleable castings plant, and aërated water-works. On the fringe of the town is the beautiful Rideau lake, a favourite summer resort. A weekly newspaper (*Record-News*) is published. Pop. (1931), 7,108.

Smith sound, a body of water at the northern end of Queen Charlotte sound, off the Coast district of British Columbia, midway between the 51st and 52nd parallels of latitude. It was discovered and named by Capt. James Hanna in the snow *Sea Otter* in 1786.

Smith sound, the passage from Baffin bay to Kane basin, lying between Ellesmere island and Greenland. It was discovered by William Baffin (q.v.) in 1615, and was named by him after Sir Thomas Smith, first governor of the Company of Adventurers for the discovery of the north-west passage.

Smithville, a village in Lincoln county, Ontario, on the Twenty-Mile creek, and on the Toronto, Hamilton, and Buffalo Railway, 20 miles south-west of Hamilton. It is in the heart of a fruit-growing district, and has in addition grist and saw mills, a creamery, and plating works. It has a high school, a public library, and a weekly newspaper (*Review*). Pop. (1931), 800. See Frank E. Page, *The story of Smithville* (Welland, Ontario, 1923).

Smoky river rises in the Rocky mountains, along the boundary between British Columbia and Alberta and near the 54th parallel of north latitude, and flows in a north-easterly direction to its junction with the Peace river between the 56th and 57th parallels. It was discovered in 1792 by Alexander Mackenzie (q.v.) on his journey to the Pacific. The name, which is the translation of an Indian word, refers to smouldering coal beds along the river banks. The Smoky is 245 miles long, while its principal tributary, the Little Smoky, is 185 miles in length.

Smooth Rock Falls, a village in the Timiskaming district, Ontario, on the transcontinental line of the Canadian National Railway, midway between Cochrane and Kapuskasing. It was incorporated as a town in 1929. Pop. (1935), 890.

Smoothstone lake is in central Saskatchewan, south-east of Lac la Plonge, between the 54th and 55th parallels of north latitude. It has an area of 110 square miles.

Smyth, Sir David William, Bart. See **Smith, Sir David William, Bart.**

Smyth, George Stracey (1767?-1823), lieutenant-governor of new Brunswick (1817-23), was born in England about 1767, and at an early age he entered the British army. He attained the rank of major-general in 1812, and in that year he was appointed president and commander-in-chief of New Brunswick, in the absence of the lieutenant-governor, Thomas Carleton (q.v.); and on Carleton's death in 1817, he became himself lieutenant-governor of the province. He died at Government House, Fredericton, on March 27, 1823. See J. W. Lawrence, *The judges of New Brunswick and their times* (Saint John, New Brunswick, 1907).

Smyth, John Paterson (1852-1932), clergyman and author, was born in Ireland in 1852, and was educated at Trinity College, Dublin. He was ordained a priest of the Church of England in 1881. He came to Canada in 1907; and he was rector of St. George's Church, Montreal, from 1907 to 1926. He died in Montreal on February 14, 1932. In 1883 he married Annie Josephine, daughter of the Rev. Hugh Ferrar, fellow of Trinity College, Dublin; and by her he had three sons and three daughters. He was the author of *How we got our Bible* (London, 1886), *The old documents and the new Bible* (London, 1890), *How God inspired the Bible* (London, 1893), *The Bible for the young* (London, 1901), *Truth and reality* (Edinburgh, 1901), *The gospel of the hereafter* (London, 1910), *The Bible in the making* (London, 1914), *A Syrian love story* (London, 1915), *God and the war* (London, 1915), *The story of St. Paul's life and letters* (London, 1917), *A people's life of Christ* (London, 1921), *On the rim of the world* (London, 1922), *God, conscience, and the Bible* (London, 1924), *Myself, and other problems* (New York, 1927), *A boy's and girl's life of Christ* (London, 1929), *The highlands of Galilee* (London, 1930), and *Marriage and romance* (London, 1930). A number of his books went into many editions, and were translated into several languages.

Smythe, William (1842-1887), prime minister of British Columbia (1883-7), was born at Whittington, Northumberland, England, on June 30, 1842. He was educated at Whittington, England, and was for a time a merchant at Newcastle-upon-Tyne. He emigrated to British Columbia before Confederation in 1871, and was for a time a road commissioner of the colony. From 1871 to 1887 he represented Cowichan continuously in the legislature of British Columbia; and in 1875 he was chosen leader of the Conservative opposition. From 1876 to 1878 he was minister of finance and agriculture in the Elliott administration; and in 1883 he became prime minister of the province. He died in office, at Cowichan, British Columbia, on March 29, 1887. In 1873 he married Martha, daughter of A. R. Kier.

Snakes. Nearly twenty species of snakes occur in Canada. Of these only the rattlesnakes are poisonous, and fatalities from the bite of these are very rare. The Missisauga rattlesnake (*Sistrurus catenatus*) is found in the Bruce peninsula, around the southern Georgian bay region, and in a marsh in Welland county, Ontario. Rattlesnakes proper (*Crotalus confluentus*) occur in southern Alberta and southern British Columbia. The most widely distributed snake is the garter snake (*Thamnophis*), which occurs right across Canada, north-westward to the Yukon. At least three species occur. In the east the ribbon snake (*Thamnophis sauritus*) is found. It is striped like the garter snake, but is a much more slender snake with a longer tail. The hog-nosed snake or blowing adder (*Heterodon contortrix*), the smooth green snake (*Liopeltis vernalis*), and the little red-bellied snake (*Storeria occipito-maculata*) occur in Ontario and Manitoba. The water snake (*Natrix sipedon*), the fox snake (*Elaphe vulpina*), the milk snake (*Lampropeltis triangulum*), and De Kay's little brown snake (*Storeria dekayi*) are all fairly common in Ontario. The ring-necked snake (*Diadophis punctatus*) and the queen snake (*Natrix septemvittata*) are more local. Various forms of the racer (*Coluber constrictor*) occur in southern Ontario and British Columbia; the bull snake (*Pituophis*) occurs in southern parts of some of the western provinces, including British Columbia, and the pilot snake (*Elaphe obsoleta*) in southern Ontario. The Pacific rubber boa (*Charina bootae*) is confined to southern British Columbia. The belief that the poisonous copperhead occurs in Canada is erroneous. The fox snake, which is commonly called copperhead, is an entirely harmless species. Some snakes produce eggs; in others the young are born alive. The egg-laying species include the milk snake, fox snake, hog-nosed snake, green snake, and ring-necked snake.

Snakeweed. See **Hemlock, Poison.**

Snipe (*Capella delicata*) is a small marsh or wet-meadow game bird belonging to one of the shore bird families, *Scolopacidae*, to which also belong the woodcock and sandpipers. This bird is intricately marked with a delicate pattern in rich dark browns, rufous and buff. Its proportionately long, rather flexible bill is a specialized organ for probing in mud for its soft-bodied worm and insect food. The mating flight of Wilson's snipe (a more exact designation) is a characteristic performance in spring. The bird flies in wide circles over the nesting area, and at short intervals produces a peculiar quavering sound with its wings.

Snively, Mary Agnes (d. 1933), nurse, was born in St. Catharines, Ontario, and was educated there and at the Bellevue Training School in New York. She was for many years a school-teacher; but in 1884 she was appointed superintendent of the Training School for Nurses at the Toronto General Hospital. She remained in charge of this school until her retirement on pension in 1910; and she was the moving spirit in the organization of the Canadian Nurses Association, of which she was elected first president in 1911. She died at Toronto on September 26, 1933.

Snodgrass, William (1827-1905), principal of Queen's University, Kingston (1864-77), was born at Cardonald Mills, Paisley, Scotland, on September 4, 1827, the son of John Snodgrass. He was educated at the University of Glasgow (D.D., 1865); and became a clergyman of the Church of Scotland. From 1852 to 1856 he was minister of St. James Church, Charlottetown, Prince Edward Island; and from 1856 to 1864 of St. Paul's Church, Montreal. In 1864 he was appointed principal of Queen's University, Kingston, with the chair of divinity; and he retained this post until 1877. He then returned to Scotland; and for the remainder of his life he was minister of Canonbie, Dumfriesshire. He died at Riversdale, Kilmacolm, Scotland, on July 22, 1906. He published a number of sermons and addresses.

Snow, Charles Hammett (1862-1931), pomologist, was born in 1862, and became a civil servant in the department of agriculture in Ottawa. He was responsible for the development of the "Snow" apple, a famous Canadian variety. He was an inspector in the fruit branch of the department of agriculture when he died at Ottawa on July 1, 1931.

Snowball, Jabez Bunting (1837-1907), lieutenant-governor of New Brunswick (1902-7), was born at Lunenburg, Nova Scotia, on September 24, 1837, the son of the Rev. John Snowball. He was educated at Mount Allison College, Sackville, New Brunswick. He engaged in business and became president and general manager of the Canada Eastern Railway. From 1878 to 1882 he represented Northumberland in the

Canadian House of Commons as an independent; and in 1891 he was called to the Senate of Canada. In 1902 he was appointed lieutenant-governor of New Brunswick; and he died in office, at Fredericton, New Brunswick, on February 24, 1907. He married (1) in 1858, Margaret, daughter of John McDougall, and (2) in 1873, Maggie, daughter of the Rev. Robert Archibald.

Snowberry (*Symphoricarpos racemosus* Michx., *Caprifoliaceae*), a low shrub with oblong-round, entire leaves, green on both sides and downy beneath. The flowers are in ones or twos, or in short interrupted spikes at the ends of the branches; the corolla is white, tinged with rose, bell-shaped, and bearded inside. The fruit is a white berry. This plant is common on dry limestone ridges and banks from Quebec to Alaska, blooming in June or July. A variety is often cultivated in gardens.

Snow Bunting. See **Snowflake.**

Snow Dome, mount, is on the boundary line between British Columbia and Alberta, at the head of Bush river, in the Rocky mountains. It is in lat. 52° 11', long. 117° 19', and has an altitude of 11,340 feet.

Snowflake (*Plectrophenax nivalis*), a white, black, and buff bird belonging to the family *Fringillidae*, to which belong the sparrows, grosbeaks, and buntings. In size it is about equal to the common sparrow. Snowflakes are Arctic tundra inhabitants in summer, but flocks of them visit settled portions of Canada in the late autumn and in winter. At such times they may be found in bleak snow-covered fields, where they are seeking seeds from the exposed tops of weed-stocks. The species is also known as the snow bunting.

Snowshoe, a contrivance formed of a racket-shaped frame of wood, strung with thongs or cords of gut, and lashed to each foot to enable travellers to walk over deep, soft snow, into which without it they would sink. Primitive forms of the snowshoe have been reported in Norway, Siberia, Japan, Korea, and the Caucusus; but these have been merely emergency types, and the finished article was developed among the Indians of Canada. The form of snowshoe varied greatly among the various Indian tribes; but it generally conformed to the general type of an oval frame with a web of gut, and with two cross-pieces dividing it into heel, foot, and toe. It was borrowed by the white man, and played a not unimportant part in Canadian history. It was used on military expeditions, both by the Indians and the white man, when travel would otherwise have been impossible; it played a part in the exploration of Canada second only to that played by the canoe; it was employed by the engineers who surveyed the routes of the transcontinental railways; and it was for many years a means of sport and exercise in winter. Forty or fifty years ago there were snowshoe clubs in most of the important centres of eastern Canada; but with the moderation of the winter climate of southern Canada these clubs disappeared. See T. Drummond, *The Canadian snowshoe* (Trans. Roy. Soc. Can., 1916).

Soapstone. See **Talc.**

Soapwort. See **Bouncing Bet.**

Social Credit. Public attention was focussed on the Social Credit scheme by the decision of the province of Alberta to offer itself, in 1935, as a subject for economic experiment. As a result of the provincial election in the summer of 1935, William Aberhart, leader of the Social Credit party at the election, accepted office as premier of Alberta, the party having won 56 out of the total of 63 seats in the legislature. Every member of the Aberhart cabinet and of the victorious party was a new-comer to parliament. The programme of the party included the issue of at least $25 of "social dividend" every month to every natural-born inhabitant.

The Social Credit scheme is directed towards the alleviation of poverty in countries where mass production in field and factory is not accompanied by mass consumption, many of those anxious to consume being short or void of the recognized claims upon the products of industry. These claims are represented by money, and the essence of the Social Credit scheme is the provision of a steady and permanent flow of newly created money into consumers' purses to supplement the deficiency. Hitherto, according to the advocates of the scheme, land, labour, and capital have been recognized as responsible for production, two essential factors being thus omitted or overlooked. These unrecognized factors are the cultural heritage and Social Credit. Cultural heritage is the product of human ingenuity embodied in machines, and of human discoveries transmitted in books, which together have made plenty for all a possibility. Natural-born inhabitants inherit *per capita* as tenants for life equal inalienable shares in this heritage, and each tenant for life is entitled to receive a dividend.

Social Credit is credit based on the strength of the resources of society, enabling it to create "faith-money", which causes industry to function and to produce dividends. The advocates of Social Credit argue that society owns both these factors, and has taken a share of the cultural heritage in the form of taxes, thereby effecting a redistribution of income; but the reward for Social Credit has hitherto been wholly appropriated by the banks in their issue of the "faith-money", by which most business transactions are conducted, and as "faith-money" can only be created as a result of Social Credit the banks are issuing what belongs not to them but to society. The advocates of the scheme say that the State prohibits private mints. It punishes those who make and pass into currency coins or bills. Yet the banker is permitted to create and issue money, and is allowed to make a charge for the use of what it has issued. Moreover, they argue, the "faith-money" created by the banker does not get into effective circulation, nor does it enable consumers to buy goods; for the book entries made by the banker represent no real productive power. The interest on the "faith-money" created is added to costs, and therefore to price; and, instead of getting permanently into the hands of consumers, it is cancelled when the producer repays his loan to the bank. For example: John Dow, a builder, whose tender for a new bridge has been accepted, is known to his neighbours to be a sound man; but this reputation is not sufficiently widespread to satisfy the merchants from whom the materials for the construction will be obtained, nor can it be used to enable his workmen to subsist during the building of the bridge. *His* credit is not money. A banker's credit, on the contrary, *is* money; for when a banker undertakes to honour his customer's cheques up to $50,000, that customer has command over the market as really as if the banker had handed him $50,000. By a stroke of the pen, it is contended, the banker has created this money, and then proceeds to charge interest upon it. The advocates of the scheme want to know to whom does the money thus created, and the interest gained by it, belong. And from this reasoning they arrive at the conclusion that banks have usurped Social Credit, which should be distributed among consumers who need it so urgently.

Under the Social Credit scheme, society becomes a giant joint-stock company, the natural-born inhabitants holding the stock, which is inalienable and unsaleable. The stock carries a dividend with which the inhabitants can buy all the products of industry beyond what is necessary to maintain production. The continuous appreciation of this stock, its constant growth in dividend-earning capacity, will be a result and a mirror of the growth in the credit of the community. Every natural-born inhabitant will, by the dividend allotted to him, obtain his due as a tenant for life in the benefits of the country's cultural heritage. Salaries and wages will still persist, but as the dividends from Social Credit grow ever larger, they will be of diminishing importance.

The issue represents "the present measure of the earning capacity of the cultural heritage handed down to each natural-born inhabitant of Alberta", and the advocates of Social Credit predict that the dividend will increase as time goes on; for each individual is vitally interested in the cultural heritage, and will be intent upon preserving and enhancing its value.

Although adopted by the leader of the party victorious at the provincial election in Alberta, the "Social Credit scheme, or any scheme which envisaged uncontrolled inflation of the currency" was rejected by the Right Hon. R. B. Bennett, prime minister of Canada, at the Dominion general election in October, 1935. At the Federal elections, the Social Credit party repeated in Alberta the success achieved in the Provincial elections, gaining 15 out of 16 seats, but it obtained only two other members (in Saskatchewan), so that in the Federal parliament it had only a representation of 17 members. See C. H. Douglas, *The Douglas manual* (London, 1934); C. H. Douglas, *Social credit* (London, 1934); E. S. Holter, *The ABC of social credit* (New York, 1934), and W. Tutte, *Douglas social credit for Canada* (Vancouver, 1934).

Social Sciences. The formal study of the social sciences in Canada is almost a development of the last half century. Before this a good deal of thought was devoted to political and economic problems; and some notable advances were made in the practical solution of such problems, especially in working out the application of responsible or parliamentary government to the British North American colonies, and in constructing the edifice of Confederation. But there were no outstanding contributions to political and economic thought, with the exception of Lord Durham's *Report on the affairs of British North America;* and even Confederation produced no Canadian *Federalist.* In the curricula of Canadian universities and colleges, natural science obtained a lodgment long before political or economic science. It was not until 1878 that Professor John Watson, of Queen's University, Kingston, inaugurated in that university a course in political economy, in the department of mental and moral philosophy; and it was not until 1889 that Professor W. J. (later Sir William) Ashley was appointed to a chair of "political economy and constitutional history" in the University of Toronto. Since then, however, the study of the social sciences has steadily grown in importance in Canadian universities and colleges. Not only have the courses in the social sciences attracted increasingly greater numbers of students; but the content of the courses has greatly expanded. A notable development has been the addition of "commerce courses", giving a professional business training, in most of the larger universities; and these have become a recruiting ground for many of the larger financial and industrial corporations in Canada. Another development has been the increasing utilization of the services of trained economists in the public service and in private research. Of recent years, moreover, Canadian students of the social sciences have established *media* for the publication of their researches such as did not exist earlier. First, through the *Studies* published by several Canadian universities, through such periodicals as the *Canadian Historical Review*, the *University Magazine*, *Queen's Quarterly*, and the *Dalhousie*

Review, as well as in the journals published by the American Economic Association and the American Political Science Association, Canadian students found an outlet for the results of their work in the social sciences; and secondly, since the reorganization of the Canadian Political Science Association in 1929, they have had a vehicle of publication of their own, first in the *Papers and Proceedings* of the Association, and since 1934 in the *Canadian Journal of Economic and Political Science.* See O. D. Skelton, "Fifty years of political and economic science in Canada" in *Royal Society of Canada: Fifty years' retrospect* (Toronto, 1932).

Société de Géographie de Quèbec, a society founded in Quebec in 1879 to encourage the study of geographical and economic science. In 1880 it commenced the publication of the *Bulletin,* containing its transactions, which was suspended during the years 1898-1907, but then resumed publication.

Société Historique de Montréal, a society founded at Montreal in 1857. During the years from 1859 to 1922 it published 12 volumes of historical memoirs and documents, and in 1926 an account of a *Semaine d'histoire de Montréal: Compte rendu et mémoires* (Montreal), which had been held in November, 1925, under the auspices of the society.

Société Historique de Saint Boniface, a society organized at St. Boniface, Manitoba, in 1902. From 1911 to 1915 it published five volumes of a *Bulletin.*

Société St. Jean Baptiste. The festival of St. John the Baptist on June 24 was observed in New France from a very early date, generally with a *feu-de-joie;* it shared with the festival of St. Joseph on March 19 the character of a popular *fête.* The festival of St. Joseph, the patron saint of New France, came to have in time, however, a purely religious aspect; while that of

St. Jean Baptiste preserved a somewhat popular aspect. When, therefore, the *patriotes* of Lower Canada, before the rebellion of 1837, cast about for a national holiday, similar to St. George's day, St. Andrew's day, and St. Patrick's day (the national holidays of the English, the Scots, and the Irish in Canada), they chose the festival of St. Jean Baptiste. It was in 1834 that Ludger Duvernay (q.v.) founded in Montreal the Société St. Jean Baptiste de Montréal. A similar society was founded in Quebec in 1843. Since that date, the observance of the festival, half religious, half popular, has spread to all parts of the province of Quebec, and to those districts in other provinces chiefly inhabited by French Canadians. It has become the national holiday of the French-Canadian people. At first the Société St. Jean Baptiste adopted as its emblems the beaver and the maple leaf; but since the maple leaf has come to be adopted as the emblem of Canada as a whole, it has, somewhat unfortunately, adopted the tricolour of France as its flag. This does not mean that the French Canadians are in sympathy with modern France; but it gives that impression to English Canadians and others who see the French tricolour displayed in French Canada on June 23. See H. J. J. B. Chouinard, *Fête nationale des français-canadiens* (Quebec, 1881); B. Sulte, *La Saint-Jean-Baptiste* (Trans Roy. Soc. Can., 1916), and *Processions de la Saint-Jean-Baptiste* (Montreal, 1926).

Société Trifluvienne d'Histoire Régionale, a society founded at Three Rivers, Quebec, in 1926, with a view to encouraging the study of local history and the collection of documents. It has a depository of documents, archives, maps, photographs, etc., at the Séminaire des Trois Rivières. The society has published volumes i and ii of a series of *Cahiers.*

Society of Jesus. See **Jesuits.**

Society of the Catholic Teaching Ladies (Dames Institutrices Catholiques) also known under the name of Daughters of the Immaculate Heart, is an order of sisters formed to further the education of Indian children. The Society, working under the federal department of Indian Affairs, has representatives in the following localities: Wikwemikong, Spanish Station, Cape Croker, Garden River and Nipigon, Ontario. Founded in 1862, the Society now numbers 50 members.

Society of Marie-Reparatrice, a religious order for women, founded in 1857 by a Belgian lady, Émilie d'Oultremont, Baroness d'Hooghvorst, known in religion as Mother Mary of Jesus, to make reparation for the sons of man by means of prayer and other devotional exercises. A convent of this Society was established in Montreal in 1910 at the time of the Eucharistic Congress.

Society of the Sacred Heart of Jesus, an institution of religious women taking perpetual vows and devoted to the work of education, was founded in Paris on November 21, 1800, by Ste. Madeleine Sophie Barat, who was canonized by Pope Pius XI on May 24, 1925. The first school was opened at Amiens in 1801, and before the death of the foundress on May 25, 1865, there were 85 houses of the Society, spread throughout France, in many other European countries, and in both Americas. In 1818 the Ven. Philippine Duchesne, one of the earliest companions of Ste. Madeleine Sophie, founded the first house of the Society in North America at St. Charles, Missouri, and from this centre the order rapidly spread, and houses were opened in many of the large cities of the United States and Canada. The first foundation in Canada was made at the request of Bishop Bourget (q.v.) of Montreal, at Saint Jacques de l'Achigan, but was later transferred to its present location at Sault-au-Recollet. There are 32 houses in the United States and Canada, and 150 scattered throughout the world in France, Italy, Spain, Austria, Hungary, Germany, Poland, Holland, Belgium, England, Ireland, Scotland, Australia New Zealand, Egypt, Malta, Belgium Congo, North and South America, West Indies, Japan, and China.

In 1826 Pope Leo XII gave his approbation to the constitutions and rules of the Society of the Sacred Heart. These rules were inspired by those of the Society of Jesus, but were adapted to the requirements of an order for women. The end proposed to the members is primarily the spread of devotion to the Sacred Heart of Jesus and the Immaculate Heart of Mary. The means employed are fourfold. (1) First was the education of girls in boarding and day schools, an education based essentially on religion and character-training. In many places colleges for the higher education of women have been opened, and houses of studies for the religious have now been established at Oxford, Louvain, and Munich. (2) Where practicable parochial schools, schools for the children of the poor, popular works, night schools etc., have been established, and a further field of work has been added in several training colleges for Catholic teachers of elementary schools. (3) The work of spiritual retreats, under the recent pronouncements of Pope Puis XI, has taken on a new impetus. (4) Congregations of Children of Mary, living in the world, have by word and example striven to win souls to the knowledge and love of the Sacred Heart of Jesus.

Sockeye, one of the species of Pacific salmon (q.v.).

Sodalite, a rock-forming mineral nearly related to the feldspars, but containing less silica, and characterized by the presence of chlorine. It crystallizes in the isometric system, but is more commonly found massive or as grains disseminated in the rock. The common colour is blue, and when found in sufficiently large pieces it is utilized as an ornamental stone. One variety of sodalite, when freshly broken, exhibits a carmine colour, which on exposure to sunlight disappears in a few seconds, leaving the material nearly pure white. This variety is called hackmanite. Sodalite is characteristically found with nepheline syenite, and when disseminated in the rock gives the variety known as ditroite. A large deposit of blue sodalite has been exploited near Bancroft, Ontario, and a beautiful mottled ditroite occurs on the Ice river, British Columbia.

Sœurs. See **Sisters.**

Sœurs Compassionistes Servites de Marie. This Congregation was founded at Scanzano, Italy, in 1869, by the Rev. Mother Madeleine Starace, with the collaboration of Mgr. Sarnelli, archbishop of Naples. Its life is both contemplative and active; and it maintains schools, orphanages, and homes. It opened at Montreal in 1926 an establishment in which Italian orphans are cared for.

Soldiers' Civil Re-establishment, a department of the Canadian government formed in February, 1918, for the purpose of rehabilitating in civil life the soldiers discharged from the military forces of Canada who had served in the World War. It took over the work begun by the Military Hospitals Commission appointed in 1915; but it went far beyond the requirements of returned soldiers in the way of hospitalization. It undertook the supervision of the return to civil life of the Canadian army on demobilization; it offered vocational training to those returned soldiers who desired it, and assumed the administration of the Returned Soldiers' Insurance Act, under which policies totalling over $82,000,000 were issued; it supervised the payment of pensions to returned soldiers; and it undertook the work of relief to deserving applicants. The comparative ease with which Canada's military forces were, after the

World War, absorbed into civilian life was in no small measure due to the work of the department of Soldiers' Civil Re-establishment. In 1928 it was merged with the department of Health, under the general name of "the department of Pensions and National Health."

Soldier Settlement. See **Land Settlement Branch.**

Sole, an European food-fish (*Solea vulgaris*), which is not represented in Canadian waters. The name, however, is applied there to other species of flatfish (q.v.).

Solomon's Seal (*Polygonatum biflorum* (Walt.) Ell., *Liliaceae*), one of the early spring-flowering perennials with simple, slender, curving stems rising from creeping rootstocks. The stem is naked below, but above bears nearly sessile, half-clasping, ovate-lanceolate leaves, pale beneath. The axillary flower stalks are slender and are mostly 2-flowered, the flowers nodding and greenish, with bell-shaped perianth. The fruit is a dark blue berry. This plant grows on wooded slopes from New Brunswick to western Ontario.

Sombra, a village in Lambton county, Ontario, on the St. Clair river, and on the Père Marquette Railway, 19 miles south of Sarnia. Pop. (1934), 400.

Somenos, a village in the Somenos district, Vancouver island, British Columbia, on the Canadian Pacific Railway, 3 miles north of Duncan. Pop. (1930), 500.

Somerset, a village in Manitoba, on the Carman-Hartney branch of the Canadian National Railway, 87 miles south-west of Winnipeg. It was originally settled by natives of Somersetshire, in England. It is in a farming district, and has four grain elevators, a creamery, and a grist mill. There is a weekly newspaper (*Somerset News and Swan Lake Echo*). Pop. (1934), 500. There is also a village of this name in King's county, Nova Scotia, 3 miles from Berwick, the nearest railway station. Pop. (1934), 300.

Somerset island lies north-west of Baffin island, at the head of the gulf of Boothia in the Franklin district of the North West Territories. The Bellot strait separates it from Boothia Felix. It has an area of 9,000 square miles, and lies mostly between lat. 73° and 74° and west of long. 90°. Peel sound separates it on the west from Prince of Wales island; while Cockburn island lies to the east. It was discovered by Sir E. Parry (q.v.) in 1819, and was named by him in 1820 after his native county in England.

Somerville, Alexander (1811-1885), soldier and journalist, was born at Springfield, Oldhamstock, East Lothian, Scotland, on March 15, 1811. In 1831 he enlisted in the Scots Greys; and from 1835 to 1838 he served with the British Auxiliary Legion in Spain. He then became a journalist, and wrote under the pen-name, "The whistler at the plough." He came to Canada in 1858, and in 1863 he became the editor of the *Canadian illustrated news* (Hamilton). In 1866 he served in the militia during the Fenian invasion, and was present at the engagement at Ridgeway. He died in Toronto on June 17, 1885. He published *The autobiography of a workman* (London, 1849); *The whistler at the plough* (Manchester, 1852); *Conservative science of nations, being the first complete narrative of Somerville's diligent life in the service of public safety in Britain* (Montreal, 1860), *Canada a battleground* (Hamilton, 1862), and *A narrative of the Fenian invasion of Canada* (Hamilton, 1866).

Somme, Battle of the. See **World War.**

Sommerville, William (1800-1878), clergyman and author, was born in Ireland in 1800, and was educated at Glasgow University (M.A., 1820). He was ordained a minister of the Reformed Presbyterian Church in 1831, and he was stationed in King's county, Nova Scotia, from 1833 to his death in 1878.

He was the author of *The Psalms of David designed for standing use in the church* (Halifax, 1834), *Antipedobaptism* (Halifax, 1838), *A dissertation on the nature and administration of the ordinance of baptism* (Halifax, 1845), *The exclusive claims of David's Psalms* (St. John, New Brunswick, 1855), *The study of the Bible* (St. John, New Brunswick, 1858), *The rule of faith* (Halifax, 1859), and *Southern slavery not founded on scripture warrant* (St. John, New Brusnwick, 1864).

Sophiasburg, a township in Prince Edward county, Ontario. It was organized in 1788, and was also known as the "Sixth Town". It was named after the Princess Sophia (1777-1848), daughter of King George III. Pop. (1931), 1,700.

Sorel, a city and port in Richelieu county, Quebec, situated on the St. Lawrence river at the mouth of Richelieu river near its confluence with lake St. Peter, and on the Canadian National Railway, 45 miles north-east of Montreal. Sorel commemorates Pierre de Saurel, who in 1672 obtained a concession of lands surrounding Fort Richelieu, the building of which he had superintended in 1665. A monument now marks the old fort. In 1787 the name was changed to William Henry, in honour of Prince William Henry, later King William IV. The name Sorel was never quite disused, and eventually replaced William Henry. The city was incorporated in 1889. It still has some eighteenth-century houses, as well as a fine new church built in 1928, a convent, two colleges, a normal school, a court house, and government offices. Sorel is a shipping and shipbuilding city, is the headquarters of the government dredging fleet that maintains the St. Lawrence channel for shipping, and is a good seaport with a deep water front. There are engine and machine shops, saw and grist mills, tanneries, shirt factories and furniture factories. Two weekly newspapers (*Le Courrier de Sorel* and *Le Sorelors*) are published. Pop. (1931),

10,320. See Abbé A. Couillard-Després, *Histoire de Sorel* (Montreal, 1926).

Sorrel. See **Dock, Sheep Sorrel,** and **Wood Sorrel.**

Soudan Expedition. See **Nile Expedition.**

Soulanges, a county in Quebec, facing the St. Lawrence river, above Montreal, and bounded by the province of Ontario on the west, and Vaudreuil county on the north and east. It is traversed by the Canadian Pacific and Canadian National Railways. Chief town, Coteau Landing. Pop. (1931), 9,099.

Soulanges Canal. See **Canals.**

Sour Gum. See **Black Gum.**

Souris, a town in the Brandon district of Manitoba, on the Souris river, and on the Estevan branch of the Canadian Pacific Railway, 25 miles south-west of Brandon. It is a railway centre, and has large railway shops. The chief industries are a creamery, a foundry, and flour mills. There is in the town a collegiate institute, a high school, and a weekly newspaper (*Plaindealer*). Pop. (1931), 1,661.

Souris, a town in Kings county, Prince Edward Island, on the east coast of the island, on Colville bay, and on the Canadian National Railway, 52 miles north-east of Charlottetown. It is the centre of a farming and fishing district, and was formerly a shipbuilding port. It is also a port of entry. Pop. (1931), 1,063.

Souris river rises in the south-east corner of Saskatchewan, crosses the boundary into the United States near the 102nd meridian of west longitude, enters Manitoba near the 101st meridian, and flows in a north-easterly direction until its junction with the Assiniboine, south-east of Brandon. The name, which means "mouse", is probably a translation of the river's Indian name. It is 450 miles in length.

South African War. In September, 1899, the unsatisfactory relations that had long existed between Great Britain and th Dutch-speaking republics of the Transvaal and the Orange Free State in South Africa came to a head, and war was declared. The declaration of war produced in Canada a division of opinion. The English-speaking parts of the country demanded that Canada should come to the help of the mother-country, and should thus demonstrate the solidarity of the British Empire; a large element in French-speaking Canada, believing that the struggle had nothing to do with Canada, and sympathizing perhaps with the South African Dutch, fighting against a powerful adversary, opposed, under the leadership of Henri Bourassa, participation in the conflict. The government in power in Canada at the time was that of Sir Wilfrid Laurier (q.v.). Laurier had no precedent to follow, for Canada had never before officially sent a contingent to take part in an imperial war. Volunteers had been raised in Canada for the Crimean war, and in 1884 a force of Canadian *voyageurs* had been raised for service in the Soudan; but the government had in these cases taken no official action. Laurier compromised by authorizing the dispatch of a contingent of 1,000 men from the Canadian militia, and this contingent, which was recruited from Halifax to Vancouver, sailed from Quebec on October 30, 1899; but as soon as it reached South Africa, it was taken over by the British War Office, and ceased to be a charge on the Canadian exchequer. Later, a second contingent, composed of mounted rifle and artillery units, about 1,320 in number, was sent; and in 1900 a regiment of 500 "Rough Riders" was raised and equipped in Canada at the expense of Lord Strathcona (q.v.), after whom it was named Strathcona's Horse. The only other contribution made by Canada to the prosecution of the war was that

Canada undertook to garrison Halifax, thus releasing the British troops there for service in South Africa. The South African war was thus the occasion for the departure of the last British troops from Canadian soil.

In South Africa, the Canadian contingents, small as they were, gave a good account of themselves. The troops composing the first contingent suffered severely at Paardeberg on February 18, 1900, when they made an attempt, with a British regiment, to rush General Cronje's position; but a subsequent attack, on February 27, brought about Cronje's surrender. A battery from the second contingent took part in the relief of Mafeking on May 17, 1900; and in the later stages of the war the Canadian Mounted Rifles did useful service. See W. Sanford Evans, *The Canadian contingents and Canadian imperialism* (London, 1901); G. P. Labat, *Le livre d'or (The golden book) of the Canadian contingents in South Africa* (Montreal, 1901), and John Stirling, *The colonials in South Africa* (Edinburgh, 1907).

Southam, William (1843-1932), journalist, was born in Montreal on August 23, 1843, the son of William and Mercy Southam. He was educated in London, Ontario, and became first a printer and then a journalist. He became the president and founder of the Southam chain of newspapers in Canada. He died in Hamilton, Ontario, on February 27, 1932.

Southampton, a town in Bruce county, Ontario, on lake Huron, at the mouth of the Saugeen river, and on the Canadian National Railway, 32 miles north-west of Walkerton. The first settlers arrived in 1848; and the settlement was incorporated as a village in 1858, and as a town in 1904. It has furniture and veneer factories, saw and grist mills, a foundry, a high school, and a weekly newspaper (*Beacon*). Pop. (1931), 1,489.

Southampton, a village in Maccan township, Cumberland county, Nova Scotia, 10 miles from Springhill. The name of the village was originally Maccan, from a Micmac word signifying "fishing-place"; but it was changed by Act of parliament in 1872, after the English port of this name. The nearest railway is at Springhill. Pop. (1934), 775.

Southampton island is a large island in the northern part of Hudson bay, south of Melville peninsula, in the Keewatin district of the North West Territories. It is about 212 miles in length, and about 150 miles at its widest part, and covers an area of about 19,100 square miles. It was named after the third Earl of Southampton (1573-1624) by Luke Foxe (q.v.).

South Branch House, a Hudson's Bay Company post on the south branch of the Saskatchewan river, about 60 miles above the Forks. It was built before 1790, was destroyed by the Indians in 1794, and was re-built in 1805 about 6 miles above the previous site. The name was also applied to the North West Company's post built in 1791 near the Hudson's Bay Company post. This was attacked by the Indians in 1794, and though the attack was repulsed, the post was soon afterwards abandoned. In 1805, however, it was re-built 6 miles upstream, near the new Hudson's Bay Company fort; and on the union of 1821 the Hudson's Bay Company took over this post, and it was in operation until about 1870.

South Edmonton. See **Strathcona.**

Southern Indian lake is in northern Manitoba, in the basin of the Churchill river, about the 98th meridian of west longitude. It is so called as the lake of the southern Indians or Crees. The Cree name for it is "big lake". It has an area of 1,200 square miles.

Southesk, James Carnegie, Earl of (1827-1905), author, was born in Edinburgh, Scotland, on November 16,

TOWN OF KASLO (ABOVE), NELSON (BELOW)
SOUTH KOOTENAY PASS, BRITISH COLUMBIA
Photographs by Canadian Pacific Railways

1827, the eldest son of Sir James Carnegie, Bart. He was educated at the Edinburgh Academy and Sandhurst, and in 1849 succeeded his father in the baronetcy. In 1855 he obtained an Act of parliament reversing the attainder of his great-grandfather, James Carnegie, fifth Earl of Southesk, who had been implicated in the Jacobite rebellion of 1715, and became sixth Earl of Southesk *de facto* and ninth *de jure*. In 1859-60 he undertook an expedition through some of the least known parts of western Canada; and he published an account of this expedition under the title *Saskatchewan and the Rocky mountains* (Edinburgh, 1875). His later years were devoted to the writing of poetry and to antiquarian research. He died at Kinnaird Castle, Brechin, Scotland, on February 21, 1905. In 1869 he was made a K.T., and a peer of the United Kingdom, with the title Baron Balinhard of Farnell; and he was an LL.D. of St. Andrews University (1872) and of Aberdeen University (1875). See J. N. Wallace, *Southesk's journey through the west* (Geographical Journal, 1925).

South Kootenay pass is in the Rocky mountains, 8 miles north of the international boundary, and is at the head of the Kishinena creek, in the Kootenay district of British Columbia. It has an elevation of 6,903 feet. It has been from time immemorial one of the chief routes used by the Indians in crossing the mountains, and was until recent times used by the Kutenai in crossing the mountains to hunt the buffalo on the Great Plains. Blakiston, of the Palliser expedition, crossed it in 1858 from the east to the west, and though he makes no claim to have been the first white man to do so, his is the first recorded crossing.

South Nahanni river, in the North West Territories, flows in a southeasterly direction and empties into the Liard river between the 123rd and 124th meridians of west longitude. It is 250 miles in length.

South River, a village in the Parry Sound district of Ontario, on the South river, and on the Canadian National Railway, 40 miles north of Parry Sound. It is a lumbering village, and has a continuation school. Pop. (1934), 600.

South Stukely, a village in Shefford county, Quebec, on the Canadian Pacific Railway, 6 miles from Waterloo. It is named after the village of Stukely, in Huntingdonshire, England, Pop. (1934), 300.

Sovereign Bank, a bank established in 1901, with head offices at Toronto. To an unusual extent it was the creation of one man, D. M. Stewart, its general manager. The collapse of the bank was inevitable, since it accepted business of a questionable character, in the effort to exhibit a prosperous spirit and rapid growth. Strenuous efforts were made, during 1907, to restore the credit of the bank, under a new management. F. G. Jemmett, who had been appointed joint general manager in May, 1907, recommended that the bank should appropriate the whole reserve fund to cover its losses. In the face, however, of effective competition from the other banks, it was found impossible for the Sovereign Bank to live down its past record. In 1908, in order to avoid injury to the general credit of the banking system, the leading banks were forced to take in hand the affairs of the Sovereign Bank. It was eventually wound up with as little disturbance to credit conditions as possible.

Sovereign Council. This was a body set up in New France in 1663, when the colony came under royal government, in imitation of the *parlements* or sovereign councils found at that time in the provinces of France. It was composed of the governor, the bishop, and five councillors, one of whom was the attorney-general. The number of councillors was increased to seven in 1674, and to eleven in 1703. The Sovereign Council was not only a court of justice and of registration, but it had legislative and administrative powers at first as well. These powers gradually passed, however, into the hands of the intendant; and in 1674 the name of the Sovereign Council was changed to that of Superior Council. Its judgments and deliberations have been published in six large volumes under the title *Jugements et délibérations de la Conseil Souverain de la Nouvelle France* (Quebec, 1885-9). See R. D. Cahall, *The Sovereign Council of New France* (New York, Columbia University Studies, 1915); and J. Delalande, *Le Conseil Souverain de la Nouvelle France* (Revue Trimestrielle Canadienne, 1927).

Sower, Christopher (1754-1799), first printer in New Brunswick, was born at Germantown, Pennsylvania, on January 27, 1754, of German descent. He took the loyalist side in the American Revolution, and in 1784 was appointed king's printer and postmaster-general for New Brunswick. On October 11, 1785, he began in Saint John the publication of the *Royal Gazette and New Brunswick Advertiser;* and the same year he published the first almanac to appear in New Brunswick. In 1799 he went on a visit to Philadelphia and Baltimore, and had completed arrangements with his brother, Samuel Sower, for a co-partnership in a type foundry, when he died suddenly on July 3, 1799.

Sow Thistle (*Sonchus oleraceous* L., *Compositae*), a leafy-stemmed coarse annual weed. The leaves, clasping the stem by a heart-shaped base, are sharply lobed, the lobes pointing backwards. The flowers are pale yellow, in clustered heads which become slightly swollen at the base, and are surrounded by a downy involucre. They bloom during the summer and autumn, and are common in waste places, and in manured soil around dwellings. This is one of the most troublesome of Canadian farm weeds.

Spanish river, in the Sudbury and Algoma districts of Ontario, rises in Biskatasi lake and flows into the north channel of lake Huron. The river was so named by H. W. Bayfield (q.v.), the Admiralty surveyor, in 1819-22, from its having been once occupied by Spanish Indians. Its banks are heavily wooded. It is 153 miles in length.

Spark, Alexander (1762-1819), Presbyterian minister, was born in the parish of Marykirk, Scotland, in January, 1762, and was educated at the University of Aberdeen (LL.D., 1804). He came to Canada in 1780, and in 1784 he became tutor to Sir John Caldwell (q.v.). In 1795 he became minister of St. Andrew's Church in Quebec; and he continued in this charge until his death on July 7, 1819. Between the years 1791 and 1819 he published in Quebec a number of sermons. See the Rev. W. Gregg, *History of the Presbyterian church in the Dominion of Canada* (Toronto, 1885).

Sparrow, a word commonly applied to almost any of the more dully coloured, seed-eating birds that are members of the family *Fringillidae*. The term is most frequently applied specifically to the so-called English or house sparrow (*Passer domesticus*), an old world species, introduced into North America in 1850, which is in reality a weaverbird, not a sparrow. Many members of the family *Fringillidae* have the term "sparrow", with an appropriate prefix, as their common English name. Examples among some of the more common and widely distributed kinds in Canada are the song sparrow (*Melospiza melodia*), the vesper sparrow (*Pooecetes gramineus*), the chipping sparrow (*Spizella passerina*), and the white-throated sparrow (*Zonotrichia albicollis*).

Sparta, a village in Elgin county, Ontario, 11 miles from St. Thomas, and 7 miles from Whites, the nearest railway station. Pop. (1934), 300.

Speakers. The office of Speaker of the House of Commons in England goes back to the fourteenth century, when the Speaker was chosen by the Commons and approved by the Crown as the spokesman of the House of Commons, and indeed the sole medium of communication at that time between the Commons and the Crown. Since the advent of parliamentary government and the growth of the office of prime minister, he has ceased to be the real medium of communication between the Commons and the Crown; but he is still the presiding officer of the House of Commons, and the first duty of a newly elected House of Commons is to choose its Speaker. The office was perpetuated in the Legislative Assemblies and the Legislative Councils established in the provinces of British North America; and it has been inherited thus by the Dominion of Canada and the Canadian provinces. The presiding officers both of the Canadian House of Commons and Senate and of the legislatures of the nine provinces of Canada (including the Legislative Council of Quebec) are all designated Speakers, and perform the same functions as the Speaker of the House of Commons at Westminster. The term employed to designate the Speaker in French is "Orateur". The Speakers of the Canadian House of Commons and those of the Canadian Senate since Confederation have been as follows:

HOUSE OF COMMONS

James Cockburn (1867-74).
Timothy Warren Anglin (1874-8).
Joseph Goderic Blanchet (1879-82).
George Airey Kirkpatrick (1883-7).
Joseph Alderic Ouimet (1887-91).
Peter White (1891-6).
Sir James David Edgar (1896-9).
Thomas Bain (1899-1900).
Louis Philippe Brodeur (1901-4).
Napoléon Antoine Belcourt (1904).
Robert Franklin Sutherland (1905-8).
Charles Marcil (1909-11).
Thomas Simpson Sproule (1911-5).
Albert Sévigny (1915-7).
Edgar Rhodes (1917-21).

Rodolphe Lemieux (1921-30).
George Black (1930-35).
James Langstaff Bowman (1935).
Pierre François Casgrain (1935—).

SENATE

Joseph Edouard Cauchon (1867-72).
Pierre Joseph Olivier Chauveau (1873-4).
David Christie (1874-8).
Robert Duncan Wilmot (1878-80).
Amos Edwin Botsford (1880).
Sir David Macpherson (1880-3).
William Miller (1883-7).
Josiah Henry Plumb (1887-8).
George William Allan (1888-91).
Alexandre Lacoste (1891).
John Jones Ross (1891-6).
Sir Charles Alphonse Pantaléon Pelletier (1896-1901).
Lawrence Geoffrey Power (1901-5).
Raoul Dandurand (1905-9).
James Kirkpatrick Kerr (1909-11).
Auguste Charles Philippe Robert Landry (1911-7).
Joseph Bolduc (1917-22).
Hewitt Bostock (1922-30).
Arthur C. Hardy (1930).
Pierre Edouard Blondin (1930-36).
William Edward Foster (1936—).

The Speakers of the Canadian House of Commons and of the Canadian Senate are termed "Honourable" for life; but the Speakers of the Legislative Assemblies of the Canadian provinces are termed "Honourable" only during their tenure of office.

Spearmint (*Mentha spicata* L., *Labitae*), a nearly smooth odorous herb, with square stem and oblong to ovate-lanceolate leaves, which are wrinkled and veiny. The flowers are small, pale purple to whitish, and borne in slender terminal spikes; the calyx is 5-toothed; the corolla is 4-lobed, the upper lobe the broadest; and the stamens are 4. It is commonly found growing in wet places.

Speckled trout (*Salvelinus fontinalis*). This is the commonly accepted name of a char (q.v.) native to eastern

North America. Its beautiful coloration and fine game qualities combine to render it one of the most highly regarded of game species. The coloration of the speckled trout varies widely, depending on the conditions under which the fish lives; in clear, cool waters it is light olive-green in general tone; in dark peat-stained water it is brownish; in the sea, silvery. The sides bear beautiful blue-ringed red spots. The size to which the speckled trout grow also varies with conditions. In small brooks they mature when seven or eight inches long; in larger waters they reach a weight of several pounds. The largest specimen of which there is authentic record was taken in Rabbit rapids, in the Nipigon river, in 1915; it weighed 14½ pounds. The speckled trout was confined originally to eastern North America, but it has been widely distributed beyond this area through artificial means. While generally found in streams, it sometimes inhabits lakes. In large lakes it is confined to the shoal water near shore. Among sportsmen fly-fishing is regarded as the only approved way of taking the speckled trout. Many, however, are caught on worms and grasshoppers. Spawning occurs in the autumn, usually in October. The speckled trout, is found only in the purer and colder waters, disappearing from streams in which the summer temperature is too high or the oxygen content too low. It, therefore, tends to disappear from settled districts and industrial areas, since clearing the land reduces stream flow, thus raising the water temperature in summer, and many industrial plants pollute the waters with their waste products.

Spedon, Andrew Learmont (1831-1884), author and journalist, was born in Edinburgh, Scotland, on August 21, 1831. He came to Canada with his parents in early life, and for a number of years taught school at Châteauguay, Lower Canada. He published *The woodland warbler* (Montreal, 1857), *Tales of*

the Canadian forest (Montreal, 1861), *Rambles among the Blue Noses* (Montreal, 1863), *Canadian summer evening tales* (Montreal, 1867), *Sketches of a tour from Canada to Paris by way of the British Isles* (Montreal, 1868), and *The Canadian minstrel* (Montreal, 1870). His health failing, he removed to Bermuda; and there he died on September 26, 1884.

Speed river, a tributary of the Grand river, in Ontario, which rises in Erin township, Wellington county, Ontario, and joins the Grand river at Preston.

Speedwell (*Veronica officinalis* L., *Scrophulariaceae*), a perennial herb with prostrate pubescent stem, rooting at the base. The leaves are short-stalked, oblong to elliptical, and toothed. The flowers are borne in dense clusters in alternate leaf axils; the corolla is wheel-shaped and pale blue. The fruit is a flattened triangular capsule, notched at the tip. It grows on dry hills and in open woods from Newfoundland to Ontario, blooming from May to August.

Spence, Robert (1811-1868), postmaster-general of Canada (1854-8), was born at Dublin, Ireland, in 1811, and came to Canada at an early age. He was, successively, an auctioneer, a school teacher, and a journalist. He edited a newspaper in Dundas, Upper Canada, which supported the Baldwin-Lafontaine and Hincks-Morin administrations; and in August, 1854, he was elected to the Legislative Assembly of Canada for North Wentworth. A month later he was included in the MacNab-Morin administration as postmaster-general; and he continued to be a member of the succeeding Liberal-Conservative governments until 1858. He was then compelled to resign from office because of the loss of his seat in the Assembly in November, 1857. At the same time he was appointed collector of Customs at the port of Toronto; and this post he held until his death at Toronto on February 25, 1868.

Spencer, Hiram Ladd (1829-1915), journalist and poet, was born at Castleton, Vermont, on April 28, 1829. He became a journalist, and in 1857 he came to Saint John, New Brunswick, where he edited the *Maritime Monthly* (1863-70). He retired from journalistic work in 1903, and he died at Saint John, New Brunswick, on October 15, 1915. He was the author of *Poems* (Boston, 1848), *Summer saunterings away down east* (Boston, 1850), *A son of the years, and a memory of Acadia* (Saint John, New Brunswick, 1889), *The inglenook philosopher of Kennebecasis bay* (Saint John, New Brunswick, 1905), and *The fugitives, a sheaf of verses* (Saint John, New Brunswick, 1909).

Spencerville, a village in Grenville county, Ontario, on the Petite Nation river, and on the Canadian Pacific Railway, 9 miles north of Prescott. It is named after Peleg Spencer, who settled here with his four sons about 1800. Pop. (1934), 400.

Spermophiles. The spermophiles or ground squirrels are small western rodents belonging to two genera. The ground squirrels belonging to the genus *Callospermophilus* are small animals somewhat resembling the Eastern chipmunk in appearance, but considerably larger. They are to be found in British Columbia and Alberta. The ground squirrels of the genus *Citellus* are to be found through the prairie provinces and north into the barren grounds west of Hudson bay. There are half a dozen different forms of this ground squirrel found over this vast range. Ground squirrels, as the name indicates, are ground-living animals, and are seldom found far from a burrow to which they run at the first sign of danger. Ground squirrels store up food in their burrows, and in agricultural districts sometimes destroy crops. Because of their abundance they often do a great deal of

harm, and are persistently trapped and hunted. They are very prolific, having from five to fourteen young in a litter. These animals hibernate early in the season, usually at the first approach of cold weather. See H. E. Anthony, *Fieldbook of North American mammals* (New York, 1928).

Sperrylite. See **Platinum.**

Sphalerite. See **Zinc.**

Spice Bush (*Benzoin aestivale* (L.) Nees., *Lauraceae*), a nearly smooth shrub with oblong leaves pale beneath, and lateral clusters of honey-yellow flowers which appear before the leaves. Petals are wanting; sepals are 6, petal-like; stamens, 9. The fruit is a one-seeded red drupe. It grows in damp woods from Maine to Ontario, blooming in early spring.

Spikenard (*Aralia racemosa* L., *Araliaceae*), an herb, with large, spicy, aromatic roots, and widely-branched stems, 2-3 feet high. The leaves are very large, and 2-compound; the leaflets are heart-shaped to ovate, pointed, doubly toothed and slightly hairy; the flowers are greenish-white, small flat-topped clusters uniting to form a large compound cluster. The fruit is dark purple or black and berry-like. It may be found in rich woodlands blooming in July, but is more conspicuous by its fruit in the autumn.

Spillimacheen river, a tributary of the Columbia river which joins it at Galena, in the Kootenay district of British Columbia. It has a length of 50 miles.

Spilsbury, Francis B. (1756-1823), surgeon, was born in London, England, in 1756 the eldest son of Dr. Francis Spilsbury. He studied medicine at St. Bartholomew's Hospital, and entered the British navy as an assistant surgeon in 1778. He served throughout the Napoleonic Wars, and in 1813 he was sent to Canada as surgeon attached to the fleet of Sir James Yeo (q.v.). He took part in all the naval engagements on the Great lakes during the later stages of the War of 1812; and in 1815 he retired on half-pay. He practised medicine in Kingston, Upper Canada, until his death there in 1823. In addition to some medical papers, he was the author of *The art of etching and aquatinting* (1794). His only son, Francis B. Spilsbury (1784-1830), also served in the British navy during the Napoleonic Wars and during the Canadian War of 1812. He returned to Canada in 1819, and settled near Colborne, Upper Canada, in 1821. He was the Tory candidate for the district of Newcastle in the House of Assembly of Upper Canada in 1830; but was defeated. Shortly afterwards, on October 6, 1830, he died at his residence Osmondsthorpe Hall, near Colborne. See W. Canniff, *The medical profession in Upper Canada* (Toronto, 1894).

Spinney, Edgar Keith (1851-1926), politician, was born at Argyle, Yarmouth county, Nova Scotia, on January 26, 1851, the son of Harvey Spinney. He became a merchant in Yarmouth, and in 1917 was elected to represent Yarmouth and Clare as a Liberal-Unionist in the Canadian House of Commons. In 1920 he was appointed a minister without portfolio in the Meighen government; but was defeated in the general elections of 1921. He died at Yarmouth, Nova Scotia, on May 13, 1926. In 1872 he married Emma, daughter of Capt. E. Anderson, of Annapolis; and by her he had four children.

Spiritwood, a village in Saskatchewan, on the Canadian National Railway, 80 miles west of Prince Albert. It is in a general farming and lumbering district, has four grain elevators and two lumber yards, and has a weekly newspaper (*Herald*). Pop. (1931), 200.

Split cape, a promontory at the southern entrance to the basin of Minas in Nova Scotia. It was called by Champlain (q.v.) "*cap fendu*", of which

its present name is an English translation.

Spodumene. See **Lithium.**

Sponges. The familiar bath-sponge is merely the dried internal skeleton of this animal. Tiny perforations on the surface communicate with cavities lined by living cells. Through the action of these cells currents of water carrying food materials are made to circulate through the cavities of the sponge. In some sponges the skeletal parts, instead of being formed of elastic fibres, are composed of calcareous or siliceous material. Those found in Canadian waters are of this latter type, and no sponges of commercial value occur. About forty species have been recorded from the Atlantic coast and gulf of St. Lawrence. Of these about half the number have a very wide distribution extending by way of Greenland to Great Britain and Norway. One or two of the species are found also in southern waters, off the Cape of Good Hope and Brazil, and one or two on the western coast of Canada. On the west coast there are also about forty species recorded. There is one group of freshwater sponges comprising the family *Spongillidae*, inhabiting clear streams and lakes where they adhere in masses or crusts to the bottom of floating objects. The skeletal parts of these species are formed of siliceous material, and the sponges themselves are frequently green. *Cliona*, one of the sponges, bores into oyster shells, rendering them unfit for the manufacture of buttons. See Lawrence M. Lambe, *Sponges from the Atlantic coast of Canada* (Trans. Roy. Soc. Can., 1896).

Spotted Cowbane. See **Hemlock, Water.**

Spotton, Henry Byron (1844-1933), botanist, was born at Port Hope, Ontario, in 1844, and was educated at the University of Toronto (B.A., 1864; M.A., 1865). He became a schoolteacher, and in 1906 was appointed inspector of high schools in Ontario. He died at Galt, Ontario, on February 24, 1933. In 1879 he was elected a fellow of the Linnaean Society; and he was the author of *The commonly occurring wild plants of Canada* (Toronto, 1888), of which the most recently revised edition has appeared under the title *Wild plants of Canada: A flora* (Toronto, 1935).

Spragge, John Godfrey (1806-1844), chief justice of Ontario (1881-4), was born at New Cross, Surrey, England, on September 16, 1806, the son of Joseph Spragge. He was brought to Canada by his parents at an early age, and was educated under his father, who became headmaster of a school in York (Toronto), and under the Rev. John Strachan (q.v.). He was called to the bar of Upper Canada in 1828, and in 1850 he became treasurer of the Law Society of the province. In 1851 he was appointed vice-chancellor of Upper Canada, and in 1869 chancellor. In 1881 he became chief justice of the province, and president of the Supreme Court. He died at Toronto on April 20, 1884. He married Catherine Rosamund, daughter of Dr. Alexander Thom, medical superintendent of the military settlements of the Rideau. See D. B. Read, *The lives of the judges of Upper Canada and Ontario* (Toronto, 1888).

Spring Beauty (*Claytonia virginica* L., *Portulacaceae*), one of the loveliest of Canadian early spring flowers. The stems are simple and fleshy, bearing a pair of opposite elongated-linear leaves, and a loose terminal cluster of flowers; the petals are a pale rose pink with deeper rose veining. It is found in rich moist woods from Nova Scotia to Saskatchewan.

Springfield, a village in Annapolis county, Nova Scotia, on the Canadian National Railway, 9 miles north of New Germany. Pop. (1934), 320.

Springhill, a town in Cumberland county, Nova Scotia, on the Cumberland Railroad and Coal Company's line, 5 miles south of Springhill Junction, on the Canadian National Railway, 18 miles south-east of Amherst. The name is derived from the fact that the town is situated on a hill, and has a number of natural water springs. Coal was discovered here in 1834, and the town has been for many years an important coal-mining centre. It has also machine shops, wood-working factories, and bottling works, as well as a public hospital and a weekly newspaper (*Springhill Record*). Its shipping port is Parrsboro, which is connected with Springhill Junction by a railway operated by the Dominion Coal Company. Pop. (1931), 6,355.

Sproat, Gilbert Malcolm (d. 1913), author, was born in Scotland, the son of Alexander Sproat and Hectorine Shaw; and was educated at Halton Hall, Dumfries, and at King's College, London. He was appointed in 1860 government agent on the west side of Vancouver island, and for half a century was intimately connected with British Columbian affairs. From 1866 to 1870 he was chairman of the committee on British Columbian affairs in London; and from 1872 to 1875 he was the first agent-general for the province in London. From 1885 to 1890 he was government agent and gold commissioner in the Kootenay district; and later he was interested in real estate in British Columbia. He died at Victoria on June 4, 1913. He was the author of *Select odes of Horace in English lyrics* (London, n.d.), *Scenes and studies of savage life* (London, 1868), *The education of the rural poor in England* (London, 1870), *On the poetry of Sir Walter Scott* (London, 1871), and other books. See T. A. Rickard, *Gilbert Malcolm Sproat* (British Columbia Historical Quarterly, 1937).

Sproatt, Henry (1866-1934), architect, was born in Toronto, Ontario, in 1866, and was educated in Collingwood, Ontario. He returned to Toronto, however, in 1882; and he studied architecture in New York, in France, and in Italy. He became the senior partner of the firm of Sproatt and Rolph, architects; and he designed such notable buildings as Hart House, Burwash Hall, and Trinity College, in the University of Toronto, Bishop Strachan School, Ridley College Chapel, the head office of the Manufacturer's Life in Toronto, and the National Research Council Building in Ottawa. He was a widely recognized authority on Gothic architecture; and from 1926 to 1929 he was president of the Royal Canadian Academy of Arts. He died at Toronto on October 4, 1934. In 1920 the University of Toronto conferred on him the degree of LL.D.

Sproule, Thomas Simpson (1843-1917), speaker of the Canadian House of Commons (1911-17), was born in the township of King, York county, Upper Canada, on October 25, 1843, the son of James Sproule, of Tyrone, Ireland. He was educated at the University of Michigan and at Victoria University, Cobourg (M.D., 1868). He practised medicine at Markdale, Ontario, and at the same time engaged in farming and stock-raising. In 1878 he was elected as a Conservative to represent East Grey in the Canadian House of Commons, and he represented this constituency continuously for the rest of his life. From 1901 to 1911 he was grand master of the Orange Association of British North America; and from 1911 to 1917 he was speaker of the House of Commons. He died at Markdale, Ontario, on November 10, 1917. In 1881 he married Mary Alice, second daughter of William Kingston Flesher, of Flesherton.

Spruce, the name of the trees belonging to the genus *Picea* Link. of the family *Pinaceae*. Thirty-eight species have been described, five of which occur in Canada. Engelmann spruce (*P. engelmannii* Engelmann) and Sitka spruce (*P. sitchensis* (Bongard) Carri-

ère) are confined to the west; red spruce (*P. rubra* Link.) is confined to the Maritime provinces and eastern Quebec; and the other two, black spruce (*P. mariana* (Miller) Britton, Sterns and Poggenberg) and white spruce (*P. glauca* (Moench.) Voss), are to be found from the Atlantic westward and northward to the mouth of the Mackenzie river on the Arctic ocean. Spruce trees are evergreens, with short, sharp-pointed, rigid, singly placed leaves, and can be readily distinguished from all other evergreens in that the leaves are borne on a tiny, woody, peg-like projection which persists at almost a right angle to the shoot after the leaves have fallen. Flowers appear in the spring and are of the pine type, but differ in that the male and female flowers are on different branches of the same tree appearing in the leaf axils of the previous year's shoots. The fruits, likewise after the pine pattern, are all pendulous, ripening during the first autumn, when they liberate their seeds, but they themselves remain on the tree for some time after the seeds have fallen.

Sitka spruce, confined to the coastal region in British Columbia, is the largest and most imposing of the spruces, mature trees being usually from three to six feet in diameter and up to 175 feet high, but may reach heights of 250 feet. The leaves are flat and with stomatic lines on the inner surface only, in this character differing from the other four species, which have four-angled leaves bearing stomata on all four surfaces. Black spruce is the smallest tree, in the extreme north of its range being but a mere shrub. It can be recognized best by its fruit, which persists for several years, and is almost spherical in shape when open and about one inch long, the cone scales stiff and toothed on the margin. White spruce, a fairly large tree, has a cylindrical cone, around two inches in length with cone scale margins entire, and the cones fall from the tree soon after the seed is released. The red spruce lies somewhat between black and white spruce in its characters, and is identified with difficulty unless one has fruit; the cone scales are somewhat toothed on the margin, and the cone is slightly shorter than that of white spruce, and ovoid in shape rather than cylindrical. Engelmann spruce resembles the white spruce most, and is frequently mistaken for it; the fruit is the best means of recognition, fruit scales being flexulose and soft with a ragged margin. In many cases the spruces are difficult to distinguish, particularly in western Canada, where engelmann and white are mixed; but also in the north, where black and white grow together, and in the east, where red, black, and white are found.

The wood of the different spruces is very similar, and of light weight, resembling somewhat that of the soft pines. Its light colour, freedom from resin, and long fibres make it the premier pulp-wood of the world. Being odourless it is favoured for food containers, and in addition is widely used in construction, for interior finish, and for many specialty purposes. Sitka spruce may be obtained in greater dimensions clear of defects, and is especially desirable in aëroplane construction.

Spruce Budworm. This is the most destructive insect enemy of the balsam pulpwood forests of eastern Canada. It has killed more than 200 million cords of balsam and red spruce during the last twenty years. The moths fly in July, and lay their eggs on the needles of balsam and spruce. The caterpillars hatch in about a week, and spin small silken cases in crevices on the twigs near the buds, under which they pass the winter. The following spring these caterpillars begin to feed upon the foliage for about five weeks, after which they pupate in loose cocoons of silk spun in the foliage on which they have been feeding. Out-

breaks may be prevented by the rapid utilization of overmature stands. The oldest stands should be cut first in order to produce fast-growing balsam forests managed on a short rotation.

Spuzzum, a village in the Yale district of British Columbia, on the Fraser river, and on the main line of the Canadian Pacific Railway, 11 miles north of Yale. Pop. (1930), 200.

Squair, John (1850-1928), educationist and author, was born at Bowmanville, Ontario, in 1850. He was educated at the University of Toronto (B.A., 1883), and from 1883 to his death was first lecturer and then professor in French in University College, Toronto. In 1924 the French government awarded him the cross of the chevalier of the Legion of Honour. He died at Toronto on February 15, 1928. He was the author of *The study of the French-Canadian dialect* (Toronto, 1888), *Problems in the study of language* (Toronto, 1924), *The history of the townships of Darlington and Clarke* (Toronto, 1927), and *The autobiography of a teacher of French* (Toronto, 1928); and with W. H. Fraser (q.v.) he was joint author of a *French grammar* (Toronto, 1900), which has gone into many editions.

Squamish, a town in the New Westminster district of British Columbia, at the mouth of the Squamish river on Howe sound. It is the southern terminus of the Pacific Great Eastern Railway, 38 miles from Vancouver. Pop. (1934), 600.

Squaw, an Indian woman. The word is derived from the Narraganset *squaw*, meaning a woman, and is cognate to the word for woman in several other Indian languages. The use of the term has spread all over North America, and is even in use by the Indians of the Canadian west.

Squawfish, a large coarse fish of the minnow or carp family, found in the fresh waters of southern British Columbia and the United States to the south.

It is an enemy of salmon and trout, devouring considerable numbers of the young of those species.

Squids, rapid-swimming predaceous molluscs which are very valuable bait for cod in the gulf of St. Lawrence and on the Atlantic seaboard. So important is this organism as bait that in its absence the success of the cod fishery is seriously impaired.

Squirrel. To the scientist all members of the family *Sciuridae* are "squirrels", but in popular usage squirrels are the "tree squirrels". The tree squirrels are represented in Canada by four well-defined groups. The red squirrels or chickarees (genus *Sciurus*) are found throughout the forested areas of Canada. The gray squirrels (genus *Sciurus*), of which the black squirrels are a colour variety, are found in Canada in southern Ontario, occasionally in the Rainy river section of Ontario, and in New Brunswick. The fox squirrels (genus *Sciurus*) reach only the extreme southern part of Ontario. The flying squirrels (genus *Glaucomys*) are found in the forested area of Canada from Atlantic to Pacific. The chickaree is usually the commonest tree squirrel, and its size, reddish colour, and inquisitive noisy behaviour serve to distinguish it from its quieter and more timid relatives, the gray and fox squirrels, in the areas where all three are found. The gray and black squirrels are the common squirrels of parks. In many sections hunters have almost exterminated this squirrel. The fox squirrel is the largest North American squirrel, and as it is known to occur only in extreme southern Ontario, it is not likely to be confused with either of its relatives. The flying squirrel is a timid animal, active only at night, and provided with loose skin between front and hind limbs, which acts as a sort of parachute allowing it to glide in a long swoop from tree to tree. All these squirrels, except the flying squirrel, are active during the day, and consequently are well known in areas which they inhabit, particularly the red squirrel, whose insatiable curiosity and noisy chatter make it a conspicuous animal. They prefer hollow trees as nesting sites and make leafy nests high up in tree crotches. Their food consists of nuts and seeds, fruits, grains, insects, young birds, eggs, etc. The chickaree is the most carnivorous of the squirrels, and has built up a bad reputation as a destroyer of birds and eggs. On the credit side of the squirrel's ledger is his fondness for tree seeds, and his habit of burying them in the ground is a valuable aid in reforestation. This habit of storing up supplies for the winter is a well-known habit of squirrels, since they do not hibernate, but are active all winter. See H. E. Anthony, *Fieldbook of North American mammals* (New York, 1928); and A. H. Howell, *Revision of American flying squirrels* (North American Fauna, No. 44, U.S. Dept. of Agriculture, 1918). See also **Spermophiles.**

Squirrel Corn (*Dicentra canadensis* (Goldie) Walp., *Fumariaceae*), a low, stemless perennial with thrice-divided, linear-lobed leaves arising from subterranean shoots which bear scattered grain-like tubers resembling grains of corn. The flowers are in few-flowered, nodding clusters, and have the fragrance of hyacinths; the corolla is heart-shaped, with very short, rounded spurs, greenish-white with rose. It may be found growing in rich woods from Nova Scotia to Ontario, blooming in April or May.

Stadacona, the name of the Algonkian village that Jacques Cartier (q.v.) found in 1535 on the site of the present city of Quebec. The origin of the word is disputed. The Abbé Ferland (q.v.) derived it from an Algonkian word meaning "a wing", the angle formed by the St. Charles and St. Lawrence rivers having the shape of a bird's wing; but others have derived it from a Montagnais word meaning "the place where they pass on a collection of logs as on a bridge."

Stafford, Ezra Adams (1839-1891), clergyman and author, was born in Elgin county, Ontario, in 1839, and in 1860 entered the Methodist ministry. Later he graduated from Victoria University, Cobourg (B.A., 1880; M.A., 1883; LL.B., 1884; LL.D., 1890). He died at Hamilton, Ontario, on December 21, 1891. He was the author of *Recreations* (Toronto, 1883) and *Ecclesiastical law* (Toronto, 1888).

Staghorn Sumach. See **Sumach.**

Stamford, a village in Welland county, Ontario, on the Michigan Central Railway, 3 miles from Niagara Falls. It was named in 1792, by Simcoe (q.v.) after Stamford, in Lincolnshire, England. Pop. (1934), 300. See Ernest Green, *Township No. 2—Mount Dorchester—Stamford* (Ont. Hist. Soc., Papers and Records, 1929).

Stamps. See **Philately** and **Post Office.**

Standard Bank of Canada, a bank founded at Toronto in 1871, as the St. Lawrence Bank. It began business in 1873, with J. C. Fitch as president and John Cowan as vice-president. After having attempted a too rapid development, it was reorganized, in 1876, under a new management, as the Standard Bank of Canada. After 1880 the Standard Bank began a steady development. In 1908-9 it purchased the business of the Western Bank of Canada and acquired 27 new branches. In June, 1913, the directors decided to increase the capital of the bank to 3 million dollars. Owing to losses in western Canada, the bank, in 1923, reduced its dividend rate from 14 to 12 per cent. and its rest account from 5 million dollars to $1,250,000. In 1924, however, the Standard acquired the assets and business of the Sterling Bank of Canada, by the payment of 8,234 shares of Standard stock. In 1928 the Standard Bank merged with the Canadian Bank of Commerce, which had offered to exchange Standard for Commerce stock, on the basis of share for share. The Bank of Commerce therefore acquired 220 additional branches. At the time of the merger, the total assets of the Standard Bank were over 103 million dollars. See A. St. L. Trigge, *A history of the Canadian Bank of Commerce*, vol. iii (Toronto, 1934).

Stanbridge, a village in Missisquoi county, Quebec, on the Canadian Pacific and Central Vermont Railways, 43 miles south-east of Montreal. It is named after the village of Stanbridge, in Bedfordshire, England. With Stanbridge East, on the Pike river, 3 miles distant, it has a population of 900.

Stanfield, Frank (1872-1931), lieutenant-governor of Nova Scotia (1930-31), was born at Truro, Nova Scotia, on April 24, 1872. He was a member of the Legislative Assembly of Nova Scotia from 1911 to 1928; and in 1930 he was appointed lieutenant-governor of Nova Scotia. He died, soon after taking office, on September 25, 1931.

Stanfold. See **Princeville.**

Stanley, Sir Charles, fourth Viscount Monck. See **Monck, Sir Charles Stanley, fourth Viscount.**

Stanley Baldwin, mount, in the Cariboo district of British Columbia is in the Cariboo range of mountains, between the headwaters of Tête creek and McLellan river. It has a height of 10,900 feet.

Stanstead, a county in south-eastern Quebec, bounded on the south by the international boundary, on the west by Brome county, on the north by Sherbrooke county, and on the east by Compton county. It is named after one of the three villages named Stanstead in England (in Essex, in Sussex, and in Suffolk). Chief town, Stanstead. Pop. (1931), 25,118.

Stanstead, a village and parish in Stanstead county, Quebec, a short distance from lake Memphramagog and from the Vermont boundary. It is an agricultural community, and has granite quarries. Pop. (1930), 780.

Stanstead Wesleyan College, a co-educational institution at Stanstead, Quebec, founded in 1872 under the auspices of the Wesleyan Methodist Church. Since 1925 it has been conducted under the auspices of the United Church of Canada; but it has no religious tests, and both pupils and teachers are drawn from other denominations. It is a "consolidated school", teaching all grades from primary to senior matriculation. Its present enrollment (1937) is 325 pupils, of whom 60 are in residence; and it has a staff of 22 teachers and instructors. Its present principal is the Rev. Errol C. Amaron, B.A., B.D.; and the lady principal is Mrs. Errol C. Amaron, B.A., M.S.P.E. See *Stanstead Wesleyan College, Stanstead, Quebec* (Municipal Review of Canada, May, 1932).

Stanton, Robert (1794-1866), printer and publisher, was born at St. John's, Lower Canada, on June 6, 1794, the son of William Stanton, afterwards deputy assistant commissary-general in Upper Canada. He was educated at the Home District Grammar school in York; and on August 19, 1826, he was appointed King's printer for Upper Canada. From 1826 to 1843 he was the editor and publisher of the *Upper Canada Gazette;* from 1843 to 1849 he was collector of customs at Toronto; and from 1849 to his death he was an officer of the law courts at Osgoode Hall, Toronto. He died in Toronto on February 24, 1866.

Star City, a town in Saskatchewan, on the Saskatchewan and Carrot rivers, and on the Canadian National Railway, 75 miles east of Prince Albert. It is in a prosperous farming district, and has five grain elevators, a high school, and a weekly newspaper (*Echo*). Pop. (1931), 558.

Starfish. These comprise one section of the Echinoderms, a group of strictly marine animals which inhabit the littoral zone of the ocean bed. There are about sixty species (including the brittle-stars) in Canadian waters. Of these about forty are confined to the west coast; about one-third of this number are confined to the Atlantic coast; and about seven are known to be common to both coasts, and are probably circumpolar in distribution. Starfish, although very slow-moving creatures, form a serious menace to oyster beds, attacking the oysters, slowly pulling open their shells to feed on the soft parts within

Star Flower (*Trientalis americana* Pursh, *Primulaceae*), a low, smooth, spring-flowering perennial, with simple erect stem, bearing a few minute scale leaves below and a whorl of thin veiny leaves at the summit. The leaves are lanceolate and taper at both ends. The flowers are borne on slender stalks, one or more arising from the whorl of leaves; they are delicate, white, with 7 spreading, pointed petals. This plant grows in moist woods and thickets from Labrador to Manitoba.

Star Grass (*Hypoxis hirsuta* (L.) Colville, *Amaryllidaceae*), a small stemless herb arising from a solid bulb. The leaves are linear and grass-like, longer than the flowering stalk which bears a cluster of greenish flowers; the perianth is composed of 6 hairy divisions, greenish on the outside and yellowish within; there are 6 stamens. It grows in meadows and open woods from New Brunswick westward.

Stark, Mark Young (1799-1866), clergyman, was born in Dumfermline, Scotland, on November 9, 1799, and was educated at the University of Glasgow. He was sent to Canada in 1833 by the Glasgow Colonial Society; and from 1833 to 1863 he was the Presbyterian minister at Ancaster and Dundas, Upper Canada. In 1844 he was elected moderator of the Presbyterian synod of Canada. He died on January 24, 1866. Some of his sermons were afterwards published, with a memoir by the Rev. William Reid (Toronto, 1871).

Starling (*Sturnus vulgaris*), an European bird, somewhat smaller than a robin, which was introduced into North America in 1890. In summer the starling is nearly black, with colourful prismatic reflections to the feathers and occasional creamy spots on the back. In winter the plumage is rather profusely spotted, above and below, and the bill changes from a horn colour to a clear yellow. The starling's spread into Canada was first made into southern Ontario. It has not as yet occupied the full extent of territory apparently acceptable to the species. Flocks of thousands which congregate, in the autumn, in southern Ontario, now exceed any similar aggregation of native birds. For a study of this species in Ontario, see Harrison F. Lewis, *A distributional and economoc study of the European starling in Ontario* (Toronto, University of Toronto Studies, Biological series, No. 30).

Starr, George Lothrop (1872-1925), clergyman and author, was born at Brockville, Ontario, in 1872, a grand-nephew of Sir Daniel Jones (q.v.). He was educated at Trinity University, Toronto (B.A., 1895; M.A., 1896), and was ordained a priest of the Church of England in 1896. In 1901 he became vicar of St. George's Church, Kingston, and later dean of Ontario. He died at Boston, Massachusetts, on November 19, 1925. He was the author of *Old St. George's* (Kingston, 1913).

Statistics. A beginning was made with the collection of Canadian statistics long before the Dominion of Canada came into existence. The first scientific census of modern times was that taken in New France in 1666; and it was repeated fourteen times before the British conquest. Early Acts in the British

North American provinces provided for the registration of births and deaths; and the Statistical Act of 1848 in united Canada made provision for a decennial census. The monthly bank statement in united Canada dates from 1856; and Canadian insurance records go back as far as 1815. It was not, however, until after Confederation that any systematic development in Canadian statistics took place. The British North America Act placed "census and statistics" among the subjects falling under federal jurisdiction. A Dominion Census Act was passed, and under this the census of 1871 was taken. The report in 1871 of the first census commissioner contains a convenient summary of the results achieved before this date. In 1876 an Act was passed providing for the regular collection of criminal statistics; and in the same year a beginning was made with the setting up of railway statistics. In 1885 a General Statistics Act was passed, and under this Act the *Statistical year book* was instituted in 1886 on an official basis—superseding the *Year book and almanac of Canada* published under private auspices, but with official patronage, before this date. In 1890 there was passed a Labour Statistics Act, which covered a wider range than its title would suggest; but the depression of the 'nineties, with its consequent economies, rendered this Act largely abortive.

Not until the dawn of the twentieth century did the modern era of statistical progress dawn in Canada. In 1900 the Canadian government instituted a department of labour; and this department set up a series of records hitherto nonexistent. In 1905 the Census Office was placed on a permanent basis; and the Census Act, the General Statistics Act, and the Criminal Statistics Act were consolidated in a single statute. Finally, in 1912, Sir George Foster (q.v.), then minister of trade and commerce, had the wisdom to appoint a departmental commission to inquire into the whole statistical situation; and the result of this commission's enquiries was the appointment of a Dominion statistician in 1915 and the creation of a central statistical office in 1918, to be known as the Dominion Bureau of Statistics. This Bureau has, under the amazing administrative genius of R. H. Coats, who has been Dominion statistician since 1915, co-ordinated the statistical activities of the provinces with those of the Dominion, eliminated the over-lapping of statistical activities in the departments of the Dominion government, and produced in the *Canada Year Book* and the *Monthly Review of Business Statistics* a statistical record not inferior to that published in any other country. See R. H. Coats, "Fifty years of Statistical Progress", in The Royal Society of Canada, *Fifty years' retrospect* (Toronto, 1932); G. E. Jackson, *Statistics in Canada* (Can. hist. rev., 1921); and the *Canada Year Book* (1871—). See also **Census.**

Statute of Westminster. See **Law, Constitutional.**

Staveley, a town in Alberta, on the Canadian Pacific Railway, 74 miles south of Calgary. It was named after Alexander Staveley Hill (d. 1905), the author of *From home to home* (London, 1884). It has a weekly newspaper (*Advertiser*). Pop. (1931), 303.

Stayner, a town in Simcoe county, Ontario, on the Canadian National Railway, 25 miles north-west of Barrie. It was founded in 1854, and was named Nottawasaga Station, when the Ontario, Simcoe, and Huron Railway passed through it; but in 1862 the name was changed to Stayner, in honour of Sutherland Stayner, the owner of a large amount of land in the vicinity. It was incorporated as a village in 1872, and as a town in 1888. It is in a farming district, and has stock-yards, a cider mill, a chopping mill, a continuation school, and a weekly newspaper (*Sun*). Pop. (1931), 1,019.

Steele, Sir Samuel Benfield (1849-1919), soldier, was born at Purbrook, Simcoe county, Canada West, on January 5, 1849, the fourth son of Capt. Elmes Steele, R.N., and Anne Macdonald. He obtained a commission as an ensign in the 35th Regiment of Militia in 1866, and he served during the Fenian Raid of 1866, and in the Red River expedition of 1870. In 1873 he became a troop sergeant-major in the Royal North West Mounted Police; and in 1885 he became superintendent in command of this force. He commanded the cavalry during the North West rebellion of 1885. During the South African War he commanded Strathcona's Horse; and from 1901 to 1906 he was in command of the South African constabulary. In 1907 he returned to Canada and in 1915 he was appointed to the command of the Second Canadian Contingent in the Great War, with the rank of major-general. In 1916 he was made general officer commanding in the Shorncliffe area; and he died at London, England, on January 30, 1919. In 1890 he married Marie Elizabeth, daughter of Robert W. Harwood, seignior of Vaudreuil. In 1900 he was created a C.B., and in 1917 a K.C.M.G. He published his reminiscences under the title *Forty years in Canada* (Toronto, 1915). See R. G. MacBeth, *Sir Samuel Benfield Steele* (Can. mag., 1919).

Steele, a town in the Kootenay district of British Columbia, at the confluence of the Kootenay and St. Mary rivers, and on the Canadian Pacific Railway. It was formerly known as Fort Steele. Pop. (1930), 250.

Steelhead (*Salmo iridens* or *gairdneri*), a fish of the trout group, native to western North America. In habits it resembles a salmon, spawning and undergoing its early growth in fresh water, and then resorting to the sea, where most of its growth occurs. Steelheads make excursions into fresh water at times other than their spawning

seasons. For instance, some commonly accompany one or more species of Pacific salmon on their spawning migrations. In the sea, steelheads are bluish above, but on entering fresh water assume a greenish coloration. At spawning time in early spring they develop a red lateral band, and are then known as rainbow trout. Most of the rainbow trout which have persisted after artificial plantings in eastern waters are of this species. The steelhead is very highly regarded as a game species.

Steenwyck, Cornelis (d. 1684), Dutch governor of Nova Scotia and Acadia, was a native of Holland who emigrated to New Amsterdam (New York) about 1652. He became a prominent merchant, and in 1676 the Dutch West India Company appointed him "governor of Nova Scotia and Acadie", which had been overrun by a force under Dutch auspices in 1674-5, and re-named New Holland. He made no attempt to assert his authority, and in three or four years the French were again in occupation of Acadia. He died in New York in 1684. See J. C. Webster, *Cornelis Steenwyck*, *Dutch governor of Acadie* (Shediac, New Brunswick, 1929).

Steeves, William Henry (1814-1873), one of the fathers of Confederation, was born at Hillsborough, New Brunswick, on May 20, 1814. He went into business, and became a member of the firm of Steeves Brothers. From 1846 to 1851 he represented Albert county as a Liberal in the Legislative Assembly of New Brunswick, and from 1851 to 1867 he was a member of the Legislative Council of the province. He was a member of the executive council of New Brunswick almost continuously from 1857 to 1865, holding the portfolio of surveyor-general from 1854 to 1855, and that of commissioner of public works from 1855 to 1856 and from 1857 to 1863. He was a delegate from New Brunswick at the Intercolonial Railway conference in Quebec in 1862, at the Charlottetown Confer-

ence on maritime union in 1864, and at the Quebec Conference on British North American union later in the same year. On the completion of Confederation in 1867, he was called to the Senate of Canada; and he remained a member of the Senate until his death at St. John, New Brunswick, on December 9, 1873.

Steinbach, a village in Manitoba, 32 miles south-east of Winnipeg, and 7 miles south-west of Giroux, the nearest railway station. It is in a mixed farming district settled originally by Mennonites from Steinbach, in Russia. It has a weekly German newspaper (*Die Post*). Pop. (1934), 750.

Steinhauer, Henry Bird (1804-1885), missionary, was born in the Ramah Indian settlement, Lake Simcoe, Upper Canada, in 1804, a pure-blooded Indian of the Chippewa tribe. He received the name of Steinhauer from a German family that adopted and educated him. In 1840 he accompanied the Rev. James Evans (q.v.) to the North West, and settled at Norway House. Here he remained until 1855 assisting in the elaboration of the Cree syllabic characters. In 1858 he was ordained a minister of the Methodist Church, and was stationed at Whitefish Lake, North West Territories. Here he died on December 29, 1885. He translated into Cree a large part of the Old and the New Testaments.

Stella, a village in Lennox county, Ontario, on Amherst island, in the bay of Quinte, 3 miles from Ernestown, the nearest railway station. Pop. (1934), 200.

Stellarton, a town in Pictou county, Nova Scotia, is situated on the East river, about 3 miles from New Glasgow, on the Canadian National Railway, of which it is a divisional point, having large railway yards, roundhouse, and machine shops. Following the discovery of coal, near where the Albion mines are located, in 1798, and the beginning of coal mining, a village came into being.

Until 1889 the community was known as Albion Mines. It was incorporated as a town in that year, and was given the name of Stellarton, to commemorate the discovery of the so-called Stellar coal which lies under the town, and which is so rich in oil that during combustion it emits short bright flames, resembling stars. Pop. (1935), 5,400.

Stephansson, Stephan Gudmundsson (1853-1927), poet, was born in Iceland on October 3, 1853, and emigrated to the United States in 1873. He engaged in farming, first in Wisconsin, then in North Dakota, and finally in the Canadian North West. In 1889 he settled in what is now Alberta, near Innisfail; and here he lived until his death on August 10, 1927. He became a poet "unsurpassed by any other Icelandic poet since the Middle Ages". His first volume of verse was published in Reykjavik, Iceland, in 1898; and other volumes followed in 1900, in 1909-10, in 1914, in 1917, and in 1920. All his work was in Icelandic. See Watson Kirkconnell, *Canada's leading poet: Stephan G. Stephansson* (Univ. of Toronto Quarterly, 1936).

Stephen, Sir George, Bart., afterwards **Baron Mount Stephen** (1829-1921), financier, was born at Dufftown, Banffshire, Scotland, on June 5, 1829, the son of William Stephen and Elspet Smith. He received a grammar school education, and emigrated to Canada in 1850. He entered the firm of William Stephen and Co., manufacturers of woollen goods, Montreal; and ultimately purchased a controlling interest. In 1873 he was elected a director of the Bank of Montreal, and from 1876 to 1881 he was its president. Together with his relative, Lord Strathcona (q.v.), he was a member of the syndicate which took over the St. Paul and Manitoba Railway, and in 1880 of the company which undertook the construction of the Canadian Pacific Railway. He was president of the Canadian Pacific Railway Company from 1881 to 1888.

In 1888 he went to live in England, and his later years were largely occupied with philanthropy. He died at Brocket Hall, Hatfield, Herefordshire, England, on November 29, 1921. He was twice married, (1) in 1853 to Annie Charlotte (d. 1896), daughter of Benjamin Kane, London, England; and (2) in 1897 to Gian, daughter of Capt. Robert George Tufnell, R.N. In 1886 he was created a baronet of the United Kingdom; in 1891 Baron Mount Stephen, in the peerage of the United Kingdom; and in 1905 a G.C.V.O. In 1911 he was made an LL.D. of Aberdeen University.

Stephen, mount, is in the Kootenay district of British Columbia, immediately east of Field in Yoho Park in the Rocky mountains. It is in lat. 51° 24', long. 116° 26', and has an altitude of 10,485 feet. It was named after Sir George Stephen (q.v.), later Lord Mount Stephen, president of the Canadian Pacific Railway (1881-88).

Stephens, William A. (1809-1891), poet, was born in Belfast, Ireland, in 1809, and came to Canada in early youth. He contributed verse to many early Upper Canadian newspapers, and was one of the earliest writers of verse in the province. He died on March 21, 1891, at Owen Sound, Ontario, where he had been for many years collector of customs. He was the author of *Hamilton, and other poems* (Toronto, 1840), *A poetical geography, and Rhyming rules for spelling* (Toronto, 1848), *Hamilton, and other poems and lectures* (Toronto, 1871), and *The Centennial: An international poem* (Toronto, 1878).

Sterling Bank of Canada. The first suggestion of the establishment of this bank dates from a meeting of two friends, who were dining in the National Club, Toronto. Others became interested; a charter was granted in 1905, and the bank began business in 1906, with head office in Toronto. The bank shares were soon subscribed. An ambitious programme was adopted, involving the early starting of many branches. Times were prosperous and hopes were high. Early difficulties were overcome, capital was increased, deposits and reserves grew large. The failure of the Home Bank of Canada in 1923, and unfavourable financial conditions in Canada about that time, however, weakened public confidence in the smaller banks. The Sterling Bank sought and obtained a successful merger with the Standard Bank; and this was carried into effect in December, 1924, two shares of the enlarged Standard being given for three shares of the Sterling. The full story is told in A. St.L. Trigge, *History of the Canadian Bank of Commerce*, vol. iii (Toronto, 1934).

Stettler, a town in Alberta, on the Canadian Pacific and Canadian National Railways, 50 miles east of Lacombe, and 100 miles south-east of Edmonton. It was known as Blumenau until 1906; but was in that year renamed after Carl Stettler, a native of Berne, Switzerland, who emigrated to the United States in 1887, and came to Canada in 1903. It is the centre of an excellent wheat-growing district; and has the advantage of large deposits of coal near it. It has four grain elevators, a high school, and a weekly newspaper (*Independent*). Pop. (1931), 1,219.

Stevens, Paul (1830-1882), author, was born in Belgium in 1830. He emigrated to Canada as a young man, and became the editor, first of *La Patrie*, and then of *L'Artiste*, in Montreal, Lower Canada. He published *Fables (en vers)* (Montreal, 1857) and *Contes populaires* (Ottawa, 1867). He died at Coteau du Lac, Lower Canada, where he was a tutor to the Beaujeu family, in 1882.

Stevenson, John (1812-1884), speaker of the Legislative Assembly of Ontario (1867-71), was born in Hunterdon county, New Jersey, on August 12, 1812, the son of Edward Stevenson. He came to Canada with his parents at an early age, and went into business in

the bay of Quinte district. In 1863 he became the first warden of the united counties of Lennox and Addington; and in 1867 he was elected to represent Lennox in the Legislative Assembly of Ontario. Though without parliamentary experience, he was chosen the first speaker of the Assembly, and he presided over it until his defeat in the elections of 1871. He died at Napanee, Ontario, on April 1, 1884. In 1841 he married Phoebe Eliza Hall; and by her he had seven children, two of whom died in infancy. See W. S. Herrington, *Some notes on the first Legislative Assembly of Ontario and its speaker, Hon. John Stevenson* (Trans. Roy. Soc. Can., 1915).

Stevensville, a village in Welland county, Ontario, on the Canadian National and Michigan Central Railways, 11 miles south-east of Welland. Pop. (1934), 500.

Steveston, a town in the New Westminster district of British Columbia, on Lulu island, at the mouth of the Fraser river. It is the terminus of the Vancouver-Steveston branch of the British Columbia Electric Railway, and has connection by ferry with Vancouver island. It has churches and a school. Pop. (1930), 1,000.

Stewart, Alexander (1794-1865), politician and judge, was born in Halifax, Nova Scotia, on January 30, 1794, the son of the Rev. James Stewart. He was educated at the Halifax grammar school, and was admitted an attorney-at-law in Halifax in 1821. In 1826 he was elected to represent Cumberland in the Nova Scotia House of Assembly, and he sat in this House until he was appointed a member of the Legislative Council in 1837. Throughout his political career he was a prominent Reformer; but in 1840 he was sworn a member of the Executive Council of the province. In 1846 he resigned from the Legislative and Executive Councils, to accept appointment as master of the rolls in Nova Scotia; and he occupied this position until the abolition of the court of chancery in 1855. He continued a judge of the vice-admiralty court until his death at Halifax on January 1, 1865. In 1856 he was created a C.B. See C. J. Townshend, *Life of Honorable Alexander Stewart, C.B.* (Coll. Nova Scotia Hist. Soc., vol. xv, 1911).

Stewart, Alexander (*fl.* 1796-1840), fur-trader, entered the service of the North West Company as an apprentice clerk in 1796. In 1806 D. W. Harmon (q.v.) met him at Fort des Prairies. Later, he was placed in charge of a post on Lesser Slave lake; and in 1812, though still a clerk, he was placed in charge of the Athabaska River department. He was made a partner of the North West Company in 1813; and was transferred to the Columbia, where he was present at the capture of Fort Astoria. In 1815 he returned to Lesser Slave lake, and there he remained for several years. At the time of the union of 1821, he was made a chief factor of the Hudson's Bay Company. From 1821 to 1823 he was in charge at Fort William; from 1823 to 1826, at Island lake; from 1826 to 1830, at Fort Chipewyan; and from 1831 to 1832, at Moose Factory. He was granted furlough in 1832; and he retired from the Company's service in 1833. He died in May, 1840. His name is frequently misspelled "Stuart".

Stewart, Andrew (1789?-1822), fur-trader, was born in Glasgow, Scotland, about 1789, and entered the service of the Hudson's Bay Company in 1811, as a writer at Moose Factory. In 1814-5 he was the master at Moose, and in 1815-6 at Missakami lake. In 1816-7 he was at Kenogamissee; and from 1817 to 1821 he was at Michipicoten. He was promoted to the rank of chief trader in 1821; and he died at Osnaburgh House on May 24, 1822.

Stewart, Charles James (1775-1837), Anglican bishop of Quebec (1826-37), was born at Scotland, on April 15, 1775, the fifth son of John Stewart, seventh Earl of Galloway. He was educated at Oxford University (M.A., 1799), and took holy orders in the Church of England. He came to Canada in 1808 as a missionary under the Society for the Propagation of the Gospel, and was stationed in St. Armand in the Eastern Townships. In 1819 he was appointed visiting missionary in the diocese of Quebec; and in 1826 he succeeded Bishop Mountain as bishop of Quebec. He died at London, England, on July 13, 1837. In 1817 he was made a D.D. of Oxford University. Besides several sermons and missionary reports, he published *A short view of the present state of the Eastern Townships* (Montreal, 1815) and a *Letter on the differences of opinion respecting the clergy reserves and other points* (Quebec, 1827). He was not married. See Rev. J. N. Norton, *Life of Bishop Stewart of Quebec* (New York, 1859); and Rev. W. J. D. Waddilove, *The Stewart missions* (London, 1838).

Stewart, George (1848-1906), journalist and author, was born in New York city, on November 26, 1848, the son of George Stewart and Elizabeth Dubuc. He came to Canada with his parents in 1851, was educated at London, Upper Canada, and at Saint John, New Brunswick, and became a journalist. In 1867 he founded and edited *Stewart's Literary Quarterly Magazine* (1867-72), and he was subsequently editor-in-chief of *Rose-Belford's Canadian Monthly* (Toronto, 1878). From 1879 to 1896 he was editor of the Quebec *Daily Chronicle*. He was a voluminous contributor to periodicals, encyclopedias, and biographical dictionaries; and he was the author of the following books: *The story of the great fire in St. John, New Brunswick* (Montreal, 1877), *Canada under the administration of the Earl of Dufferin* (Toronto, 1878), *An account of the public dinner to H. E. the Count of Premio Real* (Quebec, 1881), *Essays from reviews*

(Quebec, 1892; 2nd series, 1893). In 1882 he was made a charter member of the Royal Society of Canada; and he was the recipient of honorary degrees from Laval University, McGill University, Bishop's College, Lennoxville, and King's College, Nova Scotia. He died at Quebec, on February 26, 1906.

Stewart, Harriet (1862?-1931), feminist, was born about 1862, and was educated at Mount Allison University, New Brunswick (B.A., 1882). She was reputed to be the first woman in the British Empire to receive the degree of bachelor of arts. She died at Regina, Saskatchewan, on November 1, 1931.

Stewart, James D. (d. 1933), prime minister of Prince Edward Island (1923-7 and 1931-3), was born at Lower Montague, Prince Edward Island, and was educated at Prince of Wales College, Charlottetown, and at Dalhousie University. He was called to the bar; and in 1917 he was elected a member of the Legislative Assembly of Prince Edward Island for South Kings. He sat continuously in the Assembly until his death; and in 1921 he was elected leader of the Conservative opposition. From 1923 to 1927 and from 1931 to 1933 he was prime minister and attorney-general. He died on October 10, 1933.

Stewart, John (1758?-1834), author, was born about 1758, and settled in Prince Edward Island in 1778. He was speaker of the House of Assembly from 1795 to 1798, and again from 1824 to 1830; and he died on the island in 1834. He was the author of *An account of Prince Edward Island, in the gulf of St. Lawrence* (London, 1806).

Stewart, John (1794?-1858), legislative and executive councillor of Lower Canada, was born in Quebec about 1794. During the war of 1812 he was deputy paymaster-general of the Lower Canadian militia. In 1825 he was appointed a member of the Legislative Council of Lower Canada, and in 1826

a member of the Executive Council. At the time of the outbreak of the rebellion of 1837, he was acting as president of the Executive Council. He ceased to be a legislative councillor in 1838, and an executive councillor in 1841. He died at Quebec on January 5, 1858.

Stewart, John Alexander (d. 1922), minister of railways and canals for Canada (1921), was born at Renfrew, Ontario, the son of Robert Stewart. He was educated at Ottawa University, studied law at Osgoode Hall, Toronto, and was called to the bar in Ontario. He practised law in Perth, Ontario; and from 1918 to 1922 he represented Lanark in the Canadian House of Commons. From September 21, to December 28, 1921, he was minister of railways and canals in the Meighen administration. He died at Montreal on October 7, 1922. In 1907 he married Jessie Mabel, daughter of J. T. Henderson, of Perth, Ontario.

Stewart, McLeod (1847-1926), lawyer and author, was born in Bytown (now Ottawa) on February 6, 1847, the eldest son of William Stewart, who represented Bytown in the Legislative Assembly of United Canada. He was educated at the University of Toronto (B.A., 1867; M.A., 1870), and was called to the Ontario bar in 1870. He practised law in Ottawa, and in 1887-8 he was mayor of Ottawa. He died at Ottawa on October 9, 1926. In 1874 he married Linnie Emma, eldest daughter of Colonel Walker Powell. He was the author of several pamphlets, *Ottawa an ocean port* (Ottawa, 1893), *Fifty years of the Ottawa Board of Trade* (Ottawa, 1908), and *The first half-century of Ottawa* (Ottawa, 1910).

Stewart, Thomas Brown Phillips (1864-1892), poet, was born in Ontario, Canada, and was educated at the Brampton High School and at the University of Toronto (B.A., 1888) LL.B., 1891). He died at Toronto, on

February 2, 1892, leaving bequests to the Library of the University of Toronto and to the Library of Osgoode Hall. A writer of occasional verse, he published one volume of *Poems* (London, 1887).

Stewart, William (1835-1912), clergyman and editor, was born in Ecclefechan, Scotland, in 1835, and was educated at Glasgow University. He emigrated to Canada in 1856, and in 1859 he was ordained a minister of the Baptist Church. From 1894 to 1906 he was principal of the Toronto Bible Training School; and for several years he was editor of the *Canadian Baptist*. He died at Toronto on March 5, 1912.

Stewart, a town in the Cassiar district of British Columbia, 125 miles north of Prince Rupert, is situated at the mouth of Bear river, at the head of Portland canal (q.v.). Its location was visited during the Yukon gold rush of 1898 by a number of adventurers in search of a new placer field, and the townsite was staked out under United States pre-emption laws. Later the Alaska boundary award placed it in Canada. It was named after its first postmaster and mining recorder, R. M. Stewart. It is a port of call for steamers trading along the coast, and has an airport, a school, a hospital, and government offices. Pop. (1935), 500.

Stewart river, in the Yukon territory, rises in the Rocky mountains near the headwaters of the Peel and Gravel rivers, flows westward, and enters the Yukon river 10 miles below the mouth of the White river. Its principal tributary is the McQuesten river. The Stewart was discovered in 1850 by Robert Campbell (q.v.) of the Hudson's Bay Company, and was named by him after his friend and assistant, James G. Stewart. The river flows at first swiftly and then with a quieter current through extensive wooded or grassy plains. Except for a break at Fraser rapids, it is navigable for small

steamers from its mouth almost to its source. In the early days, placer gold was taken from its bars; but it now is noted for lead-ore, brought down from Mayo, 188 miles from its mouth. It is 320 miles in length, and drains a basin of 21,900 square miles.

Stewiacke, a village in Colchester county, Nova Scotia, on the Stewiacke river, and on the Canadian National Railway, 17 miles south of Truro. The name is from a Micmac word signifying either "oozing from dead water" or "whimpering as it goes out." Its port is Maitland, 12 miles down the Stewiacke river. It is in a general farming district. Pop. (1934), 850.

Stibnite. See Antimony.

Stickleback. The sticklebacks are small fishes characterized by a series of free spines on the back and in front of the dorsal fin, and by having the ventrals reduced to a sharp spine. The three species of sticklebacks found commonly in Canada are the two-spined stickleback, the five-spined or brook stickleback, and the nine-spined stickleback. The two-spined species is found in the sea on both the Atlantic and Pacific coasts. It also enters fresh water, being found as far inland as the head of lake Ontario in the east. The other two common species are inland in their distribution. The sticklebacks are interesting little fishes, but have a rather truculent disposition, attacking other fishes viciously and using their spines as weapons of offence. They build nests for the protection of their eggs, which the males guard during incubation.

Stikine river flows south-west through the Cassiar district of British Columbia, enters Alaska and empties into Dry strait, at the head of Frederick sound, immediately north of Wrangell. It was discovered in 1834 by John McLeod (q.v.) of the Hudson's Bay Company. The name is an Indian word meaning "great river". In 1862, after gold discoveries in this area, the

Stikine territory was formed, with the governor of British Columbia as joint administrator; when the discovery proved of minor importance the territory reverted to British Columbia in 1863. The river is navigable for about 130 miles to Glenora and Telegraph creek, and is the route for reaching the Cassiar mining district in the vicinity of Dease lake. The river is 335 miles in length, and drains an area of 20,300 square miles.

Stimson, Elam (1792-1869), physician and author, was born at Tolland, Connecticut, on October 4, 1792. He served in the American forces during the War of 1812, and later studied medicine at Yale University and at Dartmouth College, Hanover, New Hampshire (M.D., 1819). He came to Canada in 1823, and settled as a practitioner in Galt, Upper Canada. Later, he removed to the London district, and then to the village of St. George, where he died on January 1, 1869. He was the author of one of the earliest medical treatises published in Canada, *The cholera beacon, being a treatise on the epidemic cholera as it appeared in Upper Canada in 1832-4* (Dundas, 1835).

Stinging Nettle. See **Nettle.**

Stirling, Sir William Alexander, Earl of (1567?-1640), poet and colonizer, was born at the manor house of Menstrie, in the parish of Logie, Scotland, about 1567, and was probably educated at the Stirling grammar school. He became tutor to the Earl of Argyle, and later to Prince Henry, son of James VI of Scotland and I of England. He became a distinguished poet of the time and a favourite with James I. In 1621 James made him a grant of Nova Scotia, or "New Scotland", and later this grant was extended to a large part of what is now Canada. This carried with it the right of creating baronets of Nova Scotia (q.v.). In 1625 the grant was confirmed by Charles I; and in 1628 a band of Scot-

tish colonists was sent out to Port Royal. The difficulties facing colonization proved, however, almost insuperable; and the Scottish colony in Acadia gradually died out. In 1626 Sir William Alexander was appointed secretary of state for Scotland; in 1630 he was created "Lord Alexander of Tullibody and Viscount Stirling", and in 1633 the Earl of Stirling, with the additional title of Viscount Canada. He died at London, in great pecuniary difficulties, on September 12, 1640; and was succeeded in the title by his infant grandson. See G. P. Insh, *Scottish colonial schemes* (Glasgow, 1922) and *Sir William Alexander's colony at Port Royal* (Dalhousie Review, 1930).

Stirling, a village in Hastings county, Ontario, on Rawdon creek, and on the Canadian National Railway, 16 miles north-west of Belleville. Its manufactures are cheese, boxes, baskets, veneer, and flour. It has a high school, a public library, and a weekly newspaper (*News-Argus*). Pop. (1931), 938.

Stirling. See **St. Thomas.**

Stisted, Sir Henry William (1817-1875), lieutenant-governor of Ontario (1867-8), was born at St. Omer, France, in 1817, the son of Lieut.-Col. Charles Stisted, of the 3rd Hussars, and Eliza, daughter of Major-Gen. Burn. He was educated at Sandhurst, entered the British army as an ensign in the 2nd Foot in 1835, and eventually rose to the rank of lieutenant-general. He saw service in Afghanistan and Persia; and in 1857 he commanded the advance guard of Havelock's force at the relief of Lucknow. In 1864 he became a major-general, and in 1866 he was appointed divisional commander of the troops in Upper Canada. In 1867 he was sworn in as first lieutenant-governor of Ontario; and he held this office until the appointment of Sir William Howland (q.v.) as lieutenant-governor in 1868. Shortly afterwards he returned to England; and he died at Wood House,

Upper Norwood, Surrey, on December 10, 1875. In 1845 he married Maria, daughter of Lieut.-Col. Burton. He was created a C.B. in 1858, and a K.C.B. in 1871.

Stittsville, a village in Carleton county, Ontario, on the Canadian Pacific Railway, 15 miles south-west of Ottawa. Pop. (1934), 250.

Stobo, Robert (*fl.* 1727-1770), soldier, was born in 1727, the son of William Stobo, a merchant of Glasgow, Scotland. He emigrated to Virginia when a youth; and in 1754 he was appointed a captain in the Virginia regiment. When Washington was compelled to surrender Fort Necessity in 1755, Stobo was handed over to the French as an hostage. He was taken to Quebec, where he was condemned to death as a spy, having sent to the English a plan of Fort DuQuesne. He escaped, however, in the spring of 1759, and made his way to Louisbourg, whence he was sent back to Quebec to aid Wolfe (q.v.) in the capture of the fortress. He afterwards asserted that he gave Wolfe the idea of landing at Wolfe's cove. In 1760 he was given a commission as captain in the 15th Regiment of Foot; and his name appears in the *Army List* as late as 1770. He then disappears from view. His own account of his life was afterwards published under the title *Memoirs of Major Robert Stobo, of the Virginia Regiment* (Pittsburgh, 1854); but the details of his story lack corroboration. His adventures were the basis of Sir Gilbert Parker's *Seats of the mighty* (London, 1896).

Stonewall, a town in the Selkirk district of Manitoba, on the Canadian Pacific Railway, 20 miles north-west of Winnipeg. It was named in 1878 after "Stonewall" Jackson, famous Confederate general in the American civil war; but the name has reference probably also to the limestone quarries in the neighbourhood. It has a high school

and a weekly newspaper (*Argus*). Pop. (1913), 1,031.

Stoney Creek, Battle of, an engagement in the War of 1812 which took place at the south-west end of lake Ontario. On June 5, 1813, a British force of 700 men, under Colonel (afterwards Sir) John Harvey (q.v.), made a night attack on a force of over 2,000 invading Americans under Generals Chandler and Winder, camped on the east side of Stoney creek. The attack resulted in the rout of the American force and the capture of the two generals, and was a turning-point in the campaign of 1813. See Sir C. P. Lucas, *The Canadian war of 1812* (Oxford, 1906), W. Wood (ed.), *Select British documents of the Canadian war of 1812* (4 vols., Toronto, 1920-28), and E. Cruikshank (ed.), *The documentary history of the campaign on the Niagara frontier* (9 vols., Welland, Lundy's Lane Historical Society, 1896-1908).

Stoney lake is in Peterborough county, Ontario, at the head of the Otonabee river. It abounds in maskinonge, trout, and bass, and its scenery is similar to that of the Thousand islands in the St. Lawrence. Steamers run upon it. It is 20 miles long and from 1 to 3 miles wide.

Stonies. See **Assiniboin.**

Stony Mountain, a village in Manitoba, on the Teulon branch of the Canadian Pacific Railway, 14 miles north of Winnipeg. It is the site of the Stony Mountain Penitentiary. Pop. (1934), 250.

Stony Plain, a town and Cree Indian reserve in Alberta, on the Canadian National Railway, 22 miles west of Edmonton. The origin of the name is generally attributed to the region having been the former camping ground of the Stoney or Assiniboin Indians; but Hector (q.v.) wrote in 1858 that the plain "well deserves the name from being covered with boulders." It has five grain elevators, a high school, and a weekly newspaper (*Sun*). Pop. (1931), 497.

Stormont, a county in Ontario, is one of the "united counties" of Stormont, Dundas, and Glengarry. Its southern boundary is the St. Lawrence river, and it is bounded by Dundas on the west, Glengarry on the east, and by Russell and Prescott counties on the north. It was called after the Viscount Stormont whose estates were near Perth in Scotland, and was one of the original 19 counties set apart by Simcoe (q.v.) in 1792. The first settlers were United Empire Loyalists who had fought under Sir John Johnson (q.v.) in the Royal New York Regiment in the Revolutionary War. The county town is Cornwall. The area of the county is 261,760 acres. Pop. (1931), 32,524. See *Souvenir of Stormont, Dundas and Glengarry* (Cornwall, 1906); *Illustrated historical atlas of the counties of Stormont, Dundas and Glengarry* (Toronto, 1879); and *Standard-Freeholder, Souvenir edition* (Cornwall, 1934).

Stouffville (stō′-vĭl), a village in York county, Ontario, on the Canadian National Railway, 29 miles north-east of Toronto. It was named after Abraham Stouffer (or Stauffer), who moved here from Pennsylvania in 1806, and bought part of the land on which the village is situated. It was incorporated as a village in 1817, and is in a rich agricultural district. It has a continuation school, a public library, and a weekly newspaper (*Tribune*). Pop. (1931), 1,155.

Stoughton, a village in Saskatchewan, on the Souris-Regina branch of the Canadian Pacific Railway, 85 miles south-east of Regina. It is in a wheat-growing district, and has a weekly newspaper (*Times*). Pop. (1931), 373.

Stowe, Mrs. Emily Howard, *née* **Jennings** (1831-1903), physician and feminist, was born in South Norwich, Upper Canada, in 1831. She became a school-teacher; but in 1856 she married John Stowe, of Norwich, and after her marriage she graduated from the New York College of Medicine for Women (M.D., 1867). She returned to Canada, and after a long fight was admitted in 1880 a member of the College of Physicians and Surgeons in Ontario. She was the first woman authorized to practice medicine in Canada. She became a leading female suffragist, and in 1893 she organized the Dominion Woman Suffrage Association, of which she became the first president. She died in Toronto on April 30, 1903.

Strachan, John (1778-1867), first Anglican bishop of Toronto (1839-67), was born at Aberdeen, Scotland, on April 12, 1778, the son of John Strachan and Elizabeth Findlayson. He was educated at the Universities of Aberdeen (M.A., 1796), and St. Andrews, and for three years taught school. In 1799 he came to Canada, to take charge of a college projected by Simcoe (q.v.) in Upper Canada. The proposed college was not founded at that time; and for twelve years Strachan taught school at Kingston and Cornwall. In 1803 he took orders in the Church of England, and was appointed rector of Cornwall. In 1812 he became rector of York (Toronto), and in 1813 he played a conspicuous part during the American occupation of York. In 1818 he was appointed a member of the Executive Council, and in 1820 of the Legislative Council, of Upper Canada; and during the years that followed he was one of the pillars of the "Family Compact". In particular, he distinguished himself by his advocacy of the right of the Church of England to sole enjoyment of the Clergy Reserves. In 1836, however, he resigned from the Executive Council, and in 1841 he ceased to sit in the Legislative Council.

In 1825 he was appointed archdeacon of York, and in 1839 he became bishop of the newly created diocese of Toronto. Henceforth he took little part in politics, and devoted himself to religious and educational work. He became in 1827 the first president of King's College, Toronto; but when King's College was reorganized in 1850 as the University of Toronto, he withdrew from all connection with it, and founded, in 1851, the University of Trinity College, Toronto. Of this university he was the first chancellor.

He died at Toronto on November 2, 1867. In 1807 he married the widow of Andrew McGill of Montreal; and by her he had four sons and four daughters. In 1807 he was made an LL.D. of the University of St. Andrews, and in 1811 a D.D. of the University of Aberdeen.

See A. N. Bethune, *Memoir of the Right Rev. John Strachan* (Toronto, 1870); H. Scadding, *The first bishop of Toronto* (Toronto, 1868); and A. H. Young, *John Strachan* (Queen's Quarterly, 1928).

Strachan, mount, is in the New Westminster district of British Columbia, at the head of Strachan creek, north-west of North Vancouver. It is in lat. 49° 25', long. 123° 12', and has an altitude of 4,769 feet. It was named by Captain Richards, Admiralty surveyor about 1860, after Admiral Sir R. J. Strachan (1760-1828). There is also a mount Strachan on the boundary line between British Columbia and Alberta, in the Rocky mountains, in the Kootenay district, in lat. 50° 22', long. 114° 48', and with an altitude of 8,800 feet.

Strahan, mount, is in Alberta in the Rocky mountains. It is in lat. 51° 47', long. 116° 50', and has an altitude of 9,960 feet. It was named after Dr. Aubrey Strahan, director of the Geological Survey of Great Britain.

Straith, John (1826-1885), clergyman and author, was born in Aberdeenshire, Scotland, in 1826. He emigrated to Canada, and after studying theology at Knox College, Toronto, was ordained a minister of the Presbyterian Church in 1857. He died at Sherburne, Ontario, on January 10, 1885. He was the author

of *Fidelity of the Bible* (Ingersoll, Ont., 1864).

Strange, Sir Thomas Andrew Lumisden (1756-1841), chief justice of Nova Scotia (1789-98), was born on November 30, 1756, the second son of Sir Robert Strange, the engraver. He was educated at Christ Church, Oxford (B.A., 1778; M.A., 1782); and he was called to the bar at Lincoln's Inn in 1785. In 1789 he was appointed chief justice of Nova Scotia, and he retained this position until 1798, when he was appointed recorder and president of the court of the mayor and aldermen at Madras, India. In 1800 he became chief justice of the Supreme Court of the presidency of Madras; and he remained in India until 1817. He then returned to England, and devoted himself to the completion of his *Elements of Hindu law* (2 vols., London, 1825). He died at St. Leonard's, England, on July 16, 1841. He was knighted in 1798; and in 1818 he was made a D.C.L. of Oxford University. He was twice married; and by his second wife, Louisa, daughter of Sir William Burroughs, Bart., he had a numerous family.

Strange, Thomas Bland (1831-1925), soldier, was born at Meerut, India, on September 15, 1831, the second son of Colonel H. F. Strange and Letitia, daughter of Major N. Bland. He was educated at the Edinburgh Academy and at the Royal Military Academy, Woolwich; and he obtained a commission in the Royal Artillery. He served in the Indian Mutiny, and was present at the siege and capture of Lucknow. In 1871, he was appointed inspector of artillery in Canada; in 1882 he was placed on the reserve of officers, with the rank of major-general; and in 1885 he commanded the Albert field force in the second North West rebellion, and was in command at the engagement of Frenchman's Butte. During his later years he lived in England. He died on July 9, 1925. He was twice married, (1) to Elinor Maria

(d. 1917), daughter of Capt. Robert Taylor, and (2) in 1918 to Janet, daughter of the Rev. J. A. Fell, and widow of Col. F. C. Ruxton; and by his first wife he had two sons and three daughters. In addition to some publications on military subjects, he published his autobiography under the title *Gunner Jingo's jubilee* (London, 1894).

Strasbourg, a village in the Regina district, Saskatchewan, on the Pheasant Hills branch of the Canadian Pacific Railway, 45 miles north-west of Regina. It is in a general farming district, has a high school, and has a weekly newspaper (*Mountaineer*). Pop. (1934), 500.

Stratford, a city in Perth county, Ontario, situated on the Avon river and on the Canadian National Railway, 88 miles west of Toronto. The site of the city was so named by the Canada Company in 1831. It took its name from Stratford-on-Avon, England, the birthplace of Shakespeare; it became a town in 1853, and was incorporated as a city in 1885. Stratford is a divisional point on the Canadian National Railway, which maintains there locomotive repair-shops. It has several furniture factories, a pork-packing house, a dairy products packing-house, clothing factories, knitted goods factories, and bridge and iron works. The city has fourteen churches, seven public and two separate schools, a domestic science school, a manual training school, a collegiate institute, a provincial normal school, and five parks. Stratford is the shire-town of Perth county. There is a daily newspaper (*Beacon-Herald*). Pop. (1931), 17,742.

Stratford and Huron Railway, a line built from Stratford to Listowel, Ontario, in 1877, and taken over by the Port Dover and Huron Railway in 1880.

Stratford Centre, a village in Wolfe county, Quebec, on the Maskinongé river, 9 miles from St. Gérard on the Quebec Central Railway. It is in a farming and dairying district, and has some saw-mills. Pop. of the parish of Stratford (1930), 950.

Strathcona, Sir Donald Alexander Smith, first Baron (1820-1914), Canadian high commissioner in England (1896-1914), was born at Forres, Morayshire, Scotland, the son of Alexander Smith, of Archieston, and Barbara, daughter of Donald Stuart, of Leanchoil. He was educated in Scotland; and in 1838 he entered the service of the Hudson's Bay Company. From 1838 to 1868 he was stationed on the Labrador coast. In 1869 he was appointed in charge of the Company's Montreal office, and here he rose in the service of the company until he became resident governor and chief commissioner in Canada. He first came into public notice in 1869, when he was appointed by the Canadian government a special commissioner to inquire into the troubles connected with the North West rebellion of 1869-70; and his courage and tact had much to do with the settlement of these troubles. From 1870 to 1874 he represented Winnipeg in the Legislative Assembly of Manitoba, and from 1870 to 1880 he represented Selkirk in the Canadian House of Commons. In 1873, at the time of the "Pacific Scandal", his declaration that he could no longer "conscientiously" support the government, of which he had hitherto been a supporter, was partly responsible for the fall of the Macdonald administration. He was out of parliament from 1880 to 1887; but in 1887 he was elected to the House of Commons for Montreal West, and he continued to represent this constituency until 1896. During this period he gave the Conservative government an independent support. In 1896 he was appointed by the government of Sir Charles Tupper (q.v.) Canadian high commissioner in London; and this position he filled, with great acceptance, for the rest of his life.

A man of great wealth, the foundation of his fortune was laid in 1879, when he became, with George Stephen (q.v.),

J. J. Hill (q.v.), and Norman Kittson (q.v.), one of the syndicate that purchased the St. Paul, Minneapolis, and Manitoba Railway, which first gave access by railway to the Canadian North West; and he continued for many years to be closely associated with railway development in Canada. In 1880 he was an important member of the group that organized the Canadian Pacific Railway Company; and during the years that followed it was mainly his courage and resource which enabled the company to survive the difficulties of the period of construction. In 1885 he was fittingly chosen to drive the last spike of the railway at Craigellachie in the Rockies. He was also an outstanding figure in Canadian finance. In 1887 he was elected president of the Bank of Montreal; and in 1905 he became its honorary president. For many years he was governor of the Hudson's Bay Company. His benefactions were almost without number. McGill University and the Royal Victoria Hospital, Montreal, Aberdeen University, the Young Men's Christian Association, and King Edward's Hospital Fund benefited especially from his munificence; and during the South African War he outfitted at his own expense a Canadian mounted force, known as "Strathcona's Horse".

He died in London, England, on January 21, 1914. In early life he married Isabella Sophia, daughter of Richard Hardisty, of the Hudson's Bay Company; and by her he had one daughter. He was created a K.C.M.G. in 1886, a G.C.M.G. in 1896, and a G.C.V.O. in 1908; and in 1897 he was raised to the peerage of the United Kingdom as Baron Strathcona and Mount Royal. In 1896 he was sworn of the Privy Council for Canada, and in 1904 of the imperial Privy Council. He was a D.C.L. of Oxford, Dublin, and Durham Universities, and an LL.D. of Cambridge, Yale, Aberdeen, Laval, Toronto, Queen's, Ottawa, Glasgow,

and Manchester Universities. In 1889 he was elected chancellor of McGill University, and in 1899 lord rector, and in 1903 chancellor, of Aberdeen University. In 1908 he was elected a fellow of the Royal Society.

See J. Macnaughton, *Lord Strathcona* (Toronto, 1926); B. Willson, *The life of Lord Strathcona and Mount Royal* (London, 1915) and *Lord Strathcona, the story of his life* (Toronto, 1902); W. T. R. Preston, *The life and times of Lord Strathcona* (London, 1914); J. W. Pedley, *Biography of Lord Strathcona and Mount Royal* (Toronto, 1915); G. Bryce, *The real Strathcona* (Can. mag., 1915); and S. Macnaughton, *Lord Strathcona* (Living Age, 1914).

Strathcona, a suburb of Edmonton, Alberta. Originally known as South Edmonton, it was incorporated as a municipality, under the name Strathcona, given in honour of Lord Strathcona (q.v.). In 1912 it was united with Edmonton.

Strathlorn, a village in Inverness county, Nova Scotia, on the Big river, and on the Canadian National Railway, 5 miles from Inverness, and 20 miles from Port Hood. Pop. (1934), 400.

Strathmore, a town in the Bow river valley, Alberta, is situated on the main line of the Canadian Pacific Railway, 30 miles east of Calgary. It is largely a Canadian Pacific Railway town. It has the headquarters of the company's irrigation system, and the Strathmore Supply Farm is also conducted by the Company. The name was probably given the town by John Ross, a superintendent of construction on the Canadian Pacific Railway, after the Strathmore district in Forfarshire, Scotland. It has a weekly newspaper (*Standard*). Pop. (1934), 523.

Strathroy, a town in Middlesex county, Ontario, on the Sydenham river, and on the Canadian National Railway, 20 miles west of London. A saw-mill was built here as early as 1832, but the town-site was not laid out until 1850. It was not, however, until the coming of the railway in 1856 that growth really began. The village was originally known as Strath Valley or Red Valley; but was named Strathroy after 1832, when the site of the water-mill was transferred to John Stewart Buchanan, who came from Strathroy, a small seaport on the north-east coast of Ireland. It was incorporated as a village in 1859, and as a town in 1870. It is in a diversified farming district; and it has woollen and flour mills, and furniture, handle, and canning factories. There is in the town a well-known collegiate institute, a public library, and a weekly newspaper (*Age-Dispatch*). Pop. (1935), 2,964. See S. Cuddy, *Strathroy, 1832-1925* (Transactions of the London and Middlesex Historical Society, 1927).

Stratigraphy, the study of the strata of the earth's surface. The foundations of this study were laid in Canada by Sir William Logan (q.v.), the first director of the Canadian Geological Survey, between his appointment in 1843 and his retirement in 1869; and the beginnings of Canadian palæontology are due to Elkanah Billings (q.v.), who was palæontologist to the Geological Survey from 1856 to 1876. In the Maritime provinces mention should be made also of the work of David Honeyman (q.v.) and Sir William Dawson (q.v.). In the West, important work was done at an early date by G. M. Dawson (q.v.) and A. R. C. Selwyn (q.v.). The results achieved by these pioneers has been extended and corrected by a large number of stratigraphers and palæontologists, among whom may be mentioned especially W. A. Parks (q.v.), D. B. Dowling, and R. W. Ells. To-day we have a fairly comprehensive picture of the various strata of the earth's surface in Canada, resulting from the geological action of the various periods in the earth's history; and this has proved of the greatest value in the development of the mining industry in Canada, including not only the precious metals, but also coal and oil. See F. H. McLearn, "Trends in fifty years of Canadian stratigraphy", in *Royal Society of Canada: Fifty years' retrospect* (Toronto, 1932) and W. A. Parks, *The development of stratigraphic geology and palæontology in Canada* ('Trans. Roy. Soc. Can., 1922).

Straton, Barry (1854-1906), poet, was born in Fredericton, New Brunswick, in 1854. He was educated at the Collegiate Institute, Fredericton; and studied law. But, finding law uncongenial, he turned to farming; and in the intervals of farming he wrote poetry. He published *Lays of love, and miscellaneous poems* (Saint John, New Brunswick, 1884), *The building of the bridge: An idyll of the St. John* (Saint John, New Brunswick, 1887), and *The hunter's handbook* (Boston, 1885). He died at Fredericton, New Brunswick, in 1906.

Stratton, James Robert (1857-1916), provincial secretary of Ontario (1900-05), was born at Millbrook, Canada West, on May 3, 1857, the son of James Stratton. He was educated at the Peterborough Collegiate Institute, became a journalist, and owned and published the Peterborough *Examiner*. From 1886 to 1905 he represented West Peterborough, as a Liberal, in the Legislative Assembly of Ontario; and from 1900 to 1905 he was provincial secretary in the Ross administration. Charges of political corruption made against him had much to do with the defeat of the Ross government in 1905. From 1908 to 1911 he represented West Peterborough in the Canadian House of Commons; but thereafter he retired to private life. He died at Hot Springs, Virginia, on April 19, 1916.

Strawberry (*Fragaria virginiana* Duchesne, *Rosaceae*), a stemless perennial, developing lateral runners which root to produce new plants. The leaves are all radical, 3-parted, the leaflets wedge-shaped, firm and horny of texture, coarsely toothed and somewhat hairy. The flowers are white, 5-petalled, and borne in flat-topped clusters. They bloom in spring and early summer. The so-called fruit is conical, pulpy, and scarlet when ripe, and consists of the much enlarged flower receptacle bearing the true seed-like fruits in pits on its surface. It may be found from Nova Scotia to Manitoba.

Streetsville, a village in Peel county, Ontario, on the river Credit, and on the Canadian Pacific Railway, 20 miles west of Toronto. Settlement began about 1820, and the village was named after Timothy Street, who built the first grist and saw mill here. In its early days, Streetsville was a place of some importance; but its importance has declined. It was incorporated as a village in 1857. It has now factories of pickles, pumps, and windmills, as well as flour and wood-working mills; and it has a high school, a public library, and a weekly newspaper (*Review*), founded in 1846. Pop. (1931), 661.

Strickland, Samuel (1804-1867), author, was born at Reydon Hall, Suffolk, England, in 1804, the son of Thomas Strickland, and the brother of Mrs. Moodie (q.v.), and Mrs. Traill (q.v.). He came to Canada in 1825, entered the employ of the Canada Company, and ultimately settled at Lakefield, Upper Canada. Here he died in 1867. He was the author of *Twenty-seven years in Canada West* (2 vols., London, 1853).

Strikes. Ever since labour began to organize in unions in Canada, strikes and other industrial disturbances, such as lock-outs, have not been uncommon; but in the twentieth century Canada has been fairly free from serious industrial disturbances, partly owing to Conciliation Act passed by the Canadian parliament in 1900, which was followed by the Industrial Disputes Investigation Act passed in 1907. The scope of this last Act has been seriously diminished by a decision of the Judicial Committee of the Privy Council in 1925; but the boards of conciliation and investigation appointed under its provisions have generally succeeded in bringing employers and employees together. The great proportion of industrial disputes dealt with under the Act have resulted in an amicable settlement. Canada has not adopted a system of compulsory arbitration of industrial disputes, but merely a system of compulsory investigation. See B. M. Selekman, *Postponing strikes: A study of the Industrial Disputes Investigation Act of Canada* (New York, 1927), and T. T. Ko, *Governmental methods of adjusting labor disputes in North America and Australasia* (New York, 1926).

Stringer, Isaac O. (1862-1934), archbishop of Rupertsland, was born near Kincardine, Ontario, in 1862, and was educated at the University of Toronto (B.A., 1891) and at Wycliffe College, Toronto. He was ordained a priest of the Church of England in 1893; and for ten years he was a missionary in the Mackenzie River diocese, first at Peel river, and then at Herschel island. In 1905 he was elected bishop of Selkirk (later Yukon); and in 1931, archbishop of Rupertsland. He died at Winnipeg, Manitoba, on October 30, 1934.

Strong, Sir Samuel Henry (1825-1909), chief justice of the Supreme Court of Canada (1892-1902), was born at Poole, Dorsetshire, England, on August 13, 1825, the son of the Rev. Samuel Spratt Strong and Jane Elizabeth, daughter of John Gosse, of Poole. He came to Canada with his parents in 1836, and was educated at Quebec. He studied law at Bytown (Ottawa) and Toronto, Upper Canada, and was called to the bar of Upper Canada in 1849 (Q.C., 1863). From 1869 to 1874 he was a judge of the Court of Chancery of Ontario, and from 1874 to 1875 a judge of the Supreme Court of Ontario. In 1875 he was appointed a puisne judge of the Supreme Court of Canada, on its organization; and in 1892 he became chief justice of the Supreme Court. In 1897 he was sworn of the Imperial Privy Council, and became a member of the Judicial Committee of the Privy Council. He retired from the bench in 1902; and he died at Ottawa on August 31, 1909. In 1850 he married Elizabeth Charlotte Cane; and by her he had two children. He was created a K.B. in 1893.

Stuart, Andrew (1785-1840), solicitor-general of Lower Canada (1837-40), was born in Kingston, Upper Canada, in 1785, the fifth son of the Rev. John Stuart (q.v.). He was educated at Kingston, under the Rev. John Strachan (q.v.), and was called to the bar of Lower Canada in 1807. From 1814 to 1837, except in 1835, he was one of the members for Quebec in the Legislative Assembly of Lower Canada. Though at first a member of the popular party, he broke with Papineau (q.v.) and became his chief antagonist in the Assembly. In 1837 he was appointed solicitor-general of Lower Canada; but he died, in office, at Quebec on February 21, 1840. He was twice married. By his first wife, Marguerite Dumoulin, he had two sons; and by his second wife, Jane Smith, he had three daughters and one son. He was the author of *Notes upon the south-west boundary line of the British provinces* (Quebec, 1830, and Montreal, 1832), *A review of the proceedings of the legislature of Lower Canada* (Montreal, 1832), and, with William Badgley, *An account of the endowments for education in Lower Canada* (London, 1838). He contributed also several papers to the *Transactions* of the Literary and Historical Society of Quebec.

Stuart, Sir Andrew (1812-1891), chief justice of the Superior Court of Quebec (1885-91), was born in Quebec on June 16, 1812, the eldest son of the Hon. Andrew Stuart (q.v.). He was educated at a private school at Chambly, Lower Canada, and was called to the bar of Lower Canada in 1834 (Q.C., 1854).

In 1860 he was appointed a puisne judge of the Superior Court of Lower Canada, and in 1885 he became chief justice of this court. He died in Quebec on June 9, 1891. In 1842 he married Elmire-Charlotte, third daughter of Philippe-Joseph Aubert de Gaspé; and by her he had five sons and five daughters. In 1887 he was created a knight bachelor.

Stuart, David (1765?-1853), fur-trader, was born in Callander, Perthshire, Scotland, about 1765. He is said to have been the son of that Alexander Stuart who was the successful opponent of the famous Rob Roy; and he was a cousin of John Stuart (q.v.) of the North West Company. He emigrated to Canada, and lived in Montreal before the close of the eighteenth century. His obituary notice in the *Detroit Daily Advertiser*, October 19, 1853, is authority for the statement that "for a time he was an agent of the Hudson Bay Company on the Atlantic Coast, in Nova Scotia, and elsewhere"; but this is almost certainly a mistake, for the Hudson's Bay Company had no posts in these districts at that time. It is possible that he was employed by the North West Company at the King's Posts or in the Maritime provinces. In 1810 he became a partner in John Jacob Astor's American Fur Company; and he was one of the founders of Astoria. He remained with the American Fur Company for many years; but he retired from the fur-trade about 1833, and went to live with his nephew, Robert Stuart (q.v.), in Detroit, Michigan. Here he died, at the house of his nephew's widow, on October 18, 1853, aged 88 years.

Stuart, George Okill (1776-1862), clergyman, was born at Fort Hunter, New York, on June 29, 1776, the eldest son of the Rev. John Stuart (q.v.). He was educated at King's College, Windsor, at Union College, Schenectady, and at Harvard University (B.A., 1801). He was ordained a priest of the Church of England; and was rector of York

(Toronto) from 1801 to 1811, and of Kingston from 1811 to 1862. In 1821 he was made archdeacon of Upper Canada, in 1827 archdeacon of Kingston, and in 1862 dean of Ontario. He died on October 5, 1862. See A. H. Young, *The Rev. George Okill Stuart* (Ont. Hist. Soc., Papers and Records, 1927).

Stuart, Sir James, Bart. (1780-1853), chief justice of Lower Canada (1841-53), was born at Fort Hunter, New York, on March 2 (or 4), 1780, the third son of the Rev. John Stuart (q.v.). He was educated at Kingston, Upper Canada, under the Rev. John Strachan (q.v.), and at King's College, Windsor, Nova Scotia; and he was called to the bar of Lower Canada in 1801. In 1805 he was appointed solicitor-general of Lower Canada; and from 1808 to 1820 he was one of the members for Montreal in the Legislative Assembly of the province. From 1825 to 1827 he was also member for Sorel. In 1825 he was appointed attorney-general; but in 1831 he was suspended from office by Lord Aylmer (q.v.). In 1838 he was appointed by Lord Durham (q.v.) chief justice of the court of Queen's Bench at Montreal; in 1839 he became president of the Special Council of Lower Canada; and he had much to do with the framing of the Act of Union, 1840. In 1841 he became chief justice of Lower Canada; and he occupied this position until his death at Quebec on July 14, 1853. In 1818 he married Elizabeth, daughter of Alexander Robinson of Montreal; and by her he had three sons and one daughter. In 1827 he was made a D.C.L. of King's College, Windsor; and in 1840 he was created a baronet. The baronetcy became extinct with the death of his third son in 1915. See F. J. Audet, *Sir James Stuart* (Les Annales, Ottawa, 1924).

Stuart, John (1740-1811), clergyman, was born at Paxton, Pennsylvania, on March 10, 1740, the son of Andrew Stuart. He was educated at the College of Philadelphia, later the University of Pennsylvania (B.A., 1763; M.A., 1770; D.D., 1799), and was ordained a priest of the Church of England in 1770. The same year he was appointed missionary to the Mohawks at Fort Hunter, New York; and during the American Revolution he came to Canada. From 1781 to 1785 he taught school at Montreal; in 1785 he became the first Church of England missionary in the "Western Settlements", and from that date until his death at Kingston, Upper Canada, on August 15, 1811, he was rector of St. George's Church, Kingston. In 1775 he married in Philadelphia Jane Okill (d. 1821); and by her he had five sons and three daughters. See A. H. Young, *The Revd. John Stuart, D.D., U.E.L., of Kingston, Upper Canada, and his family* (Kingston, 1921).

Stuart, John (1779-1847), fur-trader, was born in Strathspey, Scotland, in 1779, the son of Donald Stuart of Leancholl. His sister Barbara was the mother of the first Lord Strathcona (q.v.). He entered the service of the North West Company in 1799, and was sent to the Peace River district. In 1806 he accompanied Simon Fraser (q.v.) on his descent of the Fraser river to the Pacific. He was placed in charge of New Caledonia in 1809; and in 1813 he became a partner of the North West Company. At the union of 1821, he was commissioned a chief factor of the Hudson's Bay Company; and he remained in charge in New Caledonia until 1824. He retired from the service of the Hudson's Bay Company in 1839, and returned to Scotland. He died at his place, Springfield House, near Forres, Scotland, on January 14, 1847. His will is on file at Hudson's Bay House, in London. Stuart Lake, in British Columbia, is named after him.

Stuart, Robert (1785-1848), fur-trader, was born in Callander, Perthshire, Scotland, on February 19, 1785, the nephew of David Stuart (q.v.). He emigrated to Canada in 1807, and in 1810 he joined John Jacob Astor's Pacific Fur Company. He was one of the founders of Astoria; and in 1812-13 he made the overland journey back from Astoria to St. Louis. In 1819 he went to Michilimackinac, as the agent of the American Fur Company; and he remained there until 1834. He then retired from the fur-trade, and settled in Detroit, Michigan. He died at Chicago, Illinois, on October 28, 1848. His son, David, born at Brooklyn, New York, in 1816, became a member of Congress for Detroit, and commanded a brigade under General W. T. Sherman in the American Civil War. Robert Stuart's narrative of his overland journey in 1812-3 has been edited by P. A. Rollins, under the title *Discovery of the Oregon trail* (New York and London, 1935).

Stuart lake is in the Coast district British Columbia. The lake, at lat. 54° 124° N.W., is drained by the Stuart river, which flows in a south-easterly direction into the Nechako, a tributary of the Fraser. Both were named after John Stuart (q.v.) of the North West Company, who accompanied Simon Fraser (q.v.) in 1806 when he ascended the Stuart river and founded a trading post at the lake. The lake is 48 miles long, from 1 to 5½ miles wide, and has an area of 138 square miles. The Stuart river is 68 miles in length.

Stukely. See **South Stukely.**

Sturgeon. The sturgeons are large fish characterized by a long, pointed snout, overhanging a protractile mouth and by a body covered with a series of large, sculptured, bony plates. Most of them are marine, but ascend rivers to spawn. Some kinds never leave fresh water. Three species occur commonly in Canadian waters. The lake sturgeon (*Acipenser fulvescens*) is found in the Great lakes, and in the larger rivers and lakes of Manitoba. It sometimes reaches a weight of one hundred pounds or more, but the average weight of those taken in most waters now is nearer fifty pounds. It is a fish of con-siderable commercial importance, but its numbers rapidly decline under intensive fishing. In this sturgeon the bony plates which are evident in the young become embedded in the skin, so that the adult appears almost smooth. The Atlantic sturgeon (*Acipenser sturio*) enters some of the rivers of the Atlantic coast, but it is not sufficiently abundant to be a fish of any commercial importance. The same species enters the rivers of northern Europe. It sometimes reaches a length of 12 feet. The Pacific sturgeon (*Acipenser transmontanus*) is taken in the Fraser river and southward. It reaches a very large size, sometimes exceeding a thousand pounds in weight. The flesh of the sturgeon now brings a very high price in comparison with that of most other fish, although it was once destroyed as of no value. From the roe, or eggs, caviare is made.

Sturgeon Falls, a town in the Nipissing district of Ontario, on the Sturgeon river, about 3 miles from lake Nipissing, and on the Canadian Pacific Railway, 24 miles west of North Bay. It is named after the Sturgeon river, which got its name from the sturgeon that formerly abounded in it. It is an industrial centre, with pulp-and-paper mills, flour and grist mills, and lumber mills; and there is good fishing and hunting in the neighbourhood. The town was incorporated in 1895. Pop. (1931), 4,234.

Sturgeon lake, in the basin of the English river, is on the boundary between Thunder Bay and Kenora districts, northern Ontario. It has an area of 110 square miles.

Sturgeon lake, in Victoria county, Ontario, is one of the group known as the Kawartha lakes. The river Fenelon flows through this lake, which has an area of 18 square miles.

Sturgeon Point, a village in Victoria county, Ontario, on Sturgeon lake, 6 miles from Fenelon Falls, the nearest railway station. It is an old settlement, but is now mainly notable as the centre of a summer colony. Pop. (1931), 475.

Sturgeon river, in Timiskaming, Sudbury, and Nipissing districts, Ontario, flows south-east into lake Nipissing. Its principal tributaries are the Timagami, Tomiko, and Smoke rivers. It is 110 miles in length.

Stutfield peak is in Alberta at the headwaters of the Athabaska river, in the Rocky mountains. It is in lat. 52° 15', long. 117° 29', and has an altitude of 11,320 feet. It was named after Hugh G. M. Stutfield, a member of the English Alpine Club, and joint author with J. N. Collie of *Climbs and explorations in the Canadian Rockies.*

Subercase, Daniel d'Auger de (1663-1732), last French governor of Acadia (1706-10), was a native of Béarn, and in October, 1684, was a captain in Brittany. On February 3, 1687, he came to Canada with fifty soldiers. In 1690 he was commandant at Verdun, and in the same year he took part in the defence of Quebec. In 1694 he became a major, and took part in Frontenac's expedition against the Iroquois in 1696. On April 1, 1702, he was chosen to fill the governorship of Terre-Neuve, and in 1704-5 he destroyed the English habitations on the island. On April 10, 1706, he became governor of Acadia, and defended the province against several attacks by the British, but was compelled to yield in October, 1710, owing to lack of troops. Following the surrender of Port Royal, he returned to France, and arrived at Nantes on December 1, 1710. He died at Cannes, France, on November 19, 1732. See B. G., *Daniel Auger, Sieur de Subercase* (Bull. rech. hist., vol xvi).

Sucker. With the exception of two species, the suckers are confined to America, where about sixty species are found. In Canada about a dozen species occur, but only half of them are common or widely distributed. The common sucker (*Catostomus commersonii*) is wide-

ly distributed, occurring in nearly all waters from the Maritime provinces to the North West Territories. It is not highly regarded as a food fish, but in the spring, when it resorts to rivers to spawn, and when the water is cold, it is taken in considerable numbers and is relished by some. A very similar, though different species, *C. macrocheilus*, replaces this in southern British Columbia. A fine-scaled, long-nosed species is found in the larger and deeper lakes, especially northward. The red-horses are a group of large, coarse-scaled suckers, less common, but more highly regarded as food fishes than the common suckers.

Sudbury, a district in northern Ontario, is bounded on the north by Algoma and Timiskaming districts, on the east by Timiskaming and Nipissing districts, on the south by the Georgian bay and French river, and on the west by Algoma district. It was formed of part of the district of Nipissing in 1914, and was made a provisional judicial district. The richest nickel deposits in the world were uncovered in this district in the 1880's, when the Canadian Pacific Railway was being built. Pop. (1931), 58,251.

Sudbury, a city in the Sudbury district of Ontario, on the main line of the Canadian Pacific Railway, of which it is a divisional point, 85 miles west of North Bay. It is served also by the Canadian National Railway, the Algoma Eastern Railway, and the Temiskaming and Northern Ontario Railway. It was named, in the winter of 1882-3, by James Worthingdon after Sudbury, in Suffolk, England, the birthplace of his wife. The city is the centre of the vast Canadian nickel industry. All about it are productive mines, producing 90 per cent. of the world's nickel supply. The International Nickel Company, the Mond Nickel Company, and the British-American Nickel Company, with their headquarters, smelters, and refining works, are all within a few miles of the centre of the city. There are also gold and copper mines in the vicinity. The city has a foundry and machine shops, sash-and-door factories, a brewery, and brick works; and in it are public, separate, and high schools, a new technical and mining institute, and several newspapers—a Finnish daily newspaper (*Vapaus*), a Finnish semiweekly (*Vapaa Sana*), an English semiweekly (*Star*), and an English semimonthly (*Nickel District Advertiser*). Pop. (1931), 18,518.

Suffrage. See **Election Laws.**

Sullivan, Edward (1832-1899), Anglican bishop of Algoma, was born at Lurgan, Ireland, on August 18, 1832. He was educated at Trinity College, Dublin (B.A., 1857), and emigrated to Canada in 1858. In 1859 he was ordained a priest of the Church of England; and he served successively in charges at London, Montreal, Chicago, and again at Montreal. In 1882 he was elected bishop of Algoma, and he remained in charge of this diocese until ill-health compelled his retirement in 1896. He was then appointed rector of St. James Church, Toronto; and he died in Toronto, on January 6, 1899. In 1866 he married Frances Mary, daughter of Edouard Renaud, of Neufchâtel, Switzerland; and by her he had several children. He was an S.T.D. of Chicago, a D.C.L. of Lennoxville, and a D.D. of Trinity University, Toronto. See Rev. C. H. Mockridge, *The bishops of the Church of England in Canada* (Toronto, 1896).

Sullivan, Robert Baldwin (1802-1853), politician and judge, was born at Bandon, near Cork, Ireland, on May 24, 1802, the second son of Daniel Sullivan and Barbara Baldwin, sister of William Warren Baldwin (q.v.). He came to Canada with his parents in 1819; and in 1828 he was called to the bar of Upper Canada. In 1835 he was elected mayor of Toronto, and in 1836 he was appointed by Sir F. Bond Head (q.v.) a member of the Executive Council of Upper Canada. In 1839 he was appointed also a member of the Legislative Council of the province, and as such he played an important part in helping Charles Poulett Thomson (q.v.) to bring about the union of Upper and Lower Canada in 1840. In 1841 he was appointed a member of the Legislative Council of united Canada; and he became president of the council in the first government of the united province. He continued to occupy this office in the first Baldwin-Lafontaine administration; but in 1844 he resigned with his colleagues, as a protest against the policy of Sir Charles Metcalfe (q.v.). In connection with the resignation of the ministry, he engaged in a newspaper controversy with the Rev. Egerton Ryerson (q.v.); and his contribution to the controversy was published under the pen-name of "Legion", with the title, *Letters on responsible government* (Toronto, 1844). In 1848 he was included in the second Baldwin-Lafontaine administration, as provincial secretary; but later in the same year he was appointed a puisne judge of the court of Queen's Bench. In 1850 he was transferred to the court of Common Pleas, and he sat in this court until his death at Toronto on April 14, 1853. He was twice married, (1) in 1829 to Cecelia Eliza (d. 1830), daughter of Capt. John Matthews, R.A., and (2) in 1833 to Emily Louisa, daughter of Lieut.-Col. Philip Delatre, of Stamford, Upper Canada, who survived him, and who married secondly, in 1875, the Hon. Sir Francis Hincks (q.v.). By his second wife he had four sons and seven daughters. See D. B. Read, *Lives of the judges of Upper Canada* (Toronto, 1888).

Sullivan, Timothy. See **Sylvain, Timothée.**

Sullivan, Sir William Wilfred (1843-1920), prime minister of Prince Edward Island (1879-89), and chief justice (1889-1917), was born at New

London, Prince Edward Island, on December 6, 1843. He was educated at St. Dunstan's College, and was called to the bar in 1867 (Q.C., 1876). From 1872 to 1889 he represented Kings county in the Legislative Assembly of the Island; and from 1879 to 1889 he was the provincial prime minister. From 1889 to 1917 he was chief justice of Prince Edward Island; and in 1914 he was created a knight bachelor. He died at Memramcook, New Brunswick, on September 30, 1920.

Sullivan lake, in Alberta, lies east of the Red Deer river and south of the Battle river, about the intersection of the 52nd parallel of north latitude and the 112th meridian of west longitude. It has an area of 62 square miles.

Sullivan, mount, is in Alberta, south-east of Mount Lyell, at the headwaters of the North Saskatchewan river in the Rocky mountains. It was named after John W. Sullivan, the secretary of the Palliser expedition in 1857. Sullivan's peak is on the Palliser expedition map of 1859.

Sullivan, mount, is in the Cassiar district of British Columbia, on the west side of Dease lake, in lat. 58° 39', long. 130° 07', and with an altitude of 4,870 feet. It was named after J. M. Sullivan, first gold commissioner of the district, who was lost in the wreck of the *Pacific* in 1875.

Sulpicians. The Sulpician Order (P.S.S.), known as the Company of St. Sulpice, was founded at Vaugirard, near Paris, in 1641, by Jean-Jacques Olier, for the training of candidates for the priesthood, in accordance with the directions of the Council of Trent. A few years previously, Jean-Jacques Olier, a zealous missionary, had, in co-operation with a layman of La Flèche named La Dauversière, laid the bases of another company, known as "La Compagnie des Messieurs et Dames de Notre-Dame de Montréal". In fact, towards the end of the year 1641, the latter organization had sent to New France a number of settlers under the command of Paul Chomedey de Maisonneuve (q.v.), in order to found a city on the island of Montreal consecrated to the Virgin Mary. This was done in May, 1642. For fifteen years the settlers at Ville-Marie were looked after, in so far as their spiritual needs were concerned, by the Jesuit Fathers. But in 1657, shortly before his death, Olier decided to send to Ville-Marie four priests of his modest order: Messrs. de Queylus, Sovart, d'Allet, and Galinier.

Their first task was to organize parochial life; and in course of time, the parish priests of Ville-Marie became the *seigneurs* of the island of Montreal. The seigniory, at first granted to Jean de Lauzon (q.v.), had passed into the hands of he Compagnie de Notre-Dame de Montréal. Afterwards it was acquired, upon the dissolution of that company, by the superior of St. Sulpice. The new seigniors continued granting lands to settlers, a policy inaugurated by Maisonneuve. They caused mills to be built all around the island; they opened the main streets of the city, this work being principally performed by Dollier de Casson (q.v.); they started the construction of a canal to facilitate boat traffic between Montreal and Lachine; and, between the years 1670 and 1683, they erected on the top of the hill, on the street bearing the same name, the church of Notre Dame. Until 1829, this church, to which several additions and improvements were made, served as parochial church to the people of Montreal. Immediately after taking possession of the Notre Dame church, the Sulpicians started the construction of their house, which is still standing, and is now the oldest building in Montreal.

As might be expected in a country where the population consisted mainly of Indians, the Sulpician Fathers also carried their activities in the missionary field. On their arrival at Ville-Marie, they found there Indians belonging to various tribes who allowed themselves to be instructed in the Gospel. The Fathers soon planned to group these Indians together. With this in view, the authorities of St. Sulpice set aside, in 1676, a substantial piece of land situated on the slope of the mountain, where they contemplated building a *manoir* for the missionaries, as well as a number of houses which would afford protection to those Indians who chose to come and live there. This plan was soon carried out, and a Sulpician Father was appointed to perform missionary work among the Indians of this reserve. He taught classes to the children, while the Sisters of "La Congrégation Notre-Dame" looked after the young Indian girls. In 1694, a drunken Indian set fire to the establishment. Vachon de Belmont, superior of the mission, re-built the manor and the walls in stone. The two round towers, which can still be seen in front of the seminary, on Sherbrooke street, date back to that period. The evil use of spirituous liquors, through which the whole fabric of the institution had already been imperilled, caused the Sulpicians to transfer the Indians, in 1696, to Sault-au-Récollet, where they remained until 1720.

At that time, the Seminary obtained from the French king a new seigniory on the shore of the lake of Two Mountains, with a view to establishing there the Indian mission, as it was thought to be still too near the city. In 1721, Oka was founded, and both Algonkin and Iroquois lived there peacefully under the paternal vigilance of the missionaries, most of whom went down in history as truly remarkable men: for instance, to mention only one name, the great François Picquet (q.v.), the "Father of the Five Nations", as Montcalm called him.

The Sulpician Fathers also preached the Gospel in a section of Ontario. In the year 1672, at the request of the Indians themselves, they established a missionary post somewhere in the Quinte peninsula. From there they covered the north shore of lake Ontario as far as the head of the lake. Nevertheless, in 1680, they were forced to abandon such missions, since the Indians continually moved their camps.

In the latter part of the seventeenth century, the Sulpician Order had also been requested to send missionaries in Acadia. The Sulpician Fathers covered the whole of the Maritime provinces, in St. John island (Prince Edward Island), Cape Breton, Nova Scotia, and New Brunswick. At the time of the dispersion of the Acadians, they shared the unfortunate fate of their flock.

The call of remote regions would have caused the Sulpician Fathers to travel to more distant parts had Providence not decided otherwise. In 1668, François Dollier de Casson left Montreal to preach the Gospel to the Indians along the shores of the Mississippi river. Going up lake Ontario, he reached, through Grand river, lake Erie, where he spent the winter at Port Dover. In the spring he resumed his journey; but one of his canoes was destroyed during a storm, and part of his baggage was lost. He was then forced to return to Montreal. Having been told by Joliet (q.v.) that a water route existed between lake Erie and Sault Ste. Marie, Dollier de Casson travelled up the river St. Clair and lake Huron, and reached the mission of Sault Ste. Marie. From there he returned to Montreal by way of the Nipissing and Ottawa rivers, after a year's absence. This fearless explorer, who was to write shortly afterwards the first history of Montreal, kept a record of his voyage; and this record, along with the maps drawn by Galinée (q.v.), his companion, constitutes one of the most precious and invaluable sources of information on the early history of Canada.

Soon after their arrival at Ville-Marie, the Sulpicians organized classes at the Seminary, and a number of

Sulpicians were proud to be known as school-teachers. After the year 1680, this educational work was carried on in a building on Notre Dame street which was given by the Sulpicians for that special purpose. Year after year the classes progressed until the number of pupils increased to such an extent that it became necessary in 1837 to call upon the Brothers of the Christian Schools for assistance.

In addition to providing primary education for their pupils, the Sulpicians also taught Latin, and this as early as the seventeenth century. The beginning of the Montreal College, or Seminary, must be traced back to that period. This educational system remained in force until the cession of New France to Great Britain. Afterwards, in the latter part of the year 1766, a Sulpician, Curateau de la Blaiserie, established a classical college in the rectory at Longue Pointe. In 1774, at the request of the citizens of Montreal, he came to that city and organized classes in the Château Vaudreuil. After the Château was burned in 1803, the Sulpicians erected, in 1806, a college on St. Paul street, outside the McGill street walls. They remained there until 1860, when the building had to be given over to the garrison troops. The College was then transferred to the Theological Seminary situated on the mountain, where activities were carried on for a few years. Finally, in 1870, the College was built on its present site.

The Theological Seminary was opened in 1840, although plans for its establishment had been made in the seventeenth century. At first the seminarists received accommodation at the college situated on St. Paul street, and later, towards the year 1857, moved to the new building specially erected for them at the foot of the mountain, on the very spot where, in 1676, stood the Indian mission.

Since then, the activities of the Sulpician Fathers along educational lines have shown great progress, as can readily be seen by the numerous institutions which in the course of time came to life: such as the Canadian College at Rome, in 1888; the Seminary for the study of philosophy, on Côte-des-Neiges road, in 1896; the school of St. John the Evangelist, now the Externat Classique, in 1911; the St. Sulpice Library, in 1915; to say nothing of the important part the authorities of St. Sulpice have played in the establishment of a university in Montreal, in 1876 and in 1920.

A word about the parishes in charge of the Sulpicians might also be of interest. Until the middle of the nineteenth century, there was only one parish in Montreal, that of Notre Dame. To accommodate the ever increasing population, the authorities of St. Sulpice erected, between 1824 and 1829, the large church which can be seen on the Place d'Armes. Nevertheless, it soon became necessary to build throughout the city chapels which were annexed to the main church. Mgr. Bourget (q.v.), second bishop of Montreal, changed these chapels into distinct parish churches. It remains true, however, that the Seminary of St. Sulpice was originally at the head of several parishes both inside and outside the city limits.

The Company of St. Sulpice, after struggling during three-quarters of a century for its very existence, was officially recognized as "an Incorporated and Ecclesiastical Community" by Lord Sydenham (q.v.), in 1841. To-day the Sulpician Order carries on the work assigned to it by its founder—that is to say, teaching through the order's seminaries and colleges, parochial ministry at the churches of Notre Dame, St. James, and Oka, and missionary activities at Oka and in Japan. See H. Gauthier, *Sulpitiana* (Montreal, 1926); O. Maurault, *Marges d'histoire*, vol. iii (Montreal, 1930), and Jean Monval, *Les Sulpiciens* (Paris, 1934).

Sulte, Benjamin (1841-1923), historian, was born at Three Rivers, Lower Canada, on September 17, 1841, the son of Benjamin Sulte and Marie Antoinette Lefebvre. He was educated at Three Rivers and at the Royal Military School, Quebec; and from 1860 to 1867 he was a journalist. He then entered the civil service of Canada, as an assistant translator in the House of Commons, and later he became an official in the department of militia and defence. In 1902 he retired from the civil service on pension; and he died at Ottawa on August 6, 1923. In 1871 he married Augustine, daughter of Étienne Parent (q.v.), under-secretary of state for Canada.

For over sixty years he was an indefatigable student of Canadian history. His most ambitious work was his *Histoire des canadiens-français* (8 vols., Montreal, 1882-4); but he published also the following works: *Histoire des Trois-Rivières* (Montreal, 1870), *Mélanges d'histoire et de littérature* (Ottawa, 1876), *Chronique trifluvienne* (Montreal, 1879), *La poésie française au Canada* (Montreal, 1881), *Album de l'histoire des Trois-Rivières* (Montreal, 1881), *Histoire de St. François-du-Lac* (Montreal, 1886), *Pages d'histoire du Canada* (Montreal, 1891), *Histoire de la milice canadienne-français* (Montreal, 1897), *La langue français au Canada* (Lévis, 1898), and *La bataille de Châteauguay* (Quebec, 1899). To newspapers and other periodicals he contributed innumerable articles on historical matters; and the more important of these have been collected and edited by Gérard Malchelosse under the title *Mélanges historiques* (21 vols., Montreal, 1918-34). He published also two volumes of verse, *Les Laurentiennes* (Montreal, 1870) and *Les chants nouveaux* (Ottawa, 1876); and he was the author of a French translation of "God Save the King." In 1882 he was appointed a charter member of the Royal Society of Canada, and in 1904 he was elected its president. See G. Malchelosse,

Cinquante-six ans de vie littéraire (Montreal, 1916); and F. J. Audet, *Benjamin Sulte* (Bull. rech. hist., 1926).

Sumach, a tree. Nearly all of the species of sumach (*Rhus* Linnaeus) found in Canada are shrubs. One species, staghorn sumach (*R. hirta* (Linnaeus) Sudworth), becomes a straggling tree with very crooked branches and a characteristic flat crown. It is common on thin, sandy to gravelly soils from lake Huron eastward. The leaves are made up of several leaflets attached to a central stalk (pinnate), one to two feet in length, with twigs, stalks and leaflets very hairy. In the autumn the leaves turn a scarlet or purple colour and with the cone-shaped, crimson fruit clusters at the twig ends present a striking picture. Two of the shrubby sumachs are poisonous to many persons. They are readily identified by their fruits, which are small ivory berries. The most dangerous is the poison sumach, oak, dogwood, elderberry, or poison ivy as it is sometimes called (*R. vernix* Linnaeus). It has fewer leaflets (seven to thirteen) than has staghorn sumach, and these are not toothed; moreover, the twigs are glabrous (not hairy). The common poison ivy (*R. toxicodendron* Linnaeus) has but three leaflets, and is a low growing form.

Sumas lake, a former body of water in the New Westminster district of British Columbia, on the south side of the Fraser river, about 7 miles south-west of Chilliwack. This lake, covering an area of 10,000 acres, has been reclaimed by the government of British Columbia, and has been subdivided into 40-acre lots.

Summerland, a town in the Osoyoos district of British Columbia, on the west side of Okanagan lake, 7 miles north of Penticton. It has a high school and an hospital; and it is the site of an experimental farm of the Dominion government. The municipal district of which it is the centre has a population of 2,000.

Summerside, the county town of Prince county, Prince Edward Island, on Bedeque bay, and on the Canadian National Railway, 18 miles from Port Borden. It is a summer resort, a port of entry, and an important shipping port for the agricultural products of the surrounding district. It is in particular a shipping port for seed potatoes; and it is the centre of the fox-farming industry of Prince Edward Island. The Dominion Fox Experimental Station is located here. It has excellent schools, a convent, and four weekly newspapers (*Island Farmer, Summerside Journal, Pioneer,* and *Prince Edward Island Agriculturalist*). Pop. (1931), 3,759.

Summerstown, a village in Glengarry county, Ontario, on the north bank of the St. Lawrence river (lake St. Francis), and 3 miles from Summerstown station, on the Canadian National Railway. Pop. (1934), 200.

Sunbury, a county in New Brunswick, bounded on the south by Charlotte county, on the west by York county, on the north by Northumberland county, and on the east by Queen's county. A township and county of this name were created in 1765; but the present county, with new limits, was established in 1785. The origin of the name is unknown, but possibly the county was named after Sunbury, a village near London, England. It is traversed by the St. John river, and by the Canadian National and Canadian Pacific Railways. County town, Oromocto. Pop. (1931), 6,999.

Sunday Schools. Robert Raikes of Gloucester, England, is recognized as the founder of the modern Sunday school; his first experiment in this direction was in 1781. It is interesting to note that in 1783—only two years later—the Church of England is said to have opened a Sunday school in Halifax, Nova Scotia. In 1781 the Rev.

William Smart (q.v.), who had just arrived from Haddington, Scotland, organized a "Sabbath school" at what is now Brockville, Ontario; and to the Rev. A. J. Parker, minister of the Congregational Church, Danville, Quebec, belongs apparently the honour of having formed, in 1828, the first Sunday school in that province. Notwithstanding a belief on the part of many that this movement infringed upon the duties of parents, it spread quickly in the various centres of population, both urban and rural. In 1836, the "Canada Sunday School Union" was organized in Montreal, "to promote the establishment of Sunday schools"—a co-operative movement, which made all Canada east of the Great lakes its field of operations. Out of this effort to promote religious instruction in needy districts, which was definitely missionary in its character, came the conviction that the teachers and officers of the schools should have some opportunity provided for consultation together as to methods and aims in their work. Thus it happened that at Hamilton, Ontario, "The Sunday School Association of Canada" was formed in 1865, to secure "mutual counsel in the great work of the religious training of the young." In due time the movement took root in the Western provinces—associations being formed in Manitoba (1877), British Columbia (1907), and in sections of the vast country between at other times. An important step was taken in 1872, at a great convention at Indianapolis, U.S.A., when it was agreed to inaugurate the system of a series of uniform Bible lessons. Thus came into being the "International Lessons", which were adopted by most of the Sunday schools of the Protestant English-speaking world.

In the Roman Catholic Church all the teaching orders give religious instruction in the regular schools, hence Sunday schools have not been developed so fully. But as the subject of Christian doctrine is so essential, it has many Sunday schools and not a few training classes for the teachers. For fuller information, consult the "Religious Education Boards" of the various churches.

Sundew (*Drosera rotundifolia L., Droseraceae*), one of the most interesting of Canadian bog plants. It is a low glandular-hairy herb with a rosette or tuft of round leaves, clothed with reddish glandular hairs, and narrowing abruptly into a hairy petiole. The naked flower-stalk bears a one-sided, nodding cluster of white flowers, the tip of the stalk being so bent that the most recently opened flower is at the top of the stalk. The glands of the leaf hairs exude drops of clear gelatinous fluid, which sparkle in the sunlight and give the plant its common name. They also serve to attract insects; these become entangled by the sticky liquid, and the leaf folds over their bodies and digests them. It is found quite commonly in peat bogs from Labrador to Alaska, and flowers from June to August.

Sundridge, a village in the Parry Sound district, Ontario, on Stony lake, and on the Canadian National Railway, 12 miles north of Burk's Falls. Near it, on the opposite shore of Stony lake, is the Glen Bernard summer camp for girls. Pop. (1931), 357.

Sunfish, a general name for several species belonging to the freshwater bass family (q.v.). The sunfishes differ from the black bass proper in being of chubbier build, less gamey, and not reaching as large a size. Included in this group are the pumpkin seed (a very brilliantly coloured little fish characterized by a red spot on the edge of the gill cover), rock bass (generally reddish brown in general coloration, with the eye of the same colour), calico bass, and bluegill. These fishes were originally confined to eastern North America, but some of them have been introduced to other waters artificially.

Sunflower (*Helianthus annus L., Compositae*), a coarse stout annual with alternate, ovate, 3-ribbed leaves, and solitary heads of flowers surrounded by an involucre of lanceolate long-pointed bracts. The ray-flowers of the head are a brilliant yellow, the disk-flowers brownish. They are in bloom in late summer, and are common in rich soil, escaped from cultivation.

Sunnybrae, a village in Pictou county, Nova Scotia, on the East river, and on the Canadian National Railway, 20 miles south of New Glasgow. Pop. (1934), 425.

Superior Council. See **Sovereign Council.**

Superior, lake, the most northwesterly of the five Great lakes, and the largest body of fresh water in the world. It was discovered in 1623 by a French explorer Étienne Brûlé (q.v.); Radisson (q.v.) and Groseilliers (q.v.) were at the Sault Ste. Marie in 1659, and in 1661 made extensive explorations on the south shore of the lake. It is situated between 46° 35' and 49° north lat., and between 84° 30' and 92° 20' west long., and is bounded on the east and north by Ontario, on the west by Minnesota, and on the south by Wisconsin and Michigan. Its form is that of an irregular crescent with its convexity on the north and its concavity on the south. The lake is about 383 miles long and 160 miles wide at its greatest breadth; and its greatest depth is 1,180 feet. Its area is 31,810 square miles, of which 11,200 are in Ontario. The international boundary follows a median line from the south-eastern extremity of the lake to about mid-lake, curves north-westward to include Isle Royal in the United States, and continues near the north shore to the mouth of the Pigeon river, which it follows westward.

The lake is situated in a basin of 80,900 square miles (including its own surface), and is fed by more than 200 rivers, almost all of which are very swift and interrupted by rocks and rapids. The principal tributaries, all from the north, are the Pigeon, Kaministikwia, Nipigon, Pic, White, and Michipicoten. The lake is joined at its eastern extremity by the river St. Mary to lakes Huron and Michigan. Around the rapids at Sault Ste. Marie, have been constructed canals on both the Canadian and American shores. The central part of the lake is comparatively free from islands which, however, are numerous both towards the north and south sides. The principal ones are Isle Royal, Michipicoten in the eastern part, St. Ignace off the mouth of the Nipigon river, Grand island in the south-east, Manitou island off Keewenaw point, and the Apostle group in the south-west. The water of the lake is deep, clear, and extremely cold; even in summer its temperature does not rise far above freezing point, although the lake never freezes over. In autumn the lake is subject to violent gales. It abounds in fish, of which the most plentiful are trout, whitefish, and sturgeon.

The north shore is indented with deep bays surrounded by high cliffs, which vary in height from 300 to 1,500 feet. The south shore is, in general, low and sandy, although interrupted occasionally by ridges. Of these, the most famous are the "Pictured Rocks", of red sandstone, 300 feet high, extending for about 14 miles, and so called from the effect of wave action upon them. The region around the lake is rich in minerals, of which the chief are iron, native silver, as well as silver ore around Thunder bay, nickel in the country north of the lake, and copper on the south shore.

The principal harbours on the Canadian side are Fort William, at the mouth of the Kaministikwia, and Port Arthur, an artificial harbour, four miles distant. They are the respective lake terminals of the two great Canadian trans-continental railways. Of the immense trade which is carried on over the lake, the principal eastward cargoes are flour, wheat, and other grains, shipped through Fort William and Port Arthur from the Canadian prairies and through Duluth and Superior from the United States, lumber produced on the tributary rivers, iron ore in large quantities from both shores and copper ore from the mines on the south shore. The principal west-bound cargo is coal. See T. Morris Longstreth, *The lake Superior country* (Toronto, 1924), and J. W. Hall, *Lake Superior* (Thunder Bay Historical Society, 1924-5).

Surf-fish, a family of spiny-finned, marine fishes of the Pacific coast of America, sometimes known collectively as viviparous perch, since all bring forth their young alive. They are somewhat distantly related to the fresh-water perch. They inhabit the shallow waters on sandy beaches, and are rather inferior as food fishes. Five or six species occur in British Columbia waters.

Surgery. See **Medicine.**

Susa, Treaty of. This was a treaty signed by France and England on April 24, 1629, by which peace was declared between these two countries, and by which it was agreed that all places captured by either country after the conclusion of peace should be restored to the former owner. It was as a result of this treaty that Quebec, which was captured by the English under Kirke (q.v.) later in 1629, was handed back to France by the Treaty of St. Germain-en-Laye in 1632.

Sussex, a town in Kings county, New Brunswick, on the main line of the Canadian National (Intercolonial) Railway, 42 miles north-east of Saint John. The parish in which it is situated was created in 1786, and was named probably after the Duke of Sussex, one of the sons of George III. It is the centre of a rich agricultural district, noted especially for its milk, butter and cheese; and it has a variety of industries, such as plants for the manufacture of refrigerators, tinware, farm implements, furniture, aërated waters, and ice cream. It has a high school and a weekly newspaper (*Kings County Record*); and it is the place of publication of the semimonthly *Maritime Farmer*. Pop. (1935), 2,252.

Sutherland, Alexander (1833-1910), clergyman and author, was born near Guelph, Upper Canada, on September 13, 1833. He was educated at Victoria College, Cobourg, and was ordained a minister of the Methodist Church in 1859. For 36 years he was foreign mission secretary of the Methodist Church in Canada. He died at Toronto on June 30, 1910. He was the author of *A summer in prairie land* (Toronto, 1882).

Sutherland, Daniel (1756?-1832), deputy postmaster-general of British North America (1817-28), was born in Scotland about 1756, and came to Canada as a young man. He appears as a merchant in Montreal as early as 1778, and for a number of years he was engaged in the fur-trade. He was one of the partners of the North West Company in 1790. In 1812 he was appointed postmaster at Montreal; and in 1817 he succeeded George Heriot (q.v.) as deputy postmaster-general of British North America. He retained this post until 1828, when he was succeeded by his son-in-law, T. A. Stayner (q.v.). He was a promoter of the Montreal Water Works Company in 1800, and of the Bank of Montreal in 1817. From 1818 to 1824 he was cashier of the Bank of Montreal at Quebec. He died of cholera at Quebec on August 19, 1832. In 1771 he married in Montreal, Margaret Robertson; and by her he had several children. See R. W. McLachlan, *Two Canadian golden wedding medals* (Canadian Antiquarian and Numismatic Journal, 3rd series, vol. iii).

Sutherland, George (1830-1893), clergyman and author, was born in New Glasgow, Nova Scotia, in 1830, and was educated at the Presbyterian College, Halifax. He was for many years pastor of the Presbyterian church in Charlottetown, Prince Edward Island; but in 1867 he went to New Zealand, and thence to Australia. He died at Sydney, New South Wales, in 1893. Besides a number of publications on religious subjects, he was the author of *A manual of the geography and natural and civil history of Prince Edward Island* (Charlottetown, 1861), and *The Magdalen islands* (Charlottetown, 1862).

Sutherland, James (1777?-1844), fur-trader, was born at Ronaldshay, in the Orkney islands, about 1777, and entered the service of the Hudson's Bay Company in 1797. He was first employed as a writer at York Factory. From 1808 to 1813 he was master at Cumberland House; and in 1816 he was made a prisoner by the Nor'-Westers, during the Selkirk troubles. From 1819 to 1821 he was in charge of the Swan River district; and he was promoted to the rank of chief factor in 1821. He retired from the Company's service in 1827; and he died at the Red River Settlement on September 30, 1844. He is to be distinguished from an earlier servant of the Hudson's Bay Company, named James Sutherland, who died while in charge of Brandon House in 1797.

Sutherland, James (1849-1905), minister of public works for Canada (1902-5), was born in the township of Ancaster, Upper Canada, on July 17, 1849, the son of Alexander Sutherland and Alison Renton. He was educated at the grammar school, Woodstock, Ontario, and entered business as a grocer and crockery merchant in Woodstock. From 1880 to 1905 he represented North Oxford in the Canadian House of Commons; in 1892 he was appointed chief "whip" for the Liberal party in the Commons; and in 1902 he became minister of public works in the Laurier government. He died at Woodstock, Ontario, on May 3, 1905. He was not married.

Sutherland, John Campbell (1860-1936), author, was born in Galt, Ontario, on December 4, 1860. He was educated at the Galt Collegiate Institute under Dr. Tassie (q.v.) and at Queen's University, Kingston (B.A., 1901). In 1911 he was appointed inspector-general of Protestant schools in the province of Quebec; and he held this post until his death at Quebec on April 10, 1936. He was the author of *Canadian rural education* (Quebec, 1913), *The province of Quebec: Geographical and social studies* (Montreal, 1922), and *The romance of Quebec* (Toronto, 1934).

Sutherland, Robert Franklin (1859-1922), speaker of the Canadian House of Commons (1905-9), was born at Newmarket, Ontario, on April 5, 1859, the son of Donald Sutherland and Jane Boddy. He was educated at the University of Toronto and Western University, and was called to the bar of Ontario in 1886 (Q.C., 1899). He practised law at Windsor, Ontario; and from 1900 to 1909 he represented North Essex in the Canadian House of Commons, as a Liberal. From 1905 to 1909 he was speaker of the House, and in 1909 he was sworn of the Canadian Privy Council. In 1909 he was appointed a judge of the High Court of Justice of Ontario; and he retained this position until his death, at Toronto, on May 23, 1922. In 1888 he married Mary Bartlett, of Windsor, Ontario.

Sutherland, a town in Saskatchewan, on the Minnedosa-Saskatoon-Edmonton branch of the Canadian Pacific Railway, 5 miles east of Saskatoon. It was named after the Hon. W. C. Sutherland, who owned a farm east of the town-site, and who was speaker of the provincial legislature when the town was laid out. Pop. (1931), 1,148.

Sutton, a village in Brome county, Quebec, on the north branch of the Missisquoi river, and on the Canadian Pacific Railway, 59 miles south-east of Montreal. It was incorporated as a village in 1896, and was named after the township in which it is situated. Pop. (1931), 967.

Sutton, a village in York county, Ontario, on the Black river, 2 miles south of Jackson's Point on lake Simcoe, and on the Canadian National Railway, 54 miles north of Toronto. It was founded in 1830, and was formerly known as Sutton West, to distinguish it from Sutton, Quebec. Pop. (1931), 788.

Suzor, Louis Théodore (1834-1866), soldier and author, was born in Lower Canada in 1834, and entered the Canadian volunteer militia in 1855. He rose to the rank of lieut.-colonel; and at the time of his death at Quebec, on August 18, 1866, was deputy assistant adjutant-general of the militia. He was the author of *Aide-mémoire de carabinier-volontaire* (Quebec, 1862), *Tableau synoptique des mouvements d'une compagnie* (Quebec, 1863), *Tableau synoptique des mouvements de bataillon* (Quebec, 1863), *Exercices et évolutions d'infanterie* (Quebec, 1863), *Code militaire* (Quebec, 1864), *Maximes, conseils, et instructions sur l'art de la guerre* (Quebec, 1865), *Guide théorique et pratique des manœuvres de l'infanterie* (Quebec, 1865), and *Traité d'art et d'histoire militaires* (Quebec, 1865).

Sverdrup, Otto (1855-1930), Arctic explorer, was born at Harstad Farm, Helgeland, Norway, in 1855. He went to sea in 1872; in 1888 he accompanied Nansen in his first crossing of Greenland; and from 1893 to 1896 he was captain of the *Fram* on Nansen's famous attempt to reach the North Pole. In 1898 he took the *Fram* on a second expedition, this time as leader, with the object of exploring round the north of Greenland He extricated himself from the ice only in 1902; but in the interval he discovered vast areas of unexpected new land west of Ellesmere island—new land of almost greater area than that uncovered by the combined efforts of the Franklin search expeditions. In 1914-15 and in 1920 he led Arctic expeditions to the Kara sea; but his fame as an explorer rests chiefly on his expedition of 1898-1902. He died on November 26, 1930. His expedition of 1898-1902 was described in his *New land: Four years in Arctic regions* (tr. by H. H. Hearn, 2 vols., London, 1904).

Swallow, a name applied to several species of small birds, with long, pointed wings and small feet, which constitute the family *Hirundinidae*. The largest member of the group is the purple martin (*Progne subis*). The barn swallow (*Hirundo erythrogastra*) is a familiar and wide-ranging species. It makes its nests of mud, straw, and feathers against the beams of barn-yard buildings throughout settled parts of Canada. This species is characterized by its long forked tail. The bank swallow (*Riparia riparia*), another common species, burrows in the crest of vertical sand banks. Suitable situations regularly attract large colonies of these birds. Several other species occur more or less commonly in Canada.

Swamp Sumach. See **Poison Sumach.**

Swan, a name used, with prefixes, for two species of large white birds closely allied to the geese and ducks, and with them constituting the family *Anatidae*. The trumpeter swan (*Cygnus buccinator*) was formerly an inhabitant of the whole of western Canada, but of recent years it has become nearly extinct. A few are still known to survive as nesting birds on certain lakes in British Columbia. The whistling swan (*Cygnus columbianus*), a slightly smaller species, is still not uncommon in certain regions, though its numbers have been greatly decimated. It nests in the far north and migrates through Ontario on its journey to and from the Atlantic coast.

Swan Lake, a village in Manitoba, on the Brandon branch of the Canadian Pacific Railway, 95 miles west of Winnipeg. It is adjacent to a Chippewa Indian reserve. Pop. (1934), 300.

Swan river rises on the boundary between Manitoba and Saskatchewan, between the 52nd and 53rd parallels of north latitude, flows south through Saskatchewan, and enters Manitoba a little south of the 52nd parallel. Curving to the north-east, it flows into Swan lake, which is drained by the Shoal river into the north-west part of lake Winnipegosis. A tributary of the main Swan river, also known as the Swan, rises in Marquette county, and flows in a north-easterly direction to its junction with the main river.

Swan river, in Alberta, flows north and enters Lesser Slave lake on its south side, between the 115th and 116th meridians of west longitude.

Swan River, a town in the Nelson district of Manitoba, on the Swan river, and on the Canadian National Railway, 275 miles north-west of Winnipeg. It is in a mixed farming and lumbering district; and it has a weekly newspaper (*Star and Times*). Pop. (1934), 968.

Swansea, a suburb of Toronto, in York county, Ontario, on the Canadian National Railway. Pop. (1931), 5,000.

Swastika, a village in the Timiskaming district, Ontario, on the Temiskaming and Northern Ontario Railway, 50 miles north of New Liskeard. It is the junction for the branch line leading to the Kirkland lake and Noranda mining region. Pop. (1931), 335.

Sweaburg, a village in Oxford county, Ontario, 3½ miles south of Woodstock, the nearest railway station. It is named after the fortress of Sviaborg, in the gulf of Finland, which was bombarded by the British fleet in 1855, during the Crimean war. Pop. (1934), 250.

Sweatman, Arthur (1834-1909), Anglican archbishop of Toronto (1906-9), was born in London, England, on November 19, 1834, the son of Dr. John Sweatman, of the Middlesex Hospital, London. He was educated at Christ's College, Cambridge (B.A., 1859; M.A., 1862; D.D., 1879), and was ordained a priest of the Church of England. He came to Canada in 1865 as headmaster of the Hellmuth Boys' College, London, Ontario; and in 1879 he was chosen bishop of Toronto. In 1906 he became archbishop of Toronto, and primate of all Canada; and he died at Toronto on January 24, 1909. He married Susanna, daughter of Robert Garland, of Islington, England; and by her he had several children. See Rev. C. H. Mockridge, *The bishops of the Church of England in Canada* (Toronto, 1896).

Sweeny, Robert (d. 1840), poet, was a native of Ireland who settled in Montreal about 1820. He was killed in a duel with Major Ward, of the Montreal garrison, in Montreal in 1840. He married Charlotte, daughter of Robert Emmett Temple, of Rutland, Vermont, afterwards the wife of Sir John Rose, Bart. (q.v.). He published in 1826 a small volume of verse entitled *Odds and ends.* See Æ. Fauteux, *Le duel au Canada* (Montreal, 1934).

Sweet Brier. See **Eglantine.**

Sweet Cicely (*Osmorhiza longistylis* DC., *Umbelliferae*), a smooth-stemmed perennial with thick aromatic roots. The leaves are 3-compound, and sparingly pubescent, the leaflets ovate. The inconspicuous white flowers are borne in loose flat clusters. It is very often confused with the water-hemlock, which is very poisonous. It may be found growing in rich woods from Quebec westward.

Sweet Fern (*Myrica asplenifolia* L., *Myricaceae*), a low shrub with sweet-scented fern-like leaves, pinnately lobed, the lobes rounded. The flowers are borne in short scaly catkins, the fertile catkins being globular in shape. It is found growing in sterile soil especially in pine barrens, from New Brunswick to Saskatchewan.

Sweet Flag (*Acorus calamus* L., *Araceae*), a perennial aquatic or marsh plant, with sword-like leaves rising from thick aromatic rootstocks. The flowers are borne in a compact spike of spadix on the side of the flattened leaf-like flower stalk, which projects far beyond the flower-cluster, forming a sort of spathe. There are 6 sepals, and 6 stamens. The fruit is a dry cone-like structure. This plant is found along the margins of streams and swamps.

Sweetsburg, a village in Missisquoi county, Quebec, on the south branch of the Yamaska river, 2 miles from Cowansville, on the Canadian Pacific Railway, and 57 miles south-east of Montreal, is the county seat of the judicial district of Bedford, comprising the counties of Missisquoi, Brome, and Shefford. It was incorporated as a village in 1875. First known as Churchville, it was afterwards named after Gardner Sweet, the first postmaster and one of the early settlers. Pop. (1931), 400.

Swift, a generalized name for four species of small birds superficially resembling the swallow, but more nearly allied to the whip-poor-will and the nighthawk. They are members of the bird family *Micropodidae*, a name which has reference to the small legs possessed by swifts. These are pre-eminently birds of the air, never normally coming to the ground. The chimney swift (*Chaetura pelagica*) is sooty black, and is further characterized by the spiny ends of the short tail feathers, which serve as spiked props in clinging to vertical surfaces. The species formerly nested in hollow trees, but it has adopted disused chimneys of man in preference to natural nesting sites. It occurs throughout Canada. The three additional species occur in the western part of Canada.

Swift Current, a city in Saskatchewan, is situated on the Swift Current river, 110 miles west of Moose Jaw. It is the commercial and distributing centre for south-western Saskatchewan, and is served by the Canadian National Railway, and the Canadian Pacific (Moose Jaw-Neidpath line), which in addition to the main line has five branch lines radiating into the surrounding country. An industrial centre, it has grain elevators, flour mills a wool preserving company, etc. It is surrounded by a rich grain-growing and mixed-farming district. In 1920 the Dominion government established at Swift Current an experimental farm of 700 acres, and this has proved of inestimable value to every branch of agriculture. It has 7 grain elevators, a high school, a hospital, a meteorological station, and two weekly newspapers (*Herald* and *Sun*). Pop. (1931), 5,296. The population of the dependent district is over 125,000.

Sycamore, a tree. There are six species of sycamore recognized as members of the genus *Platanus* Linnaeus, but one only occurs in Canada (*P. occidentalis* Linnaeus). It is also known as buttonwood and plane-tree; it is the largest of southern Canadian hardwoods, but is limited in its range to southern Ontario. The leaves resemble somewhat a maple leaf, being indistinctly three- to five-lobed, each lobe wavy-toothed. Its most distinctive character is that the end of the leaf stalk is funnel-like, a feature which readily separates it from other trees. The fruits form ball-like structures, one inch across, which hang on long stalks and persist throughout the winter. The wood is not of great importance, but is used locally for cabinet work and interior finish.

Sydenham, Charles Poulett Thomson, first Baron (1799-1841), governor-general of Canada (1839-41), was born at Wimbledon, England, on September 13, 1799, the son of J. Poulett Thomson, a merchant. He was

privately educated, and at the age of sixteen entered the St. Petersburg office of his father's firm, where he spent a number of years. From 1826 to 1830 he represented Dover in the House of Commons, and from 1830 to 1839 he represented Manchester. In 1830 he was appointed vice-president of the Board of Trade and treasurer of the navy in Earl Grey's administration; in 1834 he became president of the Board of Trade; and, except for an interval of a few months in 1834-5, he occupied this office until his appointment as governor-general of Canada in 1839, in succession to Lord Durham (q.v.).

A Liberal with a business training, he was sent to Canada to carry into effect Lord Durham's recommendations with regard to the union of the Canadas and the introduction of responsible government and municipal institutions. The union of the Canadas he achieved, with adroit diplomacy, by obtaining the assent of the Special Council of Lower Canada and the legislature of Upper Canada; and in 1840 the Act of Union passed the British parliament. Municipal institutions he succeeded in introducing into Upper Canada in 1841; and responsible government he introduced into the legislature of united Canada in a partial degree. He set up the machinery of responsible government with an executive council composed of heads of departments with seats in the legislature, and in harmony with the majority in the legislature. But he was his own prime minister; he himself presided over the meetings of council; and he took the view that "the Council was a council to be consulted, and no more." His régime was admirably suited for bridging over the period of transition to full responsible government; but it may be doubted whether it could have survived long, since it depended for its success on his finding a Council in harmony both with himself and the majority in the Assembly.

It was perhaps, therefore, fortunate

for his reputation that his period of office was cut short. On September 19, 1841, he died at Kingston, Upper Canada, as the result of a fall from his horse; and he was succeeded in office by Sir Charles Bagot (q.v.). In 1840 he had been created, for his services, Baron Sydenham of Kent in England and Toronto in Canada; and in 1841 he was made a G.C.B. But he died unmarried, and the peerage expired with him.

See G. Poulett Scrope, *Memoir of the life of Charles, Lord Sydenham* (London, 1844); A. Shortt, *Lord Sydenham* (Toronto, 1908); and J. L. Morison, *British supremacy and Canadian self-government* (Toronto, 1919).

Sydenham, a village in Frontenac county, Ontario, on the Canadian National Railway, 20 miles north of Kingston. It was named after Lord Sydenham (q.v.). Pop. (1934), 600.

Sydenham river, in Kent county, Ontario, flows into the St. Clair river below Wallaceburg. It has a length of about 100 miles. There is also a Sydenham river which rises in Grey county, Ontario, and flows into the Georgian bay.

Sydney, a city in Cape Breton county, Nova Scotia, is situated at the head of the south arm of the deep and commodious Sydney harbour, Cape Breton island, 276 miles north-east of Halifax. Situated on the harbour are also the towns of North Sydney and Sydney Mines. Sydney was established in 1783 by Governor Des Barres (q.v.) and named after Thomas Townshend, first Viscount Sydney (1733-1800). Champlain's map of 1632 calls Sydney harbour *Gran Sebon*, meaning "Great river". In 1788 the harbour was named Prince William Henry sound by Governor McCormick, in honour of Prince William Henry, later King William IV. This name appears in many old documents, but did not survive. Sydney was incorporated as a town in 1886, and as a city in 1903. It is the eastern

divisional terminus of the Canadian National Railway, and the terminus of the Sydney and Louisbourg Railway. An electric line runs to Glace Bay and Dominion, and there is regular steamship connection with all important Canadian Atlantic ports.

Sydney is noted for its coal trade and for its extensive production of iron and steel. The occurrence of iron ore in proximity to coal has made the city a manufacturing centre. There is a large tar and chemical plant, a marine ship foundry, sash-and-door factories, a biscuit factory, and a brick-works. The coal mines of the district have been developed to produce 5,000,000 tons annually. The other minerals found are gypsum, fire-clay, marble, limestone, dolomite, and silica. The forests contain spruce, hemlock, birch, fir, and beech. The city has eighteen churches, twelve public schools, a high school and a school of science. The picturesque Bras d'Or lakes are fashionable summer resorts, where the fishing and shooting are excellent. A daily newspaper (*Post-Record*) is published. Pop. (1932), 23,089.

Sydney Mines, a town in Cape Breton county, Nova Scotia, on the north side of Sydney harbour, 5 miles north of Sydney, and 3 miles from North Sydney, its shipping port. It was incorporated as a town in 1890. It is the centre of an extensive coal-mining industry; and has blast furnaces, coke-ovens, foundries, and machine shops. Pop. (1934), 8,500. North Sydney, which is connected with it by electric railway, has a hospital, a convent, and a weekly newspaper (*Herald*); and it is also the winter shipping port of Cape Breton's fishing industry. Pop. (1934), 6,000.

Syenite, a plutonic rock consisting of orthoclase and either hornblende, biotite, or augite. In texture it is granitoid. It differs from granite in the absence of quartz and from nepheline syenite by the absence of nepheline, being about midway mineralogically and

SYDNEY, NOVA SCOTIA

chemically between these two. It is an excellent building stone, and a variety found in Norway, known as laurvikite, is noted for the wonderful play of iridescent colours which it exhibits.

Sykes, Frederick Henry (1863-1918), educationist and author, was born at Queensville, Ontario, on October 21, 1863. He was educated at the University of Toronto (B.A., 1885; M.A., 1886), and at Johns Hopkins University (Ph.D., 1894). From 1895 to 1897 he was professor of English and history at the Western University, London, Ontario; but he then went to the United States, and after occupying several academic positions, he became, in 1903, professor of English literature and director of extension teaching at Columbia University. From 1913 to 1917 he was president of the Connecticut College for Women. He died at Cambridge, Massachusetts, on October 14, 1917. In addition to editing a large number of college text-books, he was the author of *French elements in middle English* (Oxford, 1899), *Elementary English composition* (Toronto, 1902), *Syllabus of lectures on Shakespeare* (New York, 1903), *Syllabus of lectures on the history of English literature in the nineteenth century* (New York, 1904), and *Public school English composition* (Toronto, 1908).

Sylvain, or **Sullivan, Timothée** (1696-1749), physician, was born in the parish of St. Philibert, Cork, Ireland, the son of Daniel Sullivan, a lieutenant-general in the army of James II. He came to Canada in 1718, and practised medicine in Montreal for many years. He died at Montreal on June 16, 1749. See Ægidius Fauteux, *Un médecin irlandais à Montréal avant la conquête* (Bull. rech. hist., 1917).

T

Tabaret, Joseph Henri (1828-1886), founder of the University of Ottawa, was born in France in 1828, and entered the Oblate order in 1845. He was sent to Canada, and was ordained a priest in 1850. In 1853 Mgr. Guigues (q.v.) placed him in charge of the college which he had established at Ottawa, as superior, and this college grew into the University of Ottawa. He died at Ottawa, on February 28, 1886. See G. Simard, *Le Père Tabaret et son œuvre d'éducation* (Ottawa, 1928).

Taber, a town in the Lethbridge district of Alberta, on the Canadian Pacific Railway, 75 miles west of Medicine Hat, and 32 miles east of Lethbridge. It is in an irrigated farming and ranching district; and there are a number of coal mines in its vicinity. It has a weekly newspaper (*Times*). Pop. (1931), 1,279.

Tabletop, a mountain in the Gaspé district, Quebec. The altitude of its highest point (mount Jacques Cartier) is 4,350 feet, and it is in lat. 48° 59' 42'', long. 65° 56' 27''. The name is descriptive of the flat, plateau-like summit.

Taché, Alexandre Antonin (1823-1894), Roman Catholic archbishop of St. Boniface, was born at Rivière du Loup, Lower Canada, on July 23, 1823, the son of Charles Taché, eldest brother of Sir Étienne Paschal Taché (q.v.), and Henriette Boucher de la Broquerie. He was educated at the College of St. Hyacinthe and the Theological Seminary of Montreal; and in 1844 he became a novice in the Oblate order. In 1845 he went as a missionary to the Red River; in 1851 he was consecrated coadjutor bishop of St. Boniface; in 1853, on the death of Bishop Provencher (q.v.), he became second bishop of St. Boniface; and in 1871 he was created archbishop and metropolitan of St. Boniface. During the Red River rebellion of 1869 he was absent from the country; but he returned at the request of the Canadian government, and was greatly influential in restoring order. Unfortunately, his promises to the rebels, made in excess of his instructions, gave rise to much controversy. This controversy he dealt with in two pamphlets entitled *L'amnistie* (Montreal, 1874) and *Encore l'amnistie* (St. Boniface, 1875). He played also an important part in the earlier stages of the Manitoba separate schools controversy; and in this connection he published *Denominational or free Christian schools in Manitoba* (Winnipeg, 1877), *Les écoles separées de Manitoba* (St. Boniface, 1890), *Un page d'histoire des écoles de Manitoba* (Montreal, 1894), and *Mémoire sur la question des écoles* (Montreal, 1894). He published also *Vingt années de missions dans le Nord-Ouest de l'Amérique* (Montreal, 1866), *Esquisse sur le Nord-Ouest de l'Amérique* (Montreal, 1869; tr. by Capt. D. R. Cameron, Montreal, 1870; new ed. by Mgr. Langevin, Montreal, 1901), and *La situation au Nord-Ouest* (Quebec, 1885). He died at Winnipeg on June 22, 1894. See Dom Benoit, *Vie de Mgr. Taché* (2 vols., Montreal, 1904); L. O. David, *Mgr. A. A. Taché* (Montreal, 1883); and *Vingt-cinquième anniversaire de l'épiscopat de Sa Grandeur Monseigneur Taché* (Montreal, 1875).

Taché, Sir Étienne Paschal (1795-1865), statesman, was born at St. Thomas, Lower Canada, in 1795, the third son of Charles Taché of Montmagny, and through his paternal grandmother a descendant of Louis Jolliet (q.v.). He was educated at the Quebec Seminary; and he fought on the British side throughout the War of 1812. He then studied medicine, and for many years was a country doctor in his native parish. In 1841 he was elected to the Legislative Assembly of Canada for the county of L'Islet, and he sat for this county until 1846. From 1846 to 1848 he was deputy adjutant-general of militia for Lower Canada, with the rank of colonel; but in 1848 he re-entered political life as commissioner of public works in the Baldwin-Lafontaine administration, and was appointed a member of the Legislative Council. In 1849 he changed his portfolio for that of receiver-general; and this portfolio he retained in the successive Baldwin-Lafontaine, Hincks-Morin, MacNab-Morin, MacNab-Taché and Taché-Macdonald administrations until his retirement from office in 1857. From 1856 to 1857 he was also technically prime minister, though the real head of the government was John A. Macdonald (q.v.). From 1857 to 1864 Taché continued a member of the Legislative Council; and in 1858 he was created a knight bachelor, and in 1860 an aide-de-camp of the Queen, with the honorary rank of colonel in the British Army. In 1864, however, he was called from his retirement to become again prime minister in the second Taché-Macdonald administration; and, on the defeat of this government in June, 1864, he was pressed into service as the technical prime minister in the "Great Coalition." As such, he presided at the Quebec Conference; but before Confederation had been accomplished, he died at St. Thomas on July 30, 1865. He wrote *Quelques réflexions sur l'organisation de volontaires* (Quebec, 1863). See M. O. Hammond, *Confederation and its leaders* (Toronto, 1917).

Taché, Joseph Charles (1820-1894), journalist and author, was born at Kamouraska, Lower Canada, on December 24, 1820, the son of Charles Taché and of Henriette Boucher de la Broquerie. He was educated at the Quebec Seminary, and became a physician and surgeon. From 1847 to 1857 he sat in the Legislative Assembly of Canada, first for Rimouski, and then for Témiscouata. From 1857 to 1859 he was editor of *Le Courrier du Canada;* in 1860 he became professor of physiology in Laval University; and in 1864 he was appointed deputy minister of agriculture for Canada. This office he continued to hold after Confederation until his retirement in 1888. He published many books and pamphlets on a wide variety of subjects; but his chief publications were *Esquisse sur le Canada* (Paris, 1855), *Des provinces de l'Amérique du Nord et d'une union féderale* (Quebec, 1858), *Trois légendes de mon pays* (Montreal, 1876), *Forestiers et voyageurs* (Montreal, 1884), and *Les sablons* (Montreal, 1885). He died at Ottawa on April 16, 1894. In 1847 he married Françoise Lepage; and by her he had six children. See P. G. Roy, *La famille Taché* (Levis, 1904).

Taché, Louis Hyppolite (1859-1927), author, was born at St. Hyacinthe, Quebec, on August 30, 1859, the son of Antoine-Louis-Jean-Étienne Taché and Marie-Charlotte Beaudet. He was called to the Quebec bar in 1883, and for several years was private secretary to Sir J. A. Chapleau (q.v.). He died at Montreal on May 22, 1927. He was the author of *La poésie française au Canada* (St. Hyacinthe, 1881), *A legal hand-book and law-list for the Dominion of Canada* (Toronto, 1888), and the *Montreal citizen's directory* (Montreal, 1893); and he edited the *Nouvelles soirées canadiennes* (Quebec and Ottawa, 1882-8), and *Men of the day* (Ottawa and Montreal, 1890-94).

Tadoussac, a village in Saguenay county, Quebec, situated at the east entrance of the Saguenay river, a short distance above its confluence with the St. Lawrence, 25 miles north of Rivière du Loup across the St. Lawrence, and 120 miles north-east of Quebec. The settlement was founded in 1599 by Pierre de Chauvin. Cartier (q.v.) had been in the locality in 1535. Tadoussac is an Indian word for which many meanings have been given, such as "hills", "steep rock", "mouth of river full of rocks". It was one of the chief fur-trading posts in Quebec, and about the year 1648 huge profits were made. A very old church is still standing here; it was built in 1747. Tadoussac is picturesquely situated, and is a favourite watering-place for summer tourists. A ferry boat runs to Rivière du Loup, daily from June 15 to September 30, connecting with main rail lines. Steamers from Montreal and Quebec call daily during the summer. Salmon and other fish are plentiful in the neighbourhood. Pop. (1931), 695. See George Tremblay, *Monographie de Tadoussac, 1535-1922* (Quebec, 1923), and J. E. Roy, *In and around Tadoussac* (Lévis, 1891).

Taffanel, Jacques-Pierre, Marquis de La Jonquière. See **La Jonquière, Jacques-Pierre Taffanel, Marquis de.**

Tagish lake is on the boundary between British Columbia and Yukon territory, west of Atlin lake, and between the 134th and 135th meridians of west longitude. It is 78 miles long, from 1 to 2 miles wide, and has an area of 114 square miles, of which 69 are in British Columbia and 45 in the Yukon.

Tahltan, a tribe of the Nahani, a division of the wide-spread Déné race, whose hunting grounds are on the Stikine river and its tributaries, Dease lake and river, and the sources of the Nass and Taku rivers. They adjoin the Tlingit on the west. They are hunters and trappers, only fishing in the summer when the pursuit of the fur-bearing animals is without profit. Their fishing camps are of posts bound together with bark or roots and roofed with bark; but their permanent homes are sheds of bark and brush, laid upon poles and set opposite each other, with a central fire. Their tribal arrangements show Tlingit influence, and with this tribe they have inter-married. The Tahltan are composed of two clans, the Wolf and the Raven, divided into four families. They reckon descent in the female line—the mother being the head of the household or family. They are exogamous—only one of the Raven can marry a Wolf, and *vice versa*. They are an adaptable people, and readily accept civilized manners and customs. Their two main villages show the effects of contact with the whites. On the whole, they are an honest, agreeable, kindly people, hospitably inclined and dignified in bearing. See G. T. Emmons, *The Tahltan Indians* (Philadelphia, 1911).

Tailhan, Jules (1816-1891), priest and historian, was born in France in 1816, entered the Society of Jesus, and was ordained a priest about 1850. In 1858 he came to Canada as professor of philosophy at Laval University, Quebec; but he returned to France in 1860. He died in Paris on June 26, 1891. He edited and annotated the *Mémoire sur les mœurs, coûtumes, et religion des sauvages de l'Amérique septentrionale* of Nicolas Perrot (Paris, 1864).

Taillon, Sir Louis Olivier (1840-1923), prime minister of Quebec (1887 and 1893-6), was born at Terrebonne, Lower Canada, on September 26, 1840, the son of Aimé Taillon and Marie Josephte Daunais. He was educated at Masson College; and was called to the bar of Lower Canada in 1865 (Q.C., 1882). He practised law in Montreal, and in 1892 was *bâtonnier* of the Quebec bar. He represented Montreal East in the Legislative Assembly of Quebec from 1875 to 1886, Montcalm from 1886 to 1890, and Chambly from 1892 to 1896. From 1882 to 1883 he was speaker of the Legislative Assembly; from 1884 to 1886 he was attorney-general in the Ross administration; and in 1887, and again from 1893 to 1896, he was prime minister of the province. In 1896 he became postmaster-general in the Tupper administration at Ottawa; but he was defeated in the general elections later in the year, and thereupon retired to private life. He died at Montreal on April 25, 1923. He was a D.C.L. of Bishop's College, Lennoxville (1895) and an LL.D. of Laval University (1901); and he was created a knight bachelor in 1917.

Tait, Sir Melbourne McTaggart (1842-1917), chief justice of the Superior Court of Quebec (1906-12), was born at Melbourne, Lower Canada, on May 20, 1842. He was educated at McGill University (B.C.L., 1862), and was called to the bar of Lower Canada in 1863 (Q.C., 1882). He was for many years the law partner of Sir John Abbott (q.v.). In 1887 he was appointed a judge of the Superior Court of Quebec; from 1894 to 1906 he was assistant or acting chief justice of this court; and from 1906 to 1912 chief justice. He died in Montreal on February 10, 1917. He was twice married, (1) in 1863 to Monica, daughter of James Holmes, of Montreal, and (2) in 1878 to Lily, daughter of Henry B. Kaighn, of Newport, Rhode Island. He was a D.C.L. of McGill University (1891) and of Bishop's College, Lennoxville (1891).

Takla lake, in the Cassiar district of British Columbia, north-east of Babine lake, has an area of 98 square miles, and is 57 miles long, with a maximum width of 2 miles.

Takulli, a group of Athapaskan tribes, inhabiting the upper branches of the Fraser river, in British Columbia, between the 52nd and 56th parallels of north latitude and the 120th and 127th parallels of west longitude. Their name means "people who go upon the water".

They are the most numerous and important of all the northern Athapaskan tribes. They were first visited by Sir Alexander Mackenzie (q.v.), who traversed their country in 1793 on his overland journey to the Pacific; and the first trading-post on the Pacific slope was established amongst them by Simon Fraser (q.v.) in 1805. They are a semi-sedentary tribe, having fixed homes in villages which they leave at regular seasons for fishing and hunting; and they are now concentrated in Indian agencies at Babine and Williams lakes and on the upper Skeena river. They have borrowed many of their customs from the Coast Indians, especially from the Tsimshian and the Heiltsuk. From the Tsimshian they acquired the practice of wearing wooden labrets; and from the other coast tribes they derived the custom of burning the dead. A widow was obliged to carry the ashes of her deceased husband with her for three years, before she was permitted to marry again; and from this custom the tribe came to be known as Carriers. They have no head chiefs, and are exogamous, all property rights descending through the mother. They have a society composed of hereditary "noblemen", or landowners, and a lower class who hunt with or for these; but slavery, as practised among the other Athapaskan tribes, has been unknown amongst them. They are not so numerous now as formerly. In 1835 their number was estimated at 5,000; but in 1889 Father Morice gave their number as 1,600. They now number over 1,000.

Taku river, in the Cassiar district of British Columbia, flows into Taku or Graham inlet in Alaska, and has a length of 36 miles.

Talbot, Edward Allen (1801-1839), journalist and author, was born in Tipperary county, Ireland, in 1801, the son of Richard Talbot. He emigrated to Upper Canada with his father in 1818, and settled in the county of Middlesex. For a time he taught school, and then he became a journalist. In 1831 he founded the *London Sun*, and later the *Freeman's Journal*. He sympathized with the rebels of 1837, and in 1838 he left Canada for the United States. He died in the poor house at Lockport, New York, on January 9, 1839. He was the author of *Five years' residence in the Canadas, including a tour through part of the United States of America, in the year 1823* (2 vols., London, 1824).

Talbot, Thomas (1771-1853), the founder of the Talbot settlement in Upper Canada, was born on July 17, 1771, at Castle Malahide, county Dublin, Ireland, the son of Richard Talbot of Malahide. He entered the British army in 1782, and in 1790 he came to Canada as a subaltern in the 24th Regiment. In 1792 he was appointed private secretary to Lieut.-Col. John Graves Simcoe (q.v.), lieutenant-governor of Upper Canada, and with Simcoe he visited the western part of the province. He returned to England in 1794, became lieut.-colonel commanding the 5th Regiment of Foot, and spent several years in active service on the continent. On the conclusion of the Peace of Amiens, however, he sold his commission, and returned to Upper Canada. Here he obtained a grant of many thousand acres, with a view to founding a settlement. He established himself at Port Talbot, on lake Erie, and here he lived, governing his settlers in almost patriarchal state, for nearly fifty years. From 1822 to 1832 he was a member of the Legislative Council of Upper Canada; but he took little interest in politics, and never attended the meetings of the Council. He died in London, Upper Canada, on February 6, 1853. He was a bachelor, and he bequeathed his estate to his servants. See C. O. Ermatinger, *The Talbot régime* (St. Thomas, Ontario, 1904); E. Ermatinger, *The life of Colonel Talbot* (St. Thomas, Ontario, 1859); L. C. Kearney, *Life of Col. Thomas Talbot* (pamphlet, 1857);

and J. H. Coyne, (ed.), *The Talbot papers* (Trans. Roy. Soc. Can., 1907 and 1909).

Talc, a soft foliated mineral with a pearly lustre. It usually, when pure, is apple-green to white in colour. It has a decided greasy or soapy feel. Chemically, it is a hydrous silicate of magnesia. It is rarely found in crystals, but usually in massive form, which is commonly known as soapstone. The massive material is cut in slabs for electrical switchboard panels and acid-proof table-tops and sinks. It is also cut in blocks to be used in sulphate pulp-mills, and because of its high capacity for retaining heat, in such articles as fireless cookers. Much of the material is ground to powder which finds a great variety of uses, the bulk of the material being used in the paint, rubber, and paper industries. The principal producing region in Canada is at Madoc, Ontario. See H. S. Spence, *Talc and soapstone* (Mines Branch, Ottawa, 1922), and M. E. Wilson, *Talc deposits of Canada* (Geological Survey of Canada, Ottawa, 1926).

Talon, Jean Baptiste (1625?-1694), intendant of New France (1665-8 and 1670-2), was born at Châlons-sur-Marne, in Champagne, about 1625, the son of Philippe Talon and Anne Beuvy. He was educated by the Jesuits in Paris, and about 1653 he entered the French administrative service. After serving as commissary of war in Flanders, and as intendant of Hainaut, he was appointed in 1665 intendant of New France. He came to Canada with Courcelles (q.v.), the first intendant under royal government who actually set foot in the colony; and he inaugurated a period of striking development. He encouraged immigration, so that the population of New France increased rapidly. He fostered the trade of New France; he was the first to build ships in the colony, and the first to establish a brewery; and he might almost be described as the first to give the colony a sound economic basis. His private affairs made necessary his return to France in 1668; but he resumed the intendancy in 1670, and held the post until 1672. On his return to France in the autumn of 1672, he was appointed *secrétaire du cabinet* and *valet de chambre* of the king; and he died in Paris on November 24, 1694. See T. Chapais, *Jean Talon, intendant de la Nouvelle-France* (Quebec, 1904) and *The great intendant* (Toronto, 1914); R. Roy, *Jean Talon* (Bull. rech. hist., vol. vii), and *Les intendants de la Nouvelle-France* (Trans. Roy. Soc. Can., 1903), with portrait; and G. Parizeau, *Un grand intendant de la Nouvelle France* (Revue Trimestrielle Canadienne, 1927).

Tamarack. See **Larch.**

Tamworth, a village in Addington county, Ontario, on the Salmon river, and on the Canadian National Railway, 20 miles north of Napanee. It was first settled about 1845. Pop. (1935), 550.

Tanager, a name applied, with a prefix, to members of the bird family *Uhraupidae,* which is largely represented in tropical America. Tanagers are allied to the sparrow family, and approximate them in size. Three species are recorded from Canada. The best known is the scarlet tanager (*Piranga erythromelas*). The male is rich, bright scarlet with black wings, and the female is greenish in colour. Males moult in August, and acquire a plumage similar to that of the female. This species occurs in the southern portion of Canada, from the bald prairie east to the Atlantic.

Tancook Island, a fishing village in Lunenburg county, Nova Scotia, 6 miles from Chester, the nearest railway station. The name is from the Indian *Uktankook,* meaning, "facing the open sea". Pop. (1935), 600.

Tangier, a fishing village and port in Halifax county, Nova Scotia, about 70 miles east of Halifax. It is said to have been named after a schooner

wrecked there in 1830. Fish is the principal export. Pop. (1935), 500.

Tanguay, Cyprien (1819-1902), priest and genealogist, was born in Quebec, Lower Canada, on September 15, 1819, the son of Pierre Tanguay and Reine Barthell. He was educated at the Quebec Seminary, and was ordained a priest of the Roman Catholic Church in 1843. From 1843 to 1865 he served in various parishes in the province of Quebec. Then he entered the service of the Canadian government, and was attached to the department of agriculture until a few years before his death, when he was retired on pension. He died at Ottawa on April 28, 1902. In 1883 he was given the honorary degree of Litt.D. by Laval University; and in 1887 he was created a *prélat romain* by the Pope. He was one of the charter members of the Royal Society of Canada in 1882. The latter part of his life was devoted to the compilation of his monumental *Dictionnaire généalogique des familles canadiennes* (7 vols., Montreal, 1871-90) He published also a *Répertoire général du clergé canadien* (Quebec, 1868-9; new ed., 1893), *Monseigneur de l'Auberivière* (Montreal, 1885), and *À travers les régistres: Notes recueillies* (Montreal, 1886).

Tansy (*Tanacetum vulgare* L., *Compositae*), an acrid, bitter, strong-scented herb, with a smooth stem, 2-4 feet high. The leaves are divided into toothed leaflets, and the flowers are borne in flat-topped clusters of yellow heads. It is escaped from old gardens, and is to be found along roadsides near dwellings. It has been used in medicine since the Middle Ages.

Tantramar river, a tidal stream in New Brunswick, which empties into Cumberland basin. The word is a corruption of the French *tintamarre,* meaning "a thundering noise", which has reference either to the noise of the tides or to the noise made by the flocks of ducks and geese which frequent the rich marsh lands along its banks. These marshes, having been dyked, produce great quantities of hay.

Tape Grass. See **Eel Grass.**

Tara, a village in Bruce county, Ontario, on the Aux Sables river, and on the Canadian National Railway, 28 miles north of Walkerton, and 18 miles south-west of Owen Sound. It was incorporated as a village in 1881. It has a continuation school, a free library, and a weekly newspaper (*Leader*). Pop. (1931), 461.

Tardivel, Jules Paul (1851-1905), author and journalist, was born at Covington, Kentucky, on September 2, 1851, the son of Claudius Tardivel and Isabella Brent. He came to Canada in 1868, and was educated at the College of St. Hyacinthe. In 1874 he joined the staff of *Le Canadien;* and in 1881 he founded *La Vérité* at Quebec. He was strongly clerical and ultramontane in politics, and advocated the independence of French Canada. He died at Quebec on April 24, 1905. In 1874 he married Henriette Brunelle, of St. Hyacinthe, Quebec. He was the author of a *Vie du Pape Pie IX* (Quebec, 1878), *Borrowed and stolen feathers* (Quebec, 1878), *L'-anglicisme voilà l'ennemi* (Quebec, 1880), *Mélanges* (Quebec, 1887), *Notes de voyage* (Montreal, 1890), *La situation religieuse aux États-unis* (Lille, 1900), *La langue française au Canada* (Montreal, 1901), and a novel entitled *Pour la patrie* (Montreal, 1895). See Mgr. J. Fèvre, *Vie et travaux de J. P. Tardivel* (Paris, 1906).

Tare. See **Vetch.**

Tariffs. Up to 1846 there were two tariffs applicable to imports into Canada, an imperial tariff on foreign goods only, and a colonial tariff fixed by the colonial legislature, levied on all imports, and limited to a maximum of 5 per cent. In the earlier years of the nineteenth century no duties were levied on the land frontiers of Canada, and even when such duties were legally imposed there was little attempt to enforce or collect them. Much of the supplies for the western pioneers in Ohio, Indiana, and Michigan came through Montreal, and considerable quantities of American produce were exported *viâ* the St. Lawrence, and accepted in Great Britain as Canadian in origin. During the 1820's and 1830's the definition of "Canadian" produce was more strictly drawn, but American raw materials processed in Canada were still admitted into England as Canadian goods. When in 1846 the repeal of the Corn Laws swept away the preferences on which so much of the St. Lawrence trade had come to be based, desolation stalked in Montreal.

1846-1866. The repeal of the Corn Laws almost necessarily involved the granting of full autonomy to Canada in tariff matters, and in 1847 a Canadian tariff, with a prevailing rate of 10 per cent., took the place of the old imperial and colonial tariffs. A second inevitable result of 1846 was the negotiation of a commercial treaty with the United States. Negotiations began in 1848, and following a difficult and complicated course were successfully concluded in 1854. The Reciprocity Treaty of 1854 in effect traded navigation and fishing privileges for free entry of all natural products of the farm, forest, mine, and sea. The treaty remained in force for twelve years, but was abrogated in 1866 at the instance of the United States. The Canadian prosperity which coincided with the period of reciprocity was due in no small measure to the free access to the American market. Especially during the Civil War did Canadian producers profit by the high prices and insatiable demand of the United States. And, in its turn, the denunciation of the treaty was an important influence underlying Confederation.

In the meantime, a protectionist movement had begun to develop in Canada. In response to the growing agitation of the small manufacturers, the Cayley tariff of 1858 and the Galt tariff of 1859 raised the duties on manufactured goods from an average of about 10 per cent. to one rather over 20 per cent. While the government defended the increases as necessary revenue measures, it is clear that it was accepting in principle a policy of moderate protection. The Cayley and Galt tariffs aroused a storm of protest in England, but the despatches, speeches, and memoranda in this connection belong to constitutional rather than economic history. They also occasioned a good deal of resentment in the United States, where they were regarded as a breach of the spirit of the Reciprocity Treaty, and this resentment was added in 1865 to the other interests demanding the abrogation of the Treaty.

1866-1879. In 1867 the normal rate of the Canadian tariff was reduced from 20 per cent. to 15 per cent. This reduction was a compromise between the moderately protectionist policy of the Canadas and the more or less free-trade policy of the Maritimes, but it was also a reply to the abrogation of Reciprocity. With the United States market largely closed, it was necessary "to make Canada a cheap country to live in and to produce in".

During the first ten years of Confederation, the tariff was not a divisive factor in politics. It was regarded primarily as an instrument of revenue, conferring, it is true, "incidental protection". The economic depression that began in 1873 created budgetary difficulties, and in 1874 the general rate was increased to 17½ per cent. In 1876 a further increase to 20 per cent. was proposed, but was rejected by the government. As the depression deepened, Canada became a slaughter market for the surplus stocks of British and American manufacturers. Attempts at relief through a new reciprocity treaty failed. After some hesitation the Conservative party, then in opposition, adopted its "National Policy", a policy

of high protection and concentration on the home market. In the general election of 1878 the Conservatives were victorious, and the new government at once put its policy into practice.

1879-1897. The budget of 1879 and its successors amply fulfilled the pre-election promises of the National Policy. Duties on manufactured goods were raised from 17½ per cent. to 30, 35, and in some cases 45 per cent., and the free list was considerably reduced. Cottons, woollens, furniture, and iron manufactures were especially favoured. In 1883 the production of pig-iron and steel was further encouraged by the introduction of a system of bounties.

The prosperity of 1879-1883, which came to Canada as it did to the rest of the world, gave a somewhat fictitious prestige to the National Policy. Undoubtedly the history of modern manufacturing in Canada dates from 1879, but after 1883 the era of the National Policy was largely one of difficulty and depression. Industry became stagnant, and emigration assumed alarming proportions. The Canadian political Scriptures, it was said, "began with Exodus and ended in Lamentations."

By 1890 the seven lean years had begun to produce a reaction. The reviving political power of the Democrats in the United States offered some hope of freer trade relations with that country. The publicity given to the growth of monopolies and trusts in Canada was turned into an effective argument against high tariffs. The government met this shift in opinion by lowering a few duties here and there, especially on articles used chiefly in the farming industry. The election of 1896 was fought on a complexity of issues, but of these the tariff was one of the most important. The Liberals roundly attacked the whole National Policy, and, against a rather disorganized Conservative party, won handsomely.

1897-1911. In spite of the Liberal professions when in opposition, the first Liberal budget of 1897 made no radical changes in the tariff. Indian corn, binder twine, barbed wire, pig-iron, and sugar were added to the free list; there was some simplification of rates and classifications; and the duties on a few items were raised.

The most significant item in the Budget of 1897 was the introduction of the principle of the British preference. It took the form of a rebate of ⅛th of the general rate on imports from countries granting at least as favourable rates to Canada. It was intended and expected that this rebate would apply only to the United Kingdom and certain of its colonies, but it was found to be legally impossible so to confine it, because the British treaties with Belgium (1862) and the German Zollverein (1865) specifically bound the colonies. In practice, therefore, the lower rates had to be extended to all countries within the world-wide network of the British most-favoured-nation treaties. The United States was the only important country that failed to qualify. At the Colonial Conference of 1897, Great Britain was persuaded to denounce the Belgian and German treaties, and in 1898 Canada was free to grant special preferences to British and Empire goods. This she at once did, at the same time increasing the rebate to ¼, a rebate further increased to ⅓ in 1900. In 1904 the flat rate preference was abandoned in favour of a two-column tariff, the British preferential column being in most cases substantially lower than the general column.

The inauguration of Imperial Preference may be attributed to several factors. It was supported by Liberal free-traders as an ingenious flank attack on the policy of protection. In part it reflected Canadian resentment to the McKinley and Dingley tariffs of 1890 and 1897; and it was in part a product of imperial emotion associated with the Diamond Jubilee. Opinion in Canada divided only on the question of whether the concessions should be conditional or unconditional. In practice they were accorded unconditionally to Great Britain and conditionally to other parts of the Empire. By 1904 preferential treatment had been extended to India, South Africa, British West Indies, and New Zealand; and by 1913 to practically the whole of the dependent Empire. In 1923 the Irish Free State was included, and in 1928 Newfoundland. Trade relations with Australia have never been governed by the preferential tariff, but since 1925 they have been the subject of a special trade agreement.

The development of imperial preference aroused some misgivings in foreign countries, but Germany was the only country to take retaliatory action by withdrawing from Canada its conventional tariff and imposing its maximum rates. Canada replied in 1903 with a surtax of 33⅓ per cent. against German goods. Not until 1910 was a settlement reached, when Germany accorded her minimum rates to the principal Canadian exports, and Canada withdrew the special surtax.

In 1904 the anti-dumping clause was introduced into the Canadian tariff. This clause provides that when the export price to Canada is lower than the domestic price in the exporting country an extra duty equal to the difference in these prices is levied. This anti-dumping clause was a Canadian invention, and has been widely copied by other countries.

In 1907 there was a complete revision of the tariff, and the well-known "three-column tariff" was introduced; that is, for each item three rates of duty are provided, the British preferential rate, the intermediate rate, and the general rate. The intermediate rate is the bargaining rate, and the general rate applies to all countries with which Canada has no most-favoured-nation agreement. Broadly speaking, the 1907 revision left the preferential and general rates unchanged, but introduced the new intermediate rates, slightly lower than the general rates.

Between 1907 and 1911 Canada built up a net-work of most-favoured-nation agreements with a large number of foreign countries. It has already been noted that Canada received autonomy in tariff-making in 1846, but freedom to negotiate commercial treaties came much later. In 1877 Great Britain adopted the practice of inserting a clause in all new commercial treaties making the adherence of the self-governing colonies optional. But treaties affecting Canada were still negotiated through the Foreign Office, though the practice slowly developed of including a Canadian as an associate in the diplomatic pourparlers. In 1883 Sir Charles Tupper (q.v.) was appointed joint-plenipotentiary with the British ambassador in Paris for the purpose of negotiating a commercial agreement. Not until 1907 did Canadian plenipotentiaries conduct the whole of the negotiations, and even then the British ambassador put his signature to the final document. Only in 1923 did the Canadian government secure recognition of the right to sign exclusively on behalf of the Crown.

Commercial agreements were signed with France in 1907, and with Italy, Germany, Belgium, and Netherlands during the next few years. In addition, by adherence to British treaties, Canada entered into most-favoured-nation relations with most of the other European countries, with several South American countries, and with Japan.

The pre-war history of the Canadian tariff naturally concludes with the struggle over reciprocity. In 1909 the Payne-Aldrich tariff had for the first time given the United States a two-column tariff, the punitively higher rates to be used against countries which discriminated against the United States. The United States raised no official objection to the preferential tariffs, but did demand, in return for its "minimum" tariff, the concession of not only the whole intermediate column, but also certain special rates conceded to France in the 1907 agreement. A very generous compromise was reached in March, 1910, by which Canada made a few very minor concessions, and in return received the whole minimum schedule.

The negotiations leading up to this settlement had, however, given rise to discussions of a much broader nature. Both governments were facing regional political revolts on the tariff question, and a sympathetic understanding of each other's difficulties led them to accept the broad objective of reciprocally lower tariffs. A draft agreement, to be given effect by concurrent legislation, was completed in January, 1911. This agreement placed most natural products on a reciprocal free list, and provided for substantial reductions on a long list of manufactured products. The agreement passed Congress, though not without difficulty, but in the Canadian parliament the Conservative opposition vigorously and successfully insisted on an appeal to the people. In the election that followed the Liberals received only 88 seats to the Conservatives' 133. The Liberals carried the Maritimes and the West; Quebec divided largely on the nationalist and naval questions; Ontario went almost solidly to the Conservatives. In the popular vote the Conservative majority was about 40,000 in a poll of 1,300,000. Both parties, however, accepted the 1911 verdict as a definitive rejection of special tariff relations with the United States, and regarded the issue as closed.

1911-1930. This period was marked by frequent changes in tariff detail, but no significant change in policy or in trend. During the Great War, a horizontal increase in all tariffs was made by imposing a special surtax on all imports, 5 per cent. on the British preference, and 7½ per cent. on the intermediate and general rates. In 1919 the tariff question was forced into political discussion once more, but the division of opinion remained strongly regional, and both national parties, in the attempt to remain national, had to compromise. Though the government changed in 1921, and for the first time a large farmers' party arrived at Ottawa, no real change in tariff policy can be observed. Duties on agricultural machinery and on automobiles were reduced in 1924 and 1926, but the rates on many iron and steel items were increased. The most numerous changes came in the Dunning budget of 1930. The number of items on the British free list was greatly increased, largely by the addition to it of items under which little was imported or in which Canadian production hardly existed. The 1930 budget completely re-wrote large sections of the tariff, but the work was really one of long overdue reclassification, and the net effect on the margin of protection was negligible. The Dunning budget did, however, introduce a new tariff device, the seasonal tariff in a wide range of fresh fruits and vegetables.

The years 1923-1928 saw renewed activity in the negotiation of trade agreements, the more important being with France, Italy, Australia, Netherlands, and the British West Indies. By exchange of notes or order-in-council, most-favoured-nation treatment was still further extended. After a short lapse this movement was renewed after 1933, and by 1937 Canada had commercial agreements either of a special nature or of the general most-favoured-nation type with all the important countries of the world except China.

An Advisory Board on Tariff and Taxation was created in 1926. For some time there had been discussion of "taking the tariff out of politics," or of applying scientific methods, or at least "open diplomacy", to tariff changes. The Board of 1926 was empowered to study and report on any question referred to it by the minister of finance.

During the four years of its life it received nearly 200 references. Its most important achievement was the complete revision and reclassification of the iron-and-steel schedules. The Board was dissolved after the general election of 1930, but a new Board was constituted in 1933. The new Board not only reports on any matter referred to it by the minister of finance; it also deals with matters arising out of Articles 10 to 15 of the United Kingdom-Canada Trade Agreement (1932); and it hears and decides appeals from the rulings of the Department of National Revenue with respect to appraisals, valuations, and the classification of imports.

1930-1937. Immediately after the general election of 1930 a special session of parliament was called to deal with unemployment, and as part of the relief programme a drastic upward revision of the tariff was undertaken. Duties were increased all along the line; and in many cases, especially in textiles, heavy specific duties were superimposed upon the increased *ad valorem* rates. Canada stepped directly into the ranks of the definitely high tariff countries. At the same time, the Customs Act was amended, giving the government broad powers to impose arbitrary valuations and drastic anti-dumping duties by ministerial decree, and to impose what were in effect almost prohibitive duties on imports from countries with depreciated currencies. The special powers thus conferred were freely used between 1930 and 1933. Partly as a result of the Ottawa Conference and partly as a result of the passing of the acute stage of the depression, these powers were more moderately exercised after 1934.

In 1931 the new powers were used to prohibit the importation of coal, lumber, asbestos, and certain other products from Russia. In retaliation the Soviet government practically ceased making purchases in Canada. Normal trade relations, however, were resumed in 1936.

A short tariff war with Japan occurred in 1935. Japan took the view that the Canadian "administrative protection" constituted in fact discrimination against Japanese trade. Negotiation failing to resolve the issue, Japan imposed a surtax of 50 per cent. on the more important exports from Canada, and Canada replied with a surtax of $33\frac{1}{3}$ per cent. on all Japanese goods. Five months later an amicable settlement was effected.

In 1932 the Imperial Economic Conference was held at Ottawa. For thirty years the principle of imperial preference had been spreading in the British Dominions, but so long as Great Britain remained a free-trade country it was impossible for it to reciprocate. During and immediately after the war Great Britain imposed protective customs duties on a few commodities—the McKenna and Key Industries duties—and in these she conceded a $33\frac{1}{3}$ per cent. rebate on imports from Empire countries. During the winter of 1931-2, however, Great Britain definitely abandoned her free-trade policy, and imposed, first, a general tariff of 10 per cent. (subject to some important exemptions), and later a more complicated tariff with rates as high as 25 and 35 per cent. In all cases imports from Empire countries were admitted free of duty pending the results of the Ottawa Conference. At this Conference a comprehensive series of bilateral agreements were negotiated. Canada signed agreements with the United Kingdom, South Africa, the Irish Free State, and Southern Rhodesia. Agreements were already in effect with Australia and New Zealand. India and Newfoundland remained the only parts of the Empire with which Canada had no special agreement.

The agreement with the Irish Free State accorded Canada most-favoured-nation treatment, and in return Canada gave the same rates of duty accorded to the United Kingdom. The agreements with South Africa and Southern Rhodesia exchanged preferences on specified lists of goods, chiefly Indian corn, fruits, nuts, and sugar, on the one hand, and wheat, apples, lumber, paper, hosiery, rubber goods, electrical appliances, and various kinds of machinery, on the other.

The Canada-United Kingdom Agreement was more comprehensive. Great Britain undertook to continue the preferences already existing under the Import Duties Act, and in addition created new preferences chiefly in wheat, dairy products, meat, fruits, and tobacco. Great Britain further undertook to secure for Canada extensive preferences in the non-self-governing Empire. In return Canada increased the margin of preference on 223 items, 133 by lowering the preferential rate, and 90 by raising the intermediate and general rates. The principal groups benefited were textiles, iron and steel, and chemicals. Canada also increased the margins of preference on various commodities largely produced in the dependent Empire.

In addition to the tariff schedules, Canada agreed to a number of broad principles governing the administration of her tariff. Chief of these were undertakings to accord protection only to industries with reasonably sound prospects of success; to limit the height of the tariff by considering the differences in the costs of efficient production in the two countries; to provide machinery for impartial settlement of disputes over tariff administration; and to abolish as soon as possible the exchange dumping duties.

The Agreement ran for five years, and was replaced by a new Agreement in 1937. The new Agreement involved no significant changes, but accorded slightly lower rates of duty on a long list of commodities, the most important being in the textile group.

In November, 1935, Canada signed a trade agreement with the United States which for the first time in seventy years placed Canadian-American trade on a negotiated foundation. The agreement exchanged unconditional most-favoured-nation treatment (the United States excepting Cuba, and Canada excepting the British preferential rates). The United States further reduced by 20 to 50 per cent. the duties on 63 items including lumber, cattle, fish, cheese, cream, apples, and certain chemicals. The United States undertook to keep twenty-one items on the free list, including newsprint, shingles, wood-pulp, and agricultural implements. For five items the tariff concessions were applicable only to reasonably generous quotas, all imports above the quota being subject to the old rates of duty. Canada in return extended the entire intermediate tariff to the United States, a reduction of $2\frac{1}{2}$ to 5 per cent. on the great majority of the items in the tariff. On fruits, vegetables, magazines, farm implements, and a wide range of industrial machinery, new rates were established considerably below the old intermediate rates. Canada also agreed to amend the Customs Act to eliminate much of the arbitrary control of customs valuations, and agreed specifically to reduce by at least 20 per cent. the special seasonal duties on fresh fruits and vegetables.

The net effect of the agreement was to put the general level of duties in both countries back to about the level prevailing in 1929, that is, before the introduction of the Hawley-Smoot and Bennett tariffs of 1930.

Summary. Beginning in 1867 with a low tariff, Canada became in 1879 a country of moderately high tariffs. Since 1879 the general level has been fairly constant, with perhaps a slight downward trend. The only important break in this policy was in 1930-35, when Canada was definitely in the high tariff class. Since about 1904, Canada has become steadily more conscious of the growing importance of trade with countries other than Great Britain and

the United States, and this has been reflected in the growth and development of a net-work of commercial treaties. Since 1890 there has been no politically significant group in Canada committed to a free-trade policy. Low tariff sentiment is strong on the Prairies and in the Maritimes; high tariff sentiment dominates the industrialized central provinces; and the national policy has remained a somewhat uneasy compromise between the two.

Bibliography. See E. Porritt, *Sixty years of protection in Canada* (London, 1908); O. D. Skelton, "General economic history, 1867-1912", in A. Shortt and A. G. Doughty (eds.), *Canada and its provinces*, vol. ix (Toronto, 1914); W. A. Mackintosh, "Canadian tariff policy", in *Canadian papers*, Banff Conference, I. P. R. (Toronto, 1933); K. W. Taylor, "Tariff administration and non-tariff methods of trade control", in *Proceedings of the Conference on Canadian-American affairs, Canton, New York, 1935* (New York, 1936); and H. Feis, "A year of the Canadian Trade Agreement" (*Foreign Affairs*, 1937). See also *Canada Year Book* and contemporary government documents on Reciprocity, the Imperial Economic Conference, etc. Full details of all rates of duty, as well as the text of all trade agreements in force, are to be found in *The customs tariff of Canada* (Office consolidation).

Tarte, Joseph Israel (1848-1907), minister of public works for Canada (1896-1902), was born at Lanoraie, Berthier county, Lower Canada, on January 11, 1848, the son of Joseph Tarte, an *habitant*. He was educated at L'Assomption College, and was admitted to practice as a notary public in 1871. He very soon, however, drifted into journalism, and here he quickly made his mark. For over twenty years he was the editor of *L'Evènement* of Quebec; and in 1897 he acquired *La Patrie*, of Montreal. From 1877 to 1881 he represented Bonaventure in the Legislative Assembly of Quebec; and in

1891 he was elected to represent L'Islet in the Canadian House of Commons. Though elected as a Conservative, he took a foremost part in pressing the charges of corruption against Sir Hector Langevin (q.v.) and Thomas McGreevy (q.v.), and went over to the Liberal opposition. In 1896 he played an important part in determining the Liberal policy in regard to separate schools in Manitoba, and in organizing the Liberal forces in the province of Quebec. On the return of the Liberals to power, he was rewarded with the portfolio of public works in the Laurier government; and his administration of his department was most effective. He was, however, unlike his colleagues, a high protectionist; and his public advocacy of higher tariffs in 1902 brought about his dismissal from the government. He thereupon assumed the editorship of *La Patrie*, of Montreal; and he died in Montreal on December 18, 1907. He was twice married: by his first wife, Georgiana Sylvestre, he had three sons and three daughters; and by his second wife, Emma Laurencelle, he had one daughter.

Taschereau, Antoine Charles (1797-1862), politician, was born at Quebec on October 26, 1797, the son of the Hon. Gabriel Elzéar Taschereau (q.v.) and his second wife, Louise-Françoise Juchereau Duchesnay. He represented Beauce in the Legislative Assembly of Lower Canada from 1830 to 1838; and in 1834, as chairman of the select committee appointed to report on the state of the province, he presented in the House the famous Ninety-two Resolutions. From 1841 to 1844 he represented Dorchester in the Legislative Assembly of united Canada. In 1849 he was appointed collector of customs at Quebec. He died at Deschambault, Lower Canada, on June 11, 1862. In 1819 he married Adelaide Elizabeth, daughter of Louis Fleury de la Gorgendière, seignior of Deschambault; and by her he had twelve children.

See P. G. Roy, *La famille Juchereau Duchesnay* (Lévis, 1903).

Taschereau, Elzéar Alexandre (1820-1898), cardinal archbishop of Quebec, was born at Ste. Marie de la Beauce, Lower Canada, on February 17, 1820, the son of the Hon. Jean Thomas Taschereau (q.v.) and Marie, daughter of the Hon. Jean Antoine Panet (q.v.). He was educated at the Quebec Seminary, and was ordained a priest of the Roman Catholic Church in 1842. For nearly thirty years he was connected with the Quebec Seminary, first as a professor, then as director, and finally as superior. In 1862 he was chosen as vicar-general of the diocese of Quebec, and in 1871 he was consecrated sixteenth bishop and sixth archbishop of Quebec. In 1886 he was created a cardinal of the Roman Catholic Church, being the first Canadian to attain this honour. He retired from the administration of his diocese in 1894; and he died at Quebec on April 12, 1898. He was the author of *Remarques sur les mémoires de l'évêque de Trois-Rivières sur les difficultés religieuses en Canada* (Quebec, 1882). See Mgr. T. E. Hamel, *Le premier cardinal canadien* (Quebec, 1886); and Mgr. H. Têtu, *S. E. le Cardinal Taschereau* (Quebec, 1898).

Taschereau, Gabriel Elzéar (1745-1809), legislative councillor of Lower Canada, was born at Quebec on March 27, 1745, the son of Thomas-Jacques Taschereau, a member of the Superior Council of New France, and Marie-Claire Fleury de la Gorgendière. He remained in Canada after the conquest, and took part in the defence of Quebec against the Americans in 1775. In 1777 he was appointed a judge of the court of common pleas for Montreal, but resigned soon afterwards. From 1792 to 1796 he represented the county of Dorchester in the Legislative Assembly of Lower Canada; and in 1798 he was appointed to the Legislative Council. From 1794 to 1802 he was *grand voyer* of the district of Quebec; and in 1802 he was appointed deputy postmaster-general of the province, in succession to Hugh Finlay (q.v.). He died at his manor house at Ste. Marie de la Beauce, on September 18, 1809. He was twice married, (1) in 1773 to Marie-Louise-Elisabeth Bazin (d. 1783), by whom he had eight children, and (2) in 1789 to Louise-Françoise Juchereau Duchesnay (d. 1841), by whom he had three children. See P. G. Roy, *L'hon. G. E. Taschereau* (Bull. rech. hist., 1902).

Taschereau, Sir Henri Elzéar (1836-1911), chief justice of the Supreme Court of Canada (1902-6), was born at Ste. Marie de la Beauce, Lower Canada, on October 7, 1836, the son of Pierre Elzéar Taschereau and Catherine Hénédine, daughter of the Hon. Amable Dionne. He was educated at the Quebec Seminary, and was called to the bar of Lower Canada in 1857 (Q.C., 1867). He sat in the Legislative Assembly of Canada for Beauce county from 1861 to 1867. In 1871 he was appointed a judge of the Superior Court of Quebec; and in 1878 a judge of the Supreme Court of Canada. In 1902 he became chief justice of this court; and, as such, he was appointed for a short time in 1904 administrator of the government of Canada. He retired from the bench in 1906, and he died at Ottawa on April 14, 1911. He was twice married, (1) in 1857 to Marie Antoinette, daughter of the Hon. R. U. de Lotbinière Harwood, by whom he had two sons and three daughters; and (2) in 1897 to Marie Louise, daughter of Charles Panet, of Ottawa. He was created a knight bachelor in 1902, and a privy councillor in 1904. He was the author of several legal works.

Taschereau, Sir Henri Thomas (1841-1909), chief justice of the court of King's Bench of Quebec, was born in Quebec on October 6, 1841, the son of the Hon. Jean Thomas Taschereau (q.v.) and Louis Adèle, daughter of the Hon. Amable Dionne. He was educated at the Quebec Seminary and at Laval University (B.L., 1861; B.C.L., 1862), and was called to the bar of Lower Canada in 1863. From 1872 to 1878 he represented Montmagny in the Canadian House of Commons; and in 1878 he was appointed a judge of the Superior Court of Quebec. In 1907 he was made chief justice of the court of King's Bench at Quebec; and he died at Montmorency, near Paris, France, on October 11, 1909. He was twice married, (1) in 1864 to Marie Louise Séverine (d. 1883), daughter of E. L. Pacaud, of Arthabaska, and (2) in 1885 to Mme. Marie Masson. By his first wife he had nine children. He was created a knight bachelor in 1908.

Taschereau, Jean Thomas (1778-1832), judge of the court of King's Bench at Quebec (1827-32), was the son of the Hon. Gabriel Elzéar Taschereau (q.v.). From 1800 to 1808, and from 1820 to 1827, he was a member of the Legislative Assembly of Lower Canada. In 1806 he was one of the founders of *Le Canadien*, and in 1810 he was arrested and imprisoned by order of Sir J. Craig (q.v.), but was released on promise of good behaviour. In 1827 he was appointed a judge of the court of King's Bench at Quebec; and from 1828 to 1832 he was a member of the Legislative Council of Lower Canada. He died at Quebec on June 14, 1832. He married Marie, daughter of the Hon. Jean Antoine Panet (q.v.). See P. G. Roy, *Les juges Taschereau* (Bull. rech. hist., 1897).

Taschereau, Jean Thomas (1814-1893), puisne judge of the Supreme Court of Canada (1875-8), was born at Quebec on December 12, 1814, the son of the Hon. Jean Thomas Taschereau (q.v.) and Marie, daughter of the Hon. Jean Antoine Panet (q.v.). He was educated at the Quebec Seminary, and was called to the bar of Lower Canada in 1836 (Q.C., 1860). He practised law in Quebec, and in 1865 was appointed a judge of the Superior Court of Quebec. In 1873 he was transferred to the court of Queen's Bench in Quebec; and in 1875 he was appointed a judge of the newly formed Supreme Court of Canada. Ill-health compelled his retirement from the bench in 1878; and he died at Quebec on November 9, 1893. He was twice married, (1) in 1840 to Louise Adèle (d. 1861), daughter of the Hon. Amable Dionne, and (2) in 1862 to Marie Josephine, daughter of the Hon. René Edouard Caron (q.v.).

Taschereau, Joseph André (1806-1867), solicitor-general of Lower Canada, was born at Ste. Marie de la Beauce on November 30, 1806. He represented Beauce in the Legislative Assembly of Lower Canada from 1835 to 1838, and Dorchester in the Legislative Assembly of united Canada from 1845 to 1847; and during this latter period he was solicitor-general of Lower Canada, though without a seat in the Council. In 1847 he was appointed a judge of the Superior Court of Lower Canada for the district of Kamouraska; and he died at Kamouraska on March 30, 1867.

Taschereau, a village in Abitibi county, Quebec, named after the Hon. L. A. Taschereau, prime minister of Quebec (1920-36). Pop. (1931), 639.

Tassé, Joseph (1848-1895), author and politician, was born in Montreal on October 23, 1848. He was educated at Bourget College, Rigaud, Lower Canada, and became a journalist. From 1869 to 1872 he was associate editor of *La Minerve*, Montreal. Later he became editor of *La Minerve*. From 1878 to 1887 he sat in the Canadian House of Commons for Ottawa; and from 1891 to 1895 he sat in the Senate of Canada. He died at Montreal on January 18, 1895. He was a charter member of the Royal Society of Canada; and he was the author of *Philemon Wright, ou colonisation et commerce en bois* (Montreal, 1871), *Le chemin de fer Canadien Pacifique* (Montreal, 1872), *La vallée de l'Outaouais* (Montreal, 1873), *Les canadiens de l'ouest* (2 vols., Montreal,

1878), and *Le 38ème fauteuil, ou souvenirs parlementaires* (Montreal, 1891). He edited also the *Discours de Sir Georges Cartier* (Montreal, 1893).

Tassie, William (1815-1886), educationist, was born at Dublin, Ireland, on May 10, 1815. He emigrated to Canada with relatives in 1834, and was educated at University College, Toronto (M.A., 1858). In 1853 he became headmaster of the grammar school at Galt, Upper Canada, and under him the school acquired a national reputation. Later he was headmaster of the Collegiate Institute at Peterborough, Ontario; and here he died on November 21, 1886. In 1871 he was made an LL.D. of Queen's University, Kingston. See James E. Kerr, *Recollections of my schooldays at Tassie's* (Waterloo Historical Society, 3rd Ann. Report, 1915), and J. C. Sutherland, *At Doctor Tassie's* (Can. mag., 1924).

Tatamagouche, a village in Colchester county, Nova Scotia, at the junction of the Waugh and French rivers, and on the Picton branch of the Canadian National Railway, 30 miles west of Pictou. The name is a corruption of a Micmac word meaning "the place where two rivers meet", or (alternatively) "barred across the entrance with sand". A variant of the name is found as early as 1738. Pop. (1934), about 1,000. See F. H. Patterson, *A history of Tatamagouche, Nova Scotia* (Halifax, 1917).

Tavistock, a village in Oxford county, Ontario, on the Buffalo and Goderich branch of the Canadian National Railway, 10 miles south-east of Stratford. It was named in 1849, when a post-office was opened here, after Tavistock in Devonshire, England. It has flour and textile mills, a cheese and butter factory, and some other small industries; and also a continuation school, a public library, and a weekly newspaper (*Gazette*). Pop. (1931), 1,029.

Taxation. Under the French régime in Canada there was no general system of taxation; temporary and local assessments were, in a few instances, levied for special purposes. A customs tax on liquors and tobacco brought in a fairly regular revenue, and a royalty exacted on all pelts yielded considerable sums from the fur-trade. In the early days of English rule, any definite organization of sources of revenue came about slowly, the main source for many years being certain seigniorial dues and the proceeds of the sale of government timber and land. The right of levying taxes and of regulating the trade of the colony was vested in the British parliament, at first for Imperial revenue, but, after 1778, for defraying the expenditures of colonial administration. Upper Canada passed the first assessment Act in 1793, which provided for the taxation of householders according to the value of property. As the definition of taxable property was vague, this was followed by various amending Acts, determining a fair valuation of property and the rate of taxation. The first assessment Act in Lower Canada was passed in 1796, when the French system was, for the most part, continued, as there was persistent opposition among the French-Canadians to any form of direct taxation. The collection of customs duties in Lower Canada and the retention of a large share for its own treasury enabled the legislature to undertake many local works which in later times would have been left to the municipalities. In 1831 the British parliament resigned its control of the customs duties to the legislatures of the British North American colonies; and the advent of responsible government completed the transfer of taxation from the mother country to the colonies. The first general property tax of Upper Canada was instituted in 1853, when an Act provided that all land and personal property should be taxed, including in the latter category all property except land and the improvements thereon. This Act, with various amendments, served as the basis of local assessment in Upper Canada for many years. In both Nova Scotia and New Brunswick the definition of taxable property included personalty. As early as 1763 an assessment Act in Nova Scotia provided for taxation of real and personal property, and an Act of 1856 defined personality to include personal chattels, stock-in-trade, money, and ships. Various New Brunswick Acts dealt also with property taxation. Lower Canada thus remained the only province with no tax on personal property, but dependent on indirect taxation; this was due to the French dislike of a direct tax, while Ontario had early been forced to it by financial straits, and the Maritime provinces had assumed it naturally through their association with the New England states and through their large United Empire Loyalist population.

When representatives from the provinces were in conference prior to Confederation, the matter of public finance for the new Dominion came up for discussion. One of the chief sources of revenue of the provinces had been customs and excise duties. It was decided that these revenues were henceforth to be taken over by the Dominion government, which had in return to assume the existing provincial debts and to provide definite cash subsidies for the support of the provincial governments. The British North America Act allowed the Dominion government to raise money "by any mode or system of taxation", but for many years, until the Great War made new and greater demands, the Dominion levied practically no other taxes than customs and excise duties. Apparent exceptions to this were such receipts as post office and railway revenues, but in reality these were absorbed by the expense of administering these services. This method of taxation met with general approval; it was an indirect tax, and hence did not seem an undue burden; it could be utilized to protect manufacturing interests, and afforded a large return and easy administration.

Dominion expenditures increased greatly after 1913, due to the war and consequent burdens of interest, pensions, and soldiers' civil re-establishment, as well as other less direct resulting deficits. These debts were met by loans raised during the war, and at intervals since that time; these necessitated new taxation both to meet the interest charges upon the loans and to provide a sinking fund for their ultimate payment. The first war taxation was an increase in customs and excise duties on certain commodities, provided in a amendment to the Customs Act, passed a few days after the outbreak of war. The 1915 session of parliament passed legislation imposing additional duties of 5 per cent. *ad valorem* on commodities imported under the British preferential tariff, and 7½ per cent. *ad valorem* on commodities imported under the intermediate and general tariffs, certain commodities being excepted. New internal taxes were also imposed on bank circulation, on income of trust and loan companies, on insurance in other than life and marine companies, on telegrams and cablegrams, railway tickets, sleeping-car berths, etc., also on cheques, postal notes, money orders, and letters. By the next year it was evident that further taxation was required to maintain the finances of the Dominion, and the Business Profits War Tax Act was passed, imposing a tax of 25 per cent. of the amount by which the profits earned in a business owned by an incorporated company exceeded 7 per cent. per annum. An amendment the following year provided for a tax of 50 per cent. on profits in excess of 15 per cent. per annum. and a tax of 75 per cent. on profits in excess of 20 per cent. per annum. Amendments of the next two years extended the operation of the Act to businesses with smaller capital. In 1920, however, exemptions

were raised and rates decreased, and the next year the tax was dropped entirely for other more satisfactory taxation.

A new source of revenue was instituted when, in 1917, the Income War Tax Act was passed. As each year has seen some amendment to this Act, the developments will here be traced to the present time. The original Act imposed a tax of 4 per cent. on incomes exceeding $2,000 in the case of unmarried men and childless widows and widowers, and on incomes exceeding $3,000 in the case of other persons. A super-tax was also imposed progressing from 2 per cent. to 25 per cent. on very large incomes. The first change was to lower the exemption to $1,000 and $2,000, respectively, and to increase the super-tax. This was followed by an increased general rate of taxation and an increase of taxes paid by corporations to 10 per cent. of net income in excess of $2,000. The amendment of 1920 empowered the minister to determine deficits and losses, taxed dividends or shareholders' bonuses, taxed incomes from an estate or accumulating in trust, increased the surtax on incomes of $5,000 or more, required that one-quarter of the tax be forwarded with the return, and imposed penalties for default. In 1923 exemption from taxation was granted the incomes of consuls and other officials of foreign countries whose duties required them to reside in Canada, provided such countries granted reciprocal privileges to resident Canadian officials. The following year the administration of the Act was transferred from the department of Finance to the department of Customs and Excise. From 1926 to 1930 the exemptions were raised to $1,500 and $3,000, the rate of taxation for individuals and for corporations was reduced, and such deductions as government annuities and donations to charity were allowed on taxable income. This relief to the tax-payer was of short duration, however, for since that time the trend has steadily been in the direction of a higher rate of taxation and lower exemption, the latter in 1936 being $1,000 and $2,000. Two of the disadvantages in the administration of the income tax have come from the possibility of evasion and from the difficulty in obtaining an accurate estimate of the incomes of farmers.

In 1920 another tax was proposed, a tax of 1 per cent. on the sales of all manufacturers, wholesale dealers, jobbers, and importers. This sales tax was put into operation, and was payable by the purchaser to the wholesaler or manufacturer at the time of sale, and by the latter then to the government. Although criticized because it was a form of taxation hitherto unknown in Canada, it met with general favour because it gave a tangible basis of taxation, *viz.*, the expenditures of a whole people, and its collection was simple and automatic. Each year saw an increase in rate, and a growing dissatisfaction with the method of determining amounts; in 1923, therefore, it was adjusted to a uniform tax of 6 per cent. imposed at the source, "at the first stage of business operations". There was a long list of exemptions, especially of essential foodstuffs. From that year there was a steady reduction in rate until 1930, when it was again 1 per cent.; this was followed by a steady increase again to 8 per cent., as at present, on both imported goods and goods produced or manufactured in Canada. Before leaving the subject of Dominion taxation, it should be repeated that the most important source of revenue is still customs and excise duties, the constant changes in which, however, are too numerous to follow in detail here.

Mention should be made of the relations between Dominion and provincial finances in the matter of subsidies and loans. Since Confederation the Dominion government has paid to all provinces over 500 million dollars in subsidy allowance. This is by virtue of the British North America Act and its revisions, especially that of 1907, which fixed the grant, according to population, at 80 cents per capita of the population population up to 2,500,000 and 60 cents per capita above that number. Additional special grants have been given at times, *e.g.*, to British Columbia from 1907 to 1917, to each of the Maritime provinces since 1928 pending reconsideration of subsidies, and to Manitoba as provided for in the Manitoba Natural Resources Act, 1930.

These Dominion subsidies, together with revenues from the natural resources of the provinces, forest, fisheries, and mineral deposits, sufficed for many years to cover the expenses of the provincial governments. With the increasing demand for more attention to matters concerning the public welfare, provincial expenditure increased and, in consequence, provincial taxation. By the terms of the British North America Act, the provinces were permitted to levy "direct taxation within the province in order to the raising of a revenue for provincial purposes, and shop, saloon, tavern, auctioneer, and other licenses in order to the raising of a revenue for provincial purposes". This right had to be claimed as increased revenue was needed for education, for health and sanitation enterprises, for highways and public works. Each province has developed its own system and sources of taxation to suit its own needs and preferences.

A corporation tax was one means adopted. Early tax laws made no mention of corporations, for they were few in number, and it was assumed they would be taxed on their property. A moderate tax was first imposed on corporations in Quebec in 1882; Ontario followed with a similar tax in 1899. All provinces now impose the tax, but by widely differing methods. The province with the most consistent system of taxation is British Columbia. The bases of taxation vary, authorized capital, paid-up capital, amount of capital invested, net earnings, volume of business transacted, and, most general of all, gross earnings. In the present day of amalgamations and mergers, increasing numbers of corporations are becoming extra-provincial, and must make returns in all provinces where they are located. The corporation tax is to-day one of the large sources of revenue in all the provinces. Real and personal property taxes vary greatly in the different provinces, and do not exist at all in Quebec. In four of the provinces, the mines contribute to the revenues; in some cases there is a provincial income tax in addition to that of the Dominion. At the present time it is, generally, the western provinces that collect an income tax, and the eastern provinces that do not do so. Ontario, between the two groups geographically, is also between them in policy, in that incomes are taxed, but the collection is made in conjunction with the Dominion income tax. During the years 1892 to 1894 all seven of the existing provinces adopted their first measures for the taxation of inheritances. Quebec based its system on death duties as they existed in France, while Ontario followed the practice in England. These succession duties are still collected in all provinces, each having, by its own enactments, determined certain details of rates, exemptions, etc. The tax, as a general rule, is on property; it accrues at the death of the owner, and all matters in relation to the taxation are determined by the facts then existing; for instance, the value of the property is the estimated value on the market at the time. The rate of taxation varies with the aggregate value of the property bequeathed and with the relationship of the beneficiaries. A general and most remunerative tax has of recent years resulted from the increase in the use of automobiles; large revenues are paid for motor licences and permits, and

almost the largest revenues received in all provinces come from gasoline taxes. Most of the provinces impose an amusement tax.

Frequent duplication in federal and provincial taxation has raised protests, and of late years interprovincial conferences have been held in an effort at co-operation, by means of a standardization of report forms, a greater uniformity in tax legislation, and even a unification of the tax-collecting machinery.

Municipal districts vary in nature and in name in different parts of Canada. In Ontario and the eastern provinces there are cities, towns, villages, townships, and counties, while in the prairie provinces the unit of administration is the rural municipality. Local government was carried on by the provinces in early days, but after 1900 urban populations increased rapidly, and it became necessary to furnish costly public services, water supply, roads, police and fire protection, sanitation and sewage, education and public health. This led inevitably to increased taxation. The one general basis of municipal finance in Canada is the assessed value of taxable property; the provinces differ only on the question of the taxation of improvements. The next most general form of municipal taxation is the business tax, determined on the kind of business, on rental value of premises, or on floor space occupied. In many municipalities a personal property tax is still retained. Ontario, Saskatchewan, Prince Edward Island, and Nova Scotia permit their municipalities to collect income taxes for local purposes. Other occasional forms of taxation are the poll tax and special franchise taxes.

See H. R. Kemp, *Dominion and provincial taxation in Canada* (Annals of the American Academy of Political and Social Science, May, 1923); H. L. Brittain, *Municipal taxation in Canada* (Annals of the American Academy of Political and Social Science, May, 1923);

Solomon Vineberg, *Provincial and local taxation in Canada* (New York, 1912); T. M. Gordon, *Canadian sales tax* (McGill University Economic Studies, No. 11); A. W. Boos, *Financial arrangements between the provinces and the Dominion* (McGill University Economic Studies, No. 12); J. H. Blumenstein, *Taxation of corporations in Canada* (McGill University Economic Studies, No. 3); W. P. M. Kennedy and D. C. Wells, *The law of the taxing power in Canada* (University of Toronto Studies in Law, Toronto, 1931); *Canada Year Book*, especially 1926, 1930 and 1936. *Heaton's Commercial Handbook* and the *Canadian Almanac* contain synopses of the Acts relating to taxation.

Taylor, Henry (*fl.* 1780-1860), author, was probably born in England, and was at school in England about 1780 with Sir Isaac Brock (q.v.) and with James Hughes (q.v.), the Nor'Wester. He emigrated to Canada prior to 1836, and he wrote in Canada books which he himself peddled about the country. He must have been a very old man when he died. He died between 1860 and 1866; H. J. Morgan (q.v.) says in his *Bibliotheca canadensis* (Ottawa, 1867) that he "died recently". He was the author of *Considerations on the past, present, and future condition of the Canadas* (Montreal, 1839), *An attempt to form a system of the creation of our globe* (Quebec, 1840), *Journal of a tour from Montreal, thro' Berthier and Sorel, to the eastern townships* (Quebec, 1840), *On the forthcoming union of the two Canadas* (Montreal, 1841), *A system of the creation of our globe, planets, and sun* (Quebec, 1841), *The present condition of united Canada* (Toronto, 1850), and *On the intention of the British government to unite the provinces of British North America* (Hamilton, 1857; new ed., Toronto, 1858).

Taylor, John Fennings (1817-1882), author, was born in London, England, on March 14, 1817, and was educated at Radley College, England. He came to Canada in 1836, and was appointed a clerk of the Legislative Council of Upper Canada. In 1841 he was transferred to the office of the Legislative Council of the united provinces, and in 1867 to that of the Senate of Canada. He was the author of *Portraits of British Americans* (3 vols., Montreal, 1867-8), *Thos. D'Arcy McGee, sketch of his life and death* (Montreal, 1868), *The last three bishops appointed by the Crown for the Anglican Church in Canada* (Montreal, 1870), and *Are legislatures parliaments?* (Montreal, 1879). He died at Old Point Comfort, Virginia, whither he had gone for his health, on May 4, 1882.

Taylor, Thomas (1778-1838), judge and law reporter, was born in St. Pancras, England, in 1778. He became an officer in the British army, and in 1809 was sent to Canada as an ensign in the 41st Regiment. He served on the Niagara frontier during the War of 1812, and was seriously wounded at the battle of Stoney Creek in 1813. He returned to England with his regiment in 1815, was placed on half-pay in 1817, and in 1819, having in the meantime been called to the bar by the Middle Temple, he came back to Canada, and was appointed judge of the Gore District Court. In 1823 he was appointed official reporter for the court of King's Bench in Upper Canada; and he was the author of the first volume of law reports issued in Upper Canada (York, Upper Canada, 1828; new ed., 1862). See W. R. Riddell, *The first law reporter in Upper Canada and his reports: An address* (Toronto, 1916).

Taylor, Sir Thomas Wardlaw (1833-1917), chief justice of Manitoba (1887-99), was born at Auchtermuchty, Fifeshire, Scotland, on March 25, 1833, the eldest son of the Rev. John Taylor, D.D., and Marion Antill, daughter of John Wardlaw, of Dalkeith, Scotland. He was educated at Edinburgh University (B.A., 1852) and at the University of Toronto (M.A., 1856); and he was called to the bar of Upper Canada in 1858 (Q.C., 1881). From 1872 to 1883 he was a master in chancery in Ontario; and in 1883 he was appointed a puisne judge of the court of Queen's Bench in Manitoba. In 1887 he became chief justice of this court, and he presided over it until his retirement in 1899. He then returned to Ontario, and he died at Hamilton, Ontario, on March 2, 1917. He was twice married, (1) in 1858 to Jessie (d. 1863), daughter of John Cameron, of Wilmington, Delaware, and (2) to Margaret, daughter of Hugh Vallance, of Hamilton, Ontario. In 1897 he was created a knight bachelor. He was the author of several legal works.

Tay river, in Lanark county, Ontario, is a tributary of the Rideau river, which it joins near the lower end of Lower Rideau lake. On it is situated the town of Perth, 8 miles above its mouth.

Teal. See **Duck.**

Tecumseh (1768-1813), Indian chief, was born on the banks of the Mad river, a tributary of the Ohio river, in 1768, the son of Puckeshinwau, a chief of the Shawnee tribe. He gained a great ascendancy over the Indians of the Old North West; and in the War of 1812 he espoused, with his Indians, the British cause. He was present at the capture of Detroit in 1812; and he was with the British during the operations on the Detroit frontier in the spring and summer of 1813. He fell, however, in the battle of Moraviantown on October 6, 1813, and was buried by his braves in an unknown grave near the battlefield. He was a man of high ideals and statesman-like views. See E. Eggleston, *Tecumseh* (New York, 1918); N. S. Gurd, *The story of Tecumseh* (Toronto, 1912); Ethel T. Raymond, *Tecumseh* (Toronto, 1915); and B. Drake, *Life of Tecumseh and of his brother the prophet* (Cincinnati, 1850).

Tecumseh, a town in Essex county, Ontario, on the Canadian National Railway, 8 miles east of Windsor. It is connected with Windsor also by an electric railway. It has a mitt factory and other industrial establishments, and a weekly newspaper in French and English (*La Feuille d'Erable*). It is named after the Indian chief Tecumseh (q.v.). Pop. (1931), 2,129.

Teeple, Peter (1762-1847), loyalist, was born near Trenton, New Jersey, on July 14, 1762, and served as an officer in the New Jersey Volunteers in the American Revolutionary War. He settled at Turkey Point (now Charlotteville) on the north shore of lake Erie in 1793; and in 1800 he was created a justice of the peace for the newly created London district. He died at Centreville, Oxford county, Ontario, in 1847. See W. B. Waterbury, *Sketch of Peter Teeple, loyalist and pioneer* (Ont. Hist. Soc., Papers and Records, vol. i, 1899).

Teeswater, a village in Bruce county, Ontario, on the Teeswater river, 17 miles south-west of Walkerton, and on the Wingham-Teeswater branch of the Canadian Pacific Railway, of which it is the terminus. It has flour, saw, and planing mills, a foundry, a creamery, carriage-works, a grain elevator, a public library, and a weekly newspaper (*News*). It is named after the Tees river, between the counties of York and Durham, in England. Pop. (1935), 900.

Tegakouitha, Catherine. See **Tekakwitha, Catherine.**

Teidemann, mount, is in Range 2 of the Coast district, British Columbia, north-west of the confluence of the Homathko river and Mosley creek. It was named after H. O. Teidemann, an engineer who explored the Homathko river in 1862 and 1872. It has an altitude of 12,000 feet.

Tekakwitha, Catherine (1656-1680), Indian saint, was born in an Iroquois village in northern New York in 1656, the daughter of an Iroquois father and a Christian Algonkian mother.

She was converted to Christianity and was compelled to flee to Canada, where she took the vows of a religious, and came to be regarded as a saint. She died at Caughnawaga, Canada, on April 17, 1680; and after her death her grave became a place of pilgrimage. Many miracles are said to have been wrought at her tomb or by her relics. See Claude Chauchetière, *La vie de la B. Catherine Tegakoüita* (Manate, 1887); N. V. Burtin, *Vie de Catherine Tekakwitha, vierge Iroquoise* (Quebec, 1894); Édouard Lecompte, *Catherine Tekakwitha* (Montreal, 1927); R. Rumilly, *Kateri Tekakwitha* (Paris, 1934); and D. Sargent, *Catherine Tekakwitha* (New York, 1936).

Telegraphs. A new era of rapid communication began with the advent of the telegraph. Professor Morse's experiments of years culminated in the transmission of a message over the line between Baltimore and Washington in 1844. This was followed quickly by the introduction of the telegraph for commercial use and its spread over all the eastern states. Canada was not slow in realizing the importance of a quick connection between all parts of the country as well as with the United States. In December, 1846, the first electric telegraph communication was accomplished in Canada, when messages were exchanged between Toronto and Hamilton, on a line laid and operated by the Toronto, Hamilton, Niagara and St. Catharines Electro-Magnetic Telegraph Company. The next year was a memorable one in the founding of telegraph systems in Canada. This company was duly incorporated by Act of parliament with T. D. Harris as president and P. B. Marling as secretary, and with a capital stock of $16,000; a line was laid between Queenston and Niagara, and thence to Buffalo, establishing a connection with all points in the United States; and by the autumn a line from Hamilton to London was completed. A second company incorporated the same year was the British

North American Electric Association, of which F. N. Gisborne (q.v.) was the leading spirit. This was a Quebec organization formed with the intention of connecting that city with the Atlantic coast, but for some years the line reached only to Rivière du Loup, with a temporary extension to Father Point with the object of reporting vessels passing up and down the St. Lawrence. In 1851 this extension was taken down and another made to Woodstock, New Brunswick.

The Montreal Telegraph Company was also incorporated in 1847; it completed a line from Toronto to Montreal by August, and east to Quebec by the end of the year, with 540 miles of wire, over which 33,000 messages had passed in that time. The construction of the line in both material and workmanship was long held as a model for other builders. This company became one of the leading institutions in Canada; much of its success was due to the early officials of the company. H. P. Dwight was an operator at the outset and showed ability and initiative in Montreal and later when he was sent to take charge of the Toronto branch. His career of 56 years in telegraph work is a record of continued service and achievement. O. S. Wood, who had studied with Morse, was the first superintendent. Sir Hugh Allan (q.v.) was president from 1851, and it was due largely to his enterprise that some of the extensions were made to remote parts of the country. It was this policy of extension that made the Montreal company more successful than some of its smaller competitors, and in the course of the next few years there was a general consolidation of these rival companies within the Montreal company. The pioneer telegraph, the Toronto, Hamilton, Niagara, and St. Catharines Company, made the mistake of confining itself to too small a field, and had to sell to the Montreal company in 1852. The British North American Company

THE BELL HOMESTEAD, BRANTFORD, ONTARIO
Birthplace of the Telephone

1875
The First
Telephone

put up a struggle; but, because of financial difficulties, it had to amalgamate in 1856. The line built by the Montreal and Bytown Telegraph Company in 1850, the first telegraph to Ottawa, operated only a few years when it was secured by purchase. The Montreal and Troy Telegraph Company, organized by E. and A. Cornell, and the Provincial Telegraph Company, which built a line from Quebec to Buffalo, were unable to finance their projects and were also absorbed by the Montreal company. The Grand Trunk Telegraph Company offered stronger opposition than the others before it too was compelled to sell; it had been organized in 1852, had built a line from Quebec to Buffalo, and had shown considerable enterprise in its business. The Montreal Telegraph Company had thus a remarkable growth, from 500 miles in 1850 to 20,000 miles in 1870, and 30,000 in 1880.

In 1868 the Dominion Telegraph Company was organized with a capital of $700,000, and soon had lines to all important points between Detroit and Quebec. After a reorganization three years later, it became the chief competitor of the Montreal company; by a further Act of 1874 it was granted rights to extend lines to the Maritime provinces, and under a management characterized by enterprise and aggressiveness it had 490 offices and about 9,000 miles of wire in 1880. At this point, however, the management followed the mistaken policy of making undue reductions in rates as a bid for popularity; at the same time there was a collapse of some of its United States connections, and the company faced financial failure.

It was in this same year, 1880, that an Act was passed to incorporate the Great North Western Telegraph Company of Canada "to establish and work telegraph lines in the North West Territories, the district of Keewatin, and the provinces of Manitoba and British Columbia, and in connection with the province of Ontario." The president, E. Wiman, saw in the financial difficulties of the Dominion Telegraph Company an opportunity for the new company to assume control by lease of its lines and equipment. With a shrewd knowledge of the advantage of removing competition, he also entered into negotiations with the Montreal Telegraph Company to lease and control its system. The next year the amalgamation was effected, H. P. Dwight became general manager, and extensions commenced which were eventually to cover central, eastern, and parts of western Canada. Economies were effected by the closing of offices where the two lines overlapped. The monopoly thus brought about did not last long, for the charter of the Canadian Pacific Railway gave it power to carry on a commercial telegraph business along all its railway lines. These were being constructed from 1880 to 1885, and under the able management of C. R. Hosmer lines eventually reached from Halifax to Vancouver. In 1902 the Canadian Pacific system had 9,736 miles of line over which more than 2,000,000 messages were sent during the year. In consequence of the completion of this system through British Columbia certain government lines in that province decided to accept the offer of purchase made by the Canadian Pacific Company. This system has increased in extent and efficiency, and now has over 17 thousand miles of line, sending nearly 5 million messages in a year.

The Maritime provinces initiated telegraph systems at an early date. In 1848 a line was built from Calais, Maine, to Saint John, New Brunswick, by an organization later incorporated as the New Brunswick Electric Telegraph Company. This line was gradually extended to reach many points in the province and to Amherst, Nova Scotia. The government of Nova Scotia erected a line from Amherst to Halifax in 1849,

thus affording fairly complete telegraphic connection between the Maritime provinces and other points in Canada and the United States. The lines of the New Brunswick company were leased in 1856 to the American Union Telegraph Company, and about ten years later to the Western Union Telegraph Company. The government line between Halifax and Amherst was sold in 1851 to the Nova Scotia Electric Telegraph Company, which extended it to Pictou, Sydney, and Yarmouth. This too was leased to the American Union Telegraph Company in 1860, and six years later, like the New Brunswick lines, to the Western Union Company, which purchased the lines outright in 1872.

Control of the Great North Western Company was acquired in 1915 by the Canadian Northern Railway, which had already an extensive commercial telegraph system. Together they became a Dominion-wide organization. Three years later, with subsidiaries, they came into the hands of the government; with other co-ordinations in a short time they formed the system now known as the Canadian National Telegraphs. Ten years later the Grand Trunk Pacific Telegraph Company, previously operated independently, merged with the Canadian National, and the next year, 1929, after lengthy negotiations, the government also acquired control over the complete land mileage of the Western Union in the Maritime provinces. The Canadian National system now operates on about 24,000 miles of poles. The Temiskaming and Northern Ontario Railway Commission operates about 600 miles.

There is one other telegraph service in Canada, that of the Dominion government, operated by the Telegraph Branch of the Department of Public Works. Its object is to furnish communication for outlying and sparsely settled districts where the amount of business is so small that commercial companies will not build lines, but where public interest requires such service. Some of these lines are in Cape Breton, cable service to Grand Manan and other islands in the bay of Fundy, to Prince Edward Island, the Magdalen islands and Anticosti, to Manitoulin island and the Peace river country, to Vancouver island and settlements in Yukon. These services comprise nearly 9,000 miles of poles. The Canadian telegraph system, in proportion to population, is one of the most extensive in the world, and is operated under considerable climatic and geographic disadvantages; its service to railway, press, and market are invaluable.

See *Sketch of the Canadian telegraph system, its rise and development* (Toronto, 1883); John Murray, *A story of the telegraph* (Montreal, 1905); Ernest Green, *Canada's first electric telegraph* (Ontario Historical Society, Papers and Records, vol. xxiv, 1927); J. E. Middleton, *The municipality of Toronto*, vol. ii (Toronto, 1923); J. C. Hopkins, *Canada, an encyclopaedia of the country*, vol. vi (Toronto, 1900).

Telephones. The invention and development of the telephone is of particular interest to Canadians because it had its origin in this country. Alexander Graham Bell (q.v.) was born in Edinburgh, but, because of ill-health, came to Canada in 1870 with his parents, who bought the now well-known Bell homestead at Brantford, Ontario. He had followed the same studies as his father, Alexander Melville Bell. who had written ably on the physiology of speech, and was working on an invention to help the deaf. The young man regained his health and was able to accept a position as teacher in a school for deaf mutes in Boston. In addition, a good deal of time was spent in experiments with the transmission of sounds, and the summers spent at Brantford afforded an opportunity for the labour and genius which were to result in the invention of the telephone. Bell himself

fixed the date and place of the invention as the summer of 1874 at his father's Brantford home, but it was two years later on August 10, 1876, that the famous first telephone message was sent a distance of 8 miles over wires lent by the Dominion Telegraph Company. The transmitter instrument was in Paris, the receiver in Brantford, and the battery on the circuit in Toronto, about 60 miles away. Transmission went one way only, but human voices were understood distinctly. The first reciprocal communication was between Bell in Boston and his assistant in Cambridge in October of the same year.

With the formation of the Bell Telephone Company in the United States and the plans for the use of the telephone for commercial purposes, there arose the fundamental question of sale or lease of instruments. The unity and efficiency of the telephone system to-day is due, in a measure, to the decision in favour of the lease basis of distribution. The next problem which Bell faced was that of some means of intercommunication, by which lines could be connected in some central office, establishing direct communication between any two places. The first exchange in Canada was opened in 1878 in Hamilton, where H. C. Baker and K. J. Dunstan did pioneer work in developing the exchange idea, in arousing the interest of subscribers, and in studying means of extending the clearness and distance of messages. From this office to one in Dundas was laid the first long-distance line erected for commercial purposes. It consisted of two single grounded wires strung on poles along the local steam road, and was used largely for despatching trains. There was confusion in conversation on the two lines; Bell came to Hamilton to make tests of means to overcome the difficulty, but success was not attained until 1888 on the line between Hamilton and Toronto, when the ground wire was abandoned and the metallic circuit substituted.

The Bell telephone patent in Canada belonged to Melville Bell, to whom the inventor had assigned all rights in 1877. Several offers were made to him, but with other far-seeing men he determined to form an organization along national lines. Application was made to parliament for a charter, and in 1880 the Bell Telephone Company of Canada was incorporated. It extended its organization to every part of the Dominion except British Columbia; by the end of the century, then, the Bell Telephone Company and its associates had a virtual monopoly of the business in Canada, with four submarine telephone cables, the first laid in 1883, connecting Windsor and Detroit. It still owns and operates the principal systems in Ontario and Quebec, serving a population of six and a half million; interchange arrangements are made with a large number of local companies in these provinces. Latest available reports give over a million telephones in use in Canada, rather more than half of them Bell telephone lines.

In Nova Scotia an interest was early shown in the telephone. G. G. Hubbard, to whose financial support Bell owed much, was interested also in mining in Cape Breton. On his visit there in 1877 he took some instruments with him and set up telephone communication between surface and underground workers in the collieries at Glace Bay. Bell later accompanied him, bought a home at Baddeck, and carried on further experiments there until his death in 1922. There was a rapid growth in private companies in the Maritime provinces until 1888, when the lines of the Bell Telephone Company were disposed of to the Maritime Telegraph and Telephone Company in Nova Scotia, and to the New Brunswick Telephone Company in New Brunswick. To-day, in addition, the former controls the Island Telephone Company of Prince Edward Island, and has a 99-year lease of submarine cables between Nova Scotia and Prince Edward Island.

The history of the telephone in the western provinces has been unlike that of the east. The Bell Telephone Company had laid plans for lines as far as the Rocky mountains, and had at an early date established offices and lines in many of the larger centres of the prairie provinces. The use of the telephone, however, grew rather slowly up to about 1900, two of the reasons being the high cost and the fact that exchanges were, for the most part, in the larger towns only. Agricultural settlements were spreading over a wider area and were demanding telephone connection. Several municipalities, notably Neepawa, approached the Manitoba government with a request for municipal ownership; and in 1899 the legislature passed an Act enabling municipalities to own and operate local exchanges. As this did not give the desired connection with long-distance telephones, it was followed by an investigation in 1905 into the whole matter of telephone ownership in the province. The result of this was an extensive policy of government ownership undertaken by the province, by which the local exchange service was to be operated by the municipalities and the long distance lines by the government; a bill providing for this was passed in 1906. It was realized that the most economical plan to effect the change would be to secure the properties and equipment already existing, and, as a consequence, negotiations were at once entered into with the Bell Telephone Company, and a purchase made the following year, for the sum of $3,300,000. A commission of three, appointed by and responsible to the government, was to operate the system; the men in the first commission were all expert telephone men from the Bell company. Assurances were given that operation would be free of all political influence, that rates would be materially reduced, and that the system

would be self-supporting. The years that followed gave evidence of the difficulties of inaugurating government ownership in an industry requiring a highly trained technical staff; the division of powers between the commission and the government was constantly in question; accounts were not kept separate from general government accounts; eventually an investigation was called for, and the commissioners resigned in 1912. Accounts were examined, plants inspected, and witnesses questioned; in the end the report recommended the telephone be placed under a provincial Public Utilities Commission, and under an improved management free from all political pressure. During the war years expansion was restricted and economy enforced; but very early in the post-war period definite growth manifested itself in financial position, in expansion of lines into rural areas, in the adoption of new inventions and improvements such as the automatic exchange.

The establishment of government ownership of telephones in Saskatchewan was similar in many respects to that of Manitoba. A Telephone Act was passed in 1908 providing for the construction of long-distance lines by the province to serve local exchanges owned by the municipalities. In 1909 the government bought the Bell Telephone system and two smaller organizations. Difficulties in financing the municipal systems were met by an Act in 1913 which regulated rural debentures.

At the meeting of the first legislature of Alberta, following the creation of that province in 1905, the government passed a vote of money to construct long-distance lines and passed an Act to empower municipalities to construct and operate local lines. The Bell Telephone system was purchased in 1908, and expansion was steady in rural districts. Until about 1926 rates were low, hence there were not adequate reserves;

various means were resorted to in order to improve financial conditions.

The Bell Telephone Company had found it impracticable to carry its lines over the mountains into British Columbia, but that province had one of the first telephone exchanges in Canada. A line had been in use some time in Victoria before it was formally incorporated in 1880 as the Victoria and Esquimault Telephone Company. In 1904 the British Columbia Telephone Company absorbed this organization and several smaller ones, and the telephone cable laid *viâ* the Gulf islands connected the mainland and Vancouver island. It has a perpetual franchise to operate in British Columbia and owns practically all lines in the southern part of the province.

Every year sees some advance in the telephone in Canada. Research laboratories and skilled workers all over the country have improved instruments and transmission. Beginning in 1924, exchanges have gradually introduced the automatic dialing system. In 1928 an all-Canadian line between Montreal and Winnipeg was completed. The year before, a telephone service between Canada and Great Britain was inaugurated by a conversation between Prime Minister Baldwin in London and Prime Minister King in Ottawa, *viâ* New York. The year 1929 was memorable in the history of telephone development; a conversation was carried on between London and Ottawa on an all-Canadian line; the first telephone connection between Canada and Europe was completed; communication was first held to and from a moving train, a Canadian National train out from Toronto; and a service was inaugurated with a number of large ships at sea. In 1933 a new achievement in long-distance telephoning was reached when, by a direct channel between Montreal and London, a trans-Atlantic service to Europe, Asia, Africa, and Australia was estab-

lished and an improved service to and from ships at sea.

See Catherine Mackenzie, *Alexander Graham Bell, the man who contracted space* (Boston, 1928); William Patten, *Pioneering the telephone in Canada* (Montreal, 1926); *Lectures on the telephone business*, delivered in the University of Toronto (Toronto, 1927); H. A. Innis, *Problems of staple production in Canada* (Toronto, 1933); James Mavor, *Government telephones, the experience of Manitoba, Canada* (New York, 1916); G. E. Britnell, *Public ownership of telephones in the prairie provinces* (M.A. thesis, University of Toronto, 1934); John Quinpool, *First things in Acadia* (Halifax, 1936).

Telkwa, a town in Range 5 of the Coast district, British Columbia, at the confluence of the Bulkley and Telkwa rivers, and on the Canadian National Railway, 9 miles south-east of Smithers. It has a school and some government offices. Pop. (1935), 250.

Témiscamingue, a town in Témiscamingue county, Quebec, at the southern end of lake Timiskaming, and on the Canadian Pacific Railway, 138 miles south of Rouyn. It was incorporated in 1920 under the name of Kipawa; but this name was changed in 1920 to Témiscamingue or Temiskaming. Pop. (1931), 1,855. See Rev. R. S. Booy, *Temiskaming, garden city of the north* (Municipal Review of Canada, 1934).

Témiscouata, a county in Quebec, bounded on the north-west by the St. Lawrence river, on the north-east by Rimouski county. on the south-east by Madawaska county, New Brunswick, and on the south-west by the state of Maine and Kamouraska county. It is traversed by the Canadian National Railway, Chief town, Rivière du Loup. Pop. (1931), 50,294.

Témiscouata lake lies in the county of the same name in Quebec, 130 miles north-east of Quebec, and 35 miles from the right bank of the St. Lawrence. The name is from an Indian word meaning "it is deep everywhere". The lake is surrounded by wooded mountains, and is 30 miles long and 2 miles in width. In prehistoric days, with the Madawaska and St. Francis rivers, it formed an important link of communication between the Indian tribes of Canada and those of the United States. During the French period, this route was used by distinguished *voyageurs* in their journeys, and the Marquis de la Jonquière (q.v.) constructed a road from the St. Lawrence to the upper St. John *viâ* lake Témiscouata. Having been improved by Haldimand (q.v.) in 1783, the road served as a valuable military communication during the War of 1812. It was made into a splendid thoroughfare after 1840, and its term of prolonged service ended only with the construction of the Intercolonial Railway in 1876. See Marius Barbeau, *Rocher-Malin—Témiscouata* (Canadian Geographical Journal, October, 1933).

Témiscouata Railway, a line of railway opened in 1889 between Edmundston, New Brunswick, and Rivière-du-Loup, Quebec, and extended in 1891 from Edmundston to Connor's. It has a total length of 112 miles, and is still under independent management.

Temiskaming. See **Timiskaming.**

Temiskaming and Northern Ontario Railway. The building of this railway was undertaken by the government of Ontario in 1902, with the object of linking southern Ontario with the "clay belt" over the height of land, in the watershed of Hudson bay. By successive extensions northward from North Bay, it reached the Canadian National Railways (Grand Trunk Pacific) at Cochrane; and finally, in 1931, it reached tidewater, at Moosonee, on an estuary of James bay, thus giving Ontario access by railway to a seaport of its own. If the railway had been dependent on the agricultural develop-

ment of the "clay belt", its progress would have been slow; but fortunately, in 1903, while it was still under construction, silver was discovered at Cobalt, on lake Timiskaming; and the development of the famous silver-mining camps in this area not only provided the railway with business, but the mining camps provided the farmer with a convenient market. A few years later gold was discovered in the Porcupine and Kirkland Lake areas in Ontario and in the Rouyn district in Quebec; and branch lines were built serving these and other mining areas as well. Since the completion of the line to Moosonee, the depression has severely curtailed the operation of the line between Cochrane and Moosonee; but the southern portion of the line has proved to be a successful example of the operation of a government-owned railway. The railway is under the operation of a board of commissioners appointed by the government of Ontario. See Arthur A. Cole, *Ontario's route to the sea* (Can. Geog. Journal, 1932).

Temple, Sir Thomas, Bart. (1614-1674), governor of Nova Scotia (1657-70), was born at Stowe, Buckinghamshire, England, in January, 1614, the second son of Sir John Temple, of Stanton Bury, and grandson of Sir Thomas Temple, Bart., of Stowe. He seems to have taken the parliamentary side in the Civil War; and in 1657 he was appointed by Oliver Cromwell governor of Nova Scotia, which had been conquered by the English in 1654. He succeeded in retaining his governorship at the time of the restoration of Charles II in 1660; and in 1662 he was created a baronet of Nova Scotia. In 1667 Nova Scotia was ceded to France by the treaty of Breda; the actual surrender of the province did not take place until 1670, but with the cession Temple's commission ceased. He died in London on March 27, 1674.

Templeman, William (1844-1914), minister of inland revenue for Canada

(1906-11), was born at Pakenham, Upper Canada, on September 28, 1844, the son of William Templeman and Helen Taylor. He was educated in the public schools, and became a printer and journalist. In 1867 he founded the Almonte *Gazette*, and in 1884 he removed to Victoria, British Columbia, and became connected with the Victoria *Times*. Of this paper he became editor and proprietor. In 1897 he was called to the Senate of Canada, and from 1902 to 1906 he was a member of the Laurier government without portfolio. In 1906 he became minister of inland revenue, and the same year, having resigned from the Senate, he was elected to the House of Commons for Victoria. In 1909 he was elected for Comox-Atlin; but was defeated in 1911. He died at Victoria on November 15, 1914. In 1869 he married Eva Bond (d. 1914), of Almonte.

Templeman, mount, is in the Kootenay district of British Columbia, and lies west of Duncan river, between Stevens and Hall creeks, in lat. 50° 42', long. 117° 13'. It has an altitude of 10,000 feet.

Temple, mount, is in Alberta in lat. 51° 21', long. 116° 12', and has an altitude of 11,626 feet. It was named after Sir Richard Temple, leader of the excursion party of the British Association to the Rockies in 1884.

Templeton, a village in Hull county, Quebec, on the southern slope of the Laurentian mountains, 7 miles east of Hull. Market-gardening is carried on; and the exploitation of neighbouring silica beds for the manufacture of glass contributes a great deal to the village's industrial activity. It was incorporated in 1920. The village was formerly known as Templeton East, as Point Gatineau was originally known as Templeton, after the township, named from Templeton, a village in Devonshire, England. Pop. (1931), 822.

Tent Mountain pass is in the Rocky mountains, on the boundary between British Columbia and Alberta, just north of the 49th parallel of latitude. It has an altitude of 4,800 feet.

Tern, a name applied generally to a group of sea or inland water birds belonging to the family *Laridae*, to which also belong the gulls. Terns have long, pointed, swallow-like wings and small feet. They are remarkably graceful birds when on the wing. Most of the Canadian species are light blue-gray above, with black caps, and entirely white below. They frequent the shores of the larger lakes, nesting either on sandy beaches or on rocky islands. One species, the black tern (*Chlidonias nigra*), is a marsh-dwelling bird. It is dark gray above and black on the head and underparts.

Terrace, a town in Range 5 of the Coast district, British Columbia, on the Skeena river, and on the Canadian National Railway, 95 miles east of Prince Rupert. It has a high school and some government offices. Pop. (1935), 1,000.

Terrebonne, a county in Quebec, fronting on the river des Mille-Îles, north of Montreal, and lying between Argenteuil and Two Mountains counties on the one hand and Montcalm and L'Assomption counties on the other. It is traversed by the Canadian Pacific and Canadian National Railways. Chief town, St. Jérôme. Pop. (1931), 38,611.

Terrebonne, a town of Terrebonne county, Quebec, situated on the river des Mille-Îles and on the Canadian Pacific Railway, 24 miles north of Montreal. Tradition says that Daulier des Landes, to whom the seigniory was granted in 1673, gave it this name on account of the fertility of the soil. The parish was established in 1727, and the town was incorporated in 1860. In 1927 the town celebrated the two hundredth anniversary of its founding. Terrebonne possesses a beautiful church, a commercial college, and a convent. The chief industrial establishments manufacture shoes, woollens, agricultural machinery, tobacco, and butter. Pop. (1931), 1,955.

Terrill, Timothy Lee (1815-1879), provincial secretary for Canada (1856-7), was born in the township of Ascot, Lower Canada, on March 12, 1815, the son of Joseph Hazzard Terrill. He was called to the bar of Lower Canada in 1840 (Q.C., 1854), and from 1853 to 1861 he represented Stanstead in the Legislative Assembly of Canada. In 1856 he became provincial secretary in the Taché-Macdonald administration; but his health gave way, and he was compelled to resign in 1857. In his later years he devoted himself to farming in the Eastern Townships. He died on August 26, 1879.

Teslin lake, a long narrow body of water on the boundary between British Columbia and the Yukon, about the 132nd meridian of west longitude. Its width varies from 3½ to ½ miles, and it has a length of 76 miles, of which 29 are in British Columbia. Its area is 246 square miles.

Tessier, François Xavier (1800-1835), physician, was born at Quebec in 1800, and died at Quebec on December 24, 1835. He was educated at Quebec and at New York, and was admitted to practice medicine in Lower Canada in 1823. He founded the first medical journal published in Canada, *Le Journal de Médecine de Québec* (1826-7); and he was the author of *The French practice of medicine* (2 vols., New York, 1829).

Tessier, Ulric Joseph (1817-1892), judge, was born at Quebec, Lower Canada, on May 4, 1817. He was admitted to the bar of Lower Canada as an advocate in 1839 (Q.C., 1863), and practised law in Quebec. From 1851 to 1854 he represented Portneuf in the Legislative Assembly of Canada, and from 1858 to 1867 he was an elected member of the Legislative Council. In 1861-2 he was commissioner of public works in the Macdonald-Sicotte government; and from 1863 to 1867 he was speaker of the Legislative Council. In 1867 he was called by royal proclamation to the Senate of Canada. He resigned from the Senate to accept appointment as a judge of the superior court of the province of Quebec in 1873, and in 1875 he was transferred to the court of Queen's Bench. He died at Quebec on April 7, 1892. In 1859 he founded La Banque Nationale; and he was dean of the faculty of law in Laval University. He married in 1847 Adèle Drapeau Kelly, granddaughter of Joseph Drapeau, seignior of Rimouski and the Isle of Orleans.

Tête-à-gauche river, a stream in Gloucester county, New Brunswick, which has its outlet in the bay of Chaleur above Bathurst. The name is a gallicized corruption of the Micmac *Too-doo-goosk'*, meaning probably "a small river", the length of the river being only 25 miles. The local pronunciation is as if the word were spelled "Tattygoosh".

Tête Jaune Cache, a village in the Cariboo district of British Columbia, on the Fraser river, immediately east of the mouth of the McLennan river, and on the Canadian National Railway. It is named after a *cache* of the fur-traders crossing the Yellowhead pass. Pop. (1935), 300.

Tête Roche mountain is on the boundary between British Columbia and Alberta, north of Yellowhead lake in the Cariboo district. It is in lat. 52° 54', long. 118° 34', and has an altitude of 7,932 feet. The name was suggested by *Tête Jaune*, which is French for Yellowhead, and was the nickname of a trapper who used to cache his furs west of the summit of the pass called after him. According to Malcolm McLeod (q.v.), this trapper was François Decoigne, who was in charge of Jasper House, Brulé lake, in 1814.

Têtes des Boules, the name applied to a tribe of wandering hunters that formerly roamed over an extensive region on the Ottawa, St. Maurice, and Gatineau rivers. The name is a French equivalent of "round heads". They belonged to the Chippewa family of Indians. They depended chiefly on rabbits for food and clothing, built mere brush windbreaks for shelters, and placed small piles of firewood near the bark-covered graves of their dead for the use of the spirits. They have been reduced in numbers by smallpox and the advance of civilization in the Ottawa valley until there are only a few of them left on a reservation on the St. Maurice river, in Champlain county, Quebec.

Têtu, Henri (1849-1915), priest and historian, was born at Rivière Ouelle, Quebec, on October 24, 1849, the son of Dr. Ludger Têtu and Clémentine Dionne. He was educated at the College of Ste. Anne de la Pocatière, and was ordained a priest of the Roman Catholic Church in 1873. In 1887 he was appointed *camérier secret* to Pope Leo XIII, and in 1889 a prelate of the Holy See. He died at Quebec on June 15, 1915. He was the author of *Monseigneur de Laval* (Quebec, 1887), *Les évêques de Québec* (Quebec, 1889), *S. E. le Cardinal Taschereau* (Quebec, 1891), *David Têtu et les raiders de St. Alban* (Quebec, 1891), and *Histoire du palais épiscopal de Québec* (Quebec, 1896). He also edited, with Mgr. C. O. Gagnon, *Les mandements des évêques de Québec* (8 vols., Quebec, 1887-1896).

Têtu, Horace (1842-1915), author, was born at Quebec, Lower Canada, on July 14, 1842, the son of Vital Têtu, M.P., and Virginie Ahier, and was educated at the Quebec Seminary. He died, unmarried, at Quebec on March 31, 1915. He devoted himself to the study of the history of journalism in the province of Quebec, and he published *Historique des journaux de Québec* (Quebec, 1875; new ed., 1889), *Journaux et revues de Québec* (Quebec, 1881; 3rd ed., 1883), *Journaux et revues de Montréal* (Quebec, 1881), and *Journaux de Lévis* (Quebec, 1890; 3rd ed., 1898). He published also *Souvenirs inédits de l'abbé Painchaud* (Quebec, 1894), *Doyens du clergé canadien de la province civile de Québec* (Quebec, 1896), *Résumé historique de l'industrie et du commerce de Québec* (Quebec, 1899), *Livre d'or du clergé canadien* (Quebec, 1903), *Édifices religieux érigés dans la province de Québec sous la domination française* (Quebec, 1903; new ed., 1910), and *Oiseaux de cage* (Quebec, 1906).

Teulon, a village in the Selkirk district of Manitoba, on the Canadian Pacific Railway, 40 miles north-west of Winnipeg. Pop. (1931), 680.

Textile Industries. There are two branches of the textile industry. The primary group includes all operations concerned with the manufacture of yarns and fabrics from raw materials, such as wool, cotton, and silk; the secondary consists in the making of clothing and allied products from these fabrics. Canada is dependent on imported raw materials for all cotton and real silk products, but has abundant material for artificial silk, and has wool, except for certain fine grades of woollen yarns.

Canadian manufacture of cotton goods dates from 1844, when, with a capital of £12,000, a mill was established at Sherbrooke, Quebec, with a capacity of 1,200 spindles. Three years later at Thorold in Upper Canada a mill with 20 looms was making gray sheetings and cotton batting. The first large-scale mill began operation at Merritton in Upper Canada in 1860, equipped with 12,000 spindles and 260 looms. The next year the industry extended to the Maritime provinces, when William Parks and Son established a mill at Saint John, New Brunswick, one which operated longer than probably any other in Canada. The census of 1871 showed 8 mills in the Dominion, 5 of which were in Ontario; 745 were employed, and the capacity was about 95,000 spindles. According to the next census, in 1881, there were 19 mills, employing 3,527, operating 243,000 spindles, and producing goods to the value of four million dollars. For a time the industry was threatened by reason of the large investment of capital in mills equipped for a production beyond the domestic demand. In order to keep their mills running profitably, owners were compelled to import machinery to diversify the kinds and improve the quality of goods produced. This enabled them to develop an export trade; a new mill at Montmorency Falls was used expressly for this trade. Another new use was made of the surplus supply of gray cotton at Magog, Quebec, where a factory for cotton print goods was built in 1884. This mill has gained an extensive reputation for its fast prints, and is now operating as part of the Dominion Textile Company.

Circumstances had led to the cotton industry being made up of many separate units, each striving to produce every line of fabric for which orders could be secured. Specialization was impossible; there was waste due to constant changing of looms and machinery; diversification of product resulted in inefficiency and extravagance. The logical step of amalgamation was taken by two men prominent in the textile industry, Alexander Gault and David Morrice. The first of their syndicates was the Dominion Cotton Mills Company, which, with a capital of $5,000,000, in 1890 consolidated several mills in Ontario, Quebec, and the Maritime provinces. The new company operated about one-third of the cotton-spinning equipment in Canada at the time, and, because of the consequent economy of production, could more satisfactorily compete with importers of fabrics. A change of government and of tariff regulations, however, made the beginning of the century a

difficult time in the textile industries, and a financial reorganization was effected under C. B. (later Sir Charles) Gordon. The Dominion Textile Company thus came into being in 1905, and, with subsequent additions, has now become one of the most extensive manufacturers of cotton goods in Canada. It has buying agencies in the Southern States for the purchase of raw cotton, and in Manchester for mill supplies; its output consists of a large range of yarns and fabrics, the latter used by other manufacturers for oilcloth, rubber footwear, artificial leather, and cotton clothing of all kinds. The second great consolidation effected by Gault and Morrice was that of six Ontario mills and one in New Brunswick as the Canadian Coloured Cotton Mills Company. These mills had been operating as separate units, some as long as 30 years, but with small profit because of size, location, or equipment. A plan of more specialized production was followed, and the whole placed under unified management. In 1910 a further reorganization took place, and the present company, Canadian Cottons, was formed by the addition of still other plants. This company specializes in many lines of woven coloured cotton goods, such as ginghams, denims, shirtings, and cotton blankets.

The immediate result of the outbreak of the Great War in 1914 was a short period of comparative inactivity in the cotton industry. Soon, however, elimination of foreign competition, the interruption to British industry, and an increased civilian and military demand created a sudden expansion, and the last years of the war saw boom conditions. This continued for only a few years. Gradually the textile industries in Great Britain and the United States resumed a normal output, and a period of great economic stress followed in Canada. Through able management and sanity of policy, a condition of some stability had been reached before the

SCENES IN A TEXTILE FACTORY

general depression of 1929. During 1935 there were 20,248 persons directly employed in 106 establishments of the cotton industry; the gross value of production was $68,917,349. As well as cotton yarn and cloth, this group of the textile industry produces curtains, comforters, bedding, quilted goods, etc.

The woollen industry in Canada had its beginnings practically from the arrival of the early colonists. Pioneer life and climatic conditions made rough, warm clothing a necessity, and the Canadian housewife at her spinning wheel and loom was the first in a long line of operators in one of the most important industries of the country. The organized manufacture of textiles in Canada began in custom carding and fulling mills which existed at numerous points in Upper and Lower Canada and the Maritime provinces in the beginning of the nineteenth century. These were frequently operated in connection with grist-mills or saw-mills. About the middle of the century, the extent of home industry is shown by a census which reveals that New Brunswick, Nova Scotia, and the Canadas produced over six and a half million yards of home-made woollen cloth in one year. At the same time there were in the same district about 385 carding and fulling mills and about 250 establishments where weaving was done. The use of power looms began at an early date; near Georgetown, Ontario, in 1820, a woollen mill was operated by the Hon. James Crooks (q.v.), and later by Barber Brothers, who moved it to Streetsville; at L'Acadie, Quebec, a mill was built by Mahlon Willett in 1827. From the middle of the century, the factory system grew, while the production of handmade cloth declined. About this time also knitting mills were opened, the Paton mills at Galt in 1854, one at Ancaster in 1859, Penman's mill at Paris in 1870, and others at Cobourg and Carleton Place. Distribu-

tion was often made by salesmen who went through the country from farm to farm, trading the cloth for wool, farm produce, or grain, but seldom for money, which changed hands little at this time. The industry reached considerable magnitude to meet the increasing demand for woollen yarn and goods. Towards the end of the century custom mills gave place to larger and more progressive mills with up-to-date machinery producing a better class of materials. From this point the changes of fortune in the woollen industry followed those of the cotton industry, except that the former reached greater extremes in each case. In the depression following the granting of a preferential tariff rate to British woollen importers more than 150 woollen mills were compelled to close between 1897 and 1907. During the war, production, sales, and employment soared to great heights; new mills were built, and old mills reequipped; the knitting industry expanded by 100 per cent.; there was an enormous demand for all kinds of woollen goods for military purposes. The post-war slump followed quickly, in 1920 and 1921. In the years since then, there has been a steady, if slow, improvement, achieved, for the most part, by introducing new processes— for instance, a new spinning frame for producing a soft yarn of a kind obtained on the mule. Other improvements have increased speed, and have allowed intricate patterns and special effects from mixture yarns; progress has been made in the art of dyeing and finishing. During 1935 there were 148 establishments in Canada engaged in the woollen textile industries; 11,159 persons were employed; and the gross value of production was $36,906,786. These statistics cover woollen yarn, woollen cloth, carpets, hosiery, blankets, etc.

One of the most remarkable developments in Canadian industry of recent years has been the manufacture of artificial silk. Canadian viscose rayon originated in the enterprise of the English firm of Courthaulds in establishing branches in centres where they had built up good markets. Cornwall, Ontario, was selected because of its proximity to suitable water, power, and railway facilities. In the ten years since the establishment there of Courthaulds (Canada) in 1926, its equipment has increased almost five-fold, with a proportionate increase of production. The raw cellulose material used is supplied in wood-pulp sheets, manufactured entirely from Canadian spruce by the sulphite process. In addition to the use of Canadian raw materials and the large number directly employed in the Cornwall plant, a still greater contribution is made to Canadian industry in that rayon yarn made by this plant is sold to manufacturers all over the country, to knitting mills and clothing factories, and the indirect employment resulting can hardly be estimated. The other main source of artificial silk in Canada is the Canadian Celanese plant in Drummondville, Quebec. In 1928 cellulose acetate yarn was first produced here in conjunction with weaving and knitting operations. The remarkable expansion of the celanese plant has been possible through the variety of their production, for, unlike Courthaulds (Canada), which produces rayon yarn only, the output of the Drummondville factories consists of all types of woven and knitted fabrics for the dress, lingerie, and other trades. The weaving, dyeing, and finishing departments have practically doubled; the organization and merchandizing have grown in efficiency; and direct employment reached 2,500 in 1935. The phenomenal growth of these two companies can be seen from their statistics for 1935: Courthaulds (Canada) produced 8,500,000 pounds of viscose yarn for the weaving and knitting trades; and Canadian Celanese produced 4,250,-000 pounds of acetate yarn for use in their own weaving and knitting plants. For the two-fold reason that the raw

materials are abundant within the country and that the fabrics can be so cheaply and attractively made, there would seem to be a promising future for the artificial silk industry in Canada. The value of real silk fabrics produced in Canada in 1935 was over four and a half million dollars, while that of artificial silk fabrics in the same year was twenty-five million dollars. There were 10,088 persons employed in 33 establishments, 22 in Quebec and 11 in Ontario; all but 2 of these were making real silk. Of recent years there has been some growth in employment and in sales in real silk factories, owing, among other causes, to the fall in the price of raw silk, to the large demand for silk hosiery, and to the opening of plants in new centres.

The clothing industry as it exists now is a comparatively recent development. In pioneer days in Canada it was a household industry, as were spinning and weaving. Even fifty years ago the work was done by tailors and dressmakers, and the sale of goods by the yard the principal form of merchandizing of textiles. The initial step in the factory system was in the manufacture of men's clothing, and in Canada the earliest record of such an establishment is in 1868. The first census that mentions clothing factories is that of 1901. To-day there are over 1,000 clothing factories; public demand is almost wholly for factory-made clothing, and machine and mass production have grown to meet this demand. If the statistics of all the needle trades in Canada were considered together, it would be seen that, from the standpoint of employment and sales, the production of wearing apparel is almost the most important industry in Canada. The clothing group in 1934 gave employment to 40,313 workers; and the total cost of fabrics, cotton, wool, and silk was 65 million dollars, over two-thirds of which was paid for Canadian primary products. The general level of quality of textiles is high; in the case of woollen clothing, Canadian fabrics are largely used; machines and equipment are constantly improving. There is, however, a certain degree of instability and excessive competition resulting from the large number of small units comprising the industry; some small progress has been made to better this condition.

With the exception of artificial silk, and perhaps hosiery and knitted goods, the textile industries present a steady rather than a spectacular growth. One reason for this may be that the cotton and woollen industries reached an advanced and stable stage earlier than other industries. The only radical changes recently are in improved processes, in higher speed machinery, and in reduced cost of manufacture.

See *Canada Year Book*, 1922-3 and 1924; *Manual of the textile industry of Canada*, published by the Canadian Textile Journal Publishing Company (Montreal, 1936); and J. A. Coote, *Graphical survey of the Canadian textile industries* (McGill Social Science Research Series, No. 4, 1936).

Thain, Thomas (d. 1832), fur-trader, was born in Scotland, the son of a sister of the Hon. John Richardson (q.v.). Through his mother he was related to the Phyns, the Ellices, and the Forsyths. He came to Canada prior to 1804, for in that year Thomas Verchères de Boucherville met him on lake Superior, evidently as a clerk in the employ of the XY Company. In 1804 he was appointed, with John Ogilvy (q.v.), an agent to represent at Grand Portage the interests of Sir Alexander Mackenzie and Company in the reorganized North West Company; and in 1813 he became a partner in the firm of McTavish, McGillivrays, and Company. In 1822 he became also a partner in the firm of McGillivrays, Thain, and Company, which was formed to wind up the affairs of McTavish, McGillivrays, and Company. From 1821, when McTavish, McGillivrays, and Com-

pany became the Montreal agents of the Hudson's Bay Company, he was the virtual manager of the Montreal office and head of the Montreal department. Shortly before McTavish, McGillivrays, and Company and McGillivrays, Thain, and Company were forced into insolvency in 1825, he left Canada suddenly, in ill health, leaving the accounts of these firms in great confusion; and soon afterwards he was reported as being "confined as a lunatic in an asylum in Scotland". He died at Aberdeen, Scotland, on January 6, 1832. His brother, Alexander Thain, of Montreal, died at Liverpool, England, on April 1, 1825, as he was about to board a vessel for Canada, possibly in order to come to his brother's assistance. Another brother, John Richardson Thain, of Edinburgh, acknowledged on January 20, 1835, the receipt of moneys received from Samuel Gerrard (q.v.) and George Gregory, "trustees to the estate of McGillivrays, Thain, and Co.", advanced by him for account of his "late brother", Thomas Thain. John McLean (q.v.) described him as "a man of rather eccentric character, but possessed of a heart that glowed with the best feelings of humanity".

Thames, Battle of. See **Moraviantown.**

Thamesford, a village in Oxford county, Ontario, on the middle branch of the Thames river, and on the Canadian Pacific Railway, 12 miles west of Woodstock, and 13 miles east of London. It is the centre of a rich farming and dairying district. Pop. (1935), 500.

Thames river rises in Perth county, in western Ontario, flows in a southwesterly direction, and enters lake St. Clair at its south-east corner. The river, which is 160 miles in length, flows through extremely fertile country. On it are located the cities of Stratford, London, and Chatham. It is navigable for boats from its mouth to Chatham. In 1812, during the war with the United

States, General Hull sent raiding parties up the Thames from Detroit. On October 5, 1813, at Moraviantown, near Chatham, the American general Harrison, defeated Col. Procter (q.v.) and his ally, the Indian chief, Tecumseh (q.v.).

Thamesville, a village in Kent county, Ontario, on the river Thames, and on the Canadian Pacific, Canadian National, and Wabash Railways, 16 miles north-east of Chatham. It has flour and saw mills, brick and tile works, a poultry station, and a creamery; and it has also a continuation school, a public library, and a weekly newspaper (*Herald*). Pop. (1931), 797.

Theatre. Canada has never had a professional theatre. In spite of this, for many years the people were provided with abundant theatrical fare of good, and sometimes excellent quality. Travelling companies brought English, American, and French actors to the chief cities, among them such celebrities as Madame Sarah Bernhardt and Sir Henry Irving. During the latter decades of the 19th and early years of the 20th century Canada formed an integral part of the American system of touring theatrical companies. This provided the larger centres with an abundance of good, well-acted plays. To supplement these, troupes of "barnstormers" visited the smaller towns and villages. These were sometimes companies of native talent, of whom the Marks brothers, which played throughout Canada, were a typical example. Occasionally stock companies played in the cities during the summer season.

In the collapse of "the Road", as the theatrical touring system was called, Canada shared. This began about 1910, and was due to several causes. The rise of the "star" system in the theatre, and the increasingly high salaries paid these stars resulted in their being sent on tour with poor supporting companies. There was a consequent decrease in theatre attendance, and the Road be-

came less profitable to the booking agencies who, by this time, were in control. To the mounting cost of play production, which reached its height shortly after the war, was added the increased cost of railway transportation. The competition offered by moving pictures was another vital element, and when a moving picture company acquired control of practically all the theatres in Canada, about 1929, and refused to lease their theatres to companies for legitimate stage productions, the collapse of the Road in this country was complete. Since then only one or two cities have had the opportunity of seeing good professional productions, and even these have had but a meagre six to eight plays a season.

During the declining years of the Road, repertory took its place in some cities. From 1921 to 1928, for example, a series of stock companies, usually of English, sometimes of American actors, played in Toronto. Vaughan Glaser's Company was the most permanent. Starting in 1921, they played for six successive years. The Cameron Matthews English Players played for two seasons from 1923 to 1925. Some of these English actors joined the Maurice British Players for the season 1923-4. They were followed by Charles Hampden's British Players in 1925-6, the English Repertory Company, backed by the newly formed Theatre Guild of Canada, and the New Empire Company in 1927-8. In all these companies, the small groups of professional actors were often supplemented by experienced amateur actors. The first group to make a definite attempt to use amateurs, in the effort to build a Canadian National Theatre, was the Theatre Guild of Canada. The venture was premature.

It brings to light, however, the fact that there were amateur players considered capable of acting with members of professional stock companies. Interest in the amateur theatre had been growing as the entertainment on the professional stage was dwindling.

For many years amateur "theatricals", as they were called, were purely social. They centred around the garrisons, and church, school, and literary societies. There were a few groups whose interest in the theatre was more serious, and to these "Earl Grey's Musical and Dramatic Trophy Competition" made a special appeal. In the spring of 1906 Earl Grey (q.v.), then governor-general, conceived the plan of an annual music and drama festival. When he officiated at the opening of the parliament buildings of the newly created province of Alberta one of the features of the ceremony was a trained chorus. He was struck by the excellent work of this chorus in an outpost town of about 10,000 people, and he decided to stimulate effort by an annual musical trophy. Having from boyhood been an enthusiast for the theatre, he included drama also.

The annual festival competitions were inaugurated at Ottawa in 1907. Five were held, two at Ottawa, one at Montreal, one at Toronto, and the final one at Winnipeg in 1911. Winning teams were the Winnipeg Dramatic Club, 1907, Ottawa Thespians, 1908, John Beverley Robinson Amateur Players of Toronto, 1909, Dickens Fellowship, Toronto, 1910, and the Edmonton Dramatic Club, 1911. The dramatic part of the festival died in 1911. Presumably, enthusiasm for the amateur theatre was not keen enough at that time to overcome the difficulties and expense of operating an annual national competition, when the impetus given by its originator was withdrawn. In any case, shortly after Lord Grey's return to England, the idea was dropped.

Although competitions were discontinued, interest in the amateur theatre survived. The years from 1914 to 1918 brought closer familiarity with the English stage to many people. There was a good deal of active participation

in concert parties in the war areas, and patriotic entertainments at home. The emotional stimulus of those times fostered an urge for self-expression to which the theatre was a natural outlet. More dramatic societies were formed, and many are still flourishing.

Prominent among the early groups was the Ottawa Drama League, which held its twenty-fifth season in 1936-7, and grew from a membership of about 50 in 1913 to over 1,700 in 1928, when it acquired its present Little Theatre. The Players Club of the University of British Columbia was organized in 1915. The Players Club of Toronto was begun by a group of University dons in 1916. Among them was the Hon. Vincent Massey, who was responsible for building Hart House Theatre at the University of Toronto in 1919. This is one of the most completely equipped Little Theatres on the continent, and has been the scene of many splendid productions. The Winnipeg Little Theatre completed its sixteenth season in the spring of 1937. The Montreal Repertory Theatre, under the guidance of Martha Allan, has had many successful years. This theatre has stressed the production of French, as well as English plays, and has also made a determined effort to encourage Canadian playwrights. Carroll Aikins's Home Theatre at Naramata, British Columbia, started in 1920, brought the stage to the fruit-growers of the Okanagan valley. Societies, such as the Dickens Fellowship of Toronto, and the Arts and Letters Clubs of Toronto and Montreal have sponsored play production for many years.

Since 1925 hundreds of dramatic clubs have been formed. Some of these are community organizations. Others centre around the Universities, churches, schools, libraries, and commercial institutions. Many of these later societies have become as widely known in the Little Theatre world as the older groups which survive. It may be pointed out that this dramatic activity has not been confined to English-speaking Canadians. French groups have been formed not only in the province of Quebec, but in cities such as Winnipeg and Edmonton.

Some groups have sent their more successful plays on tour to neighbouring towns. The Players Club of the University of British Columbia makes an annual tour. Hart House Theatre players for several seasons, from 1928 to 1931, brought Shakespeare to the schools of Toronto, and other cities in Ontario. The Edmonton Little Theatre made a Peace River tour in 1930.

Instruction in all phases of the theatre has become increasingly available. Schools, like the Margaret Eaton School of Toronto, which gave a course in literature and dramatic art from 1906 to 1926, and departments attached to Conservatories of Music, were in existence for some time before the Little Theatre movement had become so strong. Latterly, schools, universities and community theatres have offered courses in the drama. The Montreal Repertory Theatre runs a School of the Theatre. Hart House Theatre for several years held a summer course, and the University of Toronto had an extension course in connection with Hart House Theatre from 1929 to 1931. In 1933 a School of the Arts related to the Theatre was inaugurated at Banff during the summer season by the Extension Department of the University of Alberta. In addition, leading directors of amateur theatres have offered short courses on the theatre in various centres.

To train young players, Junior Groups were started by many clubs. The Hart House Experimental Group, formed in 1931, gave birth to the Children Players, who, under the auspices of the Toronto Kindergarten Association, give plays on Saturday mornings for children. The Ottawa Drama League has both a Junior and an Intermediate branch. The Vancouver Little Theatre, with assistance from the Board of Education, started a Junior Group in 1937.

A notable feature of this dramatic development has been the stimulation of Canadian playwrights. Many of the earlier plays were written in verse, and written for the library rather than the theatre. And playwrights were scarce. To-day plays are being written by authors who have a practical experience of the theatre, and benefit from the opportunity given to them to see their plays produced. Competitions, chiefly for one-act plays, have been held by such groups as the Canadian Authors' Association of Montreal, the Imperial Order of the Daughters of the Empire, Women's Canadian Clubs, the Department of Extension of the University of Alberta, the High School of Commerce, Toronto. The Montreal Repertory Theatre and the Sarnia Drama League have offered prizes for Canadian plays to be produced by their groups. A series of Canadian plays is being published by Samuel French. In his review of the drama in the *Survey of letters: 1935* in the *University of Toronto Quarterly*, April, 1936, W. S. Milne notes: "Many of the plays . . . show a mastery of the mechanics of the theatre, and adroitness conspicuously absent from most of the attempts of a decade ago. . . . One sees no masterpiece, but the way is being prepared. There never yet was a great playwright who was not first a man of the theatre."

It remained for another governor-general to provide the final stimulus to the amateur theatrical movement. When the Earl of Bessborough arrived in Canada, he found the country alive with dramatic activity. Always profoundly interested in the stage, he called a meeting of representatives of dramatic groups of the nine provinces. Encouraged by their enthusiasm, he organized the Dominion Drama Festival. Regional competitions were held in each province in the spring of 1933, and the winning teams from each region went to Ottawa to compete in the first finals of the Festival in May, 1933. The best production was awarded the Bessborough Trophy. The best English and the best French plays, exclusive of the winner of the Bessborough Trophy, also received awards. Later, the Sir Barry Jackson Trophy was awarded for the best production of a Canadian play, and the Festival Committee has offered a cash prize to the author of the best Canadian play. For five years the finals of the Festival have taken place in Ottawa. In 1938 they will be held in Winnipeg. To adjudicate in the regional, as well as the final competitions, a number of celebrated men of the theatre have been brought from England, and much of the success of the festivals has been due to their impartial and constructive criticism.

The Dominion Drama Festivals have provided a broadening and stimulating experience. To many of the competitors the work being done by some of the more experienced groups has been a revelation. In choice of plays, as well as in production and acting, there has been a notable advance. In many ways, the Festival has been an education. It is staggering to realize that many of the players from outlying districts have never sat as audience in a theatre in their lives. The future of the amateur theatre in Canada is unpredictable, but there is no doubt that the Dominion Drama Festival will rank as a potent force in the cultural life of the country.

There is no source-book for information on the Canadian theatre. The daily and weekly press must be consulted. *Saturday Night*, for example, contains many critical and intelligent articles. Chapters on the drama in histories of Canadian literature give a brief outline, chiefly from the literary point of view. Such books are V. B. Rhodenizer, *A handbook of Canadian literature* (Ottawa, 1930); Lionel Stevenson, *Appraisals of Canadian literature*

(Toronto, 1925); Lorne Pierce, *An outline of Canadian literature* (Toronto, 1927); and J. D. Logan and D. G. French, *Highways of Canadian literature* (Toronto, 1924). Thoughtful articles on the trend of the drama include one by Vincent Massey in *Queen's Quarterly* of December, 1922, and one by H. M. Smith in the *Canadian Forum* of March, 1930. The annual survey of *Letters in Canada* published in the *University of Toronto Quarterly* since 1936 contains a section on drama. This gives a comprehensive review of published plays, and books and articles dealing with the theatre, as well as a critical résumé of the yearly progress made in the literature of the drama. Kenneth Mac-Gowan's *Footlights across America* (New York, 1929) contains a wealth of material on the experimental theatre. Some groups have their own official publications. The Montreal Repertory Theatre, for example, publishes *The Cue*, and the *Community Playhouse News* deals exclusively with the activities of the Sarnia Drama League. The official organ of the Dominion Drama Festival is the *Curtain Call*, published in Toronto since 1929, which deals currently with the work of the amateur theatre in Canada from coast to coast.

Thedford, a village in Lambton county, Ontario, on the Canadian National Railway, 30 miles north-east of Sarnia, and 6 miles from lake Huron. There are limestone quarries in the vicinity; and the village has saw and flax mills and a sash-and-door factory. Pop. (1934), 700.

Theller, Edward Alexander (1810?-1859), filibusterer, was born in Lower Canada, of Irish parentage, about 1810, and studied and practised medicine. He went to the United States, and in 1838 he joined the American filibusters along the Canadian border. He was captured on lake Erie while in command of a privateer, was tried, and was sentenced to imprisonment. He escaped from prison at Quebec, and fled to New

York. In 1853 he went to California, where he was editor of several newspapers, and for a time was superintendent of public schools in San Francisco; and he died at Honitas, California, in 1859. He published *Canada in 1837-38, showing the causes of the late attempted revolution and of its failure, together with personal adventures of the author* (2 vols., Philadelphia, 1841).

The Pas, a town in Manitoba, on the Saskatchewan river, and on the Canadian National, Hudson Bay, and Flin Flon Railways, 400 miles north-west of Winnipeg. The origin of the name is one of the most interesting problems of western place-nomenclature. Near the town was formerly an Indian village named variously Pasquia, Paskoyac, or Basquia. This name was clearly derived from the Cree word *Opasquaow*, meaning "narrows between wooded banks", and was applied in reference to the fact that here was the natural crossing of the Saskatchewan. But as wood on the banks disappeared, the word *Opas* or *Opaw*, meaning merely "narrows", came to be applied to the place; and this word was evidently confused with the French *Le Pas*, meaning a "strait" or "crossing", as in the well-known French name for the strait of Dover, *Le Pas de Calais*. Another possible explanation is that the name is derived from the Sioux word *Opah*, meaning "red deer"; and this is supported by the application of the name "Red Deer" to the Saskatchewan by Jérémie (q.v.) in 1720. Perhaps the name is the result of confusion between two Indian words and one French word. In any case, the present name goes back at least to to 1808, when Alexander Henry the younger (q.v.) referred to it as "the Pas". It is now a centre for lumbering, fishing, mining, and fur-trading; and it has many modern facilities, such as electric light, waterworks, and sewers. There is a high school and a daily newspaper (*Northern Mail*). Pop. (1931), 4,030.

Thessalon, a town in Algoma district, Ontario, on the north shore of lake Huron, at the mouth of the river Thessalon, and on the Canadian Pacific Railway, 50 miles east of Sault Ste. Marie. It is said that the name is a corruption of a French name (not specified) which means "leaning point", applied to the place by the Jesuit missionaries. The town was founded as a lumbering village about 1870; but is also in a good agricultural district, and has extensive fisheries. It has a high school, a hospital, and a weekly newspaper (*Algoma Advocate*). Pop. (1931), 1,632.

Thessalon river, in the Algoma district, Ontario, drains 3 lakes, Ottertail, Desert, and Rock, and flows south-east into the North channel of lake Huron, between the 83rd and 84th meridians of west longitude.

Thetford Mines, a city in Megantic county, Quebec, is situated half-way between Quebec city and Sherbrooke, on the line of the Quebec Central Railway. During the last decade of the nineteenth century rich asbestos deposits were discovered in the locality, and Thetford Mines sprang into being. About 45 per cent. of the world's asbestos now comes from Thetford Mines; in 1929 the output was valued at $13,337,000. The asbestos field seems to be inexhaustible, as the deeper are the pits the more abundant is the mineral and the finer the fibre. The city is named after the borough of Thetford, Norfolk, England. Pop. (1931), about 11,000. See *Historique de la ville de Thetford Mines* (Quebec, 1910).

Thibaudeau, Isidore (1819-1893), president of the Executive Council of Canada (1863-4), was born at Cap Santé, Lower Canada, in 1819. He became head of the firm of Thibaudeau, Thomas, and Co., wholesale dry goods merchants of Quebec and Montreal. From 1863 to 1867 he represented Quebec Centre in the Legislative Assembly of Canada; and from 1863 to 1864 he was president of the council in the Macdonald-Dorion administration. In 1867 he was appointed a member of the Legislative Council of Quebec; but he resigned in 1874, and was elected a member of the Canadian House of Commons for Quebec East. He resigned his seat in 1877, and retired to private life. He died in 1893. In 1847 he married Laura, daughter of Gaspard Drolet, of Quebec.

Thibaudeau, Joseph Elie (d. 1878), minister of agriculture (1858), was born at Cap Santé, Lower Canada. He became a merchant; and from 1854 to 1861 he represented Portneuf in the Legislative Assembly of Canada. In 1858 he was president of the Council and minister of agriculture in the short-lived Brown-Dorion administration. In 1863 he was appointed registrar of the county of Portneuf; and this position he occupied until his death on January 5, 1878. See Abbé D. Gosselin, *L'honorable Elie Thibaudeau* (Bull. rech. hist., 1900).

Thibaudeau, Joseph Rosaire (1837-1910), senator of Canada, was born at Cap Santé, Lower Canada, on October 1, 1837. He became a member of the wholesale dry-goods firm of Thibaudeau, Thomas, and Co. (later Thibaudeau, Beliveau, and Archambault); and in 1878 he was called to the Senate of Canada. He was appointed sheriff of the district of Montreal in 1890, and this position he held until his death at Montreal on June 16, 1910. In 1873 he married Marguerite, daughter of Major G. LaMothe, postmaster of Montreal.

Thimbleweed (*Anemone virginiana L., Ranunculaceae*), a stout-stemmed, hairy perennial, 2-3 feet tall, branching where the cluster of stem-leaves is attached. These leaves are twice to thrice compound, the divisions toothed or cleft again. The flowers are greenish-white, borne on long slender stalks, and composed of 5 obtuse sepals and an indefinite number of stamens and pistils. The fruit is an oblong thimble-like structure, which gives the plant its common name. It is to be found growing in woods, thickets, and clearings from Nova Scotia to Alberta, flowering from May to August.

Thistle. See **Canada Thistle, Russian Thistle,** and **Sow Thistle.**

Thoalintoa lake is in the North West Territories, north-west of Hudson bay, between the 60th and 61st parallels of north latitude. It has an area of 160 square miles.

Thom, Adam (1802-1890), recorder of Rupert's Land (1838-49), was born in Scotland in 1802, and was educated at King's College, Aberdeen. He emigrated to Canada about 1832, studied law in Montreal, and was called to the bar of Lower Canada in 1837. While studying law, he engaged in journalism, and during the Rebellion of 1837 he was editor of the Montreal *Herald*. His attitude was so strongly anti-French that Lord Durham (q.v.) thought fit to attach him to his staff in 1838; and it was said that he was the author of parts of Lord Durham's *Report*. He accompanied Durham to England in 1838; but he was almost immediately appointed recorder of Rupert's Land, and he entered on his judicial duties at the Red River settlement in 1839. He became unpopular with the French half-breeds; and in 1849 he was removed from the bench, though he continued to act as clerk of the Council of Assiniboia until 1854. He then resigned his appointments, and returned to Great Britain. He died in London, England, on February 21, 1890. He published, under various pen-names, the following: *Letter to the Right Hon. E. G. Stanley, secretary of state for the colonies*, by an Emigrant (Montreal, 1834); *Remarks on the convention, and on the petition of the constitutionalists*, by Anti-Bureaucrat (Montreal, 1835); *Review of the Report made in 1828 by* *the Canada Committee of the House of Commons* (Montreal, 1835); *Anti-Gallic Letters, addressed to his Excellency, the Earl of Gosford*, by Camillus (Montreal, 1836); *The claims to the Oregon territory considered* (London, 1844); and *Chronology of prophecy* (London, 1848). He is said to have written for Sir George Simpson (q.v.) a large part of his *Narrative of a voyage round the world* (London, 1847).

Thomas, William (1800-1860), architect, was born in Stroud, Gloucestershire, England, in 1800. He became an architect, and practised his profession for some years in Leamington, England. He emigrated to Canada about 1842, and settled in Toronto. He was the architect of many of the public buildings built in Toronto in the fifties and sixties of last century, notably St. Michaels' cathedral, St. Lawrence hall, the Toronto gaol, and several churches. He died in Toronto on December 25, 1860.

Thompson, David (1770-1857), explorer and geographer, was born on April 30, 1770, in the parish of St. John the Evangelist, Westminster, England, the son of David Thompson. He was educated at the Grey Coat School, Westminster, and in 1784 he was apprenticed to the Hudson's Bay Company. He spent the years 1784-97 as a clerk in the service of the Hudson's Bay Company, either at the posts on Hudson bay, or in the interior. In 1797 he transferred his services to the North West Company, in which he became a partner, and from this date until 1812 he was continuously engaged in fur-trading and exploring on the western plains and on the Pacific slope. He was the first white man to descend the Columbia river from its source to its mouth. Wherever he went he made traverses of his course and observed for longitude and latitude; and when he left the western country in 1812, he prepared a map of it which has been the basis of all subsequent maps. He settled at Terrebonne, Lower Canada, and later,

at Williamstown, Upper Canada. From 1816 to 1826 he was employed in surveying the boundary line between Canada and the United States; and in later years he was employed on other surveys. He died, in circumstances of extreme poverty, at Longueuil, near Montreal, on February 10, 1857. In 1799, he married Charlotte Small, a half-breed; and by her he had sixteen children. His *Narrative of his explorations*, which remained for many years unpublished, has been edited, with introduction and notes, by J. B. Tyrrell (Toronto, Champlain Society, 1916). See C. N. Cochrane, *David Thompson the explorer* (Toronto, 1924); and E. Coues, *New light on the history of the North-West* (2 vols., New York, 1897).

Thompson, David (1796?-1868), author, was born in Scotland about 1796. He enlisted in the Royal Scots, and after his discharge settled in Canada. He became a school teacher in Niagara, Upper Canada; and in 1832 he published *A history of the late war between Great Britain and the United States of America* (Niagara, Upper Canada). Because of his inability to pay the cost of publication of this work, he was imprisoned. He died at Niagara, Ontario, in 1868.

Thompson, David (1836-1886), politician, was born in Wainfleet, Welland county, Upper Canada, on December 7, 1836, the son of David Thompson, M.P.P. He represented Haldimand in the Legislative Assembly of Canada and in the Canadian House of Commons from 1863 to 1886, as a Liberal. He died at Ruthven Park, Indiana, Ontario, on April 18, 1886.

Thompson, Sir John Sparrow David (1844-1894), prime minister of Canada (1892-4), was born in Halifax, Nova Scotia, on November 10, 1844, the son of John Sparrow Thompson, a civil servant, and Charlotte Pottinger. He was educated at the Free Church Academy in Halifax, and was called to the bar of Nova Scotia in 1865 (Q.C., 1879). In 1877 he was elected to the Legislative Assembly of Nova Scotia as a Liberal-Conservative for Antigonish; in 1878 he became attorney-general in the Holmes administration; and in 1882 he became prime minister. In the general elections of 1882, however, his ministry was defeated; and he himself, on his resignation, accepted appointment as a judge of the Supreme Court of Nova Scotia. After three years on the bench, he was offered by Sir John Macdonald (q.v.) in 1885 the post of minister of justice in the Dominion government; and was the same year elected to the House of Commons for Antigonish. "The great discovery of my life," said Macdonald later, "was my discovery of Thompson." As minister of justice, he handled with consummate skill the debate in 1886 on the execution of Louis Riel (q.v.), and that in 1889 on the Jesuits' Estates Act; and, on the death of Macdonald in 1891, he would undoubtedly have become prime minister, had he not been a convert to Roman Catholicism, and so not wholly acceptable to the Orange Order. Sir John Abbott (q.v.), the compromise candidate who became prime minister in 1891, resigned, however, in 1892; and Thompson then succeeded to the vacancy without opposition.

As prime minister, Thompson's tenure of office was too short to permit him to leave a deep impression on the history of Canada. Much of his time, moreover, was occupied with negotiations at the intercolonial conference in London over copyright and merchant shipping, and with his duties as the representative of Great Britain on the Behring sea arbitration at Paris. But he established his reputation as a political leader of great ability and high character; and his sudden death at Windsor Castle, England, on December 12, 1894, was regarded everywhere as a profound tragedy.

In 1870 he married Annie, daughter of Captain Affleck, of Halifax; and by her had two sons and three daughters. In 1888 he was created a K.C.M.G.; and just before his death in 1894 he was sworn of the imperial privy council.

See J. Castell Hopkins, *Life and work of the Right Hon. Sir John Thompson* (Brantford, Ontario, 1895); Senator Miller, *Incidents in the political career of the late Sir John Thompson* (pamphlet, Ottawa, 1895); Mr. Justice Russell, *The career of Sir John Thompson* (Dalhousie Review, 1921).

Thompson, Samuel (1810-1886), journalist, was born in London, England, in 1810, and came to Canada in 1833. He became a journalist, and established in 1838 the short-lived Toronto *Palladium*. He was later editor or publisher in Toronto of the *Herald*, the *Daily Colonist*, and *News of the Week*. In 1859, having obtained a contract for government printing, he removed to Quebec, and there he published in 1860 *Thompson's Mirror of Parliament*, a forerunner of Hansard. In his later years he retired from journalism, and was engaged in the insurance business. He died in Toronto on July 8, 1886. Shortly before his death he published his autobiography, under the title *Reminiscences of a pioneer* (Toronto, 1884).

Thompson, Thomas Phillips (1843-1933), journalist and author, was born at Newcastle-on-Tyne, England, in 1843, and came with his parents to Canada in 1857. He became a journalist, and he achieved a considerable reputation as a writer of humorous articles under the *nom-de-plume* of "Jimuel Briggs." He died at Oakville, Ontario, on May 22, 1933. He was the author of *The future government of Canada* (St. Catharines, Ontario, 1864), *The politics of labour* (New York, 1887), and *The labour reform songster* (New York, 1892); and in 1902 he was the organizer in Ontario of the Socialist League.

Thompson river, a tributary of the Fraser river, in British Columbia, has two branches, of which the northern rises in the Cariboo district and the southern in the Kamloops district. They unite at Kamloops, and the river then flows west through Kamloops lake into the Fraser at Lytton, in the Kamloops district. To the head of the North Thompson, the river is 270 miles in length, and drains an area of 21,800 square miles. It was discovered by Simon Fraser (q.v.), of the North West Company, on his descent of the Fraser in 1807, and was named after David Thompson (q.v.), another explorer of the North West Company.

Thomson, Charles Poulett. See **Sydenham, Charles Poulett Thomson, Baron.**

Thomson, Edward William (1849-1924), author and journalist, was born in Toronto township, Peel county, Upper Canada, on February 12, 1849, the son of William Thomson and Margaret Hamilton Foley. He was educated at Trinity College School, Weston. In 1864-5 he served in the Pennsylvania cavalry during the American civil war; and in 1866 he served in the Queen's Own Rifles during the Fenian raid in Canada. He was first a surveyor and civil engineer, and then he became a journalist. From 1879 to 1891, he was chief editorial writer on the Toronto *Globe*, and from 1891 to 1901, he was editor of the *Youth's Companion*. He then became Ottawa correspondent of the Boston *Transcript*, and devoted himself to independent journalism. He died at Boston, Massachusetts, on March 5, 1924. In 1873 he married Adelaide, daughter of Alexander St. Denis, of Port Fortune, Quebec. He was elected a fellow of the Royal Society of Canada in 1910; and he was the author of *Old man Savarin, and other stories* (Toronto, 1895; new ed., 1922), *Walter Gibbs, the young boss, and other stories* (Toronto, 1896), *Between earth and sky* (Toronto, 1897), *Smoky days*

(Boston, 1901), *Peter Ottawa* (Toronto, 1905), *When Lincoln died, and other poems* (Boston and London, 1909), and *The many-mansioned house, and other poems* (Toronto, 1909). See M. O. Hammond, *Edward William Thomson* (Queen's Quarterly, 1931).

Thomson, Hugh Christopher (1791?-1834), printer and journalist, was born in Scotland about 1791. He came to Upper Canada after the War of 1812; and in 1819 he founded in Kingston the *Upper Canada Herald*, which he edited until his death. From 1824 to 1834 he represented Frontenac in the Legislative Assembly of Upper Canada. He died at Kingston on April 23, 1834. See W. S. Wallace, *The periodical literature of Upper Canada* (Can. hist. rev., 1931).

Thomson, John (d. 1828), fur-trader, was of Scottish origin. Possibly he was a son of John Thomson, the first postmaster of Montreal. He entered the service of the North West Company before 1789, for from that year to 1791 he was in charge of a post "near the lower part of Grass river in the Port Nelson track". In 1798 he was on the Peace river; in 1799, on lake Athabaska; and in 1800 he built "Old Rocky Mountain House" on the Mackenzie river. He was stationed in the Athabaska department from 1806 to 1810, and in the English River department from 1811 to 1821. In 1804 he became a partner of the North West Company; and at the union of 1821 he became a chief factor of the Hudson's Bay Company. He retired from the service, however, on June 1, 1821; and he died on January 8, 1828, probably in the parish of Ste. Madeleine de Rigaud, Lower Canada, where he lived after his retirement. He married Françoise Boucher, and he had by her seven children.

Thomson, Robert (d. 1795?), fur-trader, was probably a brother of John Thomson (q.v.). In 1793 he had been for several years stationed in the English River district; and he was killed here in a quarrel with the Indians in the winter of 1794-5.

Thomson, Tom (1877-1917), painter, was born at Claremont, Ontario, in 1877. He was educated in the public schools of Owen Sound; and taught himself painting. He supported himself by serving as a bush-ranger in Algonquin Park, Ontario, during the greater part of the year; and here he obtained the inspiration for the pictures he painted in Toronto during the winter. These pictures are essentially Canadian, and betray a native-born genius. From them the group of Canadian painters known as "The Group of Seven" have largely drawn their ideas and style. Thomson, who was unmarried, was accidentally drowned in Algonquin Park in July, 1917. See J. M. MacCallum, *Tom Thomson* (Can. mag., 1917), and Blodwen Davies, *A study of Tom Thomson* (Toronto, 1935).

Thomson, William J. (1857-1927), engraver, was born at Guelph, Ontario, in 1857. He was apprenticed to an engraving firm in Toronto about 1872; and he studied art under John A. Fraser (q.v.) at the Toronto Art School. He was one of the organizers of the Art Students League in 1886; and was its president in 1890-91. From 1916 to 1919 he was also the first president of the Society of Canadian Painter-Etchers. He became a master of etched work; and some of his etchings are in the National Gallery at Ottawa and the Art Gallery at Toronto. He died in Toronto on May 25, 1927. See *William J. Thompson, Canada, engraver—1857-1927* (pamphlet, Toronto, 1930).

Thorburn, William (*fl.* 1789-1805), fur-trader, was a native of Scotland who entered the employ of the North West Company prior to 1789, when he was left in charge of "Finlay's old fort" on the Saskatchewan. He had become a partner of the North West Company by 1795, but had ceased to be a wintering partner by 1799. He relinquished his shares in the Company in 1805. He was in Scotland in the winter of 1793-4; and it does not appear that he ever returned.

Thornburn, a village in Pictou county, Nova Scotia, 6 miles from New Glasgow, on the Canadian National Railway. It was formerly known as Vale Colliery, from the coal-mines in the vicinity; but it was given its present name in 1886. Pop. (1935), 750.

Thornbury, a town in Grey county, Ontario, on the south shore of the Georgian bay, at the mouth of the Beaver river, and on the Canadian National Railway, 12 miles west of Collingwood. It is the centre of the Georgian bay apple-growing district, and has two apple evaporators and box and barrel factories, as well as flour and oatmeal mills and brick and tile works. It has also a high school, a public library, and a weekly newspaper (*Review-Herald*). Pop. (1934), 764.

Thorndale, a village in Middlesex county, Ontario, near the north branch of the Thames river, and on the London branch of the Canadian National Railway. Pop. (1935), 350.

Thornhill, a village in Markham township, York couty, Ontario, on Yonge street, and on the Canadian National and Metropolitan Electric Railways, 5 miles north of Toronto. It was named after an early merchant in the village named Thorne. In an agricultural and market-gardening district, it is a local distributing centre, and has a weekly newspaper (*Leader*). Pop. (1934), 850.

Thornton, Sir Henry Worth (1871-1933), president of the Canadian National Railways (1922-32), was born at Logansport, Indiana, in the United States, on November 6, 1871. He was educated at the University of Pennsylvania, and entered the engineering department of the Pennsylvania Railroad in 1894. In 1911 he was appointed general superintendent of the Long Island Railroad; and in 1914 he went to England as general manager of the Great Eastern Railway. In 1917 his services were commandeered by the British government, and he became assistant director-general of movements and railways in France, with the temporary rank of colonel. In 1919 he was appointed inspector-general of transportation, with the rank of major-general; and he retained this position until 1922, when he was appointed president of the Canadian National Railways. He resigned from this position, because of adverse criticism, in 1932; and he died at New York on March 14, 1933. He was created a K.B.E. in 1919. See D'Arcy Marsh, *The tragedy of Henry Thornton* (Toronto, 1935).

Thorold, a town in Welland county, Ontario, situated on the Welland ship canal and on the Canadian National Railway, 10 miles north of Welland. An electric railway runs to Niagara Falls (9 miles), St. Catharines (4 miles), and Port Dalhousie (7 miles). In 1788 a settlement was established here and named after Sir John Thorold (1734-1815), a member of the British parliament who opposed the war with the American colonies. The paper mills located here provide many cargoes for ships in the transport of newsprint. Thorold has several other established industries, including flour-milling, foundry and machine shops, and a macaroni factory. In the vicinity there are extensive quarries of natural cement stone. The surrounding country is highly cultivated by farmers and orchardists. The town possesses all modern municipal facilities. A weekly newspaper (*Post*) is published. Pop. (1931), 5,092. See John H. Thompson, *Jubilee history of Thorold* (Thorold, 1897-8).

Thoroughwort. See **Boneset.**

Thorpe, Robert (*fl.* 1781-1820), judge, was a native of Ireland, and was called to the Irish bar in 1781. He became a protégé of Lord Castlereagh, and as a reward for certain unknown services, probably in connection with the union of Great Britain and Ireland in 1801, was appointed in 1802 chief justice of Prince Edward Island. In 1805 he was appointed a puisne judge of the court of King's Bench in Upper Canada, and he arrived in York (Toronto), in September, 1805. He assumed an attitude of hostility to the executive authorities in Upper Canada; and in 1806 he was elected to represent Durham, Simcoe, and the east riding of York in the Legislative Assembly. He headed in the Assembly the opposition to the government, and in 1807 he was suspended by Francis Gore (q.v.) from his position as judge. On his return to England, he was appointed chief justice of Sierra Leone; but he remained in this colony for only two years. The rest of his life he spent in poverty and obscurity; and he last appears in connection with a suit for criminal libel against Francis Gore in 1820. He was the author of *A letter to William Wilberforce* (London, 1815), *Reply to the special report of the directors of the African institution* (London, 1815), and *View of the present increase of the slave trade* (London, 1818). See W. R. Riddell, *Mr. Justice Thorpe* (Can. Law Times, 1920), and D. B. Read, *Lives of the judges of Upper Canada* (Toronto, 1888).

Thousand islands is the name given to a large group of islands in the St. Lawrence river, between Kingston and Brockville. The name in its French form, "Les Mille Isles", is found on a map by Léry (q.v.), of 1727. A Jesuit missionary, named Poncet, in 1653, was probably the first white man to see the islands. After the War of 1812, Captain William Fitzwilliam Owen (1774-1857) made a survey of the upper St. Lawrence (1818), and gave to the islands names associated with the War. One group was named after officers, another after Indian leaders, others

IN THE THOUSAND ISLANDS

Yacht Club (above), Lost Channel (below) on the Canadian side of the St. Lawrence River near Alexandria Bay and in the heart of the Thousand Islands region. This Channel was named "Lost Channel" because the British boats proceeding up the St. Lawrence to attack Fort Frontenac at Kingston became lost here during the French and Indian War.

after the Admiralty and Navy. The Thousand islands are now a popular summer resort for Canadians and Americans. They are filled with traditions of heroism, intrigue, and sacrifice, and are extremely beautiful. They form the scene of Fenimore Cooper's *The Pathfinder*. The Indian name is *Manatoana*, meaning "the Garden of the Great Spirit". See John A. Haddock, *The picturesque St. Lawrence river* (New York, 1896), and G. W. Browne, *The St. Lawrence river* (New York and London, 1905).

Thrasher, a name for two species of Canadian birds which are closely allied to the well-known southern mockingbird. They are approximately of the size of a robin, but more slender, and may further be characterized by their long tails and decurved, wren-like bills. The brown thrasher (*Toxostoma rufum*) is yellowish brown above and creamy white with heavy streaks below. It is sometimes incorrectly called the "brown thrush". The brown thrasher inhabits the southern border of Canada from the Rocky mountains to Quebec. This bird is one of the finest of Canadian songsters. Its habitat is in and around thickets of bushes and vines in cultivated areas. The sage thrasher (*Oreoscoptes montanus*), a less strikingly coloured form, occurs locally in arid sections of southern British Columbia.

Three Hills, a village in the Red Deer district of Alberta, on the Canadian National Railway, 70 miles northeast of Calgary. It is in a farming and stock-raising district, and there are coal-mines in the vicinity. It has grain elevators and a weekly newspaper (*Capital*). Pop. (1931), 581.

Three Rivers (Les Trois Rivières), a city in St. Maurice county, Quebec, is situated at the confluence of the St. Lawrence and St. Maurice rivers. It has excellent deep water facilities, accessible timber, and abundant hydroelectric power near at hand. An indus-trial centre, it has lumber mills, cotton mills, pulp-and-paper mills (including one of the largest newsprint mills in the world, producing 700 tons of newsprint per day), boot-and-shoe factories, etc. It is on the Canadian Pacific Railway, and during the summer has a daily steamship service. It is the second oldest city in Canada, having been founded in 1634 by the Sieur de Laviolette. It is thus spoken of by Father Le Jeune (q.v.) in his *Relations* of 1635: "The French called this spot Trois Rivières, because a beautiful river here enters the great St. Lawrence by three main branches." During the French régime it was an important port; explorers, missionaries, and fur-traders used it as a point of departure into the western wilderness, and in its earliest days Indians flocked to it to trade. It was incorporated as a city in 1857. It is the seat of a Roman Catholic cathedral, and among its educational institutions is the provincial technical school. Three newspapers are published in French (*Le Nouvelliste, Le Bien Public*, and *La Chronique*), and one in English (*St. Maurice Valley Chronicle*). Pop. (1931), 35,450. See A. Tessier, *Les Trois-Rivières* (Three Rivers, 1934), and B. Sulte, *Trois-Rivières d'autrefois* (Montreal, 1933).

Thrush, a name applied with descriptive prefixes to most of the members of the bird family *Turdidae*. Thrushes are characterized by the high development of their vocal equipment and by certain other characters, such as the unscaled bare portion of their legs. None of the Canadian thrushes are larger than a robin (*Turdus migratorius*), a bird which belongs to the group. Most of them are olive brown in colour, and are streaked or spotted on the breast. The hermit thrush (*Hylocichla guttata*) is often considered the finest of Canadian songsters. Such matters, however, depend upon personal taste, and is quite possible for several of the Canadian thrushes to be so ranked. The veery (*Hylocichla* *fuscescens*) has a remarkably pleasing but weird metallic song, which may be described as descending in pitch spirally.

Thunder bay, an indentation on the north shore of lake Superior, on which are situated Port Arthur and Fort William. It was called by the Indians *Animikie wekwed*, meaning "thunder bird bay", the thunder bird being an imaginary creature that causes thunder in the folk-lore of some primitive peoples.

Thunder Bay, a district in northern Ontario, is bounded on the north by Patricia district, or the Albany river, on the west by Kenora and the Rainy River districts, on the east by the Algoma and Cochrane districts, and on the south by lake Superior, and a corner of the state of Minnesota. It was made a territorial district by proclamation in 1871, but did not become a judicial district until 1914. Fort William, at the mouth of the Kaministikwia river, was of great importance in the early days of the fur-traders. Lake Nipigon is in the middle of the district. Pop. (1931), 65,118. See the publications of the Thunder Bay Historical Society, and the souvenir edition of the *News-Chronicle* (Port Arthur, 1934).

Thunder Bay Historical Society, a society founded at Fort William, Ontario, on October 2, 1908. It possesses a small historical collection, which is stored in the Public Library at Fort William. It has published its *Annual Report*, including historical papers, since the year of organization.

Ticonderoga, a fort built by the French in 1755-6 on a promontory at the southern end of lake Champlain, with the object of guarding the approach to Canada by way of lake Champlain and the Richelieu valley. It was named by the French Carillon, but among the English it was known by the Indian name of Ticonderoga, meaning "the meeting or confluence of three waters."

It was the scene of a disastrous defeat of a British force under James Abercromby (q.v.) on July 8, 1758, when Montcalm's troops repelled repeated attacks of some of the finest regiments in the British army; but in the summer of 1759 Amherst (q.v.) captured it, after the French under Bourlamaque (q.v.) had withdrawn to the northern end of lake Champlain. In 1775 it was captured by an American force under Ethan Allen, who summoned it to surrender "in the name of the Great Jehovah and the Continental Congress"; and it remained in the hands of the Americans until it was recaptured by Burgoyne in 1777. When the boundary between Canada and the United States was settled in 1783, it was found to be south of the 45th parallel of latitude, and was handed over to the state of New York. See Helen J. Gilchrist, *The history of Fort Ticonderoga* (Quarterly Journal of the New York State Historical Association, July, 1922), and S. H. P. Pell, *Fort Ticonderoga* (Journal of the Society of Army Historical Research, April, 1928).

Tidnish river, a small stream in Cumberland county, Nova Scotia, near the eastern entrance of the Baie Verte canal. It is navigable for only a short distance even by small vessels.

Tiedemann, mount. See **Teidemann, mount.**

Tiffany, Gideon (1774-1854), printer, was born in 1774. In 1794 he became the printer of the *Upper Canada Gazette* at Newark (Niagara), Upper Canada; and he published it until 1797. In 1799, with his brother Silvester, he founded at Niagara the *Canada Consultation*, and he published this journal until toward the end of 1800. He then deserted printing and journalism for farming; and he died on his farm in Middlesex county, Ontario, in 1854. See W. S. Wallace, *The periodical literature of Upper Canada* (Can. hist. rev., 1931).

Tignish, a town in Prince county, Prince Edward Island, on the Canadian National Railway, 68 miles north of Summerside. Pop. (1935), 500.

Tilbury, a town in Kent county, Ontario, on the Michigan Central and Canadian Pacific Railways, 34 miles east of Windsor. It was named after Tilbury, on the Thames, in England. It has several important industries, notably a factory for automobile tops and bodies and a brick and tile company; and it has a high school and a weekly newspaper. Pop. (1931), 1,992.

Tilley, Sir Samuel Leonard (1818-1896), statesman was born at Gagetown, New Brunswick, on May 18, 1818, the son of Thomas Morgan Tilley and Susan Ann Peters. He was educated at the Gagetown grammar school, and in 1831 began to earn his own livelihood as a clerk in an apothecary's office in Saint John, New Brunswick. In 1838 he went into business for himself, as a partner in the firm of Peters and Tilley. He was a member of the Legislative Assembly of New Brunswick from 1850 to 1851, from 1854 to 1856, and from 1857 to 1865. In 1854 he became provincial secretary in the Fisher administration, and from 1861 to 1865 was leader of the government. In 1864 he was a delegate to the conferences at Charlottetown and Quebec to discuss Confederation; and in 1866 he was a delegate to the London Conference, at which the British North America Act was drafted. The ministry of which he was a member was defeated in 1865 on the issue of Confederation, but was returned to power in 1866. In 1867 Tilley resigned from the New Brunswick cabinet, and became minister of customs in the first cabinet of the Dominion of Canada. This portfolio he retained until 1873, when he became minister of finance in the Macdonald government. On the fall of the government a few months later, he was appointed lieutenant-governor of New Brunswick; and his tenure of this office coincided with the period of office of the Mackenzie government. In 1878, therefore, he was free to become minister of finance in the second Macdonald government, and it fell to him to inaugurate the National Policy. Failing health compelled him to resign his portfolio in 1885, and he was then appointed lieutenant-governor of New Brunswick for a second term. This second term of office lasted until 1893; and on June 25, 1896, he died at Saint John, New Brunswick.

He was twice married, (1) to Julia Anna, daughter of James T. Hanford, of Saint John, and (2) in 1867 to Alice, daughter of Z. Chipman, of St. Stephen. He was created a C.B. (civil) in 1867, and a K.C.M.G. in 1879. See J. Hannay, *The life and times of Sir Leonard Tilley* (Saint John, New Brunswick, 1896), and *Sir Leonard Tilley* (Toronto, 1907).

Tilley, mount, is in the Kootenay district of British Columbia, about 5½ miles south-west of Revelstoke, between mount Begbie and mount MacPherson. It is in lat. 50° 58', long. 118° 06', and has an altitude of 8,064 feet. It was named after Sir Leonard Tilley (q.v.), lieutenant-governor of New Brunswick.

Tillsonburg, a town in Oxford county, Ontario, on the Canadian National, the Canadian Pacific, the Michigan Central, and the Wabash Railways, 25 miles south-east of London. The place was founded in 1825, and takes its name from George Tillson, who built a saw-mill and a forge on the site. The locality was known as Dereham Forge until 1836, when a village site was surveyed and the name Tillsonburg given to it. Tobacco-growing, dairying, and fruit-growing are the chief industries in the district. The town has shoe-factories, a tobacco-factory, creameries, flour-mills, harvest-tool factories, and two foundries. Large quantities of bricks are made from clay found in the vicinity. A weekly newspaper (*News*) is published. Pop. (1931), 3,385.

Timagami lake is in the Nipissing district, Ontario, north-west of North Bay in the Timagami forest reserve. The name is an Indian word meaning "deep water". This region, which has been withdrawn from settlement by the Ontario government and constituted a forest reserve, is a resort of sportsmen and campers. The reserve embraces a series of lakes including, besides Timagami, Lady Evelyn, Obabika, Matawabika, Bay, Rabbit, Anina, and many smaller sheets of water, which cover an area of 60 miles from east to west and 50 miles from north to south. The region abounds in fish and game of all kinds, and is rich in minerals and timber, including red and white pine, spruce, tamarack, and poplar. The area of the lake is 90 square miles.

Timiskaming, a district in northern Ontario, is bounded on the north by the district of Cochrane, on the west by the district of Sudbury, on the south by the districts of Sudbury and Nipissing, and on the east by the province of Quebec. It formed part of the districts of Nipissing and Sudbury until the Act of April, 1912, which created it. Originally a fur-trading district, it is now chiefly notable for its gold and silver mines. Pop. (1931), 37,043.

Timiskaming lake is on the boundary between Timiskaming district and county in Ontario and Quebec respectively, in the basin of the Ottawa river, and in latitude 47° 30', and longitude 80°. The name, an Indian word meaning "at the place of deep, dry water", refers to the clay flats in the north-eastern portion of the lake, which are dry at low water. In 1685 a Frenchman, coming south from the Abitibi river, descended the Ottawa, *via* lake Timiskaming, to Montreal. In the following period (1686-1697), this route was utilized by the French in their attacks on the Hudson's Bay Company's trading posts. The lake has an area of 110 square miles, of which 55 are in Ontario and 55 in Quebec.

Timmins, Noah A. (1867-1936), mining operator, was born at Mattawa, Ontario, on March 31, 1867. He was educated at St. Mary's College, Montreal, and became interested in mining. In 1903 he and his brother acquired the LaRose mine at Cobalt, and in 1909 he, with his associates, developed the Hollinger mine in the Porcupine country. He was president of the Hollinger mine from its inception; and became a man of great wealth. He died at Palm Beach, Florida, on January 23, 1936. The town of Timmins is named after him.

Timmins, a town in the Cochrane district, Ontario, on the Mattagami river, and on a branch of the Temiskaming and Northern Ontario Railway, 75 miles north-west of Haileybury. It is the centre of the Porcupine gold-mining area, and the Hollinger properties are actually within the town limits. Besides gold-mining, other industries are the manufacture of railway ties, pulpwood, lumber, and beer. The town has four public schools, four separate schools, a high school, a technical school, a business college, a hospital, and three weekly newspapers, two in English (*Advance* and *Timmins Press*) and one in French (*Le Nord Ontarien*). Pop. (1934), 14,200.

Tinneh. See **Athapaskans.**

Tionontati. See **Tobacco Nation.**

Tipi, the conical skin dwelling usual among the Indians of the prairies and some of those living farther to the north-west. It consisted of a circular framework of poles brought together near the top, and covered with dressed buffalo skins sewn together so as to form a single piece. It had at the base a diameter of about 15 feet, and it averaged 25 feet in height. It must be distinguished from the wigwam (q.v.) of eastern Canada, which was a conical dwelling covered with bark. For a detailed description of the tipi, see

The handbook of the Indians of Canada (Ottawa, 1913).

Tisdale, David (1835-1911), minister of militia for Canada (1896), was born in Charlotteville, Norfolk county, Upper Canada, on September 8, 1835, the son of Ephraim Tisdale. He was educated at Simcoe grammar school, and was called to the bar of Upper Canada in 1858 (Q.C., 1872). In 1887 he was elected to represent South Norfolk in the Canadian House of Commons, and he held this seat continuously until his retirement from public life in 1908. On May 1, 1896, he became minister of militia in the Tupper administration, but he retired from office with his colleagues the following July. He died at Simcoe, Ontario, on March 31, 1911. In 1858 he married Sarah Araminta, daughter of James Walker; and by her he had two sons and two daughters.

Tisdale, a town in Saskatchewan, on the Winnipegosis branch of the Canadian National Railways, and on the Prince Albert branch of the Canadian Pacific Railway, 80 miles southeast of Prince Albert. It was named after Frederick W. Tisdale, who, at the time of the naming of the townsite, was station agent for the Canadian Pacific Railway. It is in a mixed farming district, and has four grain elevators, a high school, and a weekly newspaper (*Recorder*). Pop. (1931), 1,069.

Titanium, an element nearly related to silicon and zirconium. It occurs in many minerals, but principally in rutile, brookite, ilmenite, titaniferous magnetite, and sphene. It is used chiefly in the steel industry, and in the production of white non-poisonous paints. Various compounds of titanium are employed in the ceramic, textile, and leather industries. Titanium tetrachloride is used in making smoke screens. Rutile is an oxide of titanium. It occurs in tetragonal crystals, and as disseminated grains in rock. It is an important rock-forming mineral, with an adamantine lustre and a colour range from reddish-brown to black. It is used to some extent as a gem stone, but is more important in the manufacture of titanium compounds. Much of the titanium used commercially is obtained from ilmenite and titaniferous magnetite. The chief source of the titanium ores in Canada is near St. Urbain, Quebec, where the titaniferous ore contains great quantities of rutile needles intermingled with ilmenite. See A. H. A. Robinson, *Titanium* (Mines Branch, Ottawa, 1923).

Tithe. The introduction of the tithe (*la dîme*) in New France goes back to the period of the organization of the hierarchical organization of the Roman Catholic Church under Laval (q.v.). It was the royal edict of 1663, which gave civil confirmation to the creation of the Quebec seminary, that granted legal authority for the collection of the tithe in Canada. This was fixed at first at a thirteenth of the crops; but when complaints were made that this proportion was excessive, the tithe was reduced by Laval to a twentieth, and in 1667 the government of New France reduced it still further to one twenty-sixth, for a period of twenty years. This proportion was ratified in 1679, and again in 1707, though usage confined it to one twenty-sixth of the grain crops; and this proportion has continued unchanged until the present day. In 1760 the articles of the capitulation of Montreal assured to the French Canadians the free exercise of their religion; but whether this assurance carried with it the authorization of the tithe was doubtful, and from 1760 to 1774 the collection of the tithe had perhaps only a customary basis. In 1774, however, the Quebec Act ensured to the Roman Catholic clergy "their accustomed dues and rights, with respect to such persons only as shall profess the said religion"; and this definitely restored the tithe as a feature of the government of the old province of Quebec. The payment of the tithe was continued as an obligation on Roman Catholics in the province of Lower Canada in 1791, and in the new province of Quebec in 1867; and it is still a legal obligation in the province of Quebec to this day, so far as those who adhere to the Roman Catholic Church are concerned. See Mgr. L. A. Paquet, *La dîme* (Trans. Roy. Soc. Can., 1912); P. Lavoie, *La dîme dans le province de Québec* (Revue Trimestrielle Canadienne, 1925); A. Gosselin, *Etablissement de la dîme au Canada* (Bull. rech. hist., 1929); O. Lapalice, *La dîme à Montréal* (Bull. rech. hist., 1929); and P. P. Viard, *La dîme ecclésiastique dans les colonies françaises* (Revue d'Histoire Moderne, 1928).

Titles of Honour. The granting of titular honours in Canada has a long history. Titles of honour were freely granted in Canada during the French régime, partly (though not wholly) in connection with the system of seigniorial tenure. But after the British conquest, these titles almost wholly disappeared, for the simple reason that nearly all those who bore these titles returned to France. A single exception was the barony of Longueuil, which descended to Charles William Grant (q.v.), and which was confirmed by the British government. After the British conquest, titles of honour were very sparingly awarded in Canada, and were confined mainly to chief justices of provinces and other officers of government. By the Constitutional Act of 1791 it was apparently intended to confer titles of honour on members of the Legislative Councils of Upper and Lower Canada; but this feature to the Act was vigorously attacked by Charles James Fox and others, and remained a dead letter. "Are those red and blue ribbons," asked Fox, "which have lost their lustre in the Old World to flash forth again in the New?" Not until Confederation did the custom of granting titles of honours to Canadians receive any considerable impetus. Then knighthoods were conferred

on several of the Fathers of Confederation; and from that time it became usual to confer the honour of knighthood on lieutenant-governors of provinces, chief justices, and prominent politicians and industrialists. Hereditary honours began also to be given, such as the baronetcies conferred on Sir George Cartier (q.v.) in 1868 and Sir Charles Tupper (q.v.) in 1888, and the peerages conferred on Lord Mountstephen (q.v.) in 1891, and on Lord Strathcona (q.v.) in 1897. Sir Wilfrid Laurier (q.v.) sought to control the granting of honours in Canada by urging that they should be granted only on recommendation of the Canadian government; and while his request was not formally acceded to, it did become customary to grant titles of honour in Canada generally on the recommendation of the Canadian government. The result was that after Sir Wilfrid Laurier's defeat in 1911, and especially during the World War, there was a great increase in the number of honours granted, some of which were of an hereditary character. Public opinion on the matter crystallized; and in 1919 the House of Commons of Canada memorialized the King, requesting him to refrain from granting titular honours in future to Canadian citizens.

In 1933 the Bennett government took the view that the resolution of 1919 was not binding on future parliaments; and it recommended a number of honours which were awarded on New Year's Day, 1934. Further honours were granted in 1935; but with the defeat of the Bennett government in 1935, and the accession to power of the Mackenzie King government, the award of titles of honour has again ceased in Canada.

See C. E. Lart, *The noblesse of Canada* (Can. hist. rev., 1922) and D. W. Thomson, *The fate of titles in Canada* (Can. hist. rev., 1929).

Tiverton, a village in Bruce county, Ontario, near lake Huron, and 9 miles north-east of Kincardine. It is named after the village of Tiverton in Devonshire, England, or else after that in Cheshire. Pop. (1935), 450.

Tiverton, a fishing village in Digby county, Nova Scotia, on the north end of Long island, in the bay of Fundy. It is a port of call for vessels plying between Yarmouth and Saint John, and has a government wharf. Pop. (1935), 550.

Tlingit, a branch of the Kolushan family of Indians, inhabit the extreme north-western coast of British Columbia, the adjacent islands, and the Alaskan coast. The name "Kolosh" or "Kolushan" means "a little trough" or "a dish", alluding to the concave dish-shaped labrets worn by the Tlingit women. Their territory lies immediately north of the Tsimshian (q.v.). There are many resemblances between the legends, totemic organization, and language of the Tlingit and Haida that afford basis for the belief in their near relationship and close intercourse at a remote period. Their organization into phratries, totems, and sub-totems has been only slightly influenced by adjacent tribes, and all bear a distinct and original stamp. They consist of two exogamous groups, or phratries, the Raven and the Wolf; but these are divided into many totems and sub-totems. Amongst the Tlingit, as amongst the Haida and Tsimshian, society is based on mother-right; rank, wealth, property, etc., are received through the mother. The family is the sociological unit. There is no absolute chiefship. The head of the prominent family is nominally the chief of the village. Aside from wealth, good birth, and family influence, his position rests on his own personal or masterful qualities. The other chiefs are the heads of the principal clan totems or households of the village. The Tlingit are expert basket-makers. From time immemorial they have possessed the art of weaving twisted bark thread and the wool of the mountain goat into blankets, commonly called Chilkat blankets. Like the Haida and Tsimshian,

they are inveterate gamblers. Their burial practices were not uniform. The southern Tlingit interred their dead; the northern cremated them, believing that thus their spirits would be made very comfortable in the spirit world. The bodies of their medicine men were never cremated, because of a superstition that fire would not touch them, but were deposited within an enclosure of logs elevated a few feet above the ground. See Albert P. Niblack, *The Coast Indians of southern Alaska and northern British Columbia* (House of Representatives, Misc. Docs., No. 142, Washington, D.C., 1890).

Toadflax. See **Butter and Eggs.**

Toads. There is no sharp distinction between frogs and toads. In general, however, the term "frog" is applied to the more slender, smooth-skinned species, and "toad" to those of squat appearance and warty skins. On this basis the frogs and toads of Canada may be rather sharply distinguished, although the so-called tree-toads or tree-frogs are intermediate in some respects. The common toad (*Bufo americana*) is found throughout Canada from Alberta eastward and north at least to James Bay. In a few isolated localities along the north shore of lake Erie, Fowler's toad (*Bufo fowleri*) is found. From the Rocky mountain region westward the north-western toad (*Bufo boreas*) is the common species. Two or three other species have been reported as occurring locally in southern Alberta and British Columbia.

Tobacco Industry. Tobacco is native to North America; and it is probable that it was grown in Canada before the coming of the white man, for the Indians in what is now Canada smoked it and traded it, though it is possible that they obtained it from tribes farther south. It was certainly grown in Canada during the French régime; for in 1721 the tobacco crop in New France was about 48,000 pounds, and

both during the French period and
during the early British period in
Canada tobacco continued to be an
item of trade with the Indians. But it
is only in recent times that the tobacco
industry in Canada has become of
economic importance. This development has been connected with the rise
to popularity of the cigarette, which is
made generally of the yellow Virginia
or bright flue-cured tobacco. The pioneer
crop of this leaf was grown in Canada
shortly after the turn of the twentieth
century, near Ruthven, in Essex county,
Ontario; and for nearly two decades
the growth of this type of tobacco leaf
in Canada was confined to the district
about Ruthven and Leamington, in
Essex county. In 1919, however, a
farmer near Lynedoch in Norfolk county, planted five acres of flue-cured
tobacco; and the success of his venture
induced the experts at the Ontario
Agricultural College in Guelph, Ontario,
to make a survey of the possibilities of
Norfolk county as a tobacco-growing
area. The light, sandy soils of this
county had proved unsuitable to grain-
growing; but it was found that they
were eminently suitable to the culture
of tobacco, and the result of the survey,
which was completed in 1927, was that
large areas in Norfolk county, as well
as in adjoining counties, were diverted
to the growth of tobacco. By 1932 there
were 850 farms in what came to be
known as the "New Belt", as distinct
from the Leamington or "Old Belt",
producing over 25 million pounds of
tobacco leaf. The "New Belt" has, in
fact, out-distanced the "Old Belt" in
the production of tobacco; and the
total production in Canada, including
production in Quebec and in British
Columbia, has reached large figures.
An increasing proportion of Canadian-
grown flue-cured tobacco is used in
cigarettes and tobacco in the Canadian
market; and the reception of Canadian-
grown tobacco in the British market
has been especially encouraging. Many

million pounds of Canadian-grown tobacco are now exported annually to
Great Britain. The value of Canadian
exports of tobacco leaf have increased
from about $200 in 1890 to more than
$2,000,000 in 1936. See J. E. T. Mus-
grave, *Canadian tobacco* (Can. Geog.
Journal, 1934). For statistical details,
see the *Canada Year Book*.

Tobacco Nation, the name of an
Iroquoian tribe which was akin to the
Hurons and Neutrals, but remained
outside these confederacies of tribes.
In 1640 it had nine villages in what are
now the counties of Grey and Simcoe,
in Ontario; but like the Hurons and
Neutrals it was partially exterminated
in 1649 by the Iroquois. The name by
which the tribe was known arose from
the fact that it grew and traded tobacco
in large quantities. It was also known
as the Petun tribe, and as the Tionontati. The remnants of the tribe were
ultimately absorbed in what were known
as the Wyandot (q.v.).

Tobermory, a village in Bruce county, Ontario, at the northern end of the
Bruce peninsula, 50 miles north-west
of Wiarton, the nearest railway station.
It has saw-mills. Pop. (1935), 250.

Tobique river, a tributary of the St.
John river, in Restigouche, Northumberland, and Victoria counties, New Brunswick. It rises in Nictor lake, Restigouche
county, and flows in a south-westerly
direction to its entry into the St. John,
about 50 miles above Woodstock. It
was probably named after an Indian
chief, Tobec, who lived at its mouth.
Its chief tributary consists of two
branches, the Campbell and Serpentine
rivers, which flow through very rugged
country and unite 10 miles before their
entry into the Tobique. Below this point
of junction the Tobique flows through
a rich and fertile country. For about
2 miles from its discharge, it flows with
great rapidity through a rocky gorge.
Its banks are wooded with red pine, and
present some of the most picturesque

TOBACCO CULTURE

scenery in the province. It abounds with salmon and trout of the largest size. The Tobique is 62 miles in length from the entry of the Campbell to its mouth.

Tobique Valley Railway, a short line of railway opened in 1893 between Perth Junction and Plaster Rock, in New Brunswick. It was leased to the Canadian Pacific Railway in 1897. See *Report of the Public Accounts Committee with reference to the Tobique Valley Railway* (Ottawa, 1895).

Tod, John (1791-1882), fur-trader, was born at Lochleven, Dumbartonshire, Scotland, in 1791. He entered the service of the Hudson's Bay Company and was for many years in charge of the Thompson River district in British Columbia. He retired from the company in 1849, and he was a member of the first council of Vancouver Island. He died at Victoria, British Columbia, on August 31, 1882.

Todatorn lake is on the boundary between Manitoba and the North West Territories. It has an area of 241 square miles, of which 156 are in Manitoba and 85 in the North West Territories.

Todd, Alpheus (1821-1884), librarain, was born in London, England, on July 30, 1821, the son of Henry Cooke Todd (q.v.). He came to Canada with his family in 1832, and in 1836 was employed as an assistant in the Library of the House of Assembly of Upper Canada. In 1841 he was appointed assistant librarian to the Legislative Assembly of Canada, and in 1854 librarian. In 1870 he was placed in charge of the Parliamentary Library at Ottawa; and he occupied this position until his death at Ottawa on January 22, 1884. In 1881 he was created a C.M.G., and he was given the degree of LL.D. by both Queen's University and McGill University. Though self-educated, he became the leading authority of his day on the law and custom of the Canadian constitution. He was the author of *The*

practice and privileges of the two houses of parliament (Toronto, 1839); *Brief suggestions in regard to the formation of local governments for Upper and Lower Canada, in connection with a federal union of the British North American provinces* (Ottawa, 1866); *On parliamentary government in England* (2 vols., London, 1867); *A constitutional governor* (Ottawa, 1878); and *Parliamentary government in the British Colonies* (Boston 1880). See E. R. Cameron, *Alpheus Todd* (Canadian Bar Review, 1925).

Todd, Henry Cooke (d. 1862), author, was born in England, and was educated at Oxford University. He came to Canada with his family in 1832, and he died in 1862. He published, under the pen-name of "A Traveller", *Notes upon Canada and the United States, from 1832 to 1840, much in a small space, or a great deal in a little book* (Toronto, 1840); and, under the pen-name of "One in Retirement", *Items (in the life of an usher) on travel, anecdote, and popular errors* (Quebec, 1855).

Tofield, a town in the Vegreville district of Alberta, on the Tofield-Calgary branch of the Canadian National Railway (of which it is the terminus), 45 miles north-east of Edmonton. It was named after Dr. James H. Tofield, an early homesteader from Edmonton, and was incorporated as a town in 1909. It is the centre of a grain-growing and dairy-farming district, and there are coal-mines in the vicinity. It has a weekly newspaper (*Mercury*). Pop. (1931), 497.

Toledo, a village in Leeds county, Ontario, 20 miles north-west of Brockville, and 8 miles south-west of Jasper, the nearest railway station. It was named after Toledo in Spain at the time of the Peninsular Wars. Pop. (1935), 400.

Tolmie, William Fraser (1812-1886), chief factor of the Hudson's Bay Company, was born at Inverness, Scotland, on February 3, 1812. He studied medicine at the University of Glasgow (M.D., 1832), and entered the service of the Hudson's Bay Company as a surgeon. He arrived at Fort Vancouver, British Columbia, in 1833; and from that date until his retirement in 1870 occupied various posts in the service of the company on the Pacific slope. In 1843 he became chief factor of the company's posts on Puget Sound; in 1855 he was chief factor at Fort Nisqually; and in 1859 a member of the Hudson's Bay Company board of management at Victoria. From 1861 to 1866 he was a member of the Legislative Assembly of Vancouver Island; and from 1874 to 1878 he represented the district of Victoria in the Legislative Assembly of British Columbia. In 1870 he took up farming, and he was the first to introduce thoroughbred stock into British Columbia. He died at Victoria, Vancouver island, on December 8, 1886. In 1850 he married Jane, eldest daughter of John Work (q.v.); and by her he had seven sons and five daughters. One son, Simon Fraser Tolmie (d. 1937), became prime minister of British Columbia. He was much interested in the ethnology and linguistics of the Pacific coast Indians; and, with George M. Dawson (q.v.), he published *Comparative vocabularies of the Indian tribes of British Columbia* (Montreal, 1884). Part of his diary for 1833 has been published by E. S. Meany (Washington Historical Quarterly, 1932).

Tomison, William (*fl.* 1739-1811), fur-trader, was born in South Ronaldshay, an island of the Orkney group, in 1739, and was apprenticed to the Hudson's Bay Company in 1760. In 1767 he was sent inland to lake Winnipeg to counteract the influence on the Indians of the "Canada pedlars", and for over a third of a century he was foremost among the Hudson's Bay Company's servants in combating the encroachments of the traders from Canada. In 1777 he was placed in charge of Cumber-

land House; and in 1786 he was appointed "inland chief" from York Factory. He returned to England in 1811, and would appear to have died not long afterwards. See R. H. G. Leveson Gower, *William Tomison* (Beaver, 1934).

Tompkins, a village in the Maple Creek district of Saskatchewan, on the main line of the Canadian Pacific Railway, 55 miles south-west of Swift Current. It is in a farming district, and has a weekly newspaper (*Progress*). Pop. (1931), 379.

Tonty, or **Tonti, Henri de** (1650?-1704), explorer, was born at Gaeta, Italy, about 1650, the son of Lorenzo Tonty, or Tonti, an Italian banker who invented the "tontine". He entered the French army in 1668. In 1677 he lost his right hand in an action in Sicily, whence came his nickname of "Main-de-Fer". In 1678 he was recommended to La Salle (q.v.) as a lieutenant in his explorations, and he served under La Salle until the death of the latter in 1687. He remained in the Illinois country until the year 1700, and then he placed himself in the service of Iberville (q.v.) in Louisiana. He died at Mobile, Louisiana, in September, 1704. See B. Sulte, *Les Tonty* (Trans. Roy. Soc. Can., 1893); Henry E. Legler, *Chevalier Henry de Tonty* (Parkman Club Publications, No. 3, Milwaukee, 1896); and P. Margry, *Relations et mémoires inédites* (Paris, 1865).

Toothwort, or Pepper-root (*Dentaria diphylla* Michx., *Cruciferae*), a perennial herb growing in damp woodlands. It is developed from a long fleshy crinkled rootstock, which has a pleasant pungent taste. The stem is stout, and bears 2 opposite compound leaves, the leaflets are oblong-ovate and coarsely toothed. The white flowers are in loose clusters, the 4 petals twice as long as the sepals. It extends from eastern Quebec to southern Ontario, blooming in April and May. The root tastes like water cress, and may be used in place of it.

Torbrook, a village in Annapolis county, Nova Scotia, 3 miles from Wilmot, the nearest railway station, and 8 miles from Kingston. Pop. (1935), 750.

Tornado mountain is in the Rocky mountains, on the boundary between British Columbia and Alberta, at the head of Tornado creek, in lat. 49° 58′. It has an altitude of 10,169 feet. Adjoining it is the Tornado pass.

Toronto, the capital of the province of Ontario, with a population (including greater Toronto) of over 850,000, is situated on the north shore of lake Ontario about forty miles from its western extremity. The natural entrance to the Huron country, from which region it derives its name, Toronto was barred to the French by the hostility of the Iroquois, but soon became after the expulsion of the Hurons and the opening of lake Ontario an important centre of the fur-trade. Various meanings have been assigned to the name: "place of meeting", "trees in the water", "lake opening", all more or less conjectural. The name has also been traced to that of Atironta, chief of the Arendaronons, to the word Arendaronons itself, of which Lahontan's *Torontogueronons* is a variant, and to the word *Tarontorai*, meaning "between the lakes". The name "Tarantou" appears for the first time on Sanson's map of 1656.

The advantages of its situation made Teiaiagon (the crossing), the Seneca village of the seventeenth century, on the site of the city of Toronto, a place of importance; the trail along the north shore from Montreal to the Mississippi crossed at this point the trail to Michillimackinac. Traders and explorers from Montreal and Albany were frequent visitors at Teiaiagon and when the Missisauga about 1690 replaced the Iroquois, the trade continued to follow the old routes and became firmly established at the mouth of the Toronto or Humber river. A century later roads and railways followed the aboriginal trails,

and when schooners and steamboats replaced the canoe they found the commodious harbour at Toronto the best shelter on the lake. Toronto is to-day the natural entrance to the vast regions of northern Ontario, with which it communicates directly by highways, railways, and aeroplane, and is well adapted by its central situation to claim a large share of transcontinental aerial traffic.

The first settlement on the site of the city of Toronto was that of the Sulpician missionary Père Joseph Mariet at Teiaiagon in the latter part of the seventeenth century. "La grace de Saint-Sulpice est la vie caché", and little is known of this episode. Between 1720 and 1730 there was a trading post known as "le poste du fond du lac" or "le poste de Toronto" for the trade with the Missisauga; this was a dependency of Fort Niagara. About the same time the name Toronto is to be found in the plural form "Torontaux", since there were three trails in the neck of land between lake Simcoe and lake Ontario running respectively to the mouths of the Humber, the Don, and the Rouge rivers. In 1750, acting under instructions from La Jonquière (q.v.) the Sieur de Portneuf built a small fort on the banks of the Toronto river (the Humber). This fort bore the name of Fort Toronto; and since it proved quite inadequate to the trade, a new and larger building was constructed during the winter of 1750 and 1751 some three miles to the east, on the point of land forming the entrance to the harbour. This second fort (the fourth French settlement at Toronto), called Fort Rouillé in honour of the French minister, continued to be known commonly as Fort Toronto. In 1759 Fort Toronto was burned by the commandant Captain Alexandre Douville, and Sir William Johnson (q.v.) immediately took possession. In 1787, on the suggestion of the fur-traders in Montreal and of the Chevalier de Rocheblave (q.v.) Lord

11

Dorchester (q.v.) purchased from the Missisauga's land at Toronto, and on both sides of the communication to lake Huron, with the intention of diverting the route from Montreal to the west. In 1788 a town plot was surveyed, but the project was deferred and actual settlement was delayed till 1793, when Governor Simcoe (q.v.) garrisoned the place, laid off a new town, changed the name to York in honour of the Duke of York and explored the communication. The fur-traders of the North West Company did not resume their project until the eve of the War of 1812; and by 1825 the North West Company had ceased to exist, and the Montreal trade had been ruined.

On February 27, 1798, Simcoe wrote to the Duke of Portland that York was to become for the present the seat of government, and that plans had been made for buildings for the use of the legislature, which met for the first time in York in 1797. Alone in the wilderness, with no neighbouring settlements east or west, York grew slowly. There were twelve houses in the little village in June, 1797, and at the outbreak of the War of 1812 the population did not exceed 800. Simcoe's York consisted originally of ten four-acre blocks. Simcoe, who favoured an aristocracy had distributed all the land north of these as far as the third concession among officials of the government and personal friends; special streets in York were reserved for inferior trades. The Yonge street settlement on the other hand was to be open to all loyal settlers, and was soon occupied. Simcoe also favoured an established church, but his efforts to obtain a resident clergyman were unsuccessful. York had no settled incumbent till the arrival of the Rev. George Okill Stuart (q.v.) in 1800, and no church building of any kind till 1807; the Yonge street settlement early became the scene of the activities of the Methodist circuit riders, and to this

region many of those who had at first settled in York removed. Society in York was composed of government officials and their wives, the officers attached to the garrison, professional men and the more successful merchants and became brilliant for a brief period during the residence of the French émigrés at Windham. Little York was the object of much ridicule and jealousy for the first twenty years of its existence, but in spite of unpaved and muddy streets it soon assumed some of the characteristics of a capital. It was from York that Sir Isaac Brock (q.v.) set out during the War of 1812 for the capture of Detroit and the battle of Queenston Heights. In 1813 the town was occupied by the Americans, and the government buildings were burned.

Between the conclusion of the War of 1812 and the Rebellion of 1837 immigration into Upper Canada increased. In 1834 with a population of 9,254 York was incorporated as a city with William Lyon Mackenzie (q.v.) as its first mayor, and the name was changed again to Toronto. At this time the control of the government was largely in the hands of the "Family Compact", most of whose members resided in Toronto, which now became the centre of the agitations preceding the Rebellion. With such leaders as Strachan (q.v.), Ryerson (q.v.), and Mackenzie it is not surprising that collisions of opinion were frequent and violent; responsible government and religious equality were debated with great earnestness. Toronto had many citizens who favoured reform, but few who supported republicanism. The battle of Montgomery's tavern in 1837 and the execution of Lount and Matthews extinguished the movement in the direction of separation from the Empire, but proved the prelude to a new basis of colonial administration.

With the Act of Union in 1840 and the consequent removal of the capital to Kingston, Toronto suffered a de-

TORONTO, ONTARIO: THE DOWNTOWN SECTION

VIEWS OF THE CANADIAN NATIONAL EXHIBITION, TORONTO, ONTARIO

pression. On the return of the government in 1849, with the building of railways and the conclusion of the Reciprocity Treaty with the United States, prosperity revived. During the Civil War in the United States, Toronto became the place of residence of many refugees from the South. Under Confederation in 1867 a new era began; the province of Ontario replaced Upper Canada, and the provincial government was finally re-established in its original seat. With the extension of the province northward to Hudson bay and westward to the borders of Manitoba, Toronto has become the capital of an area twice as large as the combined area of France and Germany, containing a population of more than a quarter of the inhabitants of the Dominion. During the seventy years since Confederation the city has gradually extended itself over a wide area. With 571 miles of streets, Toronto occupies 34 square miles with a frontage of 15 miles on lake Ontario, extending from Scarborough heights on the east to beyond the mouth of the Humber on the west. The island which forms the harbour has been reserved for residences and public parks and has now become the site of a new air port. The lake beaches east and west of the city provide unique facilities for bathing. The city occupies a level area sloping gently back to an escarpment of some height about three miles from the lake shore. The Don river on the east and the Humber on the west intersect this region with picturesque ravines; north of this escarpment lie the newer parts of the city, where many beautiful residences are a proof of the wealth which has in recent years poured into Toronto from the mining region of northern Ontario. Toronto has one hundred and six park and playground areas and three zoological collections of great interest. High Park is a region of over four hundred acres maintained as nearly as possible in its natural state. Three race-courses, base-ball grounds,

and the Maple Leaf Gardens (with a capacity of 13,500 seats) provide for varied amusements. The annual Skating Club Carnival is unrivalled.

Foremost among the educational institutions of the city is the University of Toronto, the state university of the province founded in 1827 under the name of King's College and placed under the direction of the Church of England. Freed from ecclesiastical control in 1850, the University of Toronto is now a non-sectarian degree-conferring body, including a number of federated and affiliated universities and colleges, of which Victoria College (United Church of Canada), Trinity College (Anglican), and St. Michael's College (Roman Catholic), as well as University College, give instruction in courses leading to degrees in Arts. There are also affiliated theological colleges and professional schools giving instruction in medicine, dentistry, engineering, applied science, mining engineering, architecture, music, forestry, social science, agriculture, and a variety of other subjects. The buildings of the University are numerous and well equipped, and include among the more recent additions an observatory which contains one of the largest telescopes in the world. Important contributions to the progress of science have been made in the various laboratories, more especially the discovery of insulin by Sir Frederick Banting and the preparation of serums and vaccines in the Connaught Laboratories. Closely associated with the University are the Royal Ontario Museum, one of the largest museums in America, which possesses many unique collections, and the Toronto General Hospital, a thoroughly modern institution. The library of the University and the Toronto Public Library are modern and efficient.

Secondary education in Toronto began with the founding of the Toronto Grammar School in 1807 and Upper Canada College in 1827. Free schooling in primary schools dates from 1850. There are now about 150 public and separate (Roman Catholic) schools of all kinds, with an annual estimated expenditure of more than $40,000,000. This expenditure is administered by a Board of Trustees elected annually by the citizens; a separate board is elected by the Roman Catholic ratepayers. There are also a number of private residential schools.

Toronto is also the musical and artistic centre of the Dominion. The Conservatory of Music, founded in 1886, is now included in the faculty of music of the University of Toronto, and with a staff of notable artists and musicians under the principalship of Sir Ernest Macmillan enjoys a wide reputation. The Mendelsshon Choir, which gave its first concert in 1895, has brought choral singing to a high pitch of excellence, and has given concerts in conjunction with all the great American orchestras, in Canadian and American cities. The Hart House quartette and the Conservatory quartette have made chamber music popular. During the winter a series of concerts is given by the Toronto Orchestra, and during the summer promenade concerts by a full orchestra under the direction of Reginald Stewart attract large audiences. A musical competition and the singing of a chorus of two thousand voices form part of the annual Canadian National Exhibition.

The Ontario Society of Artists, with headquarters in Toronto, was founded in 1872, and is the oldest body of its kind in the Dominion. The Ontario College of Art, now in its sixtieth year, has provided training for many Canadian artists. The Toronto Art Gallery, which is the finest in the Dominion, was opened in 1916; exhibitions of old masters and modern painters are held throughout the year. An original contribution to the progress of art in Canada has been made by the efforts of a group of local artists known as "the Group of Seven". W. S. Allward, Tom Thomson (q.v.), Sir Wyly Grier, Lawren Harris, A. Y. Jackson are among the more eminent of Toronto's painters and sculptors. The School of Architecture established in the University of Toronto in 1890 is the oldest in the Empire, and Toronto possesses many beautiful buildings in varied styles: University College, St. James Cathedral, Osgoode Hall, the Bank of Commerce, and the Union Station may be mentioned among public buildings; and examples of good architecture are numerous among the private homes of the citizens. "Casa Loma", the palatial chateau erected by Sir Henry Pellatt on the escarpment overlooking the city, is now public property; the wonders of this enormous structure attract thousands of tourists.

In the last decades of the nineteenth century, Toronto possessed the highest steeple in America. The spire of St. James and the Norman tower of University College no longer dominate the horizon; in their place the eye is carried upward by the soaring structures of the Bank of Commerce and the Royal York Hotel, the loftiest buildings of their class in the British Empire. Toronto is still, however, a city of churches, among which may be mentioned St. Paul's (Anglican), which with its huge organ and richly decorated windows approaches a cathedral rather than a parish church; St. Michael's Cathedral (Roman Catholic), which for many years possessed the largest stained glass window in America; the Metropolitan Church (United Church of Canada); and Yorkminster (Baptist). There are over three hundred church buildings in Toronto, which is an archiepiscopal see of both Anglican and Roman Catholic Churches, and the residence at the moment of the primate of All Canada of the English Church in Canada; it is also the headquarters of the United Church of Canada and a stronghold of other religious denominations, including the Salvation Army. The Anglican Church is the most numerous, with a membership of over 190,000; the United Church of Canada has over 118,000, and is followed by the Presbyterians, the Roman Catholics, the Jews, and the Baptists in the order named. The influence of the Orange Order established in Toronto for over a hundred years is very strong, and the annual procession of the Order on the twelfth of July is only rivalled by the parade of the Roman Catholic Society of the Holy Name. It should be noted that Toronto is an English-speaking city, where the foreign element is relatively small.

Every year in the end of August the Canadian National Exhibition is held in Toronto. Tracing its history to the early days of Governor Simcoe, this institution began as an itinerant fair held in successive years at various points in the province; in 1879 it became the Toronto Industrial Exhibition, with permanent headquarters at Toronto; in 1912 it assumed the name of the Canadian National Exhibition. Originally intended for the encouragement of agriculture, industry, and the arts in a young country, the Exhibition has expanded in all directions, embracing all the countries of the British Empire, as well as many of the leading agricultural and industrial countries of the world. A special park is reserved on the lakeshore for its use; more than $21,000,000 are invested in grounds and equipment; the variety of exhibits and entertainment provided is very great; the attendance in a single year has been as high as two millions. The Canadian National Exhibition returns an annual surplus to the city of Toronto and is maintained without cost to the citizens. As an annual exhibition it has no rival. In November of each year a second fair known as the Royal Agricultural Fair is held in special buildings in Exhibition Park; this fair is devoted to agriculture and live-stock of all kinds and to industries allied to agriculture; it includes a horse-show and a dog-show,

and has now grown to international importance.

Under the direction of the Toronto harbour commissioners, commencing in 1914, the water-front of the city for a distance of seven miles has been transformed; nearly 45,000 lineal feet of wharves have been constructed, with navigable depth ranging from 22 to 26 feet; an excellent but inadequate harbour has become one of the most modern and efficient on the Great lakes; Toronto now ranks third in cargo tonnage among Canadian lake and seaports; and it is anticipated that with the deepening of the St. Lawrence canals Toronto will become an ocean port in reality. This work has been accomplished with the cooperation of the Dominion government. Much valuable land suitable for parks and industrial purposes has been reclaimed; a splendid highway has been constructed for the distance of seven miles along the water-front, and an amusement section known as Sunnyside Beach, with accommodation for nearly 8,000 bathers and amusement devices of all kinds, has been added to the city's numerous places of recreation. A breakwater provides a sheltered course for aquatic contests always popular since the days of Edward Hanlon (q.v.) in Toronto. The Yacht Club on the island is the centre of great activity in yachting and dinghy sailing. The Argonaut Rowing Club frequently competes at Henley.

Financially, commercially, and industrially Toronto occupies a leading position; it is the headquarters of five of the ten chartered banks in the Dominion, the Canadian Bank of Commerce, the Bank of Toronto, the Dominion Bank, the Bank of Nova Scotia, and the Imperial Bank; of several of the largest Insurance Companies, including the Canada Life, the Manufacturers' Life, the Confederation Life, and the North American Life. Toronto has the largest mining exchange in the world, and has recently opened a new stock exchange, which is regarded as the most perfectly equipped building of its kind in existence. Toronto has more than 2,627 manufacturing establishments, is the headquarters of the Canadian Manufacturers' Association, and is the centre of the automobile industry in Canada. The departmental stores conducted by the T. Eaton Company and the Robert Simpson Company are amongst the largest of their kind in existence, and have secured by means of branches in other cities of the Dominion a very large proportion of the Canadian retail trade. Through the Toronto Hydro-Electric System, which is owned by the municipality, electric power is distributed for industrial purposes and illumination at an unusually low rate. Through the Toronto Transportation Commission the city owns and operates its own street railways within the municipality and bus lines radiating to long distances in the surrounding country.

Bibliography. Many books have been written about the history of Toronto. The chief general accounts are H. Scadding, *Toronto of old* (Toronto, 1873); J. Timperlake, *Illustrated Toronto, past and present* (Toronto, 1877); W. Canniff, *Atlas of York county* (Toronto, 1878), C. P. Mulvany, *Toronto, past and present* (Toronto, 1884); G. Mercer Adam, *Toronto, old and new* (Toronto, 1891); J. E. Middleton, *The municipality of Toronto: A history* (3 vols., Toronto, 1923); Blodwen Davies, *Storied York* (Toronto, 1931); E. C. Guillet, *Toronto from trading-post to great city* (Toronto, 1934); T. A. Reed, *The story of Toronto* (Ont. Hist. Soc., papers and records, 1934); A. H. Young, *Toronto: How and why it grew* (Ont. Hist. Soc., papers and records, 1934). A vast collection of material relating to the history of Toronto is to be found in J. Ross Robertson, *The landmarks of Toronto* (6 vols., Toronto, 1894-1914); and books dealing with special phases of Toronto's history are Percy J. Robinson, *Toronto*

during the French régime (Toronto, 1934); James Edmund Jones, *Pioneer crimes and punishments in Toronto and the Home district* (Toronto, 1924); Alden G. Meredith, *Mary's Rosedale and gossip of little York* (Toronto, 1928); O. C. J. Withrow, *The romance of the Canadian National Exhibition* (Toronto, 1937); and W. S. Wallace, *A history of the University of Toronto* (Toronto, 1927).

Toronto and Nipissing Railway, a line of railway opened in 1872 between Toronto and Coboconk, Ontario. In 1877 it acquired a line from Stouffville to Jackson's Point on lake Simcoe, built by the Lake Simcoe Junction Railway Company. It was acquired by the Midland Railway in 1882, and by the Grand Trunk Railway in 1884.

Toronto, Grey, and Bruce Railway, a line built between Toronto and Owen Sound, Ontario, as a through line for traffic from lake Superior, during the years 1871-4, with branch lines from Orangeville to Arthur, and from Arthur to Teeswater. It was leased in 1883 to the Ontario and Quebec Railway, and in 1884 to the Canadian Pacific Railway.

Toronto, Hamilton, and Buffalo Railway. This railway company was incorporated by Act of the legislature of Ontario in 1884, and in 1891 by Act of the parliament of Canada. It was authorized to build lines in Ontario from Welland to Hamilton, from Hamilton to Brantford, and from Hamilton to Toronto. The road from Hamilton to Brantford was completed in 1895, and that from Hamilton to Welland in 1896; but the line from Hamilton to Toronto has not been built, except a section of 1½ miles from Hamilton to a junction with the Canadian National Railways, north of the Desjardins canal, known as the Toronto extension, which is leased to the Canadian Pacific Railway. A line built by the Brantford, Waterloo, and Lake Erie Railway from Brantford to Waterford was acquired by the Toronto,

Hamilton, and Buffalo Railway in 1892; and another line, built by the Erie and Ontario Railway Company from Smithville to Port Maitland was acquired in 1914. The entire stock of the Toronto, Hamilton, and Buffalo Railway is now owned by the New York Central Railroad and the Canadian Pacific Railway; but the company has always been, and still is, operated as an independent railway.

Toronto, University of. See **University of Toronto.**

Torrington, Frederic Herbert (1837-1917), musician, was born at Dudley, Worcestershire, England, on October 20, 1837. He came to Canada in 1857, and settled in Montreal. From 1869 to 1873 he was organist of King's Chapel, Boston, Massachusetts; but in 1873 he returned to Canada as organist and choirmaster of the Metropolitan Church, Toronto. In 1886 he organized the first musical festival in Toronto; and in 1888 he founded the Toronto College of Music. He died in Toronto on November 19, 1917. In 1902 he was honoured by the University of Toronto with the degree of Mus. Doc.

Totem, a term denoting, among the North American Indians, the tutelary spirit or guardian of an individual or of a group of individuals, such as a clan or tribe, and hence the name, crest, brand, or symbol of an individual or a group of individuals. "One part of the religious superstition of the savages," wrote John Long (q.v.) in his *Voyages and travels*, "consists in each of them having his *totem*, or favourite spirit, which he believes watches over him. This *totem* they conceive assumes the shape of some beast or other." The word is derived from the Algonkian *ototeman*, signifying "kinship" or "consanguinity", and has reference to the fact that the totem was usual¹y the badge of a clan or tribe, known consequently as the tribe of the Bear, or some such animal. Among the Indians

of the north Pacific coast, the practice existed (and still exists) of erecting totem-poles—tall cedar poles elaborately carved with representations of tutelary spirits. See W. M. Halliday, *Potlatch and totem* (London, 1935); and *Handbook of Indians of Canada* (Ottawa, 1913).

Tottenham, a village in Simcoe county, Ontario, on the Nottawasaga river, and on the Canadian National and Canadian Pacific Railways, 40 miles north of Toronto. The first store was opened in 1835, and the post-office in 1858; and the name was given in honour of Alexander Totten, the owner of the store, who was instrumental in obtaining the post-office. The village was incorporated in 1884. It is in an agricultural and dairying district, and has three grain elevators, a continuation school, and a weekly newspaper (*Sentinel*). Pop. (1931), 566.

Touch-me-not, or Jewel-weed (*Impatiens biflora* Walt., *Balsamaceae*), a smooth herb with crisp succulent stems, oval to ovate, coarsely-toothed leaves, and nodding orange-coloured flowers, thickly spotted with reddish brown. The flowers are irregular in shape; the sepals are 4 in number, the anterior one notched, the posterior one, the largest, forming a spurred sac; the petals are 2, 2-lobed. The fruit is a pod, which bursts elastically when touched and discharges the seeds with considerable force, giving the plant its common name. It grows in cedar swamps and along streams from New England westward, blossoming from July to September.

Tourmaline, a rock-forming mineral found chiefly near the margin of masses of granite, in pegmatites, or in crystalline limestone. It is a complex silicate containing boron and aluminium with other metals. Three types are recognized: iron tourmaline, which is usually nearly black in colour; lithia tourmaline, which is usually pink or green; and magnesia tourmaline, which is commonly brown. The iron tourmaline occurs in granitic rocks and in pegmatites. The lithia tourmaline is confined almost entirely to pegmatitic masses, while the magnesia tourmaline is found in crystalline limestone. The mineral is usually crystallized in prismatic crystals which commonly exhibit a roughly triangular cross section. It is strongly pyroelectric. Several varieties which are based on differences in colour are used as gems, the pink being known as rubellite, the green as Brazilian emerald, the blue as indicolite, and the brown as dravite.

Towhee, the name applied to a bird, somewhat smaller than a robin, which is a member of the sparrow family, *Fringillidae.* It is a phonetic spelling of the notes of the species, as is also another name in common use, namely, "chewink". The red-eyed towhee (*Pipilo erythrophthalmus*) is an inhabitant of the edges or brushy hillsides of the southern forests along the settled fringe of Canada. Other species occur in the west.

Townley, Adam (1808-1887), clergyman and author, was born in England on February 11, 1808, became a Methodist minister in Lower Canada in 1833, and in 1840 became a clergyman of the Church of England in Canada. In his later years he was rector at Paris, Ontario; and here he died on February 11, 1887. He was the author of *Ten letters addressed to the Hon. W. H. Draper, M.P.P., on the Church and church establishments*, by an Anglo-Canadian (Toronto, 1839), *Denominational* schools (Toronto, 1853), *Seven letters on the non-religious common school system of Canada and the United States* (Toronto, 1853), *The sacerdotal tithe* (New York, 1856), *A report on ministerial incomes* (London, Canada West, 1859), *A letter to the lord bishop of Huron in personal vindication* (Brantford, 1862), and *Plain explanations* (Toronto, 1862 and 1865).

Townshend, Sir Charles James (1844-1924), chief justice of Nova Scotia (1907-15), was born at Amherst, Nova Scotia, on March 22, 1844, the son of the Rev. Canon Townshend and Elizabeth Stewart. He was educated at King's College, Windsor, Nova Scotia (B.A., 1863; B.C.L., 1872; D.C.L., 1908), and was called to the bar of Nova Scotia in 1866 (Q.C., 1881). He practised law at Amherst; and he represented Cumberland in the Legislative Assembly of Nova Scotia from 1878 to 1884, and in the Canadian House of Commons from 1884 to 1887. From 1878 to 1882 he was also a minister without portfolio in the provincial government. In 1887 he was appointed a puisne judge of the Supreme Court of Nova Scotia; and in 1907 he became chief justice of this court. He retired from the bench in 1915, and he died at Wolfville, Nova Scotia, on June 16, 1924. He was twice married, (1) in 1877 to Laura (d. 1884), daughter of J. D. Kinnear, and (2) in 1887 to Margaret, daughter of John Macfarlane. He was created a knight bachelor in 1911. He contributed a number of historical papers to the *Collections* of the Nova Scotia Historical Society.

Townshend, George, Marquis, (1724-1807), soldier, was born on February 28, 1724, the eldest son of the third Viscount Townshend. He entered the British army at an early age, and he saw active service at the battles of Dettingen, Fontenoy, and Culloden. When the expedition under Wolfe (q.v.) was sent to Canada in 1758, he was appointed one of Wolfe's brigadiers; and after the death of Wolfe on the Plains of Abraham in 1759, the command of the British forces in Canada devolved upon him. He returned to England, however, in the autumn of 1759, leaving General Murray (q.v.) in command. He rose to the rank of field marshal in the army, and master-general of ordnance. In 1767 he succeeded his father as fourth Viscount

Townshend; and in 1787 he was created a marquis. He died on September 14, 1807. He was twice married, (1) in 1851 to Lady Charlotte Compton (d. 1770), daughter of the Earl of Northampton, and (2) in 1773 to Anne, daughter of Sir William Montgomery, Bart., by whom he had a large family. See Sir C. V. F. Townshend, *The military life of Field-Marshal George, first Marquess Townshend* (London, 1901).

Tracadie, a village in Antigonish county, Nova Scotia, at the head of George bay, and on the Canadian National Railway, 18 miles from Antigonish. The name is a corruption of the Micmac *Tulakadik,* meaning "camping ground." It is chiefly a fishing village. Pop. (1931), 750.

Tracadie, a village in Gloucester county, New Brunswick, at the mouth of the Little Tracadie river, on the gulf of St. Lawrence, and on the Canadian National Railway, 24 miles south of Caraquet. The name is a corruption of the Micmac *Tulakadik,* meaning "camping ground". The name is found as early as 1686. Pop. (1931), 500.

Tracadie river, a stream in the northeasthern New Brunswick, falls into the gulf of St. Lawrence, 20 miles north of Miramichi bay. It is about 50 miles long.

Tracey, Daniel (1795-1832), physician and journalist, was born in Roscrea, Tipperary county, Ireland, in May, 1795, the son of Michael Tracey, a merchant. He was educated at Trinity College, Dublin, and after graduation studied medicine at the Royal College of Surgeons, Dublin. He practised medicine in Dublin for several years; but in 1825 he emigrated to Canada, and began the practice of medicine in Montreal. In 1828 he established the *Vindicator,* a Reform newspaper, and became its editor; and in May, 1832, he was elected to represent the west ward of Montreal in the Legislative Assembly of Lower

Canada. He died of cholera in Montreal on July 18, 1832. See E. J. Mullally, *Dr. Daniel Tracey* (pamphlet, Montreal, 1935).

Trachyte, a volcanic rock of porphyritic or felsitic texture, consisting essentially of orthoclase and one or more of biotite, hornblende, or augite.

Tracy, Alexandre de Prouville, Sieur de (1603-1670), lieutenant-general of the French territories in America (1663-7), was born in France in 1603, and became an officer in the French army. In 1663 he was appointed lieutenant-general of the French terrieries in North and South America; and he arrived in Canada in 1665, with military reinforcements to be employed against the Iroquois. In 1666 he made a successful expedition against the Iroquois, and thoroughly cowed them. He returned to France in 1667; and he then became, first, commandant at Dunkirk, and later governor of Château Trompette, the stronghold of Bordeaux. Here he died on April 28, 1670.

Trade, External. A young country, still in the stage of settlement, must depend for the accumulation of capital upon the exploitation of its natural resources through the medium of foreign trade, far more markedly than another which has advanced farther in its economic development. Such has always been, and still is to a large extent, the key to the evolution of Canadian economic life. With this goes an intense preoccupation in trade policies and tariff restrictions by other countries upon its exports and, conversely, the protection of infant industries against competition from countries stronger and more advanced industrially. The settler with little, or sometimes no capital, must perforce reap a crop as soon as possible in order to buy the actual necessities which he needs. He turns his hand therefore to what is easiest; in the early days of settlement to the fur trade. For his pelts he can get cash, as he can for the lumber which he cuts and the wheat he grows. A "cash crop" is of prime necessity, and the exploitation of natural resources goes ruthlessly on until the area of settlement is exhausted, when the settler moves farther to repeat the process. Thus, slowly but steadily, settlement pushes out along the paths which lead to quick returns, and population grows with the increase of trade that gives the capital without which no advance can be made. Such in a few words has been the history of Canada's foreign trade and will be, we may suppose, for some time to come. First the fur-trade; then lumber; then wheat; and to-day we are seeing the mineral resources exploited.

To go no further back than the first half of the nineteenth century, Canada, as a British colony, benefited from the preference she received under the Navigation Acts. From 1721 to 1809 Canadian lumber entered Great Britain free of duty, while that from the Baltic paid a heavy tax. During the wars with Napoleon Canadian lumbermen reaped a rich harvest, and from 1821 to 1840 the white pine of Canada provided 75 per cent. of British needs. In similar fashion Canadian wheat, after Huskisson had amended the Corn Law in 1825, paid a duty very substantially less than that from foreign countries, and in 1843 wheat and flour entered at a nominal duty of one shilling a quarter. This advantage led to a great increase of the milling industry in Montreal, American wheat being ground there and shipped as Canadian flour. But with the repeal of the Corn Laws in 1846, and the lowering of the preference on timber, furs, and potash, the advantages enjoyed were swept away, and a serious crisis ensued, which so dismayed Montreal business men that they even contemplated annexation to the United States. In 1854 through the efforts of the governor-general, Lord Elgin (q.v.), to allay the distress caused by the loss of

preference in British markets, a reciprocity treaty was effected with the United States, which granted free admission of Canadian products of farm, forest, and mine in exchange for access by American fishermen to the inshore fisheries of the Atlantic coast and entry of American ships to Canadian canals. The Crimean war, with higher prices for wheat in Great Britain, and later the civil war in the United States, both helped to encourage the Canadian exporter; but in 1866 the second heavy blow fell in the abrogation of the reciprocity treaty by the United States. With no preference for her products in British markets, and with those of the United States practically shut to her, Canada progressed but slowly, while her attempts to build up her own industries were thwarted by the competition of American manufacturers, who, in the elegant phraseology of the day, looked upon Canada as a "slaughter market," in which their products could be dumped at prices ruinous to Canadian manufacturers. The depression of 1873 hit Canada very hard, and it was with feelings closely akin to despair that, in 1879, the National Policy of high protection for industries was turned to by Sir John A. Macdonald (q.v.). At first the new policy seemed to bring prosperity; but in 1883 a further economic depression brought even greater difficulties, which lasted, with greater or less intensity, until 1896, and Canada went through the most trying times of her economic history, which turned to prosperity only with the opening of the West through the building of the Canadian Pacific Railway and the rise of prices at the end of the century. The total value of trade *per capita*, which had stood at $54.81 in 1873, had fallen to $33.87 in 1880. By 1890 it had reached $41.09, and not until 1899 had it almost reached the figure of twenty-seven years earlier at $54.53.

The turn of the century saw the great leap forward with the wheat of the prairies pouring into the markets of Europe. In the first decade the *per capita* trade increased from $64.19 to $93.91 and the coming of the Great War brought enormous increases, which touched the amazing figure of $300.60 in 1918. With Canada straining every effort to feed the allies with wheat at $2.50 a bushel, and with war orders of every kind at inflated prices to be filled, this figure is hardly to be wondered at. Although the recession after the war was severe both in volume and value due to lower prices, yet by 1929 the figure had climbed to $262.23. With the disastrous years of the great depression we will deal hereafter.

The Balance of Trade. In few countries other than Great Britain are the terms "favourable" and "unfavourable" balances of trade more misleading than in Canada. It is easy to understand how Great Britain can, year after year, buy more than she sells by reason of her great revenues from foreign investments and the carrying trade. But in the case of Canada no such explanation is possible, since both these items in her balance sheet are negligible. And yet up to the outbreak of war in 1914 Canada had a considerable "unfavourable" balance of trade, as the following figures will show.

CANADA'S BALANCE OF TRADE

Period	Excess of imports over exports	Excess of exports over imports
1868-79.....	$240 millions	
1880-81.....		$ 23 millions
1882-93.....	156 "	
1894-1903...		133 "
1904-1914...	113 "	
1915-19.....		1,803 "
1920.........	30 "	
1921-29.....		1,500 "
1930-36.....		1,134 "

The explanation is not far to seek. From 1868 to 1893, with the trifling exception of 1880-1, Canada had bought $373 millions worth of imports more

than she had sold in exports, in the form of all kinds of equipment for her factories, her railways, and all that was necessary for the building up of her national life. By 1894 this phase was temporarily over; the very great expenditure of the Canadian Pacific Railway development era were past, and for the next ten years Canada began to "cash in" on what she had so freely borrowed abroad. In 1904 began the next stage of railway development, the opening of the West, and the building of the other two transcontinental railways, and the balance of trade swung back to the "unfavourable" side once more. With the coming of the Great War, the whole scene was changed, and the enormous favourable balances that were occasioned by the war orders began. But even after the war, with the brief exception of 1920, when Canada was buying moderately abroad, the favourable balances continued. Summarizing, therefore, we find that in the sixty-two years from 1868 to 1930 Canada in balance has sold to the rest of the world over $4,000 million more in merchandise than she has bought. This fact explains the comparative ease with which heavy payments of interest on capital borrowed abroad are met year by year. It may be remarked, however, that in the long run these favourable balances constitute a passing phase in the economic evolution of a young country. They represent once more the familiar phenomenon of the "cash crop" of the settler. As Canada increases in population and consumes more of her own products, these favourable balances will sink, and the trade of the Dominion approach more nearly to that of countries which have long since emerged from the "pioneer" phase of their development. Several generations, however, may pass before that stage is reached.

Changes in Trade. During the first thirty years of the present century, it is but natural that changes should have taken place in the content of the foreign trade of Canada, the most striking of which was in its volume. Imports increased from $172 millions to $1,248 millions; exports from $183 millions to $1,128 millions. As betokening the increase in population and manufacturing, imports of coal increased from $11 to $57 millions; machinery from $5 to $69; crude petroleum from $23,244 to $51 millions; automobile parts from none to $35 millions; rolling mill products from $12 to $62 millions. These are but natural increases and the satisfaction of new wants. It is, however, in the exports that the most significant changes have taken place. Exports of wheat grew from $12 to $216 millions; newsprint paper from none to $145 millions; wood pulp from $2 to $45 millions; automobiles from none to $35 millions. The most remarkable change was in the export of base metals, iron, lead, zinc, copper, nickel, and aluminium, which grew in the aggregate from $2 to $106 millions; evidence, if any were needed, of the remarkable development of Canadian mineral resources.

One significant development has been the rising importance of the Pacific coast, which has followed largely, but not wholly, on the opening of the Panama Canal. Vancouver and other Pacific coast ports are open the whole year, while Montreal is closed in winter. Wheat can be stored and does not need quick transit; it is therefore becoming evident that, besides the movement of Canadian products to the Orient, there are possibilities in sending it to Europe through the Panama Canal. It is cheaper to ship wheat from western Saskatchewan *viâ* the Pacific route than to send it east by rail and lake freighter to the Atlantic seaboard.

The greatest problem in Canada's trade is the distance from the sea of the great wheat-producing prairies. Although her wheat is of unsurpassed excellence, it has to compete with cheap wheat from the Argentine and Australia, where the costs of getting it to tidewater are far less than in Canada. This has led to the formulation of two schemes for easier access to the sea from the prairies, the first already in existence, the Hudson Bay Railway, the second still unaccomplished, the project for deepening the St. Lawrence, and so allowing ocean-going vessels to load at Fort William and discharge at Liverpool. Of the first little can be said here, other than that the practicability of the route is still open to question from a commercial standpoint. The second is a gigantic scheme, in which international policies are involved and still are under consideration. Nature, with a fine impartiality, has given western Canada a soil and climate ideal for raising the finest wheat in the world and qualified this blessing by making the difficulties of transportation so great.

Whenever the world price of wheat rises to a figure at which Europe is unwilling to pay for the highest grade, countries where production costs are low and transportation much cheaper can compete successfully with the Canadian farmer, who is beaten in the world market. Such is, in a word, the problem that confronts the Canadian exporter and, so far, has proved insoluble.

The Depression. Canada, as depending largely for her prosperity upon her foreign trade, especially the export of raw products, was hard hit by the depression which followed on the collapse of the boom after 1929. From an all-time peak of total trade valued at $2,603 millions in 1923, it had fallen to $1,004 millions in 1933. Total imports fell to $401 millions as compared with the peak of $1,336 millions in 1920, while exports fell in 1932 to $544 millions as compared with $1,593 millions in 1917. The recovery was steady from the low of 1933, and total trade by 1936 had reached for imports $635 millions and exports $1,027 millions, almost precisely the same figures as for 1923.

Distribution of Trade. One of the most important aspects of Canadian trade is that of its distribution among the various countries of the world. The following tables exhibit the percentage of imports and exports from and to the United Kingdom and other parts of British Empire for various years.

PERCENTAGE OF TRADE WITH BRITISH EMPIRE

	Imports		Exports	
Year*	U.K.	Other Brit. Empire	U.K.	Other Brit. Empire
1886..	40.7	2.5	47.2	4.2
1906..	24.4	5.1	54.2	4.5
1921..	17.3	4.2	26.3	7.6
1930..	15.2	5.1	25.2	8.8
1935..	21.4	8.5	41.5	10.2

*Fiscal years.

It will be observed that up to 1930 the ratios of trade, both imports and exports, with Great Britain had steadily declined, while those of trade with other parts of the British Empire had slightly increased. This tendency of the proportion of Canadian trade with the United Kingdom to fall was noticeably reversed after the Imperial Conference at Ottawa in 1932, whereby preferences were given to trade within the Empire.

It will be readily seen from the above table that in exports in 1935, if the total percentage going to the British Empire was 51.7, that to foreign countries was 48.3, of which 34.1 per cent. went to the United States, and 14.2 to other foreign countries. This large proportion going to the United Kingdom is accounted for by the very large export of wheat, most of which goes to the British Isles. In imports, however, the proportion from the United States was 58.1 and from other foreign countries 12.0, together making 70.1 per cent. of all Canadian imports, while those from the British Empire were

only 29.9. This is not to be wondered at since the proximity of the United States, similarity in tastes and standards of living, all make for heavy purchases from that source. It is doubtful whether in the future these proportions will very much change.

The problems inherent in the foreign trade of Canada are formidable, perhaps even more so than those of other countries. If Canada wishes to build up her own industries, she must give them adequate safeguards against competition from other more economically advanced countries, which obviously means a system of high protection. But all trade, in the last analysis, is exchange of commodities, and if Canada is to sell to other countries she must also buy from them. The cry of the western provinces that they sell their wheat in the world market, but buy their manufactured necessities in a protected one, and that therefore both their selling and buying is dictated to them, is not without a good deal of justification. The problem of how to adjust the tariff so as to give protection to the manufacturing industries in the East without unduly burdening the West with high prices for their necessities is a delicate and complicated one, to which no final and complete answer can ever be given.

In conclusion, the following tables exhibit the values of the ten leading exports and imports for the calendar year 1936.

TEN PRINCIPAL EXPORTS

Wheat..................	$226,913,763
Newsprint paper.........	103,639,634
Gold bullion.............	71,488,985
Nickel..................	44,594,296
Planks and boards........	36,858,096
Meats..................	32,505,009
Copper bars, rods, etc.....	32,230,637
Wood pulp..............	31,246,695
Fish...................	24,022,548
Whiskey................	23,388,116

TEN PRINCIPAL IMPORTS, 1936

Crude petroleum	$39,954,488
Automobile parts	24,062,901
Raw cotton	19,337,081
Sugar for refining	17,584,838
Bituminous coal	16,377,129
Raw rubber	9,519,658
Tin plate	9,184,222
Worsted tops	6,042,681
Dyeing & tanning materials	5,837,764
Raw wool	5,309,533

Detailed statistics for the trade of Canada can be found in the *Canada Year Book* and in the numerous reports published by the Dominion Bureau of Statistics.

Traders' Bank of Canada was incorporated in 1884 by a group chiefly from Bowmanville, Ontario, which included Edmund G. Burk, John Carveth, Lt.-Col. Cubitt, and J. B. Fairburn. In 1894 the bank had a paid-up capital of $607,000. In the summer of 1912, after negotiations conducted by D. K. Ridout and A. E. Dyment of Toronto, the Traders' Bank was absorbed by the Royal Bank of Canada. The Royal Bank paid 3 shares of Royal Bank stock for 4 of Traders' Bank stock, at a value of $240 and $180 per their respective shares. At the time of the amalgamation, the Traders' Bank had assets of $53,000,000.

Trade Unions. See **Labour.**

Trail, a city in the Kootenay district of British Columbia, is situated on the Columbia river at the mouth of Trail creek. The townsite was located by Col. E. J. Topping, known as the "Father of Trail," and surveyed in 1891. The building of the Trail smelter, in 1895, by F. A. Heinze of Butte, Montana, was the cause of immediate and rapid settlement. The creek on which it is situated took its name from the trail from Hope to Fort Steele, completed in 1865 by Edgar Dewdney (q.v.); and Trail was adopted as the name of the town on its founding. It is served by the Canadian Pacific Rail-

way, and is located in the centre of one of the richest mining districts in the world, seven miles from Rossland and fifty miles south-west of Nelson. It is now the greatest smelting centre in Canada; and it has also a fertilizer plant and a sulphuric acid plant. Fruit-growing and ranching are carried on in the neighbourhood; and there is an evening newspaper (*Daily Times*). Pop. (1931), 7,573. See *Trail, B.C., a brief story of the history, etc.* (Trail Board of Trade, 1931), and P. H. Sheffield, *Trail metallurgical plant* (Can. Geog. Journal, 1932).

Trailing Arbutus. See **Arbutus.**

Traill, Mrs. Catherine Parr, *née* **Strickland** (1802-1899), author, was born in London, England, on January 9, 1802, the daughter of Thomas Strickland, of Reydon Hall, Suffolk. In 1832, she married Lieut. Thomas Traill, 21st Fusiliers, and with him emigrated to Canada, and settled near Rice lake, Ontario. Her first book was *The backwoods of Canada* (London, 1835; new ed., 1846); and this was followed by *Lady Mary and her nurse* (London, 1850), *The Canadian Crusoes* (London, 1852), afterwards published under the title *Lost in the backwoods; The female emigrant's guide* (Toronto, 1855), *Rambles in the Canadian forest* (London, 1859), *Pearls and pebbles, or The notes of an old naturalist* (Toronto, 1894), *Cot and cradle stories* (Toronto, 1895), and *Studies in plant life in Canada, or Gleanings from forest, lake, and plain* (Ottawa, 1885). She died at Lakefield, Ontario, on August 29, 1899.

Transcona, a town in Manitoba, 7 miles east of Winnipeg, on the Canadian Pacific and Canadian National Railways. The name is a combination of the words Trans-Canada and Strathcona. It is an important railway centre, having railway shops of the Canadian National Railway, employing several thousand men; and has two power stations, a tar works, a creosoting plant, a malting plant, grain elevators, and a weekly newspaper (*Eastern Manitoba News*). Pop. (1931), 5,747.

Transportation. The major force governing transportation in Canada has always been physical geography. Entrance to the country from the sea may be made on the east by the ports of the Maritime provinces or of the St. Lawrence, on the north by the ports of Hudson bay, and on the west by the ports of British Columbia. Along the southern frontier from the Atlantic to the Pacific innumerable gateways may be used, either by land or over the rivers and lakes. Once in the country, the distances are great enough to make transportation an expensive service; and this natural handicap has never been overcome by a compensating growth of population. Apart from distance, there exist obstacles, but none insurmountable. The rugged Canadian shield on the east is pierced by the St. Lawrence valley, available either for land or water transport. The mountains of British Columbia offer a more formidable barrier, but have been passed by every form of transportation. The extensive inland waterways throughout Canada have provided facilities for travel in every period of its history.

During the French régime, water transport was most commonly used both in Acadia and the St. Lawrence valley. In the former the inhabitants made use of the long coast-line for travel by boat for all but the most local affairs. In Canada proper, the technique of transportation was built up on the spread of the fur-trade toward the West and the craft known in Canada before the coming of Europeans. Of the latter the most valuable was the canoe made of birch-bark, a vessel which could be made anywhere within the area of birch trees, was light both to paddle and carry, and was not expensive. The French became as adept in the use of canoes as were the Indians who taught them. The St. Lawrence-Great-

lakes system allowed for canoe travel to the height of land near lake Superior, whence other lakes and rivers were followed to lake Winnipeg and so on to the Saskatchewan river.

At the end of the seventeenth century the employees of the Hudson's Bay Company also penetrated the same area from the ports of Hudson bay. For some years it was the policy of the company to trade with the Indians at the sea ports until competition with French traders forced them to establish posts inland. Henley House (q.v.) was thus built in 1741, but it was not until the late eighteenth century that this expansion was carried far. Both their own training and the character of the rivers flowing into Hudson bay led the English traders to utilize boats rather than canoes.

In the meanwhile, a system of transportation was being evolved for the settlements on the St. Lawrence. The river itself provided the readiest means of travel. Sailing vessels constantly plied between Quebec, the chief port of Canada, and Montreal. Local travel was by boat or canoe, and in the winter the frozen river became a road. It came to be recognized, however, that land travel was also necessary, both for continuous trips between Quebec and Montreal, and to serve the farms at a distance from the river. The main road of the period, that between Quebec and Montreal, was built in sections on the north shore, and was opened to through traffic in 1735. Parallel and cross roads were added, and either bridges or ferries thrown across the rivers. Along the south shore, sections of a road were built, but not joined, before the British conquest. No record of total mileage at that time exists.

The methods of transportation employed by the British after the cession of Acadia in 1713 and of Canada in 1763 showed at first no marked innovation. For Nova Scotia coastal schooners continued to be used, while in New

Brunswick the St. John river was valuable for water transport. In Canada a large portion of travel of all kinds was also by water. For the St. Lawrence two types of open boats—the bateau and the Durham boat—were principally used, while on the lower Great lakes sailing boats began to be numerous. The latter were built at various lake ports, and were of all types and sizes. The first marked change came with the introduction of steamboats and the construction of canals. The first steamboat, the *Accommodation*, was built at Montreal for John Molson (q.v.), and was launched in 1809. Ten years later, twelve steamships were counted in Canadian waters. By the 'thirties there were regular services on the lower lakes. Canals were a little later in appearing, but by the end of the 'forties there was uninterrupted navigation as far west as Sault Ste. Marie. In addition, there were the Rideau, the Chambly, and some minor canals.

No roads had been built in Nova Scotia before its conquest, and even by 1750 there was none fit for wheeled vehicles. Within a few years, however, a passable road existed from Halifax to Annapolis, and others were steadily opened. New Brunswick, settled later than Nova Scotia, was later too in road construction; although a report of 1849 gives 1,269 miles of main roads. In Lower Canada the roads of the French régime were improved and extended. A main road followed the bank of the St. Lawrence to Upper Canada, reaching Kingston by 1795, and Ancaster (near Hamilton) in 1801. The Dundas road and Yonge street were both pioneer roads of the same period. The condition of most Canadian roads was constantly deplored, and the introduction of plank roads (1835), and of macadam (about 1837) did no more than touch a few of the main travelled sections.

A revolutionary change in the methods of transportation in Canada came with the steam railway. As soon as railways were successfully operated in England and the United States, Canadian opinion was stirred by the possibilities that were opened up of an efficient form of land transport. Yet, in spite of enthusiasm, little was accomplished before 1850; there were built by this date the Champlain and St. Lawrence Railway around the rapids of the Richelieu (1836), another portage railway (the Montreal and Champlain) from Montreal to Lachine, and two short coal lines in Nova Scotia. Even before these local lines had been finished, there had developed plans for trunk lines that would connect the British provinces with each other, and also draw American traffic to the ports of the St. Lawrence and the Maritime provinces. The first schemes depended on either St. Andrews, New Brunswick, or Halifax as the terminus. For a time it seemed as if, with English help, the lines would be built; but negotiations broke down, and only short sections on the eastern end could be completed. The centre of interest then shifted to Canada, where the Grand Trunk Railway Company built from Montreal to Toronto (1856), and *viâ* Guelph to Sarnia (1859). On the east it reached the all-year port of Portland, Maine, by the lease of the St. Lawrence and Atlantic, a railway which had been completed, partly by Canadian and partly by American enterprise, in 1853.

Two other railways were constructed with a view to tapping the traffic of the middle western states. One of them, the Northern, was planned as a magnified portage railway to connect lake Ontario with the Georgian bay. It was completed from Toronto to Collingwood in 1855, and for many years formed a link in the communication with the Canadian West. The second of the two, the Great Western Railway, was designed to run from the Niagara river and lake Ontario ports to Windsor. By 1856 it was completed from Windsor and the

Suspension Bridge *viâ* Hamilton to Toronto. During the 'fifties a number of smaller lines were also built, particularly in Canada West.

In ten years the mileage of steam railways in the British North American provinces had increased by 2,000 miles, the total in 1860 being 2,065. For the next few years little more was accomplished. The cost of construction and equipment had been very considerable, and the expected traffic from the United States had not materialized in sufficient volume to justify the extensive system. Added to these difficulties was an economic dislocation following the Crimean War. The Grand Trunk and Great Western, and to a lesser extent the smaller railways, met with grave financial difficulties, and a halt had to be called to construction.

A new phase of railway history was linked with the federation of the provinces. The British North America Act committed the new Dominion to the construction of a railway connecting the Maritime provinces with the old province of Canada. The plan for an Intercolonial Railway was not a new one, but earlier attempts to realize it had failed with the breakdown of negotiations for a loan from the British government. After some discussion, a route was chosen which followed the coast of New Brunswick and avoided the American border. Construction and operation were undertaken by the Dominion government, and by 1876 a through line was completed from Halifax to Rivière du Loup, which the Grand Trunk had reached from the west. In 1879 the government bought the Grand Trunk's line to a point opposite Quebec, and ten years later secured an entrance to Montreal.

Even before federation had been achieved, there had been a considerable interest in the idea of extending the union as far as the Pacific ocean, and with that ambition went the project of linking the whole by means of a railway.

It was easily apparent that the system of transportation built up by the Hudson's Bay Company, well managed as it was, was inadequate for a settled country. Following the original federation of 1867 came the agreement for the addition of British Columbia as a province, involving a promise to begin within two years and complete within ten a railway to the coast. Early surveys and construction were, as in the case of the Intercolonial, undertaken by the government, following the "Pacific Scandal" and the collapse of the scheme for private ownership. When the Conservative party was returned to office in 1878, it sought to revive the original plan, and was finally successful in 1880 in making a contract with a syndicate which took the name of the Canadian Pacific Railway Company. Construction was greatly accelerated, and in spite of periodic financial crises, the line to the Pacific was ready for operation in 1885. Portions of the line built by the government were utilized, but important changes were made in the route selected by Sandford Fleming (q.v.), notably by taking a southerly course and crossing the Rockies by the Kicking Horse pass.

The first transcontinental line, thought by many contemporaries to be a reckless venture, proved to be a paying concern, and led to a rapid development of the West. The Canadian Pacific, in spite of protests from the Grand Trunk, proceeded also to build up a network of lines in the east, either by purchase or by construction. There followed a period of active rivalry between the two companies, each seeking to secure a strategic position in Ontario and Quebec, and absorbing a number of smaller companies in the process. The Grand Trunk, too, began to see the necessity of building into the West, in order to gain a share of the rapidly growing traffic there, and to obtain the advantages of long-haul freight. Such ambitions were stimulated by the coming of prosperity at the turn of the century, and the atmosphere of optimism about the future of Canada.

The situation was complicated by the existence of another railway interest in the West, the group of lines built or acquired by Sir William Mackenzie (q.v.) and Sir Donald Mann (q.v.), and being unified under the name of the Canadian Northern Railway. Attempts —the details of which are not clear— were made to secure coöperation between the Canadian Northern and the Grand Trunk, but they failed of success. The Grand Trunk then offered to build to the coast from its terminus at North Bay; but the Liberal government were seeking a complete line through northern Quebec and New Brunswick. The result was a plan by which the Grand Trunk (under the name of the Grand Trunk Pacific) was to build from Winnipeg to the Pacific, while the government was to build from Winnipeg to Moncton, under the name of the National Transcontinental. Construction on both divisions began in 1905, and the whole was opened for traffic in September, 1914.

In the meanwhile, yet a third transcontinental line was under way, for the Canadian Northern Company was determined to have a line from coast to coast, arguing that it was "bottled up" in the West. The Canadian Northern, like the Grand Trunk Pacific, followed a northern route, and both went through the Yellowhead pass. By the end of 1915 regular service was established from Quebec to Vancouver.

With the outbreak of war in 1914 it became evident that the ambitious railway plans that had been adopted were too great for the capacity or needs of the Dominion. In the first fifteen years of the century, mileage had been doubled. The boom years of the early part of the century had come to an end before war actually began, and hostilities made matters worse by raising prices and closing money-markets. The

Canadian Pacific was in a strong financial position, but the other large companies were forced to come to the government for assistance. The government decided to give temporary help, and to refer the question of a general policy to a royal commission. This latter, appointed in 1916, recommended in a majority report the uniting of the Grand Trunk, Grand Trunk Pacific, and Canadian Northern under a board of trustees constituted by parliament.

In 1917 the government acquired the balance of the stock of the Canadian Northern (it already held a portion as security), and in 1918 appointed a new board of directors, who were also charged with the management of the Canadian Government Railways. In 1919 the government also acquired the Grand Trunk and its subsidiaries. All the railways taken over, together with the Intercolonial and other government lines, were then united under the name of the Canadian National Railway Company.

The years after the war saw a rapid expansion in transportation in all its forms. The development of motor cars and trucks, together with a policy of better roads, began a marked revival of travel by road. The war hastened the development of aëroplanes, which then came to be used for civil purposes in Canada, notably in northern areas to serve the growing mining industry. At the same time the canal system was enlarged to allow for larger vessels, particularly for those carrying grain. By 1903 a depth of 14 feet had been achieved through the St. Lawrence and Welland canals, and 18 feet at Sault Ste. Marie. In 1920 the Canadian and United States governments began to investigate a further deepening and widening as a joint enterprise. The Welland canal was deepened to 25 feet by Canada in 1930, but no general plan has as yet (1937) been accepted.

No less striking was the expansion of railways. Almost the whole of the mileage was now in the hands of two companies, the competition between which was accelerated by a new period of prosperity. Branch lines on a large scale were planned, and partly built, by both companies. At the same time the area covered by railways was widened by the completion of the railway to Churchill, and of the Temiskaming and Northern Ontario to Moosonee. The total mileage increased from 40,352 in 1925 to 42,049 in 1930.

It was therefore in a period of expenditure that the railways were caught by the depression of 1929. Added to a steep decline in the volume of business offering was the growing problem of competition from motor vehicles. In 1934, for example, the number of motor vehicles registered had grown to 1,129,-532. The Canadian Pacific, because of its strong financial position and because it had been constructed as a unit, was able to weather the storm. The Canadian National, however, being a collection of railways—some governmental and some private companies—had a large and growing debt, and was unable to come within sight of meeting its obligations. Some slight improvement was effected in the following few years, but for the calendar year 1936 there was a net revenue of only $6,600,000 available to meet interest charges of $49,900,000. The burden of debt is a serious one for the Dominion, even if viewed in the perspective of the historical background of the Canadian National, and the high cost of transportation under the geographical conditions of Canada.

Bibliography: G. de T. Glazebrook, *A history of transportation in Canada* (New Haven, Conn., 1937); G. A. Cuthbertson, *Freshwater, a history and a narrative of the Great lakes* (Toronto, 1931); William Wood, *All afloat, a chronicle of craft and waterways* (Toronto, 1920); O. D. Skelton, *The railway builders* (Toronto, 1920); Norman Thompson and J. H. Edgar, *Canadian railway development* (Toronto, 1933); E. C. Guillet, *Early life in Upper Canada* (Toronto, 1933); S. J. McLean, "National highways overland", and M. J. Patton, "Shipping and canals", in Adam Shortt and A. G. Doughty, *Canada and its provinces*, vol. x (Toronto, 1914); and *The Canada Year Book*. See also **Automobile industry, Aviation, Canals, Canoe,** and the names of individual railways.

Trappistines. See **Cistercian Nuns.**

Trappists. See **Cistercians.**

Travois, a peculiar contrivance used among the Indians of the western plains for transport. It consisted of two long poles lashed one on each side of a dog or horse, and supporting a bag-net behind it for the reception of baggage. It probably originated from the custom, still common among the Eskimo, of fastening the tent poles to the backs of the dogs.

Tree-frog, or **Tree-toad.** See **Frogs** and **Toads.**

Trees. See **Forestry, Lumbering,** and the names of individual trees.

Trefoil. See **Clover.**

Treherne, a village in Manitoba, on the Winnipeg-Souris branch of the Canadian Pacific Railway, 77 miles south-west of Winnipeg. It is named after an early settler, George Treherne. It is in a farming district, has grist and flour mills, oil and gas wells, a high school, and a weekly newspaper (*Times*). Pop. (1931), 750.

Trémaudan, Auguste Henri de (1874-1929), author, was born at Châteauguay, Quebec, on July 14, 1874, the son of Auguste de Trémaudan and Jeanne-Marie Huet, both natives of France. He became a journalist, and lived during most of his life in Manitoba. He died at Los Angeles, California, whither he had gone in search of health, on October 29, 1929. He was the author of *The Hudson Bay road* (London, 1915), *Pourquoi nous parlons français* (Winnipeg, 1916), *Les précurseurs* (Winnipeg, 1917), *Le sang français* (Winnipeg, 1918), and two three-act plays, *De fil en aiguille* (Los Angeles, 1925) and *Quand même* (Montreal, 1928).

Tremblay, Jules (1879-1927), author, was born in Montreal, Quebec, in 1879. He became first a journalist, and then a translator on the staff of the House of Commons at Ottawa. He died at Ottawa on November 28, 1927. He was the author of *Des mots, des vers* (Montreal, 1911), *Du crépuscule aux aubes* (Ottawa, 1917), *Les ferments* (Ottawa, 1917), *Aromes du terrior* (Ottawa, 1918), *Les ailes qui montent* (Ottawa, 1918), *La vente de la poule noire* (Ottawa, 1920), *Trouées dans les novales* (Ottawa, 1921), *Nos lettres* (Ottawa, 1921), *Sainte-Anne d'Ottawa: Un résumé d'histoire* (Ottawa, 1925), and several other books and pamphlets. A full list of his publications will be found in the *Bull. rech. hist.*, vol. xxxiv.

Tremblay, Rémi (1847-1926), author, was born on April 2, 1847, at St. Barnabé, county of St. Hyacinthe, Quebec. When still in his 'teens, he fought in the American Civil War, and later he served in the Canadian militia during the Fenian raid. He became a journalist, and was the editor of newspapers at Quebec, at Montreal, and at Fall River and Worcester in the United States. In 1897 he entered the Canadian civil service, and was employed successively in the library of parliament and on the staff of Hansard. He retired in 1923, and he died on the island of Guadeloupe, whither he had gone in search of health, on January 31, 1926. He was the author of *Caprices poétiques et chansons satiriques* (Montreal, 1883), *Un revenant* (Montreal, 1884), *Poésies diverses: Coups d'ailes et coups de bec* (Montreal, 1888), *Boutades et rêveries* (Fall River, 1893), *Vers l'idéal* (Ottawa, 1912), *Pierre qui roule* (Montreal, 1923), and *Mon dernier voyage à travers l'Europe* (Montreal, 1925).

Tremblay. See **Ste. Anne de Chicoutimi.**

Tremolite. See **Amphibole.**

Trent Affair. This was an episode in the history of Anglo-American relations that threatened in 1861 to embroil Canada, as part of the British Empire, in war with the United States. On November 8, 1861, Captain Wilkes of the United States sloop *Jacinto* halted the British steamer *Trent*, plying between Vera Cruz and the Danish islands of St. Thomas, and removed from it two commissioners of the Southern Confederacy, James Murray Mason and John Slidell, who were on their way to Europe. The British government promptly protested against this flagrant breach of international law; and for a few weeks it looked as though the incident might lead to war. But in the end the United States government acceded to the British demands, and surrendered the two Confederate commissioners. The incident was influential in Canada in bringing about a reorganization of the Canadian militia, in hastening the construction of an intercolonial railway, and in aiding the movement toward British American union, or Confederation. See F. Landon, *The Trent affair of 1861* (Can. hist. rev., 1922).

Trent Canal. See **Canals** and **Trent river.**

Trenton, a town in Hastings county, Ontario, on the bay of Quinte, at the mouth of the river Trent, and on the Canadian National and Canadian Pacific Railways, 12 miles west of Belleville. The first settler arrived in 1790; the first store was opened in 1817; and the town was incorporated in 1857. As late as 1851, it was known as Trent Port, and the name Trenton is apparently an abbreviation of "Trent-town". The town is at the head of the Trent and Murray canals; and its chief manufactures are lumber, paper, creosote, barrels, boxes, clothing, and machines.

It is also a railway divisional point. It has a high school, a public library, and two weekly newspapers (*Courier-Advocate* and *Quinte Sun*). Pop. (1931), 6,276. See Rev. W. Bleasdell, "History of Trenton", in *Directory of the county of Hastings, 1864-5* (Belleville, 1865).

Trenton, a town in Pictou county, Nova Scotia, on the East river, and on the Pictou branch of the Canadian National Railway, 2 miles from New Glasgow. It is named after the manufacturing town of Trenton, New Jersey, from the fact that the Nova Scotia Steel and Coal Company have here their steel-manufacturing plant. Pop. (1931), 2,613.

Trent river, in Ontario, rises in Rice lake, Northumberland county, and, after a tortuous southern and eastern course, discharges into the bay of Quinte at Trenton. It is the outlet for numerous lakes situated chiefly in Peterborough county, and drained into Rice lake by the Otonabee river. The Trent river forms a part of the Trent canal, the term applied to a series of rivers and lakes connected by short canals and designed to form a continuous system of light-draught navigation between lake Ontario and Georgian bay. Six-foot navigation has now been completed to Swift rapids on the Severn river, and, upon completion of the Severn division, will be possible for the entire route. The Trent possesses fine water-power facilities, and is surrounded by a rich agricultural country. The lakes at its head abound in trout, maskinonge, pickerel, and other fish. The Trent was discovered in 1615 by Champlain (q.v.), who, with his Huron allies, was *en route* to fight the Iroquois, south-east of lake Ontario. It is 150 miles in length.

Trethewey, William Griffith (1867-1926), capitalist, was born in Muskoka, Ontario, in 1867. He discovered and developed the Trethewey mine in Co-balt, New Ontario; and acquired from it a large fortune. In 1913 he removed to England, and purchased an estate in Sussex; but in 1924 he returned to Canada, and interested himself in farming near Weston, Ontario. He died at Sarasota, Florida, on March 6, 1926. His brother, John L. Trethewey, with whom he was associated, died at Toronto, Ontario, on January 19, 1930, aged 68 years.

Trillium, Red. See **Wake Robin.**

Trillium, White (*Trillium grandiflorum* (Michx.) Salisb., *Liliaceae*), one of the early spring perennials, with simple stout stem rising from a tuber-like rootstock, and bearing at its summit a whorl of 3 broadly ovate, 3-ribbed leaves, and a large showy white flower, sometimes streaked with green and turning rose-coloured with age. The flower is lily-like in structure, with 3 green sepals, 3 white ovate petals, 6 stamens, and a 3-chambered pistil. The fruit is globular, and scarlet when ripe. It may be found in rich woods from western Quebec to Manitoba.

Tring Junction, a village in Beauce county, Quebec, on the Quebec Central Railway, 10 miles west of Beauceville. Tring township, in which it is situated, is named after Tring, a town in Hertfordshire, England. Pop. (1931), 430.

Trinitarians. The Order of the Most Holy Trinity (Trinitarians), was founded in 1194 by St. John de Matha and St. Felix de Valois, and was approved in 1198 by Pope Innocent III. Its original purpose was to engage in general works of mercy, to redeem slaves from the Moors, and to give service in hospitals and prisons. Since the abolition of slavery, the constitution of the Order has been changed to meet modern needs. The Order is now interested in the administration of charity, both spiritual and temporal, and is particularly devoted to the work of reclaiming sinners. It was established in Canada in 1924 in the parish of St.

Jean-de-Matha, in the province of Quebec.

Trinity College. See **University of Trinity College.**

Trinity College School, a residential school for boys, founded under the auspices of the Church of England, and situated since 1868 in Port Hope, Ontario. It originated in a private school for boys begun by the Rev. W. A. Johnson, a clergyman of the Church of England, in Weston, near Toronto. This school was adopted by the University of Trinity College, Toronto, as a preparatory school; and was named Trinity College School. In 1868 the school was removed to Port Hope, Ontario; and there new buildings were erected. On two occasions, in 1895 and in 1928, the school buildings suffered destruction by fire; but on both occasions the school rose from its ashes, and funds were found for the erection of buildings of a modern and more commodious character. The school still retains a connection with Trinity College, since representatives of Trinity College still sit *ex officio* on its governing body; but since 1872 it has been a separate institution, having been incorporated by Act of the Ontario legislature in that year. The headmasters of the school, since the Rev. W. A. Johnson, have been the Rev. C. H. Badgeley (1867-72), the Rev. C. J. S. Bethune (1872-99), the Rev. R. E. Jones (1899-1901), the Rev. Herbert Symonds (1901-3), the Rev. Oswald Rigby (1903-13), the Rev. F. G. Orchard (1913-33), and Philip A. C. Ketchum (1933—). See Capt. O. J. Aldom, *Trinity College School* (Municipal Review of Canada, 1934).

Tripe de roche (*Umbilicaria Dillenti*), a species of moss or lichen growing on rocks in northern Canada. It is edible, but unappetizing, and has been often used by Indians and fur-traders as a last resort against starvation.

Trochu, a village in the Red Deer district of Alberta, on the Canadian National Railway, 78 miles north-east of Calgary. It is the centre of a rich grain-growing district, and has five grain elevators, a convent, a hospital, and a weekly newspaper (*Tribune*). Pop. (1931), 506.

Trois Rivières. See **Three Rivers.**

Trotter, Bernard Freeman (1890-1917), poet, was born in Toronto, Ontario, on June 16, 1890, the son of the Rev. Professor Thomas Trotter. He was educated at McMaster University, Toronto (B.A., 1914). In 1916 he received a commission in the British army; and he was killed in France on May 7, 1917. His poems were published after his death, with an introduction by W. S. W. McLay, under the title *A Canadian twilight; and other poems of war and of peace* (Toronto, 1917).

Trout. The name trout is indiscriminately applied in North America to several species of fish that are only distantly related. The fishes so designated belong to two groups: *viz.*, the trout proper (*Salmo*), and the chars (*Salvelinus*). In England, whence these common names came, the trout and the char are sharply distinguished. The trout (in this case the brown trout) is a common game fish of England, Germany, France, and central Europe generally; the char is rare in England, being found only in the lakes of the north. It is commoner in the lakes of Scotland, and occurs also in the lakes of Switzerland and Scandinavia. The char lives in colder waters than the trout, and is more brilliantly coloured and more gamey. It is also characterized by smaller scales and by other characters too technical for description here. As the char is so rare in England, and the trout so well known, it is natural that the early English-speaking immigrants to North America should have called the beautiful game fish which they found in the waters of the eastern part of the continent, speckled trout. They should, however, have called them char, for they are much more closely related to the char of the old world. (See also **Char.**) The only close relatives of the trout of the old world are the rainbow, Kamloops, cut-throat, and steelhead of the Rocky mountains area and westward. See J. R. Dymond, *The trout and other game fishes of British Columbia* (Dept. of Fisheries, Ottawa, 1932).

Trout lake, in the valley of the English river, is in Patricia district, northern Ontario, north-east of Red lake and between the 51st and 52nd parallels of north latitude. It has an area of 156 square miles.

Troyes, Chevalier Pierre de (d. 1688), soldier, came to Canada in the summer of 1685. On his arrival, he was given command of one hundred men and sent to retake the forts on Hudson bay. The party set out from Montreal on March 20, 1686, and after three months of travel, reached their destination, where they surprised and captured Forts Monsipi, Rupert, and Albany. Troyes returned to Montreal in October, 1686; and he was one of the commanders of the regular troops in Denonville's expedition of 1687. On the return march, he was left in command at Fort Niagara, and there he died of some malignant disease, on May 8, 1688. See Abbé I. Caron, *Journal de l'expédition du Chevalier de Troyes à la Baie d' Hudson en 1686* (Beauceville, Quebec, 1918), and P. G. Roy, *Le chevalier de Troye* (Bull. rech. hist., vol. x).

Trudelle, Charles (1822-1904), priest and author, was born at Charlesbourg, Lower Canada, on January 28, 1822, the son of Jean Trudelle. He was ordained a priest of the Roman Catholic Church in 1845; and occupied many charges in the province of Quebec. He died at Quebec on July 14, 1904. He was the author of *Notes sur la famille Trudelle* (Quebec, 1875), *Trois souvenirs*

(Quebec, 1878), *Paroisse de Charlesbourg* (Quebec, 1887), and *Le Frère Louis* (Quebec, 1898).

Truro, a town in Colchester county, Nova Scotia, on the Salmon river, at the eastern end of Cobequid bay, and on the Canadian National and Dominion Atlantic Railways, 60 miles north of Halifax. It was first settled in 1761 by New Englanders and Scoto-Irish from Ulster, brought to Nova Scotia by Alexander McNutt (q.v.); and it was first known as "Cobequid". Later, it was re-named after Truro in Cornwall. The township of Truro was created in 1765. The chief industries are the manufacture of various textiles, aerated waters, lumber, machinery, metal fittings, catalogues, and calendars. It has a normal school, an agricultural college, a manual training and household science school, an evening newspaper (*News*), a semi-weekly newspaper (*Citizen-Sun*), and a weekly newspaper (*News*). Pop. (1931), 7,901.

Trutch, Sir Joseph William (1826-1904), lieutenant-governor of British Columbia (1871-6), was born at Ashcot, Somersetshire, England, in 1826, the son of William Trutch, afterwards clerk of the peace of St. Thomas, Jamaica. He was educated at Exeter, England, and became a civil engineer. In 1849 he went to California; and until 1856 he practised his profession there and in the Oregon country. He was then employed on construction work in Illinois, but in 1859 he removed to British Columbia, and settled in Victoria. He built the road from Yale to Cariboo, and the Alexandria suspension bridge over the Fraser river. In 1864 he was appointed commissioner of lands and works, and subsequently surveyor-general for British Columbia, and a member of the executive council. In 1870 he was one of the delegates chosen to go to Ottawa to arrange the terms of union between British Columbia and Canada; and in 1871 he was appointed lieutenant governor of the province. He occupied this office until 1876, and then retired to private life. He died on March 4, 1904. In 1855 he married Julia Elizabeth, daughter of Louis Hyde, of New York. In 1889 he was created a K.C.M.G.

Trutch, mount, is in the Rocky mountains, on the boundary between British Columbia and Alberta, at the head of Waitabit creek, in lat. 51° 42′. It was named after Sir Joseph Trutch (q.v.), first lieutenant-governor of British Columbia; and it has an altitude of 10,690 feet.

Tsimshian ("People of Skeena"), a small linguistic family of Indians on the Nass and Skeena rivers in British Columbia, and the coast as far south as Milbanke sound. The culture of these Indians closely resembles that of their neighbours, the Haida (q.v.) and the Tlingit (q.v.), but their language is strikingly different. The Tsimshian consist of four phratries—Raven, Wolf, Eagle, and Grizzly Bear—comprising many subdivisions based, it may be, either upon family groups or residence in various towns. They have three principal secret social fraternities, the "cannibals", the "dog-eaters", and the dancers and singers; but despite these names the members do not eat human flesh or dog meat—any such eating being a mere pretence. They have their medicine men and their totems; being fine carvers, their totem poles are works of art, though not equal to those of the Haida. Amongst them descent is reckoned in the female line. The custom of the labret, or lip-piece, prevailed amongst them. Their houses were often huge structures of cedar beams and planks, accommodating as many as thirty persons, presided over by a house chief; every family or town had its superior chief. Like other coastal tribes their food came principally from the sea and the rivers. From earliest days the Tsimshian extracted oil from the oolachan, a small, smelt-like fish which frequents the Nass river in immense shoals. This "oolachan grease" was in great demand all along the coast and was indispensable at the potlatch feasts. In 1857, William Duncan (q.v.) settled amongst them at Fort Simpson, and began the work of Christianizing and civilizing them. After five years of patient and successful effort, he induced his converts to remove to Matlakahtla, where he established a model community of civilized Tsimshian. The work prospered; the village grew; a school, store, saw-mill, and salmon cannery were established; but dissensions arose, and in 1887 Duncan, with the majority of his converts, removed to New Matakahtla, on Annette island, Alaska. See John W. Arctander, *The apostle of Alaska* (New York, 1909); Henry S. Wellcome, *The story of Metlakahtla* (London, 1887); and Franz Boas, *Tsimshian mythology* (Smithsonian Institution, Washington, 1916).

Tucker, James Alexander (1872-1903), poet and journalist, was born in Owen Sound, Ontario, on December 22, 1872; and he died at Toronto, Ontario, on December 19, 1903. He was educated at the University of Toronto, but did not graduate, having been expelled from the University in 1895 as the ringleader in the undergraduate "strike" of that year. He completed his academic course at Leland Stanford University in California (B.A., 1896); and then returned to Canada, where he entered journalism. After his death, his friends published a volume of his *Poems* (Toronto, 1904), with a prefatory memoir by Arthur Stringer.

Tucker, William Bowman (1859-1934), clergyman and author, was born in London, England, on February 27, 1859. He came to Canada in 1871, and for some years worked on a farm in Ontario. He became a school-teacher, and later, in 1885, was ordained a minister of the Methodist Church. In 1910 he resigned from the Church to become the founder and superintendent of the Montreal City Mission for "New

Canadians". This position he retained until his death in Bristol, England, on August 11, 1934. He was the author of *The Camden colony* (Montreal, 1908), republished as *The romance of the Palatine Millers* (Montreal, 1929); *Songs of the wayside* (Montreal, 1918); and *Laurentian tales* (Montreal, 1922).

Tugaske, a village in Saskatchewan, on the Canadian Pacific Railway, 53 miles north-west of Moose Jaw. It has five grain elevators and a weekly newspaper (*Globe*). Pop. (1931), 196.

Tulip, the name of the trees belonging to the genus *Liriodendron* Linnaeus. Only two species have been described, of which one occurs in Canada (*L. tulipifera* Linnaeus). It is recognized under various names; yellow poplar, whitewood, tulip tree, and white poplar are the most common of these. The range is limited to southern peninsular Ontario in Canada. The leaves of tulip are peculiar in shape, very different from those of any other tree, appearing as though cut off at the end. The flowers resemble the true tulip flower, are whitish-green and about three inches across. The fruits are two or three inches long, and are made up of winged seeds attached to a central axis, which stands erect on the branch. The tulip is a tall tree, providing a long clean bole and yielding wood of high quality, but it is a comparatively scarce tree in Canada and of minor commercial importance.

Tullibee, the name usually applied in Manitoba and north-westward to the group of fish called ciscoes (q.v.), or "herrings" elsewhere. Where a distinction is made between ciscoes and tullibees, the latter name is usually applied to the larger forms.

Tully, Kivas (1820-1905), architect, was born in Queen's county, Ireland, in 1820, the son of Commander John P. Tully, R.N. He studied architecture and civil engineering in Limerick; and in 1844 he came to Canada. For many years he practised as an architect in

Toronto; and in 1867 he was appointed architect and engineer to the department of public works in Ontario. A large number of public buildings in this province were designed by him. He died at Toronto on April 24, 1905. He was twice married, (1) in 1844 to Elizabeth Drew (d. 1847), of Drewsboro', county Clare, Ireland; and (2) in 1852 to Maria (d. 1883), daughter of Lieut.-Col. Samuel Strickland (q.v.).

Tully, Sydney Strickland (1860-1911), painter, was born in Toronto, Canada, in 1860, the eldest daughter of Kivas Tully, architect, and Maria Strickland. She was educated in Toronto, and studied art in London, Paris, and New York. In 1889 she was elected an associate of the Royal Canadian Academy; and she exhibited at the Paris Salon, the Royal Academy, the World's Fair, Chicago, and other expositions. Her most notable work was as a portrait painter. She died in Toronto on July 18, 1911.

Tumble Weed. See **Russian Thistle.**

Tungsten, a rare metal used in the manufacture of high speed steel, incandescent electric lamps, and for the manufacture of tungsten compounds, which find their application in many industries. The chief source of tungsten is found in the minerals wolframite and scheelite. Wolframite is a heavy, black mineral which crystallizes in the monoclinic system. These crystals are metallic in lustre and split easily in one direction. Chemically, it is a tungstate of iron and manganese. It is found at the Kootenay Belle Mine, near Salmo, British Columbia, and at Hardscrabble creek, Barkerville, British Columbia. Scheelite is a heavy mineral with a vitreous to resinous lustre, and is usually of a pale creamy-yellow colour. It can be readily scratched with a knife. Chemically, it is a tungstate of lime. It was mined at Scheelite, Nova Scotia, and has been found at the

Hollinger Mines, in the Porcupine district, Ontario, and near Barkerville, British Columbia. As a result of weathering, a yellow mineral known as tungstite is formed. This is the natural tungstite acid. See T. L. Walker, *Tungsten ores of Canada* (Mines Branch, Ottawa, 1909).

Tunkers. The Tunkers, known also as "Dunkards", had their origin in 1708 in Westphalia, Germany; but persecution for their religious views drove them to America. They baptize by immersion and reject infant baptism, refuse to take oaths or to fight; they will not go to law, and hold some other distinctive views. They are to be found in almost every state of the American union, though not in large numbers. They are frequently spoken of as "German Baptist Brethren", though they usually call themselves simply "Brethren". The first contingent came to Upper Canada with the Pennsylvania immigration at an early period, and settled in the Niagara peninsula. The church established there was the mother Tunker church in Canada. Others followed, establishing themselves in Markham, Waterloo, and other districts. They adopted a modified form of Congregationalism, and used the German language exclusively until some sixty years ago, when English came into general use. They are found at some twenty centres, and have three city missions, at Buffalo, Welland, and Collingwood. The number of communicant members in Ontario is approximately eight hundred. The official name of the body in Canada is "The Brethren in Christ (Tunkers)". The Tunkers are doctrinally and historically related to the Mennonites. Canadian law quite early allowed exemption from military service to Quakers, Mennonites, and Tunkers.

Tupelo. See **Black Gum.**

Tupper, Charles (1794-1881), clergyman, was born at Cornwallis, Nova Scotia, on August 6, 1794, the son of Eliakim Tupper, who came to Nova Scotia from Connecticut in 1763. He entered the Baptist ministry in 1817, and during the sixty-three years of his ministry was the pastor of a number of churches in the Maritime provinces. He died at Aylesford, Nova Scotia, on January 19, 1881. In 1818 he married Miriam, daughter of James Lockhart, and widow of John Lowe; and by her he had three sons. From 1832 to 1836 he was editor of the *Baptist Magazine;* and he was the author of *Scriptural baptism* (Halifax, Nova Scotia, 1850), as well as other theological works. Acadia College conferred on him the degree of D.D.

Tupper, Sir Charles, Bart. (1821-1915), prime minister of Canada (1896), was born in Amherst, Nova Scotia, on July 2, 1821, the son of the Rev. Charles Tupper (q.v.) and Miriam Lockhart. He was educated at Horton Academy, Wolfville, Nova Scotia, and he studied medicine at Edinburgh University (M.D., 1843). He obtained the diploma of the Royal College of Surgeons in 1843; and on his return to Nova Scotia, he practised medicine in his native town. From 1855 to 1867 he represented Cumberland in the Legislative Assembly of Nova Scotia; from 1856 to 1860 he was provincial secretary in the Johnston government; and from 1864 to 1867 he was prime minister of Nova Scotia. He took a leading part in the Confederation movement, was a delegate to the Charlottetown, Quebec, and London conferences, and replied to the anti-confederation campaign of Joseph Howe (q.v.) in his *Letter to the Earl of Carnarvon* (London, 1866). It was mainly through his efforts that Nova Scotia was brought into the union of 1867.

From 1867 to 1884 he represented Cumberland in the Canadian House of Commons. But in the first government of the Dominion he was not included, having stood aside, with T. D'Arcy McGee (q.v.), in order to make way for Edward Kenny (q.v.), a Roman Catholic from Nova Scotia. In 1868 he was instrumental in defeating the attempts of the anti-confederationists in Nova Scotia to obtain repeal of the union, and in persuading Joseph Howe (q.v.) to enter the government. In 1870 he himself entered the cabinet as president of the council; and in 1872 and 1873 he held the portfolios of minister of inland revenue, and minister of customs. From 1873 to 1878 he was the right-hand man of Sir John Macdonald (q.v.), while in opposition; and when the Conservatives were returned to power in 1878, he became minister of public works. From 1879 to 1884 he was minister of railways and canals, and as such had supervision of the arrangements for the building of the Canadian Pacific Railway. In 1883 he was appointed high commissioner for Canada in London; and, apart from a period of sixteen months in 1887-8, during which he held the portfolio of minister of finance in the Macdonald government, he retained the high commissionership until 1896. He was then recalled to Canada, and assumed the leadership of the Conservative party, shortly before the general elections of that year. Not even his dauntless energy, however, sufficed to revive the fallen fortunes of the party, and he was defeated at the polls after only six months' tenure of office. From 1896 to 1900 he led the Conservative opposition in the Canadian House of Commons; but in the general elections of 1900 he was defeated in Cape Breton, and he thereupon retired to private life.

He died at Bexley Heath, Kent, England, on October 30, 1915, the last of the "Fathers of Confederation" to pass away. In 1846 he married Frances Amelia (d. 1912), daughter of Silas Hibbert Morse, of Amherst, Nova Scotia; and by her he had three sons and three daughters. He was created a C.B. in 1867, a K.C.M.G. in 1879, a G.C.M.G. in 1886, and a baronet of the United Kingdom in 1888. He was also an LL.D. of Acadia College, of Cambridge University, and of Edinburgh University. Just before his death he published his *Recollections of sixty years* (London, 1914).

See E. M. Saunders, *The life and letters of the Rt. Hon. Sir Charles Tupper, Bart.* (2 vols., London, 1916; supplement ed. by Sir C. H. Tupper, Toronto, 1926); W. A. Harkin (ed.), *Political reminiscences of the Rt. Hon. Sir Charles Tupper, Bart.* (London, 1914); J. W. Longley, *Sir Charles Tupper* (Toronto, 1917); and C. Thibault, *Biography of Sir Charles Tupper* (Montreal, 1883).

Tupper, Sir Charles Hibbert (1855-1927), lawyer and statesman, was born at Amherst, Nova Scotia, on August 3, 1855, the second son of Sir Charles Tupper, Bart. (q.v.). He was educated at McGill University and Harvard University (LL.B., 1876), and was called to the bar of Nova Scotia in 1878 (Q.C., 1890). From 1882 to 1904 he represented Pictou in the Canadian House of Commons. From 1888 to 1894 he was minister of marine and fisheries in the Macdonald, Abbott, and Thompson governments; and from 1894 to 1896 he was minister of justice in the Bowell government. He was one of the "bolters" of January 4, 1896; but resumed office as solicitor-general in the Tupper government. In 1892 he was agent for Great Britain in the Behring sea arbitration; and he was created, for his services in this arbitration, a K.C.M.G. in 1893. In 1904 he retired from politics, and devoted himself to the practice of law in Vancouver, British Columbia. He died at Vancouver on March 30, 1927. In 1879 he married Janet, daughter of the Hon. James McDonald (q.v.); and by her he had four sons and three daughters. He edited a *Supplement* (Toronto, 1926) to the *Life and letters* of his father, by the Rev. E. M. Saunders.

Tupper, mount, is in British Columbia, north of Rogers Pass railway station, in the Kootenay district. It is one of the Hermit range in the Selkirk mountains, and is in lat. 51° 20′, long. 117° 30′, with an altitude of 9,229 feet. It was formerly known as mount Hermit, from a rock near the summit which resembles a hermit with a dog lying at his feet. It was changed to mount Tupper, after Sir Charles Tupper (q.v.), by order-in-council, on April 4, 1887.

Turcotte, Joseph Edouard (1808-1864), solicitor-general for Lower Canada (1847-8), was born at Gentilly, Lower Canada, in 1808. He was admitted to the bar in 1834 (Q.C., 1847); and he sat in the Legislative Assembly of Canada for St. Maurice from 1841 to 1844, and from 1851 to 1854; for Maskinongé from 1854 to 1857; for Champlain from 1858 to 1861; and for Three Rivers from 1861 to 1864. In 1847-8 he was solicitor-general for Lower Canada in the Draper administration; and from 1862 to 1863 he was speaker of the Assembly. He died at Three Rivers, Lower Canada, on December 20, 1864.

Turcotte, Louis Philippe (1842-1878), historian, was born at St. John, Island of Orleans, Lower Canada, on July 11, 1842, and was educated at the Quebec Seminary. In 1859 he became, as the result of falling through the ice of the St. Lawrence, an invalid for the rest of his life; and he devoted himself thenceforth to historical studies. He published first an *Histoire de l'Ile d'Orléans* (Quebec, 1867); then he brought out his best-known and most important work, *Canada sous l'union* (2 vols., Quebec, 1871-2; new ed., 1882); and after this, successively, biographies of *L'hon. R. E. Caron* (pamphlet, Quebec, 1873), and of *L'hon. Sir G. E. Cartier* (pamphlet, Quebec, 1873), *L'invasion du Canada, 1775-6* (Quebec, 1876), and *La société littéraire et historique de Québec* (Quebec, 1879). He died at

Quebec on April 3, 1878. His work, while conscientious, did not attain a high level. See Faucher de St. Maurice, *L. P. Turcotte* (Trans. Roy. Soc. Can., 1883); Henri d'Arles, *Nos historiens* (Montreal, 1921); and J. P. Tardivel, *Notice biographique sur L. P. Turcotte* (Annales de l'Institut Canadien de Québec, 1878).

Turcotte. See St. Georges.

Turgeon, Pierre Flavien (1787-1867), Roman Catholic archbishop of Quebec (1850-67), was born at Quebec on November 12, 1787, the son of Louis Turgeon and Louise Dumont. He was educated at the Quebec Seminary, and was ordained to the priesthood in 1810. From 1808 to 1820 he was secretary to Bishop Plessis (q.v.); in 1833 he was elected coadjutor to the archbishop of Quebec; and in 1834 he was consecrated titular bishop of Sidyme. He succeeded to the archbishopric of Quebec in 1850; but owing to ill-health he ceased to administer the affairs of the See after 1855, and he died at Quebec on August 25, 1867, He was conspicuously loyal to the British Crown during the rebellion of 1837-8, and he was of assistance to the government during the union period. In 1852 he was instrumental in getting a charter for Laval University; and it was he who opened it officially in 1854. See C. Legaré, *Souvenir consacré à la mémoire vénérée de Mgr. P. F. Turgeon* (Quebec, 1867).

Turkey, a well-known large bird of the fowl type, characterized by the nearly naked head, the resplendent plumage, and other features too well known to enumerate. It formerly occurred as a wild bird in southern Ontario, but it was extirpated when settlement of the area became widespread. The domestic turkey is from a racial stock different from that of the Ontario form.

Turkey Point, a settlement in Norfolk county, Ontario, on lake Erie, which once promised to be important, but which has now virtually disappeared. It was here that the first settlers in the Long Point region landed; and Colonel Simcoe (q.v.) planned to make it a military and naval station. See H. B. Donly, *Turkey Point, or Charlotteville* (Ont. Hist. Soc., Papers and Records, vol. xx, 1923). See also **Charlotteville.**

Turnagain river, a tributary of the Liard river, in the Cassiar district of British Columbia. It is 110 miles long.

Turner, John Herbert (1834-1923), prime minister of British Columbia (1895-8), was born at Claydon, near Ipswich, England, on May 7, 1834, the son of John and Martha Turner. He emigrated to Canada in 1856, and after spending several years in Prince Edward Island, he removed in 1862 to Victoria, British Columbia. From 1879 to 1881 he was mayor of Victoria; and from 1887 to 1901 he represented Victoria in the Legislative Assembly of British Columbia. He was minister of finance and agriculture in the provincial government from 1887 to 1898, and again from 1899 to 1901; and from 1895 to 1898 he was prime minister. In 1901 he was appointed agent-general for British Columbia in Great Britain; and this post he held until his death at London, England, on December 9, 1923. In 1860 he married Elizabeth Eilbeck, of Whitehaven, England.

Turner, Thomas Andrew (1775?-1834), merchant and banker, was born in Aberdeenshire, Scotland, about 1775. He emigrated to Canada, and became a partner in the mercantile house of Allison, Turner, and Co. in Montreal. He was one of the founders of the Bank of Montreal, and in 1820 he was elected president of the Bank of Canada. For a number of years he was the proprietor of the Montreal *Gazette*. He died at Montreal on July 21, 1834. He was the author of a paper on *Annexation of Canada to the United States* (Dublin University Magazine, vol. xxxv).

Turner, mount, is in Alberta, in lat. 50° 51', long. 115° 29', and has an altitude of 9,230 feet. It was named after Lieut.-General Sir R. E. W. Turner, V.C., K.C.M.G., C.B., D.S.O., who commanded one of the Canadian divisions in France during the Great War.

Turner Valley, an extensive plain and industrial area in Alberta, southwest of Calgary. Its oil-wells have become the most productive in Canada. It was named after Robert and James Turner, natives of Edinburgh, Scotland, who took out homesteads in the northern end of the valley in 1886.

Turnor, Philip (1752?-1800), surveyor, was a native of Laleham, Middlesex, England, and was born about 1752. In 1778 he was articled to the Hudson's Bay Company as a surveyor; and he served as a surveyor in the Hudson's Bay Company's territories in North America until 1792. The map of North America published by Arrowsmith in London in 1795 embodied the results of his surveys; and it is noteworthy that it was from Turnor that David Thompson (q.v.) received his instruction in surveying. He died near London, England, in the early part of 1800. He was the author of a pamphlet entitled *Result of astronomical observations made in the interior parts of North America* (London, 1794). See J. B. Tyrrell (ed.), *Journals of Samuel Hearne and Philip Turnor* (Toronto, The Champlain Society, 1934).

Turnstone, a name applied, with prefixes, to two shore birds belonging to the plover family, *Charadriidae*. The term is descriptive of the habits of these birds in flicking aside small stones along the beaches in search of food. The ruddy turnstone (*Arenaria interpres*) is an Arctic nesting species, and is found along suitable beaches throughout Canada during migration. The black turnstone (*Arenaria melanocephala*) nests in the Arctic north-west, and migrates down the Pacific coast.

Turret mountain is in the Cariboo district of British Columbia, between the headwaters of the Tonquin and Geikie creeks, at the head of the Fraser river in the Rocky mountains. It is in lat. 52° 42′, long. 118° 22′. There is also a Turret mountain in the Clayoquot district of Vancouver island, on the west side of Effingham inlet, Clayoquot sound. It is in lat. 49° 04′, long. 125° 11′, and has an altitude of 1,782 feet.

Turtleford, a village in Saskatchewan, on the Canadian National Railway, 53 miles north-west of Battleford. It has a weekly newspaper (*Sun*). Pop. (1931), 325.

Turtlehead (*Chelone glabra* L., *Scrophulariaceae*), a smooth perennial with upright branching stems. The leaves are short-petioled, narrowly to broadly lanceolate, with toothed margins. The flowers are large, white tinged with rose, nearly sessile, in spikes or clusters surrounded by bracts. The corolla is inflated-tubular, 2-lipped, the upper lip broad and arched and notched at the apex, the lower 3-lobed at the apex and woolly bearded in the throat. There are 4 stamens, with woolly filaments and woolly heart-shaped anthers. It is found in wet places during July-September, from Newfoundland to Manitoba.

Turtle Mountain, an Indian reserve and a municipality in Manitoba, 6 miles from Whitewater station on the Napinka branch of the Canadian Pacific Railway, and 9 miles from Boissevain. It is named after the neighbouring mountain, which derived its appellation, not from the tortoise, but from the turtle-bird, a variety of the dove or pigeon.

Turtles are reptiles, in which the body is enclosed between a pair of bony shields. Most of the Canadian turtles live in fresh water, but with the feet adapted for walking as well as for swimming. Most of the species are strictly carnivorous, though a few take some vegetable food also. They are useful scavengers of the waters in which they live. Although aquatic, they come on shore to lay their eggs, most in June in southern Ontario. The female digs a hole in the ground with her hind feet, and after depositing her eggs in it, covers them over with soil which is then trampled and smoothed down, leaving the nest inconspicuous. The young turtles usually hatch in the late summer of the same year, dig themselves out and make for the water. Eight species occur in Ontario, but east and west of that province the number of kinds found is fewer. The most widely distributed species is the painted turtle, of which three varieties occur: the eastern painted turtle (*Chrysemys picta picta*) in eastern Canada, the western painted turtle (*Chrysemys bellii marginata*) in Ontario, and Bell's painted turtle (*Chrysemys bellii bellii*) westward. The snapping turtle (*Chelydra serpentina*), characterized by a small lower shell and a row of tubercles on the upper surface of the tail, grows to a large size. It is commonly found in ponds and small lakes throughout southern Canada. Species with more restricted distribution include the Blanding's turtle (*Emys blandingii*), map turtle (*Graptemys geographica*), musk turtle (*Sternotherus odoratus*), spotted turtle (*Clemmys guttata*), wood turtle (*Clemmys insulpta*), and soft-shelled turtle (*Amyda spinifera*). The leather-back turtle, a large marine species found in warm seas throughout the world, occasionally strays north into Canadian waters both east and west.

Tuscarora. See Iroquois.

Tusket, a village in Yarmouth county, Nova Scotia, on the Tusket river, and on the Canadian National Railway, 10 miles from Yarmouth. Pop. (1935), 750.

Tusket Wedge. See Wedgeport.

Tuxedo, a town on the outskirts of Winnipeg, Manitoba. It was so named after the Tuxedo Park Company, which originally owned most of the land on which the town is built. Pop. (1931), 1,173.

Tuzo, mount, is in the Rocky mountains, on the boundary between British Columbia and Alberta, southeast of the headwaters of Tokumm creek, a tributary of the Vermilion river, in lat. 51° 18'. It was named after Henrietta L. Tuzo, of Warlingham, Surrey, England, who was the first to climb it, in 1906. It has an altitude of 10,648 feet.

Tweed, a village in Hastings county, Ontario, on the Moira river, and on the Canadian Pacific and Canadian National Railways, 25 miles north-east of Belleville. It was named after Tweed in Scotland. It is an industrial village, with asbestos and actinolite mines in the vicinity; and its chief manufactures are flour, lumber, leather, steel troughs and tanks, acids, and bricks. It has a high school, a public library, and a weekly newspaper (*News*). Pop. (1931), 1,271.

Tweedie, Lemuel John (1849-1917), prime minister of New Brunswick (1900-7) and lieutenant-governor (1907-12), was born at Chatham, New Brunswick, on November 30, 1849. He was educated at Chatham, and in 1871 was called to the bar of New Brunswick (Q.C., 1892). From 1874 to 1878, and from 1886 to 1907, he represented Northumberland in the Legislative Assembly of New Brunswick; and he was successively surveyor-general in the Blair administration, provincial secretary in the Emmerson administration, and from 1900 to 1907 prime minister. From 1907 to 1912 he was lieutenant-governor of New Brunswick; and he died at Chatham, New Brunswick, on July, 15, 1917. In 1876 he married Agnes, daughter of Alexander Loudoun, of Chatham, New Brunswick.

Tweedsmuir, John Buchan, first Baron (1875—), historian, novelist, and governor-general of Canada (1935—), was born in Scotland on August 26, 1875, the son of the Rev. John Buchan. He was educated at Glasgow University and at Brasenose College, Oxford (B.A., 1899; D.C.L., 1934). He was called to the bar in 1901 from the Inner Temple; and from 1901 to 1903 he was secretary to Lord Milner, high commissioner for South Africa. For many years he was vice-president of Thomas Nelson and Sons, publishers. From 1927 to 1935 he was a member of the House of Commons for the Scottish Universities; and in 1935 he was appointed governor-general of Canada. In 1932 he was created a Companion of Honour, and in 1935 a G.C.M.G. and Baron Tweedsmuir. He is the author of a number of biographies and historical works, notable among which are *Sir Walter Raleigh* (London, 1911), *A history of the great war* (London, 1921-2), *Lord Minto* (London, 1924), *Montrose* (1928), *Sir Walter Scott* (London, 1932), *Julius Caesar* (London, 1932), *The massacre of Glencoe* (London, 1933), *Oliver Cromwell* (1934), and *The King's grace* (London, 1935); and he has written a long series of novels and romances, notable among which are *Salute to adventurers* (London, 1915), *The thirty-nine steps* (London, 1915), *Greenmantle* (London, 1916), *Huntingtower* (London, 1922), *The three hostages* (London, 1924), *John Macnab* (London, 1925), *The dancing floor* (London, 1926), *Witch Wood* (London, 1927), *The Runagates' club* (London, 1928), *The courts of the morning* (London, 1929), *Castle Gay* (London, 1930), *The gap in the curtain* (London, 1932), *The magic walking-stick* (London, 1932), *A prince of the captivity* (London, 1933), *The free fishers* (London, 1934), *The house of the four winds* (London, 1935), and *The island of sheep* (London, 1936).

Twelve Apostles islands, a group of islands on the south side of lake Superior. The largest of the group is Madelaine island, which was known during the French period as St. Michel, when a French fort stood on it. Many years afterwards, Jean Baptiste Cadot (q.v.), built a fort on it also. The islands are said to have been named by Charlevoix (q.v.), on whose maps the name first appears in 1744.

Twin-flower (*Linnea borealis* L. var. *americana* (Forbes) Rehder, *Caprifoliaceae*), a slender, creeping and trailing evergreen herb, somewhat hairy, with rounded-oval evergreen leaves and thread-like upright flower-stalks, which fork at the apex and bear delicate, fragrant, nodding, twin flowers. The corolla is slender, bell-shaped, equally 5-lobed, whitish tinged or striped with rose-purple, and hairy inside. There are 4 stamens, 2 longer and 2 shorter, inserted toward the base of the corolla. This little plant grows in moist mossy woods and cold bogs from Labrador to Manitoba and in the far west.

Twining, Sir Philip Geoffrey (1862-1920), soldier, was born in Halifax, Nova Scotia, in 1862, the son of Edmund Twining and Elizabeth Whitman. He was educated at the Royal Military College, Kingston, Ontario; and in 1885 he obtained a commission in the Royal Engineers. From 1887 to 1893 he served in India and Africa; from 1893 to 1899 he was professor of military engineering at the Royal Military College, Kingston; and in 1899 he returned to the Indian army. In 1914 he went to France as C.R.E. of the Seventh Division of the Indian Expeditionary Force; and he served in France continuously until 1918, rising to the position of adjutant and quartermaster-general of the First British Army. Invalided to England in 1918, he was appointed there director of fortification and works, and as such official head of the Royal Engineers. He died at London, England, on January 15, 1920. He married Louise Daly, of Kingston. In 1919 he was created a K.C.M.G. See Mary C. Ritchie, *Major-general Sir Geoffrey Twining* (Montreal and Toronto, 1922).

Twins, mountain peaks, are in Alberta, in the Rocky mountains, in lat.

52° 13′, long. 117° 26′, and have altitudes of 11,675 and 12,085 feet. These form a double-headed mountain, which was named by J. Norman Collie in 1898.

Twisted Stalk (*Streptopus amplexifolius* (L.) DC., *Liliaceae*), an herb with rather stout zigzag stems and forked divergent branching. The leaves are smooth, taper-pointed, and strongly-clasping at the base. The flowers are greenish-white, the perianth segments wide-spreading or recurved from near the middle. The fruit is a scarlet, globose berry. It may be found in cold moist woods from Greenland to Alaska, blooming in the spring.

Twitya river, in the Mackenzie district of the North West Territories, flows north-east into the Gravel river, a tributary of the Mackenzie, between the 128th and 129th meridians of west longitude. The name is an Indian word for "river flowing from lakes".

Two Mountains, a county in Quebec, fronting on the Ottawa river and the lake of Two Mountains, and bounded on one side by Argenteuil county and on the others by Terrebonne county. Chief town, Ste. Scholastique. Pop. (1931), 14,284.

Two Mountains, lake of, an expansion of the Ottawa river near its junction with the St. Lawrence in Quebec. It was explored by Champlain (q.v.) in his journey up the Ottawa in 1613. The name is derived from two remarkable mountains near the lake. It has an area of 63 square miles.

Tyendinaga, a township in Hastings county, Ontario, organized in 1800. It takes its name from the Indian name of Joseph Brant (q.v.), which was *Thayendanegea;* and there is still an Indian reserve in this township.

Tyrrell, mount, is in Alberta, in lat. 51° 42′, long. 115° 51′, and has an altitude of 8,919 feet. It was named by George M. Dawson (q.v.) in 1885, after J. B. Tyrrell, who had been his assistant in 1883.

U

Ucluelet, a settlement in the Clayoquot district of Vancouver island, British Columbia, on the east side of Ucluelet arm, in Barkley sound, 180 miles north-west of Victoria. It has a life-saving station, and is named after the Ucluelet tribe of Indians, who live here, and whose name means "people with the safe landing-place". Pop. (1934), 200.

Ukrainians. The immigration of settlers from the Ukraine into Canada began as early as 1894 when nine families of Ruthenians or Galicians settled near Star, Alberta, not far from Edmonton. This immigration was the result of economic conditions in the Austrian provinces of Galicia and Bukovina that had brought about, previously, a considerable emigration to the United States and to South America. A second group arrived in 1896; and when the Laurier government, under the inspiration of Sir Clifford Sifton (q.v.), inaugurated an aggressive immigration policy, it found a fertile field in the Ukraine. In 1900 over 5,000 Ukrainians came into Canada, and by 1907 this figure had risen to 21,000. Between 1896 and 1914 it is estimated that no fewer than 170,000 Ukrainians (known as "Galicians", "Bukovinians", and "Ruthenians") found their way to Canada. Nor did the immigration cease with 1914. Since the Great War the immigration from the Ukraine into Canada has been perhaps greater than from any other country in continental Europe. To-day the population of Ukrainian origin in Canada is not far short of 300,000, most of whom are settled in the prairie provinces; and they are the third largest racial group in the prairie provinces, and probably the fourth largest in the Dominion. The exact numbers of the Ukrainians in Canada are difficult to determine, for the Ukrainians in Europe have never been a political unit, and Ukrainian immigrants have often been entered as Austrians, Russians, Roumanians, and Poles, as well as Galicians, Ruthenians, and Bukovinians.

The Ukrainians have been mainly agriculturists, and have settled in blocks (more or less dense) in the prairie provinces. Most of them are found in Manitoba, in scrub lands neglected by other settlers; but there are also large blocks of them on good lands in Saskatchewan, and there is a large settlement of them in the country north of Vegreville, in Alberta. Because of their settlement in separate communities, they have been slow in assimilating Canadian ideals; and education has made among them only moderate progress. But there is already a strong tendency among the second generation of Ukrainians in Canada to drift into the cities or to the United States; and already there are distinct signs that the standard of living and education among them is rising rapidly. In the earlier days of railway-building in the West, their labour was of great usefulness.

See C. H. Young, *The Ukrainian Canadians* (Toronto, 1931), with bibliography. See also **Galician Immigration.**

Ulverton, a village in Drummond county, Quebec, on the Black river, 7 miles from Richmond. It was probably named after Ulverston, a town in Lancashire, England. Pop. (1934), 300.

185

Umfreville, Edward (*fl.* 1771-1790), fur-trader, was a writer in the service of the Hudson's Bay Company from 1771 to 1782. He was captured by the French under La Pérouse in 1782, and on his release in 1783 went to Canada, where he entered the service of the North West Company as a clerk. In 1784 he was employed to discover a new route from lake Superior to lake Winnipeg; and his journal of this exploration has been edited by R. Douglas, under the title *Nipigon to Winnipeg* (Ottawa, 1929). He spent the years 1784-8 on the north branch of the Saskatchewan, but left the North West Company's service in 1788, and returned to England by way of New York. It appears from the records of the Hudson's Bay Company that he applied to be taken back into the service of this company in 1789, but failed to obtain satisfactory terms. He then published a book, entitled *The present state of Hudson Bay* (London, 1790), which was in part an attack on the Hudson's Bay Company. After this, he disappears from view.

Umiak, the large skin boat or "woman's boat" of the Eskimo. It is the name by which this boat is known among the eastern Eskimo.

Underground Railway. This was the phrase used to denote, before the American civil war, the route by which fugitive slaves from the Southern States were enabled to reach freedom in Canada. Fugitives were passed by American abolitionists from one station to another, until they reached the Canadian frontier. See W. H. Siebert, *The underground railroad from slavery to freedom* (New York, 1898), W. H. Withrow, *The underground railway* (Trans. Roy. Soc. Can., 1903), and F. Landon, *Canada and the underground railroad* (Kingston History Society, Report and Proceedings 1923).

Underwood, a village in Bruce county, Ontario, 4½ miles from Tiverton, the nearest railway station, and 12 miles from Port Elgin. Pop. (1934), 400.

Unemployment. Even in times of normal international economic balance, there must always be a considerable amount of unemployment in Canada, since the comparatively wide extremes of climate found in most parts of the Dominion make the problem of seasonal employment a matter of great concern, particularly in the more important industrial occupations, such as farming, fishing, logging, trapping, and transportation by water. From this same seasonal cause has developed the mobility of labour in Canada, which makes for a more even distribution of employment. Until a few years ago, the heavy demands for workers in the harvest fields of the western provinces took thousands of men whose ordinary work was not agricultural, and moved them hundreds and thousands of miles for only a few weeks' employment. The falling-off of activities in many fields of industry during the winter months makes it necessary for workers to seek other forms of employment, or to move to other centres for part of the year. An estimate based on the Dominion official employment index covering the period from 1924 to 1929 disclosed a 55 per cent. range between the maximum and minimum in the logging industry; and for construction work the range was about 50 per cent.

Due largely to the physical formation and peculiarities of the country, the major natural industries of Canada are largely sectional, and, when in years of depression there is very little market for many of its staple products, there is great sectional unemployment and hardship. Basic products such as wheat, lumber, pulp and paper are produced in many other parts of the world as well, and a decrease in the world market for these commodities almost invariably brings about a very drastic fall in price, which in turn brings a decided drop in the social income of the Dominion, resulting inevitably in an increase in unemployment and a lowering of the standards of living.

Due to the new industrialism, in the past few years the development of new types of labour-saving machinery and improved methods in industry have decreased the demand for certain types of workers, and even rendered some groups superfluous, greatly affecting the labour market. On the other hand, improved methods of building construction have tended to overcome a customary winter slackness in that field, but they have also done away with the need for certain groups of more highly-skilled craftsmen. Of late years changes of great significance have been made in the agricultural industry, due to the use of more highly developed farm machinery and implements and the increase in large-scale farming, and there has been a consequent decline in the amount of farm labour required. The decided increase in agricultural production has made it impossible for the small farmer, who has to employ a relatively large amount of labour, to hold his own against the large organizations which have replaced human labour by machinery, and men are driven away from the land into industrial centres, where they find it impossible to become absorbed into industry.

With the development of an advanced organization of production, agriculture in Canada has become more and more affected by the type of disturbance generally associated with industrial production. Prolonged droughts in the wheat-raising areas of the prairie provinces, where there is little or no flexibility of economic activity, have greatly reduced the numbers of employed workers. When the price of wheat rises, the farm income improves, stimulating business activity and eliminating urban unemployment, or, at least, reducing it to a marked degree.

Historical survey. Following the American War of Independence the in-pouring of about 50,000 United Empire Loyalists changed the entire economic aspect of Canada and upset her whole balance. Almost all their property and effects had been confiscated by the revolting colonies; all had lost their trades; and they came seeking food and shelter and a new livelihood in an almost undeveloped country. Their disposal was a matter of grave concern to the government of Canada, and may be looked upon as the first real problem of unemployment which this country had to face. Gradually, however, the Loyalists established themselves in their new life, most of them being transferred to the unsettled parts of the Maritimes and Upper Canada. All were allotted lands; and implements, farm animals, and rations for several years were given to each household. With this aid, the Loyalist settlements in Nova Scotia, New Brunswick, and Upper Canada, though largely cut off from markets, became in a few years self-supporting and, indeed, fairly prosperous communities—one of the earliest examples in Canada of the solution of the problem of unemployment.

During the time of the Napoleonic Wars great numbers of every social class in Europe were thrown out of employment, and there was a great flow of emigrants to the New World. The depression following Waterloo gave a new need for and impetus to emigration, and many immigrants flowed into Canada, especially into the Maritime provinces, which were quite unprepared and unable to absorb the newcomers, as the problem of the Loyalists was still a very pressing one. After the Peace of 1815 Great Britain had the problem of disbanding her army, and as a result was in the throes of great industrial distress. Many of her unemployed were encouraged to emigrate to Canada. In many cases these British emigrants came as groups, and since there was no good land left in the Maritimes for group settlement, the bulk of the immigration flowed into Upper Canada, and during the ten years between 1815 and 1825, the white population of Canada rose from about 350,000 to nearly 790,000 persons.

From 1825 to 1841 there was a period of continued immigration from Great Britain, especially of the agricultural, artisan, and labour classes. Unemployment was becoming a serious problem, as the labour market of the Dominion was overstocked, and many of the immigrants who had come to the new land full of hope and expectation were forced to live on charity. Gradually new industries began to develop, especially in Upper Canada, and the increased markets for agricultural products in the growing towns and villages provided new incentives for the development of greater agricultural activity. From time to time there were poor crops bringing inactivity of labour, and depressions such as that of 1857 which brought a distressing decline in economic activity, but with Confederation a new stage in the industrial development of Canada began.

At the time of Confederation, Canada was overwhelmingly agricultural, and life was on a modest scale. In the years immediately following 1867, a considerable revival in Canadian trade took place. Canada's products found new markets, interprovincial and British; and trade with the United States continued to expand in spite of high tariff barriers. Between 1873 and 1878 there was a world-wide industrial depression, which involved Canada's newly developing commerce to a distressing degree, affecting agriculture and manufactures alike. The lumber trade with the United States was seriously affected, and the shipping which had been engaged in the foreign carrying trade no longer found employment. Because there was no work for them in their own country, large numbers of mechanics came into Canada from the United States, adding greatly to the already alarming proportions of the unemployed

in the Dominion. With the early eighties came a certain degree of recovery, the prolonged effect of which was somewhat modified by a cycle of dry seasons between 1883 and 1895 and the world-wide slump in agricultural prices, due largely to the greatly increased amount of land being brought under cultivation. In the last years of the nineteenth century, labour activity increased greatly in the United States, and Canadian industrialism began to make itself felt, and there was a marked increase in the amount of employment available. At this time an active immigration policy was inaugurated by both Dominion and provincial governments, and there was a considerable movement of American farmers across the border to take up grants or buy lands in the prairie provinces.

With the turn of the century, the Dominion began a period of definite prosperity. New industries were developed, and foreign trade expanded greatly. Improved means of transportation, higher prices for products, a marked increase in immigration, and the opening of the West brought a great industrial expansion. With 1901 a heavy tide of immigration set in, and by 1911 the rate of increase of population had risen to 34.17 per cent., the greatest which the country had ever experienced. This meant that in a single decade Canada had to assimilate a population almost equal to 50 per cent. of her population in 1900. An artificial prosperity grew up when construction boomed; the prices of articles of general consumption increased tremendously; and an abnormal inflation in all living expenses took place. Between the years 1901 and 1917 there was a period of great railway expansion and development of elaborate irrigation enterprises and other public works, as well as of remarkable growth in the cities and towns in western Canada. At the same time, and as a result of the opening up of the western provinces, between 1901 and 1914 there was a great orgy of land speculation, which no government, Dominion, provincial, or municipal, was able to prevent, regulate, or govern in any efficacious way. In 1913 this great and abnormal land boom collapsed, and nothing could have occurred in Canada more seriously to affect the general moral tone and social and economic development of the people.

During the winter of 1912 there had been a decided drop in the price of wheat, and the situation of the western farmer had become serious. The result was that by the end of 1913 there was a considerable and growing unemployment throughout the Dominion. There was much hardship during the winter preceding the war, and it is doubtful whether the volume of unemployment in that winter had ever been exceeded in the history of Canada. The usual seasonal absorption of labour in the following spring was insignificant, and by the summer of 1914 there were alarming numbers of unemployed in all the great urban centres of the Dominion, causing a growing sense of alarm among those who had been striving to develop the great natural resources of Canada. The tremendous increase in the urban population added to the complexity of social life, and also to the general cost of living. During these years immediately before the war there was a development of trade unionism which tended to complicate the absorption of labour in the great industrial centres, and this was reflected in the problem of rural labour in the parts of the country which were distinctly agricultural.

During the war nearly half a million of Canada's male population were withdrawn from active service in industry, creating a very serious problem and necessitating the absorption of many women into almost every industry, and the reorganization of the entire economic life of the country. Thus, at the close of the war the re-absorption and re-establishment of a large proportion of

the male population of the Dominion created a problem of major importance. Even early in the war the various provincial governments found it necessary to form commissions to seek employment for men returned from overseas as soon as they were fit to work, and during the last three years of the war thousands of men were re-established in industry through the medium of these commissions. The demobilization of the Canadian forces and the suspension of all war activities created a surplus of labour throughout the Dominion which caused the Canadian government to cease to encourage or give inducements to the vast numbers of labourers available throughout the world at that time as immigrants, and a system of selective and restrictive immigration was developed which admitted to the Dominion only those fitted to take a share in developing Canada's natural resources, especially its fertile farming lands.

Agricultural countries such as Canada are mainly affected economically by the reduction of their purchasing power, which depends always upon the fall of the prices of their products. There was a considerable increase in unemployment in the Dominion resulting from the industrial uncertainty of the reconstruction period after the war, and the worldwide fall in prices which followed the short boom of 1919-20. During 1920 and 1923 immigration into the Dominion was high, especially from Great Britain and Ireland, and considerable anxiety was felt in government, as well as in industrial circles, over the high unemployment figures. In 1924 immigration regulations made conditions worse by bringing in immigrants who drifted to industrial centres as casual labourers without the possibility of employment. Between 1925 and 1929 there was again a marked decrease in the price of agricultural products because of the difficulties of finding export markets, and the result was, as usual, a surplus of farm labour, and a drifting to urban centres.

Even before the financial break of 1929 there was an increasing volume of unemployment in the principal industries in Canada. Despite the boom of 1926-9, the general index of employment showed an average gain of only 0.61 per cent. between 1919 and 1934, perhaps partly because unemployment reached alarming proportions between 1929 and 1934. The effect of the 1929 crisis in the United States was more directly and immediately felt in Canada than elsewhere because of the close financial and commercial intercourse between the two countries. The year 1929 saw an unemployment problem, a labour surplus instead of a labour deficit, in the agricultural regions of Canada for the first time, and the cessation of the regular harvesters' excursions of earlier years dates from that time. Canada has developed many of its other natural resources, but its basic industries are the production of wheat, lumber, pulp and paper, and minerals, all of which are subject to severe variations in price and for some of which, in times of world-wide depression, there is little market. To develop these basic industries Canada has had to open up vast territories of land, necessitating tremendous expenditures on transport facilities and public works of general utility, creating an enormous public debt, the interest on which has to be met. The greatly decreased prices obtained for staple products during the depression years resulted in a fall in the social income of Canada, and, since most of the major industries of the Dominion are in specialized areas, there were serious regional rises in unemployment. The purchasing power of the farmers, who represent more than 40 per cent. of the population of Canada, had been reduced by 44 per cent. in 1930, as compared with 1928. The census of 1931 showed 18.61 per cent. of all wage-earners of the Dominion not at work. In 1936-7 nearly 300,000 normally self-supporting persons required public aid in the drought areas of the prairie provinces. As a result of the drought the home markets for manufactured products dropped away, and the earlier promise of more employment in industrial and commercial activities failed to materialize. As part of the depression overhaul, many industrial plants have installed labour-saving devices, and these have thrown more people out of employment.

The recent depression has left the Dominion with a greatly increased burden of economic dependency, and there are certain groups of unemployables who, with their dependents, will form the solid nucleus of the needy for years to come. These are made up largely of the homeless men who can not be absorbed into agricultural pursuits or heavy manual labour projects because of some unsuitability, such as age or physical or mental handicap, the restless youth who have grown up during the depression days never having known employment, the increasing number of displaced, older single women, and the growing number of non-resident individuals or families who are not accepted as municipal or provincial responsibilities, and finally become a burden to emergency relief authorities or private charities. In addition, the hopelessness arising out of prolonged unemployment tends towards the deterioration of the labour force of the country, and the breaking up of groups of trained skilled workers is an element of great importance in the building up of a permanent class of unemployed and even unemployable labour.

Remedial legislation. During the period of great industrial activity and development which ended in 1913, public employment offices were opened in many parts of Canada to meet the steady demands for labour which were coming as a result of the great expansion in industrial as well as agricultural activities. As early as 1910 the legislature of the province of Quebec passed an Act respecting the Establishment of Employment Bureaux for Workmen. The labour surplus of the winter of 1913-14 drew the attention of both the Dominion and the provincial governments to the necessity for more efficient organization of the labour market. In 1916 the Commission on Unemployment, which had been set up by the Ontario government, recommended a nation-wide system of employment offices to take the place of the commercial employment agencies then in active operation. Within three or four years, almost all of these latter had been dispensed with, and a system of provincial offices established.

In 1918 the Dominion parliament passed the Employment Offices Co-ordination Act, the aim of which was to set up a Dominion-wide employment service. At the same time the Employment Service Council of Canada was formed, the duties of which were to act in an advisory capacity with regard to the administration of the Act, and also to distribute statistical information regarding employment conditions and to suggest methods of preventing unemployment in the various industries throughout the Dominion. Since that time almost all of the provinces have established public employment services which act in conjunction with the Dominion Department of Labour. Provincial Employment Service Councils have also been established which co-operate with the Dominion Council.

On September 22, 1930, the first Unemployment Relief Act came into force, empowering the Dominion government to assist the various provinces in carrying out relief measures necessary to alleviate the exceptional economic conditions which had resulted in excessive unemployment. The Unemployment and Farm Relief Act, which received royal assent on August 3, 1931, was designed to "expend such moneys as might be deemed necessary for relieving distress, providing employment, and maintaining, within the competence of parliament, peace, order, and good government throughout Canada". The subsequent sessions of parliament have re-affirmed these Acts, with certain modifications and alterations contingent upon the times and conditions of the country. Under the National Employment Commission Act, 1936, the Dominion parliament appointed the National Employment Commission "to assist the Minister of Labour in promoting co-operation between the federal government, provincial governments, municipalities, and other agencies, including employers' and employees' associations and social welfare bodies, in dealing with the problem of unemployment relief, and in an endeavour to provide work for the unemployed".

The bill cited as The Unemployment Relief and Assistance Act, 1936, was designed to "find employment on public works for relief recipients in the province where such works were being carried out", and also to provide relief measures and federal financial assistance in the form of loans in agreement with the provinces, and with corporations or individuals engaged in industry in order to increase industrial employment.

A scheme to make provision for federal aid for the aged and deserving poor in Canada was first discussed in the Dominion parliament during the session of 1906-7, and, after being in abeyance through the years of the war, a bill respecting old age pensions received royal assent on March 31, 1927, and was written into the Revised Statutes of Canada, 1927.

Another form of industrial service in Canada, which has been an important factor in stabilizing labour, is group life insurance, which was first written in Canada in 1919. The fact that employees usually contributed toward the premiums under the group sickness and disability contract tends to develop a certain responsibility on the part of employees, and thus to create a more stable type of labour.

Direct relief. Since there was no Poor Law in Canada, and no definite policy by which local authorities might be guided in administering relief, when the problem of relief became one of major importance, a few public and charitable bodies throughout the Dominion had to assume the burden of providing relief and employment for the needy.

The first real attempt to measure the problem of governmental relief was made in 1915 by the appointment of the Ontario Commission on Unemployment. As early as 1915 all the provincial governments, in co-operation with the Dominion government, had established committees to find employment for, and re-establish in industrial pursuits, men returned from active service; and immediately after the Armistice the Dominion government began to plan ways of re-absorbing the men into industry as they were demobilized. Free government employment offices were established; special preference being given to war veterans for civil service positions; and an earnest attempt was made to secure a preference for returned soldiers among the employers of labour generally.

A national system of vocational training for the returned soldier was set up by the Dominion government, with the aim that those soldiers who had been disabled might be re-established in an industry as closely allied as possible to the one of which they had formed a part before enlistment. A careful survey was made of industrial opportunities, and within four years many men were placed in active industrial service who might otherwise have been unable to re-establish themselves.

In 1917 the Soldiers' Settlement Board was organized to assist properly qualified returned soldiers who wished to settle on farms in Canada. Loans were made for the purchase of live stock and farm equipment, the erection of permanent improvements, and for clearing the lands held by war veterans.

Ever since the war the Department of Soldiers' Civil Re-establishment has maintained a system whereby light employment can be given to men who became slightly handicapped during their time of military service, and who might otherwise be almost entirely without any means of self-support and find a permanent place in the ranks of the unemployed.

During the winter of 1919-20, the government realized that a considerable amount of emergency relief would be necessary to help the discharged soldiers who had not been able to find employment, and this relief was dispensed in co-operation with the Canadian Patriotic Fund.

In the winter of 1920-21 the Dominion government first shared directly in the cost of unemployment relief with the provinces and municipalities. The government stipulated that, as far as possible, the unemployment situation should be met by the provision of work rather than relief, and that all men applying for assistance should register at one of the government's Employment Service offices.

By the autumn of 1930, the Dominion government engaged in a very extensive system of municipal and federal public works and undertakings for the re-absorption of the unemployed, and large sums of money were paid to the provincial governments for work relief. By 1932 it became necessary for the government to cut down expenditures on its general public works programme, which had given employment on a full wage basis. About this time an extensive system of land settlement was developed in British Columbia, a policy of granting free land to those who would undertake to live on and develop it.

Before 1935 labour-service relief camps were operated under the direction of the Department of National Defence to meet the problem of single, homeless unemployed men. These relief camps were closed on July 1, 1936, and determined efforts were made to secure employment for the men, and "to explore the resources of Canada, both public and private, for the purpose of developing the fields of industrial employment to absorb, as speedily as possible, into useful work at current rates of wages the men in the camps physically fit for the work".

The report of the Dominion commissioner of Unemployment Relief, dated March 31, 1937, states that "The Dominion makes grants to assist each of the provinces in discharging its responsibilities for the relief of needy persons within its borders, it being understood that the provinces are to assist the municipalities within their borders financially to such an extent as may be necessary, the Dominion contributing also to the cost of certain relief works projects proposed to be undertaken by the provinces", such as provincial highway construction, provincial and municipal works and the assistance of settlers to become established on a self-supporting basis.

Government statistical services. There are no official compilations of statistics of employment or unemployment for the Dominion prior to 1912 which are of any great value for the purposes of economic survey. The pressure of the problem of unemployment in the early years of the war became of such vital importance to the economic life of the country that a tremendous interest in employment and unemployment statistics developed, and since 1920 a monthly survey of nation-wide employment has been issued in the *Labour Gazette*. "With a view to the dissemination of accurate statistical and other information relating to the conditions of labour, the Minister of Labour shall collect, digest, and publish in suitable form statistical and other information relating to the conditons of labour, shall institute and conduct

inquiries into important industrial questions upon which adequate information may not at present be available, and issue at least once in every month a publication to be known as the *Labour Gazette*, which shall contain information regarding conditions of the labour market, and kindred subjects" (*Revised Statutes of Canada*, 1927). The *Labour Gazette* has been issued regularly since September, 1900, but the scope of its contents has broadened considerably because of the great influence of the functions and work of the Department, necessitated by the changing conditions of the industrial, economic, and social spheres.

The Dominion Department of Labour in 1918 issued the first of its series of reports on labour legislation in Canada, the reports covering Dominion as well as provincial legislation. The first volume was cumulative, and contained the text of the labour laws of the Dominion as existing December 31, 1915; and the series has been continued annually since that time, with cumulative volumes appearing occasionally. In addition, in 1919 the Department began to publish in the press a weekly series of returns from employers.

In 1919 also the newly-organized Employment Service started to collect a system of reports from every important industry in Canada and to issue statistical reports of the applications for employment as well as for the demand for labour.

Early in 1936 the Department of Labour undertook a monthly classification of those in receipt of direct relief from public authorities throughout Canada, statistics secured through this classification showing the number on relief in the foilowing categories: employable persons and their dependents, unemployable persons and their dependents, farmers' families, and transient persons.

In addition to the *Labour Gazette*, a comprehensive annual report on labour organization in Canada is compiled and published by the Labour Intelligence Branch of the Department of Labour, and a reference library on labour and kindred subjects is maintained by the Department.

Bibliography. More extensive studies of the general and historical aspects of the problems of unemployment in Canada are to be found in John Buchan (ed.), *The nations of to-day: British America, Canada* (Boston, 1923); H. M. Cassidy, *Unemployment and relief in Ontario, 1929-1932* (Toronto, 1932); H. A. Innis and A. F. W. Plumptre, *The Canadian economy and its problems* (Toronto, 1934); International Labour Office, *Unemployment—Some international aspects* (Geneva, 1929); W. P. M. Kennedy (ed.), *Social and economic conditions in the Dominion of Canada* (Annals of the American Academy of Political and Social Science, vol. cvii, Philadelphia, 1923); L. C. A. Knowles, *Economic development of the overseas Empire,* vol. ii (London, 1930); Ontario Commission on Unemployment, *Report* (Toronto, 1916); Royal Institute of International Affairs, *Report on unemployment* (London, 1935); Adam Shortt and A. G. Doughty (eds.), *Canada and its provinces,* vol. ix, "Industrial expansion" (Toronto, 1914); N. J. Ware and H. A. Logan, *Labour in Canadian-American relations* (Toronto, 1937); Quincy Wright, *Unemployment as a world problem* (Chicago, 1931).

Current statistics may be found in *Canada Year Book* (Ottawa, annual), Dominion Commissioner of Unemployment Relief, *Report* (Ottawa, annual), Department of Labour, *Labour legislation in Canada* (Ottawa, annual), Department of Labour, *Report* (Ottawa, annual), *Labour Gazette* (Ottawa, monthly), and the National Employment Commission, *Interim report* (Ottawa, 1937).

Ungava, a district of the North West Territories of Canada, was created by an order-in-council of the Canadian government in 1895, and embraced the northern part of the peninsula (commonly known as the Ungava peninsula) between Hudson bay and the coast of Labrador lying north of the general line of the Eastmain and Hamilton rivers. It disappeared when this territory was annexed to the province of Quebec in 1912, and became New Quebec.

Ungava bay, a deep indentation in the northern shore of the province of Quebec, west of cape Chidley and south of the entrance to Hudson strait. The name is an Eskimo word meaning "far away"; and an Eskimo settlement here is referred to in the *Transactions* of the Philosophical Society for 1774 as "Ungabow".

Uniacke, James Boyle (d. 1858), politician, was the fourth son of Richard John Uniacke (q.v.). He studied law at the Inner Temple, London, England, was called to the bar, and practised law in Nova Scotia. He was elected to the Legislative Assembly of Nova Scotia to represent Cape Breton, and became the Tory leader in the Assembly. In 1837 he was appointed a member of the Council of Twelve; but in 1840 he resigned from the council, and became an advocate of responsible government. Later in 1840 he re-entered the Executive Council, with Joseph Howe (q.v.); but in 1844 he and Howe resigned in protest against the action of Lord Falkland (q.v.) in appointing M. B. Almon (q.v.) to the Council. In 1848 he was invited to form a government; and from 1848 to 1854 he was nominal head of the administration, with the portfolio of attorney-general. He retired from public life in 1854, and accepted the non-political office of commissioner of crown lands. He died in March, 1858.

Uniacke, Norman Fitzgerald (1777?-1846), attorney-general of Lower Canada (1809-25), was born in Nova Scotia about 1777, the eldest son of Richard John Uniacke (q.v.). He studied law at the Inner Temple in England,

and was called to the English bar. In 1809 he was appointed attorney-general of Lower Canada. He was suspended from office in 1810, but was reinstated, and continued as attorney-general until 1825. In 1824 he was also elected to represent the borough of William Henry in the Legislative Assembly of Lower Canada; but in 1825 he resigned the attorney-generalship and his seat in the House, to accept appointment as a judge of the court of King's Bench in Montreal. He sat on the bench until about 1836; and he died in Halifax, Nova Scotia, on December 11, 1846. In 1818 he suffered the loss of a leg through amputation; and in 1819 he married Sophie Delesdernier.

Uniacke, Richard John (1753-1830), attorney-general of Nova Scotia (1797-1830), was born at Castletown, Cork county, Ireland, on November 22, 1753, the fourth son of Norman Fitzgerald Uniacke and Alicia, daughter of Bartholomew Purdon. In 1769 he entered upon the study of law in Dublin; but in 1773 he emigrated to America. In 1774 he settled in Nova Scotia, and in 1781 he was admitted to practice as a barrister and attorney in that province. From 1783 to 1793 he sat in the House of Assembly of Nova Scotia; and from 1789 to 1793 he was its speaker. In 1782 he had been appointed solicitor-general, and in 1797 he was chosen attorney-general of the province, a position he occupied for the rest of his life. In 1798 he was again elected to the House of Assembly, and in 1799 he was a second time chosen speaker of the House. In 1806 he retired finally from the legislature, and in 1808 he was appointed a member of the Executive Council. He died at Mount Uniacke, Nova Scotia, on October 11, 1830. In 1775 he married Martha Maria Delesdernier (d. 1803), by whom he had six sons and six daughters; and in 1808 Eliza Newton, by whom he had one daughter. He published *Statutes passed in the General Assemblies held in Nova*

Scotia from 1758 to 1804 inclusive (Halifax, 1805). See Hon. L. G. Power, *Richard John Uniacke, a sketch* (Collections of the Nova Scotia Hist. Soc., 1895); and R. G. Trotter, *An early proposal for the federation of British North America* (Can. hist. rev., 1925).

Uniacke, a village in Abitibi county, Quebec, on the Canadian National Railway, 12 miles from Senneterre. Pop. (1934), 100.

Union, a village in Elgin county, Ontario, on the railway between London and Port Stanley, 5 miles south of St. Thomas. Pop. (1934), 300.

Union Bank of Canada was founded in 1865 and was originally incorporated as the Union Bank of Lower Canada, with head office in Quebec city. Later, the name was changed to the Union Bank of Canada, and in 1912 the head office was moved to Winnipeg. In 1925, as a result of substantially reduced earnings, the bank was faced with the necessity of making a drastic cut in the annual dividend. This would have resulted in a substantial drop in the value of the bank's shares and might have adversely affected its general standing. The Union Bank was, therefore, absorbed by the Royal Bank of Canada, which thus gained a great accession of strength in the West. At the time of its absorption the Union Bank had a capital of $8,000,000 and a reserve of $1,750,000.

Union Bay, a village in the Nelson district of British Columbia, on Union bay, and on the Canadian Pacific Railway, 9 miles south of Courtenay. It has a steamer landing. Pop. (1930), 300.

Unionist Party, a party formed in 1917 by a union of the Liberal-Conservatives under Sir Robert Borden (q.v.) and the Liberals who broke at that time with Sir Wilfrid Laurier (q.v.) and supported compulsory military service. The party carried the elections of 1917; and the Unionist government helped to bring the World War to a successful conclusion, and represented Canada at the Paris conference, which brought the war to an end, and set up the League of Nations. The party was re-christened in 1920 the "National Liberal and Conservative Party"; but the new name never gained any currency, and gradually the Liberal Unionists either went back to the Liberal party, or were absorbed by the Liberal-Conservative party. While it lasted, however, the Unionist government had a singularly high record of pure and efficient administration. See N. W. Rowell, *One year of Union government* (pamphlet, Toronto, 1919).

Union Theological College. See **Emmanuel College** (Toronto).

Unionville, a village in York county, Ontario, on the Rouge river, and on the Canadian National Railway, 20 miles north-east of Toronto. Pop. (1934), 600.

Unitarian Church. Unitarianism derives its name from its doctrine of the single personality of God the Father, in contrast with the Trinitarian conception. This system of thought has been traced back to the "Act of Uniformity", passed in England in 1662, by which not only were many clergymen compelled to leave their pulpits, but also an impetus was given to more liberal thought, than was then prevailing. The name came later. Belief kept changing, as the basis of belief changed. In the United States, Unitarianism passed through various stages, until it seemed to accept broadly the results of the scientific and comparative study of all religions, and not a few of the clergymen of New England were preaching what was essentially Unitarianism. In 1803 W. E. Channing, a man of high character and of wide influence, became the leader of the Unitarian movement. Later, the movement became more nationalistic. Henry Adams said that in his day the leaders of thought around Boston held that a virtuous, useful, unselfish life was all

that was necessary for salvation. Unitarianism has never made much headway in Canada. The last federal census (1931) gives the number of Unitarians in the Dominion as 4,445, scarcely twice the number of 60 years before. Of these 1,244 were in Ontario, 1,178 in Manitoba, and there were smaller groups in the other provinces. The First Unitarian Church in Toronto dates from 1845; there are churches in Ottawa and Montreal also, and elsewhere.

United Church of Canada. On June 10, 1925, the United Church of Canada held its inaugural service in Toronto. (See **Church Union.**) Congregations existing at the time of Union were at liberty to retain the polity to which they were accustomed; newly formed congregations were expected to adopt a policy specially prepared for them. The government of the Church embraces the Session, the Presbytery, the Conference, and the General Council. The doctrinal basis of union had been so carefully drawn up that it is said to set forth the fundamental and essential beliefs of the churches entering into Union. The spirit of mutual understanding and goodwill has helped to clear away difficulties incident to such a combination of forces. During the ten years from 1925 to 1935, the membership increased from 600,522 to 694,374, and the persons under pastoral care from approximately 1,250,000 to 1,690,177. There are 6,000 Sunday schools, with an enrollment of 623,000. The Church's headquarters are in Toronto, where its organ, the *New Outlook*, and other papers are published, and from which the Official Board and the secretaries of the different departments, in co-operation with the various Church courts, give leadership in the far-flung congregational and corporate service. Consult the *Year book of the United Church of Canada* (Toronto, 1936).

United Empire Bank of Canada, a bank which was organized in 1905, having obtained the charter of the

Pacific Bank of Canada, and was absorbed by the Union Bank of Canada in 1910. It had in 1910 only 12 branches.

United Empire Loyalists. This term is commonly applied in Canada to those Loyalists of the American Revolution who emigrated to the British North American provinces during or immediately after the Revolution, and to their descendants. In the United States those who adhered to the royal standard during the American Revolution were, and are still, known merely as "Loyalists"; but in Canada the words "United Empire" have been added to this description, in reference to the fact that Lord Dorchester (q.v.), then governor-general of British North America, proposed in 1789 "to put a Marke of Honor upon the families who had adhered to the unity of the Empire, and joined the Royal Standard in America before the Treaty of Separation in the year 1783", and ordained that all Loyalists of this description were "to be distinguished by the letters U.E. affixed to their names, alluding to their great principle, the unity of the Empire". A list of these loyalists, known as "the Old U.E. List", was drawn up, and in Upper Canada additions to this list were made by Lieutenant-Governor Simcoe (q.v.); and it is a fact sometimes forgotten that no one is entitled to be described as a "United Empire Loyalist" one of whose ancestors is not to be found in this list. After 1789 many Americans emigrated to British North America, and especially to Upper Canada, under the offer of free lands made by Simcoe, and many of these were doubtless loyalists during the American Revolution; but neither they nor their descendants have the right to be described as "United Empire Loyalists" unless their names appear in the "Old U.E. List". They are more correctly described as "late Loyalists".

The numbers of the Loyalists in the American Revolution are difficult to determine. The historian Lecky declared that the Revolution "was the work of an energetic minority, who succeeded in committing an undecided and fluctuating majority to courses for which they had little love". The loyalists themselves sometimes maintained that they constituted an actual majority in the Thirteen Colonies. In 1779 they professed to have more troops in the field than the Continental Congress. But these statements were no doubt exaggerations. The probability is that about one-third of the people of the Thirteen Colonies were opposed to the Revolution. This was the opinion expressed on more than one occasion by John Adams, the second president of the United States; and it was also the opinion of Thomas M'Kean, one of the signers of the Declaration of Independence. During the Revolution, the Loyalist levies played an important part in the military struggle; and had it not been for the maladministration of the British military authorities in the war, it is possible that they might have played a decisive part. As it was, their efforts sank into the category of isolated raids, and full advantage was not taken of their aptitude for warfare under North American conditions.

When the War of the American Revolution came to an end with the Peace of Versailles in 1783, the lot of the American Loyalists was unenviable in the extreme. The British commissioners had done their best to protect the interests of the Loyalists in the treaty of peace; and the American commissioners had made certain promises. They had agreed that no future confiscations of Loyalist property should take place, that no further persecutions of Loyalists should take place, that Loyalists should meet with no lawful impediment to the recovery of their just debts, and that the American Congress should "earnestly recommend to the legislatures of the respective states" a policy of amnesty and restitution. But these promises were hardly worth the paper they were written on. No attempt at restitution was made, except in one or two states, and the persecution of the Loyalists continued after 1783 almost unabated. The individual states refused, almost without exception, to honour the promises of the commissioners appointed by Congress; and it became clear that large numbers of the Loyalists would have to find homes elsewhere.

In these circumstances, the British government, as it was in duty bound to do, came to the relief of the Loyalists. It arranged for the transportation of those who wished to leave the revolted colonies; it offered them homes in the provinces of Nova Scotia (which then included New Brunswick) and Quebec (which then included Upper Canada or Ontario); and it appointed a royal commission to award compensation for the losses sustained. It went even further than this; and those Loyalists who settled in Nova Scotia, New Brunswick, and Canada received assistance in the form of rations, farm stock, and farm implements, until they were able to fend for themselves.

The numbers of the Loyalists who emigrated to what is now Canada have been the subject of some speculation. In all, those who emigrated to what are now the Maritime provinces of Canada seem to have numbered about 35,000; and those who settled in what later became Upper Canada, along the north bank of the St. Lawrence, about the bay of Quinte, at Niagara, and at Detroit, seem to have numbered not many more than 5,000. The total immigration of Loyalists to what is now Canada would appear, therefore, not to have exceeded 50,000 persons. A number of those who went first to Nova Scotia and New Brunswick afterwards found their way to Upper Canada. A number of the wealthier Loyalists, of course, returned to England, and there were some Loyalists who went to the West Indies, Prince Edward Island, and Newfoundland.

The Loyalists who came to Canada exerted a profound influence on the future of the country. Until the Loyalist migration, the population of Canada was overwhelmingly French. Canada was a French colony of Great Britain; and the number of English-speaking inhabitants was infinitesimal. The influx of the United Empire Loyalists, however, completely altered the situation; and made Canada predominantly an English-speaking country. It is worthy of note, moreover, that the United Empire Loyalists were passionately devoted to "the principle of the unity of the Empire"; and their presence in the country has been a potent factor in Canadian political development. Both in the War of 1812 and in the struggle for responsible government their influence was profound; and it is not negligible to-day.

See Egerton Ryerson, *The loyalists and their times* (2 vols., Toronto, 1880), *The centennial of the settlement of Upper Canada by the United Empire Loyalists* (Toronto, 1885), C. H. Van Tyne, *The Loyalists in the American Revolution* (New York, 1902), W. S. Wallace, *The United Empire Loyalists* (Toronto, 1914), and A. G. Bradley, *The United Empire Loyalists* (London, 1932). An index to unprinted materials relating to the Loyalists is to be found in W. W. Campbell, *Report on manuscript lists relating to the United Empire Loyalists, with reference to other sources* (Ottawa, Public Archives of Canada, 1909).

United Empire Loyalists' Association of Canada, an association incorporated on December 1, 1897, as the United Empire Loyalists' Association of Ontario, with the object of uniting the descendants of the United Empire Loyalists and of preserving the historical records of these early settlers in Canada. On May 27, 1914, by special Act of Parliament, it was incorporated under its present name. Since 1898 the Association has published 7 volumes of *Transactions*.

United Empire Loyalists' Association of Ontario. See **United Empire Loyalists' Association of Canada.**

United Farmers of Ontario. See **Farmers' Movements.**

Unity, a village in the Battleford district of Saskatchewan, on the Canadian Pacific and Canadian National Railways, 120 miles west of Saskatoon. It is in a grain-growing district, and has a weekly newspaper (*Courier*). Pop. (1931), 806.

Universities. See **Education, Higher,** and the names of individual universities.

University College, the provincial or state-supported arts college in the University of Toronto. It was created by the University Act of 1853, which made the University of Toronto, like the University of London, solely an examining body, and delegated the work of instruction to University College and to any other colleges willing to be affiliated to the university. From 1853 to 1887 University College was the University of Toronto on its teaching side. But with the Federation Act of 1887, University College began to acquire a separate entity. With the inclusion of Victoria College, and later of St. Michael's and Trinity Colleges, as arts colleges in the university, it was placed on a parallel, though by no means identical, footing with them. For some years the president of the University was also the principal of University College; and the registrar of the University was also the registrar of University College. University College came, indeed, to be known as "the Main Building" of the University. To this day the University Library is the library of University College, and the bursar of the University is the bursar of University College, since the two have a common purse. But gradually the demand that University College should be something more than a name, bore fruit. In 1901 a separate principal for the

College was appointed; and in 1906 a separate registrar. In 1924 the administrative offices of the university were removed from University College to the newly-constructed Simcoe Hall; and in 1931 there was built Whitney Hall, a magnificent group of residences for the women of University College.

The principals of University College since 1901 have been Maurice Hutton (1901-28) and Malcolm William Wallace (1928—).

See W. J. Alexander (ed.), *The University of Toronto and its colleges* (Toronto, 1906), and W. S. Wallace, *A history of the University of Toronto* (Toronto, 1927). See also **University of Toronto.**

University of Alberta. The University of Alberta was created by an Act of the first session of the first legislature of the province, in 1906, which set up the legal framework on which the institution could be constructed. An amendment to the Act, in 1907, authorized the lieutenant-governor-in-council to appoint a president, and the government availed itself of this authority to select Dr. Henry Marshall Tory, who entered on his duties on January 1, 1908. Under the University Act all resident graduates of British and Canadian universities were entitled to become members of convocation by registering before a specified date, and three hundred and sixty-four persons availed themselves of this privilege. The convocation thus constituted proceeded to the election of five members of the Senate, and on the result of the poll being declared, on March 18, 1908, the government nominated its ten representatives to that body also. Mr. Justice Stuart, of Calgary, was at the same time elected chancellor. The president and Senate at their first meeting, on March 30, 1908, took the necessary steps to organize the faculty of arts and sciences, and decided to open classes in September. At a subsequent meeting, held in Calgary on July 6, four professors were appointed to chairs in the faculty. Classes were begun on September 23, with a registration of forty-five. At the second session of the second legislature, in November, 1910, a new university Act was passed, the general effect of which was to separate the business management of the university from the supervision of its educational affairs. For the control of the former a Board of Governors was constituted, to consist of the chancellor and the president *ex-officio*, and nine members appointed by the lieutenant-governor-in-council. For the latter purpose the Senate, in a considerably augmented form, was continued. Convocation was further defined to include all graduates of the University of Alberta in addition to the original members under the Act of 1906. The new Board of Governors was constituted in January, 1911, and the new Senate in March. This form of university government has remained substantially unaltered to the present, except that the lieutenant-governor-in-council nominates specifically the chairman of the board. Up to 1911 the university classes were conducted in rented premises, first in a portion of the Queen Alexandra Public School, afterwards in a part of the Strathcona High School, and it was in the latter that the first graduation exercises were held on May 16, 1911. But during the summer Athabaska Hall was erected, and became available for use—partly as classrooms, partly as dormitory—in September. This was rapidly followed by Assiniboia Hall, 1912-13, and Pembina Hall, 1914. All of these buildings, after serving for a time, both for classes and residential purposes, were finally devoted entirely to the latter. Subsequent additions to the university buildings were the Arts building, opened in October, 1915, the engineering laboratories in 1919, and the medical building in 1921, while in 1922, by an agreement with the city of Edmonton, the university secured the former Strathcona hospital. In 1929 this

hospital became an institution functioning directly under the provincial department of health, but the university's rights were fully safeguarded in respect to the composition of the governing board and the provision for clinical instruction. The affiliated theological colleges, St. Stephen's and St. Joseph's, erected buildings on university sites in 1910 and 1927, respectively. The original faculty of arts and sciences was first expanded by the creation of a department of extension in 1912, with the idea of achieving more fully the important function of reaching in its educational work the people of the province at large. In 1912 the faculty of law was created with the power of recommending to the Senate candidates for the LL.B. degree. In the autumn of 1913 the department of civil engineering and allied subjects ceased to form a portion of the original faculty of arts and sciences, and was erected into the faculty of applied science. At the same time, October, 1913, instruction began in the faculty of medicine, which finally was enabled, largely owing to the generosity of the Rockefeller Foundation in placing half a million dollars at the disposal of the university for medical teaching purposes, to offer a complete medical course in 1923. The fifth faculty of the university came into being in 1915 with the creation of the College of Agriculture, for the growing needs of which it became necessary, in the spring of 1919, to acquire a tract of six hundred acres a short distance south of the original university property. In addition to the faculties proper, provision was made for certain other branches of instruction. Dentistry was organized under the faculty of medicine in 1917, and was enabled in 1924 to offer a complete five years course leading to a degree. In 1930 dentistry was organized as a school under the faculty of medicine. Pharmacy, which began its work as a department of the faculty of medicine in 1914, was in the spring of 1917 erected into a

BUILDINGS OF THE UNIVERSITY OF BRITISH COLUMBIA,
VANCOUVER, B.C.

THE UNIVERSITY OF ALBERTA, EDMONTON
THE ARTS BUILDING (ABOVE), GENERAL VIEW (BELOW)

school of pharmacy, attached to the faculty of arts and sciences. Other schools which have grown up under the same faculty are the school of commerce (1928), the school of education (1928), and the school of household economics (1928), while the school of nursing is attached to the faculty of medicine. In 1920 the province and the university combined to form a scientific and industrial research council for the general purpose of conducting economic research into the resources of the province of Alberta, and two research professorships were created under this committee to study the question of fuels and road-materials.

The university responded in common with the country at large to the special demands of the years 1914-18, and sent into various branches of the military and naval forces of the empire, some four hundred and seventy-five representatives, of whom eighty-two died in the war. Their memory was given tangible recognition by the dedication of the alumni memorial organ and a bronze tablet in the Arts Building, on November 11, 1925, while the services of all participants were permanently recorded on the roll of honour at the entrance to Convocation Hall, opened to public inspection on November 11, 1928.

After twenty years of public service as president of the university Dr. Henry Marshall Tory resigned in April, 1928, to become chairman of the National Research Council of Canada. The government of the province nominated to succeed him, on September 1, 1928, Dr. Robert Charles Wallace, formerly professor of geology in the university of Manitoba. He resigned in 1936, to accept the principalship of Queen's University, Kingston, Ontario; and was succeeded by W. A. R. Kerr, dean of the faculty of arts and sciences. Mr. Justice Stuart, first chancellor of the university, died on March 5, 1926, after a continuous term of eighteen years in his distinguished office. He was succeeded by

Mr. Justice Beck, who filled out the balance of his term. In April, 1927, Dr. A. C. Rutherford, first premier of the province and author of the original Act establishing the university, was elected by convocation to the chancellorship. In May, 1929, the university celebrated its coming of age by appropriate ceremonies.

University of British Columbia. An Act of the provincial legislature was passed in 1890 establishing a University of British Columbia, but it lapsed in 1891. However, some of the work normally done in a university was begun in 1894, when an Act was passed which permitted the affiliation of high schools in the province with recognized Canadian universities. In 1899 the Vancouver High School was affiliated with McGill University in order to provide first year work in arts, and took the name of Vancouver College. First year work in arts was offered by the Victoria High School when it became Victoria College by affiliation with McGill University in 1902. In the same year Vancouver College undertook the second year in arts. In 1906 an Act was passed incorporating the Royal Institution for the Advancement of Learning of British Columbia, which, in the same year, established at Vancouver the McGill University College of British Columbia. The scope of the work was gradually increased to three years in arts and science, and two years in applied science. The connection with McGill was brought to a close in 1915, when the University of British Columbia, incorporated by an Act of 1908 and endowed with 2,000,000 acres of land, was opened, with provision for a complete course in arts and three years in applied science. In 1920 all lands in the province had been set aside for higher education reverted to the provincial government, but it was arranged that the net proceeds from the sale of lots or lands in an area of 3,000 acres at Point Grey should be paid into a "University Endowment Account".

14

The University site consists of 548 acres on the headland of Point Grey, 300 feet above the sea. Here a group of buildings, constructed at a cost of nearly $2,000,-000, was opened in October, 1925.

The board of governors of the University consists of the chancellor, who is elected by Convocation, the president, and nine nominees of the lieutenant-governor-in-council. The Senate consists of the minister of education, the chancellor, the president (as chairman), the deans and two professors of each faculty, three nominees of the lieutenant-governor-in-council, the superintendent of education, the principals of normal schools, one member elected by high school principals and assistants, one by provincial teachers' institute, one by each affiliated college or school in the province, and fifteen members elected by Convocation.

The university is an integral part of the public educational system of the province, and its function is to complete the work begun in the public and high schools. It is the policy of the university to promote education in general and, in particular, to serve its constituency through three channels— teaching, research, and extension work. As regards teaching, it furnishes instruction in the various branches of a liberal education, and in those technical departments which are most directly related to the life and industries of the province. The people of the province are informed of the results of special work through extension lectures given by the staff of the university at centres in various parts of the province.

The library has nearly 100,000 volumes, and regularly receives over 600 periodicals. Laboratories are available for all courses. A forest products laboratory (with equipment ranging from an Olsen universal testing machine of 200,000 lbs. to the most delicate balances) was established in 1918 by the forestry branch of the Department of the Interior as a permanent branch of the Forest Products Laboratories of Canada. There are a herbarium, botanical gardens, and an arboretum.

The faculties are Arts and Science (including Commerce), Applied Science (Civil, Electrical, Mechanical, Geological, Metallurgical, Mining and Chemical Engineering, Chemistry, Nursing and Health), and Agriculture (Agronomy, Animal Husbandry, Horticulture, Dairying, Poultry Husbandry).

Matriculation examinations, junior and senior, are arranged by the High School and University Matriculation Board of the Province, consisting of members appointed from the Department of Education and from the university. Every student is submitted to a physical examination on entrance to the university.

The degree courses are as follows: B.A., 4 years; B.Com., 4 years; B.A.Sc., 5 years; B.S.A., 4 years. The double course for B.A. and B.A.Sc. is 6 years. There are courses for the M.A., M.A.Sc., and M.S.A. The teacher training course (for graduates) is 1 year; the social service course, 2 years; the course in public health for graduate nurses, 1 year. Extra-sessional classes are held in the late afternoon and on Saturday morning. The occupational course in agriculture is 1 year. Evening courses, with summer excursions, are given in botany. Short courses in agriculture are held at the University and elsewhere. In 1922 the summer school for teachers became the summer session. Teachers and others with full matriculation standing may pursue university courses and receive credit therefor towards the B.A. degree. Scholarships to the value of $25,000.00 are awarded annually to undergraduates and graduates.

Numerous lectures are given under the auspices of the university in different centres in the province, but adult education has not yet been given the status of a department. The selection of speakers and of subjects is made by a standing committee on university extension, in consultation with various local district organizations, and provision is made for single lectures or for series of connected lectures throughout the winter. Short courses of four days' duration are sometimes conducted. The Vancouver Institute co-ordinates efforts of various organizations in the field of adult education.

University of Manitoba. The University of Manitoba was established by Act of the Manitoba legislature in 1877 "for the purpose [as the preamble states] of raising the standard of higher education in the province and of enabling all denominations and classes to obtain academic degrees". The government of the university was vested in a chancellor, a vice-chancellor, and a university council, with powers as a "body politic and corporate" to receive hold, and sell property, to arrange courses of study, to hold examinations and to grant degrees. The Act provided for the affiliation of colleges and for the granting of degrees in divinity by those colleges to students who should have obtained recognized academic standing in Arts subjects. The chancellor was to be appointed by the lieutenant-governor-in-council, and the university council was to consist of seven representatives from each of the affiliated colleges, three from convocation and two from the board of education of the province.

The three colleges already in existence in Manitoba were affiliated with the university at its inception. St. John's College, the Anglican institution, had been reorganized in 1866 by Bishop (afterwards Archbishop) Machray (q.v.), who became, in 1877, the first chancellor of the university. St. Boniface College had grown from a mission school early in the century to be the chief Roman Catholic college in the West. Manitoba College, in connection with the Presbyterian Church, had been organized in 1871. Since 1877 five colleges have been received into affiliation with the university. The Manitoba Medical College was affiliated in 1882, Wesley College in 1888, the Manitoba College of Pharmacy in 1902, the Manitoba Agricultural College in 1907, and St. Paul's College in 1931.

In 1885 an agreement between the Dominion government and the province of Manitoba provided for an endowment not exceeding 150,000 acres of land for the University of Manitoba "for its maintenance as a university capable of giving proper training in the higher branches of education". In 1900 an amendment to the University Act gave the university "power to give instruction and teaching in the several faculties and different branches of knowledge as may from time to time be directed by the Council of the university". The present site was granted by the Dominion government, and the corner stone was laid in 1900 by the Duke of Cornwall and York, afterwards King George V. Four new chairs in the natural and physical sciences were founded in 1904, and also one in mathematics and one in the combined subjects of histology, pathology, and bacteriology. The number of science chairs was subsequently increased to six, geology and mineralogy, which at the first was combined in part with botany and in part with physics, being given independent status, and as well zoölogy, which at first was attached to physiology. A department of civil engineering was organized in 1907, and departments of electrical engineering, political economy, English, and history in 1909. Departments of architecture, of French, and of German were created in 1913, and began their work in the autumn of that year. In the autumn of 1914 the following new departments were instituted: a department of pharmacy, which took over the teaching in this subject formerly done by the Manitoba College of Pharmacy; a department of mechanical engineering; and a department of classics. In addition, the work of the departments of English, French,

German, history, and political economy, which had hitherto been confined to the subjects of the third and fourth year in Arts, was extended to include those of the first and second years, and the department of mathematics, which had hitherto covered only the second, third, and fourth years, assumed responsibility for the work of the first year as well. The university thus came into the position of offering for the first time through its own faculty the full work of the course in Arts for the B.A. degree. The affiliation of the Manitoba Agricultural College with the university was terminated by an Act of the provincial legislature in 1912, but restored in 1916.

By the University Amendment Act, 1917, there was introduced into the corporation a Board of Governors of nine members, appointed by the lieutenant-governor-in-council for a period of three years, three retiring each year, and in this board is vested "the government, conduct, management and control of the university," including its lands, investments, appointments, limits of instruction, etc. The Council of the university was continued, but with a reduction in the number of its members from seventy-two to twenty-eight and a limitation of the sphere of its activity to that of "general charge of the academic work of the university". Within this range it is still subject to the plenary power vested in the Board of Governors. Its representative character is maintained, as is shown by the following composition: The chancellor, the president, four representatives from the faculty of the University, two representatives from Manitoba Agricultural College, one representative from Manitoba Medical College, one representative from the College of Physicians and Surgeons of Manitoba, six members to be appointed by the lieutenant-governor-in-council, four representatives to be elected by convocation and two representatives from each of the affiliated Arts colleges, St. Boniface, St. John's,

Manitoba, and Wesley. Definite legislative recognition is given by the practice of the submission annually to the lieutenant-governor-in-council through the minister of education of a budget of "anticipated revenues and proposed expenditures" and of the appropriation by the legislature of money for university expenditures.

During the academic session 1919-20, an agreement was reached with the faculty of the Manitoba Medical College whereby that institution passed out of existence upon the assumption by the university of responsibility for the maintenance of medical teaching in an adequate manner. In pursuance of this arrangement, a full medical faculty was appointed and a faculty organization completed. Provision was also made for the teaching by the university of philosophy, including metaphysics, ethics and psychology, and a chair of philosophy and psychology was established. The Board of Governors completed a reorganization of the university faculty, which became effective on June 1, 1921. Three faculties were established, viz., the faculty of Arts and Science, the faculty of Engineering and Architecture, and the faculty of Medicine, with a dean of each faculty. A General Faculty Council was also instituted. On March 1, 1924, by Act of the Manitoba legislature, the administration of Manitoba Agricultural College was transferred to the Board of Governors of the university, and it was arranged that in future the instructional work of the college should be carried on as a faculty of Agriculture of the university, provision being made at the same time for the appointment of an advisory council for the purpose of relating the work in agriculture to the needs of the people. This advisory council was, however, abolished in 1933.

Of the affiliated colleges, St. Boniface College, St. Boniface, is in connection with the Roman Catholic Church; St. John's College, Winnipeg, is in con-

BUILDINGS OF THE UNIVERSITY OF MANITOBA, WINNIPEG, MANITOBA

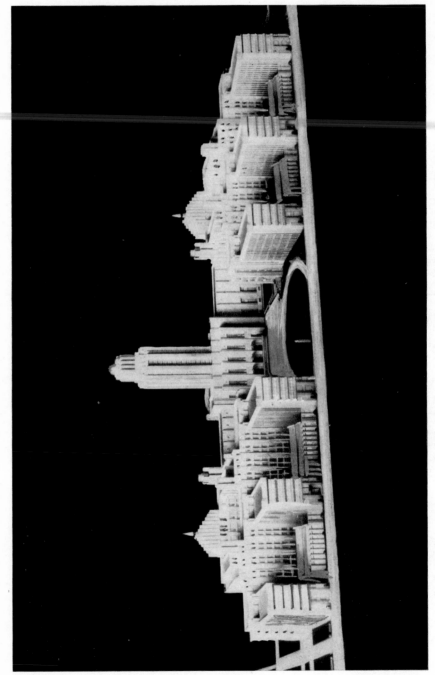

MODEL OF THE PROPOSED NEW BUILDINGS OF THE UNIVERSITY OF MONTREAL

nection with the Church of England; Manitoba College, Winnipeg, is in connection with the United Church of Canada; Wesley College, Winnipeg, is in connection with the United Church of Canada. While Manitoba College and Wesley College still retain their separate charters and separate boards of directors, they are administered by a joint Executive Committee and have a joint arts faculty, a joint theological faculty and a matriculation department, and carry on their work under the name of United Colleges.

The presidents of the University of Manitoba have been James Alexander MacLean (1913-34), and Sidney Earl Smith (1934—).

University of Montreal. This university is an offshoot of Laval University, in Quebec. In 1876, at the request of Bishop Bourget (q.v.), who was anxious to obtain the advantages of university education for the inhabitants of his diocese, the Sacred Congregation of the Propaganda at Rome proposed to the authorities of Laval University the establishment of a branch of the university at Montreal, which should give the same instruction as that given at Quebec. This instruction was begun in the faculties of theology and law in 1878; in the faculty of medicine in 1879; and in the faculty of arts in 1887. In 1889, by virtue of the apostolic constitution *Jamdudum*, the Montreal branch of Laval University became virtually independent. It received its degrees from Laval University at Quebec; but it had complete control of its local administration. In 1919 it was given complete autonomy in law and in fact; and in 1920 a charter was granted by the legislature of the province of Quebec, establishing the University of Montreal. In 1927 a rescript preparatory to a pontifical bull, granted by Rome in 1919, was followed by a definitive bull giving papal approval of the new university.

Since 1920 the growth of the Uni-

versity of Montreal has been phenomenal. By 1929 the registration at the university had risen to over 7,000 students, though over 1,500 of these were in classical colleges in Quebec affiliated with the University of Montreal. The staff in all faculties had risen to over 500. In these circumstances, the university, which had hitherto been housed in inadequate buildings in the east end of Montreal, embarked on an ambitious building scheme on Mount Royal. The depression of 1929, which began just after this building scheme was launched, severely embarrassed the university, and seriously curtailed its activities. It has carried on, under conditions which have been heart-breaking; and had it not been that the provincial legislature has come to its relief, it might have been compelled to close its doors.

The University of Montreal has embarked on an ambitious programme. In addition to the faculties of theology, law, and medicine, established before 1919, it has established faculties of philosophy, literature, science, and dental surgery; and it has brought within its organization a school of pharmacy, a school of social science, a school of optometry, a school of veterinary medicine, a school of social hygiene, and a pedagogical institute, as well as an École Polytechnique, an Institut Agricole (at Oka), a conservatory of music, a *Schola Cantorum*, and the École des Hautes Études Commerciales.

The rectors of the University of Montreal since 1920 have been Mgr. G. Gauthier (1920-3), Mgr. V. Joseph Piette (1923-35), and Mgr. Olivier Maurault (1935—).

University of New Brunswick. With the exception of the University of King's College in Nova Scotia, now federated with Dalhousie University, this is the oldest university in Canada. It was founded in 1800 by provincial charter, under the great seal of New Brunswick, as the College of New

Brunswick; and it was endowed with a grant of Crown lands in and near Fredericton, the capital of the province. Later, in 1805 and 1816, the legislature of New Brunswick passed Acts granting the College an annual sum of money from the provincial treasury. The sum of money was small; but thus early the legislature of New Brunswick acknowledged that the provincial university was a charge on its annual revenues. The College of New Brunswick was, however, slow in getting into operation. A president was appointed in 1820, but no professors; and in 1823 the governor and trustees of the College petitioned to be allowed to surrender their provincial charter, and to receive a royal charter. This charter was granted in 1828; and by it the name of the College of New Brunswick was changed to that of King's College.

Now, for the first time, the College went into operation. Professors of classics, mathematics, and theology were appointed; and instruction began, thanks to an increased grant of money from the legislature. But King's College in Fredericton underwent the same sort of experience as King's College in Toronto. Being a college in close connection with the Church of England, and the trustees and professors being compelled to subscribe to the Thirty-Nine Articles, it was the object of attack by all those elements in the population which were not Anglican; and in 1845 an Act was passed by the legislature abolishing all religious tests in the College, except in the case of the professor of theology, and suspending the operations of the College until the royal pleasure in regard to it was known. In 1854 an Act was passed empowering the lieutenant-governor to appoint a commission to enquire into the state of King's College, with a view to its improvement. The report of this commission was laid before the legislature in 1855; and in 1857 a committee appointed by the College Council, made

another report. Based largely on this second report, an Act was passed by the legislature of New Brunswick in 1859 completely secularizing King's College, and transforming it into the University of New Brunswick. It abolished the chair of theology, and it provided that the president of the university should be a layman. It created a new governing body, to be known as the Senate; and it placed in the hands of this body the appointment of professors and other officers of the University, except the president. This Act came into effect in 1860.

In 1860 the University of New Brunswick was a small arts college, with chairs in classics, mathematics, modern languages, and natural science. But gradually the curriculum has expanded. A chair in philosophy was founded in 1867, chairs in physics and civil engineering in 1889, a chair in chemistry in 1905, a chair in English and history in 1909, and a chair in forestry in 1908. Other additions have been made from time to time, and the staff now includes 19 full-time professors. In 1907 a faculty of applied science, including forestry, was organized; and in 1923 a faculty of law was established in the city of Saint John. The course in forestry, with a tract of over 3,000 acres of virgin forest as its laboratory, has already acquired an outstanding reputation, and is one of three forestry schools in Canada at which expert foresters are trained. Pre-medical courses are given, but as yet there is no medical faculty.

For many years the original building of King's College (now the Arts Building) served the University as its main home. But of recent years considerable additions have been made to the University's physical equipment. In 1923, through the generosity of the provincial legislature and the city of Fredericton, a magnificent assembly hall, known as the Memorial Hall, was built; and in 1930, through the generosity of Lord

Beaverbrook, a native of New Brunswick, a residence for men was built, known as Lady Beaverbrook's Building, and dedicated to Lady Beaverbrook's memory. In 1930 a building was erected, through a grant of the provincial legislature, to house the departments of forestry and geology; and at the same time a separate library building was opened. Of recent years, moreover, the provincial legislature, in addition to providing funds on capital account, has largely increased the annual grant.

The degrees conferred by the University are those of Bachelor and Master of Arts, Bachelor and Master of Science, Bachelor and Master of Science in Civil and Electrical Engineering and Forestry, Doctor of Science, Doctor of Literature, Bachelor and Doctor of Civil Law, and Doctor of Laws.

The presidents of the College of New Brunswick, King's College, and the University of New Brunswick have been the Rev. James Somerville (1820-29), the Rev. Edwin Jacob (1829-60), J. R. Hea (1860-61), William Brydone Jack (1861-85), Thomas Harrison (1885-92), and Cecil Charles Jones (1931—). From 1892 to 1931, there was a chancellor, but no president.

University of Ottawa, an institution of higher education founded in Ottawa (then Bytown), Ontario, in 1848, under Roman Catholic auspices, by Bishop Guigues (q.v.), as "The College of Bytown". He confided it to the care of the Oblate order, who have continued to control it to the present day. Bytown College was given a corporate existence by an Act of the parliament of United Canada in 1849; but in 1861 the name was changed to "The College of Ottawa", because of the change in name of the capital of Canada, and in 1866 the college was given by statute university powers, and was re-named the University of Ottawa. In 1889 this university was raised by Leo XIII to the rank of a pontifical university—an honour shared by only three other

universities in North America. The revised statutes of the civil charter were approved in 1933; and those of the ecclesiastical charter, amended in compliance with the Apostolic constitution "Deus scientiarum Dominus" (1931), were approved in 1934.

From the beginning, Bishop Guigues designed his institution as a bilingual college, with courses in both English and French, since his diocese contained both English-speaking and French-speaking Roman Catholics. And, except for one short and controversial period, the institution has maintained to this day its bilingual character.

On December 2, 1903, the Central Building of the university was gutted by fire; but funds were at once raised to repair the damage, and on May 24, 1904, the corner-stone was laid of a new Arts Building, which is now the chief home of the university. Plans have been drawn for the construction of a group of buildings intended to house the university; but these have so far been only partly completed.

In 1937, the University of Ottawa has the following courses and faculties: (1) A high school comprising four-year bilingual classical and commercial courses; (2) a faculty of arts offering undergraduate studies in the regular course, the night classes, the summer courses, and the correspondence courses; offering also post-graduate studies, and special courses in Italian, German, Spanish, a course in translation, a course in public administration, and a course in journalism; (3) a faculty of theology, to which is attached a new University-Seminary; (4) a faculty of canon law; (5) a faculty of philosophy, to which is attached an Institute of Philosophy. There are also special schools, such as the School of Political and Social Sciences, the School of Catholic Action, the School of Music and Elocution, the School of Nursing, and the Bilingual Normal School.

The teaching staff numbers approximately two hundred professors. There are seventeen affiliated institutions; about five thousand students follow the courses of the university at the federal capital.

Extra-curricula activities, besides participation in intercollegiate, interscholastic, and intramural athletics, are mostly centred in the following societies: (1) La Société thomiste de l'Université d'Ottawa comprises the ninety professors of theology, canon law, and philosophy of the different ecclesiastical houses of Ottawa; (2) la Société des Conférences de l'Université d'Ottawa favours the general public annually with ten lectures from outstanding Canadian orators; (3) the students' societies (la Société des débats français, the English Debating Society, the Washington Club, la Fédération nationale des Étudiants des Universités canadiennes, and la Fédération canadienne des Étudiants catholiques, affiliated to Pax Romana).

The rectors of the university since 1866 have been the Rev. Timothy Ryan (1866-7), the Rev. Joseph Tabaret (1867-74), the Rev. Antoine Paillier (1874-7), the Rev. Joseph Tabaret (1877-86), the Rev. Philémon Provost (1886), the Rev. Célestin Augier (1887-89), the Rev. James M. McGuckin (1889-98), the Rev. Henri Constantineau (1898-1901), the Rev. Joseph Edouard Emery (1901-5), the Rev. William Murphy (1905-11), the Rev. Bruno Roy (1911-14), the Rev. Henri Gervais (1914-15), the Rev. Louis Rhéaume (1915-21), the Rev. François-Xavier Marcotte (1921-7), the Rev. Uldéric Robert (1927-30), the Very Rev. Gilles Marchand (1930-35), and the Very Rev. Joseph Hébert (1936—).

The University of Ottawa has published four periodicals: The Owl (1888-1898), Revue littéraire de l'Université d'Ottawa (1900-1906), Revue de l'Université d'Ottawa, a quarterly periodical founded in 1931, and La Rotonde, the students' monthly paper founded in 1932.

See the Very Rev. Joseph Hébert, O.M.I., L'Université d'Ottawa, ses réalisations et ses espérances (Ottawa, 1937).

University of Saskatchewan. In 1903 an ordinance to establish a university for the North West Territories was passed. The ordinance contained special provisions against the introduction of sectarianism and undue political influence into the management of the university. The Act establishing the University of Saskatchewan was passed on April 3, 1907. It provided for a Convocation, consisting of all graduates of any university in His Majesty's dominions who were actually residing in the province for three months prior to the first meeting, and who applied for registration. At the first meeting of Convocation, held on October 16, 1907, the Hon. Edward Ludlow Wetmore, chief justice of the province, was unanimously chosen chancellor, and twelve members of the Senate were elected. The Senate held its first meeting on January 8, 1908, when appointments to the Board of Governors were made, and the policy of the university was discussed. The Board of Governors appointed a president in the following August, and immediately approached the difficult problems of selecting a site and determining the relation of the university to the proposed College of Agriculture. After careful inquiry, it was unanimously decided by the Senate and the governors to make provision within the university for instruction in agriculture. This decision was cordially approved by the lieutenant-governor in council and the legislature. When this question had been settled, the governors selected a site for the university in Saskatoon. Temporary quarters were secured in the Drinkle Building, and classes in arts and science were opened on September 28, 1909. Seventy students were registered. The faculty of arts and science consisted of the president and four professors.

BUILDINGS OF THE UNIVERSITY OF SASKATCHEWAN, SASKATOON, SASK.

THE ARTS BUILDING, UNIVERSITY OF OTTAWA, OTTAWA, ONTARIO

In the same year, the College of Agriculture was organized with a dean and two professors. The following year the educational work of the provincial department of agriculture was transferred to the university. The corner-stone of the first building was laid by Sir Wilfrid Laurier (q.v.) on July 29, 1910, and the buildings were opened for the admission of students in October, 1912. The College of Agriculture was opened for students in October, 1912; the School of Engineering in October, 1912; the College of Law in September, 1913; the School of Pharmacy in January, 1914; the School of Accounting in 1917; the Summer School in 1917; the School of Medical Sciences in 1926; Education in 1927; and Household Science in 1928. The University of Oxford has admitted the University of Saskatchewan to the privileges granted to colonial universities by the Statute of Affiliation.

The university has granted affiliation to Emmanuel College, St. Chad's College, St. Andrew's College, the Lutheran Seminary, the Normal Schools, the College Institutes and High Schools, the Institute of Chartered Accountants, the Pharmaceutical Association, the Association of Architects, the Dental Council, the College of Physicians and Surgeons, the Association of Registered Nurses, the Veterinary Association, the Law Society, the Optometry Associ-ation, and the Land Surveyors' Associ-ation. Emmanuel College was trans-ferred by the diocese of Saskatchewan from Prince Albert, and opened its doors on September 26, 1909. New buildings were erected on the university grounds in 1912. The General Assembly of the Presbyterian Church decided to establish a Theological Hall in affiliation with the university in 1912, and teach-ing was begun in 1914. St. Andrew's College building was opened in 1923. The university in 1924 decided to recognize the instruction of junior col-leges to the end of the second year of

the arts course. The following colleges have been recognized: Regina College, Campion College, Sacred Heart Acade-my, St. Peter's College, Luther College, Outlook College, and the Moose Jaw Central Collegiate.

Constitution. Convocation, consisting of registered graduates, elects the chancellor and twelve members of the Senate. The chancellor, the minister of education, the superintendent of edu-cation, the chairman of the Educational Council, the president, the deans of the colleges, the principals of Emmanuel and of St. Andrew's Colleges, and the principals of the normal schools, are members *ex officio.* The Senate has power to pass statutes regulating the educational affairs of the university and to exercise supervision over these affairs, to confer degrees, and to elect five members of the Board of Governors. Three other members of the Board are appointed by the governor-in-council. The Board makes appointments, and in general manages the business affairs of the university. The Council consists of the president, deans, professors, and assistant professors. It has control, subject to the supervision of the Senate, of the administration of educational matters affecting the whole university, receives the recommendations of the faculties, and makes recommendations to the Senate concerning statutes for the establishment of faculties, depart-ments, and chairs, and for the institution of degrees, scholarships, and prizes. It also recommends candidates for degrees. The faculty of a college consists of the president, dean, professors, assistant professors, lecturers, instructors, and demonstrators of more than two years' standing, and such other members as are appointed by the Senate. A faculty, according to the statutes of the Senate, has charge of matters of scholarship and discipline within its college, subject to the approval of the Council and Senate. The Advisory Council in Agriculture consists of six *ex officio* members, two members elected by the convention of agricultural societies, two members appointed by the governor-in-council, and one by the Board of Governors. The Council is required to inspect and report upon the work of the Agricultural College and Farm; its sanction is also required for the courses of study of the Agricultural College. The president is appointed by the Board of Governors, and is the administrative head of the university. Without his recommendation no appointment, promotion, or dismissal can be made. He is a member of the Senate, the Board of Governors, the Council, each faculty, and each committee *ex officio*. The dean of a faculty is appointed by the Board of Governors, and is the executive officer of his college. The revenue of the university is derived from one-third of the succession duties, one-quarter of the corporation tax, the legislative grant, fees, gifts, and the sale of the produce of the farm. The university is an integral part of the provincial system of education. The collegiate institutes and high schools prepare students for matriculation as well as for teachers' certificates.

Equipment. The university is situated on the east side of the south branch of the Saskatchewan river, opposite to the city of Saskatoon. Its site comprises 1,582 acres. About 293 acres, with a frontage of over half a mile on the river, have been set apart for a campus. A portion of the quarter-section south of the campus is devoted to plot work in field husbandry. The principal buildings, twelve in number, are of stone, a local limestone of singular beauty having been found to be appropriate to the style of architecture chosen—collegiate Gothic. These buildings include the College, now shared by arts and agriculture, later to be used solely by agriculture; the chemical, field husbandry, and physical laboratories, the latter housing biology as well; the Saskatchewan and Qu'Appelle halls of residence for students; the affiliated theological colleges, Emmanuel

and St. Andrew's; the residences of the president and the dean of agriculture; the greenhouses and the observatory. To these are to be added in the near future an Arts building. Three buildings, the first to be constructed, are of brick. The power house supplies heat, light, and power for the buildings on the campus. The engineering laboratory, rebuilt in 1925, includes machine, forge, and wood-working shops. The stock pavilion is situated near the farm buildings. The farm buildings, including a laboratory and a hospital for animal diseases, are twelve in number and are of wood. Sites of from three to five acres on the campus will be leased to affiliated colleges at a nominal rental, and subject to certain conditions of a non-burdensome character, such as the approval by the Board of Governors and university architects of the location of buildings, their style of architecture, and the material of construction. Three sites have been granted: one to Emmanuel College, one to St. Andrew's College, and one to the City Hospital.

The president of the university, from its inception to 1937, has been Walter Charles Murray, LL.D., F.R.S.C.; he was then succeeded by the Rev. James Sutherland Thomson.

University of Toronto. This university, which is now, in point of attendance, one of the largest universities in the British Empire, if not indeed the largest, had its origin in a small and desperately unpopular Church of England college, known as King's College, founded in York, Upper Canada (now Toronto) by royal charter in 1827. A charter was secured largely through the efforts of the Rev. John Strachan (q.v.). King's College had but a brief and stormy existence. The fact that all the members of its governing body and all its professors had to subscribe to the Thirty-Nine Articles of the Church of England gave it an exclusive character that subjected it from the first to attack by all the other religious denominations in the province; and the endowment of the college with public lands was one of the grievances of the rebels of 1837. It was not until 1843 that the King's College residence was completed, and that instruction began in the old parliament buildings of Upper Canada. Instruction was given in arts, divinity, medicine, and law; and a high standard was set. But already the doom of King's College was written. So great was the clamour against the endowment by public funds of a Church of England college that in 1849 Robert Baldwin (q.v.) put through the legislature of united Canada a bill secularizing King's College, and re-naming it the University of Toronto. This bill came into operation in 1850.

Seldom has a great university been launched under less auspicious circumstances. By 1850 the Methodists had already founded Victoria University in Cobourg, the Presbyterians had begun Queen's University in Kingston, the Roman Catholics had launched Regiopolis College, also in Kingston; and immediately after the secularization of King's College, Bishop Strachan organized in Toronto the University of Trinity College. There were at that time few advocates of secular education; and the new "godless university", as it was called, had few friends. It was ejected from the old parliament buildings, since the parliament of united Canada came to Toronto in 1849; and in 1853 it lost even the King's College building, which was taken over by the provincial government and used for an insane asylum—known as "the University Insane Asylum"! An Act passed by the Hincks government in 1853 attempted to mend matters by making the University solely an examining body, and by creating University College, with provision for other colleges coming into affiliation with the University. But none of the outlying colleges availed themselves of this opportunity; and since the teaching of divinity had been discontinued in

1850, and the teaching of medicine and law in 1853, University College became merely a small arts college, supported mainly by those Low Church Anglicans who were suspicious of Trinity and those Free Church Presbyterians who were suspicious of Queen's. Probably nothing but its central position in Toronto saved it from extinction. In 1860 a large part of its endowment was put into the building of the present home of University College; and once University College had a local habitation and a name, it began to grow. In 1867, moreover, on the completion of Confederation, the University of Toronto became the provincial university of Ontario; and this strengthened its position.

In the years following Confederation in Canada, great developments took place in higher education in North America. Scientific laboratories were established; new subjects invaded the curriculum; and the idea of research or post-graduate study gained ground. The resources of Canadian universities proved insufficient to meet the new demands made upon them; and in these circumstances, the idea of university federation in Ontario dawned. In 1887 the University of Toronto succeeded in persuading Victoria University to come into federation with it, under a scheme whereby Victoria, while retaining its right to grant degrees in theology, surrendered its rights in other respects, but obtained for its students access to the resources of the University in a large number of subjects, and was able to confine itself to teaching only such arts subjects (mainly languages) as it was prepared to teach. The completion of this arrangement took some time; for it was not until 1892 that Victoria was able to move from Cobourg to Toronto. But this solution of the problem of higher education in Ontario has given to the University of Toronto one of its most outstanding characteristics — a characteristic which has served as a model for many other universities, not only in Canada but also in the United States. In 1903 the University of Trinity College came into federation on the same terms as Victoria; and in 1910 St. Michael's College, which had been affiliated with the University of Toronto since 1881, and had been federated in 1887, was declared to be an arts college on the same footing as Victoria and Trinity. Queen's University, McMaster University, the University of Western Ontario, and Ottawa University have, in Ontario, remained outside the circle of university federation; but the University of Toronto has provided a shining illustration of the advantages of university federation.

In 1906 the University of Toronto was radically reconstituted, by an Act which gave it a Board of Governors appointed by the provincial government, but so constituted as to remove it from political control, and which inaugurated the remarkable development which has taken place since that time. This development was largely due to the fact that the provincial government recognized for the first time that the support of the university was a legitimate charge on the consolidated revenues of the province, just as the schools of the province were. Prior to this time, the provincial legislature had on various occasions made grants to the university for various purposes; but these grants had been niggardly and sporadic. Now it was laid down that the university should receive a fixed proportion annually of the succession duties levied by the province; and while this provision was later amended, the University of Toronto has since 1906 received an annual grant from the province which has enabled it to take its place among the great universities of the North American continent. In addition to this, it has received during this period benefactions from private sources, totalling many millions of dollars, which have effectively disproved the idea that state universities do not attract private donations.

The developments of the last thirty years are so numerous that it is difficult to describe them in detail. One of them has been the growth in the number of faculties in the university. The medical faculty had been revived in 1887, when the Toronto School of Medicine was taken over by the university, and in 1903 the Trinity Medical School was amalgamated with it; but the high reputation of the medical faculty of the University of Toronto has been achieved since 1906. In 1906 the School of Practical Science, which had been founded in 1878 in proximity to, but not in formal connection with, the university, was incorporated in the university, as the faculty of applied science. In 1907 a faculty of education was organized, and is now known as the Ontario College of Education; and at the same time a faculty of forestry was established. In 1918 a faculty of music was created, and the Toronto Conservatory of Music was handed over to the university, though it continues to have its own trustees. The development of graduate work led in 1922 to the organization of a School of Graduate Studies, as a faculty of the university. A faculty of household science, created in 1906, but discontinued in 1908, was revived in 1924. Lastly, in 1925, the School of Dentistry, founded by the Royal College of Dental Surgeons in Ontario, entered the university as the faculty of dentistry. Certain professional schools in Ontario, such as the Ontario College of Agriculture, the Ontario College of Pharmacy, and the Ontario Veterinary College, are affiliated with the University of Toronto.

With the growth of the number of faculties, there have also been created a multitude of new chairs and courses. Developments in medicine have brought about the establishment of professorships in biochemistry, zymology, hygiene, psychiatry, and medical research.

BUILDINGS OF THE UNIVERSITY OF TORONTO

BUILDINGS OF THE UNIVERSITY OF WESTERN ONTARIO,
LONDON, ONTARIO

In applied science, chairs have been created in mining, metallurgy, and aërodynamics. The demand for adequately trained graduates of the University has led to the development of a course in actuarial science, in the department of mathematics, and of a course in commerce and finance. Departments of law and psychology have gradually developed. More recently, chairs have been founded in the fine arts, in archæology, and in geography. A department of social service has been inaugurated, a School of Nursing, and the St. George's School for Child Study. These developments illustrate the expansion of the curriculum since 1906.

At the same time, there has been an amazing growth in the physical "plant" of the University. In 1906, with the exception of the School of Practical Science building (built 1878), the Biological building (1888), the Library (1892), the Mining building (1903), the Physics building (1906), and Convocation Hall (1906), the University was confined, apart from the buildings of the federated and affiliated colleges, to the historic building of University College, which actually housed the administrative offices of the University. To-day, the number of buildings under the supervision of the superintendent of grounds and buildings is well over fifty. Of these, the most notable is Hart House, built in 1913-19 through the generosity of the Massey Foundation, as a sort of students' union, comprising within its walls the non-academic activities of the men of the University, including gymnasia, natatorium, students' dining-hall, faculty club, chapel, a completely equipped "little theatre", a library, a music room, and offices of the student newspaper ('Varsity), the Athletic Association, the Students' Administrative Council, and the Student Christian Association — a building unique among academic buildings anywhere. Other notable buildings are the 'Varsity Arena, the new Botany build-

ing, with its hot-houses, and the David Dunlap Observatory near Richmond Hill, which houses one of the largest telescopes in the world. Closely connected with the university are the magnificent buildings of the Toronto General Hospital (with the Banting Institute opposite) and the Royal Ontario Museums.

The University of Toronto Press was established in 1902, and it has printed and published the *University of Toronto Studies* (q.v.) which have served as an outlet for the research work done in the University, and the *University of Toronto Monthly* (1900—). More recently the Press has published a number of important periodicals, notably the *Canadian Historical Review* (1920—), *Contributions to Canadian Economics* (1928-34), the *University of Toronto Quarterly* (1931—), the *Canadian Journal of Economics and Political Science* (1935—), and the *Canadian Law Journal* (1935—).

The presidents of King's College and of the University of Toronto have been the Hon. and Ven. John Strachan (1827-48); the Rev. John McCaul (1848-80), though from 1853 to 1880 he was styled president of University College; Sir Daniel Wilson (1880-92), though until 1887 he also was styled president of University College; James Loudon (1892-1906); Maurice Hutton, acting president (1906-7); Sir Robert Falconer (1907-32); and the Hon. and Rev. Henry John Cody (1932—).

Bibliography. Two histories of the University have been published, W. J. Alexander (ed.), *The University of Toronto and its colleges* (Toronto, 1906), and W. S. Wallace, *A history of the University of Toronto* (Toronto, 1927).

See also **Knox College, St. Michael's College, University College, University of Trinity College, Victoria University,** and **Wycliffe College.**

University of Toronto Studies, publications issued first by the Librarian of the University of Toronto, and since 1930 by the University of Toronto Press.

They consist of the following: anatomical series, 1900-25 (nos. 1-7); biological series, 1898-1932 (nos. 1-36); geological series, 1900-23 (nos. 1-35); political science, 1889-95 (nos. 1-4), continued as history and economics, new series, 1897-1930 (vols. i-vi), and Contributions to Canadian economics, 1928-33 (vols. i-vi); legal series, 1931-33 (nos. 1-2); mathematical series, 1915-21 (nos. 1-2); medical research fund series, 1915-21 (nos. 1-12); Orientals, 1931 (vol. i); papers from the chemical laboratories, 1904-25 (nos. 40-134); papers from the physical laboratories, 1903-22 (nos. 5-8, 13, 18-84); pathological series, 1906-31 (nos. 1-8); philological series, 1903-30 (nos. 1-9); philosophy series, 1914-23 (vols. i-ii); physical science series, 1903-04 (nos. 1-4); physiological series, 1899-1928 (nos. 1-98); psychological series, 1900-20 (vols. i-iv).

University of Trinity College, now one of the federated colleges of the University of Toronto, was founded in 1850 by the Right Rev. John Strachan (q.v.), after King's College, for which Strachan had obtained a royal charter in 1827, had been secularized in 1850. It was, like King's College, in close connection with the Church of England, and was designed to perpetuate the ideas embodied in the charter of King's College. The first part of the university to go into operation was the medical faculty. Earlier in 1850, the Upper Canada School of Medicine had been organized in Toronto; and this School was incorporated in the new university as the faculty of medicine before the year 1850 had closed. The remaining faculties of the university did not come into operation until the buildings of old Trinity College were erected on Queen Street West in Toronto in 1851-2. The inauguration of the University actually took place on January 15, 1852. The staff of the university were composed for many years, almost exclusively, of graduates of Oxford and Cambridge, and were members of the

Church of England. Students were expected to reside in college, except when granted special dispensation, and were to attend chapel. Even the professors were expected to live in residence, and though this did not necessarily imply celibacy, it had a tendency to do so. In 1888 a women's college, named St. Hilda's, was founded in connection with Trinity, but it was intended that this should be a separate women's college, like the women's colleges at Oxford and Cambridge; and only the lack of financial resources prevented the realization of this ideal. St. Hilda's became, in point of fact, nothing more than the women's residence at Trinity, and as such it has remained.

When university federation took place in Ontario in 1887-9, Trinity stood aloof. But gradually the logic of events made its weight felt. The endowments of Trinity had been barely sufficient to support a small arts college of the old type; but they were totally insufficient to support a university of the modern type, with well-equipped scientific laboratories and all sorts of occupational courses. An element in the college, under the leadership of Provost Macklem, came to the conclusion that the only solution lay in federation with the University of Toronto; and in 1903 Trinity finally came into federation.

Until this time, the University of Trinity College had conferred degrees in seven faculties—divinity, arts, medicine, law, music, dentistry, and pharmacy; though teaching had been confined to divinity, arts, and medicine. Under federation, the College retained control of the teaching of divinity; but the teaching in arts was divided between the College and the University of Toronto, and the Trinity Medical School was amalgamated with the faculty of medicine in the University. Except in divinity, Trinity has held in abeyance its right to grant degrees; and in return its students have had full access to the resources of the University of Toronto.

It was not without difficulty that the scheme of federation was worked out. Though situated in Toronto, Trinity was at a distance of two miles from the buildings of the University of Toronto; and it was not found possible to move immediately into closer propinquity with the University. For over twenty years Trinity continued to occupy its original home, and it became necessary for professors of the University to repeat at Trinity many lectures in "university subjects". Ultimately, however, the Trinity property was sold to the city of Toronto for a park; and funds were raised for the erection of new buildings (closely modelled on the old) on University of Toronto property, buildings which were opened for instruction in 1925. Only then, in a sense, was the effective federation of Trinity with the University of Toronto brought about.

There was, among some of the graduates and supporters of Trinity, considerable opposition to this change. The very fact that Trinity has united with the so-called "godless university", in opposition to which it was founded in 1850, might be regarded by the cynical as justification for Bishop Strachan turning in his grave. But times change; and it is by no means a foregone conclusion that Bishop Strachan, had he been living in 1903, might not have approved of the union of the two universities he had founded. The federal idea was not familiar to, or at any rate popular with, Canadians in 1850. Under it, since 1903, Trinity College has been able to retain its most essential characteristics; and at the same time it has contributed to the University of Toronto influences of great value. Indeed, by federation, the ideas of Bishop Strachan have again obtained a lodgment in the university he founded in 1827.

The provosts of Trinity have been the Rev. George Whitaker (1850-81), the Rev. C. W. E. Body (1881-94), the Rev. E. A. Welch (1895-1900), the Rev. T. C. Street Macklem (1900-1921), the

Rev. C. A. Seager (1921-6), and the Rev. F. H. Cosgrave (1926—).

See Henry Melville, *The rise and progress of Trinity College, Toronto* (Toronto, 1852); the Rev. William Clark, "The University of Trinity College, Toronto", in J. Castell Hopkins (ed.), *Canada: An encyclopædia*, vol. iv (Toronto, 1898); W. J. Alexander (ed.), *The University of Toronto and its colleges* (Toronto, 1906); and W. S. Wallace, *A history of the University of Toronto* (Toronto, 1927).

University of Western Ontario. The Church of England in Canada, through an Act of Parliament in 1863, established in London, Ontario, in the diocese of Huron, a college called Huron College, to provide facilities for training the prospective clergy of that denomination. Probably because of lack of funds, arts work was not considered until 1878, when the legislature of Ontario granted Huron College a university charter, which conferred the power to grant degrees. A new name, the Western University of London, Ontario, replaced the old name, but the new university was still under the control of the diocese of Huron.

It was not, however, until 1881 that actual instruction in arts subjects was begun, with a student body of seven, co-educational from the start. As early as 1883 there was a graduating class in both arts and medicine. There came a financial crisis in 1884, as a result of which the Senate closed the doors of the arts department in 1885, though Huron College with its original powers still existed. Though not involved directly, Huron College suffered even more painfully than the portion of the institution which had been decapitated. The future clergy turned aside to seek their theology in a centre where the arts degree also could be obtained. Huron College saw that the return to the days of the early 80's was imperative, and to this end bent its energies. In 1895, arts classes were resumed in a modest way, but at the beginning of none of the next ten or twelve years did the small but devoted staff know where the money that would be necessary to complete the year was to be secured. Had it not been for the protection of the motherly, re-affiliated Huron College, there is no doubt that the arts department would have succumbed to recurrent financial frosts. It was manifest that this sort of existence could not go on forever. With magnanimous self-effacement, the authorities of the diocese of Huron were willing to relinquish their control, provided only they could secure a guarantee that the creature of their creation would be assured a continued and abundant life. All this was safeguarded in an Act passed by the legislature of Ontario in 1908. By this Act, the university became non-denominational, and "under municipal or provincial control or both". The Western University, the name of which was changed again by an Act of the legislature on May 8, 1923, to that of the University of Western Ontario, has really a history covering only the years since 1908, although in 1928 it celebrated technically its golden jubilee.

In arts, the general or pass course has been gradually made more severe, and the honour courses have been strengthened till they are accepted by the academic bodies on this continent and in Europe as standard college courses. Up to the present time, there has been no effort to organize applied science or engineering courses, and there is no intention to launch such courses as long as other institutions show that they can easily train all the engineers that Canada can absorb. Courses with a vocational outlook are offered, however, in secretarial science, a four-year course from pass matriculation; in nursing, a five-year course, two years of which are devoted to cultural subjects; in business administration, an honour course requiring five years from pass matriculation or four years from honour matricu-

lation; and in household science, a diploma course of two years.

From the date of this rebirth in 1908, Huron College has been affiliated with the university. Other institutions, within the fourteen counties mentioned in the Acts of 1908 and 1923, have been admitted to privileges of affiliation. Two of these institutions are Roman Catholic, namely, Assumption College at Sandwich, Ontario, under the order of St. Basil, and the Ursuline College at London under the control of the Ursuline Sisters. One college is Lutheran—Waterloo College of Arts at Waterloo. One is United Church—Alma College at St. Thomas. The first three of these affiliated colleges give the complete four years' course leading to the degree of bachelor of arts. The last has junior college status, and confines its instruction to the first two years of the arts course.

The University of Western Ontario is not restricted to work in arts. Its medical faculty has had a longer unbroken existence than any other faculty, for, from 1882, when it first began instruction, to the present, it has been very much alive. From 1882 to 1913, this department was a joint stock company; but, in 1913, the Board of Governors of the university, after prolonged negotiation with the stockholders, took the medical school directly under their control, and it so continues. The medical course is of six years' duration. The registration of the first year is limited to forty. By the time the clinical years are reached, withdrawals and casualties generally reduce this number to thirty or fewer. To this number, it is possible to give in clinics almost personal attention, and personal attention is one of the things on which the administration of the university justly prides itself.

The third faculty owes its inception in 1912 to the provincial government, which erected a building for public health work and made an annual grant for carrying on the work of what was termed the Institute of Public Health. The staff was to give part of its time to teaching university students, and it was soon organized as an independent faculty of Public Health, the first of its kind in Canada, if not in North America. In addition to instruction in public health, offered to both arts and medical students, this faculty gives several courses, mostly graduate, that are distinctly its own. There is a one-year course for graduate nurses that qualifies them for public health work. There is the final year of a five-year course that leads to the degree of B.Sc. in Nursing. A one-year course, leading to the degree of doctor of public health, is offered for graduates in medicine.

The years 1910 to 1930 showed remarkable growth. In that time there was built a medical school, in the hospital area of London, at a cost of over $500,000. The campus of over 250 acres, north-west of the city, was bought, and on it were built a natural science building, an arts building (temporarily housing administration offices), a central heating plant, and a stadium, at a total cost of over $1,250,000. To provide easy access to the grounds the university built its own bridge over the Thames river, which divides the campus from the city of London, and it secured the right of way to the bridge-head on the city side. The bridge and approaches cost $125,000. Therefore, the total value of land, buildings, and equipment, now owned by the university exceeds $2,500,-000. Of this, the province of Ontario gave over $1,000,000; the city of London, $350,000; and the county of Middlesex, $100,000. The rest of the actual cost has been met by private benefaction. In the autumn of 1924, when the university moved to its present accommodations, there were 530 students in attendance. The total registration is now over three times this figure. This means that the attendance has grown

so rapidly that the material plant is crowded.

The University of Western Ontario is almost alone among Canadian universities in that it receives municipal support. Since 1908, the council of the city of London has made an annual grant towards maintenance. These grants began with the modest sum of $5,000 a year, but have expanded till the figure of $55,000 has been reached. As long as this annual grant continues, the city council is entitled to name four representatives, out of a total of sixteen, on the Board of Governors of the university. In return for this financial assistance from the city, the university agrees to rebate for one year the tuition fees of any *bona fide* London student whose parents own or occupy, inside the city limits, property assessed at $3,600 or less. The province of Ontario appoints four members of the Board of Governors and makes an annual grant toward maintenance. The rest of the money needed to balance the budget is secured from fees. Up to the present time no large gifts towards endowment have been received. A couple of bequests, in excess of $100,000 each, have been given for specific purposes to the medical school. An endowment fund campaign, undertaken several years ago, produced in cash and pledges a total of $800,000, but all this has not yet worked its way into the revenue-earning funds of the institution. Probably the best and most valuable gift that has been received is the library of the late Dr. J. D. Barnett, the well-known bibliophile and collector, who, twenty years ago, gave his collection to the university. Included in the 50,000 volumes, of which the gift consisted, were some rare Canadiana and some Shakespeare items, not duplicated in America. The Shakespeare items are not indispensable, but the Canadiana cannot be overlooked by any investigator in the field of early Canadian history. This gift is now housed in a new library building, con-

15

structed in 1934, and made possible by a bequest from the late Mrs. Lorena Lawson, supplemented by gifts from her son and daughter, and by grants from the city, the province, and the Dominion.

Until 1908 the presiding officer of the Western University was known as "provost"; and until 1902 the office of provost of the university was held by the principal of Huron College. In 1902, however, Dr. Nathaniel C. James was appointed provost, and in 1908 his official title was changed to that of president. He retired in 1914; and was succeeded by the Rev. E. E. Braithwaite, who retired in 1919. There was then a period when the office of president was vacant; but in 1927 Dr. William Sherwood Fox, who as dean of arts had been doing much of the president's work, was appointed president.

Uno Park, a village in the Nipissing district of Ontario, on the Temiskaming and Northern Ontario Railway, 6 miles north of New Liskeard. Pop. (1934), 300.

Upham, Joshua (1741-1808), loyalist, was born at Brookfield, Massachusetts, in 1741, the son of Dr. Jabez Upham. He was educated at Harvard College (B.A., 1763), and was called to the bar in Massachusetts. During the Revolutionary War he served as an officer in the King's American Dragoons; and at the close of the war he settled in New Brunswick. In 1784 he was appointed a member of the Executive and Legislative Councils of New Brunswick, and a puisne judge of the court of King's Bench. In 1807 he went on a mission to England, in connection with the salaries granted to judges in New Brunswick; and he died in England on November 1, 1808. He married (1) a daughter of the Hon. John Murray, of Rutland, Massachusetts, and (2) a daughter of the Hon. Joshua Chandler, a Connecticut loyalist. By his first marriage he had one daughter, and by his second one son and three daughters. See J. W. Lawrence, *The judges of New Brunswick* (Saint John, New Brunswick, 1907).

Upham, a village in King's county, New Brunswick, on the Canadian National Railway, 17 miles from Hampton. Pop. (1934), 200.

Upper Arrow lake. See Arrow lakes.

Upper Canada. In 1791, when the old province of Quebec was divided into two provinces, the name given to what had been "the western settlements" was Upper Canada, while the eastern province was named Lower Canada. These names ceased to have official currency after the Union of 1841, though the name Upper Canada persisted for a time in popular usage, together with that of "Canada West". The boundary line between Upper and Lower Canada was the Ottawa river, with this exception that a triangle of territory between the Ottawa and St. Lawrence rivers, with a base line on the St. Lawrence of nearly 50 miles, was annexed to the province of Lower Canada, and is still part of the province of Quebec. See **Ontario.**

Upper Canada Bible Society. The British and Foreign Bible Society, founded in London, England, on March 7, 1804, had its first touch with British North America by the publication in December of that year of a Mohawk-English edition of the Gospel of St. John, translated by Captain John Norton for the Six Nation Indians. Copies of this translation were shipped to British North America in 1805 and reached the Six Nations Indians in Upper Canada in 1806.

In a letter dated December 4, 1807, the Rev. James McGregor (q.v.) asked the British and Foreign Bible Society to send out copies of the Scriptures in Gaelic and English for the use of settlers in the Maritime provinces. In response to this and other requests 500 Gaelic Bibles and 800 New Testaments were forwarded to British North America. In 1808 Dr. McGregor founded the first auxiliary of the Society on the North

American continent in Pictou, Nova Scotia; and in the same year, influenced by the British and Foreign Bible Society, a similar society was started in Philadelphia. Auxiliary societies sprang up in the Maritime provinces and Lower Canada in 1813 at Halifax, in 1818 at Quebec, Saint John, New Brunswick, and Prince Edward Island, and in 1820 at Montreal.

In 1812 the London Committee received a communication "from a respectable Beneficed Clergyman in Upper Canada, and encouraged him to take measures to obtain the formation of a Bible Society for the Canadas, upon the principles of the British and Foreign Bible Society, by the promise of £200. should the same be effected". This grant led ultimately to the formation of an Auxiliary Society at York (Toronto) in 1818, which, operating under various names, is now known as the Upper Canada Bible Society. This Society had a certain oversight in regard to branches west of the Great lakes from time to time, as the stream of immigration moved westward. Work was also inaugurated in western Ontario in the early stages as an associate auxiliary with Upper Canada, afterwards becoming a separate auxiliary known as the Western Ontario Bible Society. As Ontario developed, an auxiliary was formed in Ottawa.

As far as the West is concerned, the work of the Society was inaugurated by the Rev. John West (q.v.), chaplain to the Hudson's Bay Company, who established an auxiliary at York Factory in 1821. At the first anniversary meeting of this auxiliary Captain (afterwards Sir) John Franklin (q.v.) attended. West afterwards visited several auxiliaries in eastern Canada, and consolidated this work in a remarkable way. From time to time agents were sent out by the parent society, who kept in touch with the various auxiliaries through personal visitation.

The next notable advocate of the Society in western Canada was Bishop David Anderson (q.v.), the first Anglican bishop of Rupert's Land. He proceeded to the Red River in 1849, and there established a depot, encouraging the work of the Society in every way.

The Society from the very beginning had the financial support of the various religious denominations which approved of the object for which the Society exists, namely "the wider circulation of the Holy Scriptures, without note or comment". Colporteurs carry the Scriptures to settlers in every part of the land, a policy which is continued in the Dominion of Canada to the present day.

In 1863 the Upper Canada Bible Society sent an agent, the Rev. Lachlan Taylor, to Vancouver Island. Travelling from Toronto by way of the Panama isthmus, in about two months' time he reached Vancouver Island. He established branches at Nanaimo, Victoria, and New Westminster. An Auxiliary Bible Society was founded for British Columbia in 1872. As the West developed the work of Scripture distribution was maintained with Winnipeg as its centre, and in 1904 a secretary for the West was appointed.

In that same year, the centenary of the Society, the auxiliaries in the Dominion of Canada agreed to federate, and a Dominion charter was obtained in 1906 for these federated Societies under the title of the Canadian Bible Society, Auxiliary to the British and Foreign Bible Society. This name was changed by an Act of Dominion Parliament in 1930 to the British and Foreign Bible Society in Canada and Newfoundland, the existing rights and privileges being confirmed in the new charter.

Gradually as the West developed auxiliaries were organized, not only in Manitoba, but in Saskatchewan and Alberta, and thus the Society operates in the Dominion and Newfoundland with 15 auxiliaries, 10 Bible houses, and depositories in various towns. It is governed by a General Board, on which representatives of its 15 auxiliaries sit, each auxiliary having oversight within a given territory. It is to be noted that from 1905 onward the parent society, the name by which the British and Foreign Bible Society is familiarly known, has appointed, with the full consent of the Board of the Society in Canada and Newfoundland, a general secretary who acts as a personal link between the parent society and the autonomous society in Canada and Newfoundland, and who also acts as its chief executive officer.

The main work of the Society in Canada and Newfoundland is the circulation of the Holy Scriptures, which are required in some 100 languages to meet the needs of the Indian and Eskimo tribes and the various nationalities which form the population of Canada.

Upper Canada College, a residential school for boys founded in York (Toronto), Upper Canada, in 1829, by Sir John Colborne (q.v.), the lieutenant-governor of Upper Canada. It took the place of the Home District Grammar School, founded in 1807; and it was intended to be a "feeder" for King's College, Toronto, then being projected. It was modelled after the great "public schools" of England; and for many years its standard was such that it was complained that only students from Upper Canada College could be expected to pass the matriculation examinations of King's College, and later of the University of Toronto. The history of its connection with the University of Toronto is complicated. Until 1850 it was under the control of the Council of King's College. By the University Act of 1850, it was cut adrift from the University of Toronto, and became a separate corporation, with a council of its own; but the University Act of 1853 placed it once more under the university, and a standing committee of the University Senate became its governing body.

This committee continued in existence until 1887, when the college was placed under the jurisdiction of a board of trustees appointed by the provincial government, and the connection of the college with the university came to an end. In 1900 the college was removed from the control of the provincial government; and since that date it has been virtually a private institution, with a board of governors of its own, most of whom are elected by the Old Boys' Association. Until 1891 the college was situated in what is now downtown Toronto; but in that year new buildings were erected in the Deer Park district of Toronto, and here the college is still situated. There have been proposals for removing it to a site outside Toronto; but removal has been postponed indefinitely. Recent additions to the buildings erected in 1891—additions largely due to the benefactions of the Massey Foundation—make removal, indeed, unlikely.

Many distinguished Canadians have been educated at Upper Canada College; and a number of distinguished Canadians have served on its teaching staff. The principals of the college have been the Rev. Joseph H. Harris (1829-38), the Rev. John McCaul (1839-43), Frederick W. Barron (1843-56), the Rev. Walter Stennett (1856-61), George R. R. Cockburn (1861-81), John M. Buchan (1881-5), George Dickson (1885-95), George R. Parkin (1895-1902), Henry W. Auden (1903-17), W. L. Grant (1917-35), and T. W. L. MacDermot (1935—).

See G. Dickson and G. Mercer Adam, *A history of Upper Canada College* (Toronto, 1893), and A. H. Young (ed.), *The roll of pupils of Upper Canada College*, (Kingston, Ontario, 1917).

Upper Houses. See **Second Chambers.**

Upper Seal lake. See **Seal lakes.**

Upsala, a village in the Thunder Bay district of Ontario, on the Canadian Pacific Railway, 75 miles north-west of Fort William. It was named after Upsala, in Sweden. Pop. (1934), 100.

Uptergrove, a village in Ontario county, Ontario, on the Canadian National Railway, 15 miles east of Orillia. Pop. (1934), 200.

Upton, a village in Bagot county, Quebec, on the Canadian National Railway, 20 miles east of St. Hyacinthe. Pop. (1931), 690.

Uranium, a hard, somewhat malleable metal, the colour of which is much like iron. It is extremely heavy, having a specific gravity of 18.68. It is alloyed with iron to make ferro-uranium, which is employed in the hardening and toughening of steel. Salts of uranium are used extensively as colouring materials in the glass and ceramic industries. They are also employed in the textile trade as dyes. Uranium is the metal from which we get much of our present conception of atomic structure. Formerly it was supposed that elements were simple substances which could not by any means be converted into simpler substances. The studies of Mme. Curie showed that uranium slowly disintegrates by an evolution of helium gas and the consequent formation of other elements, more notably radium. The end product of this disintegration is uranium lead, which has a different atomic weight from ordinary lead, but cannot be distinguished by any chemical means.

There are many uranium minerals, but the most abundant and important is uraninite or pitch-blende, which is a heavy velvet-black to pitch-black mineral with a sub-metallic to pitch-like lustre. It is opaque and has a concoidal to uneven fracture. It crystallizes in cubes and octahedra, but is more commonly found massive and in botryhoidal forms. It is the chief source both of radium and uranium.

Uraninite has been found in Canada near Murray Bay, Quebec, at Wilberforce, Ontario, where considerable mining development has been done, and near Maimanse on the east shore of lake Superior; and quite recently large deposits of uraninite and native silver have been developed on Great Bear lake in the North West Territories. See H. V. Ellsworth, *Rare-element minerals of Canada* (Geological Survey of Canada, Ottawa, 1932).

Ure, George P. (d. 1860), journalist, was a native of Scotland. He came to Canada, and became a journalist on the staff of the *North American*, and subsequently of the Toronto *Globe*. In 1859 he founded in Montreal the *Family Herald*, a weekly journal; and he died at Montreal on August 22, 1860. With A. Farewell he published *The Maine law illustrated* (Toronto, 1855), an early contribution to temperance literature; and under the *nom-de-plume* of "A member of the press", he was the author of *The hand-book of Toronto* (Toronto, 1858).

Ursulines (Quebec). The Ursulines are a religious order founded in the sixteenth century by Ste. Angela Mericia at Brescia, Italy, for the education of young girls. It was the first teaching order of women established in the church, and has adhered strictly to the work of the Institute. The approbation of Paul III was confirmed by Gregory XIII in 1572. St. Charles Borromeo was a zealous protector of the new society. The Milan foundation was the first outside of Brescia. Thence it spread to France. The first cloistered convent was founded in Paris in 1612 by Madame de St. Beuve. Nine congregations of Ursulines with three hundred convents existed before the French Revolution. The congregation of Paris was, with that of Bordeaux, the most flourishing.

In the early part of the seventeenth century an urgent appeal came from Canada for religious women to undertake the arduous task of training its Indian girls to Christian habits of life.

Madame de la Peltrie (q.v.), an opulent French widow, offered herself and all that she had to found a mission in Canada. In May, 1639, she sailed from Dieppe in company with three Ursulines and three hospital nuns. At Quebec, the latter founded the Hôtel-Dieu, and the former the first institution of learning on the American continent. At their head was Mother Marie de l'Incarnation (q.v.), a remarkable and saintly woman, who after ten years of widowhood had joined the Ursulines of Tours.

Henceforth the history of the Ursulines became one with that of New France. Its dangers, its joys, and its sorrows were theirs. When they began their first work at the foot of the mountain, Quebec was but a name. Hardly six houses stood on the site chosen by Champlain (q.v.) thirty-one years previously. At the death of Marie de l'Incarnation, in 1672, there was an upper town and a lower town—her convent, one of the finest buildings, having been destroyed by fire in 1650, and rebuilt. After the Indians were finally subjugated in 1665, the little colony was able to expand and survive even after the conquest of 1759.

The royal charter sanctioning the foundation, signed by Louis XIII, is dated 1639. Three years later, in 1642, the nuns entered the convent built on the ground they still occupy, and granted to them in 1639 by the Company of New France.

The first pupils were Indians; the nuns were soon able to teach in the Huron, Algonkian, Montagnais, and Iroquois tongues. The courageous Marie de l'Incarnation found time in the midst of her laborious days to compose a dictionary, grammars, and books of Christian doctrine in the Indian tongues, that rendered great service, even in the last century, to missionaries carrying the Gospel into the far North.

From the first years the children of the French colonists flocked to the Ursuline Seminary of New France.

There they found cultured women who taught the arts as well as the sciences of the time.

The years following the death of Mother Marie were years of hardship. The community suffered from the vicissitudes and fears caused by war and disasters. The Sisters remained at their post even during the siege of 1759. They devoted themselves to the care of the wounded soldiers of Wolfe (q.v.), lodged in a room of the convent, which remains to-day as it was then. Several bombs that fell on the convent during that terrible siege, are still kept in that room. Theirs was the only church that resisted the bombardment. Repaired by General Murray (q.v.), it served five years for both the Catholic and the Protestant services. This chapel, built in 1722, was demolished and rebuilt in 1902. The retable, pulpit and ornamentation are those of the former shrine. Not the least among its treasures is the grave of the Marquis de Montcalm (q.v.). The valuable paintings were sent from France in 1821.

The room assigned to General Murray and his staff and the legendary round table, on which many important documents were signed, may still be seen, with numbers of other historic treasures.

The first superioress after the Conquest was Esther Wheelwright, a New England captive rescued from the Abnaki by the Jesuit Bigot, and a protégée of the first Governor Vaudreuil (q.v.). Not only the French, but also the English, Irish, and Scotch have given distinguished members to the convent. Education has been bilingual since 1830.

The heartening assertion of Marie de l'Incarnation, "Canada is a country especially protected by Divine Providence," lessened the anxiety of these troubled times and inspired hope. For 176 years these words have been verified, and the development of education has kept pace with the progress of the country. The first impetus after the

Conquest was given in 1800. Half-
boarders were then received for the
first time. From 1820 and 1824 dates
the advancement of modern art and
music in all branches. Buildings have
been added, especially since 1831, in
every direction around the walls of
1651, and to-day central heating and
the modern conveniences afforded by
steam and electricity, enable the community to receive a large number of
boarders and day-scholars.

The Free School is lodged in the house
of Madame de la Peltrie, remodeled and
enlarged in 1836. In 1822, the Rev. J.
Signay applied to the Ursulines to obtain
instruction for the Irish Catholics of the
city. The Irish class was definitely
organized in 1824.

As early as 1836, the Ursulines opened
their convent to the first normal school,
and continued to receive young ladies
at the expense of the government until
normal schools were abolished by law in
1842. They were finally re-established
in 1857, and for seventy-three years the
Laval Normal School for girls was part
of the Quebec Convent. It was transferred in 1930 to the fine modern building at the entrance of the Merici
property, and is frequented by some
two hundred resident pupils and externs.

The Merici Convent was at first a
simple branch house. It was opened in
1902 on the magnificent property given
in exchange for the Plains of Abraham
(now the Battlefields Park), and adjoins
this historic field.

The convent at Three Rivers was
founded in 1697 at the request of Mgr.
de St. Valier (q.v.). He joined to the
boarding school an hospital that lasted
until 1866, and did much good work.
This convent became in turn a mother-
house, and founded convents at Grand'-
Mère, Shawinigan, and Waterville
(Maine).

The Ursuline convent of Roberval,
on the beautiful lake St. John, was
founded in 1882 at the request of Mgr.

D. Racine, first bishop of Chicoutimi.
The School of Domestic Science connected with the boarding school was
the first of the kind in the country, and
the venerable foundress, Mother St.
Raphael, who took the initiative, was
frequently praised and decorated by the
government, and encouraged by the
support of the clergy. The institution,
affiliated to Laval University, renders
important services to the region by a
superior education given at the boarding
school and by the training of excellent
housekeepers.

The Ursuline convent of Stanstead
was founded in 1884 at the request of
Mgr. Antoine Racine, first bishop of
Sherbrooke. It is ideally situated near
the frontier of Vermont, in the midst of
an English-speaking population. Pupils
from far and near follow the course of
studies and receive the diplomas given
by the institution, affiliated to Laval
University. The commercial course is
on a high footing, and is greatly appreciated. In 1921 this convent sent subjects
to open the first Ursuline convent in
Swatow, China.

The Ursuline convent of Rimouski,
perched on the heights and overlooking
the Gulf, owes its existence to Mgr.
Blais, second bishop of Rimouski, who
chose the Ursulines for the direction of
a normal school opened in 1906. It soon
gained an enviable reputation for the
intellectual and moral training of its
pupils.

In 1924 Mgr. F. X. Ross and the
Ursulines of Rimouski established the
convent of Gaspé. Its normal school
and domestic science course have already
attracted attention for educational pro-
ficiency.

At different times during its existence,
the Quebec convent has sent missionaries elsewhere to help the cause of
education—to New Orleans in 1822, to
Charlestown Heights (near Boston) in
1825, to Galveston (Texas) in 1849, to
Springfield (Illinois) in 1884, and to
Montana in 1893.

Bibliography. See *Glimpses of the monastery* (Quebec, 1897); Chapot, *Histoire de Marie de l'Incarnation* (Paris, 1892); *Ursulines de Québec* (Quebec, 1863); *Lettres de la Ven. M. de l'Incarnation* (Tournai, 1876); and Dom A. Jamet, *Marie de l'Incarnation* (Paris, 1929).

Ursulines (Saskatchewan). The Ursulines at Bruno, Saskatchewan, originally came from Haselünne, Hanover, Germany, where they belonged to an independent convent of the German Union, which followed the rule of the Bordeaux Congregation. The Canadian foundation was established in 1915, and the mother house was first stationed in Marysburg, Saskatchewan. It was then transferred to Bruno, and was there canonically erected as in independent convent, with its own novitiate, in 1919. To the mother-house is also attached an academy for young ladies, in which are taught, besides the regular high school courses, art, music, and needlecraft. The academy is affiliated with the Toronto Conservatory of Music. The community at Bruno also furnishes the various parishes in the territory of St. Peter's Abbey Nullius with qualified teachers for their schools.

Utikuma lake is in northern Alberta, north of Lesser Slave lake and between the 115th and 116th meridians of west longitude. The name is the Cree name for "whitefish". The lake has an area of 85 square miles.

Utrecht, Treaty of. This was the treaty whereby the struggle between Great Britain and France known in Europe as the War of the Spanish Succession, and in America sometimes as "Queen Anne's War", was brought to a close in 1713. By it France ceded to Great Britain her claims in North America to the Hudson bay territories, to Newfoundland, and to Acadia. But the treaty was little more than a temporary truce, for its provisions left the door open to further disputes, which ultimately culminated in the Seven Years' War. No attempt was made to define the extent of the Hudson bay territories; France retained in Newfoundland certain fishing rights, which were what she most valued; and in ceding Acadia, she did so "according to its ancient limits", which had never been laid down. She retained, moreover, the island of St. Jean (now Prince Edward Island) and the island of Cape Breton; and on the latter she proceeded to erect the fortress of Louisbourg, guarding the entrance to the gulf of St. Lawrence, and menacing Acadia itself.

Utterson, a village in the Muskoka district, Ontario, on the Canadian National Railway, 12 miles north of Bracebridge. Pop. (1934), 250.

Uxbridge, a town in Ontario county, Ontario, on the Black river, and on the Canadian National Railway, 42 miles north-east of Toronto. Settlement began in 1806; but the village was not incorporated until 1871. It was named after Uxbridge, in Middlesex, England. A rich agricultural district surrounds the town; and it has flour, oatmeal, and planing mills, as well as a foundry. It has also a high school, a public library, and a weekly newspaper (*Times-Journal*). Pop. 1931), 1,325.

V

Vail, Edwin Arnold (1817-1885), speaker of the Legislative Assembly of New Brunswick (1865-7 and 1871-4), was born at Sussex Vale, New Brunswick, on August 19, 1817, the son of the Hon. John Cougle Vail and Charlotte, daughter of the Rev. Oliver Arnold. He was educated at Edinburgh University and at the University of Glasgow (M.D., 1837), and thereafter practised medicine at Sussex, New Brunswick. From 1857 to 1867 he represented King's county as a Liberal in the Legislative Assembly of New Brunswick, and from 1865 to 1867 he was its speaker. He was a strong opponent of Confederation, and in 1867 he resigned from the legislature in protest against it; but he was again elected to the Legislative Assembly of New Brunswick for King's county in 1870, and except for the years 1874-8, he continued to represent this constituency until his death. From 1871 to 1874 he was again speaker of the Assembly; and in 1883 he was appointed a member of the executive council of New Brunswick without portfolio. He died at Sussex, New Brunswick, in August, 1885.

Vail, William Berrian (1823-1904), minister of militia and defence for Canada (1874-8), was born at Sussex Vale, New Brunswick, on December 19, 1823, the son of the Hon. John Cougle Vail and Charlotte, daughter of the Rev. Oliver Arnold. From 1846 to 1867 he carried on, with his brother, J. O. Vail, a shipping business at Digby, Nova Scotia. He was, like another brother, Dr. E. A. Vail (q.v.), an opponent of Confederation; and in 1867 he was elected, as an anti-Confederation

Liberal, to the Legislative Assembly of Nova Scotia for Digby. He continued to represent this constituency until 1874, and during the whole of this period he was provincial and financial secretary in the Annand administration. During the latter half of it he was also government leader in the lower house; and the acceptance of Confederation by Nova Scotia, on the granting of "better terms", was in part due to his influence. From 1874 to 1878, and again from 1882 to 1887, he represented Digby as a Liberal in the Canadian House of Commons; and from 1874 to 1878 he was minister of militia and defence in the Mackenzie government. His administration of this office was mainly notable for the establishment in 1876 of the Royal Military College at Kingston, Ontario. He died at Dover, England, on April 10, 1904. In 1850 he married Charlotte, daughter of Charles Jones, of Weymouth, Nova Scotia; and by her he had two daughters.

Val Barrette, a village in Labelle county, Quebec, on the Kiamika river, and on the Canadian Pacific Railway, 160 miles from Montreal, and 10 miles from Mont Laurier. It was incorporated as a village in 1914, and was named after one of the early settlers in the vicinity. Pop. (1931), 518.

Valcartier, a settlement in Quebec county, Quebec, on the Canadian National Railway, 18 miles north of Quebec city. Near it is a training camp of the Canadian militia; and this was used in 1914 as the mobilization-centre of the First Canadian Expeditionary Force. Pop. (1934), 800.

Valcourt, a village in Shefford county, Quebec, on the Noire river, and on the Canadian Pacific Railway, 40 miles from Sherbrooke. Pop. (1931), 308.

Valdes island is in the Nanaimo district of British Columbia, off the east coast of Vancouver island, between Galiano and Gabriola islands. It was named in 1859 after Commander Cayetano Valdes, of the Spanish navy, who in 1792 commanded the *Mexicana* on an exploration of the neighbourhood. It is 9 miles long and from 1 to 1½ miles wide; and has an area of 5,765 acres.

Vale Colliery. See **Thorburn.**

Valerian (*Valeriana uliginosa* (T.G.) Rydb., *Valerianaceae*), an erect herb, 1-5 feet tall, found chiefly in cedar swamps. The root-leaves are ovate to oblong, and usually entire; the stem-leaves are pinnately compound, with 7-15 leaflets. The rose-coloured flowers are borne in small clusters; the corolla is inversely conical; the stamens are 3 in number. It grows in wet ground from eastern Quebec to western Ontario, flowering from June to September.

Val Jalbert, a village in Lac St. Jean county, Quebec, on the west side of lake St. John, near the mouth of the Ouiat-chouan river, and on the Canadian National Railway, 6 miles south of Roberval. It is the site of an important lumber-dressing plant. Pop. (1931), 88.

Valleyfield (Salaberry de Valleyfield), a city in Beauharnois county, Quebec, is situated on the south bank of the St. Lawrence river at the foot of lake St. Francis, 30 miles west of Montreal. It is at the western terminus of the Beauharnois canal, and is served by the large Great Lake steamers and by the Canadian National and New York Central Railways. It is one of the most important industrial centres in Canada, having cotton mills, paper mills, artificial silk mills, flour mills, bronze powder works, machine shops, etc. There are about 3,000 employees in the cotton and artificial silk mills alone. It has a seminary, attended by about 500 pupils, a bilingual normal school, and an institute for the higher education in the English language. There is a weekly newspaper (*Progrès de Valleyfield*). Pop., about 11,000, of which 80 per cent are of French extraction. See Abbé L. Groulx, *Petite histoire de Salaberry de Valleyfield* (Montreal, 1913).

Valley Junction. See **L'Enfant Jésus.**

Vallière de Saint-Réal, Joseph Rémi (1787-1847), judge, was born at Carleton, on the bay of Chaleur, on October 1, 1787, the son of Jean Baptiste Vallière de Saint-Réal and Marguerite Corneillier dit Grandchamp. He came with his father, who was a blacksmith, to the French royalist settlement in Markham county, Upper Canada, in 1799; but at his father's death he went to Quebec, and became a protégé of Bishop Plessis (q.v.). He was called to the bar of Lower Canada in 1812; and in 1814 he was elected to the Legislative Assembly of the province for St. Maurice. He failed of re-election in 1817; but in 1820 he was elected for the upper town of Quebec, and he represented this constituency continuously until 1829. In 1823, during the absence of L. J. Papineau (q.v.), he was speaker of the House. In 1829 he was appointed a judge for the district of Three Rivers; and in 1842 chief justice at Montreal. In 1838 he was suspended from the bench by Sir John Colborne (q.v.), in consequence of his having granted a writ of *habeas corpus* to the prisoners arrested during the rebellion of 1837-8; but was restored to office by Poulett Thomson (q.v.) in 1840. He died on February 17, 1847. In 1812 he married Louise Pezard de Champlain, and in 1831 Esther Elora Hart, of Three Rivers. See F. J. Audet, *Joseph-Rémy Vallieres de Saint-Réal* (Les Annales, 1927) and P. G. Roy, *Les juges de la province de Québec* (Quebec, 1933).

Valmont, a village in Champlain county, Quebec, 8 miles from Shawinigan Falls. The name is descriptive, the village being in a valley in the Laurentian mountains. Pop. (1934), 1,000.

Van Cortlandt, Edward (1805-1875), physician and author, was born in Newfoundland in 1805, and was educated at Dr. Wilkie's school in Quebec. He studied medicine in England, and passed the examination of the Royal College of Surgeons in London in 1827. He returned to Canada in 1832, and settled in Bytown, Upper Canada (now Ottawa), where he practised medicine for the rest of his life. He died in Ottawa on March 25, 1875. He was interested in geology, mineralogy, and botany; and, in addition to papers contributed to the *Canadian Journal* and other periodicals, he was the author of several pamphlets, *Lecture on Ottawa productions* (Bytown, 1853), *Observations on the building stone of the Ottawa country* (Ottawa, n.d.), *An essay on entozoa* (Ottawa, 1865), and *An essay on the native compounds and metallurgy of iron, especially in connection with the Ottawa valley* (Ottawa, 1867). His wife, Gertrude Van Cortlandt, was author of *Records of the rise and progress of Ottawa* (Ottawa, 1858).

Vancouver, George (1758-1798), navigator, was born in 1758, and entered the navy in 1771 as an able seaman on the *Resolution*, under Capt. James Cook (q.v.). He became a midshipman on the *Discovery*, on Capt. Cook's third voyage; and in 1780 he passed his examination as a lieutenant. In 1790 he attained the rank of commander, and 1791 he was sent in the *Discovery* to take over from the Spaniards the Nootka Sound territory. He explored the Pacific coast of North America; and on his return to England in 1795 he devoted himself to preparing his journals for publication. He died, when the task was virtually completed, on May 10, 1798, at Peter-sham, England; and a few months later his brother John published his *Voyage of discovery to the North Pacific Ocean and round the world in the years 1790-1795* (3 vols., with atlas of plates, London, 1798). See G. H. Anderson, *Vancouver and his great voyage* (King's Lynn, 1923), and G. Godwin, *Vancouver: A life* (New York, 1931).

Vancouver, a city in British Columbia, situated on the Burrard inlet of the gulf of Georgia, opposite Vancouver island on the northern Pacific ocean. It is the terminus of five lines of railway: the Canadian Pacific, the Canadian National, the Great Northern, the Northern Pacific, and the Pacific Great Eastern. The Canadian Pacific Railway reached the site of the city in 1886. It was then a small collection of houses named Granville, which had had a post-office since 1874. In 1886 the city was incorporated under the name of Vancouver in honour of Captain George Vancouver (q.v.), who many years before had entered Burrard inlet, a year after the Spaniard Narvaez had discovered it in 1791.

Vancouver is the fourth largest city of Canada. It has grown rapidly in importance as a shipping port, especially since the opening of the Panama canal. The splendid natural harbour is open all the year round. It has docks on both shores of Burrard inlet; that is, both in Vancouver proper and North Vancouver. South Vancouver, which adjoins Vancouver, also has a fine series of jetties, facing on the north arm of Fraser river, making a good fresh-water harbour for large vessels. In addition to a great export trade, Vancouver is a transfer point for passengers to and from the Orient and Australia and for those crossing North America by the transcontinental railways. The coastal services are also extensive. As a port Vancouver is under the administration and direction of the Dominion government acting through the harbour commission. The harbour is nearer the

Orient than any other port in North America.

Vancouver has many interesting features, foremost of which is Stanley park, comprising about 900 acres almost surrounded by water, and containing a zoo, beautiful gardens, and an international memorial erected as a symbol of the cordial relations which exist between the United States and Canada. English park lies on the outskirts of the city. Among the public buildings are the custom house, three public hospitals, the court house, and three public libraries. The University of British Columbia is the leading educational institution of the province. A provincial normal school and an agricultural college are in Point Grey, a growing residential suburb. Vancouver is the commercial, industrial, and transportation hub of British Columbia. There is a total elevator capacity of 18,000,000 bushels, the largest on the Pacific coast. The great timber resources of the Pacific slope have provided Vancouver with an extensive industry, the products of which are exported to all parts of the world. The raw and manufactured products from the mines, fisheries, ranches, and farms of western Canada find transport by water through Vancouver. There are many industrial establishments in the city. Canned fish, lumber, shipbuilding, structural steel, and furniture are the principal industries. Three daily newspapers are published (*Province*, *Sun*, and *News-Herald*). Pop. (1931), 246,593. See T. MacInnes, *The port of Vancouver* (Canadian Geographical Journal, vol. ii, 1931); Ethel Glazier and others, *Vancouver: A short history* (Vancouver, British Columbia, 1936); and W. N. Sage, *Vancouver: The rise of a city* (Dalhousie Review, 1937).

Vancouver College. See **University of British Columbia.**

Vancouver island, a large island in the North Pacific ocean, lying off the west coast of Canada, between lat. 48° 19′ and 50° 53′ N. Its length from north-west to south-east is 285 miles; and its maximum width is 65 miles. Its area is about 20,000 square miles. With the Queen Charlotte islands, it forms part of a half-submerged mountain chain of the Corderilla, and is a continuation of the coast range of the United States. It is separated on the south from the mainland of the United States by the strait of Juan de Fuca; and on the east and north-east from the mainland of British Columbia by the gulf of Georgia and Queen Charlotte sound. Most of the island is mountainous and heavily forested: the highest summit is Victoria peak, with an altitude of 7,485 feet, in the northern district. There are no navigable rivers; but the coast-line is deeply indented with arms or fiords, which form good harbours. The harbour of Esquimalt, on the south-east coast, is one of the best on the Pacific coast, and is the chief station of the British navy in the North Pacific. The chief industries are agriculture, lumbering, fishing, and coal-mining. The coal-mines of Nanaimo provide most of the coal used in British Columbia. The climate is temperate and healthy, and is said to resemble that of England.

The island was first visited by Captain Cook (q.v.) in 1778; but it was named after Captain George Vancouver (q.v.), who explored and surveyed its coasts in 1792. In 1846, by the Treaty of Washington, the island was recognized by the United States as being British territory; and it was then granted to the Hudson's Bay Company, which undertook to colonize it. In this way the colony of Vancouver island came into existence in 1850. In 1866, however, it was united with the colony of British Columbia, which had been created in 1858; and in 1871 the united colony entered Confederation as the province of British Columbia. Victoria, at the southern extremity of Vancouver island, is the capital of British Columbia.

The population of the island, inclusive of Victoria, is about 125,000;

VANCOUVER, BRITISH COLUMBIA

and it is served by both the Canadian Pacific (Esquimalt and Nanaimo) and Canadian National Railways. There is frequent steamship service between Victoria and Nanaimo and the mainland.

See J. D. Pemberton, *Facts and figures relating to Vancouver island and British Columbia* (London, 1860), R. C. Mayne, *Four years in British Columbia and Vancouver island* (London, 1862), C. E. Barrett-Lennard, *Travels in British Columbia, with the narrative of a yacht voyage round Vancouver island* (London, 1862), D. G. F. Macdonald, *British Columbia and Vancouver island* (London, 1863), M. MacFie, *British Columbia and Vancouver island* (London, 1863), G. M. Sproat, *Scenes and studies of savage life* (London, 1868), W. G. H. Ellison, *The settlers of Vancouver island* (London 1908), C. H. Clapp, *Southern Vancouver island* (Ottawa, 1912), A. Carmichael, *Indian legends of Vancouver island* (Toronto, 1922), and C. Moser, *Reminiscences of the west coast of Vancouver island* (Kakawis, 1926).

Vanderhoof, a village in Range 5 of the coast district of British Columbia, on the Nechako river, and on the Canadian National Railway, 70 miles west of Prince George. It is in the heart of the Nechako valley, the largest agricultural area in central British Columbia, and has a weekly newspaper (*Nechako Chronicle*). Pop. (1931), 305.

VanderSmissen, William Henry (1844-1929), scholar, was born in Toronto on August 18, 1844, and was educated at the University of Toronto (B.A., 1864; M.A., 1866). In 1866 he was appointed lecturer in German at the University of Toronto, and in 1892 professor of German. From 1873 to 1891 he was also librarian. He retired from his professor's chair in 1913; and he died at Toronto on January 3, 1929. With W. H. Fraser (q.v.), he was author of *The high school German grammar* (Toronto, 1894); and he translated into English verse, with commentary and notes, *Goethe's Faust* (London, 1926).

Vandorf, a village in York county, Ontario, on the Canadian National Railway, 25 miles north of Toronto, and 4 miles from Aurora. Pop. (1934), 200.

Van Dusen, Conrad (1801?-1878), clergyman and author, was born about 1801. He became in 1829 a minister of the Methodist Episcopal Church; and in 1833 a minister of the Wesleyan Methodist Church. From 1849 to 1851 he was treasurer of Victoria College, Cobourg. He died at Whitby, Ontario, on August 18, 1878. Under the pseudonym of "Enemikeese", he was the author of *The Indian chief* (London, 1867), and *The successful young evangelist* (Toronto, 1870).

Van Egmond, Anthony (1771-1838), soldier, was born in Holland in 1771. He served as an officer in the Dutch army during the French invasion of the Netherlands in 1793-4; and later he joined the Dutch contingent under Napoleon. He served under Napoleon until after the retreat from Moscow, in which he took part; then he joined the allied armies, with the rank of colonel, and he was with Blücher at Waterloo. Soon after the close of the Napoleonic wars, he emigrated to America; and for eight years he lived in Indiana county, Pennsylvania. He then removed to Upper Canada; and he settled first in Waterloo county, and later in the Huron Tract. He took part in the rebellion of 1837, and was in command of the rebels at the engagement of Montgomery's Farm. He was captured by the loyalists, succumbed to the rigours of imprisonment in the Toronto jail, and died in hospital in the early part of 1838.

Vanessa, a village in Norfolk county, Ontario, on the Toronto, Hamilton, and Buffalo Railway, north of Waterford. Pop. (1934), 100.

Vanguard, a village in the Swift Current district of Saskatchewan, on the Noteken river, and on the Canadian Pacific Railway, 50 miles south-east of Swift Current. It is in a farming and stock-raising district, and has a hospital and a weekly newspaper (*Times*). Pop. (1931), 389.

Van Horne, Sir William Cornelius (1843-1915), president and chairman of the board of directors of the Canadian Pacific Railway (1888-1910), was born in Illinois, United States, on February 3, 1843, the son of Cornelius Covenhoven Van Horne. He became a telegraph operator on the Illinois Central Railway in 1857, and served in various capacities on American railways until 1882. He was then appointed general manager of the Canadian Pacific Railway; and it was under him that the work of construction was pushed to completion. In 1884 he was elected vice-president of the company, and in 1888 its president. In 1899 he exchanged this position for that of president of the board of directors. He retired from active connection with the company in 1910, and he died at Montreal on September 11, 1915. In 1867 he married Lucy Adeline, daughter of Erastus Hurd, Galesburg, Illinois. He was created a K.C.M.G. in 1894. See W. Vaughan, *The life and work of Sir William Van Horne* (New York and Toronto, 1920).

Van Horne range, a range of mountains in the Kootenay district of British Columbia, north-east of Golden, in the Rocky mountains.

Vankleek Hill, a town in Prescott county, Ontario, on the Canadian Pacific and Canadian National Railways, 53 miles east of Ottawa, and 58 miles northwest of Montreal. It is named after Simeon Van Kleek, a United Empire Loyalist, who after settling first in Nova Scotia, and then in Argenteuil county, Quebec, moved across the Ottawa river about 1800 to the high land south of the river, and obtained a grant of the land on which the town is now situated. It is the centre of a good agricultural district; and its chief manufactures are flour, cheese, lumber, and iron castings. It has a high school, a convent, and a weekly newspaper (*Review*). Pop. (1931), 1,380.

Vankoughnet, Philip (1790-1873), legislative councillor of Upper Canada, was born in Cornwall, Upper Canada, on April 2, 1790, the son of Michael Vankoughnet, a United Empire Loyalist. He fought in the War of 1812; and in the rebellion of 1837 he commanded the 5th Battalion of Incorporated Militia. From 1820 to 1828 he represented Stormont and Dundas in the Legislative Assembly of Upper Canada; and in 1836 he was appointed a member of the Legislative Council of the province. He died on May 7, 1873. In 1819 he married Harriet Sophia, daughter of Matthew Scott, of Carrick-on-Suir, Tipperary county, Ireland.

Vankoughnet, Philip Michael Matthew Scott (1823-1869), chancellor of Upper Canada (1862-7) and of Ontario (1867-9), was born at Cornwall, Upper Canada, on January 21, 1823, the eldest son of Philip Vankoughnet (q.v.) and Harriet Sophia, daughter of Matthew Scott, of Tipperary county, Ireland. He was educated at Dr. Urquhart's school in Cornwall, Upper Canada, and was called to the bar of Upper Canada in 1844 (Q.C., 1850). In 1849 he was one of the chief organizers of the British American League, formed to oppose the annexation movement; but he did not enter parliament until 1856, when he was returned for the Rideau division of Upper Canada to the Legislative Council, being the first elected member of the Council to take his seat. Before his election he had already replaced Sir Allan MacNab (q.v.) as president of the Executive Council and minister of agriculture in the Taché-Macdonald administration, and he immediately became the government leader in the Upper House. He resigned from office with his colleagues in 1858; but, after the collapse of the short-lived Brown-Dorion administration, he resumed office as chief commissioner of Crown lands, and this portfolio he retained until 1862. He was then appointed chancellor of the Upper Canada court of chancery; and after 1867 he became chancellor of Ontario. He died at Toronto on November 7, 1869. In 1845 he married Elizabeth, daughter of Col. Barker Turner; and by her he had two sons. See D. B. Read, *Lives of the judges* (Toronto, 1888).

Vansittart, Henry (1779-1844), naval officer, was born in Bisham Abbey, Berkshire, England, in 1779. He entered the British navy as a midshipman in 1791, and served throughout the Revolutionary and Napoleonic Wars. In 1830 he was promoted rear-admiral, and in 1841 vice-admiral. In 1834 he bought an estate near Woodstock, Upper Canada, on which he settled; and he died here in 1844.

Varennes, Pierre Gaultier de. See **La Vérendrye, Pierre Gaultier de Varennes, Sieur de.**

Varennes, a village in Verchères county, Quebec, on the south shore of the St. Lawrence river, and on the Quebec Southern Railway, 16 miles below Quebec. It is named after the seigniory granted in 1666 to René Gaultier, sieur de Varennes, a lieutenant in the Carignan-Salières Regiment. Mixed farming and market-gardening are the chief occupations of the district in which it is situated. Pop. (1931), 808.

Varna, a village in Huron county, Ontario, 17 miles south-east of Goderich, and 4 miles from Brucefield, the nearest railway station. It is named after Varna in Bulgaria. Pop. (1934), 250.

Vars, a village in Russell county, Ontario, on the Canadian National Railway, 17 miles south of Ottawa. The railway station is named Dearbrook. Pop. (1934), 300.

Vaudreuil, Philippe de Rigaud, Marquis de (1643-1725), governor of New France (1705-25), was born in France in 1643. He came to New France in 1787, as commander of the French troops in the colony, and served as chief

of staff in Denonville's expedition against the Iroquois. In 1690 he was charged with guarding the north shore of the St. Lawrence against the English, at the siege of Quebec by Phips (q.v.). He was appointed governor of Montreal in 1698, and in 1703 he became administrator of the government of Canada, on the death of Callière (q.v.). In 1705 he was appointed lieutenant-general and governor of New France; and he administered the government of the colony until his death, at Quebec, on October 10, 1725. In 1690 he married Louise Elisabeth, daughter of the Chevalier Joybert de Soulanges; and by her he had four sons. He succeeded his father in the marquisate in 1702. See P. G. Roy, *Le lieutenant-general Marquis de Vaudreuil* (Bull. rech. hist., 1929).

Vaudreuil-Cavagnal, Pierre de Rigaud, Marquis de (1704-1778), last governor of New France (1755-60), was born at Montreal in 1704, the son of Philippe de Rigaud de Vaudreuil (q.v.) and Louise Elisabeth Joybert de Soulanges. He became a captain in the *troupes de la marine*, and in 1733 was appointed governor of Three Rivers. From 1742 to 1755 he was governor of Louisiana. In 1755 he was appointed governor of New France, and he arrived at Quebec on June 23 of that year. He found Canada on the brink of war with Great Britain. He opened hostilities by sending, in March, 1756, a force to capture the forts on the road to Oswego, and in March of the following year, he sent a force against Fort William Henry, on Lake George. He became the tool of Bigot (q.v.) in his plundering of the colony; and throughout the war with Great Britain, he continually thwarted Montcalm (q.v.) and greatly hampered the conduct of the war by his vacillating policy. He was in command at Quebec during the battle of the Plains of Abraham, and on receiving the news of Montcalm's defeat, deserted the lines below the city, made a hurried retreat towards Jacques Cartier, and authorized the surrender of the city. Later in 1760, when the British were before Montreal, he himself surrendered all Canada. After the conquest, he went to France, and, with Bigot, he was tried for mal-administration, but was acquitted. He died in Paris on August 4, 1778. He married Charlotte Fleury de la Gorgendière, widow of François Le Verrier de Rousson, and had no children. His letters to the Chevalier de Lévis have been published by the Abbé H. R. Casgrain in his *Collection des manuscrits du Maréchal de Lévis*, vol. viii (Quebec, 1895).

Vaudreuil, a county in Quebec, fronting on the Ottawa river and the river St. Lawrence, west of Montreal. It is bounded on the west by the province of Ontario, and on the south by Soulanges county; and it is traversed by the Canadian Pacific and Canadian National Railways. Pop. (1931), 12,015.

Vaudreuil, a village in Vaudreuil county, Quebec, on the right bank of the Ottawa river, and on the Canadian National and Canadian Pacific Railways, 30 miles west of Montreal. It is the centre of a general farming and market-gardening district, and is also a summer resort. It was incorporated in 1850, but the church was built in 1787. Pop. (1931), 466.

Vauquelin, Jean (1728-1772), sailor, was born at Dieppe, France, in February, 1728, the son of Jean Charles Vauquelin, captain of a merchant vessel. He entered the merchant marine, and by 1750 commanded his own ship. When the Seven Years' War broke out, he was entrusted with the command of the frigate *Aréthuse;* and he greatly distinguished himself at the siege of Louisburg in 1758. He and his vessel finally escaped from the harbour, by running the British blockade; and in 1759 he was appointed commander-in-chief of the French flotilla in the St. Lawrence. He kept his flotilla intact until May 16, 1760, when he was defeated in an engage-ment with some British ships immediately above Quebec, and was taken prisoner. He was returned to France; and after serving for twelve more years in the French navy, he died at Rochefort on November 10, 1772. The statement has been made that he committed suicide; but there is doubt about this. See Æ. Fauteux, *Jean Vauquelin* (Trans. Roy. Soc. Can., 1930).

Vaux, mount, is in the Kootenay district of British Columbia, south-east of the confluence of the Ottertail and Kicking Horse rivers, in Yoho Park, and is one of the Rocky mountains. It is in lat. 51° 16', long. 116° 32', and has an altitude of 10,881 feet. The name is to be found on the Palliser expedition map, 1859.

Vavasour, mount, is in Alberta, in lat. 50° 46', long. 115° 27', and has an altitude of 9,300 feet. It is named after Lieutenant M. Vavasour, R.E., who, with Lieutenant H. J. Warre, aide-de-camp to the commander of the forces in Canada, crossed the Rockies by "the most southern British pass" (White Man pass), in 1845, on a military mission.

Veery. See **Thrush.**

Vegreville, a town in Alberta, situated in the Vermilion valley, 72 miles east of Edmonton, on the main line of the Canadian National Railway, and on a branch line of the Canadian Pacific Railway. It is a distributing point for one of the richest diversified farming regions in Canada. About 1890 Father Vegreville established a French settle-ment, named Vegreville after its founder, four miles south of the present town. On the construction of the Canadian National Railway through the district, the buildings that had been erected were moved to its present site. It has creameries, a flour mill, and a weekly newspaper (*Observer*). Pop. (1931), 1,659.

Veniot, Peter John (1863-1936), prime minister of New Brunswick (1923-5) and postmaster-general of Canada (1926-30), was born at Richibuctou,

New Brunswick, on October 4, 1863, the son of Stephen Veniot and Mary Morell. He was educated at Pictou Academy. From 1894 to 1900 he represented Gloucester in the Legislative Assembly of New Brunswick; but he resigned in 1900 to become collector of customs at Bathurst, and later secretary of the school board. In 1917, however, he was re-elected to the Legislative Assembly; and he continued to sit in it until defeated in 1925. In 1917 he became minister of public works in the Foster government; and in 1923 he succeeded W. E. Foster (q.v.) as prime minister of New Brunswick. Defeated at the polls in 1925, he was elected to represent Gloucester in the House of Commons in 1926; and later in 1926 he was sworn of the Privy Council and appointed postmaster-general in the Mackenzie King government. He resigned office with the rest of the cabinet after the general election of 1930, though he retained his seat in the House until his death at Bathurst, on July 6, 1936. In 1885 he married Catherine Melanson; and by her he had six sons. He was an LL.D. of the University of New Brunswick (1923) and of Laval University (1924).

Vennor, Henry George (1841-1884), geologist, ornithologist, and meteorologist, was born in Montreal, in 1841, the son of a hardware merchant. He was educated at the Montreal High School and at McGill University. From 1865 to 1880 he was on the staff of the Geological Survey of Canada; and his reports contained much of practical value. In 1877 he published the first of his *Vennor almanacs*, in which he ventured, with surprising success, to predict the weather. As an ornithologist, his chief work was *Our birds of prey* (Montreal, 1876). He died in Montreal on June 8, 1884.

Ventadour, Henri de Lévis, Duc de (1596-1651), viceroy of Canada (1625-31), was born in the castle of Moustier Ventadour, near Tulle, Corrèze, France,

in 1596. After serving in the army, he took holy orders; and in 1625 he bought from his uncle, Henri, Duc de Montmorency, the vice-royalty of Canada, with the object of furthering the Canadian missions. It was through him that the Jesuits came to Canada. Shortly after the Company of New France was organized in 1627, the Duc de Ventadour was compelled to relinquish his office of viceroy; but he continued throughout his life to interest himself in the Jesuit missions in Canada. He died in Paris, France, in 1651. Pointe Lévis, or Lévy, opposite Quebec, was named after him.

Verazzano. See **Verrazano.**

Verchères, Marie-Madeleine Jarret de (1678-1747), heroine, was born on her father's seigniory on the St. Lawrence river, twenty miles below Montreal, on April 17, 1678, the daughter of François Jarret and Marie Perrot. In October, 1692, when her parents were absent, a band of marauding Iroquois appeared at the fort. Madeleine at once took command, and, with the assistance of her two young brothers, two soldiers, and an old man of eighty, defended the fort for a week, when relief came from Montreal. In September, 1706, she married Pierre-Thomas Tarieu de la Pérade. In her later years she was chiefly distinguished on account of the large number of law-suits in which she engaged. She died on August 8, 1747. See P. G. Roy, *Madeleine de Verchères, plaideuse* (Trans. Roy. Soc. Can., 1921), and A. G. Doughty, *A daughter of New France* (Ottawa, 1916).

Verchères, a county in Quebec, fronting on the St. Lawrence river, and bounded on the south-west by Chambly county, and on the east by St. Hyacinthe county. Chief town, Verchères. Pop. (1931), 12,603.

Verchères, county town of Verchères county, Quebec, is situated on the south bank of the St. Lawrence river, and on the Quebec Southern Railway, 22 miles east of Montreal. It is on the site of the fort of Verchères, defended so gallantly against the Iroquois by Madeleine de Verchères (q.v.) in 1692. It is the centre of an agricultural district; but it is especially noted for the flat-bottomed boats known as "Verchères boats", which are made here, and it has also a canning factory. It has a model school directed by the Christian Brothers and a convent of the Sisters of the Holy Names of Jesus and Mary; and during the summer it is popular as a tourist resort. Pop. (1931), 722.

Verdun, a city in Jacques Cartier county, Quebec, on the St. Lawrence river and on the Canadian National Railway. It is a suburb of Montreal, with which it is connected by street-car. Verdun was first known as Côte de Gentilly, and it was given its present name later, probably by La Salle (q.v.), in honour of the historic Verdun in France. In 1830 it was named La Rivière-St. Pierre, but an Act changing the name again to Verdun was passed in 1876. The city was incorporated in 1912. Although primarily a residential suburb, west of Montreal, Verdun has a number of industrial establishments. The electric lights, water works, and fuse works are municipally owned. There are numerous churches, several theatres, a large general hospital, and a hospital for the insane. Two weekly newspapers are published in English (*Free Press* and *Guardian*), one in French (*Le Chroniqueur*), and one (*Messenger*) in French and English. Pop. (1931), 60,745.

Veregin, Peter (d. 1924), leader of the Doukhobors, was born in Russia. He became the pseudo-divine leader of the Doukhobors, a sect of Russian Quakers, and on three occasions was exiled to Siberia by the Russian government. He came to Canada in 1903, to assume control of the Doukhobor settlements which had been established in Saskatchewan shortly before; and he remained in Canada during the rest of his life. A man of great ability, he guided the destinies of the Doukhobor settlements, first in Saskatchewan, and then in British Columbia, with great success. He was killed, on November 28, 1924, by the explosion of a time bomb in a railway carriage in which he was travelling, near Grand Forks, British Columbia.

Veregin, a village in Saskatchewan, on the Canadian National Railway, 18 miles south of Yorkton. Pop. (1934), 400.

Vérendrye, mount, is at the headwaters of the Vermilion river, in the Kootenay district of the Rocky mountains, in lat. 51°, long. 116° 04'. It has an altitude of 10,125 feet; and it is named after the Sieur de La Vérendrye (q.v.).

Vergor, Louis DuPont du Chambon, Sieur de (*fl.* 1712?-1763), soldier, was born in France about 1712, the son of Louis DuPont du Chambon. He obtained a commission in the French army, and in 1751 was sent to Canada, with the rank of captain. In 1754 he was placed in command at Fort Beauséjour, and he surrendered this fort to Monckton (q.v.) on June 16, 1755, without attempting a defence. He was tried by court-martial at Quebec in 1757, but was acquitted of the charges brought against him, and returned to duty in the army. It was his misfortune that he was in command of the post at the Anse-au-Foulon (Wolfe's Cove) when the British made their landing here before the battle of the Plains. After the conclusion of peace, Vergor returned to France; but nothing appears to be known of his subsequent career. In 1752 he married Marie-Josephte Riverin; and by her he had four children, the youngest of whom was born in 1763.

Vermilion, a town in the Battle River district of Alberta, on the Vermilion river, and on the main line of the Canadian National Railway (of which it is a divisional point), 110 miles east of Edmonton. It is the centre of an excellent mixed farming district, and has a flour-mill, a creamery, and an agricultural college and demonstration farm, as well as lumber yards, a machine shop, and agricultural implement warehouses. There is a high school and a weekly newspaper (*Standard*). Pop. (1931), 1,270.

Vermilion pass is in the Rocky mountains, on the boundary between British Columbia and Alberta, at the head of the Vermilion river, in lat. 51° 09', long. 116° 07', and has an altitude of 5,376 feet. The first recorded crossing was made by Dr. James Hector (q.v.), geologist to the Palliser expedition, in 1858. The pass is now the route of the famous Banff-Windermere motor highway through the Rocky mountains.

Vermillion river, a tributary of the St. Maurice river in Quebec, the mouth of which is 93 miles north of Three Rivers. It has a length of 100 miles, and drains a basin of approximately 1,000 square miles.

Verner, Frederick A. (1836-1928), painter, was born at Trafalgar, near Oakville, Upper Canada, in February, 1836. He was the nephew of Sir William Verner, bart., and in 1856 went to England. He joined the British Legion, and served under Garibaldi in Italy in 1860. In 1862 he returned to Canada, and visited the North West. He became notable for his paintings of prairie life; and in 1880 he was elected an associate of the Royal Canadian Academy. During the latter half of his life he lived in England; and he died in London, England, on May 6, 1928.

Verner, a village in the Nipissing district of Ontario, on the Veuve river, and on the Canadian Pacific Railway, 34 miles west of North Bay, and 15 miles east of Sudbury. Pop. (1934), 700.

Vernon, Charles William (1871-1934), clergyman and author, was born in London, England, in 1871. He came to Canada in 1889, and studied at King's College, Windsor (B.A., 1896; M.A., 1901). He was ordained a priest of the

Church of England in 1896, and in 1919 was appointed general secretary of the Social Service Council of the Church of England in Canada. He died at Toronto, Ontario, on January 30, 1934. He was the author of *Cape Breton at the beginning of the twentieth century* (Toronto, 1903), *Bicentenary sketches and early days of the Church in Nova Scotia* (Halifax, 1910), and *The old Church in the new Dominion* (London, 1929).

Vernon, a town in the Yale district, British Columbia. It is the "hub" of the Okanagan fruit-growing region, and is surrounded by a picturesque lake country. The Indian name for the place was *Nintle-mooschin*, "a step-over"; to the earliest white men it was known as Priest's Valley, under which name a post office was established in 1884; in the seventies it was also called Forge Valley, and in 1885 Centreville, the name given to the original townsite. In 1887 the name was changed to Vernon, after Forbes George Vernon, at that time commissioner of lands and works for British Columbia. About it is a great fruit country under irrigation. Farming, dairying, and mining are important industries. Fish abounds in the nearby lakes, and game in the hills and forests. It is on branch lines of the Canadian National Railway and the Canadian Pacific Railway. Pop. (1931), about 4,000.

Vernon, a village in Carleton county, Ontario, 22 miles south of Ottawa, and 5 miles from Osgoode, the nearest railway station. Pop. (1934), 250.

Verona, a village in Frontenac county, Ontario, at the head of the Napanee river, and on the Canadian Pacific Railway, 25 miles north of Kingston. Pop. (1934), 350.

Verrazano, Giovanni da (1486?-1528), explorer, was born at Florence, Italy, about 1486, and about 1505 entered the maritime service of France. In 1524 he sailed from the Azores on a voyage of exploration to North America.

He made his landfall on the coast of Florida, and explored the coast northward as far as the gulf of St. Lawrence. A map or planisphere of his discoveries was drawn in 1529 by his brother Gerolamo, who accompanied him; and on this map appears for the first time the name "Gallia Nova" (New France). In 1528 Verrazano set out on a second voyage to America, but was killed and eaten by cannibals, on an island which appears to have been one of the lesser Antilles. See J. C. Brevoort, *Verrazano the navigator* (privately printed, 1874), H. C. Murphy, *The voyage of Verrazano* (New York, 1875), B. F. De Costa, *Verrazano the explorer* (New York, 1880), S. E. Dawson, *The St. Lawrence basin* (London, 1905), *New light on the Verrazzano brothers* (Geographical Journal, 1910), and *More new light on the Verrazzano brothers* (Geographical Journal, 1926).

Verreau, Hospice Anthelme Jean Baptiste (1828-1901), priest and historian, was born at L'Islet, Lower Canada, on September 6, 1828, the son of Germain Alexandre Verreau and Marie Ursule Fournier. He was educated at the Quebec Seminary, and was ordained a priest of the Roman Catholic Church in 1851. From 1851 to 1857 he was principal of the College of Ste. Thérèse, and in 1857 he became principal of the Jacques Cartier Normal School— a position he occupied for the rest of his life. In 1887 he was appointed also professor of Canadian history at Laval University. In 1873 the government of Quebec commissioned him to report on materials relating to Canadian history in the archives of Europe; and the results of his inquiry were published in the report of the minister of agriculture for 1875. Though a profound scholar, he published comparatively little. A number of his papers are printed in the *Transactions* of the Royal Society of Canada, of which he was a charter member, in the *Journal de l'Instruction Publique*, and in the *Mémoires* of the

Société Historique de Montréal. He edited also a collection of documents entitled *Invasion du Canada: Collection des Mémoires* (2 vols., Montreal, 1870-73); and he published a play, *Saint Stanislas* (Montreal, 1879). He died in Montreal on May 15, 1901. In 1878 he was made an LL.D. of Laval University.

Versailles, Treaty of, 1919. This was the treaty between Germany and the victorious Allied nations (including Canada) which brought the World War to a formal close. It was signed in the Hall of Mirrors at Versailles on June 28, 1919. The terms of the treaty affected Canada in a direct way only slightly. Canada obtained a small share of the indemnities to be paid by Germany; but otherwise she asked for, and obtained, no direct benefits from the treaty in land or money. She did benefit from it, however, in the enhancement of her national status. In the Peace Conference in Paris, Sir Robert Borden (q.v.) insisted that Canada should have the same representation as Belgium and other small countries at the Conference; and in the end Canada was given, with the other overseas Dominions, representation on the British Empire delegation to the Conference. She was given two seats in the Conference, and these were occupied alternately by Sir Robert Borden, Sir George Foster (q.v.), the Hon. A. L. Sifton (q.v.), and the Hon. C. J. Doherty (q.v.). When the Treaty of Versailles came to be signed, Borden insisted that it should be signed separately on behalf of Canada. Opposition to this proposal arose in the United States delegation, which maintained that if Canada and the other British Dominions signed separately, the British Empire would have six votes in the proposed League of Nations, whereas the United States would have only one. Eventually, the problem was resolved by having the British Empire delegation sign for Great Britain, and the representatives of the British Dominions sign underneath, the names of their respective countries being indented under that of the British Empire. Canada thus, as a result of the treaty, obtained separate representation in the Assembly of the League of Nations, and even obtained the recognition of her right to have her representative elected to the Council of the League, with the result that the representative of Canada was actually elected to the Council of the League in 1927. See also **League of Nations.**

Vespucci, Amerigo, or Americus Vespucius (1451-1512), an Italian navigator and astronomer, was born in Florence, Italy, on March 9, 1451, and died in Seville, Spain, on February 22, 1512. He made several voyages to the northern coast of South America and, in 1498, is said to have skirted the coast of North America from Florida to Chesapeake bay. He reached the mainland of America in 1497, eighteen days before John Cabot (q.v.). A geographical work published by one Waldseemüller at Freiburg, Germany, comments at some length on the discoveries of Vespucci, and in his remarks the publisher says: "Now a fourth part [of the world] has been found by Amerigo or Americus." Thus it was that the new world came to be known as America. See *The first four voyages of Amerigo Vespucci* (London, 1893).

Vetch, Samuel (1668-1732), governor of Nova Scotia (1710-17), was born in Scotland on December 6, 1668, the son of the Rev. William Vetch (or Veitch), a Covenanting minister who was compelled to flee in 1671 to England, and later to Holland. He was educated at the College of Utrecht, and returned to England in the army of William of Orange in 1688. He became an officer in the 26th or Cameronian Regiment, and served on the continent until 1697. In 1698 he took part in the unsuccessful attempt to found the Darien Colony; and in 1700 he went to New York. In 1705 he was sent on a diplomatic mission to Quebec; and in 1710 he was adjutant-general of the expedition sent to conquer Acadia. On the capture of Annapolis Royal, he was appointed the first English governor of Nova Scotia; and he administered the affairs of the province until relieved of his appointment in 1717. His later years are obscure; but he died in London, England, on April 30, 1732, in a debtor's prison. In 1700 he married Margaret, daughter of Robert Livingstone, of New York. See Rev. G. Patterson, *Hon. Samuel Vetch* (Coll. Nova Scotia Hist. Soc., 1885), and J. C. Webster, *Samuel Vetch* (Shediac, New Brunswick, 1929).

Vetch, or Tare (*Vicia angustifolia* (L.) Reichard, *Leguminosae*), an annual sprawling or climbing herb which supports itself by tendrils developed from the tips of the leaves. The stem branches, and is somewhat pubescent. The pinnate compound leaves have from 4-10 oblong to linear leaflets, borne in pairs, while the tip of the leaf develops the much-branched tendril. The flowers are borne singly or in pairs in the axils of the upper leaves. They are pea-like and purple in colour. The pods are linear and black. It is commonly found along waysides and in cereal crops in eastern Canada.

Veteran, a village in Alberta, on the Canadian Pacific Railway, 100 miles west of Lacombe. It is in a mixed farming district, and has a high school, a community theatre, and a weekly newspaper (*Post*). Pop. (1931), 180.

Veyssière, Léger Jean Baptiste Noël (d. 1800), clergyman, was a Recollet priest who, in 1769, abjured the Roman Catholic faith, and became Protestant minister at Three Rivers, Quebec. He remained in this charge until his death, at Three Rivers, on May 26, 1800. See J. E. Roy, *Les premiers pasteurs protestants au Canada* (Bull. rech. hist., 1897).

Vézina, François (1818-1882), banker, was born in Quebec on August 30, 1818. In 1849 he founded the Caisse d'Economie de Notre Dame de Québec, of which he became secretary-treasurer; and in 1859 he was appointed cashier of the Banque Nationale on its foundation. This position he occupied until his death at Quebec on January 25, 1882. He published an *Etude historique de la progression financière de la Caisse d'Economie de N. D. de Québec* (3 vols., Quebec, 1878). See J. C. Langelier, *Biographie de françois Vezina* (Quebec, 1876).

Viburnum. See **Nanny Berry.**

Victoria, a county in Nova Scotia, on Cape Breton island, lying between the counties of Inverness and Cape Breton. It was created about 1851, and was named after Queen Victoria. It faces the Atlantic ocean, and is for the most part mountainous and undeveloped. Settlement is chiefly confined to the sea-coast; but there is some agricultural land in the southern part of the county. Chief town, Baddeck. Pop. (1931), 8,009.

Victoria, a county in New Brunswick, bounded on the west by the international boundary, on the north by Madawaska and Restigouche counties, on the east by Northumberland county, and on the south by Carleton county. It was created in 1844, and was named after Queen Victoria. It is watered by the St. John, St. Francis, Madawaska, Tobique, and other rivers; and it is traversed by the Canadian Pacific Railway. Chief town, Grand Falls. Pop. (1931), 14,907.

Victoria, a county in Ontario, is bounded on the north by the district of Muskoka, on the west by Ontario county, on the east by Peterborough county, and on the south by lake Scugog and Durham county. It was part of the land bought by the government in 1818 from the Missisauga Indians, and it was for a time part of Durham county, and later part of Peterborough county; but it was given complete independence in 1863. The county was called after Queen Victoria. The first settlers were brought out from Ireland by the Hon. Peter Robinson (q.v.) in 1825. In 1833 the Trent Valley canal was begun, to connect Georgian bay with the bay of Quinte; and the large lift locks at Kirkfield are famous. The county town is Lindsay. Pop. (1931), 25,844. See Watson Kirkconnell, *Victoria county centennial history* (Lindsay, 1921).

Victoria, the capital city of British Columbia, is situated at the southern end of Vancouver island, overlooking the strait of Juan de Fuca, and the snow-capped Olympic mountains on the United States mainland, and is on the Canadian Pacific and Canadian National Railways. The nearest mainland is 20 miles south at Port Angeles, Washington. The nearest Canadian mainland is 65 miles away. Vancouver lies 82 miles to the north-east. Victoria faces United States territory to the south and east. Formerly the capital of the colony of Vancouver Island, and later of the united colonies of Vancouver Island and British Columbia, it has, since the union with Canada in 1871, been the capital of the province of British Columbia. The site was known to the Indians as Camosun or Camosack. It was named by the officers of the Hudson's Bay Company in 1843 as Fort Camosun, and later Fort Victoria, in honour of the young Victoria, Queen of England. When the site became to be laid out in streets (1851-2), the name of Victoria was adopted. It was incorporated in 1862, and the old fort was demolished in 1864. The city is noted for the architectural beauty of the government buildings. It is the site of the Dominion astrophysical observatory, one of the largest of its kind in the world. Victoria is considered one of the most English of Canadian cities, not only in climate and aspect, but in the customs and traditions of its residents. Being laid out with picturesque parks and splendid driveways, it is considered one of the most beautiful cities on the Pacific coast. It has numerous churches, public schools, private schools, high and

VICTORIA, BRITISH COLUMBIA

normal schools, an arts college, hospitals, and public libraries.

Victoria is the shipping port for Vancouver Island products, as well as a port of call for ocean liners. The Canadian Pacific Railway operates steamers daily to Vancouver (82 miles north-east), and to Seattle (80 miles south-east). Ships run to Alaska, California, Australasia, the Orient, and all the principal Atlantic and European ports. Air service is established between Victoria and the mainland. The chief industries are lumbering, fish-canning, saw-, flour-, coffee-, and oat-meal mills, boiler and machine shops, furniture factories, and a mattress factory. Victoria is a favourite resort for tourists; it has been estimated that over 300,000 visit the city for vacations during all seasons of the year. Two daily newspapers (*Colonist* and *Times*) are published. Pop. (1931), 39,082. See Edgar Fawcett, *Some reminiscences of old Victoria* (Toronto, 1912), and Lady Willison, *Victoria, B.C., city of enchantment* (Victoria, 1930).

Victoria Beach, a summer resort at the southern end of lake Winnipeg in Manitoba, near the mouth of the Winnipeg river. It is the terminus of a railway line from Winnipeg, and is mainly frequented by visitors from Winnipeg. During the summer months, it has a weekly newspaper (*Victoria Beach Herald*).

Victoria Cross, a highly prized decoration, instituted at the close of the Crimean campaign of 1856, for officers and men of the naval and military forces of the British Empire who have performed, in the face of the enemy, a signal act of valour. It was designed to take the place in the British forces which the cross of the Legion of Honour took in the French forces, during the Crimean War. It is in the form of a bronze Maltese cross, with the royal crown in the centre, surmounted by the lion, and bearing below, on a scroll, the words "For Valour". The ribbon was formerly blue for the navy and red for the army; but is now crimson for all services. The first Canadian to win the Victoria Cross was Lieut. Alexander Roberts Dunn (q.v.), who distinguished himself in the charge of the Light Brigade at Balaclava in 1856. During the South African War the Victoria Cross was awarded to three Canadians, Lieut. (later Lieut.-Gen. Sir) R. E. W. Turner, Major E. J. Holland, and Sergt. A. H. L. Richardson. During the World War the Victoria Cross was awarded to upwards of thirty Canadians. See Capt. Theodore Goodridge Roberts and others. *Thirty Canadian V.C.'s* (London, 1919).

Victoria Harbor, a village in Simcoe county, Ontario, on the south-eastern arm of the Georgian bay, and on the Canadian National Railway, 25 miles east of Orillia. Its origin dates from the building of a saw-mill here in 1869; and its chief manufactures are still lumber and shingles. It has a public school. Pop. (1931), 1,128.

Victoria island, an insular tract of land in the Franklin district of the North West Territories, lying north of the 68th parallel of latitude and between the 103rd and 110th parallels of longitude. It is separated from the mainland of Canada by Dease strait and Coronation gulf; and it comprises the territories known as Prince Albert land, Wollaston land, and Victoria land. It was discovered by Thomas Simpson (q.v.) in 1838, and was explored by Dr. Rae (q.v.) in 1851. See V. Stefannson, *Victoria island and the surrounding seas* (Bulletin of the American Geographical Society, 1913).

Victoria lake, in Pontiac county, Quebec, lies south-west of lake Abitibi. It is 32 miles long, and has a width varying from 2 to 3 miles. There is a post of the Hudson's Bay Company on its banks.

Victoria land. See **Victoria island.**

Victoria, mount, is in the Bow range of the Rockies, Alberta and Kootenay district, British Columbia, is in lat. 51° 23′, long. 116° 18′, and has an altitude of 11,365 feet. The name appears on all maps and plans since 1845.

Victoria strait, the passage between Victoria island and King William island, in the Franklin district of the North West Territories.

Victoria University had its origin in a royal charter granted in 1836 (the first granted in the British overseas dominions to a college not under the Church of England) for the establishment in Cobourg, Upper Canada, of the Upper Canada Academy, as a superior school for Wesleyan Methodists. For five years Upper Canada Academy carried on a grammar-school type of education; but in 1841, just before the opening of King's College, Toronto, the Academy obtained from the legislature of united Canada a charter entitling it, under the name of Victoria College, "to confer degrees . . . in the various Arts and Faculties". The preparatory department of the College continued in operation until 1867; but 1841 marks the beginning of Victoria College as a university. The first president of the University was the Rev. Egerton Ryerson (q.v.); but in 1844 he was appointed superintendent of education in Upper Canada, and for a few years Victoria suffered various vicissitudes. With the appointment of the Rev. Samuel Sobieski Nelles (q.v.) as president in 1850, however, a new era dawned. The new president surrounded himself with a strong staff of teachers, who set a high standard. Under him, moreover, the college, which had hitherto confined itself to Arts subjects, achieved a real university status. In 1854, the Toronto School of Medicine became the faculty of medicine in Victoria; in 1860 a faculty of law was established; and in 1871 a faculty of theology—for, though created by a Methodist communion, Victoria had been hitherto in no sense a theological school.

It was under President Nelles, also, that the negotiations were begun which culminated in 1887-92 in the federation of Victoria with the University of Toronto. From the standpoint of Victoria, federation was a perilous experiment; and even the courage of Nelles seems to have dwindled at the last moment. But in 1887 Nelles died; and he was succeeded by Nathanael Burwash (q.v.), the leading exponent in Victoria of federation. The opponents of federation in the Methodist Church appealed to the courts; but in 1889 the advocates of federation obtained a legal decision which enabled them to proceed with their project, and in 1890 Victoria was formally federated with the University of Toronto. The University of Toronto provided land on which new buildings were erected in Toronto; and in 1892 Victoria removed from Cobourg to Toronto.

Under the federation agreement, Victoria restricted its teaching to a limited number of subjects, known as "college subjects" (mainly languages), and has resigned to the University of Toronto the remaining subjects of instruction (including the sciences, history, political economy, and philosophy); and it has held in abeyance its right of granting degrees, except in theology—and these it handed over in 1928 to the newly created Emmanuel College (q.v.). That in the working out of this federal union there have not arisen difficulties, cannot be pretended. Old jealousies and suspicions did not immediately die out. But these difficulties, thanks largely to Chancellor Burwash (as he became after federation), have been smoothed out; and the University of Toronto is to-day an example of the federal idea in higher education which has attracted world-wide attention.

That federation with the University of Toronto was a sound move on Victoria's part, there are probably few among the graduates of Victoria that would now deny By it, Victoria has obtained access for its students to the laboratories of the University of Toronto, and to other resources of the University of Toronto, such as it could not hope to have provided in a small Ontario town such as Cobourg. On the other hand, it has lost none of the support which it had a right to expect from the Methodist (and since 1925 the United Church) communion. The benefactions it has received have enabled it to build a series of residences for both men and women which are the envy of other colleges in the University, as well as a great hall and a library building; and generous additions have been made to its endowment. In many ways, its entrance into federation has conferred great benefits on the University of Toronto. It has introduced into the University a healthy spirit of rivalry and emulation; in some respects, it has set the pace for the other colleges in the University; and, above all, it has enlisted in the support of the University of Toronto a large element in the population of Ontario which was formerly antagonistic to it. Many of the benefactions which have come since 1887 to the University have been, in fact, from Methodist sources.

The presidents and chancellors of Victoria University have been the Rev. Egerton Ryerson (1841-4), the Rev. Alexander McNab (1844-9), the Rev. Samuel Sobieski Nelles (1850-87), the Rev. Nathanael Burwash (1887-1912), the Rev. R. P. Bowles (1912-1930), and the Rev. E. W. Wallace (1930—).

See N. Burwash, *The history of Victoria College* (Toronto, 1927), and *On the old Ontario strand: Victoria's hundred years* (Toronto, 1936). Much information may be obtained from the college journal *Acta Victoriana* (1878—). See also **University of Toronto.**

Victoriaville, a town of Arthabaska county, Quebec, situated on the Nicolet river and on the Canadian National Railway, 32 miles north-east of Richmond and 108 miles east of Montreal.

The settlement was known as Demersville, after Modeste Demers (q.v.), until 1861, when it took its present name, in honour of Queen Victoria. The town contains several churches and schools, a convent, and an academy for boys. The manufacturing establishments include furniture factories, clothing factories, planing mills, silk mills, a toy factory, a foundry, and a machine shop. There is a weekly newspaper (*La Voix des Bois Francs*). Pop. (1931), 6,213.

Vidal, Alexander (1819-1906), senator of Canada, was born at Brocknell, Berkshire, England, on August 4, 1819, the son of Capt. Richard Emeric Vidal, R.N., and Charlotte Penrose Mitton. He was educated at the Royal Mathematical School, Christ's Hospital, London, England. In 1834 he came with his parents to Canada, and in 1835 he settled at Sarnia, Upper Canada. In 1843 he became a provincial land surveyor; but in 1853 he became the agent of the Bank of Upper Canada in Sarnia, and in 1866 the agent of the Bank of Montreal. From 1863 to 1867 he was an elected member for the St. Clair division in the Legislative Council of Canada; and he was defeated as a Conservative candidate for the Canadian House of Commons in 1867. In 1873 he was called to the Senate of Canada, and he remained a senator until his death on November 18, 1906. In 1847 he married Catherine Louisa, daughter of Capt. William Elliott Wright, R.N.; and by her he had five sons and two daughters. He was an ardent temperance and social reformer; and in 1875 he was chairman of the Dominion Prohibitory Convention at Montreal.

Vienna, a village in Elgin county, Ontario, on the Port Burwell branch of the Canadian Pacific Railway, 4 miles from Port Burwell. Pop. (1934), 350.

Viger, Bonaventure (*fl.* 1803-1838), rebel, was born at Boucherville, Lower Canada, about 1803, a near relative of the Hon. Denis Benjamin Viger (q.v.).

On November 22, 1837, he commanded the group of rebels who rescued two prisoners from a detachment of British troops on the Chambly road, and thus gave the signal for the outbreak of rebellion. He was present at the engagement at St. Charles, a few days later, and was captured by the loyalists. In 1838 he was banished by Lord Durham (q.v.) to the Bermudas; but was released later in the year, and returned to Canada after the amnesty was granted. He settled down in Boucherville, married a sister of the Abbé Trudel, and became a Conservative.

Viger, Denis Benjamin (1774-1861), president of the Executive Council of Canada (1844-6), was born at Montreal on August 19, 1774. He was educated at the College of St. Raphael, and was called to the bar of Lower Canada. He sat in the Legislative Assembly of Lower Canada for the west ward of Montreal from 1808 to 1810, for the county of Leinster from 1810 to 1816, and for the county of Kent from 1816 to 1830. In 1830 he was appointed a member of the Legislative Council of the province. He was an ardent coadjutor of his cousin, L. J. Papineau (q.v.), and in 1828 accompanied him on a mission to England to press the views of the Assembly on the Colonial Office. In 1834 he was a second time deputed to visit England as an agent of the French Canadians. In 1838 he was arrested on a charge of complicity in the rebellion of 1837, but was released without trial. From 1841 to 1845 he represented Richelieu in the Legislative Assembly of united Canada, and from 1845 to 1848 Three Rivers. He was not included in the first Baldwin-Lafontaine administration; and in 1844 he accepted office under Metcalfe (q.v.) as Lower Canadian leader of the government, with the portfolio of president of the council. He failed, however, to carry his compatriots with him, and he resigned from the government in 1846. In 1848 he was appointed to the Legislative Council, and he sat in the Council until 1858. He died at Montreal on February 13, 1861. He was the author of *Considerations sur les effets qu'ont produits en Canada la conservation des établissements du pays, les mœurs, l'éducation des ses habitants, et les conséquences qu'entraînerait leur décadence* (Montreal, 1809), *Analyse d'un entretien sur la conservation des établissements du Bas-Canada* (Montreal, 1826), *Considérations relatives à la dernière révolution de la Belgique* (Montreal, 1831), and *La crise ministérielle* (Kingston, 1844). Some poetry by him was published in *Le Spectateur* (Montreal, 1813-29). He was the first president of the Société de St. Jean Baptiste; and in 1855 he was made an LL.D. by St. John's College, New York. See J. Royal and C. S. Cherrier, *Biographie de l'Hon. D. B. Viger* (Montreal, n.d.); and *Mémoires relatifs à l'emprisonnement de l'Hon. D. B. Viger* (Montreal, 1840).

Viger, Jacques (1787-1858), antiquarian, was a cousin of the Hon. D. B. Viger (q.v.), and was born at Montreal on May 7, 1787, the son of Jacques Viger and Amaranthe Prévost. He was educated at the College of St. Raphael, became a surveyor, and in 1813 was appointed an inspector of roads and bridges at Montreal. He fought in the War of 1812 as an officer of the Voltigeurs, and was present at the capture of Sackett's Harbour. In 1832 he was elected the first mayor of Montreal. He devoted his life to the collection of materials relating to Canadian history. Of these he left twenty-nine manuscript volumes, which he called his "Sabredache", and an "Album" of original illustrations. Apart from some official reports, he was the author of only two pamphlets, *Archéologie religieuse du diocèse de Montréal* (Montreal, 1850) and *Souvenirs historiques sur la seigneurie de La Prairie* (Montreal, 1857). He died at Montreal on December 12, 1858. In 1808 he married Marie Marguerite, daughter of Lacorne de St. Luc (q.v.), and widow of Major the Hon. John

Lennox. Some of his letters to his wife were published in the *Revue Canadienne*, 1914. See E. Z. Massicotte, *Jacques Viger et sa famille* (Bull. rech. hist., 1915).

Viger, Louis Labrèche (d. 1871), journalist and politician, was born at Terrebonne, Lower Canada, and was educated at the College of Montreal. He was adopted by the Hon. Denis Benjamin Viger (q.v.), and on the death of Viger added the name of Viger to his own patronymic of Labrèche. He was successively a priest, a journalist, a lawyer, a merchant, a politician, and a company promoter. From 1861 to 1867 he represented Terrebonne in the Legislative Assembly of Canada; but he took almost no part in the debates. He died at Montreal on April 27, 1871.

Viger, Louis Michel (1785-1855), receiver-general of Canada (1848-9), was born at Montreal on September 28, 1785, the son of Louis Viger, a blacksmith, and Marie Agnes Papineau. He was called to the bar of Lower Canada; from 1830 to 1838 he represented Chambly in the Legislative Assembly of Lower Canada; and in 1837 he was implicated in the rebellion, though not actually under arms. In the Legislative Assembly of united Canada he represented Nicolet from 1842 to 1844, Terrebonne from 1848 to 1851, and Leinster from 1851 to 1854. He was one of the founders of the *Parti rouge*, and in 1848 he became receiver-general in the second Baldwin-Lafontaine administration; but in 1849 he resigned over the question of the removal of the seat of government to Toronto. He died in 1855. He was known as "le beau Viger", and for many years he was president of the Banque du Peuple. See F. J. Audet, *L'hon. Louis-Michel Viger* (Bull. rech. hist., 1927).

Viking, a village in the Camrose district of Alberta, on the Canadian National Railway, 83 miles south-east of Edmonton. It was named by Nor-

wegian settlers. Situated in a grain-growing and dairying district, it has a high school, a hospital, and a weekly newspaper (*News*). Pop. (1931), 492.

Vikings. See **Norse Voyages.**

Villebon, Joseph Robineau de (1655-1700), governor of Acadia (1690-1700), was born in Quebec, Canada, on August 22, 1655, the second son of René Robineau de Bécancour, surveyor-general of New France. He was educated in France, and joined the army. He served with a dragoon regiment for about ten years, and then returned to Canada with the rank of captain. He was sent by Frontenac (q.v.) to Port Royal in Acadia; and in 1690 he was appointed governor of Acadia, in succession to Menneval (q.v.). He was exceptionally successful in defending the province against the aggressions of the English; and he retained office until his death at Fort St. John on July 5, 1700. See J. C. Webster, *Acadia at the end of the seventeenth century: Letters, journals, and memoirs of Joseph Robineau de Villebon* (Saint John, N.B., 1934).

Ville La Salle, a town in Jacques Cartier county, Quebec, on the southern shore of the island of Montreal, at the head of the Lachine rapids, and on the Canadian Pacific Railway, 10 miles west of Montreal. It was incorporated in 1912, and was named in honour of Cavelier de la Salle (q.v.), who built a fort here. It is mainly a residential centre. Pop. (1931), 2,362.

Ville Marie. See **Montreal.**

Ville Marie, a village in Témiscamingue county, Quebec, on the east side of lake Timiskaming, and on the Canadian Pacific Railway, 53 miles north of Témiscamingue. It was formerly known as "Baie-des-Pères", from the fact that the Oblate fathers once had a residence here. It is a colonization centre for the district in which it is situated. Pop. (1931), 1,049.

Villemontel, a village and parish in Abitibi county, Quebec, on the Canadian

National Railway, 77 miles west of Senneterre. Near it is an experimental farm opened in 1915, for the internment of prisoners of war. It is named after an officer named Villemontel, who served under Montcalm (q.v.) in the Seven Years' War. Pop. (1934), 1,000.

Villeray, Louis Rouer de (1629-1700), first councillor of the Sovereign Council of New France (1663-1700), was born in Amboise, near Tours, France, in 1629, the son of Jacques Rouer de Villeray and Marie Perthuis. He came to Canada about 1650 as secretary to Lauzon (q.v.), and became a notary at Quebec. On September 18, 1663, he was chosen as the first councillor of the new Sovereign Council, and although he was expelled in 1664 by Mézy (q.v.), in 1670 by Courcelles (q.v.), and in 1679 by Frontenac (q.v.), he was in each case replaced; and he remained the first councillor until his death on December 6, 1700. He married, first, on February 16, 1658, Catherine, daughter of Charles Sevestre (d. 1670), by whom he had three children, and second, in 1675, Marie-Anne Du Saussay de Bémont. See P. G. Roy, *Louis Rouer de Villeray* (Trans. Roy. Soc. Can., 1919); P. G. Roy, *La famille Rouer de Villeray* (Bull. rech. hist., vol. xxvi); C. P. Beaubien, *Louis Rouer de Villeray* (Bull. rech. hist., vol. v); and "Ignotus", *La querelle des "institulations"* (Bull. rech. hist., vol. viii).

Villeroy, a village in Lotbinière county, Quebec, on the Canadian National Railway, 16 miles from St. Philomène de Fortierville. Pop. (1934), 300.

Vimy Ridge, Battle of. This was the engagement in which the Canadian Corps were involved, on April 9, 1917, and subsequent days, as part of the "spring drive" of the Allies on the western front in the World War. Vimy Ridge was a cardinal point on the western front. A long upland about 475 feet in height, it afforded observation of the country around in almost every direction; and it was the hinge on which the Germans had pivoted in their retirement to the Hindenburg line only a few weeks before. The Canadians attacked on a front of 7,000 yards facing the Ridge, and after a terrific bombardment took Vimy Ridge in their stride. By April 13 they had penetrated the German lines to a depth of over six miles; and only the difficulty of getting the guns and supply waggons forward stopped this advance here. The battle, although it did not eventuate in open warfare, foreshadowed the return of a war of movement on the western front. It proved the possibility of breaking through the most elaborate field fortifications, and was the most considerable success the Canadian Corps had had up to that time. It was fitting that the magnificent Canadian War Memorial in France, designed by Walter Allward, a Canadian sculptor, should have been erected later on Vimy Ridge; it was formally unveiled by King Edward VIII on July 27, 1936. See also **World War.**

Vincennes, François Marie Bissot, Sieur de (1700-1736), soldier, was born in Montreal, Canada, on June 17, 1700, the son of Jean Baptiste Bissot de Vincennes, an army officer, and Marguerite Forestier. In 1718 he joined his father as a cadet among the Miami Indians; south of lake Erie; and in 1733, having been promoted in 1730 to the rank of lieutenant, he was made commandant in the Wabash country. He re-established Fort Vincennes, which was named after him, and he has been described as "the founder of Indiana". He was burnt at the stake by the Chicacha Indians in the Wabash country on March 25, 1736. See P. G. Roy, *Le Sieur de Vincennes, fondateur de l'Indiana, et sa famille* (Quebec, 1919).

Vincennes. See **Fort Vincennes.**

Vincent, John (1765-1848), soldier, was born in England in 1765. He entered the British army as an ensign in 1781,

CANADIAN GREAT WAR MEMORIAL ON VIMY RIDGE, FRANCE

Walter Allward, Sculptor and Architect

and in 1810 reached the rank of colonel. He served in Canada during the War of 1812, and was in command at Fort George, in the Niagara peninsula, when it was evacuated in 1813. He was created a major-general in 1813, a lieutenant-general in 1825, and a general in 1841. He died in London, England, on June 21 1848.

Vincent, Thomas (1776?-1832), fur-trader, was born in England about 1776, and entered the service of the Hudson's Bay Company as a writer at Albany in 1790. In 1814 he was governor of Moose Factory and the Southern Department; and in 1821 he was made a chief factor. He retired from the service of the Hudson's Bay Company, and returned to England, in 1826; and he died in 1832.

Vinland. See **Norse Voyages.**

Vinton, a village in Pontiac county, Quebec, on the Canadian Pacific Railway, 4 miles from Campbell's Bay, and 193 miles from Montreal. It was founded in 1856 by a group of Irish settlers, and was named after a village in Iowa, in the United States, from which some of the settlers came. It is in a general farming, dairying, and lumbering district. Pop. (1934), 1,220.

Violet (*Viola* spp.). This is a large genus of early spring-flowering herbs, either stemless or with a short leafy stem, bearing in general heart-shaped leaves. There may be two types of flowers developed: the showy, petaliferous flowers, which may be white, blue, purple, or yellow, having five irregular petals, which are often spurred; and an inconspicuous flower, which remains hidden, never expands, and develops abundant seed. The bird-foot violet (*Viola pedata* L. var. *bicolor* Pursh.) is not like the plants readily recognized as belonging to this genus. The leaves are much divided into linear lobes. The flower is large and pansy-like, the upper petals being a dark violet, and the others pale lilac. The petals are beardless. It is not abundant, but

may be found in sandy soil on open sunny slopes, often blooming in late summer. The Canada violet (*Viola canadensis* L.) is a tall, leafy-stemmed form, with heart-shaped, pointed, short-stalked leaves. The petals are white inside, with a purplish tinge on the outside and purple veins; the lower petal is slightly yellow; and the laterals are bearded. The spur is very short. It is found in rich woods from Newfoundland to Saskatchewan, blooming all summer. The downy yellow violet (*Viola pubescens* Ait.) is a leafy-stemmed form, from 6 to 12 in. high, and downy. The leaves are broadly-heart-shaped, and coarsely toothed. The flowers are bright yellow, veined with purple, the spur short. It grows in dry open woods from New Brunswick to Ontario, and is the first member of the violet clan to put in an appearance in the spring.

Viper's Bugloss, or Blueweed (*Echium vulgare* L., *Boraginaceae*), a very bristly-hairy biennial weed with long black tap root and spotted, much-branched stem. The leaves are entire, oblong to linear-lanceolate, and sessile. The flowers are showy, bright blue in colour, and pinkish in the bud. They are clustered in short one-sided spikes along the upper part of the branching stem forming a large showy cluster; the whole is densely hairy. The calyx is deeply 5-parted, the corolla funnel-form, unequally 5-lobed, with 5 reddish stamens inserted on the tube. This plant is a native of Europe, but is thoroughly naturalized throughout the eastern portion of Canada, becoming a troublesome weed in some localities. It grows on limestone or gravelly soil.

Virden, a town in the Brandon district of Manitoba, on the Canadian Pacific and Canadian National Railways, 181 miles west of Winnipeg. Originally known as Gopher Creek, it was named Manchester in 1882 by the Canadian Pacific Railway officials; but the name was later changed to Virden, after Virden in Scotland, whence some of Lord Mountstephen's relatives came. It is in a grain-growing district, and has six grain elevators, a number of manufacturing plants, a collegiate institute, and a weekly newspaper (*Empire Advance*). Pop. (1931), 1,590.

Vireo, a name used, with a prefix, for any one of the members of the bird family *Vireonidae*, which is a group of inconspicuous birds slightly smaller than a sparrow and further characterized by their hooked and notched upper bill. Six species occur in Canada, the commonest of which is the red-eyed vireo (*Vireo olivaceus*). It is to be found in small groves and in the forests throughout Canada. Like the other members of the family, the species builds a slightly pensile nest at the fork of small branches in hardwood trees.

Virginia Creeper (*Psedera quinquefolia* (L.) Greene, *Vitaceae*), a woody vine climbing by means of disk-bearing tendrils and aerial rootlets. The leaves are palmately compound, with 5-7 oblong-lanceolate leaflets, decidedly pale beneath. Small greenish flowers are borne in clusters opposite the leaves. The petals are thick and concave, and drop readily. The fruit is a small black berry. This is a common plant in copses and woods in the eastern part of Canada.

Virgin's Bower. See **Clematis.**

Viscount, a village in Saskatchewan, on the Canadian Pacific Railway, 58 miles east of Saskatoon. It is in a grain-growing and dairying district, and has a weekly newspaper (*Sun*). Pop. (1931), 342.

Viscount Melville sound. See **Melville sound.**

Visitation Nuns of St. Mary, an order founded in France by St. Francis de Sales, bishop of Annecy. This old order is completely devoted to contemplative life, having no exterior occupations, and its members being cloistered. Two convents, one in Ottawa, Ontario, and the other at Lévis, Quebec, represent the order in Canada.

Vittoria, a village in Norfolk county, Ontario, on Young's creek, and on the Canadian National Railway, 5 miles south of Simcoe. It was one of the earliest settlements in this region, and was from 1816 to 1827 the judicial centre of the old London district. Pop. (1934), 400. See F. Reid, *Vittoria, the old capital of London district* (Ont. Hist. Soc., Papers and Records, 1923).

Vogt, Augustus Stephen (1861-1926), musician, was born at Washington, Ontario, on August 14, 1861, of German-Swiss parentage. He studied music in the United States and in Germany. After his return to Canada, he founded in 1894 the Mendelssohn Choir, and he directed it until 1917. In 1913 he became principal of the Toronto Conservatory of Music, and in 1919 dean of the faculty of music in the University of Toronto. He died in Toronto on September 17, 1926. He was the author of *The standard anthem book* (Toronto, 1894) and *Modern pianoforte technique* (Toronto, 1900), of which several editions have been published.

Vole, a name applied to a number of mouse-like rodents belonging to the sub-family *Microtinae*, of the family *Cricetidae*. The red backed mice (genus *Evotomys*), the meadow mice (genus *Microtus* and genus *Lagurus*), and the pine mice (genus *Pitymys*) may be, and frequently are, referred to as "voles" rather than as "mice". See also **Mice.**

Vondenvelden, William (d. 1809), surveyor, was assistant surveyor-general of the province of Lower Canada, and collaborated with Louis Charland (q.v.) in the first authoritative map of the province published in 1813. He died in the parish of St. Henri, Lower Canada, on June 20, 1809, from an accident when riding his horse. He was, with Louis Charland (q.v.), compiler of *Extraits des titres des anciennes concessions de terre en fief et seigneurie . . . dans la partie actuellement appelée le Bas-Canada* (Quebec, 1803).

Von Iffland, Anthony (d. 1876), physician, was born in Quebec, at the end of the eighteenth century, of German and French parentage. He was educated at the High School in Quebec, and studied medicine in London, Edinburgh, and Paris. On his return to Canada, he founded in 1820 at Quebec the first anatomical school in Canada; but was compelled to give up his practice in Quebec because of the rousing of public feeling against his anatomical studies. He occupied various medical positions in the public service of Quebec; but he retired from practice in 1867, and became commissary of the Marine Hospital in Quebec. He died in 1876. He was a voluminous writer; and a bibliography of his papers and articles is to be found in H. J. Morgan, *Bibliotheca canadensis* (Ottawa, 1867).

Von Shoultz, Miles Gustaf Schobtewiski (d. 1838), filibuster, was a native of Poland who took refuge in the United States. His symphathies were engaged by the filibusterers in the United States who were planning to free Canada from the British yoke; and, being an experienced soldier, he was placed in command of a force which landed near Prescott, Upper Canada, on November 12, 1838. He took up his headquarters in a stone windmill, where he held out for three or four days; but on November 16, after what was known as the battle of the Windmill, he and his companions were compelled to surrender unconditionally. He was tried before a court-martial at Kingston, and though defended by John A. Macdonald (q.v.), then a rising young lawyer, he was sentenced to death, and was hanged at Kingston on December 8, 1838. See I. E. Struthers, *The trial of Miles von Schoultz* (Can. mag., 1917).

Voyageur, the name applied to the French-Canadian canoemen or boatmen who manned the canoes or boats which carried the fur-traders of New France, and later of British Canada, across the length and breadth of the North American continent. See Grace Nute, *The voyageur* (New York, 1931).

Voyer, Pierre de. See **Argenson, Vicomte d'.**

Vulcan, a town in the Bow River district of Alberta, on the Canadian Pacific Railway, 80 miles south-east of Calgary. It is in a mixed farming district, and has nine grain elevators and a flour mill; and it is the headquarters of Vulcan Oils, Limited. It has a high school and a weekly newspaper (*Advocate*). Pop. (1931), 803.

Vulture, the name of birds closely allied to hawks and eagles, whose best known characteristic is that of eating carrion. Two species occur in Canada, the turkey vulture (*Cathartes aura*) and the black vulture (*Coragyps urubu*). Both species are large, approaching an eagle in size. The plumage of the former is dark brownish black, and the skin of the near-naked head is dull red. The latter is similarly coloured, except that the skin of the head is blackish. The turkey vulture occurs regularly, but not commonly, in southern Ontario and Manitoba; and the black vulture occurs occasionally in the Maritime provinces.

W

Wabigoon, a village in the Kenora district of Ontario, on Wabigoon lake, and on the Canadian Pacific Railway, 12 miles from Dryden. The name is an Algonkian word meaning "white feather", and is said to have reference to the fact that the lake was once covered with "white feathers" (possibly white water-lilies). Pop. (1934), 300.

Wabinosh river, a stream in the Thunder Bay district of Ontario, flows into lake Nipigon, at Wabinosh bay. It has a length of 33 miles.

Wadden, Jean Etienne. See **Wadin, Jean Etienne.**

Waddilove, William James Darley (1785?-1859), clergyman and author, was born about 1785, the son of the Very Rev. Robert Darley Waddilove, dean of Ripon. He took holy orders, and was for several years a missionary in Canada, with the Right Rev. the Hon. Charles James Stewart (q.v.), bishop of Quebec. He returned to England before 1837; and he died near Hexham, Northumberlandshire, on October 28, 1859. He was the author of *The Stewart missions* (London, 1838), *Canadian clergy reserves* (pamphlet, Newcastle-on-Tyne, 1840), and *The lamp in the wilderness* (Hexham, 1847).

Waddington, Alfred (1800?-1872), author and pioneer, was born in England about 1800. He went to British Columbia at the time of the "gold rush" of 1858, and became a merchant in Victoria. He wrote the first book published in Vancouver Island, *The Fraser mines vindicated, or the history of four months* (Victoria, 1858); and he became the leading advocate in British Columbia of the construction of a transcontinental railway. He died at Ottawa, whither he had gone to forward his plans for a railway, on February 26, 1872. See R. L. Reid, *Alfred Waddington* (Trans. Roy. Soc. Can., 1932).

Waddington, mount, is in the Coast district of British Columbia, on the west side of Homathko river, north of the headwaters of Scar creek, range 2. It is in lat. 51° 22', long. 125° 15', and has an altitude of 13,260 feet. It was named after Alfred Waddington (q.v.), a British Columbia pioneer, who in 1868, advocated a transcontinental railway through Yellowhead pass. It is sometimes called "Mystery mount", owing to its difficult ascent. See Sir N. J. Watson and E. J. King, *Round Mystery mountain* (New York, 1935).

Wade, Frederick Coate (1860-1924), lawyer, was born at Bowmanville, Ontario, on February 26, 1860, the son of William Wade. He was educated at the University of Toronto (B.A., 1882), and was called to the bar of Manitoba in 1886 (K.C., 1902). From 1897 to 1901 he was legal adviser to the Yukon Council; and in 1903 he served as one of the British counsel on the Alaska Boundary Commission. In 1918 he was appointed agent-general for British Columbia in London, England; and he died in London on November 9, 1924. In 1886 he married Edith Mabel, daughter of D. B. Read (q.v.), Toronto. He was the author of *The Manitoba school question* (Winnipeg, 1895), and a number of other pamphlets.

Waden, Jean Etienne. See **Wadin, Jean Etienne.**

Wadena, a town in the Humboldt district of Saskatchewan, on the Canadian National and Canadian Pacific Railways, 165 miles south-east of Saskatoon. It is in a fertile grain-growing district, and has a high school, a hospital, and a weekly newspaper (*News*). Pop. (1931), 582.

Wadin (Waden, Wadden, or **Waddens), Jean Etienne** (*fl.* 1761-1781) was a Swiss Protestant, the son of Adam Samuel Waddens (or Vuadin) and Bernardine Ermon, of La Tour-de-Paise, in the canton of Berne. His father is said to have been a professor at the University of Geneva; but no proof of this has been found. The son would appear to have come to Canada with the British army, and to have settled in Canada as a merchant and trader. On November 23, 1761, he married at St. Laurent, near Montreal, Marie-Joseph Deguire (b. 1739); and there is, in the register of Christ Church, Montreal, the record of the christening of a number of Wadin children after this date. On January 27, 1768, "Capt. Woden" appears in a list of signatories in the "Minutes of a general meeting of the proprietors of Canada bills", held in London, England; and in 1772 his name first appears in the fur-trade licences as trading to Grand Portage. About 1779 he formed a partnership with Venant St. Germain (q.v.); and he was one of the partners in the original sixteen-share North West Company in that year. In the winter of 1780-81, while at Lac la Rouge, he was killed in an altercation with Peter Pond (q.v.). One of his daughters, Véronique (d. 1846), married in 1782 the Rev. John Bethune; and her son, Angus Bethune (q.v.), became a partner of the North West Company. Another daughter, Josepha, married in Montreal in April, 1780, Alan Morrison; and her son, William Morrison (q.v.), became a clerk in the XY and North West Companies.

Wafer Ash. See **Hoptree.**

Wahnapitae. See **Wanapitei.**

Wainwright, William (1840-1914), railway executive, was born in Manchester, England, on April 30, 1840. He entered the service of the Manchester, Sheffield, and Lincolnshire Railway as a clerk in the accountant's office; and in 1862 he came to Canada, at the invitation of Sir E. W. Watkin (q.v.), as chief clerk in the accountant's office of the Grand Trunk Railway. In the service of the Grand Trunk he rose until he became in 1911 senior vice-president of this railway, and second vice-president of the Grand Trunk Pacific Railway. He died, after 52 years' service with the Grand Trunk Railway, at Atlantic City, U.S.A., on May 14, 1914.

Wainwright, a town in the Battle River district of Alberta, on the Canadian National Railway, 126 miles southeast of Edmonton. It was formerly known as Denwood; but the name was changed to Wainwright in 1908, in honour of William Wainwright (q.v.), second vice-president of the Grand Trunk Pacific Railway. There are crude oil and natural gas wells in the vicinity; and the town has oil refineries, as well as five grain elevators and a flour mill. It is also a divisional point of the Canadian National Railways; and it has two weekly newspapers (*Star* and *Wainwright Record*). Adjacent is a Dominion national park, with the largest herd of buffalo in existence. Pop. (1931), 1,147.

Wakashan Family, a linguistic family of North American Indians, occupying the west coast of British Columbia between lat. 54° and 50° 30′, the northern and western parts of Vancouver island, and the north-west corner of the state of Washington. The name is derived from the word *waukash* (good), which Cook (q.v.) mistook, on hearing it at Friendly cove in Nootka sound, for the name of a tribe. Their culture is similar to that of the coast Salish to the south and east of them, and to that of the Tsimshian, Haida,

17

and Tlingit to the north. In language and physical characteristics, they resemble most closely the Salish. Their two chief divisions are the Nootka (q.v.) and the Kwakiutl (q.v.). For further information, see *Handbook of the Indians of Canada* (Ottawa, 1913).

Wakaw, a village in the Prince Albert district of Saskatchewan, on the Prince Albert branch of the Canadian National Railway, 80 miles north-east of Saskatoon. It is named after the neighbouring Wakaw lake, which is the source of the Carrot river, and the name is an Indian word meaning "crooked". It has a high school and a weekly newspaper (*Recorder*). Pop. (1931), 677.

Wakefield, Edward Gibbon (1796-1862), colonial reformer, was born in London, England, on March 20, 1796. He was educated at Westminster and at Edinburgh, and entered the British diplomatic service. In 1826 he was involved in the abduction of an heiress of sixteen years of age, though he was already himself a widower; and he spent as a result three years in Newgate prison. His years in prison led to a sincere study of society, and particularly of the problems of the British Empire. He became an authority on colonization; and when Lord Durham (q.v.) was appointed high commissioner in Canada, he brought Wakefield with him, though in an unofficial capacity. Parts of Lord Durham's famous *Report on the affairs of British North America* (London, 1839) were undoubtedly his handiwork. He left Canada in 1839, but returned in 1841; and from 1842 to 1844 he represented Beauharnois in the legislature of united Canada. Under the pseudonym of "A member of the provincial parliament", he published *A view of Sir Charles Metcalfe's government of Canada* (London, 1844). After this episode, however, he transferred his activities to New Zealand; and he died in Wellington, New Zealand, on May 16, 1862. See R. Garnett, *Edward Gibbon Wakefield* (London, 1898), Ursilla M. Macdonnell,

Gibbon Wakefield and Canada subsequent to the Durham mission (Queen's Quarterly, 1924-5), A. J. Harrop, *The amazing career of Edward Gibbon Wakefield* (London, 1928), and Irma O'Connor, *Edward Gibbon Wakefield* (London, 1929).

Wakefield, a village in Hull county, Quebec, on the Gatineau river, and on the Canadian Pacific Railway, 20 miles from Hull. It is named after Wakefield, a town in Yorkshire, England. The chief industries are farming and lumbering. Wakefield lake, a short distance from the village, is a tourist resort. Pop. (1931), 296.

Wake Robin, or Red Trillium (*Trillium erectum* L., *Liliaceae*), a stout-stemmed, spring-flowering perennial, developed from a thick, short rootstock. The leaves are borne in a whorl of 3, shortly below the flower, and are dark green, broadly ovate, sharply pointed, and sessile. The flowers are borne singly, terminating the stem. They are dark purplish-red in colour and have a very unpleasant odour. The calyx consists of 3 green, pointed sepals; the corolla of 3 lanceolate to ovate, spreading petals; and there are 6 stamens. The fruit is an ovate, 6-angled, reddish berry. It may be found in thickets and woods from Nova Scotia to Ontario.

Wakomichi lake, in Mistassini territory, Quebec, south of Mistassini lake, into which it discharges, and four miles from Chibougamau lake. Its water is clear and cold. The forest around the lake has been largely destroyed by fire. The soil on the shore is good, with the exception of that on the south-east side, which is rocky. The lake is 24 miles long and from 1 to 4 miles wide.

Walbran, John T. (d. 1913), sailor and author, was born in England, and was educated at the grammar school in Ripon, Yorkshire. He became a sailor, and in 1881 obtained his certificate as master mariner. He joined the marine and fisheries service of Canada in 1891; and from this date to 1908 he commanded the government steamer *Quadra* in the lighthouse, buoy, and fishery service on the coast of British Columbia. He died at Victoria, British Columbia, on March 31, 1913. He was the author of *British Columbia coast names* (Ottawa, 1909).

Waldeck, a village in Saskatchewan, on the Swift Current river, and on the Canadian Pacific Railway, 14 miles from Swift Current. Pop. (1934), 300.

Waldemar, a village in Dufferin county, Ontario, on the Grand river, and on the Canadian Pacific Railway, 10 miles west of Orangeville. Pop. (1934), 250.

Waldheim, a village in the Prince Albert district of Saskatchewan, on the Carleton section of the Canadian National Railway, 16 miles from Rosthern. It was settled by Mennonites. Pop. (1931), 448.

Wales, William (1734?-1798), astronomer, was born about 1734, and in 1769 was sent by the British government to Hudson bay to observe the transit of Venus in that year. He afterwards accompanied Captain Cook on his second and third voyages; and on his return to England he was appointed mathematical master at Christ's Hospital. He died in London, England, in 1798. Among other works he published *General observations made at Hudson's Bay* (London, 1772).

Walkem, George Anthony (1834-1908), prime minister of British Columbia (1874-6 and 1878), was born at Newry, Ireland, on November 15, 1834, the eldest son of Charles Walkem and Mary Ann Boomer. His father came to Canada in 1847 as a surveyor on the staff of the Royal Engineers, and was employed in fixing the boundary between Canada and the United States. He was educated at McGill University; and he was called to the bar of Lower Canada in 1858. In 1862 he went to Victoria, British Columbia, and he became a Q.C. in 1873. From 1864 to

1870 he was a member of the Legislative Council of British Columbia; and in 1871 he was elected a member of the Legislative Assembly of the province for Cariboo. In 1872 he was appointed chief commissioner of lands and works in the Executive Council of the province, and in 1873 attorney-general. From 1874 to 1876 he was prime minister, and again in 1878. In 1882 he was appointed a puisne judge of the Supreme Court of British Columbia; and he continued to occupy this post until his death at Victoria on January 13, 1908. In 1879 he married Sophie Edith, daughter of the Hon. Henry Rhodes, of Victoria and Hawaii; and by her he had one daughter.

Walker, Alexander (*fl.* 1848-1867), poet, was a non-commissioned officer in the British army who came to Canada prior to 1848, when he contributed verse to the *Literary Garland* (Montreal). From 1857 to 1861 he was assistant editor of the *Quebec Gazette;* and later he was employed in the military stores department at Quebec. But after 1867 he passes from view. He was the author of *The knapsack: A collection of fugitive poems* (Kingston, 1853) and *Hours off and on sentry; or, Personal recollections of military adventure in Great Britain, Portugal, and Canada* (Montreal, 1859).

Walker, Sir Byron Edmund (1848-1924), president of the Canadian Bank of Commerce (1907-24), was born in Seneca township, Haldimand county, Upper Canada, on October 14, 1848, the son of Alfred E. Walker. He entered the service of the Canadian Bank of Commerce in 1868; in 1886 he became general manager of the bank; and in 1907 its president. He wrote a *History of Canadian banking* (Toronto, 1896); he published a large number of pamphlets and addresses on banking and kindred subjects; and he was regarded as an outstanding authority on financial questions. He had, however, a wide range of other interests. He was a well-known art connoisseur, and had much to do with establishing the National Art Gallery in Ottawa, of the board of which he became chairman; he was one of the founders of the Champlain Society, and its first president; for many years he was honorary president of the Mendelssohn Choir, of Toronto; and in 1898 he was elected president of the Canadian Institute. From 1910 to 1923 he was chairman of the board of governors of the University of Toronto; and in 1923 he was elected its chancellor. He died, at Toronto, on March 27, 1924. In 1874 he married Mary (d. 1923), daughter of Alexander Alexander, of Hamilton, Ontario; and by her he had four sons and three daughters. In 1908 he was created a C.V.O., and in 1910 a knight bachelor. In 1911 he was elected a fellow of the Royal Society of Canada. See G. P. de T. Glazebrook, *Sir Edmund Walker* (Oxford, 1933).

Walker, Hiram (1816-1899), distiller, was born in East Douglass, Massachusetts, on July 4, 1816. He emigrated to Canada in 1858, and settled on the eastern side of the Detroit river. He opened here a distillery; and about this distillery the town of Walkerville, named after him grew up. He was joined by his three sons, and the firm was known as Hiram Walker and Sons until 1890; it was then incorporated as Hiram Walker and Sons, Ltd. Hiram Walker died on January 12, 1899.

Walker, Sir Hovenden (d. 1728), rear-admiral, is said to have been born in Ireland about 1656, but was probably born later than this. He entered the service of the royal navy. On March 15, 1710-11, he was promoted to be rear-admiral of the white; and about the same time he was knighted. In 1711 he was appointed to command an expedition against Quebec, consisting of ten ships of the line, a number of smaller vessels, and about thirty transports, with 5,000 troops on board. On August 11, 1711, part of this fleet was wrecked in the St. Lawrence as a result

of fogs and gales; and Walker, after a council of war, decided that the only course open to him was to return, with the remnant of the fleet, to England. On 1715, after the accession of George I, he was dismissed from the service, ostensibly because of his conduct of the Quebec expedition, but more probably because he was suspected of Jacobite sympathies. He went to South Carolina, and became a planter; but after a few years he returned to England, and he died in Dublin, Ireland, in 1728. He was the author of *A journal or full account of the late expedition to Canada* (London, 1720).

Walker, Thomas (*fl.* 1752-1785), merchant, was born in England, possibly in 1718. He emigrated to Boston, Massachusetts, in 1752, and settled in Montreal in 1763. Here he engaged in the fur-trade. In 1764 he was appointed a justice of the peace, and shortly afterwards was the victim of an assault by the military, in which one of his ears was cut off. The incident greatly embittered feeling in the colony, and Walker became the centre of a violent agitation. In 1774, when the Americans invaded Quebec, Walker went over to them, and he left the province with them in 1776. In 1785 Pierre Du Calvet (q.v.) met him in London, England; but after that he passes from view. See L. W. Sicotte, *The affair Walker* (Canadian Antiquarian and Numismatic Journal, 1915); A. L. Burt, *The mystery of Walker's ear* (Can. hist. rev., 1922); and W. S. Wallace (ed.), *The Maseres letters* (Toronto, 1920).

Walker, William (1797-1844), lawyer and journalist, was born at Three Rivers, Lower Canada, in 1797, and was called to the bar of Lower Canada in 1819. He became a successful lawyer; and in 1835 he was sent to England, with John Neilson (q.v.), to present the views of the British constitutional party in Lower Canada to the British government. During the Sydenham administration, he was the editor of the Montreal *Times;* and he represented Rouville in the Legislative Assembly of united Canada from 1842 to 1843. He died in Montreal on April 10, 1844.

Walker, William (1793-1863), legislative councillor of Canada, was born in Scotland in 1793. He emigrated to Canada in 1815; and he became a partner in the famous mercantile house of Forsyth, Richardson, and Co., of Montreal, which later became Forsyth, Walker, and Co., of Quebec. He was part owner of the *Royal William*, the first steamship that crossed the Atlantic. In 1838 he was appointed a member of the Special Council of Lower Canada; and in 1842 he was called to the Legislative Council of Canada. He retired from business in 1848, and he died at Quebec, on May 18, 1863. He was the first chancellor of Bishop's College, Lennoxville; and he received from this college the degree of D.C.L.

Walker, mount, is one of the Rocky mountains in Alberta, and is in lat. 51° 43', long. 116° 55', with an altitude of 10,835 feet. It was named after Horace Walker, a past president of the Alpine Club, England. The name first appears on Collie's map in the *Geographical Journal* in 1899.

Walkerton, the county town of Bruce county, Ontario, on the Saugeen river, and on the Canadian Pacific and Canadian National Railways, 70 miles north-west of Guelph. It was named after Joseph Walker, who built a mill here in 1850, and was the founder of the town; and it was incorporated in 1871. Besides being the centre of a prosperous farming district, its water-power has made it an industrial town. It has a spool and bobbin factory, a furniture factory, a rattan factory, foundries, steel die works, and machine shops. It has also a high school, a public library, and two weekly newspapers (*Herald-Times* and *Telescope*). Pop. (1931), 2,431.

Walkerville, formerly a town in Essex county, Ontario, was situated on the Detroit river, opposite the city of Detroit, Michigan. It was incorporated as a town in 1890; but in 1935 it was amalgamated with the city of Windsor (q.v.). It was the centre of a manufacturing district, and produced a great variety of articles, particularly automobiles, auto accessories, and structural steel work. The shipping facilities consist of steamship lines connecting with points along the Great lakes, and with the city of Detroit by ferry service, the Ambassador Bridge (q.v.), through the town of Sandwich, three miles distant, and the Detroit and Windsor Tunnel for automobile traffic. Rail transportation is available over the Canadian National, Wabash, and Père Marquette lines, and by a terminal road through to the Michigan Central and Canadian Pacific Railways. The town was established and named by Hiram Walker (q.v.), who owned most of the farm land incorporated in the municipality, and who founded the Walker distillery. It has a collegiate institute and a weekly newspaper (*News*). Pop. (1931), 10,105. See F. Neal, *The township of Sandwich* (Windsor, Ontario, 1909).

Wallace, Francis Huston (1851-1930), theologian, was born at Ingersoll, Ontario, in 1851, the son of the Rev. Robert Wallace. He was educated at the University of Toronto (B.A., 1873; M.A., 1874), at Knox College, Toronto, and the Drew Theological Seminary, New Jersey (B.D., 1876). He was ordained a minister of the Methodist Church in 1878, and he held several pastoral charges until 1887, when he was appointed professor of New Testament literature in Victoria University. In 1900 he became dean of the faculty of theology in Victoria University; and he held this post for many years. He died at Toronto on June 2, 1930. In 1895 he was made a D.D. of Victoria University; and he was the author of

Witnesses for truth (Toronto, 1885) and *The interpretation of the Apocalypse* (Toronto, 1903). His son, the Rev. Edward Wilson Wallace, was appointed in 1930 chancellor of Victoria University.

Wallace, Michael (1747-1831), loyalist, was born in Scotland in 1747, and emigrated to America, where he established himself at Norfolk, Virginia. He lost his property during the American revolution, and removed to Halifax, Nova Scotia. He became treasurer of the province for many years, and in his later days was several times administrator of the province. He died in 1831.

Wallace, Nathaniel Clarke (1844-1901), controller of customs for Canada (1892-5), was born at Woodbridge, Upper Canada, on May 21, 1844, the third son of Capt. Nathaniel Wallace, of Sligo, Ireland. He was educated at the Weston grammar school, and for some years was a school-teacher. In 1867 he established a milling business at Woodbridge; and in 1874 he was elected a member of the county council of York. In 1878 he became warden of York county, and was elected to represent West York in the Canadian House of Commons—a constituency he continued to represent until his death. From 1887 to his death he was grand master of the Orange Association of British North America; and in 1888 he was one of the "Noble 13" who voted for the disallowance of the Jesuits' Estates Act. In 1892 he was appointed controller of customs in the Thompson government; but he retired from the government in 1895 because of his opposition to its policy in regard to the Manitoba separate school question. He died at Woodbridge, Ontario, on October 18, 1901. In 1877 he married Belinda, daughter of James Gilmour, of Ottawa. See Rev. C. E. Perry, *Hon. N. Clarke Wallace* (Mimico, Ontario, 1897).

Wallace, a village and port in Cumberland county, Nova Scotia, on an inlet of Northumberland strait, at the mouth of the Wallace river, and on the "short line" of the Canadian National Railway, 6 miles from Malagash. It was settled in 1784 by American Loyalists, and was named Ramsheg; but this was superseded in 1810 by the present name, in honour of Michael Wallace (q.v.), and the name has spread to a number of neighbouring settlements, such as Wallace Bridge, Wallace Bay, Wallace Grant, and East Wallace. The village is a summer resort. Pop. (1934), 500.

Wallaceburg, a town in Kent county, Ontario, on the Sydenham river, and on the Père Marquette Railway, 18 miles north-west of Chatham, and 12 miles east of the St. Clair river. It was originally known as "The Forks", from the fact that the north and east branches of the Sydenham river unite here; but it was later named Wallaceburg by the Scottish settlers in the neighbourhood, probably in honour of Sir William Wallace, the champion of Scottish independence. It is a port of entry; and it has shipyards, lumber mills, a hoop and stave factory, a flour mill, a glass factory, brass works, a beet-sugar factory, and a die-casting plant. It has also a continuation school, a convent, a Carnegie library, and a weekly newspaper (*News*). Pop. (1931), 4,326.

Wallacetown, a village in Elgin county, Ontario, 3 miles from Dutton, on the Michigan Central Railway. Pop. (1934), 300.

Wallbridge, Lewis (1816-1887), chief justice of Manitoba (1882-7), was born in Belleville, Upper Canada, on November 27, 1816. He was called to the bar of Upper Canada in 1839 (Q.C., 1856), and in 1857 he was elected to represent Hastings in the Legislative Assembly of Canada. In 1863 he became solicitor-general in the Macdonald-Dorion administration, and the same year he was elected speaker of the Assembly. In 1867 he retired from political life; and in 1882 he was appointed chief justice of Manitoba. He died at Winnipeg, Manitoba, on October 20, 1887.

Waller, Jocelyn (d. 1828), journalist, was the son of Sir Robert Waller, Bart., of county Tipperary, Ireland. He came to Canada in 1820, and in 1823 he founded at Montreal the *Canadian Spectator* (1823-8), a Reform journal printed in the English language. He was persecuted in the courts by the government; and he died in prison at Montreal on December 2, 1828. His eldest son, Edmund, became in 1830 fourth baronet. See Æ. Fauteux, *Jocelyn Waller* (Bull. rech. hist., 1920).

Walmsley lake, in the Mackenzie district of the North West Territories, lies north of Great Slave lake. It was named by Sir George Back (q.v.) in 1833 after the Rev. Dr. Walmsley, of Hanwell, England.

Walnut, the name of the trees belonging to the genus *Juglans* Linnaeus. Two species are known in Canada, both occurring only in the older portion of southern Ontario. Black walnut (*J. nigra* Linnaeus) may be readily separated by its foliage and fruits from its sister species, butternut (*J. cinerea* Linnaeus). The leaves of both are a foot or more long made up of eleven to seventeen leaflets, which are arranged on two sides of a central stalk, these occurring singly on the twigs. The undersurface of butternut leaflets, the leaf stalk, and the twigs are densely hairy, whereas the hairiness is insignificant in the case of walnut leaves. The fruit of the walnut is spherical in shape, whereas that of butternut is ellipsoidal. Both fruits are edible. The trees flower as they are leafing out, and since both staminate (male) and pistillate (female) flowers occur on the same tree, all walnut trees may bear fruit.

The wood of black walnut has excellent technical qualities, making it one of the most desirable woods for the manufacture of furniture and fixtures, for interior finish in offices, and for all kinds of cabinet work; butternut wood is soft, and is mainly used for small woodenware. The nut industry, centred commercially in southern California, is based on English walnut (*J. regia* Linnaeus), a native of south-eastern Europe.

Walpole island is in the north-east of lake St. Clair in Kent county at the extremity of the Ontario peninsula. It is about 10 miles long, and from 3 to 4 miles wide, and is inhabited chiefly by Indians. The island is on a chart of lake St. Clair, prepared for Commodore Sir Edward Owen in 1815, and is called St. Mary's, but the channels and a bay are called Walpole after Lieutenant Arthur Walpole, R.E., who died in 1842. He served in Canada, and prepared the Fort Erie plan in 1818-9. See B. Hudgins, *The Walpole Indian* (Trans. Roy. Soc., Can., 1936).

Walrus. The walrus (genus *Odobenus*) is the largest member of the *Pinnipedia*, a group of flesh-eating mammals highly modified for aquatic life. The Atlantic walrus (*Odobenus rosmarus*) ranges from Labrador north into the Arctic ocean. The Pacific walrus (*Odobenus divergens*) is found in the western Arctic, but does not come as far south as the coast of British Columbia. A full-grown walrus will measure ten or eleven feet and weigh more than a ton. The skin is almost hairless, thick, very wrinkled, and brown in colour. The hind flippers are free from the tail, as in the eared seals, and the upper canine teeth develop into tusks a foot to two feet in length. These animals feed on shell fish, crustaceans, and some marine plants found in the shallow coastal bays. The introduction of firearms into the Arctic and the hunting of this animal for its oil has resulted in such slaughter that to-day the walrus is but a remnant in number of what it once was.

Walsh, James Morrow (1843-1905), first commissioner of the Yukon district, was born at Prescott, Upper Canada, in 1843, the son of Lewis Walsh and Elizabeth, daughter of John Morrow. He joined the militia, and saw service in the Fenian raid of 1866. In 1873 he was appointed an inspector in the North West Mounted Police; and he served with this force until 1883, having established his reputation as an officer of great courage and firmness by his handling of the Sioux chief, Sitting Bull. In 1883 he resigned from the Police, and established the Dominion Coke, Coal, and Transportation Company; but in 1897 the discovery of gold in the Yukon brought him back to the North West Mounted Police. He was appointed a superintendent of the Police, and the chief executive officer of Canada in the Yukon, with the title of commissioner of the Yukon district. He held this post until 1898, when he retired; and he died at Brockville, Ontario, on July 25, 1905. In 1870 he married Mary, daughter of John Mowat, of Prescott.

Walsh, John (1830-1898), Roman Catholic archbishop of Toronto (1889-98), was born in the parish of Mooncoin, Kilkenny county, Ireland, on May 23, 1830, the son of James Walsh and Ellen Macdonald. He was educated at St. John's College, Waterford, and at the Seminary of St. Sulpice, Montreal, Canada. He was ordained a priest of the Roman Catholic Church in 1854. In 1867 he was consecrated bishop of Sandwich, a title changed in 1868 to bishop of London; and in 1889 he was installed as archbishop of Toronto. He died in Toronto on July 31, 1898. In 1867 he received the degree of D.D. from the Vatican.

Walsh, William (1804-1858), Roman Catholic archbishop of Halifax (1852-8), was born in Waterford, Ireland, in November, 1804. He was educated at St. John's College, Waterford, and was ordained a priest of the Roman Catholic Church in 1828. In 1834 he was appointed coadjutor vicar apostolic of Nova Scotia; in 1845 he became bishop

of Halifax; and in 1852, archbishop. He died in Halifax, Nova Scotia, on August 10, 1858. He published a number of pastoral letters, and some translations of devotional books.

Walsingham Centre, a village in Walsingham township, Norfolk county, Ontario, on Big creek, 6 miles from Port Rowan. Pop. (1934), 400.

Walton, a village in Hants county, Nova Scotia, at the mouth of the Walton river, on the south shore of the basin of Minas. It is the shipping port of the Atlantic Gypsum Products Company; and is 30 miles distant by highway from Windsor, and 50 miles from Halifax. Pop. (1934), 600.

Walton, a village in Huron county, Ontario, on the Canadian Pacific Railway, 5 miles from Brussels. Pop. (1934), 300.

Wampum, a fabric made by the North American Indians, composed by beads formed out of shells strung or woven together. The word is a contracted form of the Algonkian *Wampumpeak*, meaning "a string of white shell-beads". Wampum, often in the form of a belt, was much prized among the Indians, both for ornament and for ceremonial purposes. Among many tribes it was also a medium of exchange, and was known as "shell-money". The use of wampum in Canada was commoner among the maritime tribes than among the inland tribes; and wampum in Canada did not acquire the character of money, as it did in the colonies to the south. But it was used here both for ornament and for ceremonial purposes. An exhaustive discussion of the manufacture and use of wampum will be found in the *Handbook of the Indians of Canada* (Ottawa, 1913).

Wanapitei, a village in the Sudbury district of Ontario, on the Wanapitei river, and on the main line of the Canadian Pacific Railway, 12 miles east of Sudbury. The name is an Indian word meaning "hollow (molar) tooth". Pop. (1934), 300.

Wanapitei lake is in Sudbury district, Ontario, north-east of Sudbury. It empties by the Wanapitei river into the Georgian bay.

Wanigan, a receptacle in which small supplies or a reserve stock of goods are kept. The word is from the Abnaki *waniigan*, meaning a "trap" or receptacle into which any object strays and gets lost. It is applied to the chest in which lumbermen in New Brunswick and Maine keep their spare clothing, pipes, tobacco, etc.; and it is applied also, in a secondary sense, to the boat used on the rivers of New Brunswick and Maine for the transportation of the tools and provisions of a logging camp from one place to another. It is sometimes spelled also "wongan", "wangun", and "wangan".

Wapella, a town in the Qu'Appelle district of Saskatchewan, on the main line of the Canadian Pacific Railway, 104 miles east of Regina, and 236 miles west of Regina. It has four grain elevators and a weekly newspaper (*Post*).

Wapiti. This magnificent animal (*Cervus canadensis*), sometimes miscalled the American elk, stands five feet high at the shoulder. The wapiti is chestnut brown in colour, with a lighter patch on the rump. The males, with a set of large widely spreading antlers, present the finest appearance of any Canadian deer. The wapiti is closely akin to the red deer or stag of Europe and Asia. Once this animal ranged as far east as Ontario, but the taking over of its natural range for agriculture and excessive hunting have combined to reduce the numbers of the elk throughout Canada and to exterminate it in many areas. It is now to be found wild only in Vancouver island and in parts of British Columbia and the Prairie provinces. Any wapiti now existing in the east have been reintroduced from the western herds.

The wapiti is an animal of high ground, avoiding swamps and low situations, such as the moose delights in. Glades and mountain parks where it can graze meet its needs exactly, though it will also frequent heavily wooded areas, browsing on the foliage of the trees. Only the male has antlers, and, as with most other deer, they are shed and regrown every year. The young are spotted when born, and while one calf is the usual family, occasionally births of two or even three have been known. See E. T. Seton, *Lives of game animals* (4 vols., Garden City, New York, 1925-8).

Warbler, a word applied in Canada to any one of the members of the bird family *Compsothlypidae*, which is peculiar to the new world. The warblers constitute a large family of small birds, few of which approach the common sparrow in size. Although a great variety of colours and patterns is to be found in the numerous species and in the two sexes, greens, yellows and grays predominate. Many of the common species have the term "warbler", with a prefix, for an English name. The warblers constitute a vast army of insect destroyers which frequent the Canadian forests for half of each year.

Warburton, Alexander Bannerman (1852-1929), prime minister of Prince Edward Island (1897-8), was born at Charlottetown, Prince Edward Island, on April 5, 1852, the son of the Hon. James Warburton. He was educated at King's College, Windsor (B.A., 1874; B.C.L., 1876; D.C.L., 1897), and at Edinburgh University. He was called to the bar in 1879 (Q.C., 1897), and practised law in Charlottetown. He represented Queen's in the Legislative Assembly of Prince Edward Island from 1891 to 1898; and from 1847 to 1898 he was prime minister of the province. From 1898 to 1904 he was judge of the County Court in Queen's county, but resigned to re-enter politics. From 1908 to 1911 he represented Queen's in the Canadian House of Commons. In 1920 he was appointed surrogate and judge of probate for Prince Edward Island; and he died at Charlottetown on January 14, 1929. He was the author of *A history of Prince Edward Island* (Saint John, New Brunswick, 1923).

Warden, Robert H. (1841-1905), clergyman and financier, was born in Dundee, Scotland, on January 4, 1841, the son of Alexander J. Warden, F.S.A. He was educated at Madras College, St. Andrew's, Scotland; and in 1866 he was ordained a minister of the Presbyterian Church. The same year he came to Canada; and from 1866 to 1874 he was minister at Bothwell, Ontario. In 1875 he became agent at Montreal of the Presbyterian Church in Canada; and in 1895 he became general agent of the church, a position he occupied until his death. In 1902 he was elected moderator of the Presbyterian Church in Canada; and in 1903 he became president of the Metropolitan Bank. He died at Toronto on November 26, 1905. He married Jemima, daughter of William McCaskill, of the island of Skye, Scotland; and by her he had several children. In 1888 he was made a D.D. of the Montreal Presbyterian College.

Warden, a village in Shefford county, Quebec, on the Drummondville branch of the Canadian Pacific Railway, 2 miles north of Waterloo. Pop. (1934), 250.

Wardner, a village in the Kootenay district of British Columbia, on the Kootenay river, 3 miles south of the mouth of the Bull river, and on the Crowsnest branch of the Canadian Pacific Railway. Pop. (1934), 400.

Wark, David (1804-1905), senator of Canada, was born near Londonderry, Ireland, on February 19, 1804. He came to New Brunswick in 1825, and went into business as a general merchant. He represented Kent in the Legislative Assembly of New Brunswick from 1843 to 1851; from 1851 to 1867 he was a member of the Legislative Council of New Brunswick; and from 1867 to 1905 he was a member of the Canadian Senate. He had thus sixty-two years of continuous service in the legislatures of British North America; and he was, at the time of his death, probably the oldest parliamentarian in the world. The only period in which he held executive office was from 1858 to 1862, when he was a minister without portfolio in the executive council of New Brunswick. He died at Fredericton, New Brunswick, on August 20, 1905. Shortly after his arrival in New Brunswick he married Annie Elizabeth, daughter of Isaac Burpee (q.v.), of Sunbury; and one daughter survived him.

Warkworth, a village in Northumberland county, Ontario, 84 miles northeast of Toronto, and 10 miles from Hastings, the nearest railway station. It is in a mixed farming district, and has a cheese factory, a high school, and a weekly newspaper (*Journal*). Pop. (1934), 700.

Warman, Cy (1855-1914), author, was born at Greenup, Illinois, on June 22, 1855. He was successively a farmer, a wheat broker, a locomotive engineer, an editor, an author, and a promoter. He settled in London, Ontario, in 1898; and he lived here during most of the rest of his life. He died in Chicago, Illinois, on April 7, 1914. He was the author of *Mountain melodies* (Denver, 1892), *Tales of an engineer* (New York, 1895), *The express messenger and other tales of the rail* (New York, 1897), *The story of the railroad* (New York, 1898), *Frontier stories* (New York, 1898), *The white mail* (New York, 1899), *Snow on the headlight* (New York, 1899), *Short rails* (New York, 1900), *The last spike, and other railroad stories* (New York, 1906), *Weiga of Temagami, and other Indian tales* (New York, 1908), and *Songs of Cy Warman* (Boston, 1911).

Warman, a village in Saskatchewan, on the Canadian National Railway, 20 miles north of Saskatoon. Pop. (1934), 400.

War of 1812. See **History, Military.**

War of the American Revolution. See **History, Military.**

Warren, a village in the Nipissing district of Ontario, on the Veuve river, and on the main line of the Canadian Pacific Railway, 35 miles east of Sudbury. Pop. (1934), 600.

Warren lake, the name applied to a glacial lake which, as the ice-sheet receded, occupied the southern part of the Huron basin, the whole of the Erie basin, and extended along the south shore of the Ontario basin, the greater part of the Ontario basin being still filled with ice. Its outlet is thought to have been across Michigan toward the Mississippi. Later drainage was opened through the Mohawk valley to the Hudson river. Finally, as the waters were further lowered, lake Warren took shape as lake Iroquois (q.v.). See A. P. Coleman, *Glacial and post-glacial lakes in Ontario* (Toronto, 1922).

Warsaw, a village in Peterborough county, Ontario, 7 miles from Indian river, the nearest railway station. Pop. (1934), 300.

Warwick, a village in Arthabaska county, Quebec, on the Rivière des Pins, and on the Canadian National Railway, 8 miles south of Victoriaville. It is an industrial centre, with factories for agricultural machinery, washing-machines, overalls, cheese-boxes, and doors; and it was incorporated as a village in 1861. It is named after Warwick, in England. Pop. (1931), 987. There is also a small village of this name in Lambton county, Ontario, 6 miles from Watford.

Wasaga Beach, a summer resort in Simcoe county, Ontario, on the shore of Nottawasaga bay, 4 miles north of Stayner, the nearest railway station. The name is derived from Nottawasaga

by the elision of the first two syllables. See **Nottawasaga bay.**

Washademoak river, in New Brunswick, rises in Westmorland county, and flows south-west into the St. John river, which it enters above Belleisle. The name is the corruption of a Malecite word, the meaning of which is unknown. The river is 70 miles long, and in its lower reaches resembles a narrow lake, navigable by small steamers.

Washago, a village in Simcoe county, Ontario, on the Canadian National Railway, 13 miles from Orillia. Pop. (1934), 400.

Washington, Treaty of. This was a treaty signed in 1871 in Washington, District of Columbia, between the United States and Great Britain, whereby the differences between the two countries arising from the period of the American Civil War were settled. Because several of the points at issue affected Canada, Sir John Macdonald (q.v.), then prime minister of Canada, was appointed one of the five British commissioners. The chief points at issue were the following: (1) the indemnity to be paid by Great Britain for damages done to United States commerce by the *Alabama* and other confederate cruisers built in British ports; (2) the free navigation of the St. Lawrence by American ships; (3) the possession of the island of San Juan, in the Portland channel, on the Pacific coast; (4) the rights of American fishermen in Canadian waters; and (5) the indemnity to be paid to Canada for the damage done during the Fenian raids. The *Alabama* question, which did not concern Canada, was referred to an international tribunal, which met in Geneva, Switzerland, in 1872, and awarded the United States damages amounting to $15,500,000. The Canadian fisheries were opened to United States fishermen for a term of twelve years; and a commission which sat later at Halifax awarded Canada $5,-

500,000 as compensation for this concession. The San Juan dispute was referred to the German Emperor for arbitration; and his award was in favour of the United States. The United States was granted free navigation of the St. Lawrence; though Canada was granted free navigation of lake Michigan, of the Yukon river, and some of the rivers in the extreme north-west of the United States. The question of compensation for the Fenian raids was dropped altogether; although Canada had at least as good a claim to damages for the Fenian raids as the United States had to damages done by the *Alabama*. Macdonald, who was placed in a difficult position, complained bitterly in private that the British commissioners had sacrificed Canadian interests, "no matter what the cost to Canada"; but he signed the treaty, and defended it as necessary "for the sake of peace, and for the sake of the great Empire of which we form a part". For Macdonald's own account of the negotiations, see J. Pope, *Memoirs of the Right Hon. Sir John Alexander Macdonald* (2 vols., Ottawa, 1894).

Waskada, a village in the Souris district of Manitoba, on the Lyleton branch of the Canadian Pacific Railway, 3 miles north of the United States boundary. It has a weekly newspaper (*News*). Pop. (1934), 400.

Waskatenau, a village in the Athabaska district of Alberta, on the Canadian National Railway, 60 miles east of Edmonton. The name is an Indian word meaning "opening in the banks", from the cleft in the ridge through which Waskatenau creek flows into the North Saskatchewan. It is in a wheat-growing and stock-raising district, and has a weekly newspaper (*Witness*). Pop. (1931), 220.

Waswanipi lake lies south-east of Mattagami lake, in the basin of the Nottaway river, Abitibi territory, Quebec. The name is from the Algonkian, meaning "water where they fish with torches". The lake abounds in fish and game. It is surrounded by beautiful country, either level or gently undulating, with a rich soil and wooded with spruce, fir, tamarac, birch, and poplar. The lake has an area of 75 square miles.

Waswanipi House, a Hudson's Bay Company post at the outlet of lake Waswanipi, in northern Quebec. It is an old post, dating back possibly to the French régime, and is still in operation.

Waswanipi river, rises in the lake of the same name and flows through Gull and Olga lakes to Mattagami lake, Abitibi territory, Quebec. The river is deep and rapid, and, in certain parts, as large and powerful as the Ottawa river at the entry of the Mattawa. It is 130 miles in length and drains an area of 9,000 square miles. Auriferous quartz has been found in the valley of the Waswanipi.

Watap, a word signifying the root of the tamarack, spruce, or pine, used to sew birch-bark for canoes or for other purposes. It is a Chippewa word meaning "root of the tamarack". The word has come into English through Canadian French; and the Abbé Cuoq (q.v.) said that in 1886 the word was known from one end of Canada to the other, and deserved adoption by the French Academy.

Watchman peak is in the Rocky mountains in Alberta, in lat. 52° 02′ 30″, long. 117° 14′, and has an altitude of 9,873 feet.

Water Arum. See **Arum.**

Water Cress. See **Cress.**

Waterdown, a village in Wentworth county, Ontario, on the Canadian Pacific Railway, 5 miles north-east of Hamilton, and 31 miles west of Toronto. Its chief industries are a jam and jelly factory, a sash-and-door factory, and barrel and basket factories; and it has a high school, a convent, and a weekly newspaper (*Review*). Pop. (1931), 921.

Waterford, a village in Norfolk county, Ontario, on the Nanticoke creek, on the Michigan Central and Toronto, Hamilton, and Buffalo Railways, 8 miles north of Simcoe. It is in a mixed farming district, and has a weekly newspaper (*Star*). Pop. (1931), 1,213.

Water Hemlock. See **Hemlock, Water.**

Waterhen lake is in Manitoba, north-west of lake Manitoba, and is drained into it by the Waterhen river. The name, a translation of the Indian, is derived from the abundance of water-fowl; the western grebe breeds in the lake and river in large numbers. The lake has an area of 90 square miles.

Waterleaf (*Hydrophyllum virginianum* L., *Hydrophyllaceae*), a perennial herb with smooth, slender stems, simple or sparingly branched. The lower leaves are long-petioled, pinnately divided into 5-7 oblong to acute, sharply-pointed segments, the upper leaves are similar, but short-petioled. The flowers are white to violet in colour, and are borne in slender, stalked, nodding clusters; the corolla is bell-shaped and 5-cleft; the stamens are 5, protruding. This plant may be found in rich woods in Quebec and Ontario, growing along brooks and in moist places, and blooming from May to August.

Water Lily. See **White Water Lily.**

Waterloo, a county in western Ontario, is bounded by Wellington county on the north and Wellington and Wentworth counties on the east, by Oxford and Brant counties on the south, and by Perth county on the west. It was named after the battle of Waterloo. The county was at first part of York county; but in 1837 the district of Wellington was established, with Guelph as its county town, and this district included the present Waterloo county. In 1849 the district was divided into the counties of Waterloo and Wellington, and the united counties of Grey and Peel; but Waterloo remained part of Wellington until 1854. The first settlers were large bands of Mennonites or "Pennsylvania Dutch" who came from the United States after about 1800. The county town is Galt. Area, about 20 miles wide by 25 long. Pop. (1931), 89,852. See A. E. Byerly, *Beginning of things in Wellington and Waterloo counties* (Guelph, 1935); E. E. Eby, *Biographical history of Waterloo township* (2 vols., Berlin, Ontario, 1896); James Young, *Reminiscences of the early history of Galt and Dumfries* (Toronto, 1880); D. N. Panabaker, *Waterloo county, eighty years ago* (Waterloo Hist. Soc., 1932); and Waterloo Historical Society, *Annual reports* (q.v.).

Waterloo, the shire-town of Shefford county, Quebec, is situated on Waterloo lake, an extension of the Yamaska river, on the Canadian Pacific and Canadian National Railways, 60 miles south-east of Montreal. A mission was founded here in 1796. The settlement was named by Judge Knowlton, in 1815, after Waterloo, in Belgium. The town was incorporated in 1890. There are four churches, a high school, a convent and college, and a public library. The chief industries are toy and chair factories, a furniture factory, saw-mills, a wire-goods factory, and grist-mills. A weekly newspaper (*Journal de Waterloo*) is published. Pop. (1931), 2,192.

Waterloo, a town in Waterloo county, Ontario, adjoining Kitchener (q.v.) and connected with it by a local electric railway, is served by both the Canadian National and the Canadian Pacific Railways. It was named after Waterloo in Belgium. The district in which it has grown up was settled in the early part of the nineteenth century by Mennonites from Pennsylvania, an industrious people who carved out homes for themselves in the bush, and gradually founded industries. It was incorporated as a village in 1857. Waterloo is a busy hive of industry, having one of the largest distilleries in Canada, a flour mill, factories for the manufacture of furniture, buttons, shoes, upholstery, gloves, shirts, brooms, brushes, and threshing machines. It has a library, public and separate schools, and a weekly newspaper (*Chronicle*). Pop. (1931), 8,095.

Waterloo College, a co-educational institution of higher education, situated in Waterloo, Ontario, and affiliated with the University of Western Ontario. It is a development of the Evangelical Lutheran Theological Seminary founded in Waterloo in 1911. From the beginning a preparatory course was offered in connection with the Seminary; and this became in 1914 the Waterloo College School. Out of this developed in 1924 the Waterloo College of Arts, offering a four-year general Arts course; and in 1925 this College was formally affiliated with the University of Western Ontario. In 1929 the College School was discontinued; and in 1930 the right of the College to establish honour and specialist courses was officially recognized. The first dean of Waterloo College was Dr. Alexander O. Potter; the acting dean at present is the Rev. Dr. F. B. Clausen.

Waterloo Historical Society, a society organized in Kitchener, Ontario, in 1912. It has an historical collection in the museum of the public library at Kitchener, which includes files, practically complete, of the various newspapers of Waterloo county. Since the first year of organization it has published an *Annual report*.

Water Parsnip (*Sium cicutaefolium* Schrank., *Umbelliferae*), an erect, stout, branched, perennial herb, the lower leaves long-stalked, the upper almost sessile. The leaves are compound, the leaflets being long, narrow, sharply-pointed and saw-edged. The flowers are borne in a compound cluster subtended by numerous narrow bracts. The plant blooms from July to October in low muddy swamp-lands across the continent.

Water Plantain (*Alisma Plantago-aquatica* L., *Alismaceae*), a marsh herb, perennial from a stout bulb-like underground stem. The leaves are all radical, long-petioled, oblong to heart-shaped, with 3-9 nerves. The small white flowers are borne in a large, loose, compound cluster, which far overtops the leaves. It is common in low marshy places and shallow water across the continent.

Water-Powers. Since Jacques Cartier sailed up the St. Lawrence, the rivers of Canada have drawn the main lines of its political and economic development. They have given access to the interior, and have made it possible to carry the harvest of furs, lumber, wheat, and minerals to the seaboard for export to outside markets. In this has lain their primary importance, but since the Great War their power possibilities bid fair to overshadow transportation interests. The construction of railways, airways, highways, and the Panama canal has lessened the traditional dependence of the Canadian economy upon internal waterways, while the increasing importance, in comparison with wheat, of pulp and paper, mineral products, and the tourist trade has cut traffic routes from north to south across the east-west axis of the river systems, throwing some uncertainty upon the future pre-eminence of even the St. Lawrence outlet. The demands of these new industries for electrical energy has promoted to independent importance the power possibilities of the great rivers. Discussion of the St. Lawrence waterway has shifted from pre-occupation with the prospects of shipping to pre-occupation with plentiful supplies of hydro-electric energy, as the construction of the Beauharnois plant indicates.

The rivers of the Precambrian shield and its fringes provide over three-quarters of all the available water-power of Canada; those of the Cordilleras 15 per cent.; and those of the Appalachian region of south-eastern Quebec and the Maritime provinces, and of the Great plains of the interior, the remainder.

The rich water-powers of the Precambrian shield are due to the extent of the region, its granite and gneiss formations, and its topography and abundant precipitation. The rivers traversing the shield and skirting its edges collect the melting snow and rainfall that runs off their immense drainage basins. The St. Lawrence, Canada's chief power river, fed by the Great lakes and by a series of major tributaries from the shield to the north, such as the Nipigon, the Trent, the Ottawa, and the Gatineau, drains in all 309,500 square miles. The Nipigon has a drainage basin of 9,000, the Ottawa 56,700, and the St. Maurice and the Saguenay, emptying into the St. Lawrence below the power reach, 16,200 and 35,000 square miles, respectively. The Winnipeg river flowing westward from the St. Lawrence watershed within the shield, and then north-westward along its borders to join the Saskatchewan in lake Winnipeg, drains an area of 44,000 square miles, and the Nelson river, discharging lake Winnipeg to the north-west across the shield to Hudson bay, an area of 370,800 square miles. The fan-shaped series of rivers draining to Hudson bay, north of the St. Lawrence and east of the Nelson, includes such rivers as the Albany, draining 59,800 square miles, the Moose, with a basin of 42,100 square miles, and important power-producing tributaries such as the Abitibi and the Kapuskasing.

These great catchment areas include, especially in the case of the Nelson, and to a less extent that of the St. Lawrence, a steadying diversity of conditions. The Nelson draws tributaries not only from the shield, but also from the Rocky mountains and the Great plains, while the lesser southern tributaries of the St. Lawrence flow from the central plains and the Adirondacks.

The drainage systems of these rivers, laid down by the action of the glaciers of the Ice Age on the structural features of the continent, are new and complex. They have not yet cut gradually sloping beds in the resistant Precambrian rock, and stretches of slack water alternate with sudden falls and rapids when they spill over morainal barriers or the cuestas of pre-glacial sedimentary deposits, across which they have been diverted by the advance and retreat of the ice cap and the tilting of the continent. Thus the Niagara Falls are made by the river discharging the waters of the upper lakes, which once drained to the Mississippi, plunging 360 feet over the silurian escarpment to lake Ontario. Though the pre-glacial erosion of the shield has reduced it to a peneplain scarcely anywhere above 2,000 feet in height, this concentration in compact "heads" of the falls of its rivers makes it possible to develop almost the whole of the few hundred feet through which they descend from source to sea level. The glaciers scooped basins (notably for the Great lakes) out of softer rocks, and dammed up river outlets with debris, leaving a wealth of lakes ranging in size from the chain of giant lakes from lake Ontario to Great Bear lake fringing the shield, to the innumerable lakelets scattered through the Laurentians. They provide natural mechanical regulation for the water-flow, supplemented by the dense forest cover and swamp vegetation, which temper the violence of spring thaws and, sponge-like, hold melted snows and rainfall for a gradual discharge. The low, uneven topography of the shield and its resistant rock formations make it easy to supplement the natural controls by raising the levels of existing lakes and creating new ones, thus providing reservoirs which can be drawn on in periods of low water. The minimum flow of the Winnipeg river will eventually be raised from 11,700 c.f.s to 22,000 c.f.s., while that of the St.

Maurice and the Gatineau have been raised from 6,000 to 16,000 c.f.s. and from 3,000 to 10,000 c.f.s., respectively. Since the artificial storage basins are for the most part in wild, unsettled country, damage to other economic resources and property is negligible, except where commercial timber or patches of farm land (as on the Saguenay) may be affected, or where the level of headwaters in the United States is raised, as in the Rainy river project.

The bare rocks of the shield, scraped clear of soil by the ice-cap, are relatively impervious to moisture, so that a high proportion of rain and melted snow finds its way directly to the rivers, the forest cover preventing loss by evaporation, except from the surfaces of lakes. Precipitation is heavy in the south and east of the shield and in the St. Lawrence lowlands, increasing from less than ten inches in the tundra region north-west of Hudson bay to between 20 and 40 inches in southern Ontario and between 40 and 60 inches at Montreal and in the eastern townships of Quebec. More plentiful rain and snow provide a greater wealth of water-powers to the south and east, with a run-off increasing from less than 0.5 to 2.00 second feet per square mile of drainage area, which gives an average flow of 205,000 c.f.s. in the Niagara river and 247,000 c.f.s. in the St. Lawrence at Montreal. Precipitation is evenly distributed throughout the year, except in the far north-west, but the accumulation of snow through the winter followed by spring thaws, long delayed and lingering as these are under the protection of the forest, reduces the regularity of the run-off. In the Great lakes region and the St. Lawrence valley, there is comparatively little variation in precipitation from year to year, but the alternation of cycles of dry and wet years occasionally constitutes something of a problem in fluctuating lake levels and on the Winnipeg river. The normally dependable, regular precipitation combines with the topography and geology of the region to give a very steady rate of discharge. In the power reaches of the St. Lawrence and Nelson rivers, high water-flow is seldom more than twice as great as low water-flow; on the Winnipeg it is four times as great, and on the Ottawa fifteen times as great. On the small tributary streams not far from the height of land between the Hudson bay and the St. Lawrence drainage basins, for example, and especially where the forests have been cleared or burnt, as on the Ontario peninsula, the water-powers are small and erratic, though extremely numerous. Occasionally, they have high heads, as in the case of the Eugenia Falls (549 feet), south of Georgian bay, and the Seven Chutes (410 feet), north-east of Quebec city. Characteristically, the water-power developments of this region are low-head projects, based upon a tremendous, steady discharge of water over a comparatively short vertical drop, ordinarily of from 20 to 100 feet, though in rare cases the head is less, as at the Lachine plant (14 feet), or substantially more, as at the Queenston-Chippawa plant (305 feet) at Niagara. The power-houses are frequently built right across the natural course of the river (Abitibi Canyon), either with a simple weir-dam (Alexander Falls, Nipigon river), but more commonly with a spillway and flood-gates. In other plants the main flow of the river is diverted through power-houses, and the original course used as a spillway (Isle Maligne, Saguenay river). Rarely is the water diversion carried for long distances, though this is done in the Queenston-Chippawa and Decew plants on the Niagara escarpment and in the Beauharnois plant on the St. Lawrence.

The water-powers of the second great water-power region, in the Cordilleras, fall into two groups, one similar in character to those of the Precambrian shield, and the other in sharp contrast.

Beauharnois Power Corporation at Beauharnois Quebec
St.Lawrence River

Shawinigan Water & Power Company at Shawinigan Falls Quebec
St.Maurice River

Gatineau Power Company at Paugan Falls Quebec
Gatineau River,

Ontario Hydro-Electric Power Commission and Ottawa Valley Power Company at Chats Falls Ontario
Ottawa River

Saguenay Power Company at Isle Maligne Quebec
Saguenay River,

Alcoa Power Company at Chute-a-Caron Quebec
Saguenay River,

WATER POWER PLANTS

The first consists of powers on the great inland rivers which flow north and south for many miles along the valleys between the folded ranges before they break through the coast range to the sea. Apart from the Yukon, the most considerable are the Fraser, the Columbia, and the Kootenay, with basins respectively of 89,765, 39,722, and 14,509 square miles. These embrace both the dry plateaus and valleys of the interior, the dry eastern slopes, and the wet western slopes of the mountains. Fed by mountain streams, but flowing in deep, relatively level valleys, these rivers do not descend to sea level in continuous cascades. Quiet intervals and long narrow lakes, such as the Arrow and Slocan lakes, are interspersed with a succession of short falls and rapids where the valleys grow narrow and steep, offering sites for low-head developments.

Run-off, from the steep, rocky sides of the surrounding mountains, ranging from one to three second feet per square mile is high, especially on the western slopes, where precipitation is the heaviest. This varies from an average of over 100 inches a year on the coastal ranges to from 60 to 100 inches a year on the higher ranges of the Rocky mountains, and from 40 to 60 inches on the coastal range, to considerably less than 10 inches a year in the sheltered valleys of the Thompson and Fraser. It is most abundant in the winter on the western slopes of the mountains, where a large proportion takes the form of snow, but in the valleys it is much more nearly uniform. Irregularities in run-off are offset to some extent by the lakes on the river courses, but the accumulation of the snow and its rapid melting result in a heavy discharge in May, June, and July, from 15 to 20 times as great as low-water discharge in December, January, February, and March. Artificial regulation of river flow is possible, especially in the mountain lakes on the headwaters, but the

precipitous character of many of the high valleys and the agricultural possibilities of the land around the larger lakes in the wide valleys of the interior impose limitations upon its extension.

The second group of water-powers are those on the streams flowing from sources at high altitudes in the coast range and on Vancouver island, and from the mountains of the interior, directly to the sea or to the great rivers in the valleys. They are short and swift, plunging over mountain cliffs in high cataracts or racing down steep valleys. These waters, falling hundreds of feet in a short distance, can be used in high-head plants of considerable capacity, even though their volume is limited by the tiny catchment basins and erratic flow. Low-water discharge on these streams can be increased, in some cases, by the conservation of flood waters in artificial reservoirs, and in others by diversion schemes, common in this region, and used also to increase heads, by which the flow of several rivers is concentrated in a single outlet, as in the case of the Allouette-Stave and Buntzen-Coquitlam and Bridge River developments in British Columbia. The plentiful rainfall of the Pacific coast, with a run-off as high as 10 second feet per square mile of drainage, occur mostly in the winter, bringing winter flood and summer drought to coastal streams, such as the Jordan river on Vancouver island, with a natural flow of nearly 2,000 c.f.s. in November, and less than 50 c.f.s. in August. In the interior, where heavy winter precipitation occurs chiefly at high altitudes in the form of snow, flood water depends on spring and summer thaws, and the régime of the mountain streams is reversed; while along the frontier, where the two sets of influences meet, rivers such as the Stave have two low-water periods, one in the snowy winter and one in the dry summer. In the central range and the Rockies especially, the flow dwindles in the winter to a mere thread, though warm Chinook winds produce brief, unpredictable freshets; but in midsummer it assumes the proportions of a flood, so that the discharge on those headwaters of the Saskatchewan river which flow from the mountains fluctuate by as much as 200 to one. The flow of the Bow river, the most important of these for power purposes, with a drainage area of some 1,600 square miles above the main power reach, varies from 50,000 c.f.s. to 500 c.f.s. The power developments depend on a careful regulation of the river flow in a series of storage basins and the conservation and use of every possible drop of water; on the development of heavy summer loads; and on the use of supplementary fuel plants. Development of the characteristic waterpowers of the mountains requires diversion of stream discharge in long flumes and tunnels, sometimes many miles in length, to a point at which the highest head can be obtained. Immensely long penstocks carry the water under high pressure to the power-plant, which may be far from the natural course of the stream.

The Appalachian region includes the Maritime provinces and south-eastern Quebec, where the deeply indented coasts and the proximity of water sheds to the shore-line severely limit the size of most of the rivers. The largest, the St. John river in New Brunswick, has a drainage basin of 21,500 square miles in all. In Nova Scotia, the divide runs north-east and south-west along the length of the peninsula, making the rivers very short indeed. The ancient mountains, heavily eroded, have been worn down to elevations of 1,000 feet over most of the area, though in part of New Brunswick and in south-eastern Quebec they reach 2,000 feet, and in the Gaspé peninsula as much as 3,500 feet. In spite of the limited altitudes and small catchment areas of the rivers, there are numerous well-distributed water-powers, totalling 550,000 horse-

power, though mostly small in scale. A rough topography and glacial action in the past have created uneven watercourses rich in falls and rapids, and (except in New Brunswick) in lakes, which modify fluctuations in the discharge of the short rivers and provide sites, such as those on the St. Francis in Quebec and the North-east and Indian rivers in Nova Scotia, for artificial storage projects, which are particularly necessary in regions such as the Eastern Townships, where the forests have been cleared, and the problems of flood, erosion, and water shortage are acute. Precipitation, ranging from 30 to 60 inches a year, is heaviest in Nova Scotia, in the lower St. John and Miramichi valleys, and in the Eastern Townships. Abundant all the year round, it is heavier in the winter than in the summer except in northern New Brunswick and on the coast of Quebec. Snowfall may be substantial, characteristically bringing spring floods, while late summer and in some cases the latter part of the winter are low water periods. The erratic flow characteristic of the rivers in this region, that of the St. John varying by as much as 60 to one, limits their usefulness as a source of power, and imposes an added cost of storage systems or fuel auxiliaries upon their development.

On the Great plains, water-powers are comparatively rare, and such hydroelectric power as is used is brought from the Cordilleras in the west and the Precambrian shield in the east, as in the case of the systems of the Calgary Power Company and of the Manitoba Power Commission, fed respectively by the Bow and Winnipeg rivers. The prairie rivers have cut smooth beds for themselves down the long slope of the alluvial plains. On them there are few falls or rapids capable of power development, and the absence of hard rocks makes it difficult to find firm foundations for power-plants. To the north, river gradients are in places less even, and on such rivers as the Athabaska, the Slave, and the northern reaches of the Saskatchewan there are power possibilities amounting probably to 1,800,000 horsepower, but precipitation is everywhere light, ranging from 10 to 20 inches a year, the larger proportion falling during the early summer months in the south and the late summer in the north. Limited rainfall, high evaporation, and easily permeable soil combine to give a very slight run-off. In most of the rivers rising in the plains, this is less than 0.1 second feet per square mile, and even in those with a more highly diversified drainage system, which includes the foothills of the Rockies, not exceeding 0.2 second feet.

Severity of the winters creates special problems in the use of Canadian waterpower, though experience and improvements in technique have rendered these less formidable. Frazil ice jamming in the trash-racks of the power-plants, discharge fluctuations with ice-dams forming across river-beds and then vanishing in a sudden thaw, ice-jams backing up tail races and cutting heads, blockages caused by water freezing in flumes and penstocks, frozen flood-gates, sleet on transmission lines, (and in parts of British Columbia) snow slides must all be overcome; but nowhere, not even in the Yukon, have such obstacles proved insuperable. Increasingly, switching gear and transformers are built without housing, even in places where line patrols require dog-teams and snowshoes in winter.

The diverse demands made upon its river systems by the Canadian economy have in certain cases restricted, and in others facilitated, water-power developments, through the governmental regulation which they have called forth. The basic necessities of navigation require waterways as free as possible from obstruction and the maintenance of an adequate level of water in the navigable channels of rivers and in canals. These requirements are protected in accord-ance with its powers under the British North America Act (Section 91, s.s. 10), by the Dominion government in the Navigable Waters Protection Act (R.S.C., 1927, c. 140), which requires that all works projected upon any navigable river shall be subject to approval of the governor-in-council, and on international streams by the terms of the Boundary Waters Treaty of 1909, which gives navigation precedence over power development in competition for the use of the waters of these rivers. If impassable dams and power-houses and the diversion for power purposes of an amount of water that would threaten navigation are thus forbidden, the falls and rapids which create powersites create equally natural obstacles to navigation and improvements undertaken to overcome them have had waterpower development as a by-product on the Welland canal, on the Trent, and the Soulanges canal and elsewhere. Sometimes a power-development incidentally facilitates navigation. The full Beauharnois scheme provides for the use of the power-canal for navigation, with a series of locks past the powerhouse. As a whole, the St. Lawrence waterway project contemplates the joint production of improved navigation and water-power, with a common use by both of head-works and regulation works, storage being as important in the maintenance of water levels for navigation as in the maintenance of minimum flows for power-production, though conflicts may arise where the discharge requirements are not the same for both purposes.

The lumbering and pulp-and-paper industries depend, east of Winnipeg, on rivers for the transport of the bulk of their materials. The prior right of "floating" logs downstream from timber limits to mill is protected in the water-power legislation and regulations of Ontario, Quebec, and Nova Scotia, and by the recognition of public rights of floating in New Brunswick. Power-plants and storage-dams may be erected across "floatable" streams only when they provide suitable slides through which the logs can pass them. The water necessary for the river-drive must be provided, even though it may lessen the flow available for generating electrical power. Lumber and pulpwood interests, or their "river improvement companies", frequently must themselves construct dams to conserve part of the spring freshets for use later in the summer, and chutes to provide safe passage over destructive rapids. Storage projects undertaken on behalf of power interests (unless they flood valuable timber limits) and the construction of suitably equipped power-plants may therefore actually benefit logging interests by improving the river for floating, unless differences in flow requirements are irreconcilable.

It is harder to adapt power development to the claims of the fisheries, notably the salmon fisheries in British Columbia. Federal legislation (the Dominion Fisheries Act) and provincial (for example, the British Columbia Water Act and the Ontario regulations regarding water-power) provide protection for fishing interests. Fish ladders can be, and must be, provided where they appear to be necessary to circumvent power-works which block the river, but there is doubt in many cases as to whether the fish will or do use them. The second danger lies in the possible destruction of spawning grounds where water levels are raised. The importance of the salmon fishery on the Fraser river is so great that it may stand in the way of power developments that might endanger it.

Flooding of agricultural land, when water levels are raised, has been a problem in relatively few power projects, but the diversion of rivers may deplete underground waters, and in British Columbia especially the necessity of water for irrigation purposes has made the allocation of water privileges in that province largely a problem of irrigation

grants. Since the summer is the period of high water, there is usually plenty for both irrigation and power development, while the falling water provides in some cases a useful source of power for irrigation pumps.

Like lumbering, fishing, and agriculture, mining may interfere with power developments, just as it may stimulate and use them. Where water is scarce, its use for hydraulic mining operations, notably in British Columbia and the Yukon, may detract from power supplies, and tailings and waste frequently disturb river flows. Similarly the use of water for general industrial purposes may reduce the quantity available in certain reaches of a river for generating power.

The preservation of scenic beauty in the interests of an expanding tourist trade may limit the use of waterfalls for power purposes. Apprehension lest diversion of the waters of the Niagara river to power-plants on either side of the Falls should ruin their beauty played a large part in the restrictions imposed by the Boundary Waters Treaty in 1909.

The demands of cities for water for domestic and sanitary purposes is given precedence over all other uses under the Boundary Waters Treaty of 1909. The most serious clash between such domestic and sanitary interests and power production has arisen over the Chicago Drainage Canal, which, by diverting water from the Great lakes system into the Mississippi, to dilute sewage effluvients, reduces the flow of water available for power purposes on the Niagara and St. Lawrence rivers, as well as affecting water levels for navigation. The continued uncertainty as to what abstractions Chicago may make in the future seriously complicates the problem of further power development at Niagara Falls.

Besides the interests of other industries, water-power development involves co-operation or possible rivalry among different grantees of water privileges on the same river. Where several independent operators develop power at the same site, as in the case of the Chaudière Falls on the Ottawa river, serious disputes may arise over relative shares of the river's discharge. Since power-plants on the higher reaches of a river control the flow of water which, passing through their turbines and over their spillways, reaches the plants lower down, and since the lower plants may reduce the "head" of the plants above them by "backing up" water in the process of storage and so raising tail race levels, there is further scope for disagreement unless successive plants are under a single authority.

The problem of reconciling these conflicting and supplementary interests, of developing a systematic policy with regard to the grant of water privileges, has been solved by the gradual development of a body of law, provincial, federal, and international, and administrative machinery for its enforcement.

The delimitation of federal and provincial jurisdiction over water-powers and their respective proprietary interests in them is based on Section 91, Subsection 10, Section 92, Sub-sections 5 and 10, and Section 108 of the British North America Act. A decision of the Judicial Committee of the Privy Council in 1898 (Canada v. Ontario and others (Fisheries Case) [1898] A.C. 700) established both the right of the Dominion to exercise control, in the interests of navigation, over navigable waters, and the fact that all waters in a province (other than public harbours) not granted before Confederation are the property of that province, only *improvements* in rivers and lakes existing in 1867 having been transferred to the Dominion, along with canals, with lands and water-power connected therewith. All improvements on navigable rivers are therefore subject to federal approval, and the Dominion owns and controls the water-powers which are a by-product of canal

systems, and those situated on Dominion crown lands in the North West and Yukon Territories. The provinces own and control, subject to federal protection of navigation interests, the water-powers on provincial crown lands, Manitoba, Saskatchewan, and Alberta having in 1929 and 1930 assumed the ownership of natural resources that were previously in the hands of the Dominion. There remains some uncertainty as to whether the ownership of water-powers on navigable rivers, especially those developed as an incident of canal construction, are vested in the Crown in the right of the Dominion or in that of the provinces. Following a Dominion-provincial conference in 1927 the problem was referred to the Supreme Court of Canada, but the answers to the question in the reference were inconclusive (Canada Law Reports, Reference *re* Water and Water Powers, S.C.R. [1929], pp. 200-234), though the undisputed grant by the province of Quebec of water privileges necessary for the Beauharnois development suggests that provincial proprietary rights in such water-powers are now accepted.

By the end of the nineteenth century, the prospective importance of water-powers as a source of electrical energy was becoming apparent, as was the inadequacy of existing methods of dealing with them. Their rights once established by the decision of 1898, the provinces controlling their own natural resources proceeded each to work out a system, appropriate to its characteristic institutions and to its special economic needs, for meeting the novel problems incidental to large-scale water-power development. Existing public rights in provincial waters had to be safeguarded against possible damage by the new interests, effective use of water resources assured in the light of new possibilities, and the character and extent of those resources accurately determined, and such revenues as might be forthcoming secured for provincial treasuries. A policy was necessary both for the disposal of unalienated water-powers still included in the public domain, and for the control of hydro-electrical development of private water rights.

In Ontario, although early speculation in water-powers had by 1820 compelled special regulation to secure the actual use of suitable sites for milling purposes, riparian owners were entitled to water rights under the common law. Preliminary investigations into the extent and character of available water-powers had already been undertaken before the end of the nineteenth century. These were continued in the work of the Commission of Enquiry appointed in 1905, and carried on by the Hydro-Electric Power Commission after its creation in 1906. An Act respecting Water Powers (61 Vict., c. 8) in 1898 empowered the commissioner of crown lands to reserve from sale any water power or privilege and the land necessary for its development. Regulations for their administration were approved. The Bed of Navigable Waters Act of 1910 (1 Geo. V, c. 6) declared that water rights on navigable rivers did not belong to riparian owners except in virtue of an express grant. Water-powers so reserved, together with water-powers on as yet unalienated crown lands of a natural capacity of over 150 horsepower a year, are administered by the minister of Lands, Forests, and Mines in accordance with new regulations promulgated in 1907 under the Act respecting Water Powers (61 Vict., c. 8) later embodied in the Public Lands Act (R.S.O., 1914, c. 28, s. 58). They are leased to applicants of sufficient financial ability to carry through the projected development, when their plans have been approved. The lease runs for twenty years, with a possibility of two renewals for ten years each, and the rental, at the minister's discretion, is now usually a dollar a horse-power year of developed plant capacity, plus a charge for the use of crown lands. The whole undertaking is subject to the protection of fisheries, and floating rights, and to inspection during construction and supervision and control of rates during operation. When the lease expires, the water-power and permanent structures revert to the Crown, subject to compensation, if the lieutenant-governor-in-council so decides on the advice of the Hydro-Electric Power Commission. This commission is also authorized to carry out the necessary technical investigation and supervision at the minister's request. Special agreements govern the development of power at Niagara Falls, under the Queen Victoria Niagara Falls Power Commission.

Development of private water-powers is subject to the provisions of two Acts. The first, the Water Powers Regulation Act (6 Geo. V, c. 21), with subsequent amendments, governs the use of rivers for power purposes. To insure the most effective possible use of potential water-powers all developments are subject to inspection by any person or commission designated by the lieutenant-governor-in-council. Improvements in structure may be required; new works, alterations, and extensions must be approved; and the amount of water to be used and the quantity of power to be developed by each water-power owner determined. The second, the Lakes and Rivers Improvement Act (R.S.O., 1927, c. 40), consolidates legislation specifying the conditions under which water may be used for every purpose. Dams on all lakes and rivers covered by the Act must be approved by the lieutenant-governor-in-council, who may appoint officers to regulate the use of water and all modifications of flow and water levels. The minister of Lands and Forests may determine the respective rights of different users, and owners of water privileges are given the necessary powers to obtain such lands as are necessary for their development.

In Quebec, under article 400 of the Civil Code, a distinction is made, not only between navigable and non-navigable rivers, but also between floatable (capable of floating logs in the form of rafts) and non-floatable rivers. Grants of crown lands on navigable and floatable rivers even prior to 1884 did not include the bed of the stream, which remained vested in the Crown. From 1884 onwards grants of land even on non-floatable streams have been subject to the reservation of a strip of land along the water's edge. An Act (9 Geo. V, c. 31, s. 1a) passed in 1919 made it clear that these reserves remain crown property, as by another Act (8 Geo. V, c. 72) do all water-powers, including those on non-navigable streams, bordering lands granted since February 9, 1918, and all waters on lands as yet unalienated.

Data as to available water-powers have been accumulating since 1897, collected by the department of Lands, Forests, and Mines, through its Hydraulic Service, and, since its creation in 1910, by the Quebec Streams Commission. A systematic policy as to their disposal has been gradually evolved, based not on any general water Act or formal regulations, but on cumulative administrative practice. Before 1907 a number of water-powers were sold outright, with or without stipulations as to how much power was to be developed or capital expended within a certain period. Since then the custom has become established of disposing of rights to all but very small water-powers at public auction on the basis of an emphyteutic lease running for a period ranging from 20 to 99 years, but most commonly for 75 years. The standard lease imposes the rental bid at the auction by the lessee, plus a royalty subject to revision at agreed intervals, based on the turbine capacity of the development, and an additional rental payable for the use of any additional crown lands. A further payment is exacted on a pro-rata basis towards the cost of works by the Quebec

Streams Commission from which the lessee benefits. The development must be carried out within a specified time limit, and surplus power be made available to any responsible applicant. Plans must be approved before construction is started and operations are subject to supervision by the minister of Lands and Forests. In accordance with the Act of 1926 (16 Geo. V, c. 26) no power may be exported to the United States, though on payment of an additional royalty it may be sold to other provinces. Subsequent legislation (25 Geo. V, c. 20) has relaxed the embargo on exportation in certain cases. Third party rights and federal and provincial laws concerning navigation, mining, fisheries, and log-driving, must not be interfered with, and suitable fishways and log-slides and booms must be provided. A deposit must be made during construction, and the lease may be cancelled if any of its conditions are broken, or charges under it are not paid. When it terminates, the water-power and permanent structures revert to the Crown. Since 1935 (25-26 Geo. V, c. 23 and 1 Geo. VI, c. 24) legislative sanction has been necessary for the alienation of all but very small water-powers.

All power developments are subject to the Water Course Act (R.S.P.Q., 1925, c. 46). Private water-powers may be developed by their owners at will, subject, since 1918 (8 Geo. V, c. 68, 69, 70), to approval by the lieutenant-governor-in-council, when the proposed works affect other property and private or public rights, and to the owners' responsibility for resulting damage. Power developments of 200 horse-power or over carry with them the privilege of expropriating property required for their use. The task of regulating river-flow has been entrusted to the Quebec Streams Commission, which has carried out storage works on the major power rivers, notably the St. Maurice and the Gatineau, on behalf of the private power companies using their waters.

In British Columbia, the necessities of placer mining and irrigation had long compelled recognition of water rights as a distinct element in the public domain. Since 1892, riparian owners as such have had no claim to the use of waters except for domestic purposes. By 1919, some 7,000 grants had been made for different purposes under the authority of different Acts, frequently without proper records being kept. A succession of Acts, dating from the Water Privileges Act of 1892 (55 Vict., c. 57), have clarified the situation, and established systematic administrative practice. This last Act affirmed that all unrecorded and unappropriated water-powers not exclusively under Dominion control (as in the "Railway Belt") were vested in the Crown in the right of the province. The Water Clauses Consolidation Act of 1897 (60 Vict., c. 45) codified scattered legislation relating to water. The Water Act of 1909 (9 Ed. VII, c. 48) divided the province into water districts, and established a board of investigation to inquire into over-lapping claims to water rights, to make exact surveys of available water resources, and to institute systematic records. The consolidating Water Act of 1924 (R.S.B.C., 1924, c. 271) confirming and extending the basic Act of 1914 (4 Geo. V, c. 81), now governs the disposal, by a comptroller of water rights, of water privileges in accordance with the long-established principle of beneficial use, under the authority of the minister of Lands. Applicants for a licence to use water for power development are required to give notice of their project, to undertake surveys, submit plans, and meet objections which may be made at a hearing on the undertaking. A conditional water licence covers the period of construction specifying the date by which it must be completed, and providing for the necessary use of crown lands and acquisition of private lands. When the completed works are approved, a final licence is issued for a maximum period of fifty years (or 99 years in the case of an electric railway). The licence lays down the terms on which the water-powers are leased in accordance with regulations under the Act. The water-powers of the province are classified according to their desirability and the rents fixed accordingly, for a maximum period of 21 years, after which they are subject to revision. To check speculation, rent is charged both during the construction period and for water granted by the licence, but not yet in use. In 1929, the Board of Investigation was transformed into the Water Board, and to its duties in regulating the use of water-powers was added the supervision of all electrical undertakings, with powers to fix rates, tolls, and conditions of service. By the agreement of 1930 British Columbia assumed control of the water-powers of the "Railway Belt" and "Peace River Block" previously in the hands of the Dominion.

In Nova Scotia, by 1910, most of the available land had been granted to private owners without any reservation of inland waters, which thus passed out of the possession of the crown, becoming private property subject only to common law rights of other riparian owners, such public rights as navigation, and statutory provisions for the unobstructed floating of timber (R.S.N.S., 1900, c. 95) and the construction of fishways under the Fisheries Act (R.S.C., 1906, c. 45). By the Crown Lands Act of 1910 (10 Ed. VII, c. 4), specific provision with regard to water rights was made for the first time, but it was not until 1919 that the Nova Scotia Water Act (9-10 Geo. V, c. 5) established a new basis for the control of water resources in the province. By this Act all water-courses and the right to use in any way the waters in them were declared to be vested in the Crown in the right of the province, regardless of any grants made in the past. Such existing uses of water as could be established were confirmed under the Act, which became the basis for the sanction of new uses. Water-power developments were to be authorized by the lieutenant-governor-in-council on the advice of the minister of Public Works and Mines, in accordance with regulations approved in 1922. Since its inception in 1920, the Nova Scotia Power Commission has given technical assistance under the Act, and responsibility for its administration was in 1926 transferred to the chairman of that body. Grants are made for from 10 to 50 years. If renewal is permitted, the original grantee is entitled to preference. The annual rental is usually one dollar per horse power of continuous capacity. Plans must be approved, and the undertaking is subject to supervision by the minister throughout its duration. Provision must be made for log-driving and fisheries.

Meanwhile, the Nova Scotia Water Power Commission had been appointed in 1914 (4 Geo. V, c. 8), to investigate the extent and nature of the province's water-power resources. In 1919, this work of enquiry was taken over by the Nova Scotia Power Commission, which has since carried it on, in co-operation with the Dominion Water Power Branch, to the expenses of which the province has contributed since 1933.

In New Brunswick, as elsewhere, water-powers had been granted with the crown lands on which they were situated, and might be exploited in accordance with the common law rights of riparian owners, subject to the important rights of navigation, log-driving, and fisheries, and, since 1921, the Dams Act (11 Geo. V, c. 16), which requires the approval of the lieutenant-governor-in-council for any works in water which may hold up the water of any stream or lake, dams on small streams and water supply reservoirs being excepted. Since 1884 (47 Vict., c. 7), a strip of land four rods in width has been reserved to the Crown along the banks of twenty of the most important rivers. No general legislation has been passed governing the development of the water rights thus retained by the Crown nor those on as yet ungranted lands, each case being dealt with on its own merits. An Act was passed in 1903 (3 Ed. VII, c. 3), authorizing the lieutenant-governor-in-council to incorporate a company to develop the Grand Falls, on the St. John river, under stipulated conditions regarding rental, and the acquisition of necessary lands and privileges. The following year these powers were extended (4 Ed. VII, c. 32) to include water-powers on other rivers, but the Grand Falls were not developed until 1926, when a subsidiary of the International Power and Paper Company Limited was incorporated by Act of the legislature (16 Geo. V, c. 45) and authorized to undertake their development. Various other powers have been developed, notably on the Musquash river, by the New Brunswick Power Commission since its inception in 1920. This body has carried on investigations into the water-power situation under a special minister in charge of the water-powers of the province.

The limited water-powers of Prince Edward Island have been developed by riparian owners. No general legislation regarding water-power development has been passed in this province.

Prior to 1930, the water-powers of the three prairie provinces were vested in the Crown in the right of the Dominion, and were administered by the minister of the Interior on the advice of the director of the Water Power Branch. The North-west Irrigation Act of 1894 (57-58 Vict., c. 30) had declared that no future grants of land should carry with them rights (other than public rights) to the use of water resources. These were to remain vested in the Crown, and rights to them could be acquired only under the Act. Existing rights had to be confirmed by licence. By section 35 of the Dominion Lands Act (7-8 Ed. VII, c. 20, amended by sec. 6, 4-5 Geo. V, c. 27) special provision was made for the sale or lease of lands required for the development of any water-power under regulations made by the governor-in-council, subject to rights already in existence or established by the Irrigation Act (R.S.C., 1906, c. 61). The foundations thus laid for a systematic policy in the administration of the water powers of the crown domain were strengthened and built upon by the Dominion Water Power Act of 1919 (9-10 Geo. V, c. 19) and the regulations approved under it on October 31, 1921. Dominion water-powers and crown lands required for their development can be leased for a specified term of years on carefully defined conditions, but they cannot be sold outright. The whole development is under close supervision, both while under construction and when in operation, with all its auxiliary works whether on Dominion, provincial, or private lands. Provision is made for the expropriation of previously alienated water-powers and lands, and for a very complete investigation of both engineering and economic aspects of stream development and of licenced undertakings. Where efficiency demands that two or more water-powers should be jointly developed under one authority, a single licence may be issued for both of them, and if necessary the development of one may be delayed to secure the necessary co-ordination of control. In general, such steps may be taken as are necessary to secure the most effective possible utilization of water resources.

When the plans filed by an applicant for a licence are approved, an interim licence is granted to cover the period of construction, subject to cancellation if the licensee fails to begin construction within a specified period. Upon completion of the plant and fulfillment of the preliminary conditions, the final licence is granted for a maximum period of 50 years, after which it may or may not be renewed. If it is not renewed, the whole development reverts to the Crown, which may in certain cases regain possession of the water-power before the expiration of the lease. Compensation is provided for. The rental, fixed for the first 20 years' operation, after which it is revised every ten years by mutual agreement or arbitration, ranges from 90 cents to 75 cents per horse-power year, decreasing with a higher load factor. A proportionate share of the cost of measures taken to regulate stream flow and conserve water may be charged to the owners and lessees of power sites. Provision is also made for the control of rates and conditions of service as well as the issue of securities. These responsibilities are ordinarily left to local authorities, though an amendment to the regulations in 1928 increased the powers of the licensing authority in determining what constitutes the "fair return" a business may earn, and added a requirement as to the payment of going rates of wages.

The whole system of administration is designed "to encourage desirable development of water-power resources; to discourage and prevent the initiation and development of uneconomic and wasteful projects; to ensure that each site developed shall utilize or provide for the future utilization of the maximum available power; to ensure that river systems are developed along comprehensive lines wherein each unit is a component link in a system; to ensure adequate storage measures in the interest of all powers effected; to prevent unnecessary and costly duplication of expenditures on the part of competing plants; to protect the public from inadvisable power schemes and ill-advised plants and dams; to safeguard the public from a monopolistic control by regulation and periodical revision of rates; to see to the early carrying into effect of agreements issued by the department for the development of power; to compel the development of existing plants to their limit when the market demands; and to promote in every way the fullest conservation of the power resources of the West" (Water Resources Paper, No. 56, p. 10).

When by agreement the Dominion transferred its natural resources to Manitoba and Alberta, in December, 1929, and to Saskatchewan in March, 1930, the existing system of water-power administration was carried on practically unchanged and without prejudice to existing rights. In Manitoba, a Water Powers Branch was created in the department of Mines and Natural Resources, through which the minister manages provincial water-powers, under the Water Power Act of 1930 (20 Geo. V, c. 46). Pending the promulgation of new regulations, use has been made under the Act of the Dominion regulations. No power generated in Manitoba from any provincial water-power may be exported, and approval of the legislature is required for all grants of an interest in a water-power capable of developing more than 25,000 continuous horse-power. Investigations were carried on by the Water Power Branch, in co-operation with the Dominion, until March 31, 1933, after which the whole responsibility devolved upon the province. Existing agreements between the Dominion, Manitoba, and Ontario governments for the control of inter-provincial rivers continue in force. In Saskatchewan, the Water Rights branch of the department of Natural Resources now administers the water-powers under the Water Powers Act of 1931 (21 Geo. V, c. 18), and the Dominion water-power regulations, which have been adopted for the time being. The staff of the department being limited, the Dominion continues to carry out necessary surveys, charging the costs to the province. In Alberta, similarly the Water Resources Act of 1931 (21 Geo. V, c. 71) and the Dominion regulations control water-power policy.

Of the water-powers remaining in the hands of the Dominion, those in the North West and Yukon Territories are still administered under the Water Power Act by the department of Mines and Resources, through the Water and Power Bureau (formerly the Water Power and Hydrometric Bureau of the Department of the Interior). A second group consists of water-powers which are the by-products of improvements undertaken for purposes of navigation. Under the control of the minister of Communications (formerly minister of Railways and Canals), many of these are leased at rentals ranging from $2.00 to $6.00 per horse-power year.

Besides controlling navigable waters and administering the water-powers in which it has proprietary rights, the Dominion government performs certain very important functions in securing and providing information regarding Canadian water resources. The records of the Meteorological Service, the reports of the Geological Survey and the Topographical Surveys Branch, together with studies made under the department of Public Works, provide much useful material. Reports on irrigation, published by the department of the Interior from 1894 onwards, contained information as to water supplies before studies of stream flow became, in 1908, the subject of separate investigation. Since then the Dominion Water-Power and Hydrometric Bureau of the department of the Interior (now the Dominion Water and Power Bureau of the Departments of Mines and Resources, Surveys and Engineering Branch) has carried out exhaustive surveys of available water-powers and published systematic records of stream-flow data. Its activities, carried on in many cases in co-operation with provincial authorities and private companies, have made possible the co-ordination throughout the Dominion of the work of gathering information. In addition, the Commission of Conservation (1909-21) carried out a series of investigations into the water resources of Canada, collecting original data and collating the scattered material already available in diverse sources. This work has been of great assistance in the development of water-powers, whether by private or public authorities.

Problems arising over the development of inter-provincial boundary waters have been dealt with in agreements between the provinces concerned and the Dominion, as in the case of the Dominion-Manitoba-Ontario agreement regarding storage on Lac Seul on the English river, and on the lake of the Woods on Rainy river. The still more difficult problems arising out of the development of water-powers flowing along the international frontier, or rising on one side of the frontier and flowing across it, have led to an important departure in international law. Following discussions in 1894-5, the International Waterways Commission was appointed in 1905 to investigate and report upon the "conditions and uses of the waters adjacent to the boundary" between Canada and the United States. Its reports showed clearly the necessity for agreement as to specific principles in accordance with which the use of such waters should be controlled and the enforcement of these principles by a permanent authority. Ensuing negotiations bore fruit in the Boundary Waters Treaty of 1909. After defining boundary waters and confirming the rights of navigation by both countries in boundary waters and on lake Michigan (Article 1), the treaty provides for the appointment of an International Joint Commission (Article 7) to control future "uses, obstructions, and diversions" of "boundary waters on either side of the line affecting the natural level or flow of boundary waters on the other side of the line", except in cases of special agreement between the two countries concerned, subject to the principle of equal division of boundary waters between the two countries, and to a stated order of precedence for conflicting uses (Article 8). Pollution is

proscribed (Article 4), the amount of water that may be diverted from the Niagara river limited (Article 5), and rules laid down for the use of the St. Mary and Milk rivers in Montana, Alberta, and Saskatchewan (Article 6). Besides exercising compulsory jurisdiction in these cases, the Commission may be called upon to inquire into and report upon questions involving differences between the two countries (Article 9), and even (though this function has never been exercised) to arbitrate matters that are under dispute between them (Article 10). The work of the Commission has been remarkably successful. It has proved itself an ideal instrument for the collection of impartial and exact legal and technical information, and a most effective authority for the settlement of conflicting claims in the interests of the advantageous and harmonious use of the resources of both countries.

For further information consult the publications of the Dominion Water Power and Hydrometric Bureau, department of the Interior, since 1936, the Dominion Water and Power Bureau of the department of Mines and Resources, Surveys and Engineering Branch. The reports pertaining to water-power are called *Water resources papers*, but see also the *Annual reports* of the department and the annual report on the *Water-power resources of Canada*. See also the publications of the Commission of Conservation, especially: L. G. Denis and A. V. White, *Water-powers of Canada* (1911), L. G. Denis and J. B. Challies, *Water-powers of Manitoba, Saskatchewan and Alberta* (1916), and A. V. White, *Water-powers of British Columbia* (1919); as well as J. T. Johnston, *Canada's water-power wealth* (Canadian Geographical Journal, September, 1937) *Hydro-electric progress* (Engineering Journal, June, 1937), and P. E. Corbett, *The settlement of Canadian-American disputes* in the Relations of Canada and the United States Series

HELL ROARING CANYON, WATERTON LAKES NATIONAL PARK

(New Haven, Yale University Press, 1937). Especial reference should be made to the two "World Power Conference" issues of the *Engineering Journal* for July, 1924, and July, 1930. See also **Hydro-Electric Power.**

Water Supply. Canada, with its lakes, rivers, springs, and wells, has never lacked an abundant water supply; but with the growth of settlement this water supply tended to become impure. The cholera epidemics of one hundred years ago, as well as other epidemics, were probably caused by impure water; and it has been one of the most important functions of local government to provide people with pure water. This has been done sometimes by private enterprise; but more frequently, and more succesfully, by civic enterprise. An illustration of this may be found in the history of the waterworks of the city of Toronto. It was not until 1843 that Toronto had a waterworks system, with underground pipes drawing the water from lake Ontario; but this system was owned by a private company, and the water-pressure was so weak that it was inadequate to put out fires. The service given was so intolerable that in 1873 the city bought the waterworks; and since that time Toronto has had a fairly satisfactory water supply. Not only has a high pressure system been put into operation which ensures a water supply sufficient to cope with fires, but a filtration plant has been established which purifies the water and has reduced such diseases as typhoid fever to a minimum. To-day there are few centres of population in Canada which lack a waterworks system. Various places obtain their water supply in different ways. Some municipalities are fortunate in having a supply of pure water on higher ground nearby, from which water will flow down by gravity alone. Fort William, in Ontario, for instance, draws its water from the beautifully clear Loch Lomond to the north, rather than from lake Superior; and Saint John, in New Brunswick, has obtained its water for nearly a century from another Loch Lomond. Other cities, such as London, Kitchener, Galt, and Three Rivers, obtain water from "artesian wells"— so-called after Artois in France, where these wells, which spout water, were first drilled. Most cities and towns in Canada, however, pump their water from nearby lakes and rivers; and this water has to be filtered or chlorinated, or both, if used for domestic purposes. Every city, town, and village has thus a problem of its own in obtaining its water supply. Some places have at hand a cheap supply of pure water, while others have to pump and purify their water at great expense. But, whatever the expense, it is now recognized that to provide an adequate supply of pure water is one of the first duties of municipal government in Canada.

Waterton Lakes National Park is in the extreme south-west corner of Alberta, adjoining the United States Glacier Park at the international boundary, and has an area of 220 square miles. It was set aside as a reserve in 1895. In 1932, by special Act of the Canadian parliament and the United States congress, it became part of the Waterton-Glacier International Peace Park. The park is roughly L-shaped, with the narrow line of the Waterton lakes, upper and lower, as its axis. Within its limits, it comprises all sorts of scenery, both flat and mountainous; and it is famous as a resort for fishermen. The Waterton lakes take their name from an English naturalist, Charles Waterton (1782-1865), who was formerly well known for his researches into the source of Indian poisons and for his ornithological studies. See D. W. Buchanan, *Waterton Lakes National Park* (Can. Geog. Journal, 1933).

Waterville, a village in Compton county, Quebec, on the Coaticook river, and on the Canadian National Railway, 10 miles south of Sherbrooke, and 24 miles from the international boundary. Pop. (1931), 850. There is also a village of this name (pop., 400) in King's county, Nova Scotia, on the Dominion Atlantic Railway, 34 miles from Windsor; and another village of this name (pop., 250) in Carleton county, New Brunswick, 9 miles from Woodstock.

Watford, a village in Lambton county, on the Sarnia branch of the Canadian National Railway, 28 miles east of Sarnia, and on the provincial highway between London and Sarnia, midway between them. It is in a rich agricultural district, and has saw, flour, and planing mills, a waggon factory, and wire works. It has also a high school, a public library, and a weekly newspaper (*Guide-Advocate*). Pop. (1931), 979.

Watkin, Sir Edward William, Bart. (1819-1901), president of the Grand Trunk Railway Company (1761-3), was born in Salford, England, on September 26, 1819, the son of Absolam Watkin. In 1845 he went into railway enterprise, and in 1853 became general manager of the Manchester, Sheffield, and Lincolnshire Railway Company. In 1861 he was commissioned by the Colonial Office to visit Canada to investigate the possibility of federating the provinces of British North America; and the same year he became president of the Grand Trunk Railway Company of Canada. He retired from this position in 1863, and the rest of his life was devoted to railway work in England. He died at Rose Hill, Northenden, Cheshire, on April 13, 1901. He was created a knight bachelor in 1868, and a baronet of the United Kingdom in 1880. Among other works, he was the author of *A trip to the United States and Canada* (London, 1851), and *Canada and the States: Recollections, 1851 to 1886* (London, 1887).

Watrous, a town in Saskatchewan, on the Little Manitou lake, and on the Canadian National Railway, 58 miles south-east of Saskatoon. It was named after Frank Watrous Morse, formerly vice-president and general manager of the Grand Trunk Pacific Railway. It is in a mixed farming district, is a divisional point on the Canadian National Railway, and has a high school, a hospital, and two weekly newspapers (*Signal* and *Watrous Manitou*). Pop. (1931), 1,303.

Watson, Albert Durrant (1859-1926), physician and author, was born at Dixie, Ontario, on January 8, 1859, the youngest son of William Youle Watson and Mary Aldred. He studied medicine at Victoria University, Cobourg (M.D., C.M., 1883), and at Edinburgh University; and he was made in 1883 a fellow of the Royal College of Physicians, Edinburgh. He practised medicine successfully in Toronto for many years; but he found time also for the writing of both poetry and prose, and in his later years he became interested in psychical research. He died at Toronto on May 3, 1926. Among his published works were the following: *The sovereignty of ideals* (Toronto, 1904), *The sovereignty of character* (Toronto, 1906), *The wing of the wild bird, and other poems* (Toronto, 1908), *Love and the universe* (Toronto, 1913), *Heart of the hills* (Toronto, 1917), *Three comrades of Jesus* (Toronto, 1919), *A dream of God* (Toronto, 1922), *Robert Norwood* (Toronto, 1923), and *The twentieth plane* (Toronto, 1925). In 1924 there was published a collected edition of his *Poetical works* (Toronto). See L. A. Pierce, *Albert Durrant Watson, an appraisal* (Toronto, 1923).

Watson, Sir Brook, Bart. (1735-1807), merchant and official, was born at Plymouth, England, on February 7, 1735. He went to sea, and at the age of fourteen lost one of his legs to a shark at Havana. He served as a commissary with Monckton (q.v.) at Beauséjour in 1755, and with Wolfe (q.v.) at Louisbourg in 1758; and from 1782 to 1783 he was commissary-general of the army in Canada. From 1784 to 1793 he was a member of parliament for the city of London; and he was the first agent in London of the province of New Brunswick, after its creation in 1783. He died at East Sheen, Surrey, England, on October 2, 1807. In 1803 he was created a baronet of the United Kingdom. See J. C. Webster, *Sir Brook Watson* (reprint from the *Argosy*, Shediac, New Brunswick, Nov., 1924).

Watson, Sir David (1871-1922), soldier and journalist, was born at Quebec on February 7, 1871, the son of William Watson and Jean Grant. He was educated in the public schools of Quebec, and became a journalist. In 1901 he became managing director of the Quebec *Chronicle*. In 1900 he was gazetted a lieutenant in the 8th Royal Rifles of Quebec, and in 1911 he became its commanding officer, with the rank of lieutenant-colonel. In 1914 he was given command of the 2nd Battalion of the Canadian Expeditionary Force; and he served throughout the Great War from 1914 to 1919. In 1915 he was promoted to be brigadier-general in command of the 5th Brigade of the Canadian Corps, and in 1916 he was given command of the 4th Canadian Division, with the rank of major-general. At the end of the war he was the senior divisional commander of the Canadian Corps. He died in Quebec on February 19, 1922. In 1893 he married Mary Browning, of Quebec; and by her he had three daughters. In 1918 he was created, in recognition of his war services, a K.C.B.

Watson, Homer Ransford (1856-1936), landscape painter, was born in Doon, Ontario, in 1856. He studied landscape painting in England and in the United States, but his first work was done without formal tuition. He became *par excellence* the painter of pioneer life in Ontario. In 1882 he was elected a fellow of the Royal Canadian Academy of Art; and from 1918 to 1922 he was its president. He was also the first president of the Canadian Art Club in 1907. Some of his landscapes are in Windsor Castle; others are in the National Gallery in Ottawa, and many are in private collections. He died at Doon, Ontario, where he had lived for virtually the whole of his life, on May 30, 1936.

Watson, Samuel James (1837-1881), author, was born in Armagh, Ireland, in 1837, and was educated at the Belfast Academy. He came to Canada in 1857, and became a newspaper reporter. In 1871 he was appointed librarian of the Legislative Library of Ontario. He died at Toronto on October 31, 1881. He was the author of a *Constitutional history of Canada*, vol. i (all published, Toronto, 1874), *The powers of Canadian parliaments* (Toronto, 1879), an historical romance entitled *The peace-killer; or, the massacre of Lachine* (published in the *Canadian Illustrated News*, Toronto, 1870), and a volume of poetry entitled *The legend of the roses; and Ravlan, a drama* (Toronto, 1876).

Watson, a town in the Humboldt district of Saskatchewan, on the Canadian National and Canadian Pacific Railways, 100 miles east of Saskatoon. It is the centre of a mixed farming district, and has five grain elevators and a weekly newspaper (*Witness*). Pop. (1931), 375.

Watson, mount, is in the Kootenay district of British Columbia, south of the confluence of Wedgwood creek and Mitchell river, in the Rocky mountains. It is in lat. 50° 53′, long. 115° 43′, and has an altitude of 9,500 feet. It was named after Major-General Sir David Watson (q.v.).

Watson, mount, is in Range one of the Coast district of British Columbia, south-west of Escape point, on the west side of Knight inlet. It is in lat. 50° 51′, long. 125° 43′, and has an altitude of 4,750 feet.

Waubashene, a village in Simcoe county, Ontario, on Matchedash bay, and on the Midland division of the Canadian Pacific Railway, 12 miles from Midland. The name is from an Indian word meaning "the Narrows". Pop. (1934), 1,000.

Wauchope, a village in Saskatchewan, on the Souris-Regina branch of the Canadian Pacific Railway, 10 miles from Carlyle. Pop. (1934), 200.

Waudby, John (d. 1861), journalist, was born in England, and came to Canada prior to 1840. He became editor, and later proprietor of the Kingston *Herald;* and in 1841 he founded, under the patronage of Lord Sydenham (q.v.), the *Monthly Review.* Later, he was appointed clerk of the peace for the counties of Frontenac, Lennox, and Addington. He died at Kingston, Upper Canada, on August 28, 1861.

Waugh, William Templeton (1884-1932), historian, was born at Manchester, England, on March 18, 1884. He was educated at Manchester University (B.A., 1903; B.D., 1906), and he became assistant lecturer in history at Manchester University in 1910, and reader in history in 1919. In 1922 he was appointed associate professor of history in McGill University, Montreal, and in 1925 professor of history and chairman of the department. He died at Montreal on October 17, 1932. He was the author of *The monarchy and the people* (London, 1913), *Germany* (London, 1915), *James Wolfe, man and soldier* (Montreal, 1928), and *A history of Europe from 1378 to 1494* (London, 1932).

Waverley, a village in Halifax county, Nova Scotia, on the Dartmouth branch of the Canadian National Railway, 11 miles from Dartmouth. Pop. (1934), 700. There is also a village of this name in Simcoe county, Ontario, 6 miles northeast of Elmvale, the nearest railway station. Pop. (1934), 200.

Wawanesa, a village in the Brandon district of Manitoba, on the Souris river, and on the Canadian National Railway, 120 miles south-west of Winnipeg. The name is the Algonkian word for "whippoor-will", a bird widely found in this locality. The village is the centre of an agricultural district, and has an intermediate school and a weekly newspaper (*Independent*). Pop. (1931), 441.

Wawanosh river, in the Thunder Bay district of Ontario, flows into the head of Wabinosh bay, lake Nipigon. It has a length of 33 miles.

Wawota, a village in Saskatchewan, on the Reston branch of the Canadian Pacific Railway, 52 miles from Reston. Pop. (1934), 200.

Waxwing, a name applied, with prefixes, to two species of Canadian birds, the term having reference to the curious expansion of the shaft of some of the wing-feathers at the tip into a flake, which appears like scarlet sealing-wax. Both species are somewhat smaller than a robin. They are in general a soft dove-gray, but possess yellow and black markings, and both have crests. The cedar waxwing (*Bombycilla cedrorum*) occurs across central and southern Canada as a common species. The Bohemian waxwing (*Bombycilla garrula*) nests in north-western Canada and occurs in the settled sections of the east, occasionally, as a winter visitant.

Way, Charles Jones (1835-1919), painter, was born in Dartmouth, England, in 1835. He studied art in the South Kensington Art School, and came to Canada in 1858. He settled in Montreal; and he was elected president of the old Society of Canadian Artists in 1870. He became a charter member of the Royal Canadian Academy in 1880; but he spent the later years of his life in Switzerland. Here he died in 1919.

Weasel. This name is restricted in popular usage to the members of the weasel family (*Mustelidae*) belonging to a sub-group of the genus *Mustela*. They are small animals, with long slender bodies, short legs, long necks, and a small head. The summer coat is brown in colour, with lighter underparts; in the winter, the entire coat is white, except for a jet black tail-tip. The smallest of Canadian weasels is the least weasel, a little creature six or eight inches long; and the largest is the black-footed ferret, a big fellow two feet long. Between these extremes are some fifteen weasels of varied size. One or another of these weasels is to be found scattered over Canada from coast to coast, and from the border up into the Arctic circle. Weasels are active, daring, and astonishingly powerful for their size, attacking and killing animals many times larger than themselves. They are essentially terrestrial, but can, when the need arises, climb swiftly and well. On the ground they can move like lightning, their long sinuous bodies slipping easily into almost any aperture. Four to eight young form the usual litter, and the den may be located in almost any situation that affords seclusion and protection. Weasels in the white winter *pelage* are the ermine of the fur-trade, and are caught in great quantities each year. See H. E. Anthony, *Fieldbook of North American mammals* (New York, 1928) and E. T. Seton, *Lives of game animals* (4 vols., Garden City, New York, 1925-8).

Weatherbe, Sir Robert Linton (1836-1915), chief justice of Nova Scotia (1905-7), was born at Bedeque, Prince Edward Island, on April 7, 1836, the son of Jonathan Weatherbe and Mary Baker. He was educated at Prince of Wales College, Charlottetown, and at Acadia University (B.A., 1858; M.A., 1861; D.C.L., 1883); and was called to the bar of Nova Scotia in 1863 (Q.C., 1876). From 1867 to 1878 he was law clerk of the Legislative Assembly of Nova Scotia; and in 1877 he represented the Dominion as counsel before the Halifax Fisheries Commission. In 1878 he was appointed a judge of the Supreme

Court of Nova Scotia; and in 1905 he became chief justice of Nova Scotia. He retired from the bench in 1907; and he died at Halifax on April 27, 1915. He was created a knight bachelor in 1906.

Webbwood, a village in the Algoma district of Ontario, on the Canadian Pacific Railway, 125 miles east of Sault Ste. Marie. It is in a district rich in timber and minerals, and with good agricultural land, fairly well settled; and it has a weekly newspaper (*Record*). Pop. (1931), 451.

Webster, Thomas (1809-1901), clergyman and author, was born at Glen Dhu, Loch Wicklow, Ireland, on October 29, 1809. He emigrated to Canada, and in 1838 became a minister of the Methodist Episcopal Church of Canada. He died at Newbury, Ontario, on May 2, 1901. He was the author of *The union considered, and the Methodist Episcopal Church in Canada defended* (Belleville, 1842; 2nd ed., enlarged, Hamilton, 1858); *History of the Methodist Episcopal Church in Canada* (Hamilton, 1870); *An essay on Methodist church polity* (Hamilton, 1871); and *The life of the Rev. James Richardson* (Toronto, 1876).

Webster's Corners, a village in the New Westminster district of British Columbia, 5 miles east of Port Haney. Pop. (1931), 300.

Wedderburn, Alexander (1796?-1843), author, was born in Aberdeen, Scotland, about 1796, and for many years was British emigration officer in New Brunswick, as well as secretary of the Agricultural and Emigration Society of Saint John. He died at Saint John, New Brunswick, about June 19, 1843. He was the author of *Statistical and practical observations relative to the province of New Brunswick* (Saint John, New Brunswick, 1836). He was not, as is stated in H. J. Morgan, *Bibliotheca canadensis* (Ottawa, 1867), and in W. G. MacFarlane, *New Brunswick bibliography* (Saint John, 1895), the author of

19

Notitia of New Brunswick (Saint John, 1838). This was written by Peter Fisher (q.v.).

Wedgeport, a village in Yarmouth county, Nova Scotia, on the Tusket river, 10 miles from Yarmouth, a station on the Dominion Atlantic Railway. It was originally known as Tusket Wedge; but the name was changed to Wedgeport in 1909. Its chief exports are lumber and lobsters. Pop. (1931), 1,294.

Weedon Centre, a village in Weedon township, Wolfe county, on the Quebec Central Railway, 34 miles north-east of Sherbrooke, and on the St. Francis river. It is in a farming and lumbering region. Pop. (1931), 784. See F. Venant Charest, *Notes sur la paroisse de St. Janvier de Weedon* (Sherbrooke, 1891).

Weekes, William (d. 1806), politician, was a native of Ireland. He emigrated to the United States, and is said to have studied law in the law office of Aaron Burr. In 1798 he came to Upper Canada, and was admitted to the provincial bar. Almost immediately he plunged into politics, and in 1800 he was the chief agent in securing the election of Mr. Justice Allcock (q.v.) to the Legislative Assembly. In 1804 he was himself elected to represent Durham, Simcoe, and East York in the Legislative Assembly; and he took a leading part in the House in attacking the administration of the province. He was, in fact, a pioneer of the Reform party in Upper Canada. In the autumn of 1806 he came into conflict with William Dickson (q.v.), while arguing a case before Mr. Justice Thorpe (q.v.) at the assizes in Niagara; and in the duel which ensued he fell, mortally wounded, on October 10, 1806.

Weir, Arthur (1864-1902), poet, was born in Montreal, Quebec, on June 17, 1864. He was educated at McGill University (B.A.Sc., 1886), and became a journalist. He was on the editorial staff of the Montreal *Star*, and later on that of the *Journal of Commerce*. He died in 1902. He was the author of three volumes of verse, *Fleur-de-lys and other poems* (Montreal, 1887), *The romance of Sir Richard: Sonnets, and other poems* (Montreal, 1890), and *The snow-flake, and other poems* (Montreal, 1897), as well as a prose volume, *A Canuck down south* (Montreal, 1898).

Weir, Robert (1809?-1843), journalist, was born about 1809; and in 1833 he purchased the Montreal *Herald*, of which he became the editor. He was one of the most vigorous upholders of the loyalist cause during the rebellion of 1837. He died at Montreal, on May 16, 1843.

Weir, Robert Stanley (1856-1926), jurist and author, was born at Hamilton, Ontario, on November 15, 1856, the son of William Park Weir and Helen Smith. He was educated at McGill University (B.C.L., 1880; D.C.L., 1897), and was called to the Quebec bar in 1881. He practised law in Montreal; in 1899 he was appointed one of the two joint recorders of Montreal; and in 1926 he was named a judge of the Exchequer Court of Canada. Beside a number of legal works, he wrote some poetry; and his version of the song *O! Canada* is the basis of that commonly used. In 1923 he was elected a fellow of the Royal Society of Canada. He died at his summer home, on lake Memphramagog, Quebec, on August 20, 1926. His legal and historical publications were *An insolvency manual* (Montreal, 1890), *Administration of the old régime in Canada* (Montreal, 1897), *The Education Act of the province of Quebec* (Montreal, 1899), *The civil code of Lower Canada and the Bills of Exchange Act* (Montreal, 1899), and *Municipal institutions in the province of Quebec* (Toronto, 1907); and he published two volumes of poetry, *After Ypres, and other verses* (Toronto, 1917) and *Poems, early and late* (Toronto, 1923).

Weir, William Alexander (1858-1929), judge, was born in Montreal on October 15, 1858, the younger brother of Robert Stanley Weir (q.v.). He was educated at McGill University, Montreal (B.C.L., 1881), and he was called to the bar of Quebec in 1881 (Q.C., 1899). He represented Argenteuil in the Legislative Assembly of Quebec from 1897 to 1910; and he was a member without portfolio of the Parent and Gouin administrations (1903-5), speaker of the Assembly (1905-6), minister of public works (1906-7) and provincial treasurer (1907-10). In 1910 he was appointed a puisne judge of the Supreme Court of Quebec. He died at London, England, on October 21, 1929. He was the author of legal treatises on *The municipal code of the province of Quebec* (Montreal, 1889) and *The civil code of the province of Quebec* (Montreal, 1890).

Welch, Edward Ashurst (1860-1932), provost of Trinity University (1895-9), was born at Orpington, Kent, England, on August 22, 1860. He was educated at Cambridge University (B.A., 1882; M.A., 1885); and in 1885 he was ordained a priest of the Church of England. In 1895 he was appointed provost of the University of Trinity College, Toronto; and he held this post until his appointment as rector of St. James Cathedral, Toronto, in 1899. In 1909, on becoming vicar of Wakefield, England, he left Canada; and he died in London, England, on August 6, 1932.

Weldon, Richard Chapman (1849-1925), lawyer and educationist, was born in Sussex, New Brunswick, on January 19, 1849. He was educated at Mount Allison University (B.A., 1866; M.A., 1870; D.C.L., 1893) and at Yale University (Ph.D., 1872). From 1875 to 1883 he was professor of mathematics at Mount Allison University; and in 1884 he was called to the bar of Nova Scotia (Q.C., 1890). In 1884 he was appointed dean of the law faculty of Dalhousie University; and he held this post for over thirty years. From 1887 to 1896 he represented the constituency of Albert, New Brunswick, in the Do-

minion parliament. He died at Dartmouth, Nova Scotia, on November 26, 1925.

Welland, a county in the Niagara peninsula of the province of Ontario, is bounded on the south by lake Erie, on the east by the Niagara river, on the north by Lincoln county, and on the west by Haldimand county. It was part of Lincoln county until the Act of 1851, which took effect in 1856. The first settlers were Loyalists from New Jersey, New York, and Pennsylvania after the Revolutionary war, including disbanded soldiers of Butler's Rangers; and the county was a battlefield in the War of 1812. The Welland canal was begun in 1824. The county has many very fruitful farms and orchards; and the famous Horseshoe Falls of Niagara Falls is on its boundary. The name was taken from the Welland river in Lincolnshire. The county town is Welland. Area, 230,000 acres. Pop. (1931), 82,731. See E. A. Cruikshank, *Century of municipal history, county of Welland* (Welland, 1892); *History of the county of Welland* (Welland, 1887); and Welland County Historical Society, *Papers and Records* (q.v.).

Welland, a city in Welland county, Ontario, is situated on the Welland river and ship canal, 40 miles southeast of Hamilton, and 25 miles northwest of Buffalo, New York. Welland is served by the Canadian Pacific, the Canadian National, the Michigan Central, the Wabash, and the Père Marquette Railways, and has electric railway connections with Port Colborne, Thorold, Niagara Falls, and Port Weller. The Welland ship canal gives water communication with the Great lakes. The site of the city was known as Merrittsville. Welland was founded in 1849, and takes its name from the nearby Welland river, which was so named in 1792 by Simcoe (q.v.) after the Welland river in Lincolnshire, England. The city lies in the heart of a good fruit and agricultural district, and has become an important railway centre, as well as a distributing and manufacturing community. There is abundant natural gas in the district, and water-power is derived from the Niagara Falls. Important among the industries are foundries, an agricultural machinery plant, carbide works, a pipe mill, steel plants, a cordage factory, cotton mills, a seamless tube mill, a flour-mill, saw and planing mills. The city has several fine churches, high, public and vocational schools, two business colleges, a county court house, a jail, a hospital, and an industrial home. Welland is the county seat, and was incorporated as a city in 1917. There is a daily newspaper (*Welland-Port Colborne Evening Tribune*). Pop. (1931), 10,709.

Welland Canal. See **Canals.**

Welland County Historical Society, a society founded in Welland, Ontario, in 1928. It has issued four volumes of publications: *Centenary of the Welland canal* (vol. i, 1924) and *Papers and records* (vols. ii-iv, 1926, 1927, and 1931).

Wellesley, a village in Waterloo county, Ontario, on the Nith river, 8 miles from Baden, the nearest railway station. Pop. (1934), 700.

Wellington, a county in Ontario, is an inland county of very irregular shape, surrounded by the counties of Grey, Dufferin, Peel, Halton, Wentworth, Waterloo, Perth, and Huron. It was part of York until 1837, when the district of Wellington was established, with Guelph as the county town. In 1849 this district was divided into the counties of Wellington and Waterloo and the united counties of Grey and Peel, by an Act which became effective in 1850; but Wellington remained part of Waterloo until 1854. The early settlers were Americans, who came up the Grand river. Guelph is the county town. The county is about 18 miles wide at its widest, and about 40 miles long. Pop. (1931), 58,164. See A. E. Byerly,

Beginning of things in Wellington and Waterloo counties (Guelph, 1935); A. W. Wright, *Pioneer journalism in the county of Wellington* (Ont. Hist. Soc., *Papers and Records*, 1933); and A. W. Wright, *Pioneer days in Nichol* (Mount Forest, 1933).

Wellington, a village in Prince Edward county, Ontario, on lake Ontario, and on the Canadian National Railway, 10 miles south-west of Picton. It is a summer resort. Pop. (1934), 800. There is also a village of this name on Vancouver island, British Columbia, on the Canadian Pacific Railway, 4½ miles north-west of Nanaimo (pop., 400), and another in Prince county, Prince Edward Island, on the Canadian National Railway, 12 miles from Summerside (pop., 100).

Wellington, channel, a body of water lying between Devon island and Cornwallis island, in the Franklin district of the North West Territories. It was named by Parry in 1819 after the Duke of Wellington.

Wellington, Grey, and Bruce Railway, a line opened between Guelph and Kincardine, Ontario, between 1870 and 1874, by way of Elora and Palmerston. It was absorbed by the Great Western Railway about 1875.

Wellington Square. See **Burlington.**

Wells, Joseph (1773?-1853), executive councillor of Upper Canada, was a veteran of the Peninsular War who was born about 1773. He entered the British army in 1798, and by 1814 had attained the rank of Lieutenant-colonel. In 1815 he came to Canada as an inspecting field officer, and was soon afterwards placed on half-pay. He settled at Davenport, near York (Toronto), and in 1820 he was appointed a member of the Legislative Council of Upper Canada; and in 1829 a member of the Executive Council. In 1836 he resigned from the Executive Council with his colleagues, as a protest against the policy of Sir F.

Bond Head (q.v.). He died at Davenport, near Toronto, on February 4, 1853. In 1813 he married Harriet, daughter of George King; and by her he had eight sons and two daughters. From 1827 to 1839 he was bursar of King's College (University of Toronto).

Wells, Rupert Mearse (1835-1902), speaker of the Legislative Assembly of Ontario (1873-80), was born near Prescott, Upper Canada, on November 28, 1835, the son of Sheriff Wells, of Prescott and Russell. He was educated at the University of Toronto (B.A., 1854), and was called to the bar in 1857 (Q.C., 1876). From 1872 to 1882 he represented South Bruce in the Legislative Assembly of Ontario; and from 1873 to 1880 he was the speaker of the Assembly. In 1882 he was elected to represent East Bruce in the Canadian House of Commons; but was defeated in 1887, and thereupon retired from politics. He practised law in Toronto, first as a partner of the Hon. Edward Blake (q.v.), and later as the solicitor in Toronto for the Canadian Pacific Railway; and he died on May 11, 1902. He was not married.

Wells, William Benjamin (1809-1881), judge and author, was born in Augusta, Upper Canada, on October 3, 1809, the son of Loyalist parents. He was educated at the Augusta grammar school, and in 1833 was called to the bar of Upper Canada. In 1834 he established at Prescott the *Vanguard*, a Reform newspaper; and from 1834 to 1837 he represented Grenville in the Legislative Assembly of Upper Canada. In 1836 he went to England, with Robert Baldwin (q.v.) and Dr. Charles Duncombe (q.v.), to make representations to the Colonial Office regarding the administration of Sir F. Bond Head (q.v.). While in England he published *Canadiana: containing sketches of Upper Canada and the crisis in its political affairs* (London, 1837). In 1837 he was expelled from the Assembly, and fled to the United States; but he returned under the amnesty, and in 1850 he was appointed judge of the united county of Kent and Lambton, and later of the county of Kent. He retired from the bench in 1878, and he died at Toronto on April 8, 1881

Welsford, a village in Queen's county, New Brunswick, on the Nerepis river, and on the Canadian Pacific Railway, 22 miles north-west of Saint John. Pop. (1934), 300.

Welsh Immigration. The total of Welsh immigration into Canada is difficult to compute; for the Canadian census returns divide the population of British origin into English, Irish, Scotch, and "Other"—and there is no way of determining what proportion of those Canadians of British origin classified as "Other" are Welsh in racial origin. It is probable, moreover, that many immigrants of Welsh origin have been in the past classified as English. Clearly, however, the Welsh element in Canada is not large. There have been no solid Welsh settlements, as there have been "Scotch blocks" and "Irish blocks"; and what immigration has taken place from Wales has been sporadic. The total population of Canada of British origin classified as "Other" in 1931 was only 62,494; and the average Welsh immigration into Canada of recent years has been less than 1,000 per annum. Perhaps the most distinguished Canadian of Welsh origin has been David Thompson (q.v.), the explorer; but there have been a number of other Welshmen who have made their mark in Canada, especially in the religious sphere.

Wentworth, Sir John, Bart. (1737-1820), lieutenant-governor of Nova Scotia (1792-1808), was born in 1737, the son of Mark Hunking Wentworth, a merchant of Portsmouth, New Hampshire. He was educated at Harvard College (B.A., 1755; M.A., 1758); and in 1766 he was appointed governor of New Hampshire. He took refuge in Boston, Massachusetts, in 1775; in 1776 he went to Halifax, Nova Scotia; and in

1778 to England. He was appointed surveyor-general of the king's woods in North America in 1783; and in 1792 he became lieutenant-governor of Nova Scotia. Though personally popular, he was accused of filling the Council with his own relatives; and he had some difficulties with the House of Assembly. He was succeeded by Sir George Prevost in 1808; and he died at Halifax on April 8, 1820. In 1795 he was created a baronet of the United Kingdom; and he received the degree of D.C.L. from Oxford University (1766), from Dartmouth College (1773), and from the University of Aberdeen (1773). See L. S. Mayo, *John Wentworth* (Cambridge, Massachusetts, 1921), and Sir A. Archibald, *Life of Sir John Wentworth* (Coll. Nova Scotia Hist. Soc., 1922).

Wentworth, a county at the head of lake Ontario, is bounded on the east by lake Ontario and Halton county, on the south by Haldimand and Brant county, on the west by Brant and Waterloo counties, and on the north by Wellington county. Part of it belonged at one time to York county and later to Halton, and the south part belonged once to Lincoln; but in 1853 it became a separate county. It was called after Sir John Wentworth (q.v.), lieutenant-governor of Nova Scotia. The earliest settlers were United Empire Loyalists. County town, Hamilton. Area, about 15 by 30 miles. Pop. (1931), 190,019. See *Illustrated atlas of the county of Wentworth* (Toronto, 1875); Mrs. Dick-Lauder and others, *Wentworth landmarks* (Hamilton, 1897); and the publications of the Wentworth Historical Society (q.v.).

Wentworth Historical Society, a society founded at Hamilton, Ontario, on January 8, 1889, with the object of prosecuting research into the history and archaeology of Ontario and into the genealogy of its inhabitants. It has published ten volumes of *Papers and records*, covering the years from 1892 to 1924 (vols. i, iii, v, entitled *Journals and transactions;* vol. ii, *Transactions*).

Wentzel, Willard Ferdinand (*fl.* 1799-1832), fur-trader, was probably the son of Adam Wentzel, a Norwegian merchant in Montreal, and Endimia Grout, who were married in Montreal in 1779. He entered the service of the North West Company in 1799; and for many years he was a clerk in the Athabaska country. He was taken over as a clerk by the Hudson's Bay Company at the time of the union of 1821; but he retired to Canada in 1825. He re-entered the Hudson's Bay Company's service in 1827, and for two years was a clerk at Mingan, on the lower St. Lawrence, but in 1829 he retired a second time, and he fell a victim to the cholera epidemic of 1832.

Wesbrook, Frank Fairchild (1868-1918), president of the University of British Columbia (1913-18), was born in Brant county, Ontario, on July 12, 1868, the son of H. S. Wesbrook, later mayor of Winnipeg, Manitoba, and Helen Marr Fairchild. He was educated at the University of Manitoba (B.A., 1887; M.D., C.M., 1890), and pursued postgraduate studies in pathology and bacteriology at McGill University, Cambridge University, King's College, London, and the Hygienic and Pathological Institute, Marburg, Germany. In 1896 he was appointed professor of pathology and bacteriology at the University of Minnesota, and in 1906 he became dean of the College of Medicine in this university. In 1913 he was offered and accepted the post of president of the new University of British Columbia, and this position he held until his death on October 20, 1918. In 1896 he married Annie, daughter of Sir Thomas Taylor (q.v.). In 1918 he was elected a member of the Royal Society of Canada.

Wesley College. See **University of Manitoba.**

West, John (1775?-1845), missionary, was born in Farnham, Sussex, England, about 1775. He was ordained a priest of the Church of England; and

in 1820 he was appointed chaplain to
the Hudson's Bay Company, and sent
out to the Red River settlement in
north-west America. He remained at
Red River until 1823; he then was employed in making a tour of inspection
of the Indian settlements in Upper
Canada and the Maritime provinces;
and after this task was accomplished, he
returned to England. In 1834 the living
of Farnham was conferred on him; and
he died here at the end of 1845. He was
the author of *The substance of a journal
during a residence at the Red River colony*
(London, 1824), a second edition of
which was published, with the addition
of *A journal of a mission to the Indians
of New Brunswick and Nova Scotia, and
the Mohawks on the Ouse or Grand River,
Upper Canada* (London, 1827). See Rev.
B. Heeney, *John West and his Red
River mission* (Toronto, 1920).

West Arichat, a village and seaport
in Richmond county, Nova Scotia, on
Madame island, 3 miles west of Arichat.
It has a government wharf. Pop. (1934),
700.

Westboro, a village in Nepean township, Carleton county, Ontario, on the
Canadian Pacific Railway, 3 miles
south-west of Ottawa. It has a weekly
newspaper (*Nepean News*). Pop. (1934),
200.

Westbourne, a village in Portage la
Prairie county, Manitoba, on the Whitemud river, and on the Canadian Pacific
Railway, 15 miles from Portage la
Prairie. It was formerly known as
Whitemud River, but was re-named in
honour of the Rev. John West (q.v.),
the pioneer of Anglican missionary
enterprise in the West. An Anglican
mission station was founded here in
1859. Pop. (1934), 250.

Western Bank of Canada. The
charter of this bank was granted in
1882. The fact that the head office of
the Ontario Bank had been already
removed from Bowmanville to Toronto,
may have had some influence in the
choice of the neighbouring town of
Oshawa as the head office of the proposed new bank. The agricultural and
manufacturing interests of the district
promised well. The name chosen would
seem to indicate that "Canada West",
the former designation of the province,
still persisted in 1882, when the charter
of the bank was granted. The bank
carried on a successful business for
twenty-seven years, having reached in
1907 some 27 centres of operation. By
this time banks were coming to the
conclusion that it was not sufficient to
serve the interests of a particular section
of country; it was therefore quite in
accord with the trend of the times,
when the Western Bank, having carefully considered the proposed agreement,
was merged, on February 16, 1909, with
the Standard Bank of Canada (q.v.).

Western Counties Railway. See
Yarmouth and Annapolis Railway.

Western University. See **University
of Western Ontario.**

West Flamborough, a village in
Wentworth county, Ontario, 7 miles
north-east of Hamilton, and 2 miles
from Dundas, the nearest railway-
station. Pop. (1934), 250.

Westlock, a village in the Peace
River district of Alberta, on the Ed-
monton, Dunvegan, and British Col-
umbia Railway, 52 miles north-west of
Edmonton. It was originally known as
Edison, but in 1913 it was renamed
Westlock, after two settlers, named
Westgate and Lockhart, from whom
the townsite was purchased in 1912.
It is in a mixed farming district, and
has a weekly newspaper (*Witness*). Pop.
(1931), 536.

West Lorne, a village in Elgin
county, Ontario, on the Michigan
Central and Père Marquette Railways,
25 miles west of St. Thomas. It is in a
rich agricultural district. Pop. (1934),
900.

Westminster Conference. This was
the final conference, held in the West-

minster Palace Hotel, in London, England, at which the details of the British North America Act were worked out. The conference began on December 4, 1866, and lasted until December 24; it re-assembled in January, 1867, and continued into February. The Canadian representatives were John A. Macdonald (q.v.), G. E. Cartier (q.v.), A. T. Galt (q.v.), William McDougall (q.v.), H. L. Langevin (q.v.), and W. P. Howland (q.v.). The delegates from Nova Scotia were Charles Tupper (q.v.), W. A. Henry (q.v.), Jonathan McCully (q.v.), Adams G. Archibald (q.v.), and J. W. Ritchie (q.v.); and those from New Brunswick were S. L. Tilley (q.v.), John M. Johnson (q.v.), Peter Mitchell (q.v.), Charles Fisher (q.v.), and R. D. Wilmot (q.v.). John A. Macdonald was elected chairman of the conference, and Lieut.-Col. H. Bernard (q.v.), secretary. The conference passed sixty-nine resolutions, and drew up no fewer than seven draft bills, the last of which was substantially in the form in which the British North America Act passed the British parliament on March 29, 1867. For some account of the deliberations of the conference, see Sir J. Pope (ed.), *Confederation documents* (Toronto, 1895).

Westminster, Statute of. See **Law, Constitutional.**

Westmorland, a county in New Brunswick, fronting on Northumberland strait, and bounded on the south by Alberta county and Nova Scotia, on the west by King's and Queen's counties, and on the north by Kent county. It was created a county in 1785, and was named possibly because it was contiguous to Cumberland county in Nova Scotia, as Westmoreland is contiguous to Cumberland in England. Perhaps also the name was suggested by the marshes in the county, reminiscent of the marshes in Westmoreland in England. It is drained by the Petitcodiac river, and it is traversed by the Canadian National Railways. County town, Dorchester. Pop. (1931), 57,506.

Westmount, a residential suburb of Montreal, lying west of Montreal, on the Canadian Pacific and Canadian National Railways. It was originally the village of Notre Dame de Grâce, and was incorporated a town in 1873, and as a city in 1908. It has an excellent public library, and other up-to-date civic services. The inhabitants are mainly English-speaking. Pop. (1931), 25,000. See also **Montreal.**

Weston, a town in York county, Ontario, is situated 3 miles north-west of the city of Toronto. The municipality dates back to its incorporation in 1881, though the community originated about a hundred years prior to that date, settlers having located and erected homes on its site before 1800. It is an industrial centre, manufacturing bicycles, motors, skates, stoves, ivory products, motor bodies, kodaks, etc. It is served by the Canadian Pacific Railway, the Canadian National Railway, electric trams, and a bus line. Pop. (1931), about 4,600.

Westport, a village in Leeds county, Ontario, on the Upper Rideau lake, and on the Canadian National Railway, 45 miles north-west of Brockville. The chief industries are flour mills, cheese factories, furniture factories, a motorboat factory, a tannery, and saw-mills; and it has a continuation school and a weekly newspaper (*Mirror*). Pop. (1931), 753.

Westport, a village in Digby county, Nova Scotia, on Brier island, off the southern shore of the bay of Fundy, and at the entrance to St. Mary's bay, 35 miles north of Yarmouth. It has a harbour, with a government wharf; and the chief industry is fishing. Pop. (1934), 565.

West Toronto, a town in York county, Ontario, and a suburb immediately adjacent to Toronto on the northwest. It is on the Canadian Pacific and Canadian National Railways, and has a great variety of industrial and manufacturing establishments. It has two collegiate institutes, a technical and commercial school, and a weekly newspaper (*West Toronto Weekly*). Pop. (1931), 7,146.

Westville, an incorporated town in Pictou county, on the Middle river, and on the Pictou branch of the Canadian National Railway, 11 miles south of Pictou, and 130 miles north-east of Halifax. It is primarily a mining town. Pop. (1931), 3,946.

Wetaskiwin, a city in Alberta, is situated on the Calgary-Edmonton branch of the Canadian Pacific Railway, 42 miles south of Edmonton, and is also the western divisional point of the branch line from Saskatoon. It was incorporated as a village in 1900, and received its charter as a city in 1906. It is the centre of a fine mixed farming, live-stock, dairying, and poultry-raising district. The claim is made that this region has never known a crop failure. There is an oil-bearing stratum a few miles to the west, and good lumbering in the vicinity. It has a flour-mill of 100 barrels' daily capacity, stockyards, creameries, and five grain elevators. The name is derived from a Cree word meaning "Hills of Peace", the Cree and Blackfoot Indians having, on one occasion, concluded a treaty on the hills north of the city. It has a hospital, a high school, an opera house, and two weekly newspapers (*Free Press* and *Times*). Pop. (1934), 2,125.

Wetherall, Sir George Augustus (1788-1868), soldier, was born at Penton, Hampshire, England, in 1788, the son of General Sir Frederick Wetherall. He entered the British army in 1803; and he served in Canada, with the rank of colonel, during the Rebellion of 1837. He was in command of the column that defeated the rebels in Lower Canada at St. Charles; and for his services was gazetted a C.B. From 1843 to 1850 he was deputy adjutant-general in Canada. He was knighted in 1856, created a lieutenant-general in 1857, and a G.C.B.

in 1865. He died at Sandhurst, England, on April 8, 1868.

Wetmore, Andrew Rainsford (1820-1892), prime minister of New Brunswick (1867-70), was born in Fredericton, New Brunswick, on August 16, 1820, the son of George Ludlow Wetmore. He was called to the bar of Nova Scotia in 1843 (Q.C., 1863). In 1865 he was elected to represent Saint John in the House of Assembly of New Brunswick as an anti-Confederation candidate; but he almost immediately seceded from the ranks of the opponents of Confederation, and in 1866 he was elected for Saint John as a confederationist. In 1867 he was entrusted with the formation of the first government of New Brunswick under Confederation, and he remained prime minister until 1870. He was then appointed a judge of the Supreme Court of New Brunswick; and he sat on the bench until his death, at Fredericton, on March 7, 1892. He married Louisa, daughter of Thomas Lansdowne, sheriff of Kent county, Nova Scotia.

Wetmore, Edward Ludlow (1841-1922), chief justice of Saskatchewan (1907-22), was born at Fredericton, New Brunswick, on March 24, 1841, the son of Charles P. Wetmore and Sarah Ketchum. He was educated at the University of New Brunswick (B.A., 1859; LL.D., 1908), and was called to the bar of New Brunswick in 1864 (Q.C., 1881). From 1874 to 1876 he was mayor of Fredericton; and from 1883 to 1886 he represented York in the provincial House of Assembly. In 1887 he was appointed a judge of the Supreme Court of the North West Territories; and in 1907 he became chief justice of Saskatchewan. He retired from the bench in 1912, and he died at Victoria, British Columbia, on January 19, 1922. In 1872 he married Eliza, daughter of Charles Dickson. In 1907 he was elected chancellor of the University of Saskatchewan.

Wetmore, Thomas (1766?-1828), attorney-general of New Brunswick (1809-28), was born in New York about

1766, the son of Timothy Wetmore, one of the first graduates of King's College, New York. He accompanied his parents to New Brunswick in 1783, and studied law in Saint John. He was called to the bar of New Brunswick in 1788, and entered into partnership with his father. In 1809 he was elected to represent Saint John in the Legislative Assembly of New Brunswick, and in the same year he was appointed attorney-general of the province. This office he held until his death at Kingswood, York county, New Brunswick, on March 22, 1828. See J. W. Lawrence, *The judges of New Brunswick* (Saint John, New Brunswick, 1907).

Weyburn, a city in the district of Weyburn in the province of Saskatchewan, on the Canadian Pacific and Canadian National Railways, 73 miles south-east of Regina. Weyburn was named in 1891 or 1892 by Sir William Whyte (q.v.), then vice-president of the Canadian Pacific Railway. The meaning of the name is obscure, but the origin generally accepted is that the name was given because of a small stream, a *wee burn*, running through the town. Weyburn contains five churches, three public schools, a collegiate institute, and a municipal hospital. The city, which was incorporated in 1913, is the business centre of a prosperous district. There are six elevators, a large flour-mill, a bottling works, a brick-and-tile factory, and two creameries. A weekly newspaper (*Review*) is published. Pop. (1931), 5,002.

Weyburn Security Bank, originally the Weyburn Security Company, was founded in the town of that name in Saskatchewan. Finding the competition of chartered banks difficult to meet, the company, in 1910, decided to secure a charter and organize under the Bank Act. Its general manager was H. O. Powell. In 1930 the bank had 30 branches, all located in southern Saskatchewan, a paid-up capital of $524,560, and a reserve fund of $250,000. In January, 1931, having felt "the stress of the times", the bank was absorbed by the Imperial Bank of Canada. The purchase was based on a cash payment by the Imperial Bank and retention, by the Weyburn Security Bank shareholders, of certain of its assets. This merger eliminated the only chartered bank controlled and operated from a head office in the west of Canada.

Weymouth, a village in Digby county, Nova Scotia, on the Sissiboo river, and on the Dominion Atlantic Railway, 30 miles east of Digby. It was probably named by some of the Loyalist settlers here, who came in 1784 from Weymouth, Massachusetts. It is in a lumbering and farming district, and has a weekly newspaper (*Gazette*). Pop. (1931), 1,848.

Whale, Robert R. (1805-1887), painter, was born at Alternun, Cornwall, England, on March 13, 1805. He studied art at the National Gallery, in London, and became a successful painter of portraits and landscapes. In 1848 he was elected an A.R.A. He came to Canada, and settled at Brantford, Ontario, in 1864; and here he pursued the occupation of a portrait-painter and a landscape-painter until his death on July 8, 1887. His son, John Claude Whale (1853-1905), was also a successful painter.

Whale. This name is used commonly for the larger members of the order *Cetacea;* but to the scientist all members of this order, whether large or small, are whales. These creatures, though fish-like in form, are mammals highly modified for aquatic life. The fore-limbs are swimming paddles; there are no external traces of hind limbs; they have a tail, and some whales have a back fin, but they all suckle their young, and, having lungs like land-dwelling mammals, must rise to the surface to breathe.

Six families of whales, differing widely in size, form, and habits, are represented in Canada's coastal waters. The family *Balaenidae* (or whalebone whales) range over the Atlantic, Pacific, and Arctic oceans. The family *Rhachianectidae* (or gray whales) are found along the Pacific coast. The family *Balaenopteridae* contains the finback whales, the rorquals, the humpback whales, and the sulphur bottom whale, which, growing to a length of over 100 feet and weighing in the neighbourhood of 150 tons, is the largest animal known, either living or extinct. The family *Physeteridae* (or sperm whales) are found in the Atlantic and Pacific oceans. It is from the sperm whale that the rare substance ambergris comes. The family *Kogiidae* (or pigmy sperm whales) are, though rare, widely distributed, and may turn up anywhere. The family *Delphinidae*, which is made up of smaller whales, includes the following: the porpoises and the dolphins, found in the Atlantic, the Pacific, and the Arctic; the grampus, the blackfish, and the white whale, found in the north Pacific and north Atlantic; the killer whale, the wolf of the seas, found in both the Atlantic and Pacific; and the narwhale, occurring only in the cold northern waters. The narwhale is remarkable for the development of a front tooth in the male into a long tusk, projecting forward like a spear. The family *Ziphiidae* (the beaked whales) are found in both the Atlantic and Pacific. See F. E. Beddard, *Book of whales* (New York, 1900).

Whale river rises in several large lakes, including Manuan, runs about midway between the Koksoak and George rivers, in the eastern part of New Quebec territory, Quebec, and discharges into the south end of Ungava bay. Of all the river mouths around Ungava bay that of the Whale appears to be the favourite resort of white whales. The salmon industry in the lower part of the river, once remunerative, has considerably declined. Codfish are also taken.

Wheat. See **Grain Trade.**

Wheatley, a village in Kent county, Ontario, on lake Erie, and on the Père Marquette Railway, 8 miles north-east of Leamington. It is in a rich agricultural district, specializing in tobacco, fruits, and early vegetables; and it has a high school and a weekly newspaper (*Journal*). Pop. (1934), 798.

Whelan, Edward (1824-1867), author, was born in county Mayo, Ireland, in 1824. At an early age, he emigrated to Nova Scotia, and entered the employ of Joseph Howe (q.v.) as a printer's devil. In 1842 he went to Prince Edward Island, and he became editor and proprietor of the Charlottetown *Examiner*. In 1858 he was appointed a member of the Legislative Council of the island; and he died at Charlottetown on December 10, 1867. He published *The union of the British provinces* (Charlottetown, 1865; new ed., Gardenvale, 1927), an account of the Charlottetown and Quebec Conferences. See P. McCourt, *Biographical sketch of the Hon. Edward Whelan* (Charlottetown, 1880); and D. C. Harvey, *The centenary of Edward Whelan* (Charlottetown, 1926).

Whip-poor-will (*Antrostomus vociferus*), a bird belonging to the family *Caprimulgidae*, to which also belong the night-hawk and other similar birds, commonly designated as goatsuckers. The name "whip-poor-will" is a satisfying interpretation of the notes of the species. The whip-poor-will is active entirely at night. During the daytime it remains quietly on the ground beneath the forest, and will take to wing only when closely approached. The species is found along the southern border of Canada from Manitoba eastward. Grazing of forest land and woodlots destroys much of the habitat of this species, and locally it is becoming increasingly rare.

Whiskey-Jack. See **Jay.**

Whitaker, George (1810?-1882), clergyman and educationist, was born in England about 1810. He was educated at Queen's College, Cambridge (B.A., 1833); and in 1834 was elected a fellow of the College. He was ordained a priest of the Church of England in 1838, and was appointed vicar of Oakington, Cambridgeshire. In 1851 he was appointed first provost of Trinity University, Toronto; and he resigned this post only in 1881. He then returned to England, and he died there on August 28, 1882. He was the author of *Two letters to the lord bishop of Toronto* (Toronto, 1860); and a volume of his *Sermons* was published posthumously (London, 1882).

Whitby, a town in Ontario county, Ontario, on lake Ontario, and on the Canadian Pacific and Canadian Northern Railways, 30 miles east of Toronto. It was founded by Peter Perry (q.v.) in 1836, and was first known as Perry's Corners. Later it was named after the township in which it is situated, which was created in 1792 and called after the sea-port town of Whitby in Yorkshire, England. It has an excellent harbour, with a long cement wharf; and its chief industries are foundries, machine shops, tanneries, a creamery, and factories for hardware, saddlery, harness, and blankets. It has a collegiate institute, a ladies' college, and a weekly newspaper (*Gazette and Chronicle*); and it is also the site of a large provincial hospital, with over 1,000 patients. Pop. (1931), 5,046.

White, Harlow (1817-1888), painter, was born in London, England, in 1817. He came to Canada in 1871, and in 1880 he was elected a member of the Royal Canadian Academy of Arts. Shortly afterwards he returned to England; and he died at the Charterhouse, in London, in 1888.

White, James (1863-1928), geographer, was born in Ingersoll, Ontario, on February 3, 1863, the son of David White and Christina Hendry. He was educated in the public schools and at the Royal Military College, Kingston; and in 1884 he joined the Geological Survey of Canada. In 1894 he was appointed geographer of the Geological Survey, and in 1899 chief geographer of the department of the Interior. In this

capacity he published *The atlas of Canada* (1906; rev. ed., 1915), which was his chief contribution to Canadian geography. From 1909 to 1913 he was secretary of the Conservation Commission, and from 1913 to its abolition in 1921 its deputy head. From 1921 to his death he was technical adviser to the minister of Justice; and in this capacity he played an important part in the litigation over the Labrador boundary between Canada and Newfoundland before the Judicial Committee of the Privy Council in 1926. In 1927 he was elected chairman of the Geographic Board of Canada, of which he had been a member since 1898. He died at Ottawa on February 26, 1928. He was the author of *Altitudes in Canada* (Ottawa, 1901), *Dictionary of altitudes in Canada* (Ottawa, 1903), *Place-names in Quebec* (Ottawa, 1910), *Place-names of northern Canada* (Ottawa, 1910), *Place-names of the Thousand Islands* (Ottawa, 1910), and *Boundaries and treaties* (Ottawa, 1913). He was a fellow of the Royal Geographical Society and of the Royal Society of Canada. In 1888 he married Rachel, daughter of Thomas Waddell and by her he had two daughters. See H. S. Spence, *James White: A biographical sketch* (Ont. Hist. Soc., Papers and Records, xxvii, 1931).

White, Peter (1838-1906), speaker of the Canadian House of Commons (1891-6), was born at Pembroke, Upper Canada, on August 30, 1838, the son of Lieut.-Col. Peter White, founder of the town of Pembroke. He was educated at the local schools; and, after a business training in Ottawa, founded a lumber business at Pembroke. In 1874 he was elected to represent North Renfrew in the Canadian House of Commons, as a Conservative; but was unseated. He was, however, again returned in 1876; and he sat for North Renfrew continuously until 1896. From 1891 to 1896 he was speaker of the House. He was defeated at the polls in 1896 and in 1900; but was again elected for North Renfrew in 1904. He died at Pembroke, Ontario, on May 3, 1906.

White, Thomas (1830-1888), minister of the interior for Canada (1885-8), was born in Montreal, Lower Canada, on August 7, 1830, the son of Thomas White, a leather merchant. He was educated at the Montreal high school, and became a journalist. In 1853 he founded, at Peterborough, Ontario, the *Peterborough Review*, and he conducted this paper until 1860. In 1864, after studying law for several years, he founded, with his brother, the *Hamilton Spectator;* in 1869 he was sent to England as an emigration agent of the Canadian government; and in 1870 he assumed control of the Montreal *Gazette*. After several unsuccessful attempts to enter parliament, he was in 1878 elected to represent Cardwell in the Canadian House of Commons as a Conservative; and he sat for this constituency for the rest of his life. In 1885 he became minister of the interior in the Macdonald government; and on him devolved the reorganization of the government of the North West Territories after the second Riel rebellion. He died at Ottawa on April 21, 1888.

White, William John (1861-1934), lawyer, was born in Peterborough, Ontario, on January 29, 1861, the son of Richard White. He was educated at McGill University (B.A., 1881; B.C.L., 1882; M.A., 1885; D.C.L., 1902), and was called to the bar in 1883 (Q.C., 1899). He became *bâtonnier* of the Montreal bar in 1901. He took an interest in Canadian history and folk-lore; and from 1889 to 1891 he published a monthly periodical, *Canadiana*. He died at Montreal, on January 22, 1934. He was the author of *A treatise of Canadian company law* (Montreal, 1901).

Whiteaves, Joseph Frederick (1835-1909), palæontologist, was born in Oxford, England, in 1835. He emigrated to Canada in 1862, and settled in Montreal. For twelve years he was curator of the museum of the Montreal Natural History Society; and then, in 1876, he was appointed to the staff of the Geological Survey of Canada as palæontologist, in succession to Elkanah Billings (q.v.). He died on August 8, 1909. He was one of the original fellows of the Royal Society of Canada; and in 1900 McGill University conferred on him the degree of LL.D. A bibliography of his scientific papers includes nearly 150 titles; his most important publications were his *Contributions to Canadian palæontology* (3 vols., Montreal, 1885-91) and his *Mesozoic fossils* (3 vols., Montreal, 1876-84).

Whiteaves, mount, is on the boundary line between British Columbia and Alberta. It is one of the Rocky mountains, and is south-west of the headwaters of the Blaeberry river in the Kootenay district. It is in lat. 51° 43', long. 116° 48', and has an altitude of 10,300 feet. It was named after J. F. Whiteaves (q.v.), sometime palæontologist of the Geological Survey.

White Daisy. See **Daisy.**

White Fathers. The society usually known under the name of White Fathers (P.B.) was founded by the first archbishop of Algiers, later Cardinal Lavigerie. The mother-house is at Maison-Carrée, near Algiers, Algeria. It is a society of secular priests, consecrated to the African missions. The White Father's costume resembles very much the dress of the Algerian Arab, and consists of a "gandoura" or cassock and of a "burnous" or mantle, both of white colour. A rosary is worn around the neck, in imitation of the "mesbaha" of the Arab Marabout. The society is composed of missionary priests and of lay-brothers, called also coadjutor-brothers. The White Fathers admit in their ranks young men of all nationalities. Houses of the society are to be found in Quebec and Montreal. There are also houses in England, France, Germany, Belgium, Italy, Holland, Switzerland, Luxembourg, and Scotland.

The society has twenty-one apostolic vicariates and prefectures, five of which are administered by Canadian bishops. In December, 1933, the number of baptized, in all the missions of the White Fathers, was 737,893, while the number of those preparing for baptism attained the respectable figure of 347,889. The good reception of the sacraments (confessions were 3,511,584, and communions 12,878,963) are a proof of the fervour of the Catholic negroes.

The White Fathers have elementary schools in all their missions, where 175,828 boys and 111,706 girls are being instructed. Fifteen small seminaries and four grand seminaries are preparing 1,392 boys for the priesthood. Over 125 priests have already been ordained and are giving full satisfaction. There are 375 native sisters also, who give the missionaries help in educating the smaller children. Congregations of native lay-brothers have recently been founded. These brothers will take charge of the elementary schools. Normal schools, where special attention is given to the forming of teachers, are rapidly spreading. Several technical schools have been established, where the coadjutor-brothers teach the young negroes trades that will be useful to them and their country, such as those of the carpenter, the black-smith, the shoe-maker, and the machinist.

Whitefish (*Coregonus clupeaformis*) is the most valuable freshwater fish of Canada. It is found in all the larger lakes from the Maritime provinces to the Yukon, and is everywhere highly regarded as a food fish on account of the delicacy of its flavour. The value of the commercial catch of this species in Canada is usually in excess of two million dollars a year. Most of the catch is taken in gill nets, but some whitefish are taken on the hook. Those commonly taken in the fishermen's nets range in weight from two to five pounds, but a weight of twelve pounds or even more is sometimes attained. A number of relatives of the common whitefish occur in Canada, which have some value as food fishes. Chief among these is the round whitefish (*Prosopium quadrilaterale*), whose distribution is similar to that of its more valuable cousin. It is seldom abundant. This form is replaced in southern British Columbia by the Rocky Mountain whitefish (*Prosopium williamsoni*). The ciscoes (q.v.) also belong to the whitefish family.

Whitehaven, a village and harbour in Guysborough county, Nova Scotia, 12 miles south-west of cape Canso. The nearest railway is at Mulgrave, 65 miles distant. Pop. (1934), 500.

Whitehead, a fishing port in Guysborough county, Nova Scotia, 12 miles south-west of Cape Canso. The nearest railway is at Mulgrave, 65 miles distant. Pop. (1934), 450.

Whitehorn mountain is in the Cariboo district of British Columbia, west of Robson river, in Mount Robson Park, in the Rocky mountains. It is in lat. 53° and long. 119°, and has an altitude of 11,101 feet.

Whitehorse, a town in Yukon territory, on the Lewes river, 460 miles south of Dawson. It is named after the Whitehorse rapids on the Lewes river. It is the terminus of the White Pass and Yukon Railway from Skagway, Alaska; and through it pass most of the exports and imports of the Yukon. The steamers of the British Yukon Navigation Company leave for Dawson twice weekly during the summer season. The town is also the headquarters for the Yukon Airways and Exploration Company and the Klondike Airways Company. It has a hospital, a post of the Royal Canadian Mounted Police, and a weekly newspaper (*Whitehorse Star*). Pop. (1931), 541.

Whitelaw, John (1774-1853), physician and school-teacher, was born at Bothwell, Scotland, in 1774. He studied medicine at Edinburgh; and for a time practised medicine in Quebec, Lower

Canada. About 1807 he removed to Upper Canada, and here he became a school-teacher. For a number of years he was headmaster of the Kingston Grammar School; but in 1830 he became headmaster of the Grammar School at Niagara. He was one of the most notable teachers during the early days of Upper Canada. He retired from teaching in 1851; and he died at Niagara on January 25, 1853.

White Man mountain is on the boundary between British Columbia and Alberta, in the Kootenay district of British Columbia, south of White Man pass, in the Rocky mountains. It is in lat. 50° 45', long. 115° 29', and has an altitude of 9,768 feet. It is called after the name of the pass, which is a translation of the Indian name.

White Man pass is in the Rocky mountains, on the boundary between British Columbia and Alberta, in lat. 50° 45', long. 115° 29', and has an altitude of 7,112 feet. It divides the waters of White Man creek, which flow into Spray river, and those of Cross river, which flow into Kootenay river; and it is in the direct line of travel between the Bow and Columbia river valleys. It appears to have been used in 1841 by a party of immigrants under a half-breed named James Sinclair; and in 1845 Father de Smet (q.v.) is believed to have crossed it on his journey from Oregon to Edmonton.

Whitemouth, a village in Selkirk county, Manitoba, on the Whitemouth river, after which it is named, and on the Canadian Pacific Railway, 60 miles east of Winnipeg. Pop. (1934), 400.

Whitemud river, in Manitoba, rises in the Riding mountains and empties into lake Manitoba, 7 miles from Westbourne. It has a length of 150 miles.

Whitemud River. See **Westbourne.**

White river, in the Yukon territory, flows in a northerly direction and turns sharply to enter the Yukon river from the west, 10 miles above the entrance of the Stewart river. It was discovered and named for its colour in 1850 by Robert Campbell (q.v.) of the Hudson's Bay Company. It is 185 miles in length, and drains an area of 15,000 square miles.

White River, a village in the Algoma district of Ontario, near the mouth of the White river, on lake Superior, and on the Canadian Pacific Railway, 150 miles west of Chapleau. It has the reputation of being one of the coldest places in Canada from which temperatures are reported. Pop. (1934), 100.

White Rock, a village and summer resort in the New Westminster district of British Columbia, on Semiamu bay and on the Great Northern Railway, immediately north of the international boundary. Pop. (1931), 600.

White Sisters of Africa. The Congregation of Sisters of Our Lady of Africa was founded in 1869 by Cardinal Lavigerie, then archbishop of Algiers, to co-operate with the Society of the White Fathers in the evangelization of the dark continent. The sisters' principal rôle is the moral education of women and children. The order depends directly on Rome, has more than 1,200 members dispersed throughout 106 houses in Africa, 20 in Europe, three in Canada, and one in the United States. Its principal means of evangelization are: (1) catechism classes and preparations of children for their first holy communion; (2) primary, grammar, and high schools; (3) workrooms for women and girls; (4) orphanages and asylums for the aged; (5) hospitals, dispensaries, and leper asylums; (6) the care of the sick in their homes and visits of charity to the natives; and (7) the training of native sisters.

White-Throat. See **Sparrow.**

White Trillium. See **Trillium, White.**

White Water Lily (*Castalia odorata* (Ait.) Woodville — Wood, *Nymphaeaceae*), an aquatic with thick horizontal rootstock, and large, round, floating leaves, green, smooth, and shining above, purple and somewhat hairy beneath. The leaf and flower stalks have 4 distinct air channels within. The flowers are white to pale pink and very fragrant. They are composed of 4 greenish sepals and numerous narrowly-oblong, blunt petals, which gradually pass into numerous yellow stamens. The fruit ripens beneath the water by coiling of the flower stalks. It flowers from June till September in ponds, lakes, and slow streams, from New-foundland to Manitoba.

White Weed. See **Daisy.**

Whitewood, a town in Saskatchewan, is situated on the Soo line of the Canadian Pacific Railway, and on the Canadian National Railway, 90 miles south-east of Moose Jaw, and is the centre of a grain-growing and mixed-farming district. It was named Whitewood by the pioneer settlers on account of the white poplars which grow in its vicinity. It has a weekly newspaper (*Herald*). Pop. (1931), 564.

Whitewood. See **Basswood** and **Tulip.**

Whitlow Grass (*Draba verna* L., *Cruciferae*), an early spring flower, low growing, found in sandy waste places and along roadsides from the Atlantic west to the Mississippi. The stem is from 1 to 5 inches high, rising from a tuft or rosette of oblong leaves, which are covered with stiff hairs. The small white flowers are cruciform in shape; the 4 petals are cleft. They are borne in loose clusters at the apex of the short stems. This little plant is very incon-spicuous, and is often entirely over-looked by the layman.

Whitney, Sir James Pliny (1843-1914), prime minister of Ontario (1905-14), was born at Williamsburg, Upper Canada, on October 2, 1843, the son of Richard Leet Whitney and Clarissa

Jane Fairman. He was educated at the Cornwall grammar school, and was called to the Ontario bar in 1876 (Q.C., 1890). From 1888 to his death he repre-sented Dundas in the Legislative As-sembly of Ontario; from 1896 to 1905 he was leader of the Conservative opposition; and from 1905 to his death he was prime minister of Ontario, with the portfolio of president of the council. During his period of office he captured the confidence of the electors by his downright, straightforward methods and by his bluff honesty; and his name be-came a talisman of success among his followers. His régime was perhaps most notable for the advance made during it in the direction of government owner-ship of public utilities, and especially for the success of the Hydro-Electric Power Commission in supplying the province with power from Niagara Falls. Whitney died at Toronto on September 25, 1914. He married in 1877 Alice, third daughter of William Park, Corn-wall; and by her he had one son and two daughters. He was a D.C.L. of Trinity University, Toronto (1902), and an LL.D. of the University of Toronto (1902) and of Queen's University, King-ston (1903). In 1908 he was created a K.C.M.G.

Whonnock, a village in the New Westminster district of British Col-umbia, on the north bank of the Fraser river, at the mouth of Whonnock creek, and on the main line of the Canadian Pacific Railway, 33 miles east of Van-couver. Pop. (1931), 250.

Whycocomagh, a village in Inver-ness county, Nova Scotia, on an arm of the Bras d'Or lakes, 7 miles from Orangedale station on the Canadian National Railway, and 30 miles north-east of Mulgrave, on the gut of Canso. The name is a corruption of a Micmac word, *Wakogumaak*, meaning "the head of the water" or "the end of the bay", or else (alternatively) "beside the sea". Pop. (1934), 400.

Whymper, mount, is in the Kootenay district of British Columbia, at the headwaters of the Vermilion river, in the Rocky mountains. It is in lat. 51° 13', long. 116° 06', and has an altitude of 9,321 feet. It was named after Edward Whymper, who made the first ascent.

Whymper, mount, is in the Cowichan lake district of Vancouver Island, in British Columbia, north of the headwaters of the Chemainus river. It is in lat. 48° 57', long. 124° 10', and has an altitude of 5,120 feet. It was named by Dr. R. Brown, in 1864, after Frederick Whymper, artist, traveller and explorer, who accompanied him on an exploring expedition on Vancouver Island.

Whyte, Sir William (1843-1914), railwayman, was born in Dunfermline, Fifeshire, Scotland, on September 15, 1843, the son of William Whyte and Christina Methven. He came to Canada in 1863, and entered the employ of the Grand Trunk Railway. In 1884 he entered the service of the Canadian Pacific Railway, as superintendent of the Ontario division. In 1901 he became assistant to the president of the Canadian Pacific Railway; and in 1904 second vice-president of the company. He retired from active business in 1911; and he died at Los Angeles, California, on April 14, 1914. In 1872 he married Jane, daughter of Adam Scott, Toronto; and by her he had two sons and three daughters. He was created a knight bachelor in 1911. See R. G. MacBeth, *Sir William Whyte, a builder of the West* (Can. mag., 1914).

Whytecliffe, a summer resort in the New Westminster district of British Columbia, on the Pacific Great Eastern Railway, and on Howe sound, 12 miles north-west of Vancouver. Seasonal pop. (1934), 500.

Whyte, mount, is in Alberta, west of lake Louise, in lat. 51° 24½', long. 116° 16', and has an altitude of 9,786 feet. It was named after the late Sir William Whyte (q.v.), second vice-president of the Canadian Pacific Railway.

Wiarton, a town in Bruce county, Ontario, is situated on Colpoy's bay, Georgian bay. The first house was built on the site of Wiarton by James Lennox, who settled there in 1866. It is a terminus of the Canadian National Railway, and has numerous industries, lumbering, fishing, the manufacture of furniture, butter, etc. It is also an important fishing and farming centre, and has a fine harbour. It has a public library and a weekly newspaper (*Canadian Echo*). It was named after Wiarton Place, Kent, England, the birthplace of Sir Edmund Walker Head (q.v.). Pop. (1931), 1,949.

Wickett, Samuel Morley (1872-1915), political economist, was born at Brooklin, Ontario, on October 17, 1872. He was educated at the University of Toronto (B.A., 1894) and at the University of Leipzig (Ph.D., 1897); and from 1897 to 1899 he was Mackenzie fellow in political science at the University of Toronto. In 1898 he was appointed lecturer in political economy in this university, and he retained this position until 1905, when he went into business. He died, suddenly, at Toronto, Ontario, on December 7, 1915. He was the author of *Canadians in the United States* (Boston, 1906) and of a series of studies of municipal government in Canada, published in the *University of Toronto Studies*. He also translated into English Karl Bücher's *Industrial evolution* (New York, 1912).

Wickham, a village in Drummond county, Quebec, on the Canadian Pacific Railway, 5 miles from Drummondville. It is named after the Right Hon. William Wickham, a British statesman and diplomat who flourished at the time of the Napoleonic wars. It is in an agricultural district. Pop. (1931), 340.

Wickson, Paul Giovanni (1860-1922), painter, was born in Toronto, Canada, in 1860, the son of the Rev.

Arthur Wickson, classical tutor in the University of Toronto, and Mary Anne Thomas. He was educated at the Toronto Grammar School, and studied art at the South Kensington School of Arts. He specialized in the painting of animal subjects; and he exhibited at the Royal Academy, London, and other galleries. He died in Paris, Ontario, on September 2, 1922. In 1884 he married Elizabeth, daughter of Norman Hamilton, of Paris, Ontario. See T. G. Marquis, *The art of Paul Wickson* (Can. mag., May, 1904), and N. MacTavish, *The fine arts in Canada* (Toronto, 1925).

Wicksteed, Gustavus William (1799-1898), civil servant and poet, was born in Liverpool, England, on December 21, 1799, the son of Richard Wicksteed and Eliza Tatlock. He came to Canada in 1821, and was called to the bar of Lower Canada (Q.C., 1854). In 1828 he was appointed assistant law clerk to the Legislative Assembly of Lower Canada; and in 1838 law clerk to the Special Council of the province. In 1841 he became law clerk of the Legislative Assembly of united Canada; and in 1867 law clerk to the Canadian House of Commons. He was superannuated in 1887; and he died at Ottawa on August 18, 1898. He married (1) the daughter of John Gray, president of the Bank of Montreal, and (2) Anna, daughter of Capt. John Fletcher, of the 72nd Regiment. He published several indexes to the statutes of Canada; and he was the author of *Waifs in verse* (Montreal, 1878).

Widgeon. See **Baldpate.**

Widmer, Christopher (1780-1858), legislative councillor of Canada, was born in England in 1780. He served in the Peninsular War as surgeon of the 14th Light Dragoons; and during the War of 1812 he emigrated to Canada, and settled in Toronto. Here he was one of the early practitioners of medicine. In 1843 he was appointed a member of the Legislative Council of Canada; and

in 1853 he was for a few weeks chancellor of the University of Toronto. He died in Toronto on May 2, 1858. See W. Canniff, *The medical profession in Upper Canada* (Toronto, 1894).

Wigle, Hamilton (1858-1934), clergyman and poet, was born in Essex county, Ontario, in 1858. He was educated at Victoria University (B.A., 1889), and for many years was a Methodist minister in Saskatchewan and Manitoba. In 1910 he went to the maritime provinces, and he remained there until his superannuation in 1932. He died at Sault Ste. Marie, Ontario, on January 7, 1934. He was the author of *The veteran, and other poems* (Toronto, 1910) and *Poems for pulpit and platform* (Toronto, 1911), and he collaborated in preparing the *History of the Wigle family* (Kingsville, Ontario, 1931).

Wigwam, the name applied to the conical dwellings of the Indians of eastern North America, built as a rule of saplings and birch-bark, as distinct from the tipis, or conical buffalo-hide dwellings, of the Indians of the western plains. The word was the Abnaki name for "dwelling", and is akin to the word used by the Micmac, the Iroquois, and the Chippewa. See *Handbook of the Indians of Canada* (Ottawa, 1913).

Wikwemikong, an Indian village on the north-eastern end of Manitoulin island, at the foot of Smith's bay, 27 miles from Little Current. The name means "Beaver bay". The village was founded in 1825 by a number of Indians, Ottawa and others, brought from Michigan by a Roman Catholic priest named Proulx. These Indians have tilled the soil, and built a saw-mill. Pop. (1934), 150.

Wilberforce, the name of a former settlement of freed negroes in Middlesex county, Upper Canada, near the site of the present village of Lucan. It was founded in 1830, and as a negro settlement lasted until quite recent times; but it has now disappeared. See

F. Landon, *Wilberforce, an experiment in the colonization of freed negroes in Upper Canada* (Trans. Roy. Soc. Can., 1938).

Wilberforce, a village in Victoria county, Ontario, on the Canadian National Railway, 12 miles from Bancroft. Pop. (1934), 200.

Wilcocke, Samuel Hull (1766?-1833), author, was born about 1766 at Reigate, Surrey, England, the son of the Rev. Samuel Wilcocke. Before coming to Canada he published *Britannia: A poem* (London, 1797), *A new and complete dictionary of the English and Dutch languages* (London, 1798), and a *History of the vice-royalty of Buenos-Aires* (London, 1807; 2nd ed., 1820), as well as translations of books in Dutch, German, and French. He seems to have come to Canada about 1817 as a hack-writer in the service of the North West Company during the Selkirk controversy. He was the author of *A narrative of occurrences in the Indian countries of North America* (London, 1817; 2nd ed., Montreal, 1818), *Report of the trials of Charles de Reinhard and Archibald M'Lellan* (Montreal, 1818), *Report of the proceedings connected with the disputes between the Earl of Selkirk and the North West Company* (Montreal, 1819), and *Report of the proceedings at a court of oyer and terminer appointed for the investigation of cases from the Indian territories* (Montreal, 1819). In 1820 he fell out with the North West Company, was arrested on a charge of forgery, and spent nearly two years in the Montreal jail. From 1821 to 1827, first at Montreal, and then at Burlington, Vermont, Rouse's Point, New York, and Plattsburg, New York, he published the *Scribbler*, a scurrilous journal in which he lampooned, under thin disguises, many of the leading people in Montreal. About 1828 he returned to Canada, and became a reporter of the debates in the Lower Canada legislature. In 1828 he published a *History of the session of the first parliament of Upper Canada, for 1828-9*, which is the first approach in Canada to Hansard. He died at Quebec on July 3, 1833. A good example of his vigorous style is to be found in the fragment from his pen on *The death of B. Frobisher*, published by L. R. Masson (q.v.) in his *Bourgeois de la compagnie du Nord-Ouest* (2 vols., Quebec, 1889-90). Further details about him may be found in A. H. U. Colquhoun, *A victim of Scottish Canadians* (Dalhousie review, 1924).

Wilcox peak is in Alberta, in the Rocky mountains, in lat. 52° 15', long. 117° 14', and has an altitude of 9,460 feet. It was named after Walter Dwight Wilcox, author of *The Rockies of Canada* (New York, 1900).

Wild, Joseph (1834-1908), clergyman and author, was born at Summit, Littleborough, Lancashire, England, on November 16, 1834, the youngest son of Joseph Wild. He came to America in 1855; and, after a course of study at the Boston Theological College, became a minister of the Protestant Episcopal Church in Canada. From 1864 to 1872 he was stationed at Belleville, Ontario; from 1872 to 1880, at Brooklyn, New York; and from 1880 to 1893 he was pastor of the Bond Street Congregational Church, Toronto. He died at Brooklyn, New York, on August 18, 1908. He was the author of *The lost ten tribes* (New York, 1878; London, 1880), *How and when the world will end* (New York, 1880), *Talks for the times* (Toronto, 1886), *The future of Israel and Judah* (London, 1886), *Songs of the sanctuary* (London, 1886), *The Bond Street pulpit* (Toronto, 1888), *Canada and the Jesuits* (Toronto, 1889), and *The origin and secrets of freemasonry* (Toronto, 1889).

Wild Bergamot. See **Bergamot.**

Wild Carrot. See **Carrot.**

Wildcat. See **Lynx.**

Wild Crab. See **Apple.**

Wild Ginger. See **Ginger.**

Wild Gooseberry. See **Gooseberry.**

Wild Grape. See Grape.

Wild Leek. See Leek.

Wild Mint. See Mint.

Wild Mustard. See Mustard.

Wild Onion. See Onion.

Wild Orange Red Lily. See Lily.

Wild Radish. See Radish.

Wild Red Raspberry. See Raspberry.

Wild Rice (*Zizania aquatica*), a seed grass which grows wild in North America, but especially in the region of the Great lakes. It was an important food with the Indians, and later with the early European fur-traders; and played an important part in the fur-trade. It was never really cultivated by the Indians, as they cultivated maize, the only other seed grass growing wild in North America. The Assiniboin used to sow a portion of the seed in the mud of thin marshes, but they allowed this to grow in its wild state. See D. Jenness, *Wild rice* (Canadian Geographical Journal, 1931).

Wild Rose. See **Rose.**

Wild Yellow Lily. See **Lily.**

Wilkes, Henry (1805-1886), Congregationalist minister, was born in Birmingham, England, on June 21, 1805. He came to Canada with his parents in 1820, and went into business in Montreal. In 1828 he entered Glasgow University (B.A., 1832), and in 1834 he was ordained a minister of the Congregationalist Church. In 1836 he became the first pastor of the First Congregationalist Church in Montreal, and he was the pastor of this church until 1870. He then became principal of the Congregational College in Montreal. In a large degree, he was the father of Congregationalism in Canada. He died in Montreal on November 17, 1886. He was the author of a large number of sermons and addresses. See Rev. J. Wood, *Memoir of Henry Wilkes* (Montreal and London, 1887).

Wilkie, Daniel (1777-1851), clergyman and educationist, was born at Tollcross, Scotland, in 1777. He was educated at the University of Glasgow (M.A., 1803; LL.D., 1837), was ordained a minister of the Church of Scotland, and came to Canada in 1803. For over forty years he conducted a famous grammar school at Quebec, Lower Canada; and he died here on May 10, 1851. Besides a number of papers contributed to the *Transactions* of the Literary and Historical Society of Quebec, he was the author of a *Letter to the Roman Catholic clergy and the seigniors of Lower Canada, recommending the establishment of schools* (Quebec, 1810).

Wilkie, Daniel Robert (1846-1914), president of the Imperial Bank of Canada (1906-14), was born at Quebec, Lower Canada, on December 14, 1846, the son of Daniel Wilkie, and the grandson of the Rev. Daniel Wilkie (q.v.). He was educated at the High School and at Morrin College, Quebec; and in 1862 he entered the service of the Quebec Bank. In 1875 he became the general manager of the Imperial Bank, on its foundation; and in 1906 its president. He died at Toronto on November 19, 1914. In 1870 he married Sarah Caroline (d. 1887), daughter of the Hon. J. R. Benson, of St. Catharines, Ontario. He was the author of a treatise on *The theory and practice of banking in Canada* (Toronto, 1889).

Wilkie, a town in the South Battleford district of Saskatchewan, on the main line of the Canadian Pacific Railway between Winnipeg and Edmonton, 96 miles west of Saskatoon. It is in a cattle-raising and grain-growing district, is a divisional point of the Canadian Pacific Railway, and has a hospital and a weekly newspaper (*Press*). Pop. (1931), 1,222.

Wilkins, Harriet Annie (1829-1888), poetess, was born in England in 1829, the daughter of the Rev. John Wilkins, a Congregationalist minister. She emigrated to Canada with her family and settled in Hamilton, Upper Canada. Here she conducted for many years a "Ladies' Seminary". In her later years she was a music teacher. She died in Hamilton on January 7, 1888. She was the author of *The holly branch* (Hamilton, 1851), *The acacia* (Hamilton, 1860; 2nd ed., 1863), *Autumn leaves* (Hamilton, 1869), *Wayside flowers* (Toronto, 1876), and *Victor Roy: A Masonic poem* (Hamilton, 1882).

Wilkins, Lewis Morris (1801-1885), politician and judge, was born at Halifax, Nova Scotia, on May 24, 1801, the son of the Hon. Lewis Morris Wilkins, a judge of the Supreme Court of Nova Scotia, and Sarah Creighton. He was educated at King's College, Windsor, Nova Scotia (B.A., 1819), was called to the Nova Scotia bar in 1823, and practised law at Windsor, Nova Scotia, until 1856. He represented Windsor in the Legislative Assembly of the province from 1834 to 1837; he was a member of the Legislative Council from 1837 to 1844; and he again represented Windsor in the Assembly from 1853 to 1856. From 1854 to 1856 he was provincial secretary and clerk of the executive council in the Young administration; and in 1856 he was appointed a puisne judge of the Supreme Court of Nova Scotia. He retired from the bench in 1878, and he died at Windsor, Nova Scotia, on March 15, 1885. He was a D.C.L. of King's College, Windsor; and he was the author of a pamphlet, *The Lord's Supper* (Halifax, 1881).

Wilkins, Robert Charles (1782-1866), legislative councillor of Upper Canada, was born in 1782, and settled in the bay of Quinte district, with his parents, who were loyalists, about 1792. Here he later engaged in timber and importing businesses. He was appointed a member of the Legislative Council of Upper Canada in 1839; but he was not re-appointed to the Legislative Council of Canada after the union of 1841. He died at Belleville, Ontario, in March, 1866. See *A brief biographical sketch of the Hon. Robert Charles Wilkins* (Belleville, 1866).

Willcocks, Joseph (d. 1814), journalist and agitator, was a native of Ireland. He was implicated in the Irish rebellion of 1798, and fled from Ireland to Upper Canada. Here he obtained the patronage of Mr. Justice Allcock (q.v.), and in 1803 he was appointed sheriff of the Home district. He was dismissed from office by Francis Gore (q.v.) in 1806 for political opposition to the government; and in 1807 he founded the *Upper Canadian Guardian, or Freeman's Journal*, the first party newspaper in Upper Canada. From 1808 to 1812 he represented Lincoln, Haldimand, and West York in the Legislative Assembly of the province; and during the session of 1808 he was imprisoned by warrant of the speaker of the Assembly for making "false, slanderous, and highly derogatory" statements about the members of the Assembly. During the War of 1812, he went over to the Americans, and he was killed at the siege of Fort Erie, on October 4, 1814, while serving as a colonel in the American army. See A. H. U. Colquhoun, *The career of Joseph Willcocks* (Can. hist. rev., 1926), and W. R. Riddell, *Joseph Willcocks* (Ont. Hist. Soc., Papers and Records, 1927).

Williams, Arthur Trefusis Heneage (1837-1885), soldier, was born at Port Hope, Upper Canada, in 1837, the son of Commander Tucker Williams, R.N., who sat in the Legislative Assembly of united Canada from 1840 to 1848. He was educated at Upper Canada College, Toronto, and at Edinburgh University. He returned to Canada, and became a gentleman farmer. He represented East Durham in the Legislative Assembly of Ontario from 1867 to 1875 and in the Canadian House of Commons from 1878 to 1885. As lieutenant-colonel commanding the 46th battalion of the volunteer militia, he served in the North West rebellion of 1885; and he died near Fort Pitt, in the North West Territories, on July 4, 1885.

Williams, David (1859-1931), Anglican archbishop of Huron, was born near Lampeter, Cardiganshire, Wales, on March 14, 1859. He was educated at St. David's College, Lampeter, and at Oxford University; and he was ordained a priest of the Church of England in 1886. He came to Canada in 1887; and from 1887 to 1892 he was a professor in Huron College, London, Ontario. In 1905 he was elected bishop of Huron, and in 1926 he became archbishop of this diocese and metropolitan of the ecclesiastical province of Ontario. He died at London, Ontario, on October 7, 1931. He was a D.D. of the Western University (1905) and an LL.D. of the University of Toronto (1907).

Williams, James William (1823-1892), Anglican bishop of Quebec (1863-92), was born in Overton, Hampshire, England, on September 15, 1825, the son of the Rev. David Williams, rector of Banghurst. He was educated at Pembroke College, Oxford (B.A., 1851), and in 1856 was ordained a priest of the Church of England. In 1857 he came to Canada to take charge of a school in connection with Bishop's College, Lennoxville; and soon afterwards he became professor of classics in Bishop's College. In 1863 he was chosen bishop of Quebec, and he continued to administer this see until his death at Quebec on April 20, 1892. He published a lecture on *Self-education* (Quebec, 1865) and several papers in the *Transactions* of the Quebec Literary and Historical Society.

Williams, Jenkin (d. 1819), judge, was a Welsh lawyer who came to Canada soon after the British conquest. His commission as barrister and attorney-at-law is dated October 16, 1767. From 1776 to 1791 he was clerk of the Legislative Council; and in 1782 he was appointed also solicitor-general for the province. In 1792 he was created a judge of the court of Common Pleas in Lower Canada; and in 1794 a judge of the court of King's Bench. In 1801 he was appointed an honorary member of the Executive Council, and in 1802 a member of the Legislative Council of the province. He retired from the bench, on account of old age, in 1812; and he died on October 30, 1819.

Williams, William (d. 1837), fur-trader, was appointed resident governor of the Hudson's Bay Company's territories, with headquarters at York Factory, at the height of the Selkirk troubles in 1818. In 1819, in consequence of the aggressions of the North West Company, he took an expedition to the Grand Rapids at the mouth of the Saskatchewan, and arrested a number of partners and clerks of the North West Company, some of whom were sent to England for trial, and one of whom, Benjamin Frobisher (q.v.), died while trying to escape. A warrant was issued for the arrest of Williams; and George Simpson (q.v.) was sent out to hold his position in case he was removed from the territories over which he was governor. At the union of 1821, he was appointed joint governor with Simpson; and in 1822 he was placed in charge of the Southern Department. He returned to England in 1826; and he died in 1837.

Williams, Sir William Fenwick, Bart. (1800-1883), lieutenant-governor of Nova Scotia (1865-70), was born at Annapolis, Nova Scotia, on December 4, 1800, the son of Commissary-general Thomas Williams, barrack-master at Halifax, and Maria Walker. He was educated at the Royal Military Academy at Woolwich, and in 1825 he received a commission in the Royal Artillery. He rose in the army to the rank of general, which he attained in 1868. In 1841 he was sent to Turkey, for employment in the arsenal at Constantinople; and in 1854 he was appointed British commissioner with the Turkish army in Anatolia. He became practically commander-in-chief of the Turkish forces; and in the Russo-Turkish war he greatly distinguished himself by his gallant, though unsuccessful, defence of Kars. From 1856 to 1859 he was general-commandant of the Woolwich garrison; from 1859 to 1865 he was commander-in-chief of the British forces in Canada; and in 1865 he was appointed lieutenant-governor of Nova Scotia. In this capacity he assisted greatly in bringing about the successful issue of the negotiations for the inclusion of Nova Scotia in the Canadian Confederation. He left Nova Scotia in 1870; and from 1870 to 1876 he was governor of Gibraltar. In 1881 he was appointed constable of the Tower of London; and he died at London, England, on July 26, 1883. In 1852 he was created a C.B. (civil), in 1856 a K.C.B., and in 1871 a G.C.B. For his services in the Russo-Turkish war he was made a baronet, "of Kars". He was not married.

Williamsburg, a village in Dundas county, Ontario, 6 miles north-west of Morrisburg, the nearest railway station. It has a cheese factory, a grist mill, and a weekly newspaper (*Times*); and it is famous for a large clinic conducted there by Dr. Mahlon W. Locke, whose reputation as an orthopædist has spread over the North American continent. Pop. (1934), 350.

Williamsburg Canals. See **Canals.**

Williamsford, a village in Grey county, Ontario, on the north branch of the Saugeen river, 5 miles south of Chatsworth, the nearest railway station. Pop. (1934), 300.

Williams Lake, a village in the Cariboo district of British Columbia, at the west end of Williams lake, and a divisional point on the Pacific Great Eastern Railway, 120 miles south of Prince George. It has a hospital and a weekly newspaper (*Tribune*). Pop. (1931), 400.

Williamson, Alexander Johnson (*fl.* 1831-1840), poet and journalist, was the author of three early volumes of Upper Canada poetry, *Original poems on various subjects* (Toronto, 1836), *There is a God, with other poems* (Toronto, 1839), and *Devotional poems* (Toronto, 1840). He appears to have been a journalist, since he founded in Belleville, Upper Canada, in 1831 a short-lived weekly newspaper named the *Anglo-Canadian;* and is said to have published also a newspaper in Ancaster, Upper Canada. In 1837 he was living in Toronto, and is described in the Toronto directory for that year as "poet, etc."

Williamson, James (1806-1895), astronomer, was born in Edinburgh, Scotland, on October 19, 1806. He was educated at Edinburgh University, and was licensed as a minister of the Presbyterian Church. In 1842 he was appointed professor of mathematics and natural philosophy at Queen's College, Kingston, Canada; and he was later professor of astronomy, director of the Kingston observatory, and vice-principal of Queen's. He died at Kingston, Ontario, on September 26, 1895. He married a sister of Sir John Macdonald (q.v.). He was given the degree of LL.D. by Glasgow University in 1855; and he was the author of *The inland seas of North America* (Kingston, 1854). See R. Vashon Rogers, *Professor James Williamson* (Queen's Quarterly, 1896).

Williamstown, a village in Glengarry county, Ontario, on the Raisin river, 4 miles north-west of Lancaster, the nearest railway station, and 12 miles north-east of Cornwall. It was founded by Sir John Johnson (q.v.), who named it in honour of his father, Sir William Johnson (q.v.); and in the early days of the Loyalist settlers, it was an important community centre. Several of the partners of the North West Company had their homes here, notable among them being David Thompson (q.v.) and Simon Fraser (q.v.), the explorers. When the railway passed it by, its importance declined. Pop. (1934), 600. There is also a small village of this name in Carleton county, New Brunswick. Pop. (1934), 100.

Willing, Thomas Nathaniel (1858-1920), naturalist, was born in Toronto, Ontario, in 1858. He went to the North West Territories as a surveyor in his youth, and settled near Calgary in 1881. In 1899 he became chief game guardian in the North West Territories; and in 1910 he was appointed a lecturer in the College of Agriculture in the University of Saskatchewan. He became professor of natural history in this University; and he died at Saskatoon, Saskatchewan, on November 30, 1920.

Willis, John Walpole (1792-1877), judge, was born in England in 1792, the son of Dr. Willis, one of the physicians to George III. He was educated at the Charterhouse School and at Trinity Hall, Cambridge; and was called to the English bar. He became an equity lawyer, and published a treatise on *Equity pleading* (London, 1820). In 1827 he was appointed by royal warrant a judge of the court of King's Bench in Upper Canada; but in 1828 he came into conflict with the attorney-general of Upper Canada, John Beverley Robinson (q.v.), as well as his brother judge, Mr. Justice Sherwood (q.v.), and was summarily dismissed from office by the lieutenant-governor, Sir Peregrine Maitland (q.v.). The Privy Council held that the removal had been too summary; but the British government did not send Willis back to Canada. He was appointed a judge in Demerara, British Guiana. Later he received an appointment as district judge in New South Wales; but in 1843 he was dismissed from this post. In 1852 he succeeded to the Wick Episcopi estates in Worcestershire; and he lived there until his death in September, 1877. In 1823 he married Lady Mary Isabella Bowes Lyon, daughter of the Earl of Strathmore. He was the author of a pamphlet, *On the government of the British colonies* (London, 1850), in which he advocated colonial representation in the British parliament. See D. B. Read, *Lives of the judges of Upper Canada* (Toronto, 1888).

Willis, Michael (1799-1879), principal of Knox College, Toronto, was born in Greenock, Scotland, in 1799, the son of the Rev. William Willis, of Greenock. He became a minister of the Presbyterian Church (Old Light Burghers); and in 1847 he came to Canada as professor of systematic theology in Knox College. Of this institution he became principal; and he continued as such until 1870, when he returned to Scotland. He died at Aberdour, Banffshire, on August 19, 1879. While in Canada he published *Collectanea, Graeca et Latina; or, Selections from the Greek and Latin fathers* (Toronto, 1865).

Willison, Sir John Stephen (1856-1927), journalist and author, was born at Hills Green, Huron county, Ontario, on November 9, 1856, the son of Stephen Willison. He was educated in the public schools, and in 1882 became a journalist From 1890 to 1902 he was editor-in-chief of the Toronto *Globe;* from 1902 to 1910 he was editor of the Toronto *News;* and in 1910 he became Canadian correspondent of *The Times*. Though a Liberal up to 1902, he became after that date more and more an exponent of the Conservative point of view in politics; and in 1913 he was made a knight bachelor, on the recommendation of the Borden government. In 1906 he was made an LL.D. of Queen's University, Kingston. He died at Toronto on May 27, 1927. He was twice married, first, in 1885 to Rachel Wood (d. 1925), daughter of Mrs. Margaret Turner, of Tiverton, Ontario; and secondly, in 1926, to Marjorie MacMurchy. His most notable work was *Sir Wilfrid Laurier and the Liberal party: A political history* (2 vols., Toronto, 1903; new and revised ed., Toronto, 1926), perhaps the most outstanding example of historical biography in Canadian literature; but he was also the author *The railway question in Canada* (Toronto, 1897), *Anglo-Saxon amity* (Toronto, 1906), *The United*

States and Canada (New York, 1908), *The new Canada* (London, 1912), *Reminiscences* (Toronto, 1919), *Agriculture and industry* (Toronto, 1920), *Partners in peace* (Toronto, 1923), and *Sir George Parkin, a biography* (London, 1929). He also founded and edited *Willison's Weekly* (1925-9). See A. H. U. Colquhoun (ed.), *Press, politics, and people: The life and letters of Sir John Willison* (Toronto, 1935).

Willow, the name of the trees belonging to the genus *Salix* Linnaeus. The willow is widely distributed in Canada, and some fifty species have been recognized. Separation is made mainly by flower and fruit characters, which are available during a short period in the spring, and the determination of the species requires considerable experience. The species also hybridize among themselves, and the varieties and crosses produced are seemingly without number. As a group, the leaves are deciduous, mostly long, narrow, pointed, and singly placed. The flowers appear before the leaves and with the fruits resemble those of the poplars (q.v.). They may be readily recognized from other trees by their winter buds, which are covered by single scales. The wood is light, soft, tough for its weight, and perishable when exposed to conditions favouring decay. It is used for artificial limbs, for cricket bats, and mainly for special purposes, but is not of commercial importance. For a conspectus of the arborescent species, consult C. S. Sargent, *Manual of the trees of North America* (2nd ed., Boston, 1930).

Willow Bunch, a village in the Willow Bunch district of Saskatchewan, on the Radville branch of the Canadian National Railway, 85 miles south of Moose Jaw. (Pop. 1931), 500.

Willow Herb. See **Fireweed.**

Wills, John (d. 1814?), fur-trader, became a partner of the XY Company shortly after 1798, and was one of the six wintering partners of the XY Company who became partners of the North West Company in 1804. Soon after 1804 he built Fort Gibraltar at the junction of the Red and Assiniboine rivers; and he remained in charge of the Red River district until 1806, when he was transferred to Rat river. He returned to the Red river, however, in 1809; and he remained in charge of this department until he was relieved, because of ill-health, by J. D. Cameron (q.v.) in the summer of 1814. He died at Fort Gibraltar, either in the latter part of 1814, or in the beginning of 1815. He was elected a member of the Beaver Club of Montreal in 1807.

Willson, David (1778?-1866), religious enthusiast, was born in Dutchess county, New York, about 1778, the son of John Willson, formerly of Carrickfergus, Antrim, Ireland. In 1801 he came to Canada, and in 1802 he settled in the township of East Gwillimbury, Upper Canada. About 1812 he organized there a religious sect known as "the Children of Peace"; and at the village of Sharon he built, between 1825 and 1831, the Temple of Sharon, which is still standing. For over fifty years he guided the destinies of the sect he had founded; and he died at Sharon on January 19, 1866. About 1801 he married Phoebe Titus; and by her he had two, or possibly three, sons. Though a man of little education, he published *The rights of Christ* (Philadelphia, 1815), *The impressions of the mind* (Toronto, 1835), *Letters to the Jews* (Toronto, 1835), *Hymns and prayers* (2 vols., Toronto, 1846-9), *Sacred impressions of the mind in praise and prayer* (Toronto, 1853), and *The practical life of the author* (Toronto, 1860). See J. Squair, *The temple of peace* (Women's Canadian Historical Society of Toronto, Transaction No. 20, 1919-20), and J. L. Hughes, *Sketches of the Sharon temple and its founder* (pamphlet, Toronto, 1918).

Willson, Hugh Bowlby (1813-1880), publicist, was born at Winona, Upper

Canada, in 1813, the son of the Hon. John Willson (q.v.). He was educated at the Gore District Grammar School, and in 1841 he was called to the bar of Upper Canada. In 1849 he was one of the founders of the *Independent*, a newspaper established in Toronto to advocate the annexation of Canada to the United States; and later he assisted in founding the Hamilton *Spectator*. He died at New York, on April 29, 1880. He published a number of pamphlets on a variety of subjects: *Great Western Railway of Canada* (Hamilton, 1860); *The military defences of Canada* (Quebec, 1862); *The science of ship-building considered* (London, 1863); *High speed steamers* (Albany, 1866); *The science of money considered* (Washington, 1869); *A plea for Uncle Sam's money* (New York, 1870); *The money question considered* (London, 1874); *Industrial crises* (Washington, 1879); and *Currency* (New York, 1882).

Willson, John (1776-1860), speaker of the Legislative Assembly of Upper Canada, was born in New Jersey, on August 5, 1776. He settled in Upper Canada in 1790, and in 1810 he was elected a member of the Legislative Assembly of Upper Canada for the West riding of York. He sat in the Assembly from 1810 to 1834; and he was the author of the Common School Act of the province. From 1824 to 1828 he was the speaker of the Assembly. In 1839 he was appointed to the Legislative Council of the province; but he was not included in the Legislative Council of united Canada in 1841. He died at his home in Ontario (now Winona), on May 26, 1860. His portrait hangs in the Toronto Public Library.

Wilmer, a mining town in the Kootenay district of British Columbia, on the west side of the Columbia river, at the north end of Windermere lake, and on the Canadian Pacific Railway, 80 miles south of Golden. Pop. (1934) 300.

Wilmot, Lemuel Allan (1809-1878), politician, judge, and lieutenant-governor of New Brunswick, was born in the county of Sunbury, New Brunswick, on January 31, 1809, the son of William Wilmot and Hannah, daughter of the Hon. William Bliss. He was educated at the College of New Brunswick, Fredericton; and in 1832 he was called to the bar of New Brunswick. In 1836 he was elected to represent York county as a Reformer in the House of Assembly of New Brunswick; and he sat in the House continuously until 1851. In 1843 he was appointed a member of the Executive Council of the province; but he resigned in 1845, with his colleagues, in protest against the action of Sir William Colebrooke (q.v.) in making appointments without reference to the Council. In 1847, however, he became attorney-general in the first "responsible government" established in New Brunswick, and he was the virtual head of the administration. He held office until 1851; and then he resigned to accept an appointment as puisne judge of the Supreme Court of New Brunswick. He sat on the bench until 1868, when he was appointed lieutenant-governor of New Brunswick His period of office terminated in 1873; and he died at Fredericton, New Brunswick, on May 20, 1878 He was twice married, (1) in 1832 to Jane (d. 1833), daughter of James Balloch, of Saint John, New Brunswick, and (2) in 1834 to Elizabeth, daughter of the Hon. William Black (q.v.). See J. Hannay, *Lemuel Allan Wilmot* (Toronto, 1907); and Rev. J. Lathern, *The Hon. Judge Wilmot, a biographical sketch* (Toronto, 1881).

Wilmot, Montague (d. 1766), governor of Nova Scotia (1764-6), was a British army officer who came to Nova Scotia about 1754. In 1755 he was appointed a member of the Executive Council of Nova Scotia; in 1763, lieutenant-governor of the province; and in 1764, governor He died on May 23, 1766.

Wilmot, Robert Duncan (1809-1891), lieutenant-governor of New Brunswick (1880-85), was born in Fredericton, New Brunswick, on October 16, 1809, the son of John M. Wilmot, and a cousin of the Hon. Lemuel Allan Wilmot (q.v.). He was educated at Saint John, New Brunswick, and entered the shipping and milling business. For a number of years he lived in Liverpool England; but in 1840 he returned to New Brunswick, and in 1846 he was elected a member of the Legislative Assembly of the province for Saint John. He continued to sit in the legislature for this constituency until 1861; and from 1851 to 1854 he was a member of the Executive Council with the portfolio of surveyor-general, and from 1856 to 1857 with the portfolio of provincial secretary. He opposed Confederation; and in 1865 he became a member of the anti-confederationist government formed by Albert J. Smith (q.v.), and was elected to the Assembly for St. John county. In 1866, however, he deserted the anti-confederationists, was elected as a confederationist, and became a minister without portfolio in the Mitchell administration. He was a delegate to the London conference of 1866; and in 1867 he was called to the Senate of Canada. In 1878 he became a minister without portfolio in the government of Sir John Macdonald (q.v.), and was appointed speaker of the Senate. In 1880 he resigned from the Senate to accept appointment as lieutenant-governor of New Brunswick; and this post he occupied until 1885. He died at Orimocto, New Brunswick, on February 11, 1891.

Wilmot, Samuel (1822-1899), pisciculturist, was born at Belmont farm, Clarke township, West Durham, Upper Canada, on August 22, 1822, the youngest son of Major Samuel Street Wilmot. He was educated at Upper Canada College, and devoted his life to agriculture and pisciculture. He was a pioneer in the artificial propagation of fish: at the beginning of his operations he had in his pond only three grilse and eight grown salmon. From these he took 20,000 eggs, and in the following year he turned out 15,000 young salmon. He became superintendent of fish culture for Canada under the Dominion government; and he supervised the establishment of fish-breeding establishments from the Atlantic to the Pacific. He died on May 17, 1899. In 1872 he married Helen Matilda, daughter of Charles Clark, of Cobourg, Ontario; and by her he had four sons and three daughters.

Wilson, Sir Adam (1814-1891), judge, was born in Edinburgh, Scotland, on September 22, 1814. He came to Canada in 1830, and for a few years was in business in Halton county, Upper Canada. In 1834, however, he entered the law office of Robert Baldwin (q.v.), and in 1839 he was called to the bar of Upper Canada (Q.C., 1850). From 1840 to 1849 he was in partnership with Robert Baldwin. In 1859 he was elected mayor of Toronto, being the first mayor elected by direct popular vote; and the same year he became the representative of North York in the Legislative Assembly. From 1862 to 1863 he was solicitor-general in the S. Macdonald-Sicotte administration; but in 1863 he was raised to the bench as a judge of the court of Queen's Bench for Upper Canada. In 1878 he became chief justice of the court of Common Pleas, and in 1884 of the court of King's Bench, in Ontario. He retired from the bench in 1887, and he died at Toronto on December 28, 1891. He married a daughter of Thomas Dalton, proprietor of the *Patriot*, Toronto; and he was created a knight bachelor in 1887. He was the author of *A sketch of the office of constable* (Toronto, 1859).

Wilson, Charles (1808-1877), senator of Canada, was born at Coteau du Lac, Lower Canada, in April, 1808, the son of Alexander Wilson. He was for many years head of a hardware firm in Montreal, and was mayor of Montreal by acclamation from 1851 to 1853. In 1852 he was appointed a member of the Legislative Council of united Canada; and in 1867 he was called to the Senate of Canada by royal proclamation. He died in Montreal early in May, 1877.

Wilson, Sir Daniel (1816-1892), president of University College, Toronto (1880-92), was born in Edinburgh, Scotland, on January 5, 1816, the second son of Archibald Wilson. He was educated at the Edinburgh high school and at Edinburgh University (B.A., 1837). He became interested in Scottish archaeology, and published *Memorials of Edinburgh* (2 vols., Edinburgh, 1848), and *The archaeology and prehistoric annals of Scotland* (2 vols., Edinburgh, 1851). In 1853 he received the appointment of professor of history and English literature in University College, Toronto, and this chair he occupied until his death. In 1880 he was appointed president of University College, and, on its reorganization in 1887, president of the University of Toronto. He died at Toronto on August 6, 1892. He was created a knight bachelor in 1888; and in 1885 he was elected president of the Royal Society of Canada, of which he was a charter member. After coming to Canada he published, in addition to many papers in learned journals, *Prehistoric man* (Cambridge, 1862), *Chatterton* (London, 1869), *Caliban* (London, 1872), *Spring wild flowers: A collection of poems* (London, 1875), *Reminiscences of old Edinburgh* (2 vols., Edinburgh, 1878), *William Nelson, a memoir* (Edinburgh, 1889), *The right hand: Left-handedness* (London, 1891), and *The lost Atlantis and other ethnographic studies* (Edinburgh, 1892).

See H. H. Langton, *Sir Daniel Wilson* (Toronto, 1929); W. Kingsford, *In memoriam—Sir D. Wilson* (Trans. Roy. Soc. Can., 1893); and *Review of historical publications relating to Canada*, vol. v (Toronto, 1901), with bibliography.

Wilson, Jean (1910-1933), skater, was born in 1910, and was the undefeated holder of the title of champion of the North American speed-skating contests at five distances, when she died at Toronto, Ontario, on September 3, 1933.

Wilson, John (1809-1869), judge, was born at Paisley, Scotland, in November, 1809, the eldest son of Ebenezer Wilson. He came to Upper Canada with his parents about 1823, and in 1835 was called to the bar of Upper Canada (Q.C., 1856). He practised law in London, Upper Canada; and in 1847, and again in 1854, he was elected to represent London in the Legislative Assembly. In 1863 he was elected for the St. Clair division to the Legislative Council; but he did not take his seat, as he was shortly afterwards appointed a judge of the court of Common Pleas for Upper Canada. He died, in office, on June 3, 1869. He married a sister of Judge Hughes of St. Thomas, Upper Canada. See D. B. Read, *Lives of the judges* (Toronto, 1888).

Wilson, Robert (1833-1912), clergyman and author, was born at Fort George, Scotland, on February 18, 1833. He was educated at Prince of Wales College, Charlottetown, Prince Edward Island, and at Chicago University (Ph.D., 1887). He was ordained a minister of the Methodist Church in 1854; and after serving in many pastorates in the Maritime provinces, he retired from the pastorate in 1905. He died at Saint John, New Brunswick, on June 24, 1912. He wrote under the *nom-de-plume* of "Mark Mapleton"; and he was the author of *Methodism in the Maritime provinces* (Halifax, 1893), as well as of two novels, *Tried but true* (Saint John, 1874) and *Never give up* (Saint John, 1878).

Wilson, mount, is in Alberta, at the head of the Howse river in the Rocky mountains. It is in lat. 52° 01', long. 116° 46', and has an altitude of

11,000 feet. It was named after Tom Wilson, a guide at Banff.

Wilson range, a range of mountains in Alberta, Canada, and Montana, United States. It was named after Lieut. C. W. Wilson, R.E., secretary of the British Boundary Commission, Pacific to the Rockies, 1858-62.

Wilson's Beach, a fishing village in New Brunswick, at the northern end of Campobello island, in Passamaquoddy bay. It has a government breakwater, with a berthing length of 300 feet. Pop. (1934), 700.

Wiman, Erastus (1834-1904), author and capitalist, was born at Churchville, Peel county, Upper Canada, on April 21, 1834. He was educated in Toronto, and became in 1854 a journalist on the staff of the Toronto *Globe*. In 1860 he joined the staff of R. G. Dunn and Co.'s mercantile agency; in 1866 he was transferred to the head office of the company in New York; and later he became its general manager. In 1881 he was elected president of the Great North Western Telegraph Company of Canada; and in 1885 he became the first president of the Canadian Club in New York. He acquired a wide notoriety as the advocate of commercial union between Canada and the United States, and may be regarded as the father of the "unrestricted reciprocity" movement of the eighties. In 1897 he became a citizen of the United States; and he died at New York on February 9, 1904. Besides a number of pamphlets on commercial union, he wrote *Chances of success: Episodes and observations in the life of a busy man* (New York, 1893). See E. Myers, *A Canadian in New York* (Can. mag., 1893), with portrait.

Winchester, a village in Dundas county, Ontario, on the Canadian Pacific Railway, 93 miles west of Montreal. It is in a farming and dairying district; and has a foundry, woollen mills, saw mills, and a furniture factory. It has a

high school and a weekly newspaper (*Press*). Pop. (1931), 1,027.

Windermere, a village in the Kootenay district of British Columbia, on the west shore of lake Windermere, 3 miles from Athalmer, the nearest railway station, and 84 miles south of Golden. Pop. (1934), 100. There is also a summer resort of this name in the Muskoka district of Ontario, on lake Rosseau.

Windermere, lake, in the Kootenay district of British Columbia, is an expansion of the Columbia river, near its headwaters, and has a length of 9 miles and an average width of about one mile. It was named after Windermere, in England, by G. M. Sproat (q.v.), when, with A. S. Farwell, he explored the Columbia valley in 1883 for the government of British Columbia.

Windflower. See **Anemone, Wood.**

Windhorst, a village in the Qu'-Appelle district of Saskatchewan, on the Canadian Pacific Railway, 130 miles south-east of Regina. It has a weekly newspaper (*Independent*). Pop. (1931), 207.

Windigo, a mythical tribe of cannibals said by the Chippewa and Ottawa Indians to inhabit an island in Hudson bay. The word means "cannibal". Some of the Chippewa on the north shore of lake Superior were also said to practice cannibalism, and the name was applied to them. By an extension, it came to mean, in the mythology of the Algonkian tribes, an evil spirit or a devil.

Windigo river, in Quebec, is a tributary of the St. Maurice river, and flows into it about 4 miles above the Grand Détour. It has a length of 65 miles.

Windle, Sir Bertram Coghill Alan (1858-1929), anthropologist, was born at Mayfield, Staffordshire, England, on May 8, 1858. He was educated at Trinity College, Dublin (M.A., 1878; M.D., 1883); and after serving on the staff of University College, Cork, and of Birmingham University, he was appointed in 1905 president of Queen's College, Cork. He retired from this position in 1919; and became professor of anthropology in St. Michael's College, Toronto. Later he was appointed special lecturer in ethnology in the University of Toronto. He died in Toronto on February 14, 1929. He was created a knight bachelor in 1912. He was the author of a large number of books and papers on anatomy, anthropology, archaeology, and religious history. Some of his lectures at the University of Toronto were published under the title *The Romans in Britain* (London, 1923). See Monica Taylor, *Sir Bertram Windle: A memoir* (London, 1932).

Windmill, Battle of the, an engagement which took place on November 13-16, at Windmill point, near Prescott, Upper Canada, between a force of American filibusters under Miles von Shoultz (q.v.) and the Canadian militia. Von Shoultz and his men were forced to surrender unconditionally.

Windsor, a city in Essex county, Ontario, on the south-east shore of the Detroit river, opposite the city of Detroit, Michigan. It is on the direct water-route of the Great lakes and the Atlantic seaboard, is served by the Canadian Pacific, the Canadian National, the Michigan Central, the Wabash, and the Père Marquette Railways, and is 230 miles south-west of Toronto. Connection with Detroit is made by ferries, by two tunnels, and by a suspension bridge. The first name of the settlement was South Side. This was given in 1745-53 to describe the location of the farms granted the early French settlers. In subsequent years the place was known at three different periods by the names The Ferry, Richmond, and South Detroit, until in 1836 it was named Windsor, after Windsor, in England. The city is an important industrial centre, with automobile and accessory factories, chemical works, salt-works, and a cereal plant. There are large deposits of rock salt in the vicinity. Windsor is a fine residential city, with a number of churches and schools, a collegiate institute, and St. Mary's Academy. There is a daily newspaper (*Windsor Daily Star*). The city was incorporated in 1892; and in 1935 the municipalities known as the "Border Cities" (East Windsor, Sandwich, and Walkerville) were united with the city of Windsor. Pop. (1935) about 100,000. See George F. Macdonald, *How Windsor got its name* (Essex Hist. Soc., vol. iii, Windsor, 1921). See also **East Windsor, Sandwich,** and **Walkerville.**

Windsor, a seaport town in Hants county, Nova Scotia, on the Avon river, 8 miles from its mouth on the basin of Minas, and on the Dominion Atlantic (Canadian Pacific) Railway, 45 miles from Halifax. It is named after the townships in which it is situated, and which was created in 1764. Its prosperity is due to a variety of industries carried on in the vicinity, such as farming, fruit-growing, lumbering, fishing, mining (especially of gypsum), and the manufacture of underwear, suspenders, furniture, plaster, fertilizer, and orchard sprays. It has a collegiate school for boys, a church school for girls, a county academy, and two weekly newspapers (*Hants Journal* and *Tribune*). From 1788 to 1923 it was the site of King's College, Nova Scotia, the oldest university in the British Dominions, which is now located in Halifax and affiliated with Dalhousie University; and it was the home of Judge Haliburton (q.v.), the author of *Sam Slick the clockmaker*. Pop. (1931), 3,032.

Windsor, an incorporated town in Richmond county, Quebec, on the St. Francis river, and on the Canadian National and Canadian Pacific Railways, 10 miles south of Richmond, and 14 miles north of Sherbrooke. It was first settled about 1803, when saw and grist mills were established here; and it was until recently known as Windsor Mills. It is named after the township

WINDSOR, ONTARIO

in which it is situated, which derived its name from Windsor, in Berkshire, England; and it was incorporated as a town in 1899. It is now the site of an important pulp-and-paper mill, run by power obtained from a hydro-electric plant on the St. Francis river; and general farming and dairying are carried on in the neighbourhood. Pop. (1931), 3,294.

Windsor and Annapolis Railway, a line of railway in Nova Scotia, opened for traffic in 1869, between Windsor and Annapolis, and taken over by the Dominion Atlantic Railway in 1895.

Windsor Mills. See **Windsor** (Quebec).

Wine Harbor, a village in Guysborough county, Nova Scotia, near the mouth of St. Mary's river, 50 miles from Antigonish, the nearest railway station. It is said to have received its name from the fact of a vessel having been wrecked there with a carge of wine. Pop. (1934), 100.

Wingfield, Alexander Hamilton (1828-1896), poet, was born in Blantyre, Lanarkshire, Scotland, on August 1, 1828. He emigrated to the United States about 1847, and about 1850 settled in Hamilton, Ontario. For many years he was a mechanic in the shops of the Great Western Railway; and in his later years he was a landing waiter in the Customs department. He died in Hamilton in 1896. He published *Poems and songs, in Scotch and English* (Hamilton, Ontario, 1873).

Wingham, a village in Huron county, Ontario, on the Maitland river, and on the Canadian National and Canadian Pacific Railway, 31 miles north-east of Goderich. Its chief industries are a stove foundry, saw and flour mills, door and furniture factories, a glove factory, and tanneries. It has a high school, a public library, a hospital, and a weekly newspaper (*Advance-Times*). Pop. (1931), 1,959.

Winisk river, in the Patricia district, Ontario, flows north-west from a series of lakes including Winisk lake, and empties into Hudson bay between the 85th and 86th meridians of west longitude. The name is an Indian word meaning "woodchuck". The river is 295 miles in length, and drains an area of 24,100 square miles.

Winkler, a village in Lisgar county, Manitoba, on the Estevan branch of the Canadian Pacific Railway, 74 miles west of Winnipeg. It is in a rich agricultural district. Pop. (1934), 800.

Winlaw, a village in the Kootenay district of British Columbia, on the Nelson-Slocan branch of the Canadian Pacific Railway, 13 miles south of Slocan. Pop. (1931), 258.

Winnipeg, the capital and largest city of Manitoba, is situated at the confluence of the Red and Assiniboine rivers, 60 miles north of the boundary line between Canada and the United States, 1,425 miles west of Montreal, and is almost midway between the Atlantic and Pacific oceans. It is the western headquarters of the Canadian Pacific and Canadian National Railways, and has direct communication with the United States by three American railways. The first settlement was made here by La Vérendrye (q.v.) in 1738, when he erected Fort Rouge, but the place was abandoned for many years. The North West Company built Fort Gibraltar in 1805, and a few years later the Hudson's Bay Company erected Fort Douglas in close proximity. There was bitter rivalry between these two companies for the control of trade in the West. In 1812 the Earl of Selkirk (q.v.) brought out some colonists from his native Scotland and settled them on and around the present site of the city. More settlers followed until a little colony was formed. The bitterness between the fur-trading companies resulted in warfare and bloodshed; but, in 1821, the two companies, after settling their grievances, were merged under the name of the Hudson's Bay Company. In the following year Fort Gibraltar was renamed Fort Garry, and it became a busy trading post. In 1835 it was rebuilt; and a colony of settlers grew up outside the walls of the fort, which was given the name of Winnipeg (Cree, *Win*, murky; *nipiy*, water). In 1870 Manitoba was admitted as a province into the Dominion, and the Hudson's Bay Company transferred the territory to the Canadian government. Winnipeg was incorporated as a city in 1873. A boom accompanied the arrival of the Canadian Pacific Railway in 1881, and when the railway was completed in 1885, Winnipeg became a great distributing centre. In recent years the remarkable railway facilities have made the city the wholesale and manufacturing point for all the western provinces, and, because also of its geographical position, the greatest wheat market on the American continent.

The city is attractively planned, with wide tree-lined streets, several parks, and magnificent buildings. The prominent public buildings are the legislative buildings and provincial offices, the law courts, the city hall, and the union station. The educational establishments include the University of Manitoba, an agricultural college, collegiate institutes, provincial normal schools, and public schools. The city has numerous churches; several hospitals, including a military hospital for disabled veterans; and a large military barracks. Winnipeg has made full use of the extensive water-power resources near at hand. The cheap and abundant electric power has brought rapid industrial development. The most important products are flour, meat-packing, iron and steel implements, paper boxes, confectionery, gypsum, and bricks. Two large railway yards and the assembling plant of a well-known motor company employ many workers. The development of the mining territory of Manitoba has aided Winnipeg by the distribution of mining machinery and goods. The city is a busy airport in commercial aviation, and it is the base for the Dominion government aviation activities for western Canada. The *Free Press* is the most important of the several newspapers published, and it has both morning and evening editions. Pop. (1931), 218,785. See T. B. Robertson, *Winnipeg, the prairie capital* (Can. Geog. Journal, 1933).

Winnipeg Beach, a village and summer resort on lake Winnipeg, and on a branch of the Canadian Pacific Railway, 47 miles north-east of Winnipeg.

Winnipeg House. See **Fort Alexander.**

Winnipeg lake, in Manitoba in lat. 50° and 54° N. and long. 96° and 99° W. The name is from the Indian word meaning "nasty water lake or sea or ocean lake", as its waters are very muddy. In the Jesuit missionary report for 1640 appears a reference to "Ounipigon" or "dirty people", so called because the word "ouinipeg", the name of the unknown sea from the shores of which they came, meant "dirty water". It was discovered in 1732-3 by Jean Baptiste de la Vérendrye, the son of the great French explorer, Pierre de la Vérendrye (q.v.). Into the lake from the east flow Berens river and the large and beautiful Winnipeg river; from the south, the Red river; and, among numerous tributaries from the west, the Dauphin or Little Saskatchewan river and the Great Saskatchewan river. The lake discharges northward, by the Nelson river into Hudson bay. It is irregular in shape and its shores are low. It is 240 miles long, 55 miles wide, and has an area of 9,398 square miles.

Winnipegosis lake, in Manitoba, about 50 miles west of lake Winnipeg. The name means "little Winnipeg". It was probably discovered by Pierre de la Vérendrye (q.v.) before 1741. It is a magnificent sheet of water and navigable for vessels drawing 10 feet. It is 125

WINNIPEG, MANITOBA

miles long, and has an average breadth of 25 miles and an area of 2,086 square miles.

Winnipeg river, in Ontario and Manitoba, drains the lake of the Woods, and flows in a north-westerly direction into the south-east arm of lake Winnipeg. To the head of its ultimate source, the Firesteel river, not far from the western shore of lake Superior, the Winnipeg is 475 miles in length, and drains an area of 44,000 square miles. For a distance of 160 miles, the river has so many rapids, falls, and cascades that it is navigable only for canoes and small boats. Its numerous rapids are being harnessed for the development of water-power. Its principal tributary is the English river, which enters from the east near the Manitoba-Ontario boundary, after a course of 330 miles. The Winnipeg was discovered about 1733 by the eldest son of La Vérendrye (q.v.) and La Jemeraye. Fort Maurepas was built near its mouth by La Vérendrye and near the same site the North West Company established a post. The Winnipeg was for many years the thoroughfare, for explorers and fur-traders, from lake Superior to the West.

Winona, a village in Wentworth county, Ontario, on lake Ontario, and on the Canadian National Railway, 10 miles east of Hamilton. It is in a prosperous fruit-growing district. It was originally known as Ontario. Pop. (1934), 200.

Winslow, Edward (1746-1815), loyalist, was born in Massachusetts about 1746, the son of Edward Winslow, and a great-great-grandson of that Edward Winslow who was governor of Plymouth Colony (1633-44). He was educated at Harvard College (B.A., 1765). During the American Revolution he was muster-master-general of the British forces in North America; and in 1783 he accompanied the loyalist refugees to Halifax, Nova Scotia. For two years he was secretary to the commander-in-chief in

North America; and in 1784 he was appointed a member of the Executive Council of New Brunswick, with the office of surrogate general. In 1806 he was appointed a judge of the Supreme Court of New Brunswick. In 1808, as senior member of the Council, he became president and commander-in-chief of New Brunswick for a few months. He died in Fredericton, New Brunswick, on May 13, 1815. See C. W. Rife, *Edward Winslow* (Canadian Historical Association Report, 1928); W. O. Raymond, *The Winslow papers* (Saint John, New Brunswick, 1901); J. W. Lawrence, *The judges of New Brunswick* (Saint John, New Brunswick, 1907).

Winslow, Joshua (1727-1801), loyalist, was born in Boston, Massachusetts, on January 23, 1727, the son of John Winslow. He served with distinction at the capture of Louisbourg in 1745, and he was commissary-general with the expedition to Nova Scotia in 1755. At the beginning of the American Revolution he removed to Halifax, and became paymaster-general of the British forces in North America. After the Revolution he settled in Quebec; and here he died in 1801. In 1759 he married his cousin, Anna Green (d. 1816), and by her he had one daughter. See Alice M. Earle (ed.), *Diary of Anna Green Winslow* (Boston and New York, 1894).

Winter Cress. See **Cress.**

Wintergreen. See **Shin-leaf.**

Wintergreen, Aromatic (*Gaultheria procumbens* L., *Ericaceae*). This plant, with its slender creeping stem bearing upright branches and alternate, oval, shining evergreen leaves, is a common feature of the northern woods of Canada. The flowers, in July-August, are mostly single, white, nodding, in the axils of the leaves. The calyx is 5-lobed; the corolla urn-shaped, 5-toothed; the stamens 10; pistil 1. The fruit is a globular red berry, and edible. It grows in cool woods, chiefly under evergreens, from Newfoundland to Manitoba. This

21

is the source of the oil of wintergreen, so widely used in liniments. The Indians first discovered its use as a medicinal herb.

Wishart, William Thomas (d. 1853), clergyman and author, was a native of Scotland, and was ordained a minister of the Church of Scotland. He came to Canada, and was stationed first at Shelburne, Nova Scotia, and then at Saint John, New Brunswick. He died at Saint John in 1853. He was the author of *The decalogue the best system of ethics* (Halifax, Nova Scotia, 1842), *Extracts of lectures on political economy* (Saint John, New Brunswick, 1845), *A series of outlines or theological essays on various subjects connected with Christian doctrine and practice* (Saint John, New Brunswick, 1847), and *Six disquisitions on doctrinal and practical theology* (Saint John, New Brunswick, 1853).

Witch Hazel (*Hamamelis virginiana* L., *Hamamelidaceae*), a shrub or small tree with scurfy twigs. The leaves are alternate, short-petioled, broadly ovate, usually blunt at the apex, and hairy when young. The flowers are borne in nearly sessile, axillary clusters, are bright yellow in colour, and appear late in the season when the leaves are falling. The fruit is a woody capsule which does not mature till the following season, and when ripe bursts elastically shooting the seeds to great distances. It grows in low woods from Nova Scotia to Ontario. The bark of this plant is used in many medicinal products. Its value as a medicine was first discovered by the Indians. The wood is not used commercially.

Withrow, William Henry (1839-1908), clergyman, author, and journalist, was born in Toronto, Upper Canada on August 6, 1839, the son of James Withrow and Ellen Sanderson. He was educated at the Toronto Academy, at Victoria College, Cobourg, and at the University of Toronto (B.A., 1863; M.A., 1864). In 1866 he was admitted

to the ministry of the Methodist Church, and in 1874 he was appointed editor of the *Canadian Methodist Magazine*—a position which he continued to occupy for more than a quarter of a century. He was a voluminous writer, and published many books of an historical or religious nature: *Worthies of early Methodism* (Toronto, 1878); *The romance of missions* (Toronto, 1879); *The history of Canada* (Toronto, 1880); *Men worth knowing, or heroes of Christian chivalry* (Toronto, 1881); *Missionary heroes* (Toronto, 1883); *Our own country* (Toronto, 1889); and *The native races of North America* (Toronto, 1893). His most important work was *The catacombs of Rome* (New York, 1874). He published also several works of fiction: *The King's messenger, or Lawrence Temple's probation* (Toronto, 1879); *Valeria, the martyr of the catacombs* (Toronto, 1880); *Neville Trueman, the pioneer preacher* (Toronto, 1880); *Life in a parsonage* (Toronto, 1882); and *Barbara Heck* (Toronto, 1895). In 1880 he was made a D.D. of Victoria University; and in 1884 he was elected a member of the Royal Society of Canada. He died in Toronto on November 12, 1908. In 1864 he married Anne, daughter of John Smith, of Simcoe, Ontario.

Woburn, a village in Frontenac county, Quebec, on the Arnold river, 18 miles from Megantic, the nearest railway station. Pop. (1934), 700.

Wolf. Canadian wolves fall into two groups, a group of large wolves (subgenus *Canis*), such as the timber wolf, and a group of small wolves (subgenus *Thos*), represented by the coyotes.

The large wolves found in widely separated areas have been given different names, as the eastern timber wolf, the gray wolf of the great plains, the northern gray wolf of the north-west territory, and the tundra wolf of the barren grounds. However, so closely related are all these large wolves that no marked differences exist between the various forms.

Wolves vary widely in colour. In the same area animals have been trapped ranging in colour from almost white, through varying gray shades, to almost black. The fur is too coarse to be valuable. The destruction of game animals by wolves for food has resulted in bounties being placed on these animals through the insistence of sportsmen who wish to kill the game animals themselves. These large wolves seldom cause much loss by killing domestic animals except in ranching districts, because of their dislike of man's presence and their habit of living in areas remote from settlements.

The coyotes or brush wolves, as they are sometimes called, have also received many names, but as in the case of the large wolves, marked differences between the forms do not exist. In colour the coyote has a tendency to a reddish tint and the fur is finer; the animal itself is slimmer and has a shorter tail. Coyotes appear to have no prejudice regarding the presence of man adapting themselves readily to living close to settlements, and consequently causing a good deal of loss through the destruction of domestic stock. These smaller wolves are gradually extending their range to the north and east, and are now to be found from eastern Ontario to the Pacific coast and north into the Yukon.

Thrilling tales of wolf-packs chasing and killing trappers and other persons may be dismissed as mythical. Wolves have devoured individuals who have succumbed for one reason or another, and perhaps would attack an incapacitated person if driven by hunger, but no authenticated case is known of a person being attacked and killed by wolves in Canada.

The dens are placed in caves, windfalls, or burrows. The pups may number from three to a dozen, and both parents take part in caring for the young. The young wolves remain with the parents until fully grown, and the wolf-packs are usually composed of a single family, though a number of families sometimes unite to form a larger pack.

Wolfe, James (1727-1759), soldier, was born at Westerham, Kent, England, on January 2, 1727, the son of Colonel Edward Wolfe. He was educated at Westerham and at Greenwich; and in 1741 he obtained a commission as second lieutenant in his father's regiment of Marines. In 1742 he was transferred to the 12th Foot; and during the next fifteen years he saw service in the Netherlands, in Germany, and in Scotland. He was present at Dettingen in 1743, and at Culloden in 1745. Promoted to be lieutenant-colonel in 1750, and colonel in 1757, he was appointed in 1758 a brigadier-general in the expedition against Louisbourg; and the capture of Louisbourg was mainly due to his dash and resourcefulness. William Pitt, disregarding the claims of senior officers, then appointed him to command the expedition against Quebec in 1759, with the rank of major-general, at the age of thirty-two years. He invested the citadel of Quebec during the summer of 1759, and on the night of September 12-13 he succeeded in placing his army on the Plains of Abraham, to the west of Quebec. The battle which followed, on the morning of September 13, resulted in the defeat of the French and the capture of Quebec. But during the battle Wolfe fell, mortally wounded, and died a few minutes later. He was not married.

See W. T. Waugh, *James Wolfe* (Montreal, 1928); F. W. Whitton, *Wolfe and North America;* B. Willson, *The life and letters of James Wolfe* (London, 1909); R. Wright, *The life of Major-general James Wolfe* (London, 1864); E. Salmon, *General Wolfe* (London, 1909); F. Parkman, *Montcalm and Wolfe* (2 vols., Boston, 1884); W. Wood, *The winning of Canada* (Toronto, 1914) and *The fight for Canada* (London, 1905); A. G. Doughty and G. W. Parmalee, *The siege of Quebec* (6 vols., Quebec, 1901);

Marquess of Sligo, *Some notes on the death of Wolfe* (Can. hist. review, 1922); A. G. Doughty (ed.), *A new account of the death of Wolfe* (Can. hist. review, 1923); J. C. Webster, *A study of the portraiture of James Wolfe* (Trans. Roy. Soc. Can., 1925) and *Wolfiana* (Shediac, New Brunswick, 1927); A. E. Wolfe-Aylward, *The pictorial life of Wolfe* (Plymouth, 1926).

Wolfe, a county in Quebec, bounded on the north-west by Arthabaska county, on the north-east by Megantic county, on the east by Frontenac county, on the south-east by Frontenac and Compton counties, and on the south-west by Richmond county. For electoral purposes it is joined to Richmond county. It is traversed by the Quebec Central Railway, and watered by the St. Francis and Nicolet rivers. Chief town, South Ham. Pop. (1931), 16,911.

Wolf-eel, a long slender relative of the wolf-fishes (q.v.), found off the Pacific coast of Canada and the United States. It sometimes reaches a length of eight feet.

Wolfe island is a large island at the entrance to the St. Lawrence river, at the north-east extremity of lake Ontario, in Frontenac county. It divides the St. Lawrence into two navigable branches, the south being the main one, and forming the boundary line between the United States and Canada. Wolfe island is the queen of the Thousand islands, its coast being very beautiful, and containing a number of picturesque bays and beaches, making it a popular summer resort. It is 21 miles long, and 7 miles at greatest width, and has about 30,600 acres of excellent land. There are evidences of Indian inhabitation. No more than 50 odd years ago, it was a thick forest, inhabited only by wild beasts, but since then extensive cultivation has taken place. There is a thriving village on it, called Wolfe Island village, and several churches, schools, etc. Fish abound in the surrounding waters. It was named by proclamation of Governor Simcoe in 1792, after General James Wolfe (q.v.), and the name appears on the Simcoe map of 1792. Pop. (1901), 1,796.

Wolfe's Cove, a recess on the north shore of the St. Lawrence river, about a mile west of Quebec, where Wolfe (q.v.) landed his army early on the morning of September 13, 1759, prior to the battle of the Plains of Abraham. The French had a post under Vergor (q.v.) at the top of the cliff overlooking the cove; but the garrison of this post was surprised and overwhelmed. The cove was known to the French as the Anse de Foulon.

Wolf-fishes, a group of large fish closely related to the blennies (q.v.), found in the north Atlantic and north Pacific. They are remarkable for their strong teeth, those in front being long and canine-like. They are large, powerful, voracious fishes, which reach a length of four to six feet.

Wolframite. See **Tungsten.**

Wolfville, a town in King's county, Nova Scotia, at the mouth of the Cornwallis river, on the basin of Minas, and on the Dominion Atlantic Railway, 18 miles north-west of Windsor. It was originally known as Mud Creek, but in 1830 the name was changed to Wolfville, in honour of the postmaster, who belonged to a well-known Loyalist family of the name of De Wolfe. It is in an agricultural and fruit-growing district, and has a creamery, a wood-working plant, and an evaporating plant for apples. It is the seat of Acadia University and Horton Academy, has a weekly newspaper (*Wolfville Acadian*), and is a summer resort. Pop. (1931), 1,818.

Wollaston lake, a large body of water in northern Saskatchewan, south-east of lake Athabaska. It has a length of 70 miles and a maximum width of 25 miles; and its waters flow into the systems of both the Mackenzie and the Churchill rivers. It was named by Franklin (q.v.) in 1821 after Dr. William Hyde Wollaston (1766-1828), a famous English chemist.

Wollaston land. See **Wollaston peninsula.**

Wollaston peninsula, the south-west portion of Victoria island, in the Franklin district of the North West Territories. It was named in 1821 by Franklin (q.v.) after Dr. William Hyde Wollaston (1766-1828), a famous English chemist. It was formerly known as Wollaston land; but the Geographic Board of Canada has ruled in favour of the name Wollaston peninsula.

Wolseley, Garnet Joseph, first Viscount Wolseley (1833-1913), soldier, was born at Golden Bridge House, county Dublin, Ireland, on June 4, 1833, the son of Major Garnet Joseph Wolseley, of the 25th Borderers. He entered the army as a second lieutenant in 1852, and saw service successively in India, in the Crimea, and in China. In 1861 he was sent to Canada as assistant quartermaster-general, and in 1865 became deputy quartermaster-general, with the rank of colonel. In 1870 he was chosen to command the force sent west to the Red river to quell the Riel insurrection; and for his services in this expedition he received the C.B. and the K.C.M.G. Later he commanded the Ashanti expedition of 1873-4, the Egyptian expedition of 1882, and the Nile expedition of 1885; and for his services in the last two expeditions he was created first a baron and then a viscount. In 1895 he succeeded the Duke of Cambridge as commander-in-chief of the British army, with the rank of field marshal; but he retired in 1899, and he died at Mentone, France, on March 25, 1913. He was the author of *The story of a soldier's life* (2 vols., London, 1903). See Sir F. Maurice and Sir George Arthur, *The life of Lord Wolseley* (London, 1924), and Sir George Arthur (ed.), *The letters of Lord and Lady Wolseley* (London, 1922).

Wolseley, a town in the Qu'Appelle district of Saskatchewan, on the Canadian Pacific Railway, 60 miles east of Regina. It is in an agricultural district, and has a high school, a convent, a public library, a provincial home for the infirm, and a weekly newspaper (*News*). Pop. (1931), 882.

Wolverine. This powerful long-haired member of the weasel family (*Mustelidae*) is often mistaken on sight for a small bear. It is the largest member of the weasels, and its sturdy low set body is in harmony with its formidable reputation. In colour, the wolverine is a dark brown, with a light patch above the dark muzzle, and broad yellowish white lateral bands from shoulder to rump.

The wolverine can climb and swim, but it is more at home on the ground. As to food, it will eat nearly anything it can catch or find, birds, animals, fish, berries, frogs. It is anathema to the trapper from its habit of destroying trapped animals, following a trap line for miles. The tales of its ferocity and astuteness are part truth and part myth, but that the wolverine has unusual strength and aggressiveness is shown by the fact that this thirty-five pound animal has been known to attack and kill deer and caribou and even moose.

The number of young in a litter is usually two or three, and they are born in early summer. The den is situated in some sheltered spot among rocks or down timber.

The wolverine is rare now in southern Canada, and probably has never been abundant anywhere. It may still be found in the northern forests and even in parts of the barren grounds. The fur is valuable, but it is as a destroyer of other fur that the trapper regards the wolverine rather than a potential source of income. See E. T. Seton, *Lives of game animals*, vol. ii.

Women's Canadian Historical Society of Ottawa, a society founded at Ottawa in 1898. Since 1901 it has published 10 volumes of *Transactions* and now issues an *Annual report*. The society has a museum at Ottawa, the Bytown Historical Museum, which also contains a valuable historical library.

Women's Rights. See **Female Suffrage.**

Women's Canadian Historical Society of Toronto, a society founded in 1895. It publishes almost every year a *Report and Transactions*, which contains also two or three articles on Canadian history.

Wongan. See **Wanigan.**

Wood, Andrew Trew (1826-1903), senator of Canada, was born at Mount Norris, Armagh, Ireland, the son of David Wood and Frances Bigham Trew. He was educated in Ireland, but came to Canada while still in his 'teens, and in 1848 entered the hardware business in Hamilton, Upper Canada. He acquired wealth, and in 1881 was a member of the Howland syndicate that offered to construct the Canadian Pacific Railway. He represented Hamilton in the Canadian House of Commons from 1874 to 1878, and again from 1896 to 1900. In 1901 he was appointed to the Canadian Senate; and he died at Hamilton on January 21, 1903. He was twice married, (1) in 1851 to Mary, daughter of William Freeman, and (2) in 1863 to Jennie, daughter of George H. White, Yorkville, Upper Canada.

Wood, Edmund Burke (1820-1882), chief justice of Manitoba (1874-82), was born near Fort Erie, Upper Canada, on February 13, 1820. He was educated at Overton College, Ohio (B.A., 1848), and was called to the bar of Upper Canada in 1848 (Q.C., 1872). From 1863 to 1867 he represented West Brant in the Legislative Assembly of Canada, and from 1867 to 1872 he represented the same constituency in both the Canadian House of Commons and the Legislative Assembly of Ontario. From 1867 to 1871 he was provincial treasurer of Ontario, in Sandfield Macdonald's "Patent Combination", and he incurred much obloquy on account of his desertion of Sandfield Macdonald (q.v.) in the crisis which led to the defeat of the government in 1871. In 1873 he re-entered the House of Commons as member for West Durham; but in 1874 he was appointed chief justice of Manitoba, and he held this post until his death at Winnipeg, on October 7, 1882. In parliament he was known by the *soubriquet* of "Big Thunder".

Wood, Joanna E. (d. 1919), novelist, was born in Lanarkshire, Scotland, and came to Canada with her parents in early life. For many years she lived at Queenston Heights, Ontario; and she died in Detroit, Michigan, in 1919. She was the author of *The untempered wind* (Toronto, 1898), *Judith Moore* (Toronto, 1898), *A daughter of witches* (Toronto, 1900), and *Farden Ha'* (London, 1902).

Wood, John Fisher (1852-1899), controller of inland revenue and customs for Canada (1892-6), was born in Elizabethtown, Upper Canada, on October 12, 1852, the son of John Wood. He was called to the bar of Ontario in 1876 (Q.C., 1890), and practised law in Brockville. He represented Brockville in the Canadian House of Commons from 1882 to his death; in 1890-91 he was deputy speaker of the house; and from 1892 to 1896 he was a member of the government, first as controller of inland revenue, and then as controller of customs. In 1896 he was one of the "nest of traitors", so called, who deserted Sir Mackenzie Bowell (q.v.). He died on March 14, 1899. He was unmarried.

Wood, Josiah (1843-1927), lieutenant-governor of New Brunswick (1912-7), was born at Sackville, New Brunswick, on April 18, 1843, the son of Mariner Wood. He was educated at Mount Allison University (B.A., 1863;

M.A., 1866; D.C.L., 1891), and was called to the bar in 1866. Later, he abandoned law, and entered his father's ship-building business, to the control of which he succeeded on his father's death. From 1882 to 1895 he represented Westmorland in the Canadian House of Commons; and in 1895 he was appointed a member of the Canadian Senate. In 1912 he was made lieutenant-governor of New Brunswick, and he retired from office in 1917. In 1912 he was made an LL.D. of the University of New Brunswick. He was for a number of years treasurer of Mount Allison University; and in 1925 he founded in connection with this university the Josiah Wood Lectures. He died at Sackville, New Brunswick, on May 13, 1927.

Wood, Samuel Casey (1830-1913), provincial secretary, commissioner of agriculture, and provincial treasurer of Ontario (1873-85), was born at Bath, Upper Canada, in 1830, the son of Thomas Smith Wood. From 1871 to 1883 he represented South Victoria in the Ontario legislature; and from 1875 to 1883 he was a member of the Mowat government. In 1883 he retired from politics, and devoted himself to business. He died at Toronto on April 11, 1913. He married in 1854 Charlotte Maria Parkinson, of Mariposa, Upper Canada; and by her had several children.

Wood, Samuel Thomas (1860-1917), journalist, was born in Wollaston township, Hastings county, Ontario, on January 16, 1860, and he was educated in Belleville, Ontario. He joined the staff of the Toronto *Globe* in 1891, and became an editorial writer. A number of his nature studies, originally published as editorials, were published under the title, *Rambles of a Canadian naturalist* (Toronto, 1915); and he was also the author of *A primer of political economy* (Toronto, 1901) and *How we pay each other* (Toronto, 1917). He died at Toronto on November 6, 1917. See Sir J. Willison and others, *A tribute to*

S. T. Wood (Toronto, 1917, privately printed).

Wood Anemone. See **Anemone.**

Wood Betony. See **Betony.**

Woodbine. See **Honeysuckle.**

Woodbridge, a village in York county, Ontario, on the Canadian Pacific Railway, 15 miles north-west of Toronto. It is the centre of a good agricultural district, and an annual agricultural fair is held here. Pop. (1934), 300.

Wood-Carving. The tradition of the French renaissance in wood-carving was imported into Canada by Mgr de Laval (q.v.), and persisted in French Canada as a local growth a century and a half after its collapse in Europe. It is exemplified chiefly in the wood-carvings in churches and other public buildings erected during the French régime, but has continued down almost to the present day—as an illustration of a native art among the people of French Canada. See Emile Vaillancourt, *Une maîtrise d'art en Canada* (Montreal, 1920) and Marius Barbeau, *Two centuries of wood-carving in French Canada* (Trans. Roy. Soc. Can., 1933).

Woodchuck. See **Narmot.**

Woodcock (*Philohela minor*), a game bird belonging to one of the shore bird families, *Scolopacidae*, to which belong the snipe and sandpipers. The species is characterized by its relatively short legs, its heavy rounded body, long bill, and large eyes, which are set well back and up on the head. In colour it is rich russet brown, delicately patterned with darker tones. This species was one of the most highly prized members of its family as a game bird, but its numbers are greatly reduced. It now sparingly inhabits swampy thickets from Manitoba eastward to the Maritime provinces.

Woodfibre, a town in the New Westminster district of British Columbia, on the west shore of Howe sound, at the mouth of Mill creek, south-west of Squamish. It is the site of the British Columbia Pulp and Paper Mills, Limited. Pop. (1930), 400.

Woodington, a summer resort in the Muskoka district of Ontario, on lake Rosseau, at the mouth of the Joseph river, 8 miles from Footes Bay station on the Canadian National Railway.

Wood Lily. See **Lily, Wild Orange-red.**

Woodpecker, a name used in a general sense for any member of the family *Picidae*, a group which is characterized by its members possessing special adaptations for securing food and making homes in wood. The flicker (*Colaptes auratus*) is perhaps the best known of the Canadian species. The largest representative in Canada is the pileated woodpecker (*Ceophloeus pileatus*); it measures nearly one and one-half feet in length. Black and white are the usual combinations of colour in this family, although red is also found, especially in the form of a mark at the back of the head on male birds.

Woods, Robert Stuart (1819-1906), judge and historian, was born at Sandwich, Upper Canada, in 1819. He served as a volunteer during the rebellion of 1837, and was present at the cutting-out of the *Caroline* at Niagara Falls. In 1842 he was called to the bar of Upper Canada (Q.C., 1872), and in 1885 he was appointed a judge of the county of Kent. This position he retained until his death at Chatham, Ontario, on November 20, 1906. He was the author of *The burning of the Caroline and other reminiscences of 1837-8* (pamphlet, Chatham, Ontario, 1896) and *Harrison Hall and its associations* (Chatham, Ontario, 1896).

Woods, William Carson (1860-1902), author, was born in 1860, the son of Alexander Woods, a merchant in Quebec. He was educated at the Quebec High School and at Stanstead College; and he entered his father's business. He lived successively in Winnipeg, Toronto, and Quebec; and he died in July, 1902. He was the author of *The isle of the massacre* (Toronto, 1901).

Wood Sorrel (*Oxalis Acetosella* L., *Oxalidaceae*), low creeping herb with sour watery juice. It is developed from a slender, scaly rootstock, covered with brownish hairs. The leaves are all radical, and are shamrock-shaped, the leaflets drooping in the evening. The flower stalks are longer than the leaves, and bear single white flowers veined with red. It may be found in deep cool woods from Nova Scotia to Saskatchewan.

Woods, lake of the, is on the international boundary line between Ontario (Kenora and Rainy River districts), Manitoba, and the state of Minnesota. The name is probably a mistranslation of an Indian word meaning "the inland lake of the hills", in reference to the range of sand hills along the south shore. The lake was discovered in 1688 by Jacques de Noyon, and was visited in 1732 by the great explorer La Vérendrye (q.v.). It became part of the great fur-trading highway between eastern and western Canada, over which travelled voyageurs, coureurs de bois and, later, traders of the North West Company. In 1870 the expedition of Sir Garnet Wolseley (q.v.), on the way to quell the Red river rebellion, followed the same route. The northern portion of the lake has an excessively irregular coastline and is thickly studded with islands; the southern part is a broad sheet of shallow water, almost free of islands, with low, sandy, and marshy shores. The lake abounds in trout, black bass, pickerel, jacks, and maskinonge. Around its shores stand pine, spruce, balsam, poplar, and birch. The lake has long been the mecca of Manitoba summer vacationists, and has now become more accessible by the completion in 1932 of the Winnipeg-Kenora section of the Trans-Canada highway. The adjacent woods are an attraction to tourists in the autumn for the hunting of red deer and moose. See Earle C. Popham, *The Lake of the Woods*

(Canadian Geographical Journal, September, 1934).

Woodstock, a city in Oxford county, Ontario, on the Thames river and the Canadian National and Canadian Pacific Railways, 27 miles north-east of London. In 1832 the district was known as Blandford, the name of the township to the east of the present Woodstock. The virtual founder of Woodstock was Admiral Vansittart (q.v.), who in 1834 opened a tavern and a store in what was, with the exception of a few homesteads, a wilderness. The settlement was named after Woodstock, Oxfordshire, England. It rapidly became a town, and was incorporated as a city in 1901. There are a number of churches, five public schools, a Roman Catholic school, a collegiate institute, a commercial college, a public library, and armouries. The city was the seat of Woodstock College. It is the geographical centre of a rich and fertile agricultural district supplying cattle, hogs, cheese, butter, wool, hides, and grain. Important among the industries are machine shops, furniture factories, farm-implement works, a pipe-organ works, textile factories, and cereal factories. There is a daily newspaper (*Sentinel-Review*). Pop. (1931), 11,395. Consult W. E. Elliott, *The parish of Woodstock* (Ont. Hist. Soc., papers and records, 1934), for the story of the parish and its environment, and of some of its early inhabitants.

Woodstock, a town in Carleton county, New Brunswick, on the St. John river, and on the Canadian National and Canadian Pacific Railways, 60 miles north-west of Fredericton, and 135 miles north-west of Saint John. The parish of Woodstock in which it is situated was created in 1786. The origin of the name is disputed. It has been explained as descriptive of the "stock of wood" which impressed the early settlers; but it was more probably suggested by its proximity to the neighbouring parish of Northampton—Woodstock and Northampton being not far apart in England.

It is in a prosperous farming and fruit-growing district, with many apple and plum orchards in the vicinity; and it has cheap electrical power from the adjacent state of Maine. Its chief manufactures are potato machinery, furniture, flour, cheese, butter, lumber, and shingles; and it has an agricultural college, a high school, an armoury, a court house, two hospitals, and two weekly newspapers (*Carleton Sentinel* and *Press*). Pop. (1931), 3,259.

Woodstock College was a residential school, latterly for boys, founded in Woodstock, Ontario, in 1857 as the Canadian Literary Institute. Its founder and first principal was the Rev. Dr. Robert Alexander Fyfe (q.v.), a Baptist minister. In 1881 the Theological Department was moved to Toronto, where it was reorganized as the Toronto Baptist College (later McMaster University); and in 1883 the Canadian Literary Institute was re-named Woodstock College. A few years later the Ladies' Department was removed to Toronto, where it was reorganized as Moulton College; and Woodstock became a school for boys. It was one of the first schools in Canada to offer manual training. Because of financial difficulties, it closed its doors in 1926.

Woodsworth, James (d. 1917), clergyman and author, was born in Toronto, the son of Richard Woodsworth, a local preacher in the Methodist Church. He was ordained a minister of the Methodist Church in 1864, and in 1882 he was sent to the Portage la Prairie circuit in the west. He remained in the west for the rest of his life, and for many years he was superintendent of north-west missions for the Methodist Church. He retired from this post in 1915; and he died in Winnipeg, Manitoba, on January 26, 1917. He was the author of *Thirty years in the Canadian north-west* (Toronto, 1917).

Woodville, a village in Victoria county, Ontario, on a branch of the Beaver river, and on the Canadian

National Railway, 17 miles north-west of Lindsay. Pop. (1931), 427.

Wooler, a village in Northumberland county, Ontario, on Cold creek, 8 miles north-west of Trenton, the nearest railway station. Pop. (1934), 400.

Woolley, mount, is in Alberta, at the head of the Sunwapta river in the Rocky mountains. It is in lat. 52° 18', long. 117° 25', and has an altitude of 11,170 feet. It was named by J. Norman Collie, in 1898, after H. Woolley, a fellow climber.

Work, John (1792-1861), fur-trader, was born in the north of Ireland in 1792. He entered the service of the Hudson's Bay Company in 1814; and for eight years he served at York Factory and other posts on Hudson bay. In 1823 he was sent to the Pacific slope; and he spent the rest of his life in this region. In 1846 he was promoted to the rank of chief factor, and from 1857 to his death he was a member of the Executive and Legislative Councils of Vancouver Island. He died at Victoria, British Columbia, on December 23, 1861. He married Susette Legace, a Spokane half-breed; and by her he had five daughters and one son. See W. S. Lewis and P. C. Phillips (eds.), *The journal of John Work* (Cleveland, 1923). Work's papers are in the Provincial Library, Victoria, British Columbia.

Workman, George Coulson (1848-1936), clergyman and author, was born at Grafton, Upper Canada, on September 28, 1848. He was educated at Victoria University, Cobourg (B.A., 1875; M.A., 1878) and at Leipzig University (Ph.D., 1889). He was ordained a minister of the Methodist Church in 1878; and in 1882 he was appointed associate professor of Hebrew in Victoria University. He was subsequently professor of Old Testament exegesis and professor of oriental languages; but he retired from the staff of Victoria in 1891. From 1904 to 1908 he was professor of Old Testament exegesis in the Montreal

Wesleyan Theological College; but after this he devoted himself to private studies. He died at Toronto, Ontario, on April 22, 1936. He was the author of *The text of Jeremiah* (Edinburgh, 1889), *The Old Testament vindicated* (Toronto, 1897), *The Messianic prophecy vindicated* (Toronto, 1899), *How to study the Bible* (Toronto, 1902), *The servant of Jehovah* (London, 1907), *Atonement; or, Reconciliation with God* (New York, 1911), *Armageddon; or, The world movement* (Toronto, 1917), *Divine healing* (Toronto, 1924); *Jesus the man and Christ the spirit* (New York, 1928), and *Immortal life* (Toronto, 1934).

Workman, Joseph (1805-1894), physician, was born near Lisburne, county Antrim, Ireland, on May 26, 1805. He emigrated to Canada with his parents in 1829, and obtained his diploma as doctor of medicine from McGill College in 1835. For a number of years he abandoned the practice of medicine, and engaged in business in Toronto, Ontario, but he resumed the practice of medicine in Toronto in 1846, and for several years he was on the staff of Dr. Rolph's Toronto School of Medicine. In 1849-50 he was a member of the Royal Commission appointed to inquire into the affairs of King's College; and the report of the Commission was largely his work. In 1854 he was appointed superintendent of the Insane Asylum in Toronto; and he retained this position until 1875. He died at Toronto on April 15, 1894. His unpublished diary, covering the years 1867 to 1894, is in the University of Toronto Library.

World War. The World War of 1914-18 was an appalling event in the history of humanity. Even those who had foreseen and prepared for it for many years had no idea how tremendous a cataclysm was to shake the world, what enormous armies would be engaged, what stupendous supplies of ammunition would be expended, how many millions of men would die.

In the pages that follow special attention has been given to the part played by Canadian forces; their operations are therefore given perhaps disproportionate prominence. Yet it is only right to recognize that, during the last few months of war, the Canadian Corps, which was then at its highest efficiency, carried out a far more important task than has been generally attributed to it.

When we look for the causes of the war, we find ourselves in a considerable difficulty. Statesmen, soldiers, and historians have been debating these for over twenty years, and still disagree. As we study the matter, it seems that there were five sets of causes, all of which had their part in bringing about the struggle.

The first and most important set of causes is to be found in the general conduct of international relations since the days of Napoleon. To the European diplomat, war was always the main feature of the outlook, just as to-day he concerns himself mainly with economics, and his calculations were aimed at getting as much force as possible on his side.

The second set of causes lay in the commercial development of European states which took place towards the end of the nineteenth century, in personal greed of gain and national projects of aggrandizement.

The third set of causes came from the actions of a controlling, or at least very influential, class to which war was normal or even desirable, the class from which both in Germany and England most of the army officers were drawn, and which was mostly made up of their friends.

The fourth set of causes consists of the sprouting, in Europe particularly, of a new "nationalist" spirit, which had for years been overlaid by the detritus of the Holy Roman Empire and monarchic ideas in general.

Finally, and least important, came the actual events of 1914. In those days these were almost all that were thought of. We realize now that they were only the culmination of a long series of other events.

Let us look a little more closely into these five sets of causes.

We cannot take them in order, for each cause had its effect on, and was mingled with, every other cause, but we shall try to differentiate them as we proceed.

When Europe settled down after the Napoleonic wars, the four principal powers were England, France, Austria, and Russia; and world diplomacy concerned itself with balancing one against the other, so that none would become too strong, maintaining a sort of equilibrium, the "Balance of Power", resulting in a relationship which was called the "Concert of Europe". This was an antiquated style of manœuvering inherited by the diplomats from their predecessors of the seventeenth century, but it did not survive long in the new world which had arisen out of the ashes of the old Europe. "Nationalism," which few had learned to call by that name, now came into the picture.

England had acquired a true national feeling some time before; it had been in existence since the Middle Ages. France learned it during the Revolution. Germany was the next. For hundreds of years the docile subjects of their kings and princes or of anyone else who wished to hire them, the Germans had never thought of themselves as a nation. But Napoleon, when he reorganized Germany planted among the wreckage the seeds of a new idea. The Prussians, who were not originally German, but had become German, and the people of the older German states became linked by a feeling of common interest; and a German nationality began to emerge.

This new element clashed with another. Austria as the centre of the "Holy Roman Empire" had always been entitled to leadership among German states. That was one of her assets in the "Balance of Power". Prussia annexed the provinces of Schleswig and Holstein, which had been ruled by Denmark; Austria challenged her right to control them; and in the war that followed Austria was deposed from her hegemony. The other states now saw the "Balance of Power" completely upset. Here was a new nation which must be dealt with. France, ignoring the strength of that national feeling which she herself had taught, attacked the newcomer, declaring war over the first question that came to hand, was terribly defeated and lost two fine provinces, Alsace and Lorraine, to the victors. The King of Prussia, his hand strengthened by this conquest, declared himself Emperor of Germany, and thus established a militarist control of the newly "nationalized" country. From that time onward, so far as Germany was concerned, "militarism" and "nationalism" worked along parallel lines.

About the same time began the epoch of secret alliances arranged by the great Prussian chancellor, Bismarck, in the course of which the statesmen of Europe involved their countries in such a network of agreements that the end could not be predicted. We cannot go into their history at length; and a brief statement must suffice. The first series were as follows: (1) a treaty, which amounted to an alliance, between the Emperors of Russia, Germany, and Austria, and which lasted from 1872 to 1878, then disappeared, and was succeeded by (2) a general alliance between Austria and Germany (1879-1919); (3) a *secret* treaty by which Russia, Germany, and Austria agreed to remain neutral in case of any war involving any one of them, and Russia agreed to respect Austria's rights in the Balkans (1881-7); (4) a *secret* treaty between Russia and Germany, in which Russia's aims in the Balkans were virtually recognized (1887-90); (5) the Triple Alliance, between Germany, Austria, and Italy—a defensive alliance designed to protect Italy and Germany against France (1882-1915); and (6) the Rumanian treaty, by which Germany and Austria became bound to

protect Rumania against Russia. How this could be reconciled with (4) is not obvious, but as it was completely secret, it did not matter!

It cannot fairly be said that these alliances themselves were productive of war; for the most part they were aimed at security. Bismarck, the great German chancellor, who was mainly responsible for them, desired nothing more than a chance for Germany to grow. But the fatal characteristic was that they were all based on the theory that war is a normal method of dealing between civilized nations; they kept the idea of war constantly in the minds of statesmen, and they made preparation for war a duty, imposed on each country by its obligation toward others.

A new problem appeared about 1870, a complication between Great Britain and Russia. It affected the Near East and Central Asia. In Asia Russia's dominions were coming nearer and nearer to Britain's Indian Empire, and Britain watched every Russian move. In the Near East, largely as a result of British action, the Turkish Sultan, who controlled the straits between Europe and Asia, held them closed against Russia. An opposing project had been in the minds of the Russian emperors for generations. It was their constant aim to take and to control Constantinople. Between Russia and Constantinople lay a number of Christian provinces of the Turkish Empire, the peoples of some of which were largely Slavonic, and therefore regarded as brothers of the Russians, while the people of another, Rumania, regarded themselves as Latins.

In 1877 Russia declared war on Turkey, but England by the presence of a huge fleet had transformed the Mediterranean into an English lake and did not want Russia on that sea, so the English fleet prevented the Russians from occupying Constantinople and closed the Bosphorus. At the same time Austria, afraid of Russian influence, and Germany, already more or less bound to Austria, made their opposition to Russia evident. In the treaty which settled matters the Turkish provinces were transformed into the Balkan states, Russia claiming a kind of vague interest which was never recognized. The Austrian Empire, as a counter to the increase of Russian influence, occupied two Turkish provinces, Bosnia and Herzegovina, which had not been made into separate states. In spite of this Austria and Russia did not at once become hostile.

Meantime, the spirit of nationalism, which had built up the new Germany, was, in Austria, operating in another direction. The Austrian Empire was made up of several racial groups, each occupying a fairly well-defined territory. The German Austrians in the west exercised control over the whole—a control which the Magyars were beginning to share. The subject peoples were Czechs and Slovaks in the north, Magyars in the centre, Rumanians in the south-east, Slavs (Serbs, Croats, and Slovenes) in the south. These subject peoples were mostly discontented; although, so far as the Magyars were concerned, their discontent was mitigated by their increasing influence. The Rumanians wished to be united with their fellows in Rumania; while the Serbs, Croats, and Slovenes along the southern border were openly rebellious, and the removal of some of their privileges, granted when they were holding the border against the Turks, made them more so. To the south of them was the kingdom of Serbia, reconstituted by the Great Powers after years of subjection to Turkey, and the Serbs of that country began to dream of a Greater Serbia which should include all the neighbouring Slav peoples, including those living in the south of the Austrian Empire. Their dream spread across the border, and became a plan, and Austrian statesmen, disturbed already by internal

dissension, took the matter very seriously. A rebellion in the south, supported by Serbia, would give an opportunity to the other "subject peoples"; the composite army could not be depended upon, and the Empire might well fly apart.

Austrian nervousness increased as time went on, until the fear of a Greater Serbia movement became an obsession, and with a good deal of reason. It was all the worse because, by the end of the century, Russian opinion had turned openly in favour of the aims of the southern Slavs, and Russia was evidently inclined to back up sentiment by force.

The result of this situation was a growing heat which was finally to burst into flame and set all Europe alight.

As the nineteenth century approaches its close, we see another series of war causes—commercial and colonial expansion. Britain and France had been first in the field, and although long before Britain had virtually ejected France from North America and India, France had latterly not done badly in Africa. Portugal had managed to get hold of some territory there, but Britain and France had the lion's share, and the newcomer, Germany, saw that there was not much left for her to seize. Britain had hitherto been the great manufacturing nation of the world. Germany, almost at a single step, caught up with her, and from an agricultural country grew into an industrial country. In 1890 her machinery exports were less than 20 per cent. of those of Britain, and Britain's were almost 60 per cent. of the world trade. By 1910 Germany's machinery exports grew to over 80 per cent. of those of Britain and 25 per cent. of the world total. By 1900 Germany had unquestioned leadership in the chemical industry. In 1889 Germany produced 93 million tons of coal per annum, less than half the production of Britain; by 1909 she was producing 239 million tons, nearly as much as Britain, and by the same time her steel exports as a whole had passed those of Britain. To support all this furious activity, Germany needed a "place in the sun", as the Kaiser put it. Other European nations depended on their colonies and on markets such as were offered by the non-manufacturing peoples of South America. Germany proceeded to seek for colonies in what was left of Africa and Oceania, and to compete strongly with Britain in South America. To transport her new goods she built up a great merchant marine, and before long had thrown down the gauntlet to Britain as a world-carrier. There is no doubt that the bitter economic struggle between the commercial magnates of the two countries prepared their minds for what was coming, and made them willing, when the time arrived, to accept the financial demands of the military authorities.

It became evident, well before 1900, that Germany, even with her new colonies, her South American trade, and her excursions into the home markets of England and France, would find it hard to discover consumers for her increasing production. With a view to obtaining these consumers, many influential Germans began to look to south-eastern Europe and beyond into the adjacent parts of Asia. Some, more politically minded, saw an opportunity for the establishment of a great "sphere of influence", extending from the North sea to the Persian gulf. They were encouraged by the weakness of the Austrian Empire, ready to break up at a touch.

So began the project of the *Drang nach Osten*, the "Storming of the East", which was during the war to develop into the policy of a German "Middle Europe". The first step towards the objective was the planning of the Baghdad Railway. Berlin was to be linked with Constantinople, and Constantinople with the Persian gulf, by a line which was to be owned and con-

trolled by German capital. The original scheme was blocked, it may be here observed, by the control of the Persian gulf established by Britain; but it had nevertheless a considerable effect in rousing hostility to Germany, especially in France and Russia. Finally, an agreement was reached with Russia, and in 1914 Britain, having been granted control of the south-eastern end of the line and places on the directorate, withdrew her opposition. Then, of course, it was too late.

Another step came with the development of very friendly relations between German and Turkish military leaders, resulting in the appointment of German officers to instruct the Turkish army.

A third and, from certain points of view, a still more significant event was the placing of a German prince on the throne of Bulgaria. Bulgaria was a Slav state, in theory at any rate (the population were half Slav, half Turk in origin, but the church was Orthodox); and it was in that section of the Balkans at which Russia aimed and where Russian interests had actually been recognized by Germany. It has never been proved that the appointment was managed by Germany, nor has it been disproved; in either case, Russia was roused to much indignation.

Europe was now ready for the new alignment which was to end with the Great War. France, left isolated by the Triple Alliance, seeing that Germany's increasing strength would block the recovery of Alsace and Lorraine, and Russia, enraged over a supposed breach of faith, and watching her plans of centuries endangered by German policies in the Near East, came almost automatically together. After three years of negotiating and jockeying, the two countries in 1894 entered into a secret treaty which in effect provided that, on mobilization by Germany or Italy directed against France or Russia, both these countries should mobilize and attack at once. Thus the alliance, while in form defensive, provided for offensive action. In 1899 its scope was extended. The two powers became still more closely attached.

The next development was curious, and took a long while to come about. During the latter part of the nineteenth century Britain and France were bitter competitors. Their enmity was historic and inherited. The French navy was the main rival to the British. Their interests in Africa were opposed. Egypt, where France had certain financial rights, was occupied by Britain; one encounter, in which British forces expelled a French expedition from Fashoda, in the area south of Egypt, brought the two countries very near to war. But the growing commercial and colonial power of Germany disturbed the minds of many Englishmen. What was the best course to follow? For years Britain had kept aloof from European diplomacy, holding her hand free to act as she pleased, and during her war against South Africa she found that she had few friends.

The British government began in 1899 by making some tentative proposals to Germany. They were still worried by the menace of Russia toward India, and this, without question, was one of their main motives. Another was the feeling that as Germany was going to expand in any case, a friendly arrangement to divide the world was desirable. (It must be remembered that these negotiations came in the heyday of the "British Empire" idea, which culminated in the South African War.) The proposals were renewed, and the plan apparently pressed, but Germany rejected the advances; and Britain, having decided to play a tune in the concert of Europe, turned from one group to the other.

This would probably never have happened but for the accession of Edward VII to the throne of England in 1901. He had always liked France—and he very soon began to make his influence felt in foreign affairs as no British monarch had done for many a long year. His first step was to visit Paris; the French president returned his visit; and in 1904 was established the relationship between the two countries which came to be known as the "Entente". Various agreements were made, which settled all the outstanding differences, and Britain and France undertook a new course of policy. Without an alliance they determined to keep their interests parallel.

This was the beginning of the "encirclement" of Germany, which was for years to be the nightmare of German statesmen. They attributed to British diplomacy the fact that they were gradually surrounded by hostile powers. As a matter of fact, the "encirclement" was less the result of any British initiative than of French and Russian action. And the "entente" between Britain and France was really the Germans' fault, for they had been warned that Britain, if her advances to Germany were neglected, would turn to France. The Kaiser disliked the English, and hated his uncle Edward VII; his advisers did not want an alliance with Britain, and did not believe that Britain and France would come together. When the unexpected happened, a new hostility to Britain began to be apparent among German statesmen, and the Kaiser became more inimical than ever. The Kaiser now tried to play a hand on his own, and in 1905 made an agreement with the Czar of Russia aiming directly at war with England. But the Entente between England and France had just been perfected in time: the hand of Edward VII reached into the cabin of the Czar's yacht where the two Emperors met. It was quite clear that the new agreement was inconsistent with the Franco-Russian treaty, and on the advice of his ministers the Czar withdrew his undertaking. In 1907 the Russian and British governments settled all their outstanding difficulties, and while they did not make any such agreement or establish any "entente", such as those which bound them respectively to France, the very fact that they were both so bound committed them to each other.

One item in the Franco-British programme, which Russia backed, was later to be of great importance. The public treaties provided that France should recognize British rule in Egypt, while both should abstain from interference in Morocco. But a secret treaty recognized that Morocco was to be partitioned, and it was understood that France was to get most of it.

While this was going on, the "encirclement" had been progressing in another direction. Italy and France had their main reasons for disagreement in North Africa, where both wished to expand. In 1900 they settled their differences, Italy consenting to keep out of Morocco, while France agreed that Italy might seize Tripoli. This the Italians did, in a campaign in which it was shown that non-combatants, women, and children, could suffer just as atrociously in modern days as ever before. This war being over, Italy and France in 1902 entered into a secret treaty by which each country was bound to remain neutral in case of a war in which the other was attacked or expected to be attacked. This was, in spirit at least, contrary to Italy's agreement with Austria and Germany (the Triple Alliance); and the truth of the matter is that, so far as Italy was concerned, the Triple Alliance was of no more use.

Europe was now hopelessly divided into two camps, and from this time on the Great War began to take shape— like an evil genie springing from a magic bottle. In the next scenes of European history, it seems as though events were the real actors, and men the puppets with which they played.

The first crisis came over Morocco. In 1905 the Kaiser himself landed at Tangiers, and announced a protectorate.

This was entirely contrary to the plans which France had been so carefully laying; France objected, and apparently the British government of those days was ready to support her even by war. The crisis was deferred, and a conference was called at Algeciras. Here for the first time Russia, France, and Britain openly stood together, and Italy, bound by her new treaty with France, still secret as far as her former allies were concerned, stood with them. For months war was in the air. The final result was that the German protectorate disappeared, and that France got the foothold in Morocco she had desired, by obtaining the right to "police" the southern section of the country.

Now we turn from tortuous diplomacy to militarism and the growth of armaments.

The alignment of Triple Alliance versus Triple Entente with Italy in both was only one reason for the increase of armed forces; the others were all those causes of war to which reference has been made. To the European diplomat, preparedness for war was the only guarantee of security.

Between 1899 and 1914 the peace strength of the French and Russian armies grew from about one and a half million to about two and a quarter million men, and the peace strength of the Central Powers from about a million to a million and a quarter. These figures, while interesting, do not tell nearly all the story. Germany's military expenditure is the key to the situation. Germany spent far more on her army than did France, largely because of her provisions of munitions and the completeness of her preparations. Russia's expenditure, as we know to-day, was largely wasted, and the enormous force she paraded largely valueless.

The increase of German strength at sea could easily be explained by the German militarists. At first they thought of protecting their new merchant marine and colonies. Then, with the growth of

CANADA'S NATIONAL WAR MEMORIAL, OTTAWA, ONTARIO

Courtesy of Toronto Star Weekly

the new European connections of Britain, they came to regard the British navy as a serious menace. At the time of the Morocco troubles, for instance, a British landing in Schleswig under the guns of the navy, whether it was a possibility or not, was seriously discussed.

In 1900 the new development of the German navy began. The law of that year called for the doubling of the fleet; and in five years such progress had been made that Lord Roberts, then the most famous of British soldiers, was foretelling a German invasion. Meantime the British navy had been lagging, but in 1906 Britain produced the Dreadnought type of battleship, and the corresponding battle cruisers. The Dreadnought relegated the German navy to obsolescence. It did the same thing to the rest of the British battleships, and so far as their largest units were concerned, therefore, the two navies started out more or less even. But this was only true as to battleships. Britain had seamen and docks for a Dreadnought fleet; Germany had not, and Britain had a long start in the necessary smaller vessels.

Here, or hereabouts, comes in the vicious influence of the armament rings. An important official of Vickers Ltd., one of the leading armament firms, upon whose opinion the British government greatly relied, informed them that Germany was building faster than was admitted or her naval laws provided. The story was incorrect, but it was good enough. The newspapers got the tale; public feeling was aroused; the government and the Opposition were united; and a huge addition to the British fleet was decided upon. The profits of the firm which started the story doubled within four years. And not only thus, but in many other ways and places, the powerful and wealthy munition-makers of every country did all they could to encourage "preparedness". Almost as strong an influence was wielded by the press of all countries, which, from the first Morocco crisis onward, used every opportunity to exploit war scares and improve circulation.

The situation was now full of risk because it was admitted that Germany was building her navy against England, and in 1909 some negotiations were begun with a view to finding some limitation. But these came to nothing, and the competition went on.

Now, although, as has already been observed, European politicians, who always thought in terms of war, were on the whole anxious for security without war, the air was just what was needed to nourish the poisonous crop of militarism, planted long before and already strong.

Militarism, the belief in war for its own sake, appeared first not as a political plan, but as a philosophy, and strangely enough it grew not in France, where one might have expected it, but in Germany. The idea did not, and this must be clearly understood, obsess the minds of the whole nation, or even of a majority, but it did seize upon an intellectual and influential group; and recent events in Russia, Germany, and Italy have shown us that a strong group with a fixed plan can swing a country where they will.

The development of the war spirit of Germany may be traced in three stages First came the idea of the superman, the doctrine of the highest good. This was the philosophy propounded by Nietszche in his *Zarathustra*. It tells us first that God is dead, then that the strongest and finest men must take the place of God, that they are to be the masters, and that all others are to be their slaves. "Ye have heard men say," says Nietszche, "blessed are the peacemakers, but I say unto you, blessed are they who make war, for they shall be called, not the children of Jahve, but the children of Odin, which is greater than Jahve."

Nietszche was succeeded by another prophet of the same doctrine, Heinrich von Treitschke, professor of history at the University of Berlin. Treitschke began his work in the new Germany, the Germany which came into existence in 1870. He saw the supermen of Nietszche in his own fellow-citizens. To thousands of young men he strove to bring home his vision of the future Germany, the Germany which was to be led by the masters of mankind, which was to unite the whole earth, for the good of the whole earth.

It is impossible to exaggerate the effect which the growth of this philosophy had on the German mind. The most brilliant youths, the greatest leaders were filled with it; it was obvious that if Germany were to conquer the world it must be by war, and if by war Germany were to conquer the world, to fulfil her destiny, then war was the most magnificent undertaking in which the German people could engage.

So we find the philosopher Hegel saying, "Just as the movement of the ocean prevents the corruption which would result from perpetual calm, so by war people escape the corruption which would be occasioned by a continuous peace."

Treitschke declares that "War is a biological necessity of the first importance—efforts directed towards the abolition of war are not only foolish but absolutely immoral, and must be stigmatized as unworthy of the human race."

General von Bernhardi, the most brilliant of German military writers, says: "I believe in the German people—I believe that a great future is in store for it, and that it has to accomplish a high calling in the development of mankind. But it can only put this task to good account if it exerts its military strength to the utmost, and if its policy, while placing its aims high and not afraid of dangerous paths, remain conscious of the fact that as in war, so also in the political intercourse of States, the will and action alone can achieve great things." And finally Treitschke says, "Then when the German flag flies over and protects this vast empire, to whom will belong the sceptre of the universe? What nation will impose its wishes on the other enfeebled and decadent peoples? Will it not be Germany that will have the mission to ensure the peace of the world?"

It need scarcely be said that the officers of the German army and navy became devoted adherents of the new religion. They were quite ready to develop into swashbucklers, and did so to some effect.

Later, when it became necessary to accustom the common people of Germany to bear the burden of immense armaments, they were inspired with the idea that England and France were plotting an attack on them, and that Germany, therefore, must strike first. A German official report of 1913 reads: "The people must be accustomed to think that an offensive war on our part is a necessity. We must act with prudence in order to arouse no suspicion." The words have been attributed to Ludendorff, chief of the German general staff, although he denies them. And it must be said, in fairness, that German officials, rightly or wrongly, had convinced themselves of what they preached: militarism had done its work.

In France at the same time there was an unrelenting desire for "revenge" in the hearts of a large part of the population. No one who lived in that country towards the end of the last century could fail to take account of the strength of this idea. The French wanted Alsace and Lorraine back, and nearly every French boy prayed for a chance to kill Germans. It is true that the Socialists, whose power was continually increasing, were opposed to war, but nevertheless the longing in the hearts of so many of the French people to regain the lost provinces was one of the main guiding forces of French policy.

Alone in Europe the people of Britain were in general opposed to war. Their leaders were not perhaps as unanimous.

And, dislike war as they might, the British people were deeply impressed by their naval traditions. They regarded naval supremacy as an essential to their very existence; they were ready to make almost any sacrifice to maintain it; and when Germany threatened it, they were, as we have seen, ready to take up the challenge.

The final arrangements which were to put Britain in a supreme strategic position, so far as naval action was concerned, were not really completed until 1912, but may as well be mentioned here. At that time, under an agreement with France by which each navy was to act for both countries, Britain, which had always maintained a strong fleet in the Mediterranean, concentrated her forces in the North sea, while France moved most of her ships to the Mediterranean. The alliance between Britain and Japan had some years before enabled most of the British ships to be withdrawn from the Far East, and when Germany increased her regular battleship squadrons to 25, Britain was able to increase hers to 49. Germany, by mobilizing her reserves, could add 13; Britain could add 16.

The position, forced on Britain by the continuous increase in German naval strength, was now more dangerous than ever. The very existence of these huge opposing forces made for war, and by this time, as will be noted, the German war plan for an attack on France *via* Belgium was well known.

Induced by two leading men of business, the British and German governments attempted to agree, first as to their naval increases, second as to their political aims. But the effort came to nothing, and things were worse than before.

It was the officers of the British and French armies who really turned the Entente into an alliance, and in doing this the soldiers had the approval, not of the cabinets, but of the war offices concerned. Informal "conversations"

began early in 1906 at which the means of meeting a German advance through Belgium were discussed, and a very general plan for the employment of a British force was outlined. While Britain was still under no formal obligation, there was thus an understanding between the war offices that if circumstances arose making such action desirable, a British army would be available in France, and the reorganization of the British army, and with it the creation of an expeditionary force, was begun. The "conversations" went on, and in 1909 we find Foch, commandant of the French War School, and Wilson, commandant of the British Staff College, discussing joint action. It is stated by some historians that these "conversations" were unknown to the British cabinet till 1912 and to the British people till 1914; but as even Canadian militia officers had heard of the "conversations" by 1911, these assertions must be taken with a grain of salt. The British army and navy, which knew all about the matter, held that they were bound to act in case of a German invasion of Belgium. The French army, and therefore French politicians, held the same view. Practically, there was a *fait accompli*, and the statements made in 1914 that Britain's hands were free did not mean much.

Historians, as a general rule, have made far too little of war spirit as a war cause. Whether they take the view that one side or the other was responsible, they fail to recreate the feeling of the armies and navies as it existed during the pre-war years, or the manner in which the contagion was spread to the public at large by a press which was quite clever enough to realize what was happening and to take advantage of it. Not politics but militarism was the the main cause of the World War. A clear sign of the coming danger came in 1911, when another crisis arose in Morocco. It will be remembered that France had been made responsible for that area.

Germany now asserted that German residents were in danger, and sent a gunboat to Agadir to protect them. Her main objective was not Morocco at all, but the French territory on the Congo, and she hoped to get it by forcing France's hand at Agadir. Britain announced that the Morocco question affected her interests, and was apparently again ready to fight over it. The dispute was ended; France got a protectorate in Morocco; Germany got some of the Congo. But public feeling had been inflamed; the French people felt that they had gained nothing in Morocco, and had been robbed of the Congo; the war came measurably nearer; the "conversations" between the British and French war staffs became more detailed, and were communicated to Russia.

Now we turn to the Balkans. Early in 1912 Serbia and Bulgaria made a treaty; soon after, Greece and Bulgaria did the same thing, and the three powers at once attacked Turkey, with a view to seizing some territory. The victory lay with the attackers, who promptly began a new war over the loot, Rumania joining in the fight in order to steal some territory from Bulgaria. Finally, a division was made, but the ill feeling and suspicion which existed between the various European powers was increased by their interests in the subsequent quarrels of these Balkan states, to which another, Albania, had now been added. Serbia wanted a port on the Adriatic. Austria, for reasons already explained, opposed her. Montenegro also wanted one, and even took Scutari; but the Great Powers—for once in agreement—"induced" the Montenegrins to withdraw. Russia favoured the Serb ambitions; France had only thoughts for Russia, just as Germany knew that she must stand with Austria. In the result it became evident to every thinking man that within a few years a Balkan quarrel would start the World War.

The "hot spot" of Europe was now the point of contact between Austria and Serbia. The reason for Austria's fear of Serbian ambitions has already been noted, and it has been made clear that the wires which attached Serbia to Russia ensured connection with Britain and France. Laudable though "self-determination" may be, few people to-day think that the birth of Jugo-Slavia was worth the awful travail of Europe and the world. As a matter of fact, few thought so then; but Russia, ready for the trial which every one by this time knew was coming, was quite ready to back the Serbs to the limit. The freeing of a Slav nation was a good enough cause to fight for, if it meant a struggle of Slav against German for control of the Near East; and if, necessarily, it meant a European war, that could not be helped.

The agitation in Serbia for the "Greater Serbia" project had been considerably increased by Austria's formal annexation of Bosnia and Herzegovina, which had taken place in 1908. This was a deadly blow at the cause of Serbian unity, and was bitterly resented by all Serbs, especially those in the annexed areas. The younger element, entirely uncontrolled, organized a secret society in Bosnia, aiming at terrorist methods, and a revolutionary movement rapidly took shape. The "hot spot" was at its hottest.

On June 28, 1914, came the flame which was to set Europe alight. The Archduke Franz Ferdinand of Austria was assassinated at Sarajevo in Bosnia, during a formal visit.

Events marched now at an almost incredible speed, and enough has perhaps been said to show that matters were far beyond any human control. Nothing but what did happen could have happened.

Austria, blaming the Serbian government for failing, as it did, to arrest the accomplices of the murderer, and for permitting the growth of revolutionary organizations, and fearing, as we have learned, the Greater Serbia movement and the overwhelming shadow of Russia in the background, began by informing Germany that she must now attempt a re-alignment in the Balkans and hinting that Serbia might be compelled to accede. There has been much dispute as to the reception of this word at Berlin, and the debates which took place on July 5 and 6; but there is no doubt that the Austrians were, in a general way, told to proceed in the assurance that they had Germany's backing.

It is quite incredible that the Kaiser and his ministers did not realize what might happen, although no trustworthy evidence has been produced to prove that at this time it was their deliberate intention to bring about a conflagration. They thought, apparently, that the conflict might be "localized".

Austria, strengthened by Germany's assurances, prepared her demands. While this was being done, the Austrian government tried hard to give the impression that they were doing nothing, although the Entente statesmen suspected what was brewing. The German government knew something of the form of the ultimatum, although they did not know the whole of it. In any case Germany did nothing to stop it.

On July 23 the ultimatum was delivered. Serbia was accused of permitting anti-Austrian propaganda, and was required to publish a statement of regret, to suppress all secret societies and propaganda, to remove all officers with anti-Austrian tendencies, to allow Austrian representatives to help in repressing the Greater Serbia movement, and to carry out a judicial enquiry under Austrian surveillance. At this same moment the President of France was in Russia, the feeling of friendship was being strengthened, and the fever of approaching conflict was at its height.

The President returned to France, but even before his arrival the Entente powers, led by Britain, joined in appealing to Berlin to request Austria to extend the time allowed by the ultimatum, in order that there might be some discussion. The Germans forwarded the request, without hurrying much, and it was refused. The Serbians, as a matter of fact, accepted most of the terms; but they could not agree to the judicial investigation under Austrian control, since that would have meant a revolution. Sir Edward Grey, the British foreign minister, now attempted to get the powers into a conference. Germany refused, and when Grey begged Germany to use her own influence, Germany did not. What Germany did do was to suggest a temporary Austrian occupation.

While all this was going on, it must be remembered that the excitement and activity among the army officers of the powers was intense, that the newspapers were becoming more and more vociferous, and that statesmen were thus faced with extraordinary difficulties.

On July 28 the Austrian government, which had never wanted a peaceful settlement, declared war, and thus put an end to the conference proposals. The Germans, too late, tried to delay the conflict by negotiations with Austria; Sir Edward Grey had by now made it clear to the German ambassador that Britain might be drawn in, and this more than anything else had forced Germany's hand.

But nothing could be done. Austrian guns bombarded Belgrade from across the Danube, and they echoed in St. Petersburg. On the night of July 29 Russia mobilized. Immediately afterwards Austria followed. Next day Germany followed suit, and despatched ultimatums to both Russia and France. France mobilized on August 1. Meantime Britain had been trying to persuade the continental powers to cease preparations. But this failed too, and here again we must not underestimate the tremendous momentum of the forces which had been unloosed. The movement of armies collecting for war cannot be stopped as water can be turned off at a main. On the evening of August 1, Germany declared war on Russia, and France accepted the obligations of her alliance.

Germany's first acts were to bring in Britain. As already mentioned, it was generally known that the German war plan involved an attack through Belgium, and the British army had based its plans on such an operation. Britain was a guarantor of Belgian neutrality, and must be ready to stand by her contract. The attack did not come at once, but what did come was a statement by Britain on August 2 that her fleet would defend the northern coasts of France. This was in accordance with the contract already mentioned. It was still not war. But on August 4 the German invasion of Belgium began. For Britain the *casus belli* had arisen, and at midnight Germany and Britain were at war.

1914

The first month of war showed the power of two great entities, each of which had been rather undervalued by those whose task was to face it, the German army and the British navy. Looked at even from the short distance of twenty odd years, the war tends more and more to appear as a combat between these two forces. From their very nature they could only meet in comparatively minor operations, yet every success of the German army was countered by British power at sea.

Active naval operations were so few by comparison with the extraordinary struggles of the armies that most writers and most readers have an entirely inadequate conception of the influence of the British fleet on the course of hostilities. Like a tremendous snake, it wrapped around the warring land forces, leaving one side free to escape from the folds as it pleased and to attack in some other quarter, constricting the other side ever more tightly.

We have already observed that the great increase in German naval strength had been followed first by the concentration of the British fleet in home waters, and second by the construction of more ships. To these British changes we must add the development of very heavy guns and the organization of a very fast subordinate fleet of battle cruisers and battleships, armed with new and powerful weapons.

The British navy in home waters was organized into three fleets, the First Fleet consisting of a flagship, four squadrons of battleships, and four squadrons of cruisers (this was to form the Grand Fleet), the Second Fleet, with two battle squadrons, two cruiser squadrons and a number of patrol flotillas, and the Third Fleet, consisting of two squadrons of older battleships and a number of cruisers destined for trade protection, this last Fleet being maintained in reserve with nucleus crews only.

The superiority of the British in guns is shown clearly enough by the following table, which includes vessels completed up to the summer of 1915:—

	15-inch	13.5-inch	12-inch	11-inch	10-inch	9.4 or 9.2-inch	Total
British.	40	172	290	...	4	116	622
German	..	...	162	102	..	46	310

An occurrence of July, 1914, had a highly important, though quite unforeseen, effect in the early days of the war. The British Admiralty determined on a test mobilization of the Third (reserve) Fleet. On July 17 and 18 the fleets in home waters were reviewed by the king, and took more than six hours to pass by the Royal Yacht at 15 knots. This mobilization, which resulted in the whole navy stationed at home being placed on a war footing, had no connection with the immediate situation in Europe, but before the test period was quite over the crisis was coming fast to a head. The necessary orders were given; the dispersal of ships and crews (which had actually begun) was stopped, and partial steps towards war mobilization were taken, to be completed on August 1. On July 29 the First Fleet left secretly for Scapa Flow; by July 30 it was safe from surprise attack and in command of the sea. This was an event of supreme importance. It secured for the British navy the incalculable advantage of the initiative. It was in a position which enabled it to assume the offensive at its own time and on its own terms, and to dictate the character of the war, not only by sea, but by land.

The German High Seas Fleet, of which so much had been expected, was paralyzed; German overseas commerce, which had been a bitter rival to British trade, completely disappeared; Germany could not raise a hand to save her overseas colonies; and at least two million Germans of military age were prevented from crossing the sea. German submarines had, at a later date, a notable success; but although they seriously restricted the flow of supplies to Britain and France, they were never able to stop it, and in the end they were practically abolished.

Britain, on the other hand, was enabled to land troops when she liked and where she liked, to import enough food for her people and her armies and to maintain her financial credit.

In the last events, as will be seen, British sea-power played a most important rôle. German morale suffered a severe setback when the German fleet proved useless; and its final destruction in 1918 was mainly the result of the British blockade, while the defeat of the German army was due in great part to the fact that British shipping was free to transport American as well as British and Dominion forces.

An impression got about during the war, largely caused by an attempt to assimilate sea to land strategy, and has been maintained since, that because the British navy did not attempt to destroy the German ships under the guns of their shore batteries and in mine-sown ports, it was on the defensive. Such was never the case. To attack the Germans in their war harbours would have been lunacy; but whenever the German fleet was outside its ports it was the British who sought it out, and it never sought the British. At the beginning of the war all local offensives were British; and Zeebrugge, the greatest of British minor operations, showed that the initiative still lay with the British at sea, though the tide was running against them on land.

It would scarcely be fair to omit mention in this place of the work done by the French fleet, which, with some help from the Japanese, maintained control of the Mediterranean, by the Japanese themselves who helped to clear the German detached forces from the Pacific, and by the Americans, whose destroyers were a valuable aid during the last stages of the submarine war. But the main burden fell on the British navy.

The first task was the destruction of the isolated German forces in various parts of the world, most of which, it may be observed, did much damage before they were put out of action. By December, 1914, this piece of work had been accomplished, and the navy could devote its energies to its main duty, the constriction of Germany by blockade.

To the Germans, the British navy was like an enemy god in the Trojan War, always in the background, always to be reckoned with, almost impossible to touch, and quite impossible to defeat. It was the ultimate force.

But if the Germans were surprised in 1914 by British sea-power, the Allies were even more surprised by the magnitude of Germany's land effort. Armies of unprecedented size advanced at unexpected speed, smashing down formidable defences without difficulty, and forcing their way onward by sheer weight of man-power. There were errors of judgment on both sides, but in the first days of fighting they were not evident; all that was apparent was the relentless advance of the Kaiser's armies.

We have already mentioned the invasion of Belgium—an essential part of the German war plan, which had been studied and perfected for years. Cavalry advances across the German-French frontier were designed apparently to lead the French general staff to think that the scheme had been materially altered, and the first faulty operations of the French armies indicate that the deception had been partly successful. The German error, fatal to their early success, was that if they did not actually alter their plans, they vacillated between two ideas.

The general scheme of the German High Command was to dispose of France by one tremendous blow, before Russia could get into action. Seven German armies, 1,500,000 strong in all, moved westward. The two armies on the right, under Von Kluck and Von Buelow, were enormously large, containing altogether 600,000 troops; their task was to pass through and crush Belgium, then to swing southwards along the short route into Paris. The Belgian army put up a stouter fight than was anticipated. Although Liège was entered on August 7, its forts did not fall until the 15th. That was, in effect, the end, so far as Belgium was concerned. The great fortress of Namur was taken without difficulty, but the delay had been useful; the French, under Marshal Joffre, had been able to complete their concentration; the British Expeditionary Force of six divisions and one cavalry division under Sir John French had been moved into France by August 13, and were concentrating on the northern border. The French staff now made one of their worst mistakes of the war, a mistake which might have had far more serious

consequences. It was bad enough that they had only five armies with which to oppose the German seven. This gave them a hard enough task, but apparently they completely misjudged the strength of the German forces in Belgium. The First French Army moved eastwards into Alsace, the Fourth north-westward against the German line of communications. Both attacks failed, the French forces lost cohesion, and four German armies thereafter held the four French armies on the right, leaving the Fifth French Army and the British expeditionary force on their left to oppose three armies on the German left, including the immense forces of Von Kluck and Von Buelow coming through Belgium. The task was impossible, although, owing to their lack of knowledge of the German dispositions, neither the British nor the French knew it was impossible.

The Belgian army, meantime, separated from the British and French, had retired on Antwerp, and from that point made two attacks, which, while they accomplished nothing in themselves, kept a certain number of German troops occupied.

It was at this time that the world first heard the stories of "atrocities" in Belgium. The actual facts will never be completely known, but there is no doubt that occasional attacks on the Germans were made by non-combatants. There is no doubt that these attacks were punished by stern, often by cruel actions; there is no doubt, finally, that many civilians suffered terribly at the hands of soldiers. The main reason for reprisals was panic; strange though it may seem in an invading army, the Germans, officers and men alike, worn out, excited, and often enough intoxicated, lost their heads. Many soldiers apparently were mentally affected; others were, as many must be in every army, criminal. Towns were looted; individuals and groups of civilians, even women and children, were shot when

no offence had been proved. Robbery
at the point of the bayonet became
common, and even worse crimes took
place. Naturally, the tales of all these
horrors drifted across the lines, and bad
enough became ten times worse. The
effect was the reverse of what might
have been expected. There were without doubt some Germans who thought
this "frightfulness" would have a salu-
tary effect; but what it did was to rouse
public opinion, especially in England,
to such a pitch that the war fever grew
beyond belief.

On August 22 the French Fifth Army
was heavily attacked by two German
armies and forced to fall back. The
Germans then turned eastward against
the balance of the French line (which
was, as we have noted, already pinned
to its ground by other German forces)
and westward against the British; on
August 23 came the first engagement
between British and German forces,
the first battle of Mons. Now the extraordinary value of the British force
became apparent. It was so small that a
German *communiqué* referred to it as
"that contemptible little army", a
phrase which has given its veterans the
proud nickname of "Old Contemptibles".
It was composed of seven-year volunteers, stiffened by highly trained non-
commissioned officers, led by officers
who had learned coolness and discipline
from their youth up; and most of its
units had seen fighting in India or
Africa. These troops met the Germans
as professionals might meet amateurs.
One company of the West Kent Regiment, to take a single instance, fought
off three battalions of Germans, only
losing about half its strength. But with
the huge German forces working around
on their left, retirement was inevitable;
and so began the famous retreat from
Mons. It is almost impossible to give
an adequate picture of the next period.
The British and the Fifth French Army,
a broken line of khaki and horizon blue,
stretched across fifty miles of front,
were moving away southwards. Against
them from the north came down column
after column of Germans, deploying
into fighting formation, advancing,
breaking under the fire of the worn-out,
but undefeated Allied infantry. First
one side, then the other gained a success,
but the Allied retreat continued.

By August 25, the Germans were
following the British so closely that a
stand had to be made, and next day was
fought the battle of Le Cateau. The
British, in an unprepared position,
resisted for a whole day, aided materially by a French cavalry corps,
which had moved across to their left.
Finally, the attackers became confused,
and broke off the battle. The British
were able to continue the retreat.

The situation was terribly serious.
More masses of Germans kept pouring
in on the west, the armies pivoting on
the left flank; the best the French and
British could do was to keep disengaging
and retiring. Before long the line of
battle was on the latitude of Paris,
then south of Paris. It was off to the
east, and the Germans did not attack
Paris, their main object being to destroy
the French armies.

But now appeared new factors in the
situation. The German armies on the
west flank had come a long way and
were no longer so mobile as they had
been. Two new French armies had been
concentrated, the Sixth on the extreme
left of the line, with the British on their
right, and the Ninth on the right of the
Fifth, which was still on the right of the
British. On the French right was the
strong fortress of Verdun, the first really
modern fortification which had stood
in the way of the Germans.

Now the Germans in their turn made
two serious errors. The first was that
they gave up, or at least wavered in,
their original plan of a main attack on
their right, in order to overwhelm
Verdun on their left, an objective in
which they never succeeded. The second
was that, thinking the British had been

put out of action at Le Cateau, and neglecting the new French Sixth Army (both of these now on the French left), they turned their two western armies towards the south-east, in order to take the Fifth French Army on its flank. This movement took them across the front of the French Sixth Army and the British, and laid them open to the attack which paralyzed their whole scheme. On September 6, began the battle of the Marne.

The French Sixth Army, which was now under Galliéni, the commander at Paris, was reinforced by the Paris garrison, sent out in taxicabs, and with the British attacked the flank of the German forces marching across their front and began to press them inward. This bold movement really decided the whole battle. Galliéni had shown a unique quality of imagination. Finally, Von Kluck's great army on the German right gave way and began to retreat, the British forcing their way between Von Kluck and Von Buelow. Now Foch, who commanded the new French Ninth Army, formed, as has been mentioned, on the right of the Fifth, had his chance to attack Von Buelow, and this he did on September 9. The Germans had to retreat again; all their armies became involved; and by September 12 their centre had fallen back fifty miles, their right more than thirty.

The battle of the Marne was one of the decisive battles of the war. It put an end once and for all to the German plan of finishing up the French in the first month or two; it put new heart into the Allied forces; it enabled them to form a strong line of defence, and thus finally determined the character of the following three years of fighting.

The Allies continued to press on the Germans, but the battle of the Aisne, on a line almost parallel to that of the Marne, was far from being a victory. When it ended, all the troops in the centre and on the Allies' right were in a stalemate. Now, perforce, the action spread to the Allies' left flank.

Starting in the last week of September, there began a gradual extension of the line towards the British channel, the Germans attempting to work northward, threatening the channel ports, the Allies shifting troops to their left to oppose the threat, a phase of the war which is generally called the "Race to the Sea". There was a good deal of vicious fighting, but it was mostly between Germans and French, for the British army was now marching around the French flank, northwards into Flanders. On the day they started their march, another event was happening three thousand miles away which was to bring into the war a factor which Germany had never contemplated: the first Canadian division, with its first reserves, was leaving Gaspé bay.

It was now evident that the left of the line of battle must reach the sea. The Allies aimed at placing it at Antwerp; the Germans hoped it would be at Havre. In a mistaken attempt to hold an impossible position, a small British force was sent to aid in the defence of Antwerp; but the city fell on October 10 after a furious bombardment by artillery of unprecedented power. The Belgian and British garrisons got safely away; and the river Yser became the general line of demarcation in the north, and by opening of sluices and damming its mouth the Belgians made it almost impassable. To the south the forces still swung this way and that. The Germans made one effort to break through the extreme left wing, but it was frustrated by the British navy, which brought three shallow draft monitors into action, and paralyzed the enemy. The Germans attacked the British at Ypres, using a completely new army, and attacked the French at Arras. Both attacks failed, but the blows at the British line were renewed again and again, and the German reserves were brought into the fighting line with complete disregard of consequences; the German High Command was making a desperate effort for victory before the year's end. Before this battle was over, the original British expeditionary force had been reduced to about the size of a single division. It had been small enough to begin with; it had never been adequately reinforced; and it had suffered 80,000 casualties. The casualties among the French and the Germans had been equally appalling. In the later days of the war commanders came to have some appreciation of the value of men, and took some pains to keep them alive. As artillery developed, it was used, as it ought to be, for the protection of attacking infantry. But in 1914 the munitions supply was appalling inadequate, and methods in attack were not much ahead of those of the Zulus. Battalions were used like projectiles, hurled against strong positions with scarcely a hope of success. The only bright spot in the picture was the almost incredible bravery and endurance shown by the fighting troops, and we must give the Germans credit for their share in the display of heroism.

But, as winter settled down, it became evident that 1914 was to bring no conclusion. By November 22 the heavy fighting ended, and the line became stabilized, as it was, for the most part, to remain for three and a half years. The trench system of the south-eastern part of the line was extended to the north-western, and the troops settled down for the first winter.

The story of the western front in 1914 has been given first, and in some detail, because, as was mentioned earlier, it was the scene of Germany's main effort. But all through those early days the Allied nations had been hoping for some great demonstration from their third ally, Russia. Germany had left only some 200,000 regular soldiers to defend her eastern front. To oppose these the Allies calculated on 1,000,000 Russian regulars, 3,000,000 first reserves, with millions of additional men available. The "Russian steam roller" was a favourite figure of speech, and both professional and amateur war critics expected it to flatten Germany and Austria out. What actually happened was something very different.

The Russians advanced into east Prussia and eastern Galicia, meeting at first with comparatively easy success. But the success did not last long. Hindenburg, a veteran who had made a careful study of the defence of eastern Prussia, came out of retirement and organized a new army. In the great battle of Tannenberg he completely annihilated the Russian right. Thousands of Russians were drowned in the Masurian swamps into which he drove them, and thousands more were captured. But as they were thus stopped on their right the Russians forced their way forward on the left into Galicia, where the Austrians, never very famous soldiers, met with one defeat after another. The loss of Galicia was serious for Germany for more reasons than one, since it exposed the rich German mineral regions of Silesia and Westphalia, and deprived Germany of most valuable oil reserves. Moreover, it established a connection between Russia and the disaffected Czechs and Slovaks who would sooner be with Russia than against her. The Germans made another attack in Poland, striking towards Warsaw, but at this stage had no very remarkable success.

The Austrians had meantime been busy with operations against Serbia, which they entered just as the Germans were destroying the forts of Liège, on August 13. This invasion was far from glorious; in spite of some successes, the Austrians suffered severely, and by August 24 their effort came to an end. In September they made another attack; this time the Serbians turned the tables, and entered Hungary. Before long they had also gone southward and taken part of Macedonia. There they stopped, and

now, so far as the Balkans were concerned, the situation was, as in the
west, a stalemate.

But other events were happening in
the Near East, which were to have a
serious effect on the whole conduct of
operations by the Allies. For many
years Germany had been establishing
herself as the most influential power at
Constantinople. The Kaiser had set
himself up as a firm friend of Mo-
hammedanism, and had even dressed
himself in oriental clothes, in the
negotiations concerning the Berlin-Bag-
dad Railway. Turkey had always been
ready to serve German interests; the
Turkish army had, as we have noted,
been trained by German officers; the
Young Turks, who formed a very important political element, were strongly
pro-German; and by the autumn of
1914 Turkey was so subservient that
meetings of the cabinet were more often
than not held in the German ambassador's house. When the international
situation became critical, the fast
German battle cruiser *Goeben* and light
cruiser *Breslau* were in the Mediterranean, and the British ships there were
ordered to shadow, although not to
attack them. The main risks were the
escape of the Germans into the Atlantic
or their attacking the French transports
leaving Algeria, and in ensuring against
these the Allied fleets almost lost sight
of the Germans altogether. Then came
the declaration of war. A lone light
cruiser, the *Gloucester*, spotted the
German cruisers off Sicily and pursued
them eastwards, apparently bluffing
them into believing she was closely
supported, so that they did not attack
her with any energy. But the Germans
were too fast for the other ships, and
finally reached the Dardanelles, proceeding towards a refuge in Constantinople. Here, in accordance with international law, they should have been
interned. Suddenly it was announced
that the two cruisers had been sold to
Turkey; and with their German admiral,

German crews and all, they became
part of the Turkish navy. If any extra
inducement were needed to bring Turkey
over to the German side, this considerable naval force at her very gates supplied it. A good deal of strenuous diplomacy was to come first, for Britain
and France, with millions of Mohammedan subjects to control, had
much to fear if a Holy War were pro-
claimed, and the Allied representatives
strained every nerve to keep Turkey
neutral. But the German influence was
too strong. On September 28 Turkey
announced that the Dardanelles were
closed; on October 29, apparently on its
own initiative, the "Turkish" fleet, with
its German admiral, officers, and crews
bombarded Odessa. Russia naturally
declared war on Turkey, and on November 5 Britain and France did the
same. Fortunately, though a Holy War
was declared by the Sheikh ul Islam,
the principal Mohammedan dignitary
of the Near East, the Mohammedan
world as a whole paid very little attention. But the existence of this hostile
power on the Mediterranean and the
Persian gulf made it essential for Britain
and France to take active steps to
protect their interests and their prestige,
and so began those campaigns which
were to be so costly in money, in energy,
and in men. They were not, however,
to come on for some time yet; the year
1914 saw only operations by the Russians south of the Caucasus.

One other series of land operations
must be mentioned before we end this
brief survey of the kaleidoscopic events
of 1914. The Union of South Africa
found itself between two colonies of
the enemy power and, in addition,
facing a large disaffected group of its
own people. A rebellion aiming at independence began on September 15. It
was shortly and sharply dealt with by
Smuts and Botha, and within three
months the threat was over. The capture
of the German colonies in south-west
Africa took some time longer, but a

joint French and British expedition seized on the Cameroons without much difficulty.

Now we come back to the story of the navy and its Allied forces, the navies of France and of Japan. There had, as we have already observed, been no threat to the safety of the first British troop transports. Nevertheless, precautions had to be taken to guard the channel; here and there, on the seven seas, were German units which must be disposed of before either transports or freighters could be secure; a watch must be kept on New York, so that German ships might not escape, and that British ships might come and go safely; and convoys must be found for troops moving by sea. There was plenty to be done, and, as already observed, we must not let the continuous violence of the war by land blind us to the extreme importance of the naval operations. From the purely economic point of view one shot at sea not only costs more than one on land, but if it hits the mark may do incalculably more damage to a hostile cause.

Next to its main duty of operating against the German fleet, the immediate task before the British navy was to protect the passage across the British channel. This was done by establishing a joint English and French guarding force in the straits of Dover and at the western entrance, with two battle squadrons in the centre. The whole channel was thus transformed into an Allied lake, and the troops passed across without danger. By August 18 most of the army had crossed, without any knowledge of the fact having reached the Germans.

The next job was the support of the army in a landing at Ostend, which had little ultimate value, and was the first sign of the differences as to policy which always existed at London. Then came the Heligoland action. This was, in a way, the result of the Ostend effort. The Admiralty expected a movement by the Germans, and an independent flotilla was ordered to prepare for an attack on the German destroyers and light cruisers, the Grand Fleet battle cruisers coming in to support them.

The Germans got news of the plan, and prepared to counter it by the use of more light cruisers. On August 28 the action began, between destroyers and light cruisers, and continued, in a good deal of confusion, owing to mist and errors in transmitting orders, for several hours, until the British flotillas were very near the enemy bases. The German cruisers fought well, and were far from losing the battle until the appearance of the battle cruisers under Admiral Beatty. That ended it, and when the engagement was over the British had lost no ships and had only 75 casualties, whereas the Germans had lost three cruisers and a destroyer, and had suffered at least 1,000 casualties. Moreover, the Germans were shown, as has already been indicated, that the British were on the offensive.

There was other work to be done by the navy, the importance of which cannot be minimized. At the declaration of war, besides the *Goeben* and *Breslau* in the Mediterranean, the Germans had a number of other cruisers in foreign waters. They were as follows: in China, the *Scharnhorst*, the *Gneisenau*, the *Emden*, the *Nürnberg*, and the *Leipzig;* in the West Indies, the *Dresden*, and the *Karlsruhe;* and in East Africa, the *Königsberg* and various gunboats. There were also a large number of merchant ships which might have been transformed into cruisers, but only two ever came into action and both were sunk, one by a cruiser, one by another merchantman, the *Caronia.*

The *Karlsruhe* gave the most immediate concern by reason of her nearness to New York, she managed to get away from the *Suffolk, Berwick,* and *Bristol,* which were all too slow for her (this indeed was the fault with most of the British cruisers on outlying stations).

but by August 14 she was chased well away from the trade routes. The *Dresden* had already gone, so the North Atlantic was cleared. The *Königsberg* was hard to find. She was like a live needle in a haystack; but at last she was discovered in an African river and blockaded.

The most important situation was in the Pacific, where besides the above-mentioned five ships there were a merchant cruiser and a gunboat; these, with the *Königsberg*, constituted a serious threat to the convoys which were beginning to leave from India.

The first operations in the Pacific were Allied successes. On August 15 Japan summoned Germany to leave Tsingtau on the Shantung peninsula, within seven days. The Germans refused to surrender; and on the 23rd Japan landed her troops, supported by her main fleet, and after a gallant resistance Tsingtau surrendered on November 7. Meantime a considerable fleet had been assembled at Sydney, made up of Australian and New Zealand vessels, later reinforced by some French ships. After various preliminary operations this fleet proceeded to capture, without any difficulty, German New Guinea and the other German possessions in the eastern Pacific. Now began the astonishing exploits of the German light cruiser *Emden*. In the middle of September she managed to get into the unguarded Indian ocean, with an accompanying merchant ship, the *Marcomannia*, captured a Greek collier and an American vessel, and sank several British vessels, all after she had transferred their crews to her consorts. She disappeared; then suddenly she came out of the blue to bombard some oil tanks at Madras. A few days later she reappeared near Ceylon, sank four merchantmen, captured two, one of which was a collier, and disappeared again. Early in October she made seven more captures, in the same area, then made off to the east, where she raided

Penang, and sank a Russian gunboat and a French destroyer. Finally, on November 9, she was run to ground and destroyed by the Australian cruiser *Sydney*, after a career which had aroused much admiration and caused an entirely disproportionate and very disturbing sensation among the public.

The northern Pacific was controlled by Japan, and an arrangement made at this time was destined to have an important effect years later. The Japanese took over the Caroline islands, which had hitherto been German, and thus extended their empire a considerable distance into the Pacific ocean.

Now came a serious setback, beginning with a bad mistake by the British admiralty. Admiral Cradock, in the south Atlantic, was ordered to seek out and destroy the main German squadron in the Pacific, which, it was supposed, would be coming south to avoid the Japanese. It had not much other option, for Esquimalt was now well protected, and the Japanese navy controlled the western Pacific. The German Pacific squadron was actually better than Admiral Cradock's, but when he ordered another cruiser to join him his orders were countermanded by the admiralty. He had one old battleship, but it was too slow to be any use. On November 1, with a fine regard for the traditions of the service, he met and tackled the enemy (*Scharnhorst, Gneisenau*, cruisers, *Leipzig, Dresden, Nürnberg*, light cruisers) off Coronel on the west coast of South America. His own ships available were *Good Hope*, cruiser, *Monmouth*, cruiser, *Glasgow*, light cruiser, and *Otranto*, a merchant cruiser, which was not in action. The Germans got to the eastward and windward, and kept out of range until the sun went down; then, when the British were silhouetted against the sky and they were themselves invisible, they went into action. There could be but one end: the *Good Hope* and *Monmouth*, refusing to surrender, were sunk with all on board;

the *Glasgow* and *Otranto* escaped. There was never a more heroic fight.

The Coronel defeat followed a good deal of other German activity. The *Emden* was still busy; a fortnight before the *Berlin* had broken out from Wilhelmshaven, laid a minefield, and so destroyed a fine battleship (*Audacious*); a German squadron had tried a raid into the North sea. More important still, the German submarines had shown that, if the rest of the navy were inactive, they were not. In September one of them had sunk three old cruisers (*Aboukir, Hogue, Cressy*), with most of their crews; in October another sank the *Hawke* near Peterhead; another attacked some of the cruisers near Scapa Flow; another was said to have actually got into the anchorage. The result was that the whole disposition of the Grand Fleet had been changed pending the establishment of a protected harbour at Scapa Flow, and their main anchorages were moved out of the North sea. There had, owing to all this submarine activity, been a good deal of anxiety as to the Canadian transports which had left Gaspé on October 3, carrying about 25,000 troops. They were convoyed by several cruisers, two battleships, and the battle cruiser *Princess Royal;* and in addition the North sea exits were specially guarded. Yet when the convoy, which was destined for Southampton, was off Ireland, a German submarine was spotted near the Isle of Wight, and the convoy was diverted into Plymouth. It must be noted that British submarines, although less advertised, had been far from inactive; some had kept a close watch on German harbours and had sunk one cruiser, while others had actually penetrated into the Baltic. E-9 played the surprising trick of taking a seaplane, which happened to land above her.

It was obviously necessary that Coronel should be avenged, and that very quickly, and no time was wasted.

Lord Fisher, now at the head of the admiralty, established a new command for the south Atlantic and Pacific, and sent out the large battle cruisers *Inflexible* and *Invincible*. On these rallied five smaller cruisers, and the squadron proceeded to the Falkland islands. On December 8 the Germans appeared, surprising the British who were coaling, but far more surprised themselves to see the big cruisers. After a long chase, the large German cruisers accepted action, in order to save the smaller ones. The fight lasted some time; the large German cruisers were sunk, and there were no British casualties. Not long after, although at widely separated spots, two other German cruisers were sunk, leaving only one, which finally escaped. Such was the battle of the Falkland islands, described as "the most decisive battle in naval history".

The first few months of war had been extraordinarily eventful, but had produced a situation which, as we shall see, was going to be hard to change. The two factors which had completely upset the German plans were the Allied success on the Marne, which gave time for the British Empire to begin a real mobilization, and the control of the sea by the British navy, which choked off practically all enemy marine activity.

1915 - 16

The following two years of the land fighting were marked by experiment and disappointment. Offensives were undertaken which could not succeed. The strategical moves showed no understanding of warfare on the scale and of the nature which was now developing. The higher commanders, for the most part, were quite lacking in those qualities of imagination which might have made up for their inexperience; and their staffs knew no more than they did. In consequence there were no successes, but only a terrible toll of killed and wounded men.

There was one bright spot. A number of younger leaders and staff officers were gaining at close quarters the kind of experience their seniors lacked and, owing to their distance from the scene of action, were never able to obtain. It was, for example, by reason of their freedom from the slavery of precedent that the Canadians were later able to develop an organization quite different from the British and particularly suited to the needs of the new warfare.

Another factor was of even greater importance. The whole German people was fully organized into a great war machine, and filled with confidence in victory; the British, at first, were not organized at all; the French only partly organized, and far from confident. While better leadership would have saved many, perhaps most, of the Allied losses in these two hard years, nothing could have brought about an Allied victory.

But during all this period there were many developments in the armies themselves, in their armament, and in methods of defence and offence; and it is necessary to make a note of some of these changes.

In all the armies the early battles had seen the growth of a new arm, which was to become more and more important, the aëroplane. It was still new at the beginning of the war. Only in 1909 had aviation begun to emerge from the stage of experiment; only in 1912 had the Royal Flying Corps been formed in England. The French Flying Corps had been formed just previously. The Germans had fewer aëroplanes, but had been successful in the construction of Zeppelins.

The British Flying Corps, when it went to France, consisted of four "squadrons", each containing three "flights" of four machines each. They were of varying types, although that did not matter much when there was no formation flying and machines worked independently. A Naval Air Service had also developed, and some progress had been made in spotting submarines and in bomb-dropping. Aërial reconnaissance began early, and although some of the reports, owing to lack of experience, were faulty, it was quite evident that troop movements in rear of the main battle line would soon be no secret. Air fighting began, although aëroplanes were not yet fitted to carry machine guns, and still used bombs and rifles; by September 7, 1914, five enemy machines had been brought down. By the time of the battle of the Marne the Allied aëroplanes were doing excellent work; not long after began the system by which aëroplanes observed the effect of artillery fire, and reported it by wireless and also undertook the task, afterwards so important, of photographing enemy positions. The Royal Naval Air Service was as active as the Royal Flying Corps. It carried on, mostly in motor cars, a series of operations in Belgium, and before the end of the year made four attacks on Zeppelin sheds at Cologne, Düsseldorf, and Friedrichshafen. It also co-operated with the fleet in the Heligoland action.

The need for improvement in machines and organization was now obvious; and before long British factories were competing with the French in the production of aëroplanes. By May, 1915, over 500 machines had been acquired, and over 2,200 were building. The strength of the Corps grew. By the middle of 1916 the number of squadrons had increased eight times, and Sir Douglas Haig, now commander-in-chief, was asking that this should be nearly doubled. Fighting between formations in the air became common, and before 1916 was over still more machines were demanded.

An even more sensational development came in guns and munitions. The British army had not enough of either when hostilities began. Infantry calling for artillery protection often received little or none. The French and Germans, while they were much better prepared, had nothing to compare with the quantities they obtained later. The increase in the production of munitions in Britain was considerable. From September, 1914, to March, 1915, the output of munitions increased 20 times, and by that time the factories were producing 15,500 shells per day. But the Germans and Austrians were producing 250,000 per day; and though the French did all they could, they could not make up the deficiency or come anywhere near doing so. Moreover, there was serious trouble in England owing to the immense profits made by the manufacturers and the high wages (which they did not think high enough) of the workers. The British government assumed control of all production, and David Lloyd George was made minister of Munitions. By December, 1915, the shell output increased twelve times, while the construction of heavy guns and machine guns was enormously accelerated. In September, 1916, the British expenditure in the field was five and a quarter million rounds. Even this was to be far surpassed; in April, 1917, the expenditure was over 8 million rounds, and in September, 1918, almost 12 million.

There was a corresponding increase in the number of guns. When the original British force went to France, it had only 504 guns, and they were inferior to the German guns. By the Armistice the British possessed over 6,000 guns; and the Canadian Corps alone often used more than 750, of which some would be Canadian, some British. Finally, the concentrations became immense, and towards the end of 1918 the Canadian Corps used in one day, for one comparatively small operation, almost as much ammunition as the whole British army used in the whole South African war.

In two points the Germans always maintained their superiority over the British: their ammunition was more uniform, and their guns had a slightly longer range. As the quantity of British supplies increased, this became less important, while the French field-gun was from beginning to end one of the most useful weapons possessed by any army. It was unfortunately a long time before the higher commanders and their staffs learned to utilize these new facilities in a scientific manner.

The Allied signal services, which supplied telephones to gun positions, had to be immensely improved; the Allies had to develop an intelligence service which located enemy guns by observing flashes from different positions, or noting the time required for the report of a gun to be heard; above all, they had to obtain sufficient artillery officers trained under active service conditions and staff officers who understood the use of guns. All this took a great deal of time, and was not accomplished without some bitter lessons.

The commanders had equally little comprehension of the value of machine-guns, which the British commander-in-chief thought "overrated", and even Kitchener rather despised. It was long before they learned from German successes, and even then the way was led by Canadian developments.

The collection of information concerning the enemy was an important matter. The aëroplane "observers" and observers in captive balloons took their photographs with such boldness that complete maps of the hostile area could be constructed. Scout officers and patrols crept out into the "no man's land" between the lines to examine the enemy wire. "Trench raids" by bold little groups forced their way into the enemy's line, bombed and bayoneted along a small section, and, before they could be counter-attacked, brought back prisoners whose uniforms could be identified. And each nation had its secret service "spies" who worked behind the lines, even in the enemy country, sometimes dressed as soldiers, sometimes as civilians (often indeed they were women), and managed to get some information out. Probably the best secret service was that of the British admiralty; next came that which the Germans had organized. It must be noted, in parenthesis, that a whole branch of the staff in every country was occupied in "counter-espionage" service, and few indeed were the agents who escaped.

Every bit of information obtained was collected and collocated, and by adding one fact to another an almost complete statement was put together. In 1917 and 1918, for instance, the British G.H.Q. was able to furnish its troops with good maps of the German lines, photographs of the barbed wire which defended them, and details as to the German troops, while hardly a German ship could move out of harbour without the knowledge of the British admiralty.

The main characteristic of the fighting on the western front during 1915, 1916, and 1917 was that it was "trench warfare". The general line stabilized towards the end of 1914 was before long marked by two opposing fortifications, extending from one end to the other. The trench system consisted of a front-line trench, numerous communication trenches running back from it, then one or two or more lines of support line trenches, and back of these again other trenches serving artillery and machine-gun positions. The infantry trenches were several feet deep, with a "parapet", a low wall of bags filled with earth built along the front, and sometimes a similar wall, a "parados", in rear.

These trenches were laid out on an irregular line, so that artillery had difficulty in ranging on them; sometimes they were divided into bays a few feet long, forming a kind of Greek key pattern; a little below the parapet was a "fire-step" on which the troops stood to fire or the sentries to watch. Here and there in the system, in key positions, were built "strong points" especially fortified, which controlled considerable areas over which the enemy must advance, and deep "dug-outs" were constructed many feet underground, in which the garrisons might take shelter while the trench was being shelled.

The Germans carried the trench system to its highest perfection. Their trenches came to be very deep, strengthened by wooden supports, strongly protected in front by rows and rows of barbed wire, dotted everywhere with concrete "pill-boxes", proof against anything but a direct hit from a heavy shell, where machine-gun crews waited to mow down an attack. Their officers' dugouts were luxuriously furnished, and the whole system seemed more like a permanent fortress than a temporary construction in the field.

The front-line and support trenches were garrisoned mainly by infantry, but with them were machine-gunners, signallers, "forward observation officers" for the artillery, and trench mortar batteries, armed with small guns which fired heavy bombs for short distances. Infantry battalions took over duty in the front line for a few days at a time, and while there the commander of each section of trench was responsible for holding his piece of line. During inactive periods sentries watched from the fire-step, or, when the enemy were very vigilant, through "periscopes", vertical boxes fitted with two mirrors in such a way that any hostile movement was reflected by the upper mirror onto the lower, and so seen by the sentry. In case of an attack the whole force mounted the fire-step to repel it. Food and water were brought up daily from the rear by the communication trenches, and ammunition when necessary the same way. This garrison work was a difficult and dangerous duty. The trenches were always subject to desultory shelling, trench-mortar bombs, and rifle fire, so that casualties were constant, although at some periods much more infrequent than at others.

A battle during this trench warfare

period was a highly complicated operation. The operation might be of a minor nature, involving the capture of some point of vantage which was useful to the enemy or might in future be useful to the attackers, or it might be a major affair, aiming at pushing back a large section of line. In either case the arrangements were much the same.

When trench warfare first began, and indeed for a long time afterwards, the importance of thorough preliminary preparation was not fully understood; the initial attacks were arranged, but the necessary follow-up details were not thoroughly worked out. Not until almost the end of the war was the possibility of using the valuable factor of surprise really considered. Only by degrees and by experience did the leaders learn. Meantime the losses went on.

The first step was the preparation of special maps showing as exactly as possible the position of the hostile trenches and wire. On these maps were marked, first, lines upon which the artillery was to fire, and second, a series of objectives for the attacking infantry. Orders were issued to the troops, some of which were to take the nearer objectives, others the more distant ones. Careful instructions were given, and often the attacking troops were practised in their duties. Stores of gun and small-arm ammunition were collected, and engineers prepared to make bridges over trenches and roads for guns. Finally, before the operation, the hostile position was bombarded for days with high explosive shell in order to destroy the wire and strong points. The hostile artillery replied to this attack by bombarding the attacking artillery; so that the duel could be heard for scores of miles. Finally, on the day appointed, as the dawn came, a heavy artillery fire, a "barrage", was laid down on a given line, and under its protection the infantry, armed with rifles, with bayonets fixed, machine-guns, and bombs, leapt from their trenches and

advanced. They were met by the fire of rifles, machine-guns, and field guns, so far as these had not been silenced. Many were killed and wounded, but the attack swept on. If it was successful, the "barrage" lifted to its next position, and another "wave" of attacking troops surged forward.

If the attack was successful, the new position had to be consolidated and quickly prepared for the inevitable counter attack. Gun positions were altered, machine-guns placed, and the captured trenches reversed so that they faced in the other direction.

It may well be imagined that after three years of this artillery warfare the ground for a long way on both sides of the front became a complete waste. In places like Ypres and Verdun, where there was much fighting, the whole surface was destroyed.

Into the northern 35 miles of the front-line sector, British and German guns fired altogether nearly 500 million shells, something like a million into each square mile. In rainy weather, the front-line area was practically impassable. The shell-holes were full of water; guns sank up to the hubs; ammunition trucks were bogged. The discomfort this mud brought to the troops cannot be pictured. Their trenches were often full of water, and movement was next to impossible. It can easily be seen that a "break-through" in winter weather was impossible; for even if the troops could move, artillery and transport could not.

The panorama of the line of battle was weird and terrible in the extreme. By day little could be seen, except the smoke of guns, the burst of shells, in the midst of a wilderness dotted by skeletons of trees, where even the towns had been pounded to pieces and nothing was left but heaps of ruins. Here and there an observation balloon hung in the air; here and there was an aëroplane surrounded by little white clouds, the bursts of anti-aircraft shells. By night the flashes of cannon were visible for miles along the lines; occasional signal rockets and lights blazed in the sky; and always, night and day, there was the sound of guns, the whistle of shells, the whining crack of bullets. Even at quiet moments the noise was bad enough, but when "active operations" were in progress it grew to a roaring and shrieking inferno of sound that was enough by itself to drive many men insane.

Yet it would be wrong to imply that the troops were entirely miserable. The Germans, on the whole, in spite of the many books produced since the war, were filled with a kind of sentimental courage; the French took discomfort as a matter of course, and rejoiced in a good wine ration and plenty of Parisian papers; the British displayed their own peculiar brand of humour by inventing songs about the war, sometimes ribald, sometimes sentimental, and sometimes very funny, which they sang loudly and on every occasion.

Behind the front line was a complicated organization, the object of which was the direction of operations or the movement and provision of men, munitions, and food. The movement of men, in accordance with the needs of the situation, was arranged by the various branches of the staff and carried out by the railways, by Army Service Corps trucks or busses, or by marches. Ammunition, supplies, and mail were taken forward by the Army Service Corps under orders of the staff and delivered to the units which expected them. For this work and for the moving of wounded there were great fleets of motor-trucks, motor-ambulances, wagons drawn by horses and mules, caterpillars for the heavy guns, besides a whole organization of special trains, for wounded, for supplies, for reinforcements, or for troops on the move.

When men were wounded they were taken back by the Army Medical Corps, through a complete organization of front-line "dressing-stations", "division-al dressing-stations", "corps dressing-stations", "casualty clearing-stations" (small field hospitals, near the front, where the wounded first met the tender care of "nursing sisters"), and "stationary hospitals" (larger field hospitals), to "base hospitals", or perhaps to hospitals in their home countries. The arrangements differed in different forces, but the main idea was to get the wounded away as quickly as possible, to get the badly wounded as far away as possible, and to save as many as possible for more fighting. Motor-ambulances and hospital-trains helped in the work, and altogether one of the most important tasks in the preparation of an attack was the medical organization.

Other arrangements had to be made for the replacement of casualties and the reconstitution of units. This was at first a very slow business, but finally a method was devised and put into practice in the Canadian Corps by which, through the use of a special organization, reinforcements were brought up to the line as regularly as ammunition.

Another organization was kept busy building or repairing railways; another, in supplying wood for necessary construction. The battalions of the Canadian Railway Troops and of the Canadian Forestry Corps were responsible for most of this work.

The Corps of Signals was responsible for providing communications, and so remarkable was its work that on many parts of the front the telephone service was almost perfect. An officer in an Army Corps Headquarters could call up an artillery observation officer in the front line or an office in London with no particular delay or difficulty. It may well be imagined that during active operations this matter of communications presented terrific obstacles, but they were almost always, though not quite always, overcome. There were many other special organizations, which can only be mentioned: the corps which provided the soldiers' pay and kept his accounts, the chaplains, the Inland Water Transport (which manned canal boats, a prosaic but useful duty), the postal corps (which carried mail), the Veterinary Service, and last, but not least, the "fighting" services, the cavalry (which had no chance during trench warfare to do anything but act as messengers, and not much chance of that), the machine gun corps (which worked with the infantry and handled those very useful weapons the heavy machine-guns), and the engineers, who were responsible for the proper construction of positions, the building of concrete emplacements for guns and machine-guns, the construction of camps behind the line, the building and maintenance of roads and railways, the explosion of mines under enemy lines, and an infinity of other jobs.

While the special arrangements for all this work varied in different armies, it all had to be done, and was done. But it was carried out in such detail only on the western front. In the eastern theatres of war, things were much more haphazard; even the Germans never organized to such a degree as they did in the west, while other forces, the Russians for instance, were little more than half-disciplined, half-fed, less than half-armed, and much less than half-trained, only notable for their blind courage.

The organization of the three great armies was more or less similar. At the head was the commander-in-chief surrounded by his staff, General Headquarters, Grand Quartier General, or Main Headquarters. This staff was divided into branches, one of which dealt with fighting, one with the supply and appointment of officers and men, and one with the supply of food and ammunition. There were many subsidiary offices to deal especially with the different services which we have mentioned above. By the end of the war there were nearly 700 officers at

British General Headquarters, and a still larger number of other ranks, clerks, signallers, servants, etc.

Directly under General Headquarters came the Air Force, the Tank Corps, except for those parts detached, as they usually were, to serve under subordinate armies and the troops on the lines of communication, and at the bases, that is, the concentration points for men, supplies, and munitions. Each of these three bodies had a commander and staff of its own.

The remainder of the troops were organized into armies, each with its own staff; each army was subdivided into army corps, each again with its own staff. Under each army corps were several "divisions", each with a commander and staff, and these were moved about as necessary from one corps to another. The composition of "divisions" varied in the different forces; in the British army they were made up of three "brigades", each consisting of four infantry battalions, with artillery engineers and other accessory troops. The German and French divisions were constituted in a slightly different manner, but in all cases the "division" at full strength amounted to about 18,000 of all ranks.

These "divisions" were the "fighting formations", being considered the largest body which could be effectively trained, moved, and handled in action as a single unit (though an exception to this rule was to appear later in the case of the Canadian Army Corps), and in calculating an army's fighting strength the question first to be answered was the number of divisions which constituted it.

The most important event of 1915, apart from actual operations of war, was the astonishing growth of the British army. Before the war both France and Germany possessed, as we have noted, huge permanent forces and a large number of reserves who had been trained during a period of compulsory military service. Britain had a small permanent army and a number of partially trained volunteer "territorial" units. Immediately after war was declared, Lord Kitchener, a soldier who had won a great reputation in Egypt and South Africa, was appointed secretary of state for war. He determined at once on the creation of a new army, and issued a call for volunteers. Before the end of the year 26 "new" divisions were in process of formation, and 27 "territorial" divisions were being organized. Where so many officers were in France or engaged with the regular reserves, the business of training this mass of new soldiers was a serious one; but by utilizing every officer and non-commissioned officer available, progress was made. Already by the autumn of 1914 "territorial" divisions were replacing regular troops in Egypt and India; in February, 1915, the First Territorial Division reached France, and by May the first of the new army divisions. By the middle of that year there were half a million British troops in France; and by the spring of 1916 the original small British force in France had grown to forty-two divisions, and more were coming.

Moreover, greatly to the surprise of the Germans, the Dominions were beginning to make large contributions. The First Canadian Division with its reinforcements and subsidiary units was in England by October 14, 1914; by February 11, it was in France. In September, 1915, the Second Canadian Division reached France; in January, 1916, the Third was formed in France; and in August, 1916, the Fourth, a Corps headquarters having been established to control the whole. Before the end of 1914 the First Australian Division was in Egypt; then it went to the Dardanelles, where the Second joined it. By the spring of 1916 they were both in France, where three more Australian divisions joined them within the year. New Zealand sent a division to the Dardanelles, and to France with the Australians. Two Indian divisions went to France, and later, with several others, served in eastern theatres.

Another important event was the accession of Italy to the Allied cause. Both the Central Powers and the Allies had used every effort to gain Italian support. Austria, pushed by Germany, offered considerable territorial concessions, but not enough. The Allied Powers promised a great deal more. In the event of their success, the eastern shore of the Adriatic was to become Italian; and they also promised more financial aid. In the end Italy declared war on Austria on May 22, and against Turkey on August 20.

Now we must turn to the general progress of the war during 1915 and 1916, and, just as the advantage in 1914 lay, surprisingly, with the Allies, we must confess that in these two years the fight, on the whole, went in favour of the Germans.

The year 1914 had shown them that, in the west, they were facing much stronger opposition than they expected. They had expected France to lose courage, but France never had more. They had expected the British Empire to fall to pieces, but the British Empire did nothing of the kind. Moreover, without the command of the sea they felt considerably hampered, though they did not realize how firmly they were encircled. Further success in the west being thus far from certain, Germany decided to direct her main effort towards the construction of a German Middle Europe reaching from the North sea to the Aegean. The first thing to do was to dispose of Russia; for Russia, as has been noted, was the main obstacle in the way of Germany's continental, as contrasted with her world, ambitions. The defeat of the Russian army, therefore, and the extension of the eastern border beyond Poland, became the main objectives of German strategy. At the same time Britain and France must be prevented from helping Russia, and the foothold already established on the English channel must, if possible, be enlarged. Therefore there was to be a violent, though (as we realize now) secondary, offensive on the west, while any Allied offensive there was to be met by well-organized defence. Russia's early movements, as we have noted, had put her army in a huge salient, of which the head was in Silesia, while one flank lay along the Carpathians. In April a great German drive, presaged by a terrific bombardment, was launched on the Russian left, north of the Carpathians. In little over a fortnight the Russians were forced back nearly 100 miles; by the end of June they were almost driven out of Galicia. Now the Russians were in a smaller salient, roughly corresponding with Russian Poland. The German armies in Galicia turned north; those in East Prussia came south; the Russians were squeezed out of Poland; and on August 5 the Germans entered Warsaw. Before the month was over, they had advanced another 200 miles, and their northern forces had gone just as far. Finally they were stopped, partly by Russian efforts, partly because they went too far and too fast for their own transport. The eastern line was stabilized. The Germans had so far failed in part of their main object, the destruction of the Russian armies; but they had carried the boundary of German "Middle Europe" several hundred miles to the east, just as they hoped to do.

The western attack, which was a short affair, was launched at about the same time as the eastern, and began with a drive towards the channel ports. The attack was on the salient east of Ypres on April 22. Here the First Canadian Division held the left of the British line. On their left again were French auxiliary troops, Turcos and Zouaves. The Germans, contrary to the Geneva agreements, began the attack by releasing a cloud of poisonous gas, which rolled over the French and some of the Canadians. The effect on those who felt its full force was appalling. Their lungs filled and burned with the fumes; gasping for breath, twisted by pain, many died on the spot. The remnants of the French colonials broke back to the rear. The Canadian line was extended to the left rear to cover the flank; then, for three days, they were on the defence, sometimes counter-attacking with incredible courage. With the help of a few British troops, the new Canadian formation stood off the immensely superior German forces. The German effort to reach the channel had failed.

This episode came in the midst of a general offensive which had been undertaken by the French in Champagne and Alsace. The British had backed them up by an attack at Neuve Chapelle. In these battles there was much more artillery preparation than had ever before been attempted, but other preparations were hopelessly inadequate, and the result was failure. At Neuve Chapelle the loss in killed and wounded was over 13,000, and the line was advanced less than a mile. The orders were that the attack was to be pushed "regardless of loss". Such an order, for such a small gain, shows little comprehension of the value of man-power in a long war. The French battle in Champagne and Alsace had very little more effect on the general situation. It was terribly costly in men, and the situation of the Germans was, if anything, better when it was over.

Another attack on the western front began later, but in the meantime came the worst error of the British government, the attack on the Dardanelles. This plan was conceived by Winston Churchill, then at the head of the British admiralty, and controversy has raged over it. If it could have been carried out successfully it would have decided the war. The "Middle Europe" scheme would have been smashed, and Russia would have been saved from isolation and from the final debacle.

But it could not have been carried out successfully without a far larger force than was ever used. Lloyd George saw this, and wanted to send the whole British army to the Balkans; but the commander-in-chief on the western front objected to any weakening of their lines, and in this he was probably quite right. It would have been possible for the Germans to disengage in the east and launch an irresistible attack on the west. Constantinople would have been a poor exchange for Paris and the channel ports.

Another point has escaped notice. A larger force would have suffered more casualties and needed more reinforcements. This business of reinforcement was never very well done on the western front; to do it in the East would have presented almost insuperable difficulties. And the difficulties in the way of efficient supply and transport would have been just as serious.

In any case the plan, conceived with doubtful judgment, was carried out, so far as the War Office was concerned, in a half-hearted fashion, which guaranteed its failure; though there was nothing half-hearted about the soldiers and sailors who tried to do the impossible.

The invasion began by a naval attack in March, 1915, which brought about nothing but a warning of British intentions and an immediate increase in the Turkish garrison. When British, Australian, New Zealand, and French divisions, five in all, were landed on April 25 at various points on the rocky and barren Gallipoli peninsula, the Turks were superior in numbers.

The story of the naval and military effort at Gallipoli is an epic of heroism which will never be forgotten, but in spite of gallant efforts and dreadful casualties, no success was possible. More British troops were sent, but by then there were more Turks. Finally, skilfully enough, the invaders withdrew on December 18 and January 8. A total of over 32,000 killed and almost 115,000

wounded was the cost of this unfortunate campaign.

The French were to make just as costly an error. Their commanders too had failed to realize that success without adequate munitions was impossible. In May and June, with some help from the British, they attacked north of Arras. The Germans, in accordance with their new plan, remained on the defensive, and the attack, after heavy casualties, petered out. In September the Allies tried again, the British at Loos, the French near Lens and in Champagne. Their general idea was, as will be seen, that which succeeded in 1918: one force working east and another working north were to squeeze out the Germans in the centre. But the attempt was on too small a scale, and the execution was ineffective. There was not nearly enough artillery; the arrangements for reinforcing the attacking troops, especially with the British at Loos, were poor and failed; and again the attacks broke down.

Meantime Italy had, without much regard for the general conduct of the war, directed her efforts towards Trieste, and commenced scattered advances eastward and northward. Neither strategy nor tactics was good, although the troops in the wild mountain regions did wonders in moving guns from peak to peak, scaling and then fortifying almost impossible heights by the aid of ropes and cableways. But they did not get very far, and when their attacks stopped they had lost over a quarter of a million men.

By autumn the Allied offensive, from which so much had been expected, wore itself out. The casualties had been far greater than those of the enemy, and nothing had been accomplished.

In July, 1915, a secret agreement was made between the Central Powers and Bulgaria, by which Bulgaria was to get considerable territorial concessions as a reward for joining in an attack on Serbia. The Allies attempted to counter this move by promising troops to Greece, which was bound to assist Serbia in case of war. But arrangements for the murder of Serbia went on without much attention to the police. Early in October the Germans attacked on the north, the Bulgarians on the south-east; and the king of Greece, a henchman of the Kaiser, kept his country neutral. The Allies landed an expedition at Salonika, but it was weak and it came late. After a campaign of atrocious cruelty Serbia was occupied, although its army and some of its people escaped. At the same time Austria seized on Montenegro. Before the new year was well begun the whole Balkan peninsula, except for the French and British troops at Salonika and semi-neutral Greece, was a German dependency. "Middle Europe" had been established.

The Germans had cause for satisfaction, the more so by reason of another British failure. The control of the head of the Persian gulf, an important oil-producing area, was essential to Britain, and a force was despatched there from India. In the summer of 1915 an inadequate little army was sent up the Tigris, and reached Kut-el-Amara. There it was besieged by a considerable Turkish force; all attempts at relieving it were defeated; and it finally surrendered in April, 1916. The force at the head of the Persian gulf remained in possession of its ground; and more was to be heard of it later.

While the command of the sea had been denied to Germany and the continuous British blockade had stopped her sea-borne trade, she had, simultaneously with her drive for victory by land, developed considerable marine activity of a new and unpleasant kind. Early in the war German submarines had attacked several merchant and passenger vessels, although without much success. In February, 1915, the German government announced that all Allied merchant vessels in the waters around Great Britain and Ireland would be sunk without warning, and that neutral ships would not be safe "in view of the misuse of neutral flags". This declaration was contrary to all established law and usage; the sinking of merchantmen, even after warning, had never been permitted by international law, except in case of extreme necessity, and the use of neutral colours by a merchantman attempting to elude capture had always been permitted. A number of ships were destroyed soon after this. In most cases there was considerable loss of life; ships were deliberately destroyed before the crew and passengers could leave, and sometimes life-boats were fired on. On May 7 the British steamship *Lusitania* was sunk without warning, and nearly 1,200 persons, among them a number of Americans, were drowned. The United States protested against such cruel and illegal behaviour, and this single act did more than any other event to bring the United States into the war, although that was not to come for two more years.

While all this was going on, two German armed merchant ships also got out safely and did a great deal of damage to Allied shipping. One returned safely, but not the other.

Meantime on March 1, 1915, Britain had declared an absolute blockade of Germany, and enforced it by establishing a cordon of vessels across the open seas. This involved a considerable extension of the rights which international law had previously allowed to belligerents, and which only permitted the holding up of certain articles called "contraband". The United States were at first very much annoyed by the British declaration, but the torpedoing of the *Lusitania* tended to smooth over the trouble. In order to mollify the Americans, the orders given to the German submarines were modified: neutral vessels were to be spared, and also all large passenger ships. Action against other vessels continued, and during the year 1915, over 1,000 were destroyed. In the beginning of 1916 the Germans again felt that the submarine weapon must be made more of. There was a renewal of the former activities, and in March a passenger steamer, the *Sussex*, was torpedoed near Dieppe, with much loss of life. But just about the same time the German fleet staged a hit-and-run raid on the east coast of England. The German government, much encouraged, began to think that its navy might do something after all, and for the time being, submarine warfare was in the background. In consequence President Wilson of the United States, by the threat of severing diplomatic relations, was able to extract from Germany a promise that merchant vessels in the war zone would no longer be sunk without warning.

The German naval activity of 1916 coincided with a new attack on France. Germany at the moment regarded England as her main enemy, and while with one hand she aimed at a stranglehold, by the use of her submarines, with the other she struck at the French army, "the sword of England", as German strategists put it. This time the High Command tried at Verdun, and the attack, which began on February 21, 1916, lasted until September. In method it showed a slight improvement on previous battles, in that it began with a tremendous bombardment, but the ground was too limited. The first attacks failed; but the bombardment continued, though the French counter-battery work was good, and many German guns and much ammunition were destroyed. The Germans used up troops without compunction. The strain on the French became terrible, but Verdun had become a symbol: "They shall not pass" was the watchword of France. In spite of appalling losses, they held on, giving a little now here, now there, until a day came when the attack petered out; the battle of the Somme had begun. As an active strategic effort Verdun did the Germans this good, that the French were too exhausted to fight much more in 1916. But otherwise it was a failure. Verdun had saved France and Britain too.

The attack on Britain by sea, the secondary attack of German strategy, had been timed with the attack at Verdun. It began, as has been noted with submarine activity and the raid on Lowestoft. It culminated—and ended —with the battle of Jutland. On May 30 the British admiralty sent out word that the German High Seas Fleet was out, and by daybreak the British battle cruisers, with a squadron of fast battleships, were cruising southward near Jutland, the Grand Fleet battleships some distance astern. The German battle cruisers were travelling north, to the eastward of the British. The light cruisers of both sides met; then the big British cruisers turned east, astern of the Germans; the Germans turned east to escape, and finally both lines of battle cruisers were heavily engaged. The battleship *Queen Mary* and the battle cruiser *Indefatigable* were both sunk; wild fighting between destroyers followed; then Admiral Beatty saw the whole High Seas Fleet. He turned away at once, to lead them towards the Grand Fleet. The British destroyers were able to ride off the enemy battle cruisers while this was happening; the British battleship squadron, which also turned, fought as a rearguard. Cruiser and destroyer fighting was going on all the time, and the boldness of the British destroyers, added to the heavy fire of the large ships, sent the German battle cruisers back to their main fleet. Finally, in a mist, the two main fleets came in sight of one another and presently were on parallel courses running south-east. Admiral Scheer's hope had been to destroy the British battle cruisers, then to tackle a section of the Grand Fleet before the latter could deploy, but Admiral Jellicoe's tactics were too fast for him; and although the battle cruiser *Invincible* was sunk in the subsequent fighting, the Grand Fleet in line was too much for his ships. The Germans turned away. Then they turned back to attack the British centre. Again the Grand Fleet was more than ready, and Admiral Scheer ran his van into a huge semicircle of battleships waiting to meet him. Again he turned away and tried to escape to the west. The British battle cruisers kept level with, and south of, the head of his line, and after a good deal of confusion the Grand Fleet came along behind them. It seemed as though the Germans were cut off from home and certain to be destroyed, but by a brilliant manœuvre Admiral Scheer turned clear around north of the British fleet, made off to the south and regained his base. So ended the battle. It was no Nelsonian victory. The German fleet was safe; the British losses were greater than the German; and for some time the public did not know who had won, but as months went by and the Germans made no other effort it became evident that, so far as the fleets were concerned, the war was over. British sea-power had again been proved, and the High Seas fleet had ceased to be a menace.

Thus ended the second stage of the war, Germany's establishment of her European empire, the first succession of costly Allied failures, and the failure of the second German attempt at a swift knockout in the west.

1916 - 17

The balance of 1916 and the whole of 1917 was marked by offensives in which the Allies battered vainly and with terrible losses against the walls of German middle Europe, by defeatism in France and Italy, by the elimination of Russia and Rumania, the appearance of America, and the return of Germany to violent submarine warfare.

By the end of 1915 the British armies in France numbered almost a million men, and were holding a line stretching from Boesinghe to near Arras, about 40 miles in all.

The commander-in-chief had been changed. Sir John French, whose tenure had been marked by a good deal of friction and not much success, had given place to Sir Douglas Haig; and a new staff had undertaken the responsibilities at British G.H.Q. The new armies were settling down and becoming inured to the excitements and discomforts of trench warfare, and there was a general expectation of a great attack.

There was a good deal of difference between British and French methods at quiet periods. The French, during active operations, fought furiously, but at other periods, abstained from much offensive action at all. The British, on the contrary, were continually "strafing", shooting up German communications, using machine-guns at long range and trench mortars at short range, snipers picking off odd stragglers. This naturally brought reprisals and resulted in continuous, though scattered, casualties. It had another result, too: it fixed firmly in the German mind the expectation of a British attack, and in consequence the Germans were well prepared.

The Somme offensive, which began on July, 1916, was not a battle, in spite of the official reports, but a series of infantry attacks, directed against the south-west corner of the battle-front. Here, as almost everywhere else along the British line, the Germans had the high ground; they held a series of ridges running roughly north-west to south-east, from which they commanded the British positions. The attack was planned for July 1. The British staff hoped that they would be able to break through the line, and had a considerable force of cavalry ready for the event. It was only a hope, scarcely an expectation. The battle began by a week's heavy bombardment, which made quite clear to the Germans what was going to happen. The result, at first, was an apparent success, the German line being driven in for a considerable distance. The French attack, timed for the same hour, was still more successful. Counter-attack followed attack; the lines swayed this way and that, sprayed by artillery fire; positions were captured only to be lost and captured again. Finally, within three weeks, one ridge was taken. But the lessons of the war had not yet been learned. When the first attack was over, others were pressed forward without adequate preparation. The wire was not always destroyed by gunfire. Infantry, instead of attacking in small groups, were ordered to move in "waves", lines in regular formation, and they suffered in consequence; the British casualties in July alone were over 180,000, greater than those of any other month in the war. The Australian Corps, which suffered particularly from the hasty methods of the commander in whose army it was, lost over 15,000; and in the whole course of the battle their casualties were over 32,000, more than half their infantry strength. One good result was obtained by the first operations: the German offensive at Verdun was stopped.

It is impossible to tell what was in the mind of the British leaders during the rest of the battle. At one time we are told that they were aiming at "attrition", in other words, at eating away the German infantry, relying on an ultimate superiority in man-power to gain the final victory. At another time they evidently thought that continued retirement would injure the German morale, and that they could break through. Probably they varied from one view to the other, but in any case the methods were not changed much. In putting the matter thus, we are placing the responsibility where it belongs. For it must be clear that even a commander-in-chief does not act alone. He forms his opinions and makes his decisions in council with his staff officers after receiving the appreciations and recommendations of his army commanders, who in turn are advised by their own staff.

August was another costly month, although not as costly as July, with almost 72,000 casualties, of which 13,000 were Australian. But the line was advanced a little further.

Words cannot describe what life in the Somme area was to the infantry officers and men. Nameless bits of a huge half-coördinated machine, they lived in a sort of bewildered nightmare of torn trees and ruined villages and harried ground, amid a rain of shells and bullets, scarcely knowing whether it was day or night, yet rising to heights of endurance and heroism such as history can scarcely parallel.

In September came the British "tanks", mobile fortresses on caterpillar wheels, armed with machine-guns. There were not enough of them; half of them did not work; but at first they were certainly useful and with their help another advance was made. By September 25 the main ridge position was gained. In this month the Canadians came on the scene, and suffered about 15,000 out of the 100,000 or so casualties.

It should have been clear enough by now that no break through was possible, and the weather was beginning to change. Nevertheless, without any good reason the attack was pressed on to the low ground beyond the ridges.

The total result of the Somme battles was an advance of about five miles on a twelve-mile front. The cost to the British armies alone was over 400,000 casualties. The final position of the British was if anything worse than the first; it was in the middle of a devastated area instead of near comfortable billets, and the front-line trenches were low and waterlogged.

While the operation was going on in France and during the few months preceding it, Russia had been having a considerable, if illusory, success on two fronts. On the Caucasus, in the spring, a determined advance had carried the Russians well into Turkish territory, they had taken Erzerum and reached Trebizond. On that line they were halted. But Russia's main effort was to come on her western front, where the Germans thought they had her stopped. In June the Russians attacked along the whole southern half of their line and broke the Austrian right, pushing their troops well forward into Austrian territory. In July they attacked in Galicia, and had another considerable success, which was more or less consolidated during August. These tremendous battles, swinging over wide spaces of territory, should receive more note; but, as will be seen, their only effect on the eastern front, in the final analysis, was to waste Russian man-power.

They did give one advantage to the Allies in the west, by keeping occupied German troops which might otherwise have been employed against Verdun or on the Somme, but it is hard to see how the Germans could have caused many more losses to the French and British than they did cause.

The Italian front, during the summer of 1916, was also the scene of some activity. The campaign began with an Austrian attack, which came to an early end. The Italians struck back quickly, and made a considerable advance, but this too gradually came to a standstill.

Not Italy but the Near East was the scene upon which the eyes of the Allies were fixed, with hopes quite unwarranted by the value of the aid which they sought. Greece, ever since the beginning of the war, had been courted by both sides, and each had a strong group of supporters—the king, a German himself, being naturally pro-German. It must be remembered that, at the beginning of the war, Greece had a treaty with Serbia, and was in possession of the district of Macedonia to the south of Serbia. The Greeks had never stood by their treaty, and in 1916 handed over to the Bulgarians a fort

which blocked the Allies' route from Salonika. This began trouble at once; German control soon spread over the whole district; and the Allies replied by a futile blockade of Greece.

This brought about a sort of revolution, although most of the country remained under the king. The pro-Ally party set up a provisional government, or the shadow of one, at Salonika, which was recognized by the Allies and declared war on Bulgaria. Its aid was, needless to say, not very valuable, and the whole episode was more important to the newspapers than to anyone else.

At the same time another Balkan state had become involved, and from its intervention great things were expected. The actual reason for Rumania's entry on hostilities has been the cause of a good deal of discussion. Some writers believe it to have been entirely the result of a plot among Germanophile politicians in Russia, who wished to destroy both their political opponents and Rumania; but this is certainly not the complete explanation. All the Entente powers used their utmost efforts towards the same end, and intrigues of every sort were going on. The Rumanian objective was Transylvania, the south-east section of Hungary, where the population was part German, part Magyar, but mainly Rumanian. Their original idea was, probably, that they would get this area at the end of the war, just as they had got some Bulgarian territory at the end of the last Balkan war, without fighting. But the Russians would have none of this; they wanted some help for their own flagging offensive, and informed Rumania that the Allies would permit annexations in Austria-Hungary only if Rumania intervened at once. This finally brought Rumania in on August 28, 1916. Her army invaded Hungary, and at first all went well. But success did not last. The Germans took this new threat very seriously, and two efficient, although not large, forces were despatched to deal with it. One of these attacked from the north, and finally forced its way into the western part of the country; the other, aided by Turks and Bulgarians, came up from the south-east. Before the autumn was over, Rumania had lost all but part of the northern province, and had ceased to be a factor of any importance; her activity had only prevented the Germans from making a counter-attack on Russia, but this may have been all that Russia expected.

In two of the outlying theatres of war the British were having better fortune than in France. At the beginning of the year the South African forces under General Smuts, having at last disposed of the rebellion and occupied German South-West Africa, were able to undertake their long-planned campaign in German East Africa. This proceeded as quickly as an operation in a huge country, opposed by a small but well-directed force, could be expected to proceed, and was finally successful after a highly picturesque campaign.

In Arabia too there were interesting developments, for in June the Sherif of Mecca, whose country had long been subject to the Sultan, began a revolt, captured Mecca, was declared "King of the Arabs", and then, by the autumn, came more or less to a standstill. He was, though he did not know it, waiting the advent of the famous "Colonel Lawrence", the Oxford student who came out of nowhere to control the tribes as they had not been controlled for centuries.

The year had not been encouraging to the Allies. The walls of middle Europe had not been breached; although the Germans had been forced back to inner defences along their eastern front, their western line had only swung back a little in one small area. Rumania had been knocked out, and the Salonika expedition looked little better than the Dardanelles. The only real gain had been the victory of Jutland; and, since the British losses had been greater than the German and there had been no time to learn that the German High Seas Fleet had lost its morale, no one was quite sure whether Jutland was a victory or not.

The British people expressed their general distrust in a characteristic way, and, largely as a result of newspaper propaganda, Asquith, who had been prime minister since the war began, gave place to Lloyd George.

There was to be one brighter spot before the year closed. On October 24, before the British attacks on the Somme were quite over, the French attacked at Verdun, and pressed the Germans back almost to the line from which they had started months before. It was a costly and, from a military point of view, not a very useful operation. But from a moral standpoint, it was most important; the confidence of the French people at large had begun to flag, and the success at Verdun renewed it for the time being.

The Germans were now in still worse case than the Entente powers. They had been "fighting blind" for some time, in the hope of a decision, and their interior arrangements were badly out of gear. The whole of Germany required new organization, if any success were to be hoped for. New arrangements had to be made for the provision of men, supplies, and munitions. The German plans for 1917 involved a general defensive, while such an organization was in progress. To facilitate this Ludendorff, now chief of the German staff, decided during the winter to shorten the line around the Somme; and, leaving a sufficient garrison to contest at first the gradual British advance, the army moved back. In their retirement the Germans systematically turned the country into a desert, wrecking the houses, destroying all trees, contaminating wells, and planting bombs everywhere.

The operation was successfully completed, and although the Allies had the satisfaction of noting the German withdrawal from a considerable section of occupied territory, they lost the chance of making an attack from the small salient into which the British had pushed on the Somme, and so enveloping part of the German force. At the conclusion of the movement, the Germans had left a dangerous, deep, and irregular salient, and held a prepared and very strong position on a long shallow curve which could be better garrisoned by fewer troops.

The Allied plans, on the other hand, called for an offensive. The British armies, by March, had risen to 1,800,000, and the French forces were still larger, while the German total in the west was about 2,500,000.

Joffre and Foch had been retired, and Nivelle had become the French commander-in-chief. His original plan was for a "pincers" operation, the British going eastward from Arras, the French northward from Champagne. The Germans had spoiled this scheme by their retirement. Nivelle, instead of reconsidering his plan, tried to carry it out, and Haig loyally played his part in it.

The Canadian Corps of four divisions, formed some time before, was the main fighting force of the British First Army, and included a large number of British troops. On April 9, at a strength of 175,000, it attacked the German positions on Vimy Ridge, north of Arras; it was successful at once, on the right, and after two days fighting on the left. At the same time the British Third Army on the right of the First attacked, and made a corresponding advance. The ground won was consolidated, and the rest of the battle of Arras (1917) was a desperate struggle for a further slice of territory, most of the fighting being south of the Canadian area. It finally came to a standstill. It was difficult and sometimes impossible to get the necessary guns and ammunition forward over the sea of mud, soaked by spring rains and pitted with huge shell holes, and the Third Army lost very heavily in constant infantry attacks. It was clear again that there was to be no "break-through", and that the hopefully waiting British cavalry were of no use.

By the end of April the total British advance was about four miles on a 15-mile front, with about 100,000 casualties, of which over 13,000 were Canadian. The First Army casualties, as contrasted with those of the Third, were low in proportion to the ground gained, over one-third of the whole, and considering the strength of the German position on Vimy Ridge. This was largely due to the careful training carried on, and the detailed arrangements made over a period of months, the light railways which had been built all over the area to facilitate movement over the muddy ground, and the very heavy bombardment. The element of surprise, which might have provided a further advantage, was lacking. A clever German agent, who had been a sergeant in a Canadian regiment, managed to get across the line with a fairly complete set of orders, and the German intelligence service broadcast these at once. In any case the long preliminary bombardment had been notice enough; it might have saved men's lives, but it set the enemy to constructing other positions which could not be reached by reason of the destruction caused by the guns themselves.

Failure to surprise the enemy had another effect. They were able to hold up the tanks by artillery fire, and between this and the difficulties of the mud the "mobile strong points" were of little use.

While all this was going on, many things had been happening far away from the western front; and first, an extension of German submarine warfare was involving the United States.

Ever since the beginning of the war the British blockade of Germany had become more and more effective. Germany had excused her submarine activities on the ground that Britain was violating the "freedom of the seas". It was a doctrine generally recognized by the nations of the world that the "open sea" as contrasted with coastal waters must be free. The Germans deduced from this that the British had no right to blockade them by stringing vessels far out in the North sea and the Atlantic, and for some time the United States, which obviously wished to trade with Germany, was inclined to agree. The Germans went farther, and suggested that no nation should be allowed to use the seas for warlike purposes at all, and the Americans were rather attracted by the idea. The German propaganda was good, and the correspondence between the United States and Britain was often rather sharp. But Germany's submarine warfare was really contrary to the doctrines she enunciated, and the United States found it hard to forgive the deaths of so many American citizens.

In 1916, as has already been mentioned, the Germans undertook to mitigate their operations, though this they intended to be temporary only. Their main reason for acceding to America's proposal was that their early U-boats were not very efficient. Meantime, however, feeling in the United States had been swinging to the side of the Allies; the most influential American citizens were pressing hard for war; and by the end of 1916, the German government faced the probability of hostilities with a huge new opponent, whose resources were practically unlimited. They had, as we have already noted, been forced to rest on the defensive on the western front, yet their only chance now was to knock out Britain and France. The answer lay in the submarine. German shipyards had now turned out many and far better boats, and the German government believed that they now had matters in their own hands. On January 31, 1917, a German note to the United States announced blockade zones around Britain, France, Italy, and North Africa, all traffic through which would be stopped. On February 3, in consequence of this notice, the United States severed diplomatic relations with Germany, and when submarine operations began in accordance with the German plan and more lives were lost, the American Congress, on April 3, declared war.

The example of the United States was followed by a number of other nations, who saw advantages which they might obtain by a formal declaration of war without the need to expend any effort in fighting. War was declared by Cuba and Panama on April 7, by Siam on July 22, by Liberia on August 4, by China on August 14, by Brazil on October 26, by Guatemala on April 23, 1918, and by Haiti on July 5, 1918. Bolivia, Honduras, Santo Domingo, Costa Rica, Argentina, Peru, Uruguay, and Ecuador at one time and another broke off diplomatic relations with Germany.

Nevertheless, in February, 1917, Germany began the warfare which was, she thought, to bring Britain to her knees. A total of 123 ships were sunk in the first five weeks, and in the next month 154. More than half as many were unsuccessfully attacked, but by no means all ships were attacked. As the year went on the number of ships attacked slightly diminished, but there is no denying that the campaign had a serious effect on British efficiency. It was conducted, as the German government had promised, in an absolutely ruthless manner. Ships bearing supplies for the starving population of the occupied areas, hospital ships, neutral merchantmen, all that could be sunk were sunk. Before the year was over, 10,000 deaths had been caused. Supplies in Britain ran low; the nation was

CANADIANS AT MONS

From the painting by Inglis Sheldon-Williams
(Courtesy of the Public Archives of Canada)

rationed, although the army was never stinted. And the sad part of it all was that the principal sufferers, in all nations, were the children, who had done no harm and could do none, yet were to be permanently injured in health.

The Germans at the same time made further efforts to destroy the morale of the civilian population. The Zeppelins had proved more or less useless. In two years they had made 42 raids and caused 1,554 civilian casualties, but a large number of the ships had been destroyed by explosive bullets. Aëroplanes had made 22 raids, and caused 687 casualties. But now large aëroplanes were built. They were copied, it is believed, from a British machine which came down behind the German lines. In 1917 and 1918, 37 raids were made on Britain; and the total of civilians killed and injured in the two years was 2,266. There were 10 more airship raids, causing in all 180 casualties. The same activity went on over France, where the raids had possibly more effect, both physically and morally.

The Allies replied by similar raids over Germany, the total casualties amounting to 2,474 persons. This does not include the civilians, German, French, or Belgian, killed in the bombing of munition works in the occupied areas.

There were at the same time a great many raids over the opposing armies. The casualties were high, and the moral effect, for some reason, much greater than that of shelling.

An important change in the general character of the fighting during the last two years of war was brought about by further developments in the air. We have already noted how machines were used for photographing enemy areas, other faster machines protecting them, and it became almost impossible to carry out any movement unseen. "Camouflage" came into use, the covering of horse lines by nets strewn with branches, the painting of

guns and huts to tone into the landscape, but the eye of the air camera often defeated it. The heroic combats between fighting machines excited even the soldiers.

The Royal Air Force grew fast. In January, 1917, there were 39 squadrons in France; by December, there were 58, with 11 in other theatres of war; in that one year 4,222 aëroplanes were sent to France, and almost 4,000 were generally available for service. But in 1918 there had to be a change, old machines had to be discarded, for they had no chance against the German ones, and it was well on in the year before the R.A.F., with 1,500 first-class ships, was again a factor in the situation. The story of air fighting is a wonderful one. In the World War the art was still in its infancy, but the moral and material value of the aëroplane became more and more evident as the struggle proceeded.

The spring of 1917 saw a tremendous event, the significance of which was scarcely realized at the time. This was the revolution in Russia. From the very beginning conditions in that country had been unsatisfactory; and we must turn back to review them. The people were very loyal to the Czar, Nicholas Romanoff, but he was far removed from them. He was surrounded by an autocracy which resented any influence but its own, and by a bureaucracy which maintained itself in power by espionage and cruel repression. The Duma, or Parliament, amounted to nothing; the people as a whole were only vocal through the unions of cities and zemstvos (country districts), and these were unrecognized. In 1914 there was a great burst of enthusiasm, religious in its fervour, but the governmental attitude was a cold douche; and that was the beginning of the end for the Romanoff dynasty.

There had been for many years various revolutionary groups working in the utmost secrecy; members had been sternly dealt with whenever they

24

could be convicted of actual sedition, but no group had ever been completely crushed. At first these revolutionaries were at one with the rest of the nation, but, as the war went on, they returned to their old attitude. It was no wonder; nothing could have been more lamentable than the management of the war by the Russian government. There was, indeed, something worse than bad management. There had always been a good deal of German influence in Russia, and it soon began to be exaggerated. Rumours spread that the hand of Germany touched the highest in the land, and the Czarina was accused of aiding the enemy. It is difficult to say now what the truth was, but certain facts cannot be disputed. The Czar dismissed those ministers who were most popular with the people, and best fitted to ensure popular co-operation. He dismissed at least one of them on the demand of the monk, Rasputin, who was, with considerable reason, believed to be in the pay of Germany, and had acquired an extraordinary ascendency over the German-born Czarina. He appointed a German, Stürmer, as prime minister. There were a number of strikes in munition works, organized by unknown persons, which were generally supposed to have been caused by German intrigue. The operations of the cities and zemstvos unions, aimed at increasing efficiency in munition works and food-supply arrangements, were frowned upon. The army was miserably supplied with munitions, again, it was generally supposed, as the result of intrigue by pro-German officials; most of its successes were obtained by the reckless expenditure of infantry, and when it was driven back in 1915 there was terrible national depression and defeatism. As a result of all this, feelings of discontent with the government spread. France and Britain became much disturbed, and in 1916 Lord Kitchener left for Russia. He never arrived. The mission was supposed to

be a secret one, but it was known of beforehand in Russia; it must have been known in Germany also, and the cruiser *Hampshire*, on which he was travelling, was sunk off the north coast of Scotland.

The offensive of 1916 renewed for a while the flagging confidence of the people, but when it came to a finish discontent was renewed. Rasputin, regarded as the centre of pro-German intrigue at the court, was assassinated at the end of 1916. In return the Czar, his entourage, and the police became more than ever opposed to the population at large. There were three groups of revolutionaries: democrats, socialists, and communists, and the situation was thus extremely confused. But one thing is now clear, that the group who were later called communists, or Bolsheviks, were successful in permeating the army.

The revolution began on March 8, 1917, with the assembling of comparatively orderly crowds in the streets of Petrograd protesting against the failure of the food supply. The police and some of the troops attempted to repress them by force; but by March 11 the Czar's government was paralysed, by March 14 that government had disappeared, and all the troops in the neighbourhood of the capital had joined the revolutionaries. A committee of democratic leaders of the Duma (parliament) was in control, as far as any organization could be in control, but a Council of Workmen's and Soldiers' Deputies was already challenging it. The army was rapidly disintegrating; thousands of soldiers were going home; others were fraternizing with the enemy. The Czar, who was the nominal commander-in-chief, set out from his army headquarters for Petrograd, but was unable to reach the city. On March 15 Nicholas abdicated in favour of his brother Michael.

But the people would have no more autocracy. They wanted democracy pure and simple, and for a while the democratic Duma committee, headed by Prince Lvoff under the surveillance of the Workmen's and Soldiers' Council, assumed control. They were greatly encouraged by American recognition, given almost at once by a nation enthusiastic over the birth of a new republic. But the Duma's power scarcely reached outside Petrograd; the army was before long in a state of chaos with councils of soldiers deciding as to whether they would obey orders or not. The socialist Kerensky now came into power: socialism, for the time being, was in the ascendant, and the central Council of Workmen and Soldiers appealed to their "comrades" of the army to fight for the freedom of Russia and the liberation of the downtrodden Europe. An attempt at reorganization was made; finally on July 1, 1917, the army stirred itself to a new attack, and without much difficulty made an advance on the Austrian front. But on July 16 the extremists in Petrograd started a new revolutionary movement, and a German attack, designedly or not, began on the same day. The Russian advance began to fail, since the rot in the Russian army was growing fast. Officers had lost all authority; everything was now decided by the soldiers' councils, and the only popular movement was retreat. A determined advance in the autumn carried the Germans well past Riga. This was almost the end. In November a new group, the Bolsheviks, or communist extremists, came into power, and on December 17 an armistice was signed, leaving Germany in easy command of a huge area including Finland, the Baltic provinces, and Poland, from which Russia was later to be excluded by a treaty of peace made on March 3, 1918. And the collapse of Russia forced Rumania also to agree to an armistice on December 10. The remainder of the history of the Russian revolution, including the futile efforts of Britain to combat the new régime in North Russia and Siberia, belongs less to the

story of the war than to general history.

In the outlying theatres of war Britain had cause for some satisfaction, and her accomplishments there had a picturesqueness which gave them a high moral value among the general population, greater indeed than was warranted by their real military importance. In Palestine, in the deserts of northern Arabia, and in Mesopotamia the early British failures against the Turks were more than redeemed, and such names as Gaza and Gadara, Baghdad and Beersheba delighted a people which knew the Bible and the *Arabian Nights*.

In Mesopotamia British arms were at last successful. The force at the head of the Persian gulf was reorganized in the autumn of 1916, and after some preliminary operations commenced an offensive towards the north. Before the end of February, 1917, Kut had been recaptured, and the Turks were in flight. By March 11 Baghdad was occupied; by May the whole surrounding area was firmly in the hands of the British; and before long they were in touch with Russian forces coming through northern Persia.

Farther to the west matters went equally well. The Arab tribes, united for the first time in centuries, waged a guerilla warfare under the newly made King Feisal and his adviser Lawrence. They operated in the desert east of the Red sea, then on northwards towards Syria and Damascus, appearing and disappearing like ghosts, harassing the Turks in every way possible, blowing up trains, cutting telegraph wires, attacking odd fragments of the Turkish armies that came their way, and finally severing the Turkish railway lines running southward into Palestine.

Nearer the Mediterranean coast, a considerable British force began, late in 1916, operations in the Sinai peninsula. By March of the next year, the British were in Palestine attacking the Turks at Gaza. This attack came to a standstill, but soon afterwards the forces in

Egypt were reorganized under General Allenby, and a determined offensive began in October. Jerusalem was captured in time for Christmas, an event which brought some badly needed cheer to the British people.

In this eastern warfare, three points were worthy of special note: first was the extraordinary adaptability and cheerfulness of the new British soldier, who took it quite as a matter of course that he should be fighting Turks in a country full of deadly snakes and poisonous insects, where blazing heat alternated with most uncomfortable cold. The second point of interest was the use of the Royal Air Force. It proved its usefulness for warfare in broken country, where units, instead of being closely packed, as in France, were scattered over wide areas. In an operation at a little later date an R.A.F. squadron caught a Turkish Army Corps in a defile, flew to and fro above them raining bombs and machine-gun bullets, and destroyed almost the whole formation. The third point has already been mentioned, the uniting of the Arabs under the strange influence of Lawrence.

But while this was going on, matters on the western front were not satisfactory, and in Italy the Allies had a bad setback.

The operations on the Arras front had been followed almost at once by a French attack along the line of the Aisne, with Laon as a final objective. Laon stands on a hill like a buttress at the northern edge of the rolling country projecting into the plain beyond, and if the French could reach it the Germans would be forced into another great retreat. But the German line, on high wooded ground north of the Aisne, was very secure, and the flank positions were exceptionally strong. The French attack made some headway, stopped, started again, but finally broke down completely; again preparations had been inadequate, and the French toll was 200,000 casualties.

France was now sunk in gloom and defeatism (there is not much doubt that the "defeatists" were made more influential by clever German propaganda), and the contagion spread to the armies. The French forces were in their own country, comparatively close to the capital, in touch with civilians and newspapers. Instead of being a separate entity like the British expeditionary force, they were an integral part of the population. In consequence, they were far more easily affected than were the British by the waves of popular feeling that carried the population of Paris alternately to the crest of optimism or the deepest valley of despair. Unrest and disobedience appeared in sixteen corps; there were thousands of desertions, troops refused to attack, and the situation became dangerous in the extreme. The government made an effort to improve matters. Nivelle was superseded by Pétain, with Foch as chief of staff, and although he could not undertake to prepare for operations on a large scale, Pétain commenced a thorough reorganization of the disorganized army which was before long effective. By August it had sufficiently recovered to put on a courageous, though fruitless, attack at Verdun.

The French difficulties at this particularly critical moment forced action on the British. Something had to be done to prevent the Germans from taking advantage of the opportunity to turn their defensive into an offensive.

On June 7 Haig tried, for one and the only time, a new kind of attack. Hundreds of tons of ammonal were exploded in mines laid under the German lines on the Messines Ridge, a very strongly held hill to the south of the Ypres area. It was by far the greatest explosion ever brought about by man, the ground shook for miles, and the report was heard in London. The preparation for this was a long and complicated matter. Engineer mining companies, formed of skilled men, were burrowing underground for months; German engineers were countermining, trying to locate the British galleries; sometimes they exploded mines themselves; and sometimes there was hand-to-hand fighting far underground. The British made a considerable advance over the mined area. The moral effect was valuable, for the Germans regarded the Messines Ridge as a key position, and felt their loss even more than the British appreciated their gain. The visible effect was to turn the triangular "Ypres salient" into a long shallow curve bent eastward, and so to facilitate the next operations.

On July 31 the British Fifth Army began the long series of attacks at Ypres. Ever since the beginning of the war, the British had held a more or less triangular salient, with Ypres at the centre of its base. By the attack at Messines the southern arm of this triangle had been pushed eastward. The key of the German position opposite was now the Passchendaele Ridge, east of Ypres, and the British staff believed that if the Germans could be driven off that point of vantage it might be possible to cut into them still farther, and make them abandon their hold on the North sea coast.

Successive attacks were made on comparatively narrow fronts after a great deal of artillery preparation, and by slow steps and at the cost of heavy casualties, the British line moved forward. But the advance was far slower than G.H.Q. had hoped. One division after another was moved into the Ypres area, took its place in the gallant succession, made its attack, suffered its losses, and went out to recover. The Germans had established a system of defence which was very difficult to deal with. "Pillboxes", machine-gun emplacements, were scattered all over the area from front to rear. They were made of reinforced concrete, and were proof against anything but a direct hit by a large shell. Apart from

these the line was very lightly held, and the defenders were in deep dugouts during all the preliminary bombardment. For months the fighting went on; gradually the British bombardment and the German counter-battery fire churned up the ground on both sides of the line into a mess of earth and broken stone.

There were two minor offensives on other parts of the line. The first, in August, 1917, was the Canadian battle of Hill 70. The public importance of this was beyond its military importance. The coal reserves of France occupied a long narrow strip of land running east and west through the area north of Arras, which the Canadians were holding, and about the city of Lens. A large portion of them were in German territory, and Hill 70, north of Lens, provided the Germans with a jumping-off point from which they might operate to seize more. And the loss of more coal, as Clemenceau, president of the Council of France, said the next year, would have finished France as a combatant. The attack on the hill, which began by a very heavy surprise bombardment, was completely successful and very costly to the enemy.

Before the second diversion, however, a blow was to fall on the Allies elsewhere. The Austrians, rendered increasingly nervous by the slowly advancing Italian armies, were anxious (notwithstanding the general plans of the German staff for a year of defence) to make an attack, and the disposition of the Italians in the autumn was highly favourable. The Italian First Army was facing north-west on the Asiago plateau. Some distance to the right of the First their Second Army was facing north in the mountains of the Tyrol, but the Austrians opposing them were still higher up. South of this a considerable sector was held by the Austrians, with a small Italian force against them. Then, further south, almost on the Austrian border and facing east, came the Italian Third Army, which had actually reached the summits and commanded the Austrian position. Although there were reserves, they were not near by.

Italy had suffered from the same defeatist troubles which had almost paralyzed France; Bolshevik envoys had been actively preaching the social revolution to rioters in Turin, and some at least of the Second Army regiments had fraternized with the rioters. How much more damage had been done by German agents it is impossible to say, but events showed that the morale of the Second Army was very low, and without doubt the Germans were well informed on the subject. On October 24 a small but efficient German-Austrian army, which had been concentrated on the Italian Second Army front, climbed the summits, attacked, and broke through to the southward at Caporetto. They were thus in rear of the Third Army, which, it will be remembered, was off to the east; and an additional menace to the Third Army was an Austrian force advancing along the north shore of the Adriatic. The men of the Second Army, which had thus been cut in two, surrendered (it is said that 200,000 were taken prisoners) or deserted. The army disappeared like snow in the sun, leaving the Third Army to get out of the trap as best it might. The Third Army was aided by good fortune. Behind it were two rivers, flowing southward, straight across the path of the enemy. As it crossed the first, the Tagliamento, torrential rains fell, and the Austrians were blocked. On the second river, the Piave, the Italians turned to bay. The operation had not taken long; it was over by November 4, stopped partly by the Italian stand, partly by the impossibility of reorganizing the German-Austrian supply and transport after so long an advance.

Italy was still in grave danger, for the left of the Third Army was in the air till the Fourth, largely made up of the youngest recruits, filled the gap as well as it could.

Events had gone so quickly that the other Allies scarcely knew the blow had fallen until they heard its far-reaching results. The impression on the French and British was very serious. Without delay British and French armies were constituted in Italy, and by December were holding the most important section of the line. The German divisions gradually withdrew, but the Austrians made a last effort; finally their converging attacks wore themselves out. By the end of the year the immediate peril was over, but the morale of the Allies took much longer to recover from the blow. What had happened once might happen again.

All through the autumn the British staff, with much perseverance, but complete lack of vision, pounded at the ridges in front of Ypres. The tremendous bombardment for months on end of an area which needed drainage gradually smashed all the drains and turned the country into a morass pitted by enormous shell holes. The roads had gone, and it was now perfectly evident to anyone who saw the area that even if the Passchendaele ridge were taken, that would be the utmost limit of advance, since supplies and ammunition could not get any farther. Moreover, the staff arrangements had not been satisfactory; some attacks were evidently made without enough preparation or protection, and some were pressed too far. Finally, the Canadian Corps was ordered to repeat its effort of April. Some time before, the command had passed to Sir Arthur Currie (q.v.), who had more than once made it clear that while he was entirely subject to the direction of Haig, he should be consulted regarding the disposal of Canadian troops. He lacked confidence in the army commander and staff who had been responsible for the Passchendaele attacks, and induced Haig to hand over that section of the front to another army. He found that half the guns which were supposed to be supporting the infantry were out of action, and refused to attack until they were replaced. Very careful arrangements were made; roads were built over the swamps; and finally the attack began. Passchendaele was duly taken, and there, as was to be expected, the advance stopped.

The original plan for an offensive had been sound enough; something, as has been observed, was necessary to raise the morale of the Allied armies and peoples. But to continue at the same spot after an advance had become impossible was clearly wrong, and the rising tide of casualties appalled the British government. Their losses were almost half a million, though the Canadian share, compared to their proportion in other operations, was small.

Now came the second of the minor offensives, which might have been much more. So far the tanks, of which so much had been expected, had not, as has been observed, done very well. They could not cross mud; they could not face prepared artillery; and there had never been enough of them. But a place was to be found where there was little mud and where the artillery were not ready. And a lesson in surprise was to be learned which was to be very useful in 1918. The battle of Cambrai was, indeed, far more important in its lessons than it ever was in fact.

The British Third Army throughout 1917 was in front of Cambrai. The ground was comparatively solid, and the German position, although strong, was obviously far from impregnable. Early in August a proposal was made to General Byng for a surprise tank raid on a large scale. He suggested changing it to an attempt at a break-through. There was a great deal of discussion: the G.H.Q. staff were set on the Ypres offensive; they believed that failure to reach Passchendaele would

have a bad moral effect, and they would not switch to Cambrai. They had still not learned the lessons of the Somme. Byng asked for reserves, in case of a break-through, but did not get them; and while the discussion went on, division after division which might have been used at Cambrai was breaking itself to pieces in front of Ypres.

The attack came off on November 20. An army of tanks, followed by lines of infantry, swept into the German lines with no long preliminary bombardment, and apart from a delay in one spot, where field guns came into action against them, went through without any difficulty and made a deep square salient in the German line. It was quite evident that, with adequate reserves, the British could have broken through. There were no reserves except a few cavalry, who fought well, but could not fight the German army; and the tanks had done all that they could. Before the new position could be consolidated, the Germans had counter-attacked. There was not enough artillery, there were not enough men to stop them, and on their left they advanced beyond their original line. Most of the ground the Germans had lost was retaken, and the British finally lost as much area as they gained. Cambrai was a lesson, but not a victory.

Why G.H.Q. did not support Byng's plan has already been stated. Why the effort was made at all, without the reserves that would have made it successful, is a question still unanswered. Perhaps the most important question is: What would the British have been able to do if they had got through? For not only had years of trench-warfare immobilized the army as a whole, but almost every division had been wrecked at Ypres.

So ended 1917. Russia was out; America was not ready; Italy had been badly defeated; the western wall of Middle Europe was intact; and the Allies had lost their supremacy in man-power on the western front. It was not a very encouraging outlook for Entente statesmen.

But there was something to be said on the other side. The German submarine campaign, while it had done terrible damage, had failed to reduce Britain to extremity. Time had proved that Jutland had been a real victory. The British stranglehold on Germany never relaxed. Lack of supplies and lack of food gradually cramped German industry, disheartened and demoralized the German people. And away in the Middle East, the British forces in Palestine and Mesopotamia were slowly but surely destroying the foundation of the whole Middle Europe plan.

1918

On January 8, 1918, President Wilson of the United States, set up "fourteen points" which he considered a proper basis for peace. Although they were not generally accepted, they have been given so important a place in literature that they must be mentioned. But, as will be seen, General Pershing, not President Wilson, had the final say as to America's proposal.

The fourteen points, summarized, were: (1) Open diplomacy; (2) freedom of the seas; (3) removal of economic barriers and the establishment of equality of trade conditions; (4) reduction of armaments; (5) adjustment of colonial rights; (6) evacuation of Russia (by the Allies); (7) restoration of Belgium; (8) evacuation of France, including Alsace and Lorraine; (9) return to Italy of territory inhabited by Italians within Austria; (10) freedom of Austria's subject races; (11) restoration of the Balkans; (12) freedom of Turkey; (13) re-establishment of Poland; and (14) setting up of a League of Nations.

There was, naturally, a great deal of discussion, but the Germans were far from consenting to the proposals as to Belgium and Alsace-Lorraine, which,

to the French and British, were vital. So the war went on.

The terrific economic cost of the struggle was beginning to appal everyone, but it was clear enough now that it must be finished. Taking one man serving one month as the unit, Britain's land effort was immense. Including only men in active theatres of war the Empire expended, up to the Armistice, 88,780,000 man-months, and in France alone 64,180,000 man-months. Canada's contribution was 4,319,000 man-months.

By the beginning of 1918 the totals were already enormous, and the financial cost of keeping these great armies supplied with food and ammunition was almost incredible. The arrangements for raising money by loans and taxes had been extremely complicated, but had mostly involved the making of "War Loans" by the issue of bonds which were generally sold in the midst of much patriotic fervour, and the control of all the money markets by the various governments. It is interesting, by the way, to note that Britain only secured about 30 per cent. of her war expenditure from taxes; all the rest came from loans. Another interesting point is that the total war borrowings of Britain in the United States were about £2,000,000,-000, of which £888,000,000 were borrowed after the United States entered war. All the proceeds of these loans were expended in the United States. Advances to Britain from Canada were $709,000,000, the proceeds of which were spent in Canada.

The cost to the main Allied nations and to the United States has been calculated as follows: Britain, $36,072,-000,000 (this figure is under rather than over the mark; the actual outlay was over $48,000,000,000, but there were some credits); the United States, $32,-000,000,000 (without credit for profit on material supplied to the Allies); France (including devastation losses), $54,000,-000,000; Canada, $1,000,000,000. The national debts of the various nations between 1913 and 1920 increased almost beyond belief; the increment for France was, roughly, 650 per cent., for Britain 1,000 per cent., for Canada 300 per cent. The figures were so stupendous that no economist could really grasp them, and these enormous debts remain with us to-day.

As for Germany, the bubble swelled to an incredible figure, and finally burst. By 1918 it was quite evident that a reckoning was coming, and now one of the main reasons for desiring victory was the hope of making the enemy pay.

What a hope it was! Could the statesmen of those days have looked ahead and seen the financial ruin of Germany which was to come so quickly after her downfall, and realized that the United States would demand payment even of advances made after they had declared war—what would they have done? It is difficult to guess.

During 1917 another important factor had become more clearly appreciated. At the beginning of the war and during the first two years the governments of the various countries made their decisions without much reference to popular feeling. They believed, at the outset, that most people would greet the outbreak with enthusiasm, and the almost unanimous support of the newspapers and the public justified them.

Censorship was used from the very beginning, not only to suppress information which might be useful to the enemy, but to magnify victories and suppress knowledge of reverses. High-pressure publicity methods, articles, speeches, and personal contacts were used by both sides in the United States and other neutral countries. While this was going on, incidentally, the newspapers had learned that their power was even more immense than had been realized, and it is no secret that Lord Northcliffe, who controlled the most influential section of the English press, wielded so much authority that he was the main factor in the replacement of

Asquith by Lloyd George. The defeatism of France in 1917, the withholding of reinforcements by the British government after the Passchendaele losses (the result of which was soon to be seen) were largely the result of press criticisms. The delay in the final decision of the United States was largely due to the attitude of a section of the sensational press that was unsympathetic to the Allies even to the end of the war. As time dragged on and people grew less enthusiastic, the governments found it necessary to increase their propaganda in order to support themselves and to keep their public nerved up to the continuous struggle. By 1918 it became evident that by the press, by addresses, by posters, and by the skilful use of censorship, the public must be impressed with a belief in victory, which would not only do good in itself, but could be communicated to the rather wearied armies. The result was such a campaign of publicity and propaganda in all countries as had never been seen before.

At the beginning of 1918, the battle-line in France and Belgium was a long, shallow curve bent south-westward. It stretched from Nieuport on the Belgian coast to Mézières, ten miles south of Metz on the Lorraine border. There were a few detachments in the Lorraine front between Mézières and Switzerland, but this section of the line had no importance. On the left of the Allies were the Belgians, holding a very small sector. Then came the British armies in the following order: Second, Fourth, First, Third, Fifth, holding about 120 miles in all. The British armies included a corps and some railway troops furnished by Portugal under an old treaty. The French, with a few Americans, held the last two hundred miles of battle-front and the quiet Lorraine sector.

The British casualties up to March, 1918, had been over two million. The French had been even greater. The Central Powers had suffered the appalling total of seven million, six hundred thousand.

It was quite evident to the German High Command that if they were going to win at all they must win early in the year before Britain had recovered from the loss and disorganization of Passchendaele and before the United States, whose mobilization was very slow, could begin to act. The British government helped them, unwittingly, by withholding from Haig the reinforcements he needed to make up for the Passchendaele losses.

During the winter the British and French governments had seen the need of co-operation between their armies and adopted the strange measure of setting up, instead of a single command, a Supreme War Council, a sort of supervising committee with no real power. Unfortunately, the British representative, Sir Henry Wilson, had had no extensive experience of the western front, and few soldiers had confidence in him. In the result, the Supreme War Council accomplished only one thing. On the insistence of Clemenceau, the British took over a section of line from the French, and the Fifth Army was entrusted with it.

The defences of the new British sector were poor; the Fifth Army was comparatively weak, with its troops strung out. It was here that Ludendorff decided to throw the main weight of his attack, while other troops advanced on the right of his line. His hope was to roll up the British armies towards the sea. And his hope was the higher in that he had 177 good divisions against 165 British and French, which were still not fully reorganized, and four large American divisions quite new to warfare.

The date, the place, and even the time of the offensive were known days before, but the fatal immobility of the Allied forces prevented them from making any adequate preparation.

On March 21 Ludendorff struck his terrific blow. Fourteen British divisions were attacked by sixty-four German divisions, and the attack was aided by a blinding fog which made the British artillery almost useless. A few machine-gunners and a small infantry force gathered at random, tried gallantly, but vainly, to stem the tide. Within a week a salient forty miles deep was driven into the Allied line.

There had been little co-ordination between British and French during the first part of the war; and there was not much now. In the battle which began on March 21, one hundred German divisions came into action, and the Allied commanders, hampered by red tape and lack of flexibility, could only put thirty-five against them. G.H.Q. announced to the troops which still held that "a new army" of French divisions was coming to help them. There was no such army, and so it never came, although a number of detached French divisions did reach the battlefield.

But Ludendorff made an error which itself prevented his plan from succeeding. He might have profited by the defeat of the Fifth Army, which was completely disorganized, and struck northward from the gap. Instead of this he attacked the Third Army near Arras. This was a different business. The Third Army had a resolute commander, Sir Julian Byng, a good staff, and a strong position. Its front bent back on the right and left, but it never broke.

The proposal for a unified command, which the French had always wanted and Haig had always successfully resisted, even against the will of Lloyd George, was now renewed, and on March 26, at a conference held just behind the line at Doullens, Foch was entrusted with the general co-ordination of the British and French forces. On April 3 at Beauvais the momentous document was signed which placed

British, French, and Americans all under the Marshal's orders.

The danger was certainly extreme. Foch's comment to Clemenceau was, "You give me a lost battle, and you ask me to win it."

On April 9 the Germans struck another blow, this time in the Lys valley, a few miles north of the Canadians. They were successful almost without fighting. The Portuguese retreated; other troops went with them. Most of the First British Army was left in a salient. And it is worth recording that during the next six weeks of the German offensive against the British, the Canadian Corps held between a fifth and a quarter of the total British and Belgian line.

The total casualties of the British armies in March and April were about 300,000, a terrible addition to the Passchendaele losses.

On May 27, forty enemy divisions drove southward at the French on the Chemin des Dames and forced them back, just as two months before they had forced back the British. The advent of a number of British divisions sent to help hold the French line was not enough to stem the flowing tide, which filled up another great salient and began to press westwards. This attack finally petered out, but the situation was still bad. The actual cessation of the operation was on June 6. Four days before, when the outcome could very well be foreseen, Clemenceau for France, Orlando for Italy, and Lloyd George for Britain, told the President of the United States that "the crisis still continues . . . . 162 Allied divisions now oppose 200 German . . . . [Marshal Foch] urges that the maximum number possible of infantry and machine gunners should continue to be shipped from America in the months of June and July to avert the immediate danger of an Allied defeat in the present campaign . . . . He represents that it is impossible to foresee ultimate victory in the war unless America is able to provide such an army [about 100 divisions]."

At the same time the neutral nations who were selling goods to the Allies refused further credits, and the commission responsible for purchases reported to Lloyd George that unless a successful attack was soon made, supplies could not be kept up.

But the United States was at last on the move. For nearly eight months after war was declared, no American divisions had reached the line. By the twelfth month there were only two divisions in the line, or the equivalent of four British. By the fifteenth month there were only five, equal to ten British. But the United States made a remarkable effort when the Allied need was the greatest. In January, 1918, at the Supreme War Council, General Bliss had promised that there would be four fully trained American divisions in the line by July, eight by October, twenty by April, 1919. Instead of this there were seventeen (equal to thirty-four French or British) in France by June, seven of them trained, and by November twenty-nine (equal to fifty-eight French or British) were trained, and twelve more in training. The news that the Americans were coming, were in France, was just as great a contribution to victory as were their battles when they did come. The Allied armies were filled with confidence, the Germans with despondency. Victory in the end was a matter of numbers, and if the Germans could not win before the full strength of the United States was in action, they could not win at all.

The original plan, acceded to by President Wilson, was to infiltrate American regiments into the Allied forces, and orders covering this were actually issued by British G.H.Q. (As a matter of fact, an American corps fought on the left of the Australians and Canadians in the battle of Amiens.) But General Pershing, the American commander-in-chief, stood out firmly against any such plan, and insisted on organizing a new force, to take over an entire sector from the hardly tried French.

The rôle of the Canadians also had been gradually increasing in importance. Up to 1918 they had, according to the casualty lists, made a much smaller contribution, relatively, than Britain, and until 1917 they had been treated as a small section of the British army. Even if the whole campaign be included, Canada only contributed about one-fifteenth of the total man-power effort of the Empire. But during the last months of war they were to play an unexpectedly important part.

The Canadian Corps was, during the summer, organized into a large homogeneous, striking force, consisting of four strong divisions, now making up about 52,000 infantry. (A Canadian division numbered 21,802, as compared with a British division of 16,035.) In addition to this, the Canadian Corps had a special and large machine-gun corps of four battalions and two mechanized brigades, a large engineer corps of four brigades, and far more mechanical transport than any other corps possessed. The various units composing it were well used to working together. It had a single staff, and functioned as smoothly as any smaller formation.

This was an entirely different plan from that which had prevailed, generally, in the British forces. A corps, as a rule, consisted of a commander and staff, a group of "corps troops", including heavy artillery, and a number of divisions. The division, as has been observed, had been the fighting unit, the corps a directing headquarters, and the divisions of a corps were withdrawn from time to time as they became depleted. In the Canadian Corps a new system was devised by which divisions were reinforced during operations; thus the organization could be kept continually in action. The value of this great machine was soon to be demon-

strated. It was just as formidable an addition to the British forces as the tank or the heavy gun.

It must be made clear that, while the main body of the Canadian Corps consisted of the four Canadian divisions with the Canadian artillery, it was far from being entirely made up of Canadians. It had several British staff officers, and frequently, on important occasions, a large number of British troops, mainly artillery. In the first battle of the Hindenburg line, for instance, its strength was 148,090, of which 46,491 were British.

At the same time every effort was bent towards reorganizing the British armies in France. Troops were brought home from the Middle East and largely replaced by regiments from the Indian Empire, which first and last supplied nearly a million men to the two Middle Eastern theatres. The composition of divisions was altered; they were reduced to nine battalions instead of twelve. This made them about equal in size to the existing German divisions, and naturally made the problem of reinforcement much simpler.

Improved aëroplanes became available, and before very long British and French machines had regained supremacy. Stores of ammunition were gathered, and by the summer the convalescent British and French forces were well on the road back to efficiency.

On July 15, 1918, the Germans launched 47 divisions in the *Friedenstürm*, the attack which was to bring the Allies to their knees, striking southward from the Aisne, and also to the east of Rheims, and reaching the Marne. This time they were checked and held east of Rheims, and on July 20 the French counter-attacked from the west and drove them back to the line of the 15th.

Meanwhile, and for some time previously, Foch and Haig had been preparing for their return blow. With the utmost secrecy, the Canadian Corps was first withdrawn into reserve, then moved quickly southward. To ensure surprise every effort was made to make the German command think that it was going north, not south. Fake telephone messages and even delusive movements of troops and hospital units ensured the secrecy of its actual move. The object of the operation now undertaken was to free the Amiens-Paris railway line, vital to Allied communications, from the persistent threat of a German attack and from artillery interference.

On August 8 the Canadians, with the Australians and an American corps on their left and French troops on their right, attacked the line in front of Amiens. This time advantage was taken of every lesson. The preliminary bombardment was very short, the surprise was absolute; a brigade of tanks cooperated; the Canadian cavalry too had, at last, their chance; and, with comparatively small losses, a fourteen-mile gain was made in a few days. Fifteen German divisions were met and defeated by the Canadians. The effect on German morale was more serious than the military result. The tide had turned, and the Germans knew it.

The Amiens operation came to an end because the troops came up against the old defences of 1915-16, which would have caused much trouble, and because the real objective had been attained. After some deliberation, and on the suggestion of Sir Arthur Currie, it was decided to begin a new operation, which later became the basis of the final attack; and the Canadian Corps was moved north again to begin the task. It was its first duty to break into the Drocourt-Quéant line (part of the Hindenburg system), a very strong position with huge trenches guarded by many lines of heavy barbed-wire and hundreds of machine-gun posts. In front of this lay two other trench systems. By now the lessons of the past four season's fighting had been learned. The Corps, owing to the new reinforce-ment arrangements, had left the Amiens area at full strength. The Arras area was quickly but carefully mapped; every enemy gun-position was "spotted", and every "machine-gun nest" that could be seen was marked. The preliminary bombardment was short, but heavy and scientifically accurate, aëroplanes marking the progressive destruction of the wire. On August 26, the infantry attacked, supported, not preceded by tanks; by the 28th the outlying position was taken. On September 2 the main attack was delivered on the Drocourt-Quéant line, which was successfully carried in a similar manner.

In these attacks the element of surprise, which had been present at Amiens, was lacking, for again secret agents had been active, but it had been replaced by highly scientific artillery preparation, and by the use of a large well-trained body at full strength, with a high morale.

The Germans now began to fear an offensive farther to the north, and on August 18 commenced to withdraw their troops in Flanders, where the retirement was quickly followed up by the British.

Soon afterwards the newly constituted American army undertook its first serious work. Ever since the early days of war the Germans had held the deep St. Mihiel salient, covering nearly 200 square miles on the east of Verdun. It was held by seven German divisions, of which four were mediocre. On September 12 after heavy artillery preparation and much aëroplane bombing, the salient was attacked from both sides by strong American forces, accompanied by small French tanks, and was captured with comparatively small loss.

The stage was now set on the western front for the final act of the great drama, but before viewing it we must turn to other theatres of war and see what was passing there.

It has already been noted that the submarine campaign of 1917 had not fulfilled German hopes. Over 900 British ships had actually been sunk during the year, but the numbers each month had been dropping. The loss of British ships during the war was over 7,000,000 tons, but ship-yards were busy all the time, and the final effect of the German effort was only to reduce the total of British shipping from 20,100,000 tons in 1914 to 16,900,000 tons at the end of 1918. The menace was combated by every possible means; seamanship and science united to fight it. The most picturesque and one of the most effective methods of beating the submarine was the "Q ship". A few resourceful naval crews were put in charge of innocent-looking merchant vessels, which were, in reality, quite adequately armed. Officers and men alike even dressed the part of merchant seamen, in order to decoy the submarines as near as possible. Sometimes there was a "panic party", which acted as a terrified crew and took to the boats, so that the submarine might think that the ship was now empty. One after another the submarines took the bait, and one after another the "Q ships" sank them. It was a heroic calling enough, for the crews were deliberately making themselves a target, but the results were highly satisfactory.

Merchant ships themselves took part in their own defence, and more than one sank the submarines which were endeavouring to sink them. Destroyers were fitted with mechanism which enabled them to locate submarines with uncanny exactness. Motor launches and destroyers as well carried "depth charges", large bombs calculated to explode at a given distance under water. Seaplanes looked down from above, spotted the "tin fish", and signalled its whereabouts; one of a swarm of small vessels dropped a depth charge; and presently a great bubble and a patch of oil announced the end of the submarine. Approximately 200 submarines, out of a total of 371 completed before and during the war, were destroyed. Finally,

the watch became so close that the submarines' only chance was to make a raid from the German ports on the Belgian coast, Zeebrugge, and Ostend, which could be reached by water from Germany.

The mouth of the canal at Zeebrugge was guarded by a large curving mole; the whole area was strongly garrisoned and protected by heavy guns. At midnight, on April 22, 1918, Zeebrugge was attacked. A cruiser and two ferryboats made fast to the outside of the mole, in spite of strong currents, and landed a large detachment which chased off the Germans; and a British submarine was exploded near the neck of the mole, and by blowing it up prevented a counter-attack. By this time the German guns and all their machine guns were firing hard, but they could not prevent what happened next. Three old cruisers, laden with concrete, made their way in towards the canal. One went ashore outside, but the other two made their way in and were sunk in the channel, their crews being taken off by motor launches. The other vessels then left, with the survivors of the attack on the mole. It was a well-organized and heroic attempt. It cost many lives, but by its blow at the submarines it saved thousands more. Zeebrugge had been rendered practically useless as a submarine base. A few days later a similar effort was made at Ostend and, in spite of a fog, was very successful. The submarine menace was to all intents ended, and Britain had no longer cause to fear shortage of food or supplies.

Meantime one after another the merchant ships which had survived the submarine campaign were crossing the Atlantic ferrying American troops, and before the spring was over seven American soldiers per minute, day and night, were landed in France.

In the Middle East the German structure was weakening fast. Nothing of any importance had happened in the Balkans since 1917, but the Allies were still holding a small territory north of Salonika. Towards the end of June they prepared to act, but it was the end of August before they set to work, and meantime some efforts had been wasted by a fruitless attack which the French and Italians made on the Austrians in Albania. On August 31, a joint attack was made on the Bulgarians by French, British, and Greeks, aided by the reconstituted Serbian forces, and the Bulgarians, with no Germans now to help them, fell away. Before September was over they were begging for an armistice, and on September 30 it was granted. At last light was breaking for the Allies and darkness falling on the other side. Ludendorff was ill with rage and despair, and on October 4 the Czar of Bulgaria abdicated.

Not long before, on September 18, a new offensive had begun in Palestine. The British forces, which had been stationary since February, advanced northwards, and while the infantry held the Turkish army in front of them, the cavalry went around the flank and cut off the Turks' retreat. Thousands of prisoners were taken, and the advance went on. The Arabs, across the Jordan, kept pace; finally British and Arabs, the latter now under Allenby's command, converged towards Damascus, turned inward on the city, and took it. Meantime, the British in Mesopotamia, who had by now established a cordon across Persia, reaching to India, having first sent a courageous but largely useless forlorn hope to Baku, attacked the Turks again, and on October 28 the Turks surrendered.

Turkey was knocked out. On October 30 an armistice was signed; the Allies were given their long-sought control over the Dardanelles; and the Persian cordon was extended to the Black sea. The death-knell to Germany's "Storming of the East" had sounded.

But on the western front all was by no means over, and it was there that the decisive blows were to be struck.

By the middle of September these were in preparation. A heavy weight of German forces was still massed against the British. Fifty-eight British and 10 Dominion divisions faced 76 German divisions, while 130 French and American divisions, the latter of double size, faced 102 German. The central sector of the curving line was to be the main battle-field. At the north-west end of this sector were the Canadians facing east. The American army was at the south-east end, and was facing north. The operations which followed were designed to cut off the whole German force between these two, and were finally settled at a conference between Foch, Pétain, and Pershing on September 2.

On September 25 the Americans were deployed west of Verdun, with their right on the Meuse, flowing through that city, and their left passing through the Argonne forest, a hilly and wooded area running north and south through the front. Their intention was to make a deep advance in the centre, while the French advanced west of the Argonne, thus forcing the enemy to evacuate it. On September 26 the battle of the Argonne began, after a rapid but heavy bombardment by nearly 3,000 guns, with nearly 200 tanks and 800 aëroplanes. In two days the Americans advanced nearly seven miles—and were then held up by the need of reorganizing their transportation arrangements. At the other end of the pincers, and twenty-four hours later, on September 27, the Canadian Corps broke through the main key position of the Hindenburg line, the Canal du Nord. This was a deep canal running north and south across the front. It was only available for crossing on a front of 2,000 yards, and the whole body had to pass over by this narrow space and fan out to 8 miles. This movement, under enemy fire, was highly complicated, and at the crucial moment of crossing the tension was high. But the preliminary arrangements had been careful; the operation was successfully completed; and the result was a considerable advance across the canal, which was continued for five days, the Germans putting up a stubborn fight all the way. Other troops immediately to the south of the Canadians had also been attacking, but had been held up, so that by this time the Canadian Corps was in a considerable salient, and as the German resistance had stiffened, operations in this area were stopped.

Farther to the north the British troops in Flanders had also begun an attack on the ridges east of Ypres, and had made very satisfactory progress, advancing, in the face of considerable German resistance, until October 10. Between the Canadians and the Americans, the British and the French were keeping up a constant pressure by continued attacks, which prevented the Germans from relieving the hard-pressed ends of the crescent.

The violence of this September fighting on the British front may be gauged by the great increase in artillery ammunition expended. In the five heaviest weeks of the attack in the Somme area in 1916 about 7½ million rounds were expended; in the five weeks of fighting which began on August 20 over 11½ million rounds were used. The casualties in the first month on the Somme had been about 200,000; in the 1918 operation two months had seen very few more.

The Americans and French were now close to the hinge on which the German armies must turn in order to escape from France; they had gone more than half-way through the defence system. On October 8 a French attack east of Verdun, preceded the day before by a delusory American advance, caused a good deal of confusion, and a general attack on October 14 went through the Hindenburg line in front of the American position. This endangered the German troops to the westward, who began to filter back to the rear.

The success of these pincer operations in France, the collapse of Turkey, and the impending collapse of Bulgaria made it clear to the Germans that they could not succeed, and on October 3 Hindenburg called for an offer of peace to be made. But what Germany expected was an "equal" peace, and that did not suit the Allies, who proceeded to continue their advance.

On October 8 the Canadian Corps attacked towards the south-east, entered Cambrai, then changing its direction towards the north-east, crossed the Canal de l'Escaut, running from Cambrai to Valenciennes. At the same time the British troops on the right of the Canadians advanced, took over Cambrai and linked up with the forces on their right.

The remainder of the 1918 campaign consisted of continuous advances at the two ends of the "pincers", the Germans putting up an unexpectedly stubborn resistance, using machine-guns and gas and high-explosive shells. The Canadians reached Valenciennes on November 1, pushed on, and by November 10 were in front of Mons. The Americans advanced towards Sedan, and by November 7 had cut the main line of German communications.

The career of the German navy was now to be ended. Late in October, the High Seas Fleet was ordered to sea, without any very clear idea of what it was to do. But revolutionary activity was now active in Germany; the propagandists had found fine material on the ships; and practically all the crews mutinied and hoisted the red flag.

At the same time, the Austrian Empire had fallen to pieces. Austria's control over the "subject races" had gone. Every nation was declaring itself independent, and only the Austrian army in Italy was intact. Nothing had happened there during the whole year except for a brief Austrian attack in the spring. On October 23 the Italians began the great battle of Vittorio

Veneto, one army attacking the mountain positions, while three, after a violent battle, got across the Piave. The lower river was a difficult problem, for the river was very wide; flat-bottomed boats had to be used, and a rainfall would have spelt disaster. But the task was accomplished. The Austrians were hopelessly beaten; more than 400,000 were prisoners; and on November 3 their commander signed an armistice which amounted to an unconditional surrender.

Germany was on her knees at last. One after another her allies had gone. The wild prophecies of her leaders of 1914 had turned to visions of despair.

On November 7 the German High Command asked for an armistice. On November 8 the German plenipo-tentiaries reached the Allied lines, and saw the terms which had been prepared. They would not sign. Foch replied by issuing an order on November 9 for a further advance. The Canadians complied by entering Mons, the Americans by reaching Beaumont, and completing their control of the Meuse line. The two ends of the "pincers", which had started 160 miles apart, were now separated by only 65 miles. The German army could not get out of the trap, and at 5 a.m. on November 11 the armistice was signed, to take effect six hours later. In the meantime, on November 9 the Kaiser had abdicated. The Great War was over.

THE ARMISTICE AND THE PEACE TREATY

The armistice terms presented to the Germans called (in summary) for the following:—

(i) Cessation of hostilities at 11 a.m., November 11, 1918.

(ii) Evacuation of invaded countries including Alsace and Lorraine.

(iii) Return of all inhabitants of invaded countries.

(iv) Surrender of most of the war *matériel* on the western front.

(v) *Evacuation of all territory on the west bank of the Rhine and of large semi-circular zones at each bridgehead on the east bank. These to be occupied by Allied and American forces.*

(vi) No damage to be done in evacuated areas, etc.

(vii) Roads, railways, and canals not to be damaged; a large quantity of rolling stock and trucks to be handed over.

(viii) All mines which may have been laid to be disclosed.

(ix) The troops occupying Germany to have the right to requisition supplies.

(x) All prisoners of war to be repatriated.

(xi) Sick and wounded prisoners to be cared for.

(xii-xvi) All non-German territory east and south of Germany to be evacuated, all German activity there to cease, and the Allies to have free access *viâ* Danzig.

(xvii) East Africa to be abandoned.

(xviii) Repatriation of all interned civilians.

(xix) *Reparation for all damages, and return of all gold taken from Russia or Rumania.*

(xx) Cessation of hostilities by sea, all prisoners to be returned.

(xxi-xxiii) All submarines to be surrendered; all other warships to be disarmed, some to be held in neutral, some in German ports.

(xxiv-xxv) The Allies to be entitled to sweep up all minefields, to have free entrance to the Baltic, and to occupy all forts covering the approach.

(xxvi) *The Allied blockade of Germany to be continued.*

(xxvii) Immobilization of naval aircraft, abandonment of all *matériel* in Belgium, evacuation of the Black sea, return of all merchant vessels, no destruction of ships, no transfers of merchant vessels to a neutral flag, all restrictions placed on neutral trade by Germany abolished.

(xxviii) *The armistice to last for thirty days, provided its terms are kept.*

The terms were severe, but hardly more severe than the Germans might have expected, in view of the bitter feelings which existed.

Following them British (including Canadian), French, and American forces commenced their long march to the

Rhine, and early in December occupied the territory on the west bank and the bridge-heads.

On January 18, 1919, the Peace Conference assembled at Versailles to convert the armistice into a permanent peace; and by February 14 President Wilson presented his plan for a League of Nations. But there were many difficulties in the way either of a League of Nations or of an agreement. Britain had no intention of giving up her navy; France wanted to hold on to the Rhine. Italy wanted to get Dalmatia; Germany hoped to get Austria, at least. President Wilson would not discuss anything until the League of Nations was agreed on, and Clemenceau is said to have remarked, "Let us give this American his League of Nations. He will go home, and then we can get on with our treaty."

The Treaty itself, a volume of 400 pages, was a compromise between many ideas, but it involved a terrible chastisement for Germany. In accordance with President Wilson's "fourteen points", the subject peoples of Russia and Austria were made autonomous. The result, in any case, was the modern map of Europe, the people of a few odd corners being given the right to choose their nation by a plebiscite. It is doubtful whether the Allies were more actuated by President Wilson's views or by their desire to make permanent the dismemberment of Austria, in order to establish Czecho-Slovakia and Poland as policemen to help control Germany, and bar out Bolshevik Russia. But the principal of "self-determination" was sometimes side-tracked altogether; Germany was cut in two at her eastern end by the "Polish Corridor", nominally because the country south of Danzig was really Polish, but in fact to enable the Allies to supply Poland with arms. The German colonies came nominally under the League of Nations, but "mandates" to govern them were given to the power in possession, so that under a new name the old system of territory-grabbing was kept up. And when German Austria, which, reduced to beggary by the loss of all her dependencies, wished to join Germany, she was not permitted to do so.

It may be that the verdict of history will support the Allies in the terms imposed up to this point. But nothing could have been more senseless than the sections of the treaty which made Germany acknowledge that she was solely responsible for the war and bound her to pay the whole cost of it. The accusation, as we all realize now, was untrue; the fine was impossible; and anyone should have known that it could not be paid. But the Allied statesmen expected to get the money, or they would even at that stage have made an effort to escape the appalling burden of their debts to America.

The treaties with Austria and Bulgaria presented fewer difficulties. Austria was left a weak inland nation, with no economic resources. Bulgaria lost her sea-coast on the Aegean, although according to "self-determination" principles, she should have kept it. Serbia, one of the victors, obtained large accessions of territory, and promptly had a bitter quarrel with Italy over the Aegean coast.

In the Middle East Britain found herself holding a "mandate" for Palestine and Mesopotamia, while France held one for Syria, which she proceeded to govern like any other colony.

The Peace Treaties have been mentioned of necessity. But they were not part of the War. They belong less to the old epoch than to the new; their details appertain to the post-war history of Europe. See **Versailles, Treaty of.**

The real story of the World War ends with the figures of the German plenipotentiaries signing the armistice before the stern figure of Foch and the fellow officers who stood beside him, while fifty miles away the pincer ends of the great offensive were coming closer and closer together, and a black cloud of despair and revolution was descending upon Germany.

Bibliography. The literature relating to the World War is of such vast extent that no attempt can be made here even to indicate its extent. It may be mentioned, however, that the Historical Section of the Committee of Imperial Defence in Great Britain has issued a *History of the Great War, based on official documents,* in many volumes (London, 1922—), and that a good account of the war for the general reader will be found in Capt. B. H. Liddell Hart, *A history of the World War* (London, 1934).

So far as Canada's war effort is concerned, reference may be made to *Report of the ministry, overseas forces of Canada* (London, 1919); I. and R. F. L. Sheldon-Williams, *The Canadian front in France and Flanders* (London, 1920); H. Steele, *The Canadians in France* (London, 1920); Sir Charles Lucas (ed.), *The Empire at war,* vol. ii (London, 1923); and G. A. Drew, *Canada in the Great War* (Toronto, 1928). The Canadian government has projected an official history of the Canadian forces in the Great War; but of this only one volume has yet been published, that on *The medical services,* by Sir Andrew Macphail (Ottawa, 1925). A remarkably full bibliography of the materials relating to Canada's part in the war is to be found in W. B. Kerr, *Historical literature on Canada's participation in the Great War* (Can. hist. rev., 1933), with a *Supplementary list* (Can. hist. rev., 1934).

Worm. The term worm is applied to a very heterogeneous group of organisms belonging to unrelated classes, having in common a cylindrical elongate body.

Tapeworms and flatworms belong to a group of animals that are largely parasitic on other animals. During the growth of the worm, two or more hosts are usually involved. There are many tapeworms found in Canada, parasites of mammals, birds, and fish. The well-known pork tapeworm belongs here, the final host being man. It is practically unknown in Canada at the present time. The liver fluke and other flukes also belong here.

Roundworms and hookworms belong to a group of elongate, unsegmented animals, many of which are parasitic in other animals. The roundworm of the pig is perhaps the best known, being found in great numbers in the small intestine of pigs in Canada. A close relative is occasionally found in humans, usually immigrants from European countries, where it is much more prevalent. Many of the round worms are free-living, a great many occurring in Canada. One group in particular has recently become important as a parasite of greenhouse plants.

Fish-worms, earthworms, and beach-worms are members of the great group of annulate or segmented worms. There are several species of earthworms found in Canada.

The caterpillars or larval stages of many insects are commonly called worms. Army-worms, cutworms, tomato-worms, cankerworms, and cabbageworms are the caterpillars of moths or butterflies. Of these there are a great many in Canada that are among the most serious pests of field and garden crops and forests.

Mealworms and wireworms are the larvae of beetles, the former doing considerable damage to stored products, and the latter destroying timber.

Caddisworms, of which there are a great many species in Canada inhabiting fresh water, are the well-known larvae of caddis flies, sometimes called shad-flies. Many of the species build protective cases around themselves made of pieces of plant material or small grains of sand, bound together with silk. They are important as a source of food for many fresh-water fishes.

Bloodworms are the larvae of midges, small mosquito-like flies which appear in certain seasons in dense swarms in the vicinity of lakes and streams. The bloodworms dwell in tubular retreats of silt in the ooze and silt at the bottom of the stream or lake.

Arrow worms are small arrow- or torpedo-shaped marine animals found usually at or near the surface of the sea, sometimes in such numbers that the sea is said to be "stiff" with them. They are an important food of fishes and other marine animals.

Wormwood (*Artemesia Absinthium L., Compositae*), a shrubby perennial herb covered with silky hairs. The stem is angular and branched, and the branches droop at the tips. The leaves are 2-3 pinnately compound, the lobes lanceolate. The flower heads are hemispherical, and grouped in a nodding cluster. This plant is a native of Europe, but is common in eastern Canada along roadsides and on dry banks.

Worrell, Clarendon Lamb (1854-1934), primate of the Church of England in Canada (1931-4), was born at Smith's Falls, Ontario, on July 20, 1854. He was educated at Trinity University (B.A., 1873; M.A., 1884; D.C.L., 1902); and was ordained a priest of the Church of England in 1884. From 1891 to 1904 he was professor of English literature at the Royal Military College, Kingston; and in 1904 he was elected bishop of Nova Scotia. In 1915 he became archbishop of Nova Scotia and metropolitan of Canada, and in 1931 primate of all Canada. He died at Halifax, Nova Scotia, on August 10, 1934.

Wottonville, a village in Wolfe county, Quebec, on an arm of the Nicolet river, and on the Canadian National Railway, 12 miles from Richmond. It was probably named after the Right Hon. William Wyndham (1759-1834), who was created Baron Grenville of Wotton. Wotton is a parish in Surrey, England. Pop. (1931), 452.

Wrangel island is in the Arctic ocean, about 100 miles off the eastern extremity of Asia. The island is barren, lies in lat. 71°, long. 179°, and is about 70 miles long, by 40 miles wide. It was first sighted by Sir Henry Kellatt in 1849, and was re-discovered in 1867 by the American Captain De Long, who named it after Baron Wrangel, the Russian Arctic explorer. Wrangel had reported the existence of the island from the accounts of Siberian natives, but was unsuccessful in finding it. After De Long's visit, it was explored in 1881 by Waring and Hunt, American officers, and finally in 1921 by an expedition organized by V. Stefansson, the Canadian Arctic explorer, which temporarily occupied it, and suffered a tragic fate. Subsequently the island was taken possession of on behalf of the Russian Soviet government. See V. Stefansson, *The adventure of Wrangel island* (New York, 1925).

Wren, a word used in a general sense for any of the members of the bird family *Troglodytidae*. Wrens are diminutive birds predominately brownish in colour and with short tails. The common house wren (*Troglodytes aedon*) occurs across Canada in the central and southern portions. It is one of the few species of birds which commonly lives about, or close to, the habitations of man. Several other species of wrens occur in the southern edge of Canada. Some of these are marsh dwellers.

Wright, Adam Henry (1846-1930), professor of obstetrics, was born at Brampton, Ontario, on April 6, 1846. He was educated at the University of Toronto (B.A., 1866; M.B., 1873). From 1887 to 1914 he was professor of obstetrics in the University of Toronto; and in 1909 he was elected president of the Canadian Medical Association. He died at Toronto on August 20, 1930. He was a M.R.C.S., Eng. (1877); and he was the author of *Lectures on obstetrics* (Toronto, 1905).

Wright, Alonzo (1825-1894), capitalist and politician, was born at Hull, Lower Canada, on February 26, 1825, the son of Lieut.-Col. Tiberius Wright and the grandson of Philemon Wright (q.v.). He was educated at the Potsdam Academy, New York, and engaged in lumbering on the Ottawa river. He represented Ottawa county in the Legislative Assembly of Canada from 1862 to 1867, and in the Canadian House of Commons from 1867 to 1891. He died on January 7, 1894. In 1850 he married Mary, daughter of Nicholas Sparks. He was nicknamed "the King of the Gatineau".

Wright, Philemon (1760-1839), pioneer, was born in 1760 in Woburn, Massachusetts, and emigrated to Canada in 1800. He settled on the site of what is now Hull, Quebec, and was known as "the father of the Ottawa". He died at Hull on June 2, 1839. He published *An account of the first settlement of the township of Hull, on the Ottawa River, L.C.* (Canadian Magazine, 1824). See J. Tassé, *Philémon Wright, ou Colonisation et commerce de bois* (Montreal, 1871), and B. Harris, *The white chief of the Ottawa* (Toronto, 1903).

Wright, Robert Ramsay (1852-1933), biologist, was born in Alloa, Scotland, in 1852, and was educated at Edinburgh University (M.A., 1871; B.Sc., 1873). He came to Canada in 1874 as professor of natural science (later, of biology) in the University of Toronto; and in 1901 he became vice-president of the University. He retired in 1912, and went to live in England. There he died, at Droitwich, Worcestershire, on September 6, 1933. He was a fellow of the Royal Society of Canada, and was in 1910 its president. In addition to numerous scientific papers, he was the author of an *Introduction to zoology for high schools* (Toronto, 1889) and a report on *The fish and fisheries of Ontario* (Toronto, 1892).

Wrigley. See **Fort Wrigley.**

26

Wrong, Edward Murray (1889-1928), historian, was born in Toronto, Canada, on April 14, 1889, the eldest son of Professor George M. Wrong and Sophia Hume, daughter of the Hon. Edward Blake (q.v.). He was educated at the University of Toronto (B.A., 1911) and at Balliol College, Oxford (B.A., 1913; M.A., 1916). In 1914 he was elected a fellow of Magdalen College, Oxford; from 1916 to 1919 he was vice-principal of the College of Technology, Manchester; in 1919 he was appointed fellow and tutor of Magdalen College, Oxford; and from 1919 to 1924 he was also Beit Lecturer in Colonial History at Oxford. He died in Oxford on February 16, 1928. In 1915 he married Rosalind, daughter of A. L. Smith, the Master of Balliol; and by her he had six children. He was the author of *Charles Buller and responsible government* (Oxford, 1926) and a *History of England, 1688 to 1815* (London, 1927); and he edited *Crime and detection* (Oxford, 1926).

Wroxeter, a village in Huron county, Ontario, on the Maitland river, and on the Canadian Pacific Railway, 28 miles north-east of Goderich, and 25 miles west of Mount Forest. Pop. (1934), 400.

Würtele, Jonathan Saxton Campbell (1828-1904), judge, was born at Quebec, Lower Canada, on January 27, 1828, the son of Jonathan Würtele, seignior of River David, and Louisa Sophia Campbell. He was educated at the High School in Quebec; and was called to the bar of Lower Canada in 1850 (Q.C., 1873). From 1873 to 1886 he represented Yamaska in the Legislative Assembly of Quebec; from 1882 to 1884 he was provincial treasurer in the Quebec government, and from 1884 to 1886 he was speaker of the Assembly. In 1886 he was appointed a judge of the Superior Court of Quebec, and in 1892 a judge of the court of Queen's Bench. He died on April 24, 1904.

Wyandots. See **Hurons.**

Wycliffe, a village in the Kootenay district, British Columbia, on the St. Mary river, and on the Cranbrook-Kimberley branch of the Canadian Pacific Railway, 8 miles north-west of Cranbrook. Pop. (1934), 500.

Wycliffe College, a theological school founded in Toronto, Ontario, in 1877, as the Protestant Episcopal Divinity School, by the Church Association of the diocese of Toronto, an association of evangelical or low-church Anglicans. The school was opened in the school house of St. James Cathedral, with the Rev. J. P. Sheraton (q.v.) as principal and sole full-time professor. In 1879 the school was incorporated as Wycliffe College; and in 1882 buildings were erected for it on the grounds of the University of Toronto, with which it became affiliated in 1885. In 1891 this site was bought back by the University of Toronto, and Wycliffe College was given the site which it now occupies. Here were erected the present buildings of Wycliffe College, and to these additions were made in 1902 and in 1928. In 1890 Wycliffe College was federated with the University of Toronto; and since that time its students have had access to the class-rooms and laboratories of the university. It was in the early days one of the mainstays of the University of Toronto; and it has played a conspicuous part in the history of the Church of England in Canada. It is a striking fact that the first foreign missionary ever sent forth by the Church of England in Canada was a graduate of Wycliffe College; and to-day nearly all of the foreign missionary bishops of the Church of England in Canada are also graduates of Wycliffe. The principals of the college have been the Rev. J. P. Sheraton (1877-1906), the Rev. T. R. O'Meara (1906-30), and the Rev. R. B. McElheran (1930—). See the *Jubilee history of Wycliffe College* (Toronto, 1927).

Wyebridge, a village in Simcoe county, Ontario, on the Wye river, 5 miles south of Midland, and 6 miles north of Wyevale, a station on the Canadian National Railway. Pop. (1934), 300.

Wye river, a stream in Simcoe county, Ontario, emptying into Matchedash bay, 2 miles east of Midland. Near its mouth was located the Jesuit mission of Ste. Marie, the ruins of which are still discernible, and are a centre of attraction to tourists and pilgrims. It is about 11 miles long.

Wylie, David (1811-1891), journalist and poet, was born in Johnstone, Renfrewshire, Scotland, on March 23, 1811. In 1825, he was apprenticed to the printing business in Paisley; and he became a journalist. In 1845 he emigrated to Canada, and from 1849 to 1878 he was editor and proprietor of the Brockville *Recorder*. In his later days he was known as "the father of the Canadian press". He died at Brockville on December 21, 1891. He contributed in his early days in Canada to the *Literary garland* (1838-51); and he was the author of *Recollections of a convict, and miscellaneous pieces in prose and verse* (Montreal, 1847) and *Metrical waifs from the Thousand Islands* (Brockville, 1869).

Wynyard, a town in Saskatchewan, on the Saskatoon branch of the Canadian Pacific Railway, 120 miles east of Saskatoon. It was so named in 1906 by an officer of the Land Department of the Canadian Pacific Railway after an estate in England belonging to his wife's parents. It is a railway divisional point, and has a weekly newspaper (*Advance*). Pop. (1931), 1,042.

Wyoming, a village in Lambton county, Ontario, on the Canadian National Railway, 12 miles east of Sarnia. It has flour mills. Pop. (1931), 504.

X

XY Company, the name popularly applied to "the New North West Company", formed in 1798 by a union of the fur-trading firms of Forsyth, Richardson and Co., of Montreal, and Leith, Jamieson and Co., in opposition to the old North West Company (q.v.). The name originated, it is said, from the fact that, while the goods of the North West Company were labelled "NW", those of the New North West Company, were labelled "XY"—these being the only two letters of the alphabet remaining after "N W". In 1800 the merger was strengthened by the inclusion of John Ogilvy (q.v.) and John Mure (q.v.), representing the firm of Parker, Gerrard, and Ogilvy, which was also interested in the fur-trade; and in 1802 it was further strengthened by the inclusion of Sir Alexander Mackenzie (q.v.), who had left the old North West Company in 1799. In 1803 Mackenzie reorganized the New North West Company under the name of "Sir Alexander Mackenzie and Company"; but in 1804, after a bitter struggle, the XY Company was absorbed in the North West Company, and was given a quarter interest in the new organization. Sir Alexander Mackenzie was "excluded from any interference in the fur-trade"; but the wintering partners of the XY Company became wintering partners of the North West Company. See W. S. Wallace (ed.), *Documents relating to the North West Company* (Toronto, The Champlain Society, 1934).

Y

Yahk, a village in the Kootenay district of New Brunswick, on the Moyie river, and on the Crowsnest branch of the Canadian Pacific Railway, 40 miles south-west of Cranbrook. Pop. (1930), 150.

Yale, James Murray (1801-1871), fur-trader, was born at Lachine, Lower Canada, in 1801. He entered the service of the North West Company about 1820, and was taken over as a clerk by the Hudson's Bay Company in 1821. He was sent to New Caledonia in 1821. He remained on the Pacific slope for the rest of his life; and he died at Saanich, British Columbia, on May 17, 1871. Fort Yale was named after him.

Yale, a village in the Yale district of British Columbia, on the west bank of the Fraser river, and on the main line of the Canadian Pacific Railway, 102 miles east of Vancouver. It takes its name from Fort Yale, which was built here by the Hudson's Bay Company in 1848, and was named after James Murray Yale (q.v.), a servant of the Company. Pop. (1930), 100.

Yamachiche, a village in St. Maurice county, Quebec, situated on the Yamachiche river, and on the Canadian Pacific Railway, 15 miles west of Three Rivers. The settlement dates from 1656, when the seigniory was granted to Pierre Boucher, governor of Three Rivers. The name Yamachiche comes from an Algonkian word meaning "muddy river". The village was organized as a municipality in 1887. It contains a beautiful old church, which is visited by numerous pilgrims. The chief occupations of the inhabitants are foundry work, general farming, dairying, and market-gardening. Pop. (1931), 831. See Raphaël Bellemare, *L'histoire d'Yamachiche* (Montreal, 1903) and Abbé N. Caron, *Histoire de la paroisse d'Yamachiche* (Three Rivers, 1892).

Yamaska, a county in Quebec, fronting on the south shore of lake St. Peter, an extension of the St. Lawrence river, and bounded by Richelieu, Bagot, Drummond, and Nicolet counties. It is named after the Yamaska river, which drains it, together with the St. Francis river; and it is traversed by the Canadian National Railway. Chief town, St. François. Pop. (1931), 16,820.

Yarker, a village in Addington county, Ontario, on the Napanee river, and on the Canadian Pacific and Canadian National Railways, 12 miles north of Napanee. Pop. (1934), 600.

Yarmouth, a county in Nova Scotia, at the south-western extremity of the province, bounded on the north by Digby county, and on the east by Shelburne county. It was first settled by returned Acadians in 1763, and later there came to it Loyalist settlers from Shelburne. It was cut off from Shelburne county, and created a separate county in 1836. Chief town, Yarmouth. Pop. (1931), 20,939. See J. R. Campbell, *A history of the county of Yarmouth, Nova Scotia* (Saint John, New Brunswick, 1876), G. S. Brown, *Yarmouth, Nova Scotia: A sequel to Campbell's History* (Boston, 1888), and E. D. Poole, *Annals of Yarmouth and Barrington in the Revolutionary War* (Yarmouth, Nova Scotia, 1899).

Yarmouth, a town in Yarmouth county, Nova Scotia, on the east side of Yarmouth harbour, at the entrance to the bay of Fundy, and on the Dominion Atlantic and Canadian National Railways, 145 miles south-west of Halifax. It is named after the sea-port town of Yarmouth, in Norfolk, England. Besides being the headquarters of an extensive fishing industry, it is an important sea-port, being a transfer point for goods and passengers between New York and Boston in the United States, on the one hand, and Nova Scotia, on the other. There is a daily steamship service to Boston during the season, and a semi-weekly service to Saint John, New Brunswick. The chief industries are shipbuilding, woodworking, cotton manufactures, and iron foundries; and the town has a hospital and three weekly newspapers (*Herald*, *Telegram*, and *Light*, of which the *Herald* and the *Telegram* are issued by the same publishers, and are really a semi-weekly). Pop. (1931), 7,055. See J. Murray Lawson, *Yarmouth, past and present: A book of reminiscences* (Yarmouth, Nova Scotia, 1902).

Yarmouth and Annapolis Railway, a line between Yarmouth and Digby, Nova Scotia, opened for traffic in 1879, and originally known as the Western Counties Railway. It was taken over by the Dominion Atlantic Railway in 1895.

Yarrow, or Milfoil (*Achillea millefolium* L., *Compositae*), a perennial herb with acrid smell, the erect simple stems bearing finely dissected fern-like leaves and flat clusters of small white flower heads. It is very common in fields and along wayside fences throughout Canada.

Yathkyed lake lies south-west of Chesterfield inlet, which is on the north-west shore of Hudson bay. The name is the Chipewyan Indian for "snow". The lake has an area of 860 square miles.

Yeigh, Frank (1861-1935), author, was born at Burford, Ontario, on July 21, 1861, and was educated in the local schools. He entered the civil service of Ontario, and from 1880 to 1896 was the private secretary of the Hon. A. S. Hardy (q.v.). He left the civil service in 1908, and devoted himself to lecturing, journalism, and social service. He died at Toronto on October 26, 1935. In 1892 he married Kate Westlake (q.v.), and on her death he married secondly Annie Louise, daughter of the Rev. Robert Laird. He was the author of *Ontario's parliament buildings, or A century of legislation* (Toronto, 1893) and *The heart of Canada* (Toronto, 1910); and for over 25 years he published an annual volume entitled *Five thousand facts about Canada*.

Yeigh, Mrs. Kate Westlake (1856-1906), novelist, was born in London, Ontario, in 1856, and became a journalist. She married Frank Yeigh (q.v.), of Toronto, in 1892; and she died at Toronto on March 4, 1906. She was the author of a novel entitled *A specimen spinster* (Toronto, 1905).

Yellow Adder's Tongue. See **Dog's Tooth Violet.**

Yellow-eyed Grass (*Xyris montana* Ries., *Xyridaceae*), a small, rush-like herb commonly found in bogs along with the sundew. The leaves are narrowly linear, sheathing the base of the slender flower stalk, which bears a compact head-like cluster of yellow flowers, usually two in bloom at the same time. It is found from Newfoundland west to the shores of lake Superior.

Yellow Grass, a village in the Weyburn district of Saskatchewan, on the Portal branch of the Canadian Pacific Railway, 75 miles south-east of Moose Jaw. It is in a rich mixed farming district, and has five grain elevators, a high school, and a weekly newspaper (*Herald*). Pop. (1931), 449.

Yellowhead pass is on the boundary between British Columbia and Alberta, in the Rocky mountains, at the head of Yellowhead creek, in Mount Robson park, and has an altitude of 3,711 feet. It was named after François Decoigne, a clerk of the North West Company, who was in charge at Jasper House in 1814, and who was nicknamed Tête-Jaune, or Yellowhead, from the colour of his hair. The pass is said to have been the spot which he used as a *cache* for his furs. The first recorded crossing of the pass took place in 1827, when George McDougall (q.v.) took the express from New Caledonia across the mountains by this route. Though only 40 miles north of Athabaska pass, it never, however, obtained much favour, and seems to have been used chiefly by the traders at the Hudson Bay Company's posts in northern British Columbia, for importing supplies of leather or dressed skins. It was sometimes called the Leather pass or the Caledonian valley. When the preliminary surveys for the Canadian Pacific Railway were being made, the route by the Yellowhead pass was favoured by Sir Sandford Fleming (q.v.), because of its easy gradients; but political and economic considerations turned the scale in favour of the Kicking Horse pass. When the second transcontinental railway was built, however, the Yellowhead pass was chosen; and the Canadian National Railway line now runs through it.

Yellowknife, a tribe of Athapaskan Indians inhabiting the country northeast of Great Slave and Great Bear lakes, in the North West Territories. Their hunting-grounds adjoin those of the Eskimo to the north and east, of the Chipewyan to the south-east, and of the Slave Indians to the west. In language and characteristic traits, they are hardly distinguishable from the Chipewyan, to whom they are akin; but they rank as a separate and independent tribe. Like the Chipewyan, they are an edge-of-the-woods people, living in skin-covered tipis, and spending the summer on the barren grounds in pursuit of the caribou and the muskox. During the last years of the eighteenth century and the first years of the nineteenth, they were at war with the Slave, Dogrib, and Hare Indians to the west and north-west of them; and about 1823 they retreated to the north-east corner of Great Slave lake. To-day they number only about 150, though their numbers were originally several times as large; and they trade at Fort Resolution. They are named after the knives of native copper which they once carried. See D. Jenness, *The Indians of Canada* (Ottawa, 1932).

Yellowknife river flows south into Yellowknife bay, the north arm of Great Slave lake, in the Mackenzie district of the North West Territories. It was named after the Yellowknife tribe of Indians.

Yellow Lady's Slipper. See **Lady's Slipper.**

Yellow Pond Lily. See **Pond Lily.**

Yellow Rocket. See **Cress.**

Yeo, Sir James Lucas (1782-1818), sailor, was born in Southampton, England, on October 7, 1782, the son of James Yeo, formerly agent-victualles at Minorca. He entered the British navy at an early age, and served throughout the Napoleonic wars. His ability won him rapid promotion; and in 1813 he was sent to Canada, with the rank of commodore, to command the British naval forces on the Great lakes during the later stages of the War of 1812. He engaged in a duel with the American commodore, Isaac Chauncey; and by the end of 1814 he had captured Oswego and bottled up Chauncey's fleet in Sackett's Harbour. On the conclusion of peace, he returned to England; and he was then ordered to duty off the west coast of Africa. He died on the voyage home from Africa, on August 21, 1818, aged only 35 years. He was created a knight bachelor in 1810. He was not married.

A SCENE IN YOHO NATIONAL PARK

TWIN FALLS IN YOHO VALLEY, YOHO NATIONAL PARK

Yeo, John (1837-1924), senator of Canada, was born at Port Hill, Prince Edward Island, on June 29, 1837. He sat in the Legislative Assembly of Prince Edward Island from 1858 to 1891, and in the Canadian House of Commons from 1891 to 1898. On three occasions he was a member of the Executive Council of Prince Edward Island. In 1898 he was appointed to the Senate of Canada; and he sat in the Senate until his death, at Charlottetown, Prince Edward Island, on December 14, 1924.

Yeoman, Eric McKay (1885-1909), poet, was born at Newcastle, New Brunswick, on October 9, 1885, and was educated at Dalhousie University, Halifax. He became a journalist, and contributed verses to various periodicals. He died in February, 1909. After his death a small volume of his *Poems* was published privately in Halifax, Nova Scotia. Some of his verses are included in Mrs. C. M. Whyte-Edgar, *A wreath of Canadian song* (Toronto, 1910).

Yew, the name of the tree belonging to the genus *Taxus* Linnaeus of the family *Taxaceae*. Seven species are known. One of tree size occurs in Canada, Pacific yew (*Taxus brevifolia* Nutall), limited in its range to the islands and mainland of the Pacific coast. It is a small tree, usually less than thirty feet high and from four to six inches in diameter, and is of no commercial importance. The leaves are evergreen, flat, sharp-pointed, lance-shaped, yellowish-green, and soft to touch. They are singly placed in a spiral arrangement on the twigs, but twisted to appear two-ranked, and resemble somewhat the foliage of fir trees and hemlock. Their sharp points and the fact that they are fairly uniformly coloured on both surfaces will readily separate them. The flowers are unisexual, male and female on different trees. The fruits are made up of an erect, bony seed, borne in a scarlet fleshy cup or aril, ripening the first year.

The wood of the yew tree is of a very high quality, but the tree is only occasionally cut, and is used for special purposes.

Ymir, a mining town in the Kootenay district of British Columbia, on the Salmo river, and on the Great Northern Railway, 18 miles south of Nelson. It has a hospital and government offices. Pop. (1930), 200.

Yoho National Park, a reservation of 507 square miles adjoining Banff National Park on the north-west, at the boundary between Alberta and British Columbia. It was set aside by order-in-council of the Canadian government in 1886. The park headquarters is Field, on the Canadian Pacific Railway; and the chief points of interest are the Yoho valley, the Takakkaw falls, the Emerald lake, the Twin falls, and the natural bridge on the Kicking Horse river. See *Banff, Kootenay, and Yoho National Parks* (Ottawa, Dept. of the Interior, 1931).

Yoho pass is in the Rocky mountains, on the boundary between Alberta and British Columbia, and between the Yoho river, in Yoho park, Kootenay district, British Columbia, and the headwaters of Emerald creek. Its name is a Cree word signifying, "How wonderful!"

Yoho peak is in the Kootenay district of British Columbia, at the head of the Yoho river, in Yoho Park, in the Rocky mountains. It is in lat. 51° 34', long. 116° 34', and has an altitude of 9,046 feet. The name, which was suggested in 1901, is the Cree exclamation of surprise.

Yonge Street, a road cut from York, Upper Canada to lake Simcoe, by order of Colonel John Graves Simcoe (q.v.), before the end of the eighteenth century. It was begun on December 28, 1795, and completed by April, 1796; and it was named by Simcoe after Sir George Yonge, then secretary of state for war, and member of parliament for Honiton, near Simcoe's family estate in Devonshire. It was one of the earliest highways in Upper Canada; and it is still one of the most important highways in Ontario, leading as it does from Toronto to the summer resorts on lake Simcoe, the Muskoka lakes, and the Georgian bay, and to the mining districts of northern Ontario.

York, a county in Ontario, is bounded on the south by lake Ontario, on the north by lake Simcoe and Simcoe county, on the east by Ontario county, and on the west by Peel county. It was known in very early days as the Toronto region. After the British conquest, it was part of the district of Nassau, and in 1793 it was given its present name by Colonel John Graves Simcoe (q.v.), the first lieutenant-governor of Upper Canada. After successive divisions of the district in 1798, 1816, 1821, 1827, 1832, and 1836, it was finally, by the Municipal Act of 1851, given its present boundaries. For a time the counties of Ontario and Peel were united with York for municipal and judicial purposes, but final and complete separation took place in 1866. Early immigration included Quakers from Pennsylvania to the townships of Whitchurch and King, Germans to Markham township, and French Royalists to the Oak Ridges, as well as United Empire Loyalists. The town of York (now Toronto) was made in 1793 the capital of the province of Upper Canada; and this fact, and the building of Yonge and Dundas Streets through the uncleared lands, gave an early impetus to colonization in the county, which is now the most populous in the province. Area, 540,271 acres, roughly 25 by 40 miles. Pop. (1931), 856,955. There are many books about Upper Canada and the early days of Toronto, and all of these contain information about York county. But see especially *Illustrated atlas of the county of York* (Toronto, 1878) and *History of the county of York* (2 vols., Toronto, 1885).

York, a county in New Brunswick, bounded on the west by Carleton county, the state of Maine, and the St. Croix river, on the north by Northumberland county, on the east by Sunbury county, and on the south by Charlotte county. It was created in 1785, and was named doubtless in honour of the Duke of York, the eldest son of George III. It is intersected by the St. John river, and traversed by the Canadian Pacific and Canadian National Railways. County town, Fredericton. Pop. (1931), 32,454.

York. See **Toronto.**

York Currency. See **Currency.**

York Factory, the central supply house of the Hudson's Bay Company on Hudson bay, situated at the mouth of the Hayes river. The first post built by the Hudson's Bay Company was a small establishment erected in 1670 at Hart's creek, but this post soon disappeared, and in 1673 the Company was trading at the place where Sir Thomas Button (q.v.) had wintered in 1612-3. In 1682 a fort was built by the Hudson's Bay Company a short distance up the Nelson river; but this fort was captured and destroyed by Radisson (q.v.) in the spring of 1683. Radisson then built a post, which he called Fort Bourbon, about 15 miles up the Hayes river. In 1684, having taken service with the Hudson's Bay Company, Radisson returned and seized Fort Bourbon for the English, renaming it Fort Nelson. In 1690 it was destroyed in order to prevent the French occupying it; and in 1691 a new fort was built by the Hudson's Bay Company about four miles from the mouth of the Nelson river. This fort, which was known as Fort York or York Factory, and which stood for nearly one hundred years, was occupied continuously by the English, except during the years 1694-6 and 1697-1714, when it was in the hands of the French and was known as Fort Bourbon. In

1782 it was captured by La Pérouse (q.v.), and was then destroyed. It was partially rebuilt by the English in 1783; but in 1788 it was abandoned, and the present fort was built about half a mile upstream, between the years 1788 and 1793. The remains of the old fort destroyed in 1782 are still visible. The present factory consists of several buildings arranged around a quadrangle, some of them being large warehouses, and some of them living-quarters; and is still the great warehouse depot of the Hudson's Bay Company, where a supply of goods is kept on hand to meet the demands of trade for two years, though since the building of the Canadian Pacific Railway its importance as a distributing centre has somewhat declined. For an account of the history of York Factory, see J. B. Tyrrell (ed.), *Documents relating to the early history of Hudson bay* (Toronto, The Champlain Society, 1931), and R. Douglas and J. N. Wallace (eds.), *Twenty years of York Factory, 1694-1714: Jérémie's account of Hudson strait and bay* (Ottawa, 1926).

York Mills, a suburb immediately north of Toronto, Ontario, on Yonge street, and on the Toronto and York Radial Railway. Pop. (1934), 100. There is also a small village of this name in York county, New Brunswick, 2 miles from Prince William, the nearest railway station.

York Pioneer and Historical Society, a society founded in Toronto, Ontario, in 1869, which claims to be the oldest of its kind in Canada, with the exception of the Literary and Historical Society of Quebec. It has published an *Annual report* since the year of its organization. The old log cabin in the Canadian National Exhibition grounds, Toronto, was erected by the society, and furnished with a collection of antiques. The society owns the Temple at Sharon, Ontario, which was erected by the Children of Peace, and which contains historical relics.

York sound, a bay on the southwest shore of Frobisher bay, in the Franklin district of the North West Territories, named after Gilbert York, captain of the *Gabriel*, in the Frobisher expedition of 1577.

Yorkton, a city in eastern Saskatchewan, on the Canadian Pacific and Canadian National Railways, 200 miles east of Saskatoon, and 290 miles northwest of Winnipeg. It was first settled in the early eighties by a colony of settlers from York county, Ontario, and was so named by them. It is the centre of one of the oldest, wealthiest, and best settled sections of Saskatchewan; and it has become an important distributing point for eastern Saskatchewan, because of the way in which railways radiate from it in all directions. Its position on the Hudson Bay Railway makes it also a distributing centre for northern Manitoba. In it are located the warehouses of many wholesale firms, two large creameries, brick and concrete block plants, a tannery, and a flour-mill. It has a collegiate institute, a Roman Catholic college, hospitals, and a weekly newspaper (*Enterprise*). Pop. (1931), 5,027.

Youghall, a village and summer resort in Gloucester county, New Brunswick, on Chaleur bay and on the Canadian National Railway, 6 miles from Bathurst.

Youmans, Mrs. Letitia, *née* **Creighton** (1827-1891), temperance reformer, was born at Cobourg, Upper Canada, in 1827, and was educated at the Cobourg Ladies' Academy and at the Burlington Academy, Hamilton, Canada West. In 1850 she married Arthur Youmans (d. 1882); and soon afterwards she became known as a lecturer on temperance reform. In 1878 she was elected president of the Ontario Women's Christian Temperance Union, and in 1883 of the Dominion temperance organization. She died in Toronto on July 19, 1891. See her autobiography, *Campaign echoes* (Toronto, 1893).

Young, Archibald Hope (1863-1935), historian, was born at Sarnia, Ontario, on February 6, 1863. He was educated at Upper Canada College and at the University of Toronto (B.A., 1887); and from 1887 to 1892 he was a master of Upper Canada College. In 1892 he was appointed lecturer in modern languages at Trinity University, Toronto, and in 1900 professor. He retired on pension in 1931; and he died at Toronto on April 6, 1935. In his later years he took a great interest in the history of the Church of England in Canada; and he was the author of *The Revd. John Stuart, D.D., U.E.L., of Kingston, Upper Canada, and his family* (Kingston, 1920), as well as of numerous historical papers contributed to the *Papers and Records* of the Ontario Historical Society, the *Canadian Churchman*, the *Canadian Historical Review*, and other periodicals. He edited *The roll of pupils of Upper Canada College, Toronto* (Kingston, 1917) and *The parish register of Kingston, Upper Canada* (Kingston, 1921). At the time of his death he was engaged on a life of Bishop Strachan (q.v.) which has not been published.

Young, Sir Aretas William (1778-1835), lieutenant-governor of Prince Edward Island (1831-5), was born about 1778, and entered the British army as an ensign in 1795. He served throughout the Revolutionary and Napoleonic Wars in Ireland, in Egypt, and in the Peninsula. In 1813 he was sent to Trinidad; and in 1820 and in 1821-3 he administered the government to Trinidad during the absence of the governor. In 1826 he was appointed protector of the slaves in Trinidad; and in 1831 he was gazetted lieutenant-governor of Prince Edward Island. This post he occupied until his death at Charlottetown, Prince Edward Island, on December 1, 1835. He married Sarah Cox, of Coolcliffe, Wexford, England; and by her he had several children, one of whom was Sir Henry Edward Fox Young, governor of South Australia (1848-55) and of Tasmania (1855-61).

Young, Egerton Ryerson (1840-1909), missionary and author, was born at Crosby, Upper Canada, on April 7, 1840, the son of the Rev. William Young and Amanda Waldron. He was educated at the Provincial Normal School, Toronto; and for several years he was a school-teacher. In 1867 he was ordained a minister of the Methodist Church; and in 1868 he was sent to the North West as a missionary. He remained in the North West until 1876; from 1876 to 1888 he served in various charges in Ontario; and in 1888 he retired from active parochial work to devote himself to writing and lecturing. He died at Bradford, Ontario, on October 5, 1909. In 1867 he married Elizabeth Bingham, of Bradford, Ontario. He wrote a number of books based on his western experiences: *By canoe and dog-train among the Cree and Salteaux Indians* (London, 1890), *Stories from Indian wigwams and northern camp-fires* (London, 1893), *Oowikapun, or How the gospel reached the Nelson River Indians* (London, 1894), *On the Indian trail* (London, 1897); *The apostle of the north* (London, 1899); *Indian life in the great north west* (London, 1900); *My dogs in the northland* (Toronto, 1902), and *Algonquin Indian tales* (Toronto, 1903). He was also the author of a number of stories for boys: *Three boys in the wild north land* (London, 1896), *Winter adventures* (London, 1899), *The children of the forest* (Toronto, 1904), *The battle of the bears* (Toronto, 1907), and others.

Young, George (1821-1910), clergyman and author, was born in Prince Edward county, Upper Canada, on December 31, 1821, of United Empire Loyalist descent. He became in 1842 an itinerant preacher in the Methodist Church, and for many years he served in various parts of eastern Canada. In 1868 he went to Winnipeg, as superintendent of Methodist missions in the

West; and he was the first president of the Manitoba and North West Conference. He was in Winnipeg throughout the North West rebellion of 1869-70, and attended Thomas Scott (q.v.) at his execution by the rebels. He was superannuated in 1884, and returned to Toronto, Ontario. Here he died on August 1, 1910. He was the author of *Manitoba memories, being leaves from my life in the prairie province* (Toronto, 1897).

Young, George Paxton (1819-1889), professor of logic, metaphysics, and ethics in University College, Toronto (1871-89), was born in Berwick-on-Tweed, England, in 1819, the son of a Scottish clergyman. He was educated at Edinburgh High School and University, and was trained for the ministry of the Presbyterian Church. In 1847 he came to Canada, and in 1850 he became minister of Knox Church, Hamilton, Upper Canada. From 1853 to 1864 he was a professor in Knox College, Toronto; and from 1864 to 1871 he was inspector of the grammar schools of Upper Canada. He was then appointed professor of logic, metaphysics, and ethics in University College, Toronto; and in this position he acquired a remarkable reputation as a teacher. He died at Toronto on February 26, 1889. He was the author of *Miscellaneous discourses and expositions of scripture* (Edinburgh, 1854); and some of his lectures were published long after his death by J. G. Hume, under the title *The ethics of freedom* (Toronto, 1911).

Young, George Renny (1802-1853), journalist and author, was born at Falkirk, Scotland, on July 4, 1802, the second son of John Young (q.v.), author of the *Letters of Agricola* (Halifax, 1822). He came to Nova Scotia with his father in 1815, and in 1824 he founded in Halifax the *Nova Scotian*, a weekly newspaper which he edited, until it was purchased by Joseph Howe (q.v.) in 1828. He then became a member of the legal profession, in partnership with his brother William Young (q.v.); and

he was for many years a prominent member of the Liberal opposition in the Legislative Assembly of Nova Scotia. In 1848 he became a member of the Uniacke administration, which marked the transition to responsible government in Nova Scotia; but he resigned in 1851 as the result of a difference with one of his colleagues. He died at Halifax, Nova Scotia, on June 30, 1853. An active writer, he published *The British North American colonies: Letters to E. G. S. Stanley, M.P.* (London, 1834), *The history, principles, and prospects of the Bank of British North America and of the Colonial Bank* (London, 1838), *The Canadian question* (London, 1839), and *Articles on the great colonial project of connecting Halifax and Quebec with a railroad* (London, 1847); but his chief work was an essay *On colonial literature, science, and education*, of which only vol. i (London, 1842) appeared.

Young, James (1835-1913), politician and author, was born at Galt, Upper Canada, on May 24, 1835, the eldest son of John Young and Janet Bell. He was educated at Galt, and from 1853 to 1863 was editor of the *Dumfries Reformer*. From 1867 to 1878 he represented South Waterloo in the Canadian House of Commons; and from 1879 to 1886 he sat for North Brant in the Legislative Assembly of Ontario. For a few months in 1883 he was provincial treasurer in the Mowat administration. In 1878 and in 1893 he was chairman of the Liberal conventions held in Toronto; and for a time he was president of the Ontario Reform Association. He died at Galt, Ontario, on January 29, 1913. In 1858 he married Margaret, daughter of John McNaught, of Brantford, Ontario. Besides a number of pamphlets and addresses on political subjects, he wrote *Reminiscences of the early history of Galt and the settlement of Dumfries* (Toronto, 1880) and *Public men and public life in Canada* (Toronto, 1902; new and enlarged ed., 2 vols., Toronto, 1912).

Young, John (1773-1837), agricultural writer, was born near Falkirk, Scotland, in September, 1773, and was educated at Glasgow University. He emigrated to Nova Scotia, with his wife and children, in 1815; and in 1818 he published in the Halifax *Recorder* a series of papers drawing attention to the backward state of agriculture in the province. These letters, which were published in book form, under the title *Letters of Agricola* (Halifax, 1822), secured the creation of a board of agriculture in Nova Scotia; and of this board Young became secretary. In 1825 he was elected a member of the Legislative Assembly of Nova Scotia; and he retained his seat until his death at Halifax on October 26, 1837. He married Agnes, daughter of George Renny, of Falkirk, Scotland; and by her he had three sons. See R. Cumming, *The Junius of Nova Scotia* (Dalhousie Review, 1933).

Young, John (1811-1878), commissioner of public works for Canada (1851-52), was born in Ayr, Scotland, on March 11, 1811. He was educated at the Ayr parish school; and in 1826 he emigrated to Canada. He went into business in Montreal, and ultimately became chairman of the board of harbour commissioners for the port of Montreal. From 1851 to 1857 he represented Montreal in the Legislative Assembly of Canada; and from 1851 to 1852 he was commissioner of public works in the Hincks-Morin administration. From 1872 to 1874 he represented Montreal also in the Canadian House of Commons. He died at Montreal on April 12, 1878. He published numerous pamphlets on Canadian trade and commerce; and he was the founder in 1846 of a Free Trade Association which published the *Canadian Economist* (Montreal, 1846-7).

Young, Sir John, Bart. See **Lisgar, Sir John Young, Bart., first Baron.**

Young, Sir William (1799-1887), prime minister and later chief justice of Nova Scotia, was born at Falkirk, Scotland, on September 8, 1799, the eldest son of John Young (q.v.), the author of the *Letters of Agricola*, and Agnes Renny. He was educated at Glasgow University (matriculation, 1813); and he emigrated with his father to Nova Scotia in 1815. In 1826 he was called to the bar of Nova Scotia; and he was a member of the Legislative Assembly of Nova Scotia from 1832 to 1860, representing Cape Breton from 1832 to 1837, Inverness from 1837 to 1859, and Cumberland from 1859 to 1860. He was a prominent supporter of Joseph Howe (q.v.). From 1843 to 1854 he was speaker of the Assembly; in 1854 he was appointed attorney-general of the province; and in 1859 he became prime minister. In 1860 he retired from political life, and was appointed chief justice of Nova Scotia, a position which he retained for twenty-one years. He died at Halifax on May 8, 1887. In 1869 he was created a knight bachelor, and in 1881 he was made an LL.D. of Dalhousie College, Halifax.

Young, a village in the Humboldt district of Saskatchewan, on the Canadian Pacific and Canadian National Railways, 140 miles north-west of Regina. It is in a farming and dairying district, and has a weekly newspaper (*Journal*). Pop. (1931), 340.

Young Men's Christian Association. This Association, which seeks to minister to the needs of young men, had its origin in London, England, in 1844. The growth of industrialism brought many young men from their homes to the crowded centres; it was primarily formed for such as were living away from home in the cities, though later it included many others. Its founder was George Williams, a dry-goods clerk, who was afterwards knighted for his service in connection with the Association, which by that time had spread to many other centres. To Montreal belongs the honour of having organized, on November 19, 1851, the first Young Men's Christian

Association on the continent of America, —though Boston followed almost immediately afterwards. Robert Baldwin, the son of the Hon. Robert Baldwin (q.v.), and others attempted to form an Association in Toronto, but owing to the churches having somewhat similar societies within themselves, organization was not formally completed until February 18, 1864. Professor (later Sir) Daniel Wilson (q.v.) was its first president. Other Canadian centres followed in quick succession, both east and west. Everywhere it was, and continues to be, a laymen's organization, though the co-operation of pastors has been an element of strength.

In the earlier years of the Canadian Associations, there were two currents of influence, one stimulated by the British Associations, which were almost exclusively evangelistic and devotional, the other much broader and more in line with the United States type, having in mind the whole man, embracing body, mind, and spirit. The latter influence would seem to have prevailed, though the former remains as the source and motive of the wider service. The Association's programme includes physical activities, educational agencies, industrial and business services, training in summer camps, and other features; but though these various activities demand much attention and effort, its avowed purpose is "to build Christian personality and a Christian society". The emphasis may be changed; but the essence remains. The Association in its methods and spheres of service tries to adapt itself to a changing social environment, but claims never to have departed from its definite purpose and spirit, of forming fellowships of men and boys, in order to develop in them a Christian personality. It does not claim to be a religious organization in any technical sense, but it does claim to be distinctively Christian in its adherence to the ideal of a Christian character.

The Canadian Young Men's Christian Association was very active in connection with the Great War. The National Council of the Canadian Associations came into being in 1912, and was thus prepared, as a unit, to serve efficiently in the War. In camps and overseas developments, in the realms of recreation, sport, education (as in the Khaki University), and religious services, its representatives ministered so acceptably as to receive from General Sir Arthur Currie (q.v.) this testimony: "The work which they did is a tribute not only to devotion and goodwill, but to organization and instruction, before the war and behind the lines, as well as on the fighting front; there was no body of men less self-seeking. The Y.M.C.A. deserves a place in the record of Canadian achievement."

The Association has found it necessary, on account of the depression, to withdraw some of its overseas staff, and at the moment has only two secretaries in India, one in Korea, and one in South America.

Seventy-nine organizations are reported in Canada for 1936 (including 61 in city and town, 16 in railways, one in a university, and the National Council) with an enrollment of 97,657 members and non-member participants, with many official workers to give leadership, and with a vast number of voluntary helpers. The National Council, at its meeting in Montreal in March, 1937, laid plans for a "Move Forward", especially in regard to young men, who because of prevailing unemployment and for other reasons were in sore need of such assistance as the Association could give.

See *Historical souvenir book, Toronto Y.M.C.A.* (Toronto, n.d.), *International survey of the Y.M.C.A. and Y.W.C.A. Associations* (New York, 1932); C. W. Bishop, *The Canadian Y.M.C.A. in the Great War* (Toronto, 1924), and *The Y.M.C.A. Yearbook* (Toronto, 1936).

Youngstown, a village in the Acadia district of Alberta, on the Canadian Pacific and Canadian National Railways, 225 miles south-east of Edmonton. It is in a grain-growing and stock-raising district, and has three grain elevators, a flour mill, a high school, and a weekly newspaper (*Plaindealer*). Pop. (1931), 372.

Young Women's Christian Association. Soon after the formation of the Y.M.C.A. in London, England, Prayer Unions for Young Women came into being, and about the same time girls coming to London to follow various trades were organized into an Improvement Association. In 1877 these two movements came together to form the Young Women's Christian Association of Great Britain. The Earl of Shaftesbury was its first president. Already, after several attempts, the Y.W.C.A. of Boston, Massachusetts, had been established (1866), having as its object "the temporal, moral and religious welfare of young women, who are dependent on their own exertion for support".

The first Canadian Association seems to have been formed in Saint John, New Brunswick (1870), primarily to meet the needs of self-supporting young women. As the Association idea developed in Canada, the purpose broadened so as to include other classes of young women and various physical and social, as well as religious, activities. The organizing of the work in its pioneer stages proved difficult, for the needs differed in the various localities; and it became necessary, for the sake of closer co-operation among the groups, to seek the formation of a "Dominion Association". Such an organization was finally formed (1893); a constitution was approved; and a travelling secretary for national work appointed. The Association in 1895 joined the World's Y.W.C.A., which already included Great Britain, Norway, Sweden, and the United States. In 1898 the Canadian Y.W.C.A. "assumed the financial support of a Y.W.C.A. worker in Foreign Fields", and the next year Miss Ruth Rouse sailed for India as its first representative. The years 1902-12 were a period of rapid expansion in city and student departments, in educational and Bible classes, and in the budget. A great variety of tasks was assumed and discharged during the Great War period. The post-war period has made great demands upon the organization's resources; but the forty Associations embraced on the National Council have continued to give leadership and valued help to hundreds of young women and girls through Canada, as well as to many in its foreign field. Meantime the Y.M.C.A. and the Y.W.C.A. have co-operated with each other, especially in regard to physical education and health programmes.

See *The story of the Y.W.C.A. in Canada*, issued by the National Council (Toronto, 1933) for a detailed and graphic account of its national work, 1893-1933.

Youville, Marie Marguerite Dufrost de La Jemmerais, Mère d' (1701-1771), founder of the Grey Nuns of Montreal, was born in Varennes, Canada, in 1701. In 1722 she married M. d'Youville; but her husband died in 1730, leaving her with two children. She then began to devote herself to charity; and in 1747 she was placed in charge of the Hôpital-Général in Montreal. Here she founded the order of Grey Nuns, or Sisters of Charity; and was thus a pioneer in organized charity in Canada. She died in Montreal in 1771. See Lady Jetté, *Vie de la vénérable mère d'Youville* (Montreal, 1900); Mgr. D. S. Ramsay, *Life of the vénérable M.-M. Dufrost de Lajemmerais, Mde d'Youville* (Montreal, 1896); Abbé Faillon, *Vie de Mme d'Youville* (Ville-Marie, 1852); and *L'Hôpital Général de Montréal (Sœurs grises), 1692-1821*, vol. i (Montreal, 1916).

Yukon river, the chief river of the Yukon territory and one of the largest

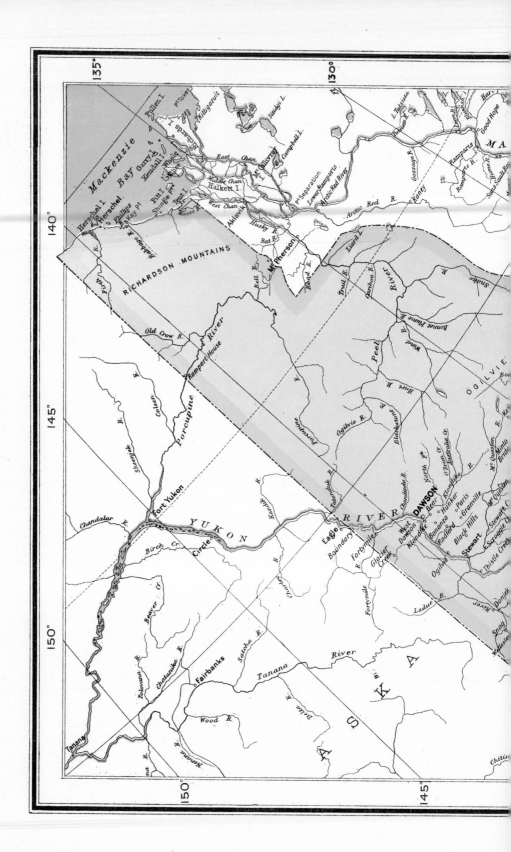

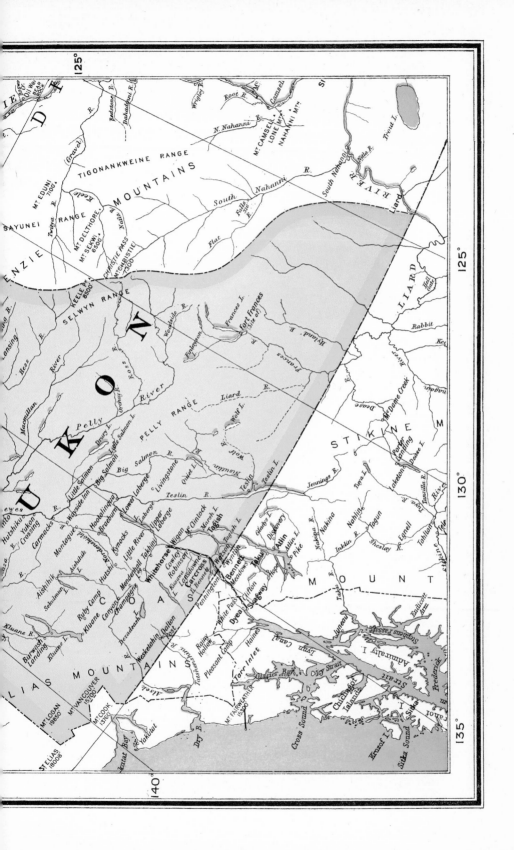

on the North American continent. It
is formed by the junction of the Lewes
and Pelly rivers, and flows in a north-
westerly direction across the international boundary into Alaska. At the
entry of the Porcupine river it turns
in a south-westerly direction and flows
eventually into the northern Pacific.
From its mouth to the head of the
Nisatlin river, the Yukon is 1,765 miles
in length, of which 655 are in Canada,
and drains a basin of 145,800 square
miles. In addition to the three already
mentioned, the river's principal tributaries are the White and the Stewart.
The head of navigation is at Whitehorse, on the Lewes river. Considerable
fur-trading is carried on at Selkirk,
opposite the mouth of the Pelly, as the
trapping is done on the Pelly and
MacMillan rivers. At the entry of the
Stewart river, the Yukon is more than
a mile wide. As one descends the river
from the Stewart to Dawson, large
islands, dividing the channel, and long,
broad stretches with majestic curves
are frequently encountered. The valley,
in this part, is wider than in the upper
reaches of the river, although the
mountains remain in sight on either
side. Since the altitude is lower than
in the upper part of the river, vegetation
becomes denser, and a large amount of
wood-cutting is done along the banks
of the river to supply the steamers.
Dawson, at the entry of the Klondike
river, has declined since the days of
its early prosperity. The river is bounded
by hills down to the Alaska boundary.
Its valley then begins to broaden, and
Circle City is on the edge of the Yukon
flats. At this point the Yukon broadens
into scores of channels, and the current
slackens visibly; it flows into the Pacific
by a number of outlets. The lower part
of the Yukon, up to the Nulato, was
explored by the Russian Glazunof in
1836-7; in 1843 another Russian, Za-
goskin, reached the mouth of the
Nowikakat. In the same year Robert
Campbell (q.v.), of the Hudson's Bay

Company, reached the head of the
Yukon by descending the Pelly river;
in 1844 John Bell (q.v.), of the Hudson's
Bay Company, explored the Porcupine
to its junction with the Yukon; and,
in 1850, Campbell descended the river
from the Pelly to the Porcupine. In
1896 George Carmacks and two Indians
made their famous discovery of gold
on Bonanza creek, a tributary of the
Klondike. In 1898 and subsequent years
thousands of prospectors flocked into
the area, around Bonanza and adjacent
creeks; within a few years the district
had produced nearly $200,000,000 worth
of gold. Small-scale gold mining is now
practically extinct; but dredge and
hydraulic mining is still carried on. See
W. K. Gibb, *Eight hundred miles on the
Yukon* (Canadian Geographical Journal,
March, 1934).

Yukon Territory. Until 1897 the
territory now known as the Yukon was
part of the North West Territories of
Canada, and was unorganized. In that
year, however, the gold rush to the
Yukon began, commonly known as the
Klondike gold rush, and the territory
was created by proclamation of the
governor-general of Canada a judicial
district. In 1898, by the Yukon Act
(61. Vict., c. 6), it was made the Yukon
Territory, with a government of its
own. It was bounded on the west, at
the 141st parallel of longitude, by
Alaska, on the north by the Beaufort
sea, on the west by the Mackenzie
district of the North West Territories,
and on the south by British Columbia,
at the 60th parallel of latitude. Dawson
was designated its capital city. The
government of the Territory was vested
in a chief executive officer, known as
the commissioner (later the comptroller)
of the Yukon, to be appointed by the
Canadian government; he was to administer the government under instructions from the minister of the
Interior, but was to be assisted by a
Council of not more than eleven
members, five of whom were to be

elected, and six appointed by warrant of the governor-general of Canada. This Council was superseded in 1909, through an amendment to the Yukon Act, by a Council of ten members, all elected, for a period of three years; but in 1919 this elective Council was reduced in number to three members. Since 1902 the Yukon has been represented by a member in the Canadian House of Commons.

The region, which is named after its chief river, the Yukon river (q.v.), was first explored by Robert Campbell (q.v.), of the Hudson's Bay Company, during the years 1842-8; and from that date until 1869 it constituted part of the fur-trading territories of the Hudson's Bay Company. In 1894 a detachment of the North West Mounted Police was sent into the region, since prospectors were invading the country; but it was not until 1897 that the gold rush began. By 1901, the population had risen to 27,219; but thereafter it began to decline, and by 1931 it had sunk to 4,230. Since 1897 it is estimated that over two hundred million dollars' worth of gold has been taken out of the Territory.

In 1937, it was announced that an agreement had been reached between the government of Canada and the government of British Columbia whereby the Yukon Territory was to be annexed to British Columbia; but opposition to this proposal developed in the Yukon Territory, and the consummation of the agreement remains a matter of the future.

The commissioners of the Yukon were Major J. M. Walsh (1897-8), William Ogilvie (1898-1901), James H. Ross (1901-3), F. T. Congdon (1903-4), W. W. B. McInnes (1905-6), Alexander Henderson (1906-12), and George Black (1912-20). Since 1920 the chief officer of the Dominion government in the Yukon has been the gold commissioner or (more recently) the comptroller.

Bibliography. See W. Ogilvie, *Information respecting the Yukon district* (Ottawa, 1897), J. N. E. Brown, *Evolution of law and government in the Yukon Territory* (in S. M. Wickett, ed., *Municipal government in Canada*, University of Toronto Studies, vol. ii, 1907), *The Yukon Territory: Its history and resources* (Ottawa, 1909), W. Ogilvie, *Early days on the Yukon* (Toronto, 1913), C. Sheldon, *The wilderness of the upper Yukon* (Toronto, 1911), and the Hon. S. Tollemache, *Reminiscences of the Yukon* (Toronto, 1912). See also **Klondike.**

Yule, Mrs. Pamelia S., *née* **Vining** (d. 1897), poetess, was born in the state of New York, and was educated at Albion College, Michigan. When the Canadian Literary Institute was founded at Woodstock, Ontario, in 1860, she was appointed instructor in English art and literature. Later, she married Professor James Cotton Yule (d. 1876), of the Canadian Literary Institute. She died at Ingersoll, Ontario, on March 6, 1897. She was the author of *Poems of the heart and home* (Toronto, 1881), and she edited *Records of a vanished life: Lectures, addresses, etc., of James Cotton Yule* (Toronto, 1876).

Z

Zealandia, a village in the Rosetown district of Saskatchewan, on the Saskatoon-Calgary branch of the Canadian National Railway, 67 miles southwest of Saskatoon. It is in an agricultural district, and has five grain elevators and a weekly newspaper (*Zealandia News*). Pop. (1934), 200.

Zeisberger, David (1721-1808), missionary, was born in Zauchtenthal, Moravia, on April 11, 1721. He emigrated to America in 1840, and became a Moravian missionary among the Delaware Indians. In 1791 he led his band of Delaware Indians into Canada, and established them on the banks of the Thames river, in Upper Canada. In 1797, the colony having been well established, he returned to minister to the Indian converts remaining in Ohio. He died at Goshen, Ohio, on November 17, 1808. See Rev. J. Morrison, *David Zeisberger and his Delaware Indians* (Ontario Hist. Soc., Papers and Records, 1914).

Zeolites, a group of minerals which are essentially hydrous silicates of alumina with lime and sodium. They are secondary minerals which fill cavities and crevices, principally in basaltic rocks. The name zeolite refers to the fact that when these minerals are heated to a high temperature they melt and bubble in their own water of crystallization. The natural zeolites are commercially of no value, but artificial zeolites have been prepared which are used to soften water. The basalts along the shores of the bay of Fundy furnish the best specimens of zeolites to be found in Canada.

Zephyr, a village in Ontario county, Ontario, on the Canadian National Railway, 15 miles north of Stouffville. Pop. (1934), 250.

Zig Zag mountains, in the Cariboo district of British Columbia, are southwest of the confluence of the Fraser and Goat rivers.

Zimmerman, Samuel (1815-1857), contractor, was born in Huntingdon county, Pennsylvania, in 1815. He came to Canada in 1842, and settled at Thorold, Upper Canada. His first undertaking was the construction of a part of the Welland Canal; and subsequently he built part of the Great Western, the Cobourg and Peterborough, the Port Hope and Lindsay, and the Erie and Ontario Railways, and the suspension and railway bridges across the Niagara river. He rapidly acquired great wealth, and was perhaps the richest man in Canada at that time. He was killed in the Desjardins Canal accident on the Great Western Railway at Hamilton on March 12, 1857. He was twice married, first to the daughter (d. 1854) of William Woodruff, of St. David's, Upper Canada, and second to a Miss Dunn, of Three Rivers, Lower Canada. See R. W. Geary, *Samuel Zimmerman* (Welland County Hist. Soc., Papers and Records, vol. iii).

Zinc, a bluish tin-white metallic element, which, when freshly cut, has a brilliant metallic lustre. It, however, soon takes on a tarnish that protects it from further oxidation. In the metallic state, it is used in the form of sheets, and is employed largely in coating iron to protect it from rusting. Large quantities are used in electrical batteries. It is alloyed with copper to make brass and certain types of bronze.

Zinc oxide is employed extensively in the manufacture of paint, and an artificial sulphide is used as a luminous paint. It is doubtful whether zinc occurs native, though there are some records which would seem to indicate this. The chief sources are the minerals sphalerite, smithsonite, and hemimorphite.

Sphalerite, the sulphide of zinc, crystallizes in the isometric system, and is characterized by a good dodecahedral cleavage. It can easily be scratched with a knife, and has a specific gravity of 4. It is characterized by a resinous to adamantine lustre, and the common colours are resin-yellow, brown, or nearly black, though it sometimes is found nearly colourless and brilliant red. The powder is pale yellow to white. Sphalerite is a common vein mineral, and is associated with galena, chalcopyrite, and silver ores, in addition to the common vein minerals calcite, dolomite, and fluorite. It has been mined in Quebec, Ontario, Manitoba, and British Columbia. The chief source at present is British Columbia, where it is obtained in great quantities at the Sullivan Mine in Kimberley.

Smithsonite, the carbonate of zinc, is rhombohedral in crystallization, and has perfect rhombohedral cleavage. It is about as hard as a knife, and somewhat heavier than sphalerite, with a specific gravity of about 4.4 The lustre is vitreous, and the colour ranges from white to gray, green, blue, and brown. It is found both in veins and beds, and usually occurs in calcareous rocks. It is probably always of secondary origin, resulting from the action of carbonated waters on sphalerite. It is a minor source of zinc in Canada, being found in the oxidized portion of some of the zinc deposits in British Columbia.

Hemimorphite, which is also known as calamine, is a basic silicate of zinc. It is frequently associated with smith-

sonite. It crystallizes in the orthorhombic system, and one end of the crystal has a different form from the other. The crystals are strongly electric after heating. It has been obtained in Canada near Salmo, British Columbia, but is not a commercial source of zinc in this country. See F. J. Alcock, *Zinc and lead deposits in Canada* (Geological Survey of Canada, Ottawa, 1930).

Zircon, a mineral having the composition of silicate of zirconium. It usually occurs in crystals which are tetragonal in form, and is an important rock-forming mineral. It is one of the extremely hard minerals with an adamantine lustre, and varies in colour from colourless to reddish-brown, brownish-yellow, and blue. When transparent, it is used as a gem stone. The principal production of zircon, however, is for use in making zirconium steel and for the preparation of zirconium oxide, which has many applications in ceramics, the electric light industry, the rubber industry, and the silk industry. The mineral is not mined commercially in Canada, but some of the largest known crystals have been obtained in Brudenell township, Ontario. See H. V. Ellsworth, *Rare-element minerals of Canada*, (Geological Survey of Canada, Ottawa, 1932).

Zoar, a Moravian mission among the Eskimo on the east coast of Labrador. It was opened in 1864 and closed in 1889.

Zoölogy. The study of zoölogy has been followed in Canada almost since the discovery of the country by Europeans. The records left by the first discoverers and colonists of Canada are full of notes on natural history; and some of the early settlers were trained observers of wild life. When universities and colleges were established, natural history was, as a rule, the first scientific subject to invade the curriculum; and later a number of learned societies were established with the object of furthering the study of natural history, and publishing papers on natural history. The first of these was the Canadian (now the Royal Canadian) Institute, which began publication of its *Journal* in 1852; the Natural History Society of Montreal began publication in 1856 of the *Canadian Naturalist;* the Nova Scotia Institute of Science, founded in 1862, began publication in 1863; and the *Naturaliste Canadien* made its appearance in 1868, the *Canadian Entomologist* in 1869, the *Transactions of the Ottawa Field Naturalists' Club* in 1879, the *Bulletin of the Natural History Society of New Brunswick* in 1882, the *Proceedings and Transactions of the Hamilton Association* in 1882, the *Transactions of the Historical and Scientific Society of Manitoba* in 1883, and the *Transactions of the Royal Society of Canada* in 1883. The work of the first zoölogists in Canada was largely descriptive; but within recent years much attention has been devoted to the conservation of the wild life of Canada. National parks and sanctuaries have been established; societies have been formed for the protection of birds; an interesting experiment has been conducted at Kingsville, Ontario, by Jack Miner, in the protection of migratory birds; the Biological Board of Canada has done a notable work in the conservation of fishery resources; and the Entomological Branch of the Department of Agriculture at Ottawa has done an equally notable work in its field. In zoölogy there has been the happiest co-operation between Canadian government departments and Canadian universities, as well as between these and scientific societies such as the Royal Society of Canada. See J. Playfair McMurrich, *Fifty years of Canadian zoölogy* (Trans. Roy. Soc. Can., 1917), and Arthur Willey, *The development of zoölogy in Canada, 1882-1932*, in *The Royal Society of Canada: Fifty years' retrospect* (Toronto, 1932).

Zorra, a township in Oxford county, Ontario, organized in 1819. The name is the Spanish word for "a female fox" or "a crafty person", and was probably suggested by Sir Peregrine Maitland (q.v.), lieutenant-governor of Upper Canada in 1819, who saw service in Spain during the Peninsular War. The township was settled chiefly by Scottish Highlanders. See W. A. MacKay, *Pioneer life in Zorra* (Toronto, 1899) and *Zorra boys at home and abroad* (Toronto, 1900).

Zurich, a village in Huron county, Ontario, 25 miles south of Goderich, and 6 miles west of Hensall, the nearest railway station. Its chief industries are a saw mill, a flax mill, and evaporator, waggon, and jam factories; and it has a continuation school and a weekly newspaper (*Herald*). Pop. (1934), 600.

FINIS